Communications in Computer and Information Science 2178

Rationale

The CCIS series is devoted to the publication of proceedings of computer science conferences. Its aim is to efficiently disseminate original research results in informatics in printed and electronic form. While the focus is on publication of peer-reviewed full papers presenting mature work, inclusion of reviewed short papers reporting on work in progress is welcome, too. Besides globally relevant meetings with internationally representative program committees guaranteeing a strict peer-reviewing and paper selection process, conferences run by societies or of high regional or national relevance are also considered for publication.

Topics

The topical scope of CCIS spans the entire spectrum of informatics ranging from foundational topics in the theory of computing to information and communications science and technology and a broad variety of interdisciplinary application fields.

Information for Volume Editors and Authors

Publication in CCIS is free of charge. No royalties are paid, however, we offer registered conference participants temporary free access to the online version of the conference proceedings on SpringerLink (http://link.springer.com) by means of an http referrer from the conference website and/or a number of complimentary printed copies, as specified in the official acceptance email of the event.

CCIS proceedings can be published in time for distribution at conferences or as post-proceedings, and delivered in the form of printed books and/or electronically as USBs and/or e-content licenses for accessing proceedings at SpringerLink. Furthermore, CCIS proceedings are included in the CCIS electronic book series hosted in the SpringerLink digital library at http://link.springer.com/bookseries/7899. Conferences publishing in CCIS are allowed to use Online Conference Service (OCS) for managing the whole proceedings lifecycle (from submission and reviewing to preparing for publication) free of charge.

Publication process

The language of publication is exclusively English. Authors publishing in CCIS have to sign the Springer CCIS copyright transfer form, however, they are free to use their material published in CCIS for substantially changed, more elaborate subsequent publications elsewhere. For the preparation of the camera-ready papers/files, authors have to strictly adhere to the Springer CCIS Authors' Instructions and are strongly encouraged to use the CCIS LaTeX style files or templates.

Abstracting/Indexing

CCIS is abstracted/indexed in DBLP, Google Scholar, EI-Compendex, Mathematical Reviews, SCImago, Scopus. CCIS volumes are also submitted for the inclusion in ISI Proceedings.

How to start

To start the evaluation of your proposal for inclusion in the CCIS series, please send an e-mail to ccis@springer.com.

Antonia Bertolino · João Pascoal Faria ·
Patricia Lago · Laura Semini
Editors

Quality of Information and Communications Technology

17th International Conference on the Quality of Information and Communications Technology, QUATIC 2024
Pisa, Italy, September 11–13, 2024
Proceedings

Springer

Editors
Antonia Bertolino
Istituto di Scienza e Tecnologie
dell'Informazione "A. Faedo"
Consiglio Nazionale delle Ricerche
Pisa, Italy

Patricia Lago
Dept of Computer Science
Vrije Universiteit Amsterdam
Amsterdam, Noord-Holland, The Netherlands

João Pascoal Faria
Faculty of Engineering
University of Porto
Porto, Portugal

Laura Semini
Dipartimento di Informatica
Università di Pisa
Pisa, Italy

ISSN 1865-0929 ISSN 1865-0937 (electronic)
Communications in Computer and Information Science
ISBN 978-3-031-70244-0 ISBN 978-3-031-70245-7 (eBook)
https://doi.org/10.1007/978-3-031-70245-7

This Springer imprint is published by the registered company Springer Nature Switzerland AG
The registered company address is: Gewerbestrasse 11, 6330 Cham, Switzerland

Preface

The International Conference on the Quality of Information and Communications Technology (QUATIC) is a forum for disseminating advanced methods, techniques, and tools to support quality ICT engineering and management approaches. Practitioners and researchers meet at the conference to exchange ideas and approaches on how to adopt a quality culture in ICT process and product improvement and to provide practical studies in varying contexts.

QUATIC 2024 was held on September 11–13, 2024, in Pisa, Italy. The organizing chairs of this 17th edition of QUATIC were Antonia Bertolino (ISTI-CNR, Pisa, Italy) and Laura Semini (University of Pisa, Italy), who hosted it locally at the Department of Computer Science of the University of Pisa. The program chairs were Patricia Lago (Vrije Universiteit Amsterdam, The Netherlands) and João Pascoal Faria (University of Porto, Portugal). Alexandra Mendes (University of Porto, Portugal) was the proceedings chair.

This volume collates the papers selected by the members of the Program Committee to be presented at the conference and published in the conference proceedings. QUATIC 2024 attracted many submissions from different areas spanning several thematic tracks proposed in the call for papers in various cutting-edge technologies of specialized focus.

The following ten Thematic Tracks (together with their track chairs) were considered in QUATIC 2024:

- Innovative Strategies for Total Quality in Business Processes and Software (Mohamad Kassab and Phillip LaPlante, Pennsylvania State University, USA)
- ICT Process Improvement, Organization, and Governance (Gleison Santos, UNIRIO, Brazil; Edna Dias Canedo, UnB, Brazil)
- Emerging Topics and Technologies in Requirements Engineering (Sallam Abualhaija, University of Luxembourg, Luxembourg; Alessio Ferrari, CNR, Italy)
- Verification, Validation, and Testing (Mercedes G. Merayo, Universidad Complutense de Madrid, Spain; Filippo Ricca, University of Genoa, Italy)
- Quality Aspects of Services and Cloud Computing (Vasilios Andrikopoulos, University of Groningen, The Netherlands; Elisabetta Di Nitto, Politecnico di Milano, Italy)
- Quality in Adaptive Software (Claudia Raibulet, Università degli Studi di Milano-Bicocca, Italy; Karthik Vaidhyanathan, International Institute of Information Technology, Hyderabad, India)
- Human Factors for Quality Software (Rodrigo Santos, UNIRIO, Brazil; Xiaofeng Wang, Free University of Bozen-Bolzano, Italy)
- Quality Aspects of Empirical Studies (Marcos Kalinowski, PUC-Rio, Brazil; Roberto Verdecchia, University of Florence, Italy)
- Quality in the Age of AI (Grace A. Lewis, Carnegie Mellon Software Engineering Institute, USA; Domenico Bianculli, University of Luxembourg, Luxembourg)
- Sustainability as a Quality Concern (Luis Cruz, Delft University of Technology, The Netherlands; Maja Hanne Kirkeby, Roskilde University, Denmark)

Main Conference Program

The Technical Program Committee of QUATIC 2024 comprised 137 international academic and industrial domain experts from organizations in 26 different countries on six continents. The best-quality papers were identified for presentation and publication based on a rigorous peer review process by the Thematic Tracks Program Committee members as reviewers. The review was carried out in a double-blind process, with at least three reviews per submission. The submitted papers came from 23 countries and the accepted papers came from 17 countries. After a discussion period and confirmation with the reviewers, out of the 50 completed submissions, 20 (40%) were accepted as full papers and 9 (18%) were accepted as short papers. While the former report novel and scientifically rigorous research contributions or relevant industrial case studies, the latter describe innovative and exploratory approaches at an early stage of investigation.

Authors of the best papers from QUATIC 2024 will be invited to submit an extended version of their work to a Special Issue on Quality Assurance in ICT-based Systems to be published in the Elsevier Journal of Systems and Software.

Invited Talks

The conference this year included two outstanding keynote speakers.

The first keynote speaker was Letizia Jaccheri. She is a Professor at the Department of Computer Science of the Norwegian University of Science and Technology, Norway. Jaccheri has been teaching courses in software engineering at various levels and acted as one of the independent directors of Reply S.p.A. From 2013 to 2017, she was the department head for the Computer Science department at NTNU. She is an ACM Distinguished Speaker since 2018. She is the recipient of two gender equality prizes for her work to attract and retain women in computer science. Letizia Jaccheri has a long record of research leadership in interdisciplinary projects with a focus on gender and software engineering. She is involved in several research projects and leads the CA19122 COST Action Gender Balance in Informatics EUGAIN with 155 members from 39 European countries. In her talk titled "For Quality in Software Engineering, We Should All Be Feminists," Letizia provided a clear definition and understanding of Software Engineering and of the role that intersectionality (interconnectedness of social differences, including gender, class, ethnicity, sexuality, and nationality) plays in improving the quality of software products and processes.

The second keynote speaker was Sigrid Eldh. She is a software industry veteran with 40 years in the field. She currently leads research in software engineering and testing at Ericsson in Stockholm (Sweden), where she has worked for 30 years. Sigrid is passionate about software quality and ways to automate software, testing, and validation, while keeping humans in charge. Her key interest is how software, which is everywhere, can aid humanity and be used in a variety of ways to solve challenging problems and improve lives. She received a PhD "On Test Design" from Mälardalen University, where she also works as a senior lecturer. She is also an adjunct professor at Carleton University in Ottawa, Canada. Sigrid served as a chair of many conferences, including ICSE-SEIP, NEXTA, AST, A-MOST, and A-Test; she has been industrial chair for ISSRE and ICST;

and she has served as a reviewer for numerous program committees and journals. She is now the Editor-in-Chief of IEEE Software Magazine. In her talk "How to Achieve System Quality in 10 Easy Steps" she built upon her experience to illustrate how to achieve quality, and provided participants with a clear strategy and a way to champion their own goals and describe what they need to overcome challenges, exploit novel technologies, and consider financial constraints. She relied on a lifetime of transforming and improving systems quality to exemplify the journey, including the best know-how from research and practice in areas from, e.g., quality metrics and automation to AI-augmentation to lead the audience to clear improvements and success.

SEDES Doctoral Symposium

In line with previous editions of the conference, there was a co-located doctoral student symposium chaired by Catia Trubiani (Gran Sasso Science Institute, L'Aquila, Italy) and Alessio Bucaioni (Mälardalen University, Sweden). They received five submissions, which were all accepted for discussion at the symposium after a double-blind review process by the SEDES Program Committee. We are particularly pleased to support this event, as doctoral students represent much of the future of our community.

Poster Track

The conference program was complemented with a special call for poster contributions, with the goal of giving researchers and colleagues the opportunity to discuss their work in progress in the community. The Poster Chairs were Guglielmo De Angelis (IASI-CNR, Rome, Italy) and José Pereira dos Reis (ISCTE-IUL, Lisbon, Portugal). Four posters were accepted for presentation during the event.

As editors of these proceedings, we thank all the people and organizations that directly or indirectly supported this event. A multi-track event such as QUATIC is the result of the coordinated efforts of many people who generously provide their expertise and time. In particular, we should mention the Thematic Track chairs, the SEDES chairs and the Posters chairs, who worked with us in coordinating the calls and review process. Also we are grateful to all members of the respective Program Committees for their thorough and constructive reviews that guaranteed the quality of the QUATIC 2024 conference. Alexandra Mendes has been extremely professional and accurate in following the complex procedures for preparing the proceedings and bridging between Springer and authors. Cristian Augusto has been quickly responsive and proactive in managing the web pages. Stefano Forti and Giovanna Broccia have been our heroes for publicity and social media.

We thank our colleagues at the University of Pisa and at ISTI-CNR for the detailed organizational support required to host the conference, as well as many colleagues at different levels in its organization. Also, special thanks to all the organizations involved in this conference, including supporters at the Vrije Universiteit Amsterdam and the University of Porto. We appreciate the generous support from Registro .it (the Registry of .it Internet domains). We also thank the Comune di Pisa for their prestigious endorsement.

Thanks to the Steering Committee members, and especially to the SC chair Fernando Brito e Abreu, for trusting us to organize the conference and for their guidance and support throughout this process. Thanks to the Comissão Setorial para as Tecnologias da Informação e Comunicações (Cs/03) from the Instituto Português da Qualidade, which has been supporting and promoting QUATIC since its inception.

Finally, a warm and kind mention to all the authors and participants of QUATIC 2024! Organizing the conference and producing these proceedings would have been impossible without their efforts and contributions. Thank you for contributing to the critical mass of researchers that keep QUATIC's history alive for what we expect to be many years to come.

September 2024

Antonia Bertolino
Laura Semini
Patricia Lago
João Pascoal Faria

Organization

Program Committee Chairs

Patricia Lago	Vrije Universiteit Amsterdam, The Netherlands
João Pascoal Faria	University of Porto, Portugal

Organizing Chairs

Antonia Bertolino	ISTI-CNR, Italy
Laura Semini	University of Pisa, Italy

Proceedings Chair

Alexandra Mendes	INESC TEC, FEUP, University of Porto, Portugal

Publicity Chairs

Stefano Forti	University of Pisa, Italy
Giovanna Broccia	ISTI-CNR, Italy

Web Chair

Cristian Augusto	University of Oviedo, Spain

Posters Chairs

Guglielmo De Angelis	IASI-CNR, Italy
José Pereira dos Reis	Iscte-IUL, Portugal

Innovative Strategies for Total Quality in Business Processes and Software (ISTQBPS)

Chairs

Mohamad Kassab	Pennsylvania State University, USA
Phillip LaPlante	Pennsylvania State University, USA

Program Committee

Giuseppe Destefanis	Brunel University London, UK
Isabel Margarido	Portugal
Joanna DeFranco	Pennsylvania State University, USA
Jeffery Voas	National Institute of Standards, USA
Johnny Cardoso Marques	Aeronautics Institute of Technology, Brazil
Maria Istela Cagnin	Universidade Federal de Mato Grosso do Sul, Brazil
Mohammad Hamdaqa	Polytechnique Montreal, Canada
Valdemar V. Graciano Neto	Universidade Federal de Goiás, Brazil
Youakim Badr	Pennsylvania State University, USA

ICT Process Improvement, Organisation, and Governance (ICTPIOG)

Chairs

Gleison Santos	UNIRIO, Brazil
Edna Dias Canedo	UnB, Brazil

Program Committee

Ana Lucila Sandoval Orozco	Universidad Complutense de Madrid, Spain
Ana Paula Chaves Steinmacher	Northern Arizona University, USA
Claude Laporte	École de technologie supérieure, Canada
Claude Tadonki	MINES Paris, France
Fabiana Freitas Mendes	UnB, Brazil
Isabel Sofia Brito	UNINOVA-CTS, Portugal
Jefferson Molléri	Kristiania University College, Norway
Káthia Marçal de Oliveira	Université Polytechnique Hauts-de-France, France

Norsaremah Salleh	International Islamic University Malaysia, Malaysia
Rahul Mohanani	University of Jyväskylä, Finland

Emerging Topics and Technologies in Requirements Engineering (ETTRE)

Chairs

Sallam Abualhaija	University of Luxembourg, Luxembourg
Alessio Ferrari	ISTI-CNR, Italy

Program Committee

Carla Silva	Universidade Federal de Pernambuco, Brazil
Elena Navarro	University of Castilla-La Mancha, Spain
Emilio Insfrán Pelozo	Universitat Politècnica de València, Spain
Farnaz Fotrousi	Mälardalen University, Sweden
Giovanna Broccia	ISTI-CNR, Italy
Henning Femmer	Qualicen GmbH, Germany
Jose Luis de la Vara	University of Castilla-La Mancha, Spain
Juan Pablo Carvallo	Universidad del Azuay, Ecuador
Julian Frattini	Blekinge Institute of Technology, Sweden
Krzysztof Wnuk	BTH, Sweden
Lidia Lopez	Barcelona Supercomputing Center, Spain
Luis Olsina	UNLPam, Argentina
Maya Daneva	University of Twente, Netherlands
Nelly Condori-Fernández	Universidad de Santiago de Compostela, Spain
Oscar Dieste	Universidad Politécnica de Madrid, Spain
Juan Carlos Trujillo	University of Alicante, Spain
Rafael Parizi	Instituto Federal Farroupilha, Brazil
Sabrina Marczak	PUCRS, Brazil
Saad Ezzini	Lancaster University, UK
Sheila Reinehr	PucPR, Brazil
Sotirios Liaskos	York University, Canada

Verification, Validation, and Testing (VVT)

Chairs

Mercedes G. Merayo	Universidad Complutense de Madrid, Spain
Filippo Ricca	University of Genoa, Italy

Program Committee

Alessandro Marchetto	Università di Trento, Italy
Ana Paiva	University of Porto, Portugal
Andreas Ulrich	Siemens AG, Germany
Andrea Stocco	Technical University of Munich, Germany
Antonio Becerra-Terón	Universidad de Almería, Spain
Boni Garcia	Universidad Carlos III de Madrid, Spain
Francesca Lonetti	ISTI-CNR, Italy
Maria José Escalona	University of Seville, Spain
Luis Llana Díaz	Universidad Complutense de Madrid, Spain
Rudolf Ramler	Software Competence Center Hagenberg, Austria
Santiago Matalonga	University of the West of Scotland, UK
Shingo Takada	Keio University, Japan

Quality Aspects of Services and Cloud Computing (QASCC)

Chairs

Vasilios Andrikopoulos	University of Groningen, Netherlands
Elisabetta Di Nitto	Politecnico di Milano, Italy

Program Committee

Daniel Feitosa	University of Groningen, Netherlands
Davide Taibi	University of Oulu, Finland
Jacopo Soldani	University of Pisa, Italy
Justus Bogner	VU Amsterdam, Netherlands
Marco Comuzzi	Ulsan National Institute of Science and Technology, South Korea
Martina De Sanctis	Gran Sasso Science Institute, Italy
Nour Ali	Brunel University London, UK
Sabrina Sicari	University of Insubria, Italy

Quality in Adaptive Software (QAS)

Chairs

Claudia Raibulet	Università degli Studi di Milano-Bicocca, Italy
Karthik Vaidhyanathan	International Institute of Information Technology, Hyderabad, India

Program Committee

Christian Krupitzer	Universität Hohenheim, Germany
Elisa Yumi Nakagawa	University of São Paulo, Brazil
Elsy Kaddoum	IRIT, University of Toulouse, France
Kenji Tei	Tokyo Institute of Technology, Japan
Maria da Loura Casimiro	University of Lisbon, Portugal
Martina De Sanctis	Gran Sasso Science Institute, Italy
Matteo Camilli	Politecnico di Milano, Italy
Mauro Caporuscio	Linnaeus University, Sweden
Mahyar Moghaddam	University of Southern Denmark, Denmark
Roberto Casadei	Università di Bologna, Italy
Sona Ghahremani	Hasso Plattner Institut for Digital Engineering, University of Potsdam, Germany

Human Factors for Quality Software (HFQS)

Chairs

Rodrigo Santos	UNIRIO, Brazil
Xiaofeng Wang	Free University of Bozen-Bolzano, Italy

Program Committee

Daniela Cruzes	NTNU, Norway
Davi Viana	Federal University of Maranhão, Brazil
Emitza Guzman	Vrije Universiteit Amsterdam, The Netherlands
Helena Olsson	Malmö University, Sweden
Jürgen Münch	Reutlingen University, Germany
Jorge Melegati	Free University of Bozen-Bolzano, Italy
Letizia Jaccheri	NTNU, Norway
Mary Sánchez-Gordón	Østfold University College, Norway

Pablo Oliveira Antonino	Fraunhofer IESE, Germany
Sergio Rico	Mid Sweden University, Sweden

Quality Aspects of Empirical Studies (QAES)

Chairs

Marcos Kalinowski	PUC-Rio, Brazil
Roberto Verdecchia	University of Florence, Italy

Program Committee

Amiangshu Bosu	Wayne State University, USA
Beatriz Bernárdez	University of Seville, Spain
Clemente Izuireta	Montana State University, USA
Gregorio Robles	Universidad Rey Juan Carlos, Spain
Guilherme Travassos	Federal University of Rio de Janeiro, Brazil
Marco Kuhrmann	Reutlingen University, Germany
Marco Torchiano	Politecnico di Torino, Italy
Maria Teresa Baldassarre	University of Bari, Italy
Maya Daneva	University of Twente, Netherlands
Michel Chaudron	Chalmers University of Technology and University of Gothenburg, Sweden
Oscar Dieste	Universidad Politécnica de Madrid, Spain
Patricia Matsubara	Federal University of Mato Grosso do Sul, Brazil
Rafael Maiani de Mello	Federal University of Rio de Janeiro, Brazil
Silverio Martínez-Fernández	UPC-BarcelonaTech, Spain
Stefan Wagner	Technical University of Munich, Germany
Valentina Lenarduzzi	University of Oulu, Finland

Quality in the Age of AI (QAI)

Chairs

Grace A. Lewis	Carnegie Mellon Software Engineering Institute, USA
Domenico Bianculli	University of Luxembourg, Luxembourg

Program Committee

Alessio Gambi	AIT, Austria
Donghwan Shin	University of Sheffield, UK
Julien Siebert	Fraunhofer IESE, Germany
Lei Ma	University of Tokyo, Japan and University of Alberta, Canada
Neelofar Neelofar	Monash University, Australia
Rachel Brower-Sinning	Carnegie Mellon Software Engineering Institute, USA
Vincenzo Riccio	University of Udine, Italy
Xiaochen Li	Dalian University of Technology, China
Xiao-Y Zhang	University of Science and Technology Beijing, China
Zhenya Zhang	Kyushu University, Japan

Sustainability as a Quality Concern (SQC)

Chairs

Luis Cruz	Delft Technical University, Netherlands
Maja Hanne Kirkeby	Roskilde University, Denmark

Program Committee

Andreas Schmidt	Saarland University, Germany
Clemens Grelck	Friedrich Schiller University Jena, Germany
Gordana Rakić	University of Novi Sad, Serbia
João Paulo Fernandes	New York University, Abu Dhabi, UAE
João Saraiva	University of Minho, Portugal
June Sallou	TU Delft, Netherlands
Jukka K. Nurminen	University of Helsinki, Finland
Kerstin Eder	University of Bristol, UK
Michael Kirkedal Thomsen	University of Oslo, Norway
Silverio Martínez-Fernández	UPC, Spain

Doctoral Symposium (SEDES)

Chairs

Alessio Bucaioni	Mälardalen University, Sweden
Catia Trubiani	Gran Sasso Science Institute, Italy

Program Committee

Amleto Di Salle	Gran Sasso Science Institute, Italy
Andrea Marin	University of Venice, Italy
Bara Buhnova	Masaryk University, Czech Republic
Barbara Re	University of Camerino, Italy
Breno Miranda	Universidade Federal de Pernambuco, Brazil
Claudio Mandrioli	University of Luxembourg, Luxembourg
Elisa Yumi Nakagawa	University of São Paulo, Brazil
Emilio Incerto	IMT Lucca, Italy
Francesco Tiezzi	University of Florence, Italy
Giovanni Quattrocchi	Politecnico di Milano, Italy
Hugo Brunelliere	IMTA, France
Ioannis Stefanakos	University of York, UK
Jacopo Soldani	University of Pisa, Italy
Jon Ayerdi	University of Mondragon, Spain
Leonardo Mariani	University of Milano-Bicocca, Italy
Luca Berardinelli	JKU Linz, Austria
Michele Tucci	University of L'Aquila, Italy
Miren Illarramendi	University of Mondragon, Spain
Roberto Natella	University of Federico II, Naples, Italy

Additional Reviewers

Joel Castaño Fernández
Samuele Giussani
Ana Lavalle
Aboua Ange Kevin N'Da
Alicia Takaoka

Steering Committee

Fernando Brito e Abreu (Chairman)	Instituto Universitário de Lisboa, Portugal
Alberto Silva	Universidade de Lisboa, Portugal
Ana C. R. Paiva	Universidade do Porto, Portugal
Ana Rosa Cavalli	Institut Polytechnique de Paris/Télécom SudParis, France
Antonia Bertolino	National Research Council (CNR), Italy
Guilherme Horta Travassos	Universidade Federal do Rio de Janeiro, Brazil
João Pascoal Faria	Universidade do Porto, Portugal
Joost Visser	Leiden University, The Netherlands
Mario Piattini Velthuis	University of Castilla – La Mancha, Spain
Martin Shepperd	Brunel University London, UK
Miguel Brito	Universidade do Minho, Portugal
Miguel Goulão	Universidade Nova de Lisboa, Portugal
Patricia Lago	Vrije Universiteit Amsterdam, Netherlands
Paulo Rupino da Cunha	Universidade de Coimbra, Portugal
Ricardo Machado	Universidade do Minho, Portugal
Valentina Lenarduzzi	University of Oulu, Finland
Vasco Amaral	Universidade Nova de Lisboa, Portugal

Contents

Quality in Organisations and Practice

On Security and Privacy

Doctoral Symposium (SEDES)

Quality of AI/ML Based Systems

A Framework for Managing Quality Requirements for Machine Learning-Based Software Systems

Khan Mohammad Habibullah(✉), Gregory Gay, and Jennifer Horkoff

Chalmers and University of Gothenburg, Gothenburg, Sweden
{khan.mohammad.habibullah,jennifer.horkoff}@gu.se, greg@greggay.com

Abstract. Systems containing Machine Learning (ML) are becoming common, and the tasks performed by such systems must meet certain quality thresholds, e.g., desired levels of transparency, safety, and trust. Recent research has identified challenges in defining and measuring the achievement of non-functional requirements (NFRs) for ML systems. Managing NFRs is particularly challenging due to the differing nature and definitions of NFRs for ML systems including non-deterministic behavior, the need to scope over different system components (e.g., data, models, and code), and difficulty in establishing new measurements (e.g., measuring explainability). To address these challenges, we propose a framework for identifying, prioritizing, specifying, and measuring attainment of NFRs for ML systems. We present a preliminary evaluation of the framework via an interview study with practitioners. The framework captures a first step towards enabling practitioners to systematically deliver high-quality ML systems.

Keywords: Quality Framework · NFR Framework · Non-Functional Requirements · Requirements Engineering · Machine Learning

1 Introduction

Software systems have become increasingly dependent on Machine Learning (ML)[1] to perform complex decision-making and prediction tasks based on large quantities of data [42]. Although the inclusion of ML advances the capabilities of such systems, it also makes the systems and their development more complex—introducing challenges related to the impossibility of exhaustive testing [20], non-determinism and potentially unsafe operations [10], unfair or unexplainable results [9], and unintended bias [28].

To ensure successful development, implementation, and operation, ML systems must satisfy certain quality requirements. In the field of requirements engineering, these quality aspects are known as "non-functional requirements" (NFRs). For ML systems, NFRs are arguably the key requirements, as it is challenging to identify functional requirements over ML components [46]. NFRs for

[1] We will use the term "ML systems" to describe such systems.

A. Bertolino et al. (Eds.): QUATIC 2024, CCIS 2178, pp. 3–20, 2024.
https://doi.org/10.1007/978-3-031-70245-7_1

ML systems have recently become a widely investigated topic, with research investigating NFR importance, definition, and measurement [20], scoping over different components (e.g., models, data, and code) [19,20,37,41], and research on specific NFR types such as explainability [11], trust [40], or safety [14].

Past research has uncovered challenges related to the difficulty in defining different types of NFRs (e.g., correctness)—including prioritization, uncertainty, domain dependence, requirement interdependence, lack of documentation, regulations, and lack of awareness among practitioners and customers—as well challenges in measuring attainment of NFRs—including lack of established practices or clear baselines, complex ecosystems, testing costs, and bias [19,20]. As ML systems contain interacting code and non-code components (e.g., models), NFRs may need to be scoped over different aspects of the system [19,20,37,41]. Further, the trade-offs between different NFRs may change with their shifting definitions and are not yet well-understood [3,19,20,25]. Practitioners agree that NFR attainment is a major contributor to the success of ML systems, but they lack knowledge, processes, and tools to help define and measure NFRs for ML systems [3,20,41,45].

Towards addressing these challenges, we propose a *framework* to help practitioners manage NFRs for ML systems. This framework, consisting of five steps, guides NFR specification from a high level—identifying, prioritizing, defining, scoping, and balancing trade-offs between *NFR types* (e.g., accuracy)—to template-based specification of low-level individual *specific NFRs* (e.g., "The lane identification model must have an accuracy of 99.99%").

Our framework could enable practitioners (e.g., ML system developers, architects, product owners, and testers) and researchers to systematically deliver high-quality ML systems by offering step-by-step guidance for defining, prioritizing, scoping, measuring, and specifying NFR types and specific NFRs during the development process. Although such a framework could be useful for NFR management in any type of system, the challenges specific to ML systems indicate that this type of guidance and management is particularly needed, and the framework has been designed with these ML system challenges in mind.

While describing our proposed framework, we use autonomous perception systems—part of driving automation systems (DAS)—as a running example [22]. Autonomous perception systems use ML, trained on complex sensor data, to identify and analyze objects within a vehicle's environment.The framework has undergone a preliminary evaluation through four interviews with five practitioners. This evaluation demonstrates the potential of this framework, and also provides feedback for future revisions.

2 Running Example

Driving automation systems (DAS)—including both autonomous driving and advanced driver assistance systems—are systems designed to augment or automate aspects of vehicle operation. Autonomous perception systems (APS)—an important element of the DAS ecosystem—are ML systems that identify and

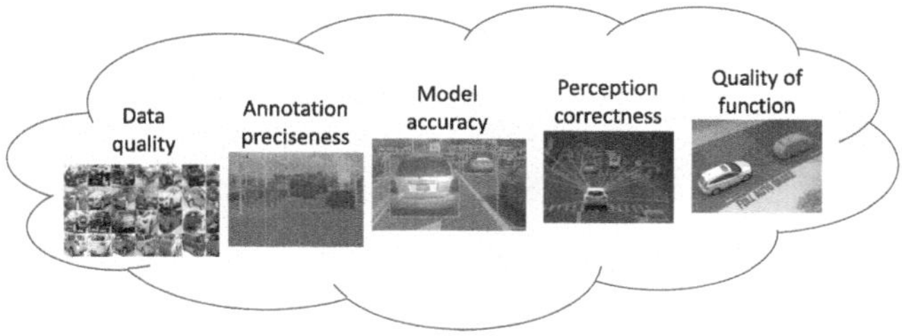

Fig. 1. Elements contributing to the quality of an APS, from [22].

analyze objects in a vehicle's environment based on sensor input. Such systems combine ML models with conventional signal processing [33].

The quality of an APS is dependent on—and must be specified at—multiple scopes within the overall system. As illustrated in Fig. 1, APS quality is determined by the quality of data collected from the operational design domain, the object detection model, functional code, and other aspects of the system.

Specifying NFRs for an APS is challenging due to the complexity of perception tasks, a dynamic environment where conditions change rapidly, uncertainty and ambiguity inherent in sensor data, real-time data processing, compliance with regulatory standards and guidelines, and ethical considerations [34].

An APS must satisfy certain NFRs (e.g., related to accuracy, safety, and performance). However, it is difficult to determine what NFR types are the most important and how to measure their attainment. Additionally, the meaning of certain NFR types needs to be better understood, and that meaning must be adapted to different scopes, as suggested in Fig. 1. For example, a practitioner may need to define broadly what "performance" means for an APS at the system level, as well as what "performance" means in regards to a model or a code component[2]. With this definition, it becomes easier to decide which measurements should be employed at each scope to assess attainment of performance requirements, or how performance should be balanced against other NFR types such as safety. Past research has shown that practitioners working in the APS domain currently lack a structured process for managing NFRs [22]. As such, we employ APS as a representative of ML systems that could benefit from our framework.

3 NFR Management Framework

Our proposed NFR management framework consists of five steps—each consisting of one or more concrete tasks—presented in Fig. 2. Although the steps are presented in an ordered sequence, practitioners can jump between steps and tasks, as it is expected that NFR identification, definition, scoping, trade-off, measurement, and specification will be iterative in nature.

[2] When discussing models, the term "performance" often is a synonym for accuracy, while for code, "performance" generally refers to execution time.

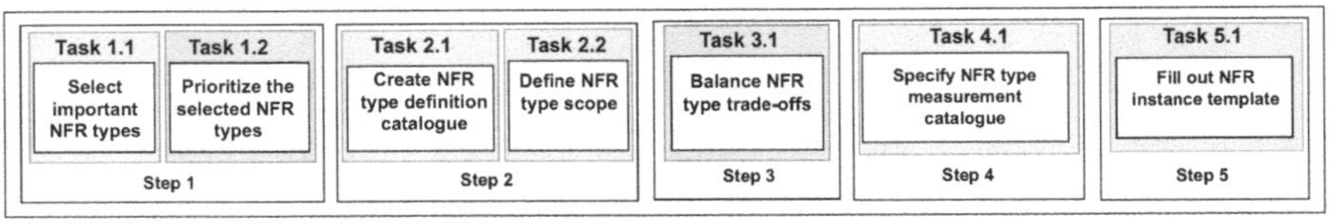

Fig. 2. Overview of the framework. Tasks in blue are performed on NFR types, tasks in red compare NFR types, and tasks in green are performed on specific NFR instances (Color figure online)

Table 1. Mapping between NFR challenges for ML systems and our framework.

Challenge	Framework Aspect
New NFR types are needed [20,24,41]	Task 1.1
NFR types change in priority for systems with or without ML [19,20]	Task 1.2
NFR type definitions need to be adjusted [20,41]	Task 2.1
NFRs type definitions need to be scoped over components [19,20,41]	Task 2.2
Trade-offs between NFR types are important and unclear [3,20,25]	Step 3
Difficulty measuring attainment of different types of NFRs [20]	Step 4
Lack of documentation [20]	Step 5
Lack of management guidance, practices, and knowledge [20,41]	All
Lack of management solutions (e.g., frameworks or tools) [3,20,45]	All

We discuss NFR management at two levels. Steps 1–4 of the framework relate to broad high-level *types* of NFRs (e.g., "performance"). Step 5 of the framework relate to *specific instances* of those types (e.g., "PE003: the object detection function should detect objects defined in the operational design domain within 0.001 s.").

We summarize how the elements of the framework address identified challenges in NFR management in Table 1. For example, "new" NFR types like fairness can be discovered and considered as part of Task 1.1—where important NFR types are identified—with the help of a list of potentially relevant NFRs.

3.1 Step 1: Select and Prioritize NFR Types

Task 1.1: Select Important NFR Types: Practitioners should first select the subset of NFR types that are potentially important for their system. By selecting important NFR types, practitioners can ensure research allocation (time, effort, and budget) more effectively, mitigate risks and prevent potential issues that could arise later, and make informed design decisions that prioritize aspects of system architecture, infrastructure, and implementation that contribute most significantly to meeting performance objectives. The importance of a particular NFR type may depend on the context or domain of the system under development. As a starting point, a set of important NFR types generally important for ML systems was identified in previous work [20]—a subset are listed in Table 2. This list must, however, be adapted to a specific domain or ML system (e.g., by discarding irrelevant NFR types or adding additional types).

Table 2. Example definitions of NFR types relevant for ML systems as identified and defined by Habibullah et al. [19,21]. Here we include only those NFR types that may be important for an APS system (12/35 identified NFR types).

NFRs	Definition
Accuracy	The number of correctly predicted data points out of all the data points of ML systems
Explainability	The extent to which the internal mechanics of ML-enabled system can be explained in human terms
Fairness	The ability of a ML system to operate in a fair and unbiased manner
Integrity	The ability of the ML system to ensure that data is real, accurate and safeguarded from unauthorised modification
Interpretability	The extraction of relevant knowledge from a model concerning relationships in the data or learned by the model
Performance	The ability of a ML system to perform actions within defined time or throughput bounds
Privacy	An ML model or ML system is private if an observer examining the output is not able to determine whether a specific information was used in the computation
Reliability	The probability of the ML system performing without failure for a specific number of uses or amount of time.
Safety	The absence of failures or conditions that render a system dangerous.
Security	Security measures ensure a ML system's safety against malicious use or sabotage
Transparency	The extent to which a human user can infer why the ML system made a particular decision or produced a particular externally-visible behaviour
Usability	How effectively users can learn and use an ML system
...	....

Running Example: In applying Task 1.1 for an APS, practitioners may identify NFR types such as accuracy, explainability, performance, reliability, safety, security, and privacy as important (as suggested in recent research [22]). For example, as a safety-critical system, understanding how the APS reaches a decision is critical, and transparency makes it easier to understand how erroneous decisions are made. Real-time performance can also be critical in a vehicle, as this ensures the system reacts swiftly to changing environmental situations. Ensuring security and privacy ensures that the APS is guarded against adversarial attacks, data manipulation, or data leaks.

Task 1.2: Prioritize the Selected NFR Types: The initial list of selected NFR types may be too large to practically manage. It is very difficult to prioritize NFR types at a general level, as significance may vary from system to system. Therefore, a practitioner may want to prioritize the NFR types based on the context of the ML system to be developed. We first recommend that practitioners rank the identified NFR types (e.g., very important, important, less important), then use that ranking to determine where to prioritize efforts. Practitioners can prioritize in an ad-hoc way, discussing among themselves and coming to understand the meaning and purpose of the NFR types, or they can use one or more established RE prioritization techniques (e.g., [2]).

Running Example: For an APS, accuracy is likely to be given the highest priority because it is essential for the system to function correctly. Safety is also likely to get high priority, as there is a risk of harm to drivers when hazards occur.

The practitioners might also prioritize performance, as the system needs to make quick decisions to avoid obstacles or accidents.

3.2 Step 2: Define NFR Types and Identify NFR Type Scope

Task 2.1: Create NFR Type Definition Catalogue: After identifying important NFR types for the ML system to be developed, we recommend that practitioners create a definition catalogue by adapting the general definitions of these NFRs (e.g., from Table 2) to their particular system. The adjustment is needed as the definition of an NFR type may vary depending on context. The resulting catalogue helps to establish a clear and shared understanding of the NFRs among the stakeholders working on a particular system, facilitate the identification and management of potential quality issues, and enable more effective decision-making and risk management [43,47].

Table 3. Definitions of important NFR Types for autonomous perception system.

NFRs	Definition
Accuracy	The ability to precisely and correctly identify objects defined in the Operational Design Domain
Reliability	The system consistently identify objects correctly and without sudden errors, ensuring the system can react appropriately to the environment
Safety	Objects are accurately identified and located—preventing collisions, accidents, and other potential hazards—even in the presence of poor visibility, occlusions, and unexpected object behaviors

Table 4. Examples of NFR scoping for an APS.

NFR	System Element the NFR Type Can be Defined Over				
	Training Data	ML Pipeline	ML Model	Results	Whole System
Accuracy	✖	✔	✔	✔	✔
Explainability	✖	✔	✔	✔	✔
Integrity	✔	✔	✔	✔	✔
Performance	✔	✔	✔	✔	✔
Reliability	✔	✔	✔	✔	✔
Safety	✔	✔	✔	✔	✔

Running Example: Example definitions for an APS are presented in Table 3.

Task 2.2: Scope NFR Types over Different Elements of ML Systems: A ML system is typically not a monolith, but different types of components working together to deliver functionality [37]. Some components relate directly to ML, while others do not. Therefore, the definitions of NFR types may differ between components or groups of components. Past research suggests one form of scoping—that NFRs could be specified over datasets, models, ML pipelines used to train models, results of executing those models, and the system code [19].

Scoping is important, as the definition, importance, and measurement of NFR types may differ depending on the components considered. For example, "usability" of a ML pipeline refers to how difficult it is to use that pipeline to train a model, "usability" of a model refers to how difficult it is to extract decisions from the model, and "usability" of results refers to how effectively users can understand and apply the model output for practical purpose.

We envision Tasks 2.1 and 2.2 to be highly iterative. Practitioners need to understand how (and which) NFRs apply to different scopes and may need to refine NFR type definitions at each scopes.

Running Example: An example of a possible scoping of NFR types for an APS is presented in Table 4. For example, when specifying accuracy, one might have requirements on the accuracy of a particular model (e.g., ability to detect particular types of objects). However, one might also specify NFRs on the meta-accuracy of the ML pipeline—that is, *any* model produced by the pipeline must meet a minimal level of accuracy. The system may have further requirements on the accuracy of broader functions that make use of these models.

Similarly, reliability at the system level refers to the ability of the code to operate correctly and without crashing, while at the training data level, this may be reinterpreted to limit the amount of corrupt or noisy data. In different scopes, reliability may refer to the ML pipeline's ability to produce models or the model's ability to produce a prediction on-demand without error. The other rows of Table 4 have similar explanations.

Table 5. Examples of NFR type trade-offs for APS Systems. The cited papers offer more discussion on the potential trade-offs.

Conflicting NFR Types	APS Example
Accuracy, Interpretability [7]	Some model architectures, e.g., deep convolutional neural networks, provide high accuracy for image recognition, but provide limited insight into how predictions are reached
Accuracy, Privacy [1]	Certain data (e.g., GPS or visual data) could enhance the accuracy of a model's predictions. However, this data is also potentially sensitive—violating the privacy of users or individuals in the APS' environment. Protecting privacy may require masking or removing sensitive information from the training data, which could negatively impact the model's accuracy
Safety, Performance [31]	Ensuring APS safety may require adding additional safeguards or constraints that could negatively impact the performance. For example, an ensemble of models may collectively produce safer verdicts than a single model, but this requires asking all models for predictions and then calculating a combined verdict

3.3 Step 3: Balance NFR Type Trade-Offs

Practitioners may observe trade-offs among different NFR types—e.g., performance, usability, and security often conflict. It is also important to note that the nature and criticality of these trade-offs may differ based on the scope within the system, or the context and domain of the system under development. For example, trade-offs between accuracy and interpretability at the ML model level may have a different weight and impact than trade-offs between the two at the result-level.

In cases where a trade-off exists, practitioners need to find a balance between the conflicting NFR types. Trade-offs can be considered in an ad-hoc way, or via more structured methods (e.g., [36]). The emphasis here is to make such trade-offs explicit and raise them for discussion and eventual resolution.

Running Example: Some examples of trade-offs among different NFR types for an APS are presented in Table 5. An appropriate balance must be found, potentially guided by standards like ISO 26262 in the automotive industry [26].

3.4 Step 4: Specify NFR Measurement Catalogue

At this stage, we suggest practitioners adapt a measurement catalogue for the selected NFR types. In future work, we aim to provide an example NFR measurement catalogue for the NFR types identified in our previous study [23]. A partial excerpt of such a catalogue is shown in the first three columns of Table 6. For each NFR type, the catalogue should record all measurements—including equations—that will be used to assess the satisfaction of each of the specific NFRs of each type at each scope in the system. Considering the scope of NFR measurement is important (see Task 2.2), as our prior work found that definition and measurement of NFR types varies depending on the scope [18].

Table 6. Example excerpt from a NFR measurement catalogue for an APS.

NFR Type	Measurement	Equation	APS Example Application
Accuracy	F-Score	$\frac{2*(Precision*Recall)}{(Precision+Recall)}$	The F-Score is the harmonic mean of a system's precision and recall, and is commonly used to assess the accuracy of an APS (e.g., when detecting pedestrians)
Reliability	Mean Time Between Failures (MTBF)	$\frac{Uptime}{Num.Failures}$	MTBF can be used to define how often an APS is allowed to fail in practice. If MTBF rises above the defined threshold, improvements must be made

Having a clear and comprehensive measurement catalogue is crucial, as it provides a systematic method to identify how to assess the attainment of each NFR. It enables identification of targets to show that an NFR is attained. It also enables detection of measurement challenges early in the development process, provides a means to group related NFRs, and enables proactive management and monitoring of NFR attainment and overall system quality.

Running Example: Table 6 illustrates an excerpt from an NFR measurement catalogue for an APS.

3.5 Step 5: Specify NFRs Using Template

In the final step, practitioners fill out a template as part of the process of specifying the low-level individual NFRs of the types selected and defined in the previous steps. Each NFR type will have many specific NFRs that must be fulfilled to ensure the overall quality is upheld. It is important that NFRs have documentation that is stable, unambiguous, and complete, so that stakeholders can form a shared understanding of the NFR and ensure that the NFR is satisfied. A template can help ensure the attainment of this goal, facilitating discussion, reducing development time, cost, and effort, and enabling verification [16].

Past research has found that the practitioners need to capture a context-aware definition of the NFR, importance (and justification for the importance), system scope, measurement method, measurement target, and trade-offs with other specific NFRs. We capture these elements in a template—presented in Table 7—inspired by existing templates such as the one offered by Volere [35].

Table 7. Template for specifying individual NFRs.

Requirement ID: A unique id.
Requirement Type: NFR Type (e.g., performance)
Definition: A context-adapted definition of the specific NFR type
Description: The primary text describing the requirement
Rationale: A justification of the requiremen.
Importance Level: The overall importance of this specific NFR for the system (e.g., very important, important, not important.
System Scope: System elements the specified NFR is relevant to
Measurement: The measurement used to assess attainment of this NFR
Measurement Target: The measurement threshold required to satisfy this NFR
Trade-Offs: IDs of other specific NFRs that conflict with this specific NFR, and explanation of the conflict
Source: Person, regulation, document, etc. that suggested the requirement
Responsible: Person responsible for managing this requirement

Table 8. An example of a specific accuracy NFR for an APS.

Requirement ID: AC001	
Requirement Type: Accuracy	
Definition: Accuracy for object detection in an autonomous perception system refers to ability to precisely and correctly identify objects defined in the Operational Design Domain	
Description: The lane identification model shall detect lane divisions on all road types with high accuracy	
Rationale: If the perception system is not accurate, it may make mistakes or incorrect decisions that could have serious consequences (e.g., accidents)	
Importance Level: Very Important	
System Scope: ML model	
Measurement: F-Score	
Measurement Target: 99.99999%	
Trade-Offs: To protect passenger privacy, the system employ object detection models that blur or anonymize faces and license plates, sacrificing some detection accuracy (requirement PR013)	
Source: Tom Robertsson (product owner)	
Responsible: Tom Robertsson (product owner)	

Running Example: Table 8 offers an example of a specific accuracy NFR for the lane detection model that is part of the overall object detection functionality of an APS. In reality, many similar accuracy requirements would need to be captured for different aspects of the system functionality and for different scopes.

4 Preliminary Evaluation

4.1 Methodology

To gain initial feedback on the framework, we conducted a qualitative interview study. We chose interviewees who had experience with NFRs and were currently working with ML in industry.

Sampling: The sampling method was a mix of convenience and purposive sampling. We contacted people in the industry who have requirements engineering and ML experience, and then asked them if they knew any qualified candidates we could contact.

Data Collection: We interviewed five practitioners over four interviews. These practitioners have 6–25 years of experience working with RE and ML. Among the five, three are from the automotive domain, one from the telecommunications and networking domain, and another from the smart home monitoring domain. Table 9 presents demographic information of the interviewees. Although the numbers of interviewees is small, this is a preliminary evaluation of our proposed framework. We believe that the background and experience of the interviewees will be valuable for refining the framework before conducting a more thorough evaluation.

The interviews lasted approximately 60 min, and were conducted between September and October 2023 via Microsoft Teams. We recorded interviews with the permission of the interviewees, then transcribed and anonymized for further analysis. During this interview, we first presented the framework steps, then asked about the utility of the overall framework, as well as each step. We asked if any elements should be removed, added, or adjusted. The interviews were semi-structured, with the ability to ask follow-up questions[3].

Data Analysis: The collected data was qualitative in nature. We applied a mixed form of thematic analysis, where we started with high-level codes based on our interview questions, then also extracted and refined additional inductive codes from the transcripts. Codes were then grouped into themes and sub-themes. The first author did the initial coding, then all codes were checked and discussed by all authors. Based on this thematic analysis, we extracted impressions and insights about the framework, as well as suggestions for future improvements to the framework.

Table 9. Interviewees' Demographic Information

ID	Field of Work	Role	Exp. (Years)	ML Exp.	NFR Exp.	Responsibilities
I1	Smart home monitoring	Software developer	6	Yes	Yes	Development and data analysis
I2	Automotive	Researcher and senior system safety engineer	8	Yes	Yes	Requirements specifications, safety functions analysis, system design
I3	Automotive	Researcher and chief safety engineer	25	Yes	Yes	Responsible for safety compliance, Fulfill stakeholder requirements by ensuring ISO 26262 standard, SOTIF standard, and cybersecurity and quality standards
I4	Automotive	Researcher and requirements engineer	14	Yes	Yes	Work with system level requirements, ensure safety compliance
I5	Telecomm-unications	Software engineer and data analyst	8	Yes	Yes	Anomaly detection, data analysis, software development

4.2 Impressions and Insights

Overall, the feedback was positive, with all interviewees suggesting the need for such a framework. The interviewees did not suggest that any steps or tasks be removed. However, they did make several observations about the individual

[3] The interview guide and presentation to the interviewees can be found at https://doi.org/10.7910/DVN/QUPD8D. Due to the sensitive nature of the collected practitioner data from the interviews, we can not share the full interview transcripts.

steps and tasks, as well as the framework as a whole. We indicate the number of interviewees supporting a particular point in parentheses, e.g., (2).

Interviewees had feedback on when the framework would be useful. Two interviewees (2) stated that our framework was potentially very useful at early stages of development—particularly tasks centered around NFR types. Furthermore, interviewees (2) suggested that the framework would be very useful for a new system or when performing a large overhaul, but that it may be less useful as part of continuous evolution.

Interviewees (2) pointed out that the framework could be used to identify important NFR types for an ML system, especially having been provided a pre-existing list of NFRs that are commonly important for ML systems. In addition, interviewees noted that creating a definition catalog could facilitate understanding of the contextual meaning and purpose of an NFR type (2), and that having a definition catalogue could improve shared understanding and facilitate discussion among stakeholders (3).

In terms of prioritization, interviewees (2) pointed out that this step should be iterative and repeated at different times and with different degrees of thoroughness. Scoping was identified as helping in prioritizing as well as identifying and discussing trade-offs (2).

Interviewees (3) had comments on measurements, pointing out that some NFR types may not be critical enough or too difficult to measure. They also noted that some measurements and targets could be extracted from standards. Finally, interviewees (2) suggested that the template was useful as a means of documenting specific NFRs. However, they also noted that it would be too much work to fill out the template for all NFRs.

4.3 Potential Future Improvements

Interviewees also pointed out many ways in which the framework can be improved. Interviewees (3) suggested that the framework should also account for stakeholder roles, it should document stakeholder roles more explicitly and at many steps as possible to facilitate discussion and negotiation.

Other interviews made suggestions concerning support for NFR breakdown and traceability. One interviewee stated that the framework should consider requirements breakdown and layering more explicitly (e.g., logical level, system level, feature level), possibly as part of—or in addition to—scoping. Interviewees (2) added that the framework should enable explicit traceability between NFR types and specific NFRs to ensure decisions made at the type level are reflected at the instance level.

In terms of process, interviewees (2) stressed that the framework must fit into their process (e.g., it may need to be adapted to work within a specific agile process). In addition, an interviewee mentioned that the framework should keep historical records of decisions (e.g., trade-offs and prioritization).

Interviewees (3) expressed that it is difficult and time consuming to fill out the template for every requirement, and we should identify when this type of documentation is needed. We should explore ways to make filling out the template easier, like identifying optional fields, populating the framework with default values, and providing examples to guide and ease application. Interviewees (2) suggested the inclusion of a default definition catalogue (including defaults for different scopes). As some scopes may not be applied to some systems, the framework must be flexible enough to function without fully scoping all NFR types. Another interviewee said that the framework could provide examples of trade-offs among NFR types. Regarding default values and measurements, interviewees (2) suggested that the framework include an extensive measurement catalogue and guidance on the most common measurements and measurement targets. Further interviewees (3) pointed out that standards (e.g., ISO 26262 [26]) could provide template defaults and guidance for certain domains, and one interviewee suggested that earlier steps regarding NFR types could populate generic default templates for those types.

Our future work includes framework tooling. An interviewee mentioned that a tool based on our framework could offer suggestions to the users of potentially incomplete or missed aspects (e.g., trade-offs, measurements, template fields), providing a type of quality or completeness check. In addition, we will explore how our proposed framework will facilitate compliance with the EU AI Act [13].

Finally, currently, we have focused on trade-offs amongst NFR types, but one interviewee rightly points out that the framework should also be able to identify potential trade-offs at the instance level and inform responsible stakeholders. We will enhance our proposed framework by incorporating the suggested improvements from the interviewees, including a detailed breakdown of NFRs, better traceability between NFR types and specific NFRs, managing historical records of decisions, flexible scoping options, and easier implementation processes.

4.4 Threats to Validity

External Validity: We used a mixture of purposive and convenience sampling as the interviews required a certain set of expertise. The number of interview participants may impact the reliability of the evaluation. In addition, three out of five interviewees were from the automotive domain. However, we selected interviewees based on deep knowledge of both NFRs and ML, and their suggestions are applicable to other domains. Importantly, the goal of this evaluation is simply to gain preliminary feedback. We plan to conduct a comprehensive assessment in the future, after incorporating some of the recommendations into the framework. Although the focus of the framework has been on ML systems, elements of the framework could be generally useful to manage NFRs for all types of systems. However, by considering ML-specific definitions, scopes, and measurements, we focus this work on the particular challenges of NFR handling in ML systems.

Internal Validity: In addition, while the evaluation analysis relies on thematic coding, potential validity threats due to the need for interpretation were addressed by having all authors review and discuss the codes.

5 Related Work

In this section, we summarize related work on NFRs, and compare the framework presented in this work to other NFR management frameworks.

NFRs: NFRs play a critical and important role in ensuring system quality [30]. However, consistent and clear approaches to eliciting, documenting, and validating NFRs are not fully established [15]. There is a lack of agreement among researchers on when and how NFRs should be considered and integrated into the overall RE process [4,12]. Stakeholders are sometimes unaware of NFRs, because of lacking background knowledge of the domain [17].

Scope of NFRs over ML Systems: ML aspects of a system are part of a larger software system, which may include components for configuration, data collection, feature extraction, analysis tools, monitoring, and glue code [37]. In addition, an interview study with four data scientists noted the increasing complexity of ML-based development processes, which require the effective use of large data sets and a reliance on NFRs and suggested that requirements engineering for ML should focus on requirements over data along with requirements for the system [45]. As part of a systematic mapping study, Habibullah et al. identified clusters of NFRs for ML systems based on shared characteristics and scoped NFRs over datasets, ML pipelines, models, results, and system code [19].

Towards Solutions for Managing NFRs for ML Systems: Recent research has reported several aspects that are required to address to manage NFRs for ML systems. The importance of identifying and extracting relevant NFRs for ML systems is reported in a survey study [39]. With an aim at constructing a quality model for ML systems, Siebert et al. emphasized the need for NFR identification, scoping, and measurement [41]. Two different systematic mapping studies pointed out the need for further research and necessity of RE techniques for managing NFRs for ML systems [3,44].

Towards establishing solutions for managing NFRs, standards define necessary quality properties of the software and its components. For example, ISO/IEC 25010 defines quality models for software and systems [27]. However, these quality models cannot be applied directly to ML systems due to the challenges identified previously (e.g., definition, scoping, and measurement differences from traditional systems) [41]. While several frameworks exists that focus on different aspects of RE for ML systems (e.g., Holistic DevOps [8], Ethics-Aware SE for analyzing ethical requirements [5], and RE4ML for requirements elicitation for ML systems [32]), few comprehensive frameworks exists for managing NFRs for ML systems.

Table 10. Comparison of select NFR frameworks to our proposed framework.

Framework	Focus	Identification	Prioritization	Definition Catalogue	Scope	Trade-Offs	Measurement Catalogue	Template and/or Documentation
[12]	Non-ML	✔	✔	✖	✖	✔	✖	✖
[38]	Non-ML	✔	✖	✖	✖	✔	✖	✔
[41]	ML	✔	✖	✖	✔	✖	✔	✔
[29]	ML	✔	✔	✔	✖	✖	✖	✖
[6]	ML	✔	✖	✖	✖	✖	✖	✔
Our Framework	ML	✔	✔	✔	✔	✔	✔	✔

We compare our framework with other NFR-related frameworks proposed from the literature in Table 10, where ✔ indicates that the framework provides capabilities or guidelines for managing the aspect specified in that column. A ✖ indicates that the study either did not discuss the activity or mentioned it only in passing, and the framework does not provide specific guidance on that aspect.

NFR frameworks have been proposed for traditional systems, including one centered around acquiring domain knowledge, identifying and decomposing NFRs, identifying operationalizations for meeting NFRs in the system, dealing with ambiguities, trade-offs, priorities, and inter-dependencies among NFRs and operationalizations, supporting decisions with rationale, and evaluating decision impact [12]. A framework has also been proposed for managing NFRs in agile development, supporting elicitation, analysis, documentation, and validation [38].

For ML systems, a quality model construction process has been proposed that includes defining a quality meta-model, defining use case and application context, identifying relevant ML quality requirements, identifying relevant entities of an ML system, identifying reference elements of an ML quality model, and instantiating the quality model for the use cases [41]. An approach has also been proposed to build quality models that focuses on definition and ordering of "characteristics" (NFRs) for AI systems [29]. In addition, templates exist for documenting NFRs for ML systems [6].

Although these frameworks overlap with ours in certain aspects, illustrated in Table 10, to our knowledge, our framework is the first to cover a wide range of steps and tasks in the management of NFRs for ML systems, addressing many of the ML system challenges identified in past studies (e.g., [3,20,22,45]).

6 Conclusion

We have proposed a framework for managing NFRs for ML systems. This framework can be used—starting from the early stages of a project—to define, scope, and prioritize the NFR types that are important to the system-under-development. It can be used to identify measurements to ensure specific NFRs of those types are satisfied to the necessary degree. Finally, the framework offers templates to specify and document individual NFRs of those types.

We conducted semi-structured interviews to offer feedback on our proposed framework. All of the participants stated that our proposed framework could be useful in their practice, and suggested how it could improve the quality of the systems they develop. However, the interviewees also recommended potential improvements. The current framework can be considered as the first iteration of a broader design science process. In future work, we will incorporate suggestions from the interviewees (e.g., explicit representation of stakeholders, default definitions and measurements, and clarifying when the template should be used).

Acknowledgement. This research is supported by a Swedish Research Council (VR) Project: Non-Functional Requirements for Machine Learning: Facilitating Continuous Quality Awareness (iNFoRM).

References

1. Abbasi, W., Mori, P., Saracino, A., Frascolla, V.: Privacy vs accuracy trade-off in privacy aware face recognition in smart systems. In: 2022 IEEE Symposium on Computers and Communications (ISCC), pp. 1–8. IEEE (2022)
2. Achimugu, P., Selamat, A., Ibrahim, R., Mahrin, M.N.: A systematic literature review of software requirements prioritization research. Inf. Softw. Technol. **56**(6), 568–585 (2014)
3. Ahmad, K., Abdelrazek, M., Arora, C., Bano, M., Grundy, J.: Requirements engineering for artificial intelligence systems: a systematic mapping study. Inf. Softw. Technol. **158**, 107176 (2023)
4. Ameller, D., et al.: Dealing with non-functional requirements in model-driven development: a survey. IEEE Trans. Softw. Eng. (2019)
5. Aydemir, F.B., Dalpiaz, F.: A roadmap for ethics-aware software engineering. In: Proceedings of the International Workshop on Software Fairness, pp. 15–21 (2018)
6. Bajraktari, E., Krause, T., Kücherer, C.: Documentation of non-functional requirements for systems with machine learning components. In: 2024 REFSQ Workshops (2024)
7. Baryannis, G., Dani, S., Antoniou, G.: Predicting supply chain risks using machine learning: the trade-off between performance and interpretability. Futur. Gener. Comput. Syst. **101**, 993–1004 (2019)
8. Bosch, J., Olsson, H.H., Crnkovic, I.: It takes three to tango: requirement, outcome/data, and AI driven development. In: SiBW 2018, Software-intensive Business: Start-ups, Ecosystems and Platforms, Espoo, Finland, 3 December 2018, pp. 177–192. CEUR-WS. org (2018)
9. Burkart, N., Huber, M.F.: A survey on the explainability of supervised machine learning. J. Artif. Intell. Res. **70**, 245–317 (2021)
10. Challen, R., Denny, J., Pitt, M., Gompels, L., Edwards, T., Tsaneva-Atanasova, K.: Artificial intelligence, bias and clinical safety. BMJ Qual. Saf. **28**(3), 231–237 (2019)
11. Chazette, L., Brunotte, W., Speith, T.: Explainable software systems: from requirements analysis to system evaluation. Requirements Eng. 1–31 (2022)
12. Chung, L., Nixon, B.A., Yu, E., Mylopoulos, J.: Non-functional Requirements in Software Engineering, vol. 5. Springer, Heidelberg (2012)

13. European Commission, Directorate-General for Communications Networks, Content and Technology: EUR-Lex - 52021PC0206 - EN - EUR-Lex. CNECT (2021). https://eur-lex.europa.eu/legal-content/EN/TXT/?uri=CELEX:52021PC0206
14. Faria, J.M.: Machine learning safety: an overview. In: Proceedings of the 26th Safety-Critical Systems Symposium, York, UK, pp. 6–8 (2018)
15. Glinz, M.: On non-functional requirements. In: 15th IEEE International requirements engineering Conference (RE 2007), pp. 21–26. IEEE (2007)
16. Gondal, M.A., Qureshi, N.A., Mukhtar, H., Ahmed, H.F.: An engineering approach to integrate non-functional requirements (NFR) to achieve high quality software process. In: ICEIS (2), pp. 377–384 (2020)
17. Gruber, K., Huemer, J., Zimmermann, A., Maschotta, R.: Integrated description of functional and non-functional requirements for automotive systems design using SysML. In: 2017 7th IEEE International Conference on System Engineering and Technology (ICSET), pp. 27–31. IEEE (2017)
18. Habibullah, K.M., Diaz, J.G., Gay, G., Horkoff, J.: Scoping of non-functional requirements for machine learning systems. In: 2024 IEEE 32nd International Requirements Engineering Conference (RE). IEEE (2024)
19. Habibullah, K.M., Gay, G., Horkoff, J.: Non-functional requirements for machine learning: an exploration of system scope and interest. In: SE4RAI Workshop, 44th International Conference on Software Engineering (ICSE 2022) (2022)
20. Habibullah, K.M., Gay, G., Horkoff, J.: Non-functional requirements for machine learning: understanding current use and challenges among practitioners. Requirements Eng. **28**(2), 283–316 (2023)
21. Habibullah, K.M., et al.: Requirements engineering for automotive perception systems: an interview study. In: Ferrari, A., Penzenstadler, B. (eds.) REFSQ 2023. LNCS, vol. 13975, pp. 189–205. Springer, Cham (2023). https://doi.org/10.1007/978-3-031-29786-1_13
22. Habibullah, K.M., et al.: Requirements and software engineering for automotive perception systems: an interview study. Requirements Eng. 1–24 (2024)
23. Habibullah, K.M., Horkoff, J.: Non-functional requirements for machine learning: understanding current use and challenges in industry. In: 2021 IEEE 29th International Requirements Engineering Conference (RE), pp. 13–23. IEEE (2021)
24. Horkoff, J.: Non-functional requirements for machine learning: challenges and new directions. In: 2019 IEEE 27th International Requirements Engineering Conference (RE), pp. 386–391. IEEE (2019)
25. Hort, M.: Investigating trade-offs for fair machine learning systems. Ph.D. thesis, UCL (University College London) (2023)
26. ISO: Road vehicles – Functional safety (2011)
27. ISO/IEC25010: Systems and software engineering systems and software quality requirements and evaluation (square) (2023)
28. Kamishima, T., Akaho, S., Sakuma, J.: Fairness-aware learning through regularization approach. In: 2011 IEEE 11th International Conference on Data Mining Workshops, pp. 643–650. IEEE (2011)
29. Kharchenko, V., Fesenko, H., Illiashenko, O.: Quality models for artificial intelligence systems: characteristic-based approach, development and application. Sensors **22**(13), 4865 (2022)
30. Kopczyńska, S., Ochodek, M., Nawrocki, J.: On importance of non-functional requirements in agile software projects—a survey. In: Jarzabek, S., Poniszewska-Marańda, A., Madeyski, L. (eds.) Integrating Research and Practice in Software Engineering. SCI, vol. 851, pp. 145–158. Springer, Cham (2020). https://doi.org/10.1007/978-3-030-26574-8_11

31. Mairiza, D., Zowghi, D.: Constructing a catalogue of conflicts among non-functional requirements. In: Maciaszek, L.A., Loucopoulos, P. (eds.) ENASE 2010. CCIS, vol. 230, pp. 31–44. Springer, Heidelberg (2011). https://doi.org/10.1007/978-3-642-23391-3_3
32. Nalchigar, S., Yu, E., Keshavjee, K.: Modeling machine learning requirements from three perspectives: a case report from the healthcare domain. Requirements Eng. **26**, 237–254 (2021)
33. Pandharipande, A., et al.: Sensing and machine learning for automotive perception: a review. IEEE Sens. J. **23**(11), 11097–11115 (2023)
34. Parekh, D., et al.: A review on autonomous vehicles: progress, methods and challenges. Electronics **11**(14), 2162 (2022)
35. Robertson, S., Robertson, J.: Mastering the Requirements Process: Getting Requirements Right. Addison-Wesley (2012)
36. Ruhe, G., Eberlein, A., Pfahl, D.: Trade-off analysis for requirements selection. Int. J. Softw. Eng. Knowl. Eng. **13**(04), 345–366 (2003)
37. Sculley, D., et al.: Hidden technical debt in machine learning systems. In: Advances in Neural Information Processing Systems, vol. 28 (2015)
38. Sherif, E., Helmy, W., Galal-Edeen, G.H.: Proposed framework to manage non-functional requirements in agile. IEEE Access (2023)
39. Shreda, Q.A., Hanani, A.A.: Identifying non-functional requirements from unconstrained documents using natural language processing and machine learning approaches. IEEE Access (2021)
40. Siau, K., Wang, W.: Building trust in artificial intelligence, machine learning, and robotics. Cutter Bus. Technol. J. **31**(2), 47–53 (2018)
41. Siebert, J., et al.: Construction of a quality model for machine learning systems. Softw. Qual. J. **30**(2), 307–335 (2022)
42. Smola, A., Vishwanathan, S.: Introduction to machine learning. Camb. Univ. UK **32**(34), 2008 (2008)
43. Supakkul, S., Hill, T., Chung, L., Tun, T.T., do Prado Leite, J.C.S.: An NFR pattern approach to dealing with NFRs. In: 2010 18th IEEE International Requirements Engineering Conference, pp. 179–188. IEEE (2010)
44. Villamizar, H., Escovedo, T., Kalinowski, M.: Requirements engineering for machine learning: a systematic mapping study. In: 47th Euromicro Conference on Software Engineering and Advanced Applications (SEAA), pp. 29–36. IEEE (2021)
45. Vogelsang, A., Borg, M.: Requirements engineering for machine learning: perspectives from data scientists. In: IEEE 27th International Requirements Engineering Conference Workshops (REW), pp. 245–251. IEEE (2019)
46. Wan, Z., Xia, X., Lo, D., Murphy, G.C.: How does machine learning change software development practices? IEEE Trans. Softw. Eng. **47**(9), 1857–1871 (2019)
47. Werner, C., Li, Z.S., Lowlind, D., Elazhary, O., Ernst, N.A., Damian, D.: Continuously managing NFRs: opportunities and challenges in practice. IEEE Trans. Softw. Eng. (2021)

An Environment for the Assessment of the Functional Suitability of AI Systems

Jesús Oviedo[1,2(✉)], Moisés Rodríguez[1,2], and Mario Piattini[2]

[1] AQCLab Software Quality, Puertollano, Spain
{joviedo,mrodriguez}@aqclab.es

[2] Instituto de Tecnologías y Sistemas de la Información y Escuela Superior de Informática, Universidad de Castilla – La Mancha, Ciudad Real, Spain
{jesus.oviedo,moises.rodriguez,mario.piattini}@uclm.es

Abstract. Artificial Intelligence (AI) is currently a fundamental part of the digital transformation of organizations and the impact of applications with AI is increasing every day. In this situation, there is a growing need for these AI systems, as software systems, to have the necessary quality characteristics to guarantee their use. This article presents a methodological and technological environment for the measurement and evaluation of AI Systems Functional Suitability. The environment proposes a set of metrics and quality properties aligned with the new ISO/IEC 25059 standard. It also includes an assessment methodology aligned with ISO/IEC 25040 and a set of automatic tools to facilitate the evaluation of the quality of AI Systems.

Keywords: ISO/IEC 25059 · ISO/IEC 25000 · Functional Suitability · Quality Artificial Intelligence · Artificial Intelligence (AI) Engineers

1 Introduction

Historically, the Software Engineering (SE) and Artificial Intelligence (AI) communities have remained poorly communicated, having their own terminologies, methods, and challenges. At the R&D level, since the early years, and still to this day, it is more common for researchers to focus on **"AI for SE",** i.e. how to use Artificial Intelligence to improve some aspects of Software Engineering, such as requirements, estimation, technical debt, defect detection, testing, etc. [1] than on using Software Engineering to improve AI. Although there were some attempts to do so [2]. However, as AI Systems are software systems, their development and maintenance have many parallels with the construction, deployment, and maintenance of software. For this reason, over the last three years there has been a similar growth in research on **"SE for AI"**, i.e. how to use Software Engineering techniques to build intelligent systems with adequate quality and productivity [3]. In fact, the "1st Workshop on AI Engineering - Software Engineering for AI" was launched by IEEE and ACM in 2021.

In terms of possible definitions, according to the SEI, this research area could be referred to as "Artificial Intelligence Engineering[1]", being the result of *"combining the*

[1] https://www.sei.cmu.edu/our-work/artificial-intelligence-engineering/.

A. Bertolino et al. (Eds.): QUATIC 2024, CCIS 2178, pp. 21–34, 2024.
https://doi.org/10.1007/978-3-031-70245-7_2

principles of systems engineering, software engineering, computer science and human-centred design to create Artificial Intelligence systems according to human needs for mission outcomes".

The use of software engineering techniques for the construction of AI systems is based on the principles established by Horneman [4], who can be called the authors of this new area, considering that AI systems are intensive systems, and that, therefore, they can be used as a basis for the construction of AI systems:

- Established principles for designing and deploying quality software systems that meet their mission objectives on time should be applied to engineering AI systems.
- Teams should strive to deliver functionality on time and with quality, design for important architectural requirements (such as security, usability, reliability, performance, and scalability), and plan for system maintenance throughout the life of the system.

While "Artificial intelligence (AI) and machine learning (ML) are ubiquitous in today's computing landscape, there is still a lack of software engineering expertise and best practices in this field" [5]. Developers of AI-intensive systems are aware of the need to organise development in a systematic way by applying engineering methods and tools, but also recognise that traditional software engineering methods and tools are neither adequate nor sufficient on their own and need to be adapted and extended [6].

Therefore, in the new area of Artificial Intelligence Engineering, challenges related to the definition and assurance of the behaviour and quality attributes of these systems and applications have arisen, which have prompted us to work on the development of an environment that allows the Assessment of Functional Adequacy in AI Systems. This environment consists of:

- A quality model consisting of characteristics, sub-characteristics and a set of metrics that are used to determine the outcome of the quality characteristics and sub-characteristics.
- An evaluation process describing the set of activities and tasks to be performed to carry out the evaluation of AI software systems.
- A technological environment consisting of the set of tools that support the measurement, the application of the evaluation criteria and the visualization of results.

Therefore, the main objective of this article is to present the components of a first version of such an evaluation environment, which will soon be used in a practical way for its validation and improvement. To this end, the rest of the article is structured as follows: Sect. 2 presents the new standard for quality assessment in AI Systems as a product. Section 3 describes the quality model where the metrics we have defined to evaluate the sub-characteristics and characteristics that has been defined for the assessment of Functional Adequacy in AI Systems. Section 4 presents how the product evaluation process is carried out, detailing the defined evaluation process. Section 5 presents the set of tools developed and adapted to carry out the assessment and the presentation of the results. And finally, Sect. 6 presents the conclusions obtained with this work and the future lines of work and research.

2 Quality in AI Systems

Quality assurance of AI-based systems is an emerging area that has not yet been well explored and requires collaboration between the Software Engineering (SE) and Artificial Intelligence (AI) research communities. Recently, as has happened in other cases: software product sustainability [7], cloud services [8], e-learning systems [9], etc., it has been necessary to adapt the quality model defined in ISO/IEC 25010 for the software product to the special characteristics of Artificial Intelligence, thus emerging the new standard ISO/IEC 25059 [10] according to the framework of the ISO/IEC 25000 standards.

2.1 New ISO/IEC 25059 Standards for Quality Assessment in AI Systems

The new ISO/IEC 25059 [10] standard for "quality for AI-based systems" was approved in July 2023 and proposes two models: a quality-in-use model and a product quality model, which is the one used for the development of the functional suitability assessment environment for AI systems presented in this article. This new quality model includes the product quality characteristics that any AI system must comply with, based on those proposed by ISO/IEC 25010, but presenting certain changes and adaptations in some of the characteristics and sub-characteristics [11], as is the case in:

- **Usability**, where two new sub-characteristics User Controllability and Transparency have been added.
- **Reliability**, where the Robustness sub-characteristic has been included.
- **Security**, where the Intervenability sub-characteristic has been added.
- **Functional Suitability**, where the Functional Correctness sub-characteristic has been modified and a new sub-characteristic, Functional Adaptability, has been included.

Figure 1 shows the proposed characteristics and sub-characteristics for the artificial intelligence system product quality model.

Although this new standard is an important starting point, the proposal made by ISO/IEC 25059 is high level and incomplete, being necessary to define a set of metrics and thresholds that allow us to determine the quality values of each of the defined subcharacteristics and characteristics to be applicable in the industry. In addition, to have an evaluation environment, it is necessary to have other elements such as the evaluation process and the technological environment to allow the collection of data necessary for the calculation of the new metrics and to obtain the quality value of each of the characteristics that make up the quality model for the AI system.

3 Functional Suitability Quality Model for AI Systems

The functional suitability model defined for AI systems is based on the ISO/IEC 25059 standard, with functional suitability being one of the characteristics that have been modified in this new standard. These changes have motivated the need to define a new model to address the quality of AI Systems, not being able to use the quality model defined by AQCLab [12] for the assessment of functional suitability in software products [13], based on ISO/IEC 25010, being necessary to address the development of a new model that can assess the functional suitability for AI systems.

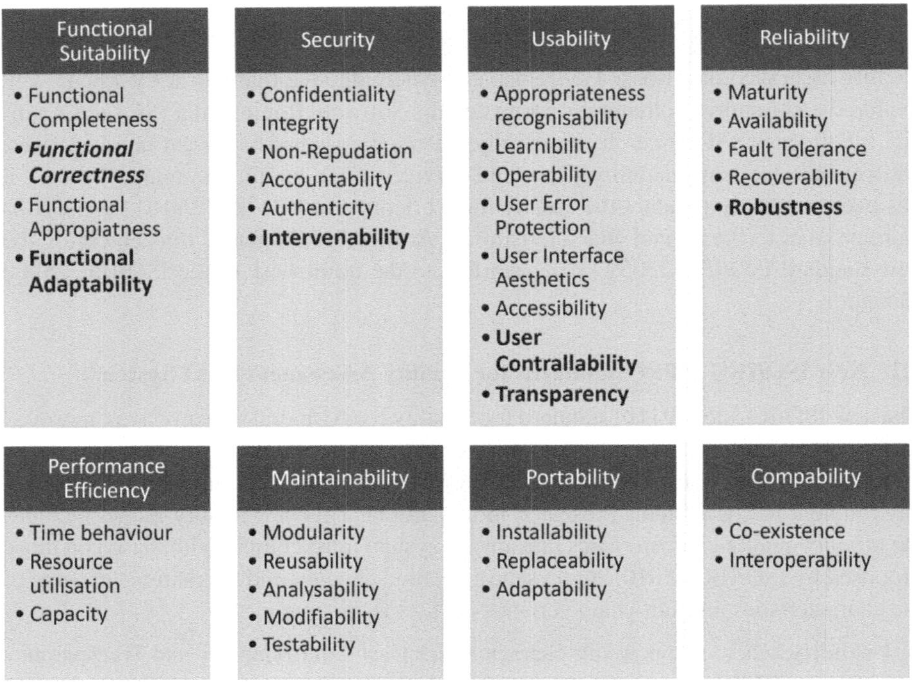

Fig. 1. Quality model for AI ISO/IEC 25059 systems (in bold the added or modified sub-characteristics).

This new model proposed in the ISO/IEC 25059 standard is based on the ISO/IEC 25010 standard and presents the same hierarchical approach where there are different levels. At the top levels of the model are the Quality Characteristic and Sub-characteristics that are defined by the standard. However, the model is incomplete, and it has been necessary to specify the quality attributes for the lower levels to make the model operational. Thus, a set of Quality Measures and Measurement Elements have been defined, which have been named in this model as **Quality Properties** and **Base and Derived Metrics**, which are the most concrete elements of the model, as can be seen in Fig. 2. It is also necessary to define the operations and functions to be applied to obtain the quality values of the upper measurement elements.

Functional Suitability in the ISO/IEC 25059 standard is defined as the degree to which an AI System provides functions that satisfy stated and implied needs when used under specified conditions and is assessed based on the evaluation of its Sub-Features (Fig. 1) using a profiling function as presented in [13]. This profiling function has been adapted to the number of sub-features presented in the ISO/IEC 25059 standard for Functional Suitability. The value of the Functional Suitability, Quality Characteristic, would be obtained, taking a discrete value between 1 and 5.

The following sections describe the metrics and functions defined by the authors to calculate the quality value of each of the Functional Suitability sub-characteristics

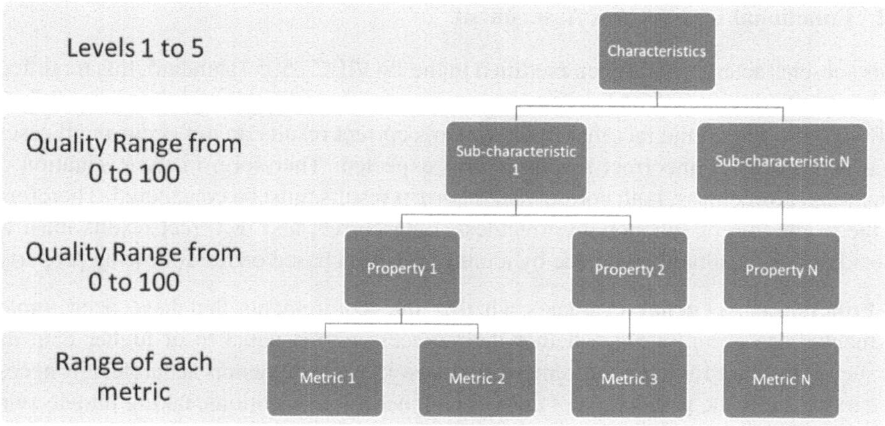

Fig. 2. Elements of a Software Quality Measurement Model.

included in the standard. The value of the Quality Sub-characteristics, which also take a value between 0 and 100, as well as the Quality Properties.

3.1 Functional Completeness Assessment

This sub-characteristic has not been modified with respect to the ISO/IEC 25010 quality model, and therefore the definition made in the AQCLAB [13] software product quality assessment model is valid for the assessment of the Functional Completeness of AI Systems. However, this sub-characteristic is defined as the degree to which the set of functions implemented in the product or system covers all functional requirements and user objectives. Therefore, Functional Completeness can be understood as the ability of the product or system to implement all specified functional requirements. Its evaluation is made by means of a weighted average based on the following properties:

- **Completeness of Functional Implementation** considers which of the specified requirements are implemented in the AI system [14]. To evaluate this property the metrics: number of requirements implemented in the AI system and the number of requirements that have been included in the AI product specification and/or indicated by the user or project owner, resulting in a list of requirements that have been implemented.
- **Completeness of Functional Tests** studies whether the requirements that have been described in the requirements specification have been subjected to a testing process. Thus, Functional Test Completeness is evaluated by comparing the requirements that have been tested against the requirements that have been implemented. If a requirement has not been tested, it is not possible to know if it has been fully implemented. To obtain the value of this Property the following metrics are necessary: number of implemented requirements together with the number of requirements that have been tested and the percentage of lines of code coverage when executing the test cases defined for the AI system requirements.

3.2 Functional Correctness Assessment

This sub-characteristic has been modified in the ISO/IEC 25059 standard, this modification is justified because in AI systems correctness is a broader concept than in traditional software [6], due to the fact that in AI systems correct results do not occur in all cases, so a percentage of incorrect results is also expected. Therefore, in the evaluation of functional correctness, both correct and incorrect results must be considered. Therefore, in the evaluation of functional correctness, both correct and incorrect results must be considered. Its evaluation is made by identity function based on the following property:

- **Functional Accuracy** evaluates whether the requirements that have been implemented are accurate, i.e. whether their success rate is equal to or higher than the success rate set for that requirement. To know if a requirement is accurate, it is necessary to know the percentage of correct and incorrect executions, taking into account false positives and false negatives [15] and that the proportion of correct executions is higher than the threshold established for that requirement to consider that its results are accurate. To calculate the value of this Property it is necessary to know the number of implemented requirements and the number of accurate requirements. To determine whether a requirement is accurate, it is necessary to perform several runs of each of the test cases associated with the requirement. The number of runs to be performed has been determined by the equation shown in Fig. 3, which provides the minimum sample size for a very large population size (Fowler, 2002)

$$n = \frac{Z_{\sigma/2}^2 * p * q}{e^2}$$

Fig. 3. Equation for determining the sample size

where the assigned values are:

- The values of p and q is 0.5 as the probability of the event (correct execution or incorrect execution) is unknown.
- The value of e corresponds to the error to be accepted: 1%, 5%, 10%, etc.
- The Z value has been obtained from normal distribution tables, depending on the selected errors. A normal distribution has been taken, because the number of times a functionality can be run is not limited. In addition, the result of the execution can be treated as a nominal distribution, the result of the functionality can be correct or incorrect.

After executing the test case the given number of times, the number of successful executions shall be obtained, considering true positives and true negatives. If the percentage of correct results in all test cases plotted against the requirement is equal to or higher than the correctness threshold set in the requirement specification, then the requirement can be considered to have been implemented correctly.

3.3 Functional Appropriateness Assessment

Functional Appropriateness is another sub-characteristic that has not been modified in the new ISO/IEC 25059 standard. Therefore, the definition made in the software product quality assessment model by AQCLAB [13] is valid for the assessment of the Functional Relevance of AI Systems. Thus, this sub-characteristic is defined as the degree to which the functions of the product or system facilitate the fulfilment of the specified tasks and objectives. Therefore, Functional Appropriateness can be understood as the ability of the product or system to implement the functional requirements of each intended use in an appropriate way. Its evaluation is made by identity function based on the following property:

- **Appropriate Functionality,** this property refers to whether the AI product meets the requirements of each type of user. The requirements of each type of user are called usage goals. In other words, it is about whether the software product provides all the expected usage goals. To obtain the value of this property, one must first identify the requirements associated with each usage target, as well as the proportion of the requirements that are accurate for each usage target. In this way, it can be seen whether the AI product is suitable for all types of users by providing them with the expected requirements.

3.4 Functional Adaptability Assessment

This is the new sub-characteristic defined in the ISO/IEC 25059 [10] model for the Functional Suitability Characteristic. This sub-characteristic is defined as the degree to which an AI system can make new predictions based on new knowledge acquired from new data and/or results of previous runs. This sub-characteristic is significantly different from other quality sub-characteristics, as an increase in Functional Adaptability does not imply an improvement in system quality, i.e. it cannot be interpreted using a linear scale. Therefore, in this model, an interpretation of Functional Adaptability has been made to allow for linearity, like all other sub-characteristics, and is only considered if the Functional Adaptability of the AI system improves the performance of the AI system. Thus, Functional Adaptability can be defined as the ability of the AI system to improve its performance based on its experience, i.e. based on new inputs and/or previous results. Its evaluation is made by identity function based on the following property:

- **Appropriate Learning,** this property examines whether the use of new data inputs generates better results from the AI model, i.e. whether the probability of incorrect results is reduced. For the analysis of this property, it is necessary to know the number of requirements that have improved their rate of correct results and the number of implemented requirements. To determine whether a requirement has improved its correct results, it must be checked, after the evaluation of the functional correctness, if the percentage of correct results of the requirement is higher than the correctness threshold defined in the requirement specification then the correctness rate of the requirement can be considered to have improved.

3.5 Case Study

The model proposed in this article has been used to perform a case study to ensure that it could be applied to assess the functional adequacy of an AI system. In addition to the main objective, the case study has an additional objective of identifying possible problems and improvements, both on the established metrics and thresholds, and on the applicability of the model to evaluate real AI systems. The product selected for this pilot project is a deterministic Artificial Intelligence system, based on fuzzy rules to determine the correction to be applied to the prediction of the total energy consumption for a type of customer, depending on the day of the year and other aspects such as the number of hours of sunshine and the weather.

The result of the assessment is shown in Table 1. After carrying out the case study, the viability and effectiveness of the implemented model was verified. On the other hand, the case study has allowed us to find some difficulties to address the evaluations of the AI Systems, such as the change of behaviour in non-deterministic systems, which makes it necessary to have a greater number of data to perform different executions of the test cases and to ensure that the results obtained are not affected by the number of executions. On the other hand, a risk in functional adequacy assessments in IA systems is that adequate documentation does not exist and must be taken into account in the planning of the assessment.

Once the model has been described, the next element is the evaluation process, which will indicate each of the activities that must be carried out in order to approach the evaluation.

Table 1. Results of the Functional Suitability Assessment for an AI System

Measurement Element		Value
Properties	Completeness of Functional Implementation	100
	Completeness of Functional Tests	0
	Functional Accuracy	100
	Appropriate Functionality	100
	Appropriate Learning	100
Sub-charcteristics	Functional Completeness	50
	Functional Correctness	100
	Functional Appropriateness	100
	Functional Adaptability	100
CHARACTERISTIC: Functional Suitability		3

4 Assessment Process

To address the assessment of the functional suitability of AI systems, a process has been defined based on the ISO/IEC 25040 standard [16], which proposes an assessment process that considers both the inputs (requirements for the assessment, specification of quality requirements, products to be assessed, etc.), and the constraints (needs, planning, etc.) and available resources (personnel, tools, IT equipment, etc.) to obtain the corresponding outputs (assessment plan, measures, decision criteria, results and assessment report, etc.). However, there are some variations in the defined procedure with respect to the standard. Figure 3 shows the activities that make up this evaluation process, which has been adapted from that defined in the standard, the details of the differences of the defined assessment process compared to ISO 25040 are as follows:

- The first task to be performed in an evaluation project, as part of the first activity ('Define the Evaluation') is to 'Establish the purpose of the evaluation'. This task in the defined process has less impact than it might have in other cases, because the purpose of the evaluation in this case has little influence as the quality aspects of the product to be evaluated, the Functional Suitability, have been predefined. However, it is necessary to know the customer's purpose in order to determine whether the assessment of the functional suitability of the IA systems performed with the laboratory environment can answer it.
- When performing the task 'Elicit quality requirements', the scope to be assessed shall be agreed with the customer and shall be aligned with the set of quality subcharacteristics defined in the model of the functional suitability of artificial intelligence systems.
- Regarding the task 'Define the rigour and formality of the evaluation', the evaluations to be carried out do not consider different levels of integrity and rigour; the same techniques are always applied and the same type of evaluation products are always produced in all projects, so it is not done specifically for each project. Therefore, this task defined in the standard as part of the first activity of an evaluation has not been included in the defined evaluation process.
- The 'Design the evaluation' activity defined in ISO/IEC 25040 does not require the depth set out in this standard, since a predefined evaluation module is always applied. This module defines the metrics to be measured, the criteria to derive the Property values from them (thresholds, evaluation functions), and likewise, the criteria to obtain the values of the sub-characteristics of the functional adequacy and with them the global result of the functional adequacy of the evaluated artificial intelligence system. Due to the above, it is not necessary in each evaluation project to perform the four tasks established in the standard for this activity as defined in the standard: 'Identify the components to be evaluated', 'Select the quality metrics (evaluation module)', 'Define the decision criteria for the metrics' and 'Define the results. In fact, the second and fourth tasks have been eliminated from the process, and the third task, 'Define decision criteria for metrics' is maintained, but not with the objective of establishing thresholds for the base metrics or evaluation functions, but rather this task will be carried out with the objective of establishing how and with which tools compliance will be checked as part of the subsequent measurement activity, which will depend on the technologies used in the implementation of the AI system to be evaluated.

- The task 'Identify evaluation activities', which is part of the activity 'Plan the evaluation', is not included in the evaluation process because the evaluations that are carried out have the same purpose and therefore always present the same work.
- In the case of the task 'Review the evaluation results', as part of the last activity of the project ('Conclude the evaluation'), this review is not carried out with the client prior to the preparation of the report. This review is done internally by the laboratory staff, to check that the results are correct. The review of results with the client is carried out once a first version has been produced. The client's comments from this review are considered when the final version of the report is drafted.

The activities of the process defined for the assessment of the functional suitability of artificial intelligence systems considering the above adaptations are detailed below (Fig. 4).

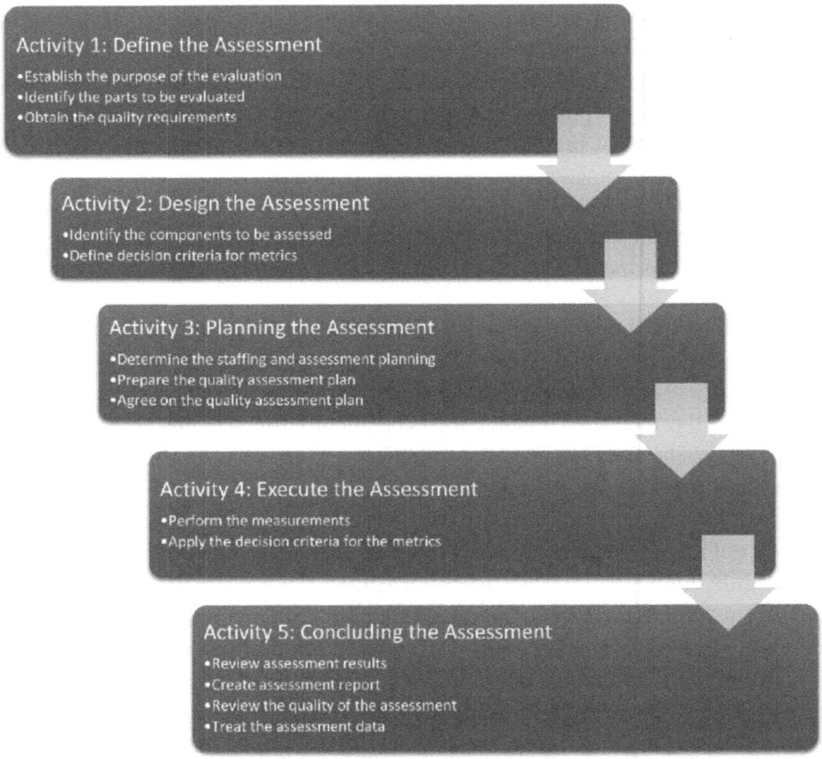

Fig. 4. Process for assessing functional suitability in AI systems

- **Define the Assessment:** This consists of establishing the customer's objective and requirements to determine whether the assessment of the functional suitability of the laboratory's AI Systems can meet them.

- **Design the Evaluation:** The components of the AI system to be evaluated are identified. However, it is not necessary to select the metrics and evaluation criteria as they are always the same, specifically the model defined in Sect. 3.
- **Planning the Evaluation:** The planning of the evaluation activities is established, determining who is going to carry out the evaluation and making the evaluation plan.
- **Execute the Evaluation:** The tasks related to the evaluation are carried out, obtaining the quality metrics, and applying the evaluation criteria to obtain the result of the functional suitability of the AI System.
- **Concluding the Evaluation:** The tasks necessary to conclude the evaluation are addressed, by producing the report of results to be delivered to the client and reviewing with the client the results obtained, as well as all internal review and closure activities.

5 Assessment Tools

The software environment for the measurement and evaluation of functional suitability in implemented AI systems (hereafter referred to as AQCLab environment) is mainly composed of four components: the measurement tool, the evaluation tool, the visualization tool, and the database, as presented in Fig. 5.

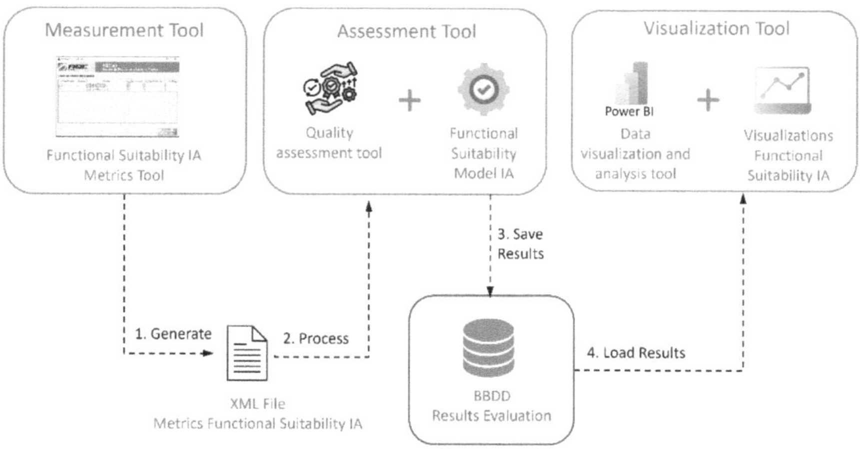

Fig. 5. Architecture Technological Environments

- **Measurement Tool** is a tool developed in Java with the objective to record information from AI Systems to obtain the metrics necessary for the assessment of functional adequacy in AI systems. The tool developed specifically to obtain metrics related to the assessment of the functional suitability of AI Systems allows to record information related to the requirements and test cases of the system, generates an XML file with the results of the metrics, which is used as input by the assessment tool.

- **Assessment Tool:** it is responsible of measuring and assessing the functional suitability of the AI systems, it is composed of two components, a standard assessment component and a specific component for assessing the functional suitability of the AI systems. This specific component includes the model for assessing functional suitability implemented in XML and a Python-implemented program that performs the necessary calculations to carry out the assessment based on the results of the measurement tool.
- **Visualization Tool.** This is a tool consisting of two components: a visualization environment provided by AQCLab in PowerBI, which is a versatile platform for the creation of different interactive reports and a specific extension dedicated to the visualization and analysis of functional fitness data in AI Systems. These reports include graphs, tables and other visual representations that clearly and effectively present the metrics, trends, and results of the functional suitability assessment of AI systems. Figure 6 shows an example of a visualization of the results of a Functional Suitability assessment of an AI system.

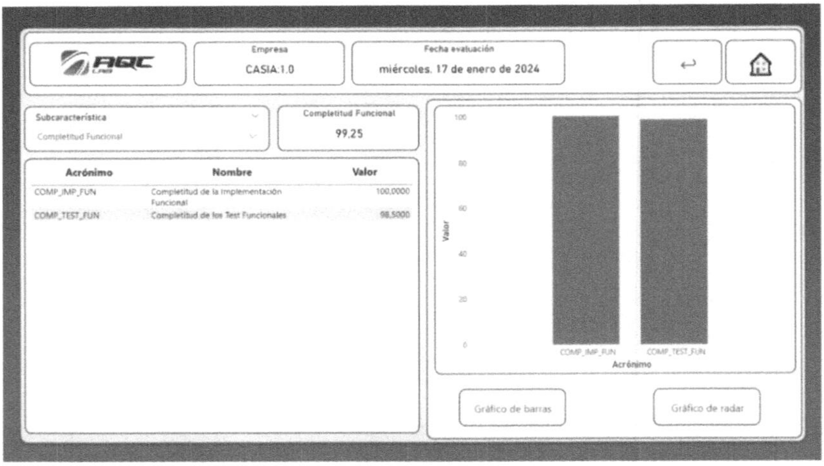

Fig. 6. Results Visualization Work

6 Conclusion and Future Work

The rise of Artificial Intelligence in all facets of everyday life makes it necessary, as in software, to use software engineering techniques, such as Quality, for the development of these systems. However, the traditional methods and tools of software engineering must be adapted to the particularities of Artificial Intelligence systems. Therefore, in this article we have presented a new environment for the evaluation of functional adequacy in AI systems, adapted to the particularities of this new technology.

In this new evaluation environment, a new quality model has been defined, aligned with the new ISO/IEC 25059 standard, in which new metrics have been analysed with which to approach the evaluation of software systems. It has also been necessary to adapt the assessment process defined in ISO/IEC 25040 to the particularities of the activities that must be carried out to assess the functional suitability of an AI system. Finally, a new measurement tool has been developed to support the collection of the new metrics. Thus, adaptations to AQCLab's evaluation and visualization tools to be able to carry out the functional suitability assessment and the presentation of its results.

Therefore, once this new evaluation environment has been developed, our main line of future work is the study of the practical application of this environment, through the evaluation of Artificial Intelligence systems. Furthermore, this practical application will allow us to validate the environment, ensuring that the values obtained in the evaluations are correlated with the Functional Suitability of the AI Systems.

Another thing to investigate is the relationship between the recent ISO/IEC 42001 standard [17] of IA management system and the quality of the IA system.

Acknowledgments. This research has been supported by ADAGIO "Alarcos' DAta Governance framework and systems generation" (SBPLY/21/180501/000061) financed by the Junta de Comunidades de Castilla La Mancha (JCCM), European Union, Ministerio de Hacienda y Función Pública and European Regional Development Fund FEDER (Programa Operativo de Castilla-La Mancha 2021–2027) and CASIA (Calidad de Sistemas de Inteligencia Artificial) financed by the Junta de Comunidades de Castilla La Mancha.

References

1. Romero, J., Medina-Bulo, I., Chicano, F.: Optimising the Software Development Process with Artificial Intelligence. Springer, Singapore (2023)
2. Ford, L.: Artificial intelligence and software engineering: a tutorial introduction to their relationship. Artif. Intell. Rev. **1**, 255–273 (1987). https://doi.org/10.1007/BF00142926
3. SEI: Architecting the future of software engineering: a national agenda for software engineering research & development (2021). https://insights.sei.cmu.edu/documents/1308/2021_014_001_741195.pdf
4. Horneman, A., Melligener, A., Ozkava, I.: AI Engineering: 11 Foundational Practises. Recommendations for decision makers from expert in software engineering, cybersecurity, and applied artificial intelligence. Carnegie Mellon University Software Engineering Institute (2019)
5. van Oort, B., Cruz, L., Aniche, M., van Deursen, A.: The prevalence of code smells in machine learning projects. In: WAIN@ICSE, pp. 35–42 (2021)
6. Lavazza, L., Morasca, S.: Understanding and modeling AI-intensive system development. In: IEEE/ACM 1st Workshop on AI Engineering - Software Engineering for AI (WAIN), Madrid, pp. 55–61 (2021)
7. Calero, C., Moraga, M., Piattini, M.: Software Sustainability. Springer, Cham (2021)
8. Navas, R.: Modelos de Calidad para servicios en el Cloud. Universidad Politecnica de Valencia, Valencia (2016)
9. Rahman, A.: Quality consideration for e-learing system based on ISO/IEC 25000 Quality Standards. In: IWESQ, pp. 12–17 (2019)
10. ISO/IEC: ISO/IEC 25059:2023. Software engineering - systems and software quality requirements and evaluations (square) - quality model for AI systems. Ginebra (2023)

11. Oviedo, J., Márquez, R., Rodríguez, M., Piattini, M.: Calidad en los sistemas IA: adaptación de modelos de procesos y productos. Actas de las XXVII Jornadas de Ingeniería del Software y Bases de Datos, Ciudad Real (2023)
12. Verdugo, J., Oviedo, J., Rodríguez, M., Piattini, M.: Connecting research and practise for software product quality evaluation and certification: a software laboratory's 25-year journey. IEEE Softw. (2024). https://doi.org/10.1109/MS.2024.3357119
13. Rodríguez, M., Oviedo, J., Piattini, M.: Evaluation of software product functional suitability. A case study. Softw. Q. Prof. **18**(3), 18–29 (2016)
14. Yahaya, J., Deraman, A.: Measuring unmeasurable attributes of software quality using pragmatic quality factor. In: 3rd IEEE International Conference on Computer Science and Information Technology (ICCSIT), Sintok, Malaysia, pp. 197–202 (2010)
15. ISO/IEC: ISO/IEC 29119-16:2023. ISO/IEC 29119-16 Testing Machine Learning Systems. Ginebra (2023)
16. ISO/IEC: ISO/IEC 25040:2023. Systems and software engineering—Systems and software Quality Requirements and Evaluation (SQuaRE)—evaluation process. International Organization for Standardization, Ginebra, Suiza (2023). https://www.iso.org/standard/35765.html
17. Fowler, F.J.: Survey Research Methods. Sage Publications, Thousand Oaks (2002)
18. ISO/IEC: ISO/IEC 42001:2023. Information technology - Artificial intelligence - Management system. International Organization for Standardization, Ginebra, Suiza (2023)

RSUTT: Robust Search Using T-Way Testing

Chisato Matsukawa and Shingo Takada(✉)

Keio University, Yokohama 223-8522, Japan
{chisato,michigan}@doi.ics.keio.ac.jp

Abstract. Recent years have seen an increase of decision-making software based on Machine Learning (ML). Multiple cases have been reported where such software are discriminatory based on attributes such as race and gender. Thus, ML-based decision making software need to be tested for discrimination, or fairness testing. One popular approach to fairness testing is to find discriminatory data items by first conducting a global search, and then searching locally near the found discriminatory data items. Aequitas, CGFT, and KOSEI are three examples taking this approach. However, there are issues in terms of stability and efficiency. We thus propose an approach called *Robust Search Using T-way Testing (RSUTT)*, which is based on CGFT for global search and KOSEI for local search. Experiments showed that RSUTT performs more efficiently compared to Aequitas, CGFT, and KOSEI.

Keywords: Fairness Test · Robustness · Machine Learning

1 Introduction

In recent years, advances in Machine Learning (ML) technology have made it possible to make predictions and decisions with greater precision and accuracy. As a result, ML models are being used in software in a variety of fields by individuals, companies, and countries. Such software include recommendations [7], loan decisions [8], and automated driving systems [5]. Ensuring fairness is critical to quality in such ML software.

There have been reports [2–4] where decisions made by ML-based software are biased. Such biases occur when two items differ only by certain attributes (called *protected* attributes) which should not cause the two items to be classified differently. There are many examples of discrimination that have been confirmed in ML-based software that are actually in use. One example is COMPAS, which is used in the courts of the United States. COMPAS calculates a risk assessment score to estimate the likelihood that a suspect will reoffend [4]. However, COMPAS tends to judge black defendants as more likely to commit crimes again compared to white defendants, i.e., it estimates a lower risk of recidivism for white defendants than for black defendants [2]. Other examples include the ML

A. Bertolino et al. (Eds.): QUATIC 2024, CCIS 2178, pp. 35–50, 2024.
https://doi.org/10.1007/978-3-031-70245-7_3

model used in Amazon's hiring practices that discriminates against women [3]. Thus, ensuring fairness is a critical component for the quality of ML software.

One approach to ensure fairness is to conduct fairness testing. Fairness testing is the process of providing pairs of items (inputs) that differ only by protected attributes, and check if the results (outputs, i.e. the classification or decision of the two inputs) are the same or not. If the outputs are different, then the pair of inputs are considered to be discriminatory.

Individual discrimination refers to the classification of two items (or *individuals*) that differ only in their protected attributes into different groups. Protected attributes are attributes that should not be discriminated against, such as age, gender, and race. As ML models are based on training datasets, if the training dataset is biased, the resulting ML models are also biased. However, even if the training dataset itself is not biased, biases can be introduced into the ML model. Therefore, it is essential to find as much individual discrimination as possible through fairness testing.

Conventional fairness testing has problems such as excessive execution time and inconsistent results from run to run. In order to discover discriminatory data items in a stable and efficient manner, we propose a method called *Robust Search Using T-way Testing (RSUTT)*, which is based on Coverage-Guided Fairness Testing (CGFT) [10] for global search and KOSEI [11] for local search. CGFT's global search finds discriminative data items by generating and testing evenly distributed data items through combinatorial testing (CT). KOSEI's local search systematically generates and tests data items in the neighborhood of discriminative data items obtained in the global search.

The main contribution of this paper is to integrate CGFT's global search and KOSEI's local search to enable more stable and efficient fairness testing.

Section 2 gives definitions of key terms used in this paper. Section 3 describes related work. Section 4 describes our proposed approach RSUTT. Section 5 evaluates RSUTT. Section 6 makes concluding remarks.

2 Definition

This paper uses the following definitions based on [10] and [11].

- Data item: Individual data contained in the dataset to be used. Each data item is based on a list of attribute values, which are limited to numerical values in our work.
- Attribute: Attributes of the data item, such as age, race, and gender.
- Protected attribute: The output should not change when only the value of a protected attribute is changed, The actual protected attributes will differ based on the software, but examples include gender and race.
- Non-protected attribute: There is no issues if changes in non-protected attribute values result in the output to change.
- Discriminatory data item: A data item for which discrimination was found to exist as a result of fairness testing.
- Seed data item: Discriminatory data items that were discovered as the result of global search. Local search is performed based on seed data items.

3 Related Work

3.1 Fairness Testing

Fairness testing has been the subject of much research [1,4,10–12,14].

Galhotra et al. [4] proposed Themis, which is a black box testing method which randomly selects values within a defined domain for all attributes and inputs them to a ML model to make a decision.

Aggarwal et al. [1] proposed SG, which uses dynamic symbolic execution and local interpretation. Their approach takes a two stage approach. In the first stage, LIME generates a partial decision tree using local interpretation based on the predictions given by the software model. In the second stage, individual discrimination is discovered using dynamic symbolic execution. Many test cases are generated by changing the constraints on the non-protected attributes.

Sharma et al. [12] proposed VBT, which uses verification techniques to detect discrimination. In VBT, a black-box model is first approximated to a decision tree. This decision tree is then converted into a logic equation, and the properties of the decision tree are checked by using a constraint solver.

Zhang et al. [15] proposed a white-box testing for deep neural network (DNN). They found individual discrimination by generating test cases using adversarial sampling, where small perturbations are applied to the input to induce the trained DNN to make incorrect predictions.

Udeshi et al. [14], Morales et al. [10], and Sano et al. [11] proposed Aequitas, CGFT, and KOSEI respectively. As our approach is based on their work, we go into more details in the next subsection.

3.2 Aequitas, CGFT, and KOSEI

Aequitas [14], CGFT [10], and KOSEI [11] all conduct black box fairness testing to detect individual discrimination. They take a two stage approach to find discriminatory data items. They first conduct global search, and then conduct local search on the discriminatory data items (i.e., seed data items) found in the global search. The main difference between Aequitas and CGFT is how global search is conducted, while the main difference between Aequitas and KOSEI is how local search is conducted.

Discrimination Evaluation. Before discussing global and local search, we first discuss discrimination evaluation, which is a key part of fairness testing. Discrimination evaluation takes a data item, and decides if it is a discriminatory data item. The basic steps are as follows:

1. Given a data item, the values of all of its attributes are converted to integers.
2. The protected attribute value is changed. Non-protected attributes are not changed.
3. The two data items (i.e., the original data item and the data item whose protected attribute was changed in the previous step) are input to the ML model, and the outputs for each are obtained.

4. The two outputs are compared. If the difference is greater than a threshold, the given data item is considered to be a discriminatory data item. (The modified data item is also a discriminatory data item).

In Aequitas and CGFT, when changing the value of a protected attribute, the minimum and maximum values of the protected attribute's domain are selected and changed. KOSEI, on the other hand, is implemented in such a way that the value of each attribute is converted to a predefined concrete value (0 or 1).

Global Search. Global search aims to discover discrimination in the entire data item space. Data items are generated, and discrimination evaluation is executed on the generated data items. This is repeated for a pre-defined number of times, resulting in a set of seed data items to be returned.

The general approach to global search is the same for Aequitas, CGFT, and KOSEI. The three differ in the way they generate data items. Aequitas and KOSEI generate data items randomly, while CGFT uses CT. Random generation can be done if the number of attributes and the attribute domain (i.e., the range of values that an attribute can take) is known, but the generated data items may be skewed. CGFT uses combinatorial t-way testing [6] to solve this issue. Combinatorial t-way testing is an example of CT and is a coverage-based data sampling method. In general, the greater the number of attributes and their values in a test, the greater the number of test cases, simply due to the number of possible combinations. By using coverage criteria, the number of test cases can be reduced.

Local Search. Local search aims to discover discriminatory data items that are *near* the seed data items that were found in the global search. The key idea behind this is to take advantage of the robustness property, where the output of a data item is similar to that of its neighbors in the input space of an ML model. Thus, discriminatory data items are likely to be in the vicinity of other discriminatory data items [14]. The basic process is to generate data items in the neighborhood of seed data items, and execute discrimination evaluation. Data items are generated by *perturbating* seed data items, specifically making small changes to the attribute values of seed data items.

The general approach to local search is the same for Aequitas, CGFT, and KOSEI. The three differ in their methods of perturbation and neighborhood search. Aequitas systematically updates the probabilities to choose an attribute for perturbation. CGFT is also based on this systematic update. On the other hand, KOSEI does not update the probability for choosing attributes for perturbation. It applies perturbation to all non-protected attributes one by one. Thus, if there are twelve non-protected attributes, 24 new data items are generated. Furthermore, KOSEI dynamically updates the seed data items, and searches the neighborhoods of discriminatory data items found by local search. This, in essence, applies the robustness property to both discriminatory (seed) data items that were found in global search as well as those found in local search.

4 Proposal: Robust Search Using T-Way Testing (RSUTT)

4.1 Overview

We propose *Robust Search Using T-way Testing (RSUTT)*, which integrates ideas from previous work, and implemented to work coherently[1]. RSUTT takes the two stage approach of global and local search, where global search is based on CGFT [10], and local search is based on KOSEI [11].

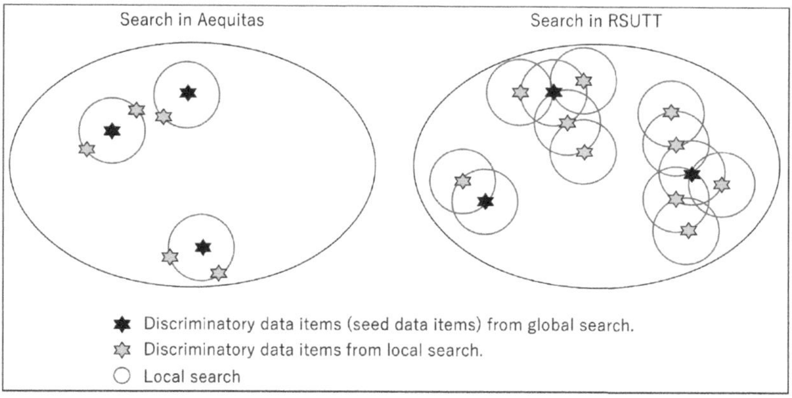

Fig. 1. Difference between Aequitas and RSUTT

Figure 1 shows the two key differences between Aequitas and RSUTT. The seed data items found in global search are more evenly spread out in RSUTT compared to Aequitas due to the use of CT. Furthermore, RSUTT uses discriminatory data items found during local search to find more discriminatory data items. This is shown in Fig. 1 with the discriminatory data items from local search, also becoming the center of another local search.

RSUTT is divided into the following four steps:

STEP 1 Global Search: Generates data items of a specified size using CT.
STEP 2 Discrimination Evaluation: Data items generated in STEP1 are checked for discrimination.
STEP 3 Local Search: The seed data items found in STEP2 are used to generate data items.
STEP 4 Discrimination Evaluation: Data items generated in STEP3 are checked for discrimination.

RSUTT was implemented using Python's scikit-learn library [9]. The rest of this section describes details of each step.

[1] The code of RSUTT as well as data from the evaluation is made available at https://github.com/mctsktw/RSUTT.

4.2 STEP 1: Global Search

In STEP 1, CT is used to generate data items of a specified size. The generation is the same as done by CGFT, and is shown in Algorithm 1. The user specifies the number of data items to be generated (N). The value of t starts from 1. If the number of data items generated by the algorithm at $t = 1$ is less than N, t is incremented and data items are generated for $t = 2$. This process is repeated until the sum of the number of data items from $t = 1$ to $t = t_{current}$ exceeds N. All of the data items from $t = 1$ to $t = t_{current} - 1$ and some of the data items at $t = t_{current}$ are used as generated data items. More details can be found in the CGFT paper [10].

Algorithm 1. Combinatorial test generation [10]

function CT_GENY(N, M)
  $TC \leftarrow \emptyset, A \leftarrow \emptyset, D \leftarrow \emptyset$
  $t \leftarrow 1$
  $N_\alpha \leftarrow 0$
  while $N > size(CT(t+1, M))$ **do**
    $t \leftarrow t + 1$
  end while
  $D \leftarrow CT(t+1, M) \setminus CT(t, M)$
  $N_\alpha \leftarrow N - size(CT(t, M))$
  $A \leftarrow N_\alpha$ $test\ cases\ from\ D\ randomly$
  $TC \leftarrow CT(t, M) \vee A$
  return TC
end function

4.3 STEP 2: Discrimination Evaluation

In STEP 2, discrimination evaluation is executed on all data items generated in STEP 1 to search for discriminatory data items (seed data items). The basic steps have already been described in Sect. 3.2, and the algorithm is shown in Algorithm 2. Although the algorithm used in RSUTT and KOSEI is the same, their implementation differs as RSUTT allows for a wide range of data sets. Specifically, KOSEI preprocesses the protected attribute values to be either 0 or 1, while RSUTT is implemented in such a way that it can handle other (numeric) values. The base implementation of RSUTT uses the minimum and maximum values of the protected attribute, but we have also implemented a version that can take other values (which we call RSUTT2 in RQ4 of Sect. 5).

4.4 STEP 3: Local Search

STEP 3 takes advantage of the robustness property in the same way as Aequitas, CGFT, and KOSEI. Algorithm 3 shows the algorithm for STEP 3 and STEP 4. Data items in the neighborhood of the seed data item are generated through perturbation. Specifically, data items are generated by incrementing or decrementing the value of the protected attribute. We do not generate data items

Algorithm 2. Discrimination Evaluation [10,11]

function EVAL_DISC($Data$)
  ▷ All values in $Data$ are converted into integers
  ▷ $\mathbf{I}^{(d)}$ extends $Data$ with all possible values of P_{disc}
  $\mathbf{I}^{(d)} \leftarrow \{Data' | \forall p \in P \setminus P_{disc}.Data_p = Data'_p\}$
  $tot\_inputs \leftarrow tot\_inputs \cup \{Data\}$
  if $\exists Data, Data' \in \mathbf{I}^{(d)}, |f(Data) - f(Data')| > \gamma$ **then**
    $disc\_inputs \leftarrow disc\_inputs \cup \{Data\}$
    return True
  end if
  return False
end function

whose attributes are outside the range of values that attributes can take, nor do we evaluate data items that have already been generated.

KOSEI implements the perturbation algorithm on a dataset-by-dataset basis because the algorithm depends on the number of parameters of the non-protected parameter. On the other hand, RSUTT unifies the implementation of perturbation by using information on the number of attributes and the protected attribute's index.

4.5 STEP 4: Discrimination Evaluation

In STEP 4, the discrimination evaluation algorithm is executed again. In STEP 2, discrimination evaluation is performed after the data item generation is completed in STEP 1. In STEP 4, on the other hand, discrimination evaluation is interleaved with STEP 3; each time a data item is generated, discrimination evaluation (STEP 4) is immediately performed for that data item. Furthermore, if a data item is evaluated as discriminatory, it is subject to perturbation in STEP 3.

5 Evaluation

We evaluate RSUTT by comparing it with Aequitas, CGFT, and KOSEI. We use three datasets and three ML models to answer the following research questions:

- RQ1 How many more seed data items did RSUTT find compared to existing methods?
- RQ2 How many more discriminatory data items did RSUTT find compared to existing methods?
- RQ3 How efficiently did RSUTT discover discriminatory data items compared to existing methods?
- RQ4 If a protected attribute can take more than two values, which values should be selected?

Algorithm 3. Perturbation [11]

```
function PERTURBATION(Data, P_non_protected)
    for param ∈ P_non_protected do
        Test ← Data
        Test[param] ← Test[param] − 1
        if Test[param] < param_min then
            continue
        else if Test ∈ tot_inputs then
            continue
        else
            Eval_Disc(Test)
        end if
        Test ← Data
        Test[param] ← Test[param] + 1
        if Test[param] > param_max then
            continue
        else if Test ∈ tot_inputs then
            continue
        else
            Eval_Disc(Test)
        end if
    end for
    return True
end function
```

RQ1 compares the number of seed data items found by Aequitas, CGFT, KOSEI, and RSUTT, i.e., discriminatory data items that were discovered by global search. RQ2 compares the total number of discriminatory data items found by Aequitas, CGFT, KOSEI, and RSUTT after executing local search. RQ3 compares the number of discriminatory data items generated per unit time (s) using the number of discriminatory data items found and the execution time of Aequitas, CGFT, KOSEI, and RSUTT. RQ4 investigates how changing the values used for discrimination evaluation affects the result.

5.1 Test Environment

The experiments were performed on a laptop computer with an Apple M1 with 16 GB of RAM, an 8-core CPU and an 8-core GPU, under macOS version 13.0. We used three datasets and three ML models described below.

Dataset. The datasets used in this experiment are Adult (A, Census Income), Statlog (S, German Credit), and Bank Marketing (BM) [13]. These data sets are commonly used in fairness testing evaluations.

Adult is used to predict whether an individual's income exceeds US$50,000 and has 13 attributes. Gender was used as the protected attribute, and the size of the training dataset was 32,562.

Statlog is used to determine good or bad credit risk based on an individual's data and has 20 attributes. Gender was used as the protected attribute, and the size of the training dataset was 1,000.

Bank Marketing is used to predict whether a client will sign up for a term deposit based on personal data, and has 16 attributes. Age was used as the protected attribute, and the size of the training dataset was 45,211 samples.

Note that the base implementation of RSUTT uses the minimum and maximum values of a protected attribute. This is not an issue for cases such as gender which has only two options. But, in Bank Marketing, age had nine categorized options. We used the minimum and maximum values for RQ1, RQ2, and RQ3. We also used other values for RQ4.

ML Model. We use the following three ML models based on Python's Scikit-learn library: (1) Decision Tree (DT), (2) Multi-Layer Perceptron (MLP), (3) Random Forest (RF).

Experimental Conditions. The number of test cases N in the global search was set to 3,000 and 7,000. The reason for this is to allow the value of t to vary in the global search. Aequitas, CGFT, KOSEI, and RSUTT were executed ten times each, and the average was used. The number of local search executions for Aequitas and CGFT was set to 2,000, while the number for KOSEI and RSUTT was set to (2,000 $\times$ the number of seed data items). The reason for the difference is to further explore the neighborhood of discriminatory data items found in the local search. We consider determining the best value to be part of future work.

5.2 Results

Tables 1 and 2 show the experimental results. This table is the average of the results of 10 executions. We now discuss each of the research questions.

[RQ1] How Many More Seed Data Items did RSUTT Find Compared to Existing Methods? Overall, Table 1 shows similar results for Aequitas and KOSEI, and for CGFT and RSUTT. This makes sense since, theoretically, the algorithms for global search are the same for Aequitas and KOSEI, and for CGFT and RSUTT.

We now compare between these two groups. The global search in CGFT is an improved version of the global search in Aequitas global search. The results given in the CGFT paper [10] shows this to be the case, i.e., the evaluation results for CGFT was better than Aequitas. From the same reasoning, RSUTT and CGFT should have better results than Aequitas and KOSEI in our experiment. However, there were quite a few cases where Aequitas and KOSEI found more seed data items than RSUTT and CGFT. We discuss this point in Sect. 6.

Table 1. Execution results

		Number of seed data items				Number of discriminatory data items			
N	DS/ML	Aequitas	CGFT	KOSEI	RSUTT	Aequitas	CGFT	KOSEI	RSUTT
3,000	A/DT	28	49	27	52	2,767	2,588	40,548	81,543
	A/MLP	375	363	363	361	7,528	7,791	521,774	492,031
	A/RF	241	282	245	280	8,411	9,967	341,223	386,786
	S/DT	52	38	49	36	4,221	1,530	68,532	50,922
	S/MLP	367	373	372	377	14,953	24,630	464,126	471,545
	S/RF	276	251	267	245	18,668	12,126	313,307	286,406
	BM/DT	728	719	758	721	6,622	4,741	1,142,000	1,095,304
	BM/MLP	230	182	226	183	1,697	1,343	201,123	168,364
	BM/RF	433	404	430	408	2,447	1,799	581,072	551,507
7,000	A/DT	62	123	61	129	3,007	4,150	93,283	200,793
	A/MLP	882	812	874	812	8,702	10,822	1,255,028	1,112,945
	A/RF	576	664	572	665	8,238	10,666	795,422	939,963
	S/DT	119	102	121	107	11,424	6,630	172,141	150,468
	S/MLP	858	864	877	871	26,777	16,909	1,092,831	1,081,530
	S/RF	625	570	633	569	19,615	21,941	730,711	666,313
	BM/DT	1,739	1,680	1,752	1,687	7,736	6,636	2,633,181	2,561,664
	BM/MLP	534	445	527	439	1,927	1,487	467,402	404,917
	BM/RF	990	941	997	937	3,757	2,848	1,340,204	1,269,559

Table 2. Number of discriminatory data items per second

N	DS/ML	Aequitas	CGFT	KOSEI	RSUTT
3,000	A/DT	49.4	26.8	6,157.2	11,061.9
	A/MLP	1.1	1.2	1,087.5	1,092.4
	A/RF	1.9	1.9	1,036.1	1,098.6
	S/DT	28.1	13.4	5,979.6	9,633.2
	S/MLP	11.0	17.7	6,662.0	7,220.7
	S/RF	2.5	1.8	837.4	928.6
	BM/DT	3.6	2.6	10,230.0	10,604.6
	BM/MLP	2.3	2.4	4,791.8	5,547.5
	BM/RF	0.3	0.2	1,024.0	1,079.3
7,000	A/DT	23.9	17.2	6,158.4	10,234.8
	A/MLP	0.5	0.7	1,099.9	1,097.1
	A/RF	0.8	0.9	1,027.2	1,128.2
	S/DT	31.8	22.0	6,163.4	9,373.2
	S/MLP	8.3	5.1	6,628.0	7,138.2
	S/RF	1.1	1.4	825.8	939.2
	BM/DT	1.6	1.6	10,161.9	10,718.8
	BM/MLP	1.1	1.1	4,843.1	5,661.1
	BM/RF	0.2	0.1	1,022.6	1,090.5

> **Answer to RQ1**
>
> As expected, RSUTT and CGFT gave almost the same results. Contrary to expectations, RSUTT did not necessarily show better results than Aequitas and KOSEI.

[RQ2] How Many More Discriminatory Data Items did RSUTT Find Compared to Existing Methods? Theoretically, since the algorithms for local search are the same for Aequitas and CGFT, and for KOSEI and RSUTT, the results should be similar. However, the local search relies on seed data items, i.e., the results of the global search. Therefore, the results cannot be naively compared as we did for RQ1, i.e., when comparing local search, we are actually comparing the entirety of global and local search.

Table 1 shows that KOSEI and RSUTT have significantly larger values than Aequitas and CGFT. The KOSEI paper [11] gave two reasons for this. First, the input space was explored multiple times with many discriminatory data items. Second, duplicate evaluations of data items are removed. These two points also hold for RSUTT.

> **Answer to RQ2**
>
> RSUTT was able to find many more discriminatory data items than Aequitas and CGFT.

[RQ3] How Efficiently did RSUTT Discover Discriminatory Data Items Compared to Existing Methods? Table 2 show the results of the number of discriminatory data items that were found per second. RSUTT clearly has the best results. There was only one case ($N = 7{,}000$, Adult, MLP) where RSUTT did not have the best result, but even in this case the difference between RSUTT and KOSEI was minimal, just 2.8 items per second. Similar to what the KOSEI paper [11] say, two reasons can be given for RSUTT's superiority over Aequitas and CGFT. First, the number of discriminatory data items found is greater. Second, the search time is reduced.

Next, as for the difference between KOSEI and RSUTT, we consider that this is due to the coverage of the data item space in global search. Compared to KOSEI, RSUTT is more likely to cover the data item space. As we discuss in Sect. 6, the stability of the global search means that seed data items are less likely to be clustered in a biased space, making it easier to find discriminatory data items more efficiently during local search.

> **Answer to RQ3**
>
> RSUTT was found to produce the best results for the number of discriminatory data items per second for most data sets and ML models.

[RQ4] If a Protected Attribute can Take More Than Two Values, Which Values Should be Selected? Discriminatory data items were defined as data items whose output differs when the value of a protected attribute is changed. In RSUTT, the discrimination evaluation uses the minimum and maximum values of a protected attribute. However, protected attributes may take other values. RQ4 considers such cases through the following three scenarios:

- SceA: The minimum value is fixed as one value of the protected attribute. The other value is randomly selected within the protected attribute's domain other than the minimum value.
- SceB: The minimum value is fixed as one value of the protected attribute. The other value changes its value from minimum to maximum within the protected attribute's domain. Once a discriminatory data item is found, no further values are checked, i.e., the discrimination evaluation terminates.
- SceC: The two values are chosen from the protected attribute's domain randomly.

The implementation of RSUTT was modified for each of the above scenarios. We call the modified version RSUTTA, RSUTTB, RSUTTC for SceA, SceB, SceC, respectively.

The experiment was done only with RSUTT under the following condition:

- Number of test cases: $N = 3,000$
- ML model: Decision Tree
- Dataset: Bank Marketing

Table 3 shows the results of the experiment for RQ4, where each result is the average of 10 executions. "All data items" denotes the total number of data items generated in both global and local search. "Discriminatory data item rate" denotes the percentage of "All data items" that were found to be discriminatory.

Table 3. Results of experiment ABC

	RSUTTA	RSUTTB	RSUTTC	RSUTT
All data items	906,205	739,002	593,804	1,435,003
Seed data items	452	735	295	716
Discriminatory data items	483,691	570,072	436,588	1,086,700
Discriminatory data item rate	53%	77%	71%	76%
Discriminatory data items per sec	7,478	6,122	9,502	10,052
Elapsed time (sec)	65	93	44	108

[SceA] Minimum Value: Random. When we compare RSUTTA and RSUTT in Table 3, we can see that RSUTTA is less efficient than RSUTT. This result suggests that the method of selecting protected attributes contributes to the efficiency of discriminatory data item discovery.

[SceB] Minimum Value: Other Than Min. When we compare RSUTTB and RSUTT in Table 3, RSUTTB showed little difference in the number of seed data items compared to RSUTT. However, the number of discriminatory data items was significantly lower. In global search, discrimination evaluation is performed after the data item is generated, so the termination condition does not affect the number of searches. Thus, the results for RSUTT and RSUTTB is basically the same.

In local search, the same data item may be evaluated multiple times as the value for the protected attribute is continually changed unless it is found to be discriminatory. For example, if a protected attribute can take ten possible values, the same data item will be evaluated up to nine times in RSUTTB, while it is only once in RSUTT. However, there is a limit in the total number of local search executions, and as a result the number of discrimination evaluations. This means that RSUTTB will evaluate fewer data items compared to RSUTT. This means that the method of selecting the protected attribute values will affect the number of data items, which in the end will affect the number of discriminatory data items to be found.

[SceC] Both Random. When we compare RSUTTC and RSUTT in Table 3, RSUTTC is less efficient than RSUTT. However, when we checked each of the ten executions, the larger the difference between the selected two values, the greater the efficiency. If we interpret robustness as a property where the further away from a data item, the more likely it is to produce a different output, we can say that the most efficient way is to run the discrimination evaluation on the minimum and maximum values.

Answer to RQ4

When selecting the protected attribute for the discrimination evaluation, it is most efficient to select the minimum and maximum values.

6 Discussion

We discuss two issues: seed data generation and data item generation efficiency. We then discuss threats to validity.

6.1 Seed Data Generation

As we have already shown in the results of RQ1, RSUTT (and CGFT) did not necessarily find more seed data items compared to Aequitas and KOSEI. This was not what we had expected, but this may have been affected by the robustness property, but in reverse. An important point of global search is to search the entire data item space. This means that RSUTT (and CGFT) will tend to generate data items that are evenly spaced out, while that may not be the case for Aequitas and KOSEI. According to the robustness property, similar results tend to be near each other. Thus, RSUTT and CGFT may actually have a higher chance of missing seed data items.

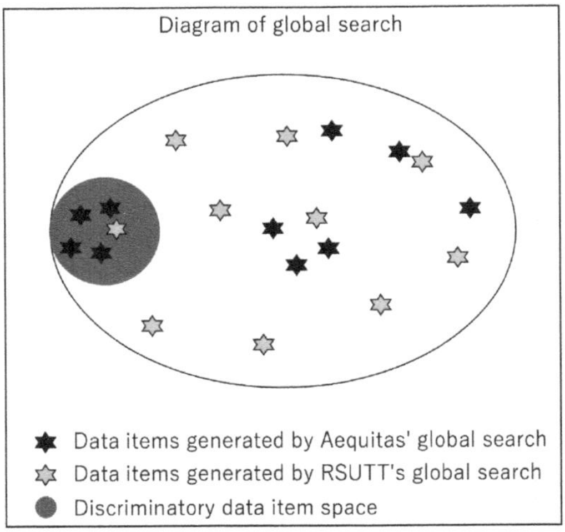

Fig. 2. Diagram of the global search for RSUTT

Figure 2 shows this schematically. RSUTT (CGFT) generates data items that are fairly evenly spaced, while data items generated by Aequitas and KOSEI may be partially bunched together. According to the robustness property, discriminatory data items will likely be near each other, and is shown as discriminatory data item space in Fig. 2. Thus, there could be cases where Aequitas and KOSEI will find more seed data items because they generated data items within the discriminatory data item space, while RSUTT (CGFT) will only find one from the same space. In the end, this should not be an issue as the discriminatory data items in this space should be found through local search in RSUTT.

6.2 Efficiency: Duplicate Data Item Generation

We discuss the efficiency of RSUTT's data item generation from the viewpoint of duplicate data item generation. Duplicate data items are data items for which a discrimination evaluation has already been used to determine whether they are discriminatory or not. We counted the number of duplicate data items that were actually generated for Aequitas, CGFT, KOSEI, and RSUTT under the following condition:

- Number of test cases: $N = 3,000$
- ML model: Decision Tree
- Datasets: Adult, Statlog, and Bank Marketing

Table 4 shows the results. For global search, duplicate data items were generated by Aequitas and KOSEI, but not CGFT and RSUTT. This is because CGFT and RSUTT use CT to systematically generate data items resulting in zero duplicates.

Table 4. Number of duplicate data items

Dataset	Aequitas	CGFT	KOSEI	RSUTT
Adult	345	0	332	0
Statlog	1,060	0	1,064	0
Bank Marketing	11,135	0	10,911	0

6.3 Threats to Validity

We used three datasets and three ML models, so this is a threat in terms of generalizability. However, many other fairness testing research use the dataset and ML model used in this experiment, and we believe they have a certain degree of reliability. Future experiments should be conducted on a larger number of data sets.

We selected gender and age as the protected attributes. Although RSUTT can be applied to any protected attribute, future work should experiment with other protected attributes for further generalization.

There may be bugs in the implementations of Aequitas, CGFT, KOSEI, and RSUTT. Although it is possible that such bugs have not been eliminated, every effort was made to debug them as much as possible.

7 Conclusions

We proposed *Robust Search Using T-way Testing (RSUTT)* to discover discriminatory data items in a stable and efficient manner. The method is based on Coverage-Guided Fairness Testing (CGFT) for global search and KOSEI for local search. CGFT's global search generates and tests evenly distributed data items by utilizing combinatorial testing. In KOSEI's local search, the neighborhoods of discriminatory data items obtained in the global search are systematically generated and tested based on the order of pre-defined order relations. Local search is also performed again on discriminatory data items obtained in local search.

Evaluation results show that, although there was no significant improvement in the number of discriminatory data items, there was a significant improvement when comparing the number of discriminatory data items found per second.

Future work includes generalizing the proposed method by using other datasets and ML models than those used in this experiment, and retraining the proposed method to reduce the number of discriminatory data items.

References

1. Aggarwal, A., Lohia, P., Nagar, S., Dey, K., Saha, D.: Black box fairness testing of machine learning models. In: Proceedings of the 2019 27th ACM Joint Meeting on European Software Engineering Conference and Symposium on the Foundations of Software Engineering, pp. 625–635 (2019). https://doi.org/10.1145/3338906.3338937
2. Angwin, J., Larson, J., Mattu, S., Kirchner, L.: Machine bias: there's software used across the country to predict future criminals and it's biased against blacks (2016). https://www.propublica.org/article/machine-bias-risk-assessments-in-criminal-sentencing. Accessed 15 Mar 2024
3. Dastin, J.: Insight - amazon scraps secret AI recruiting tool that showed bias against women (2018). https://www.reuters.com/article/idUSKCN1MK0AG/. Accessed 15 Mar 2024
4. Galhotra, S., Brun, Y., Meliou, A.: Fairness testing: testing software for discrimination. In: Proceedings of the 2017 11th Joint Meeting on Foundations of Software Engineering, pp. 498–510 (2017). https://doi.org/10.1145/3106237.3106277
5. Goodall, N.J.: Can you program ethics into a self-driving car? IEEE Spectr. **53**(6), 28–58 (2016). https://doi.org/10.1109/MSPEC.2016.7473149
6. Kuhn, D.R., Kacker, R.N., Lei, Y.: Introduction to Combinatorial Testing. Chapman & Hall (2013)
7. Mattioli, D.: On orbitz, mac users steered to pricier hotels (2012). https://www.wsj.com/articles/SB10001424052702304458604577488822667325882. Accessed 15 Mar 2024
8. Olson, P.: The algorithm that beats your bank manager (2011). https://www.forbes.com/sites/parmyolson/2011/03/15/the-algorithm-that-beats-your-bank-manager. Accessed 15 Mar 2024
9. Pedregosa, F., et al.: Scikit-learn: machine learning in python. J. Mach. Learn. Res. **12**(85), 2825–2830 (2011)
10. Perez Morales, D., Kitamura, T., Takada, S.: Coverage-guided fairness testing. In: Lee, R. (ed.) ICIS 2021. SCI, vol. 985, pp. 183–199. Springer, Cham (2021). https://doi.org/10.1007/978-3-030-79474-3_13
11. Sano, S., Kitamura, T., Takada, S.: An efficient discrimination discovery method for fairness testing. In: Proceedings of the 34th International Conference on Software Engineering and Knowledge Engineering, SEKE, pp. 200–205 (2022).https://doi.org/10.18293/SEKE2022-064
12. Sharma, A., Wehrheim, H.: Automatic fairness testing of machine learning models. In: Casola, V., De Benedictis, A., Rak, M. (eds.) ICTSS 2020. LNCS, vol. 12543, pp. 255–271. Springer, Cham (2020). https://doi.org/10.1007/978-3-030-64881-7_16
13. UCI: UCI machine learning repository. https://archive.ics.uci.edu/. Accessed 15 Mar 2024
14. Udeshi, S., Arora, P., Chattopadhyay, S.: Automated directed fairness testing. In: Proceedings of the 33rd ACM/IEEE International Conference on Automated Software Engineering, pp. 98–108 (2018). https://doi.org/10.1145/3238147.3238165
15. Zhang, P., et al.: White-box fairness testing through adversarial sampling. In: IEEE/ACM 42nd International Conference on Software Engineering, pp. 949–960 (2020)

Exploring Image Similarity-Based Splitting Techniques in Automotive Perception Systems

Md Abu Ahammed Babu[1,2](✉), Sushant Kumar Pandey[2], Darko Durisic[1], Ashok Chaitanya Koppisetty[1], and Miroslaw Staron[2]

[1] Research and Development, Volvo Car Corporation, Gothenburg, Sweden
{md.abu.ahammed.babu,darko.durisic, ashok.chaitanya.koppisetty}@volvocars.com

[2] Chalmers | University of Gothenburg, Gothenburg, Sweden
{sushant.kumar.pandey,miroslaw.staron}@gu.se

Abstract. Training object detection models for automotive perception systems is often a challenging task due to the variation in the image data used to train and test the model. The images might come from different geographic locations as well as different weather and lighting conditions. Image similarity-based split could be a safe option to keep the train and test sets as identical as possible. However, based on which similarity measure is chosen to split the data, the train and test set may not contain enough representative images of all the different situations, including seasonal and lighting variations, and hence often degrades overall performance. This study considered four different image similarity measures based on visual features and intrinsic/semantic information that come with the image data. The semantic similarity helps to avoid gathering images in the same (train/test) set that visually look similar to each other. The evaluation results show that the semantic similarity-based splits resulted in 12–47% higher performance of the object detection model in terms of mean average precision (mAP) and F1-score. Among the four similarity measures, AllClass similarity consists of the highest intrinsic information available with the image data, which also results in the highest performance of the model when used for data splitting.

Keywords: image similarity · object detection · computer vision · deep learning · automotive perception system

1 Introduction

Autonomous Driving (AD) software is typically composed of multiple perception and decision sub-systems [1]. The perception sub-systems within autonomous vehicles identify objects surrounding the vehicle by using data from the operational design domain (ODD), coming from sensors such as LiDAR, radar, camera, and ultrasound. Recently, the automotive industry has been focusing on implementing autonomous vehicles equipped with cameras as their primary sensors

A. Bertolino et al. (Eds.): QUATIC 2024, CCIS 2178, pp. 51–67, 2024.
https://doi.org/10.1007/978-3-031-70245-7_4

[2]. These cameras capture images serving rich data sources for advanced driver assistance systems. Applications of cameras include identifying potential hazards in surrounding traffic and detecting traffic lights, signs, and road conditions. All these scenarios depend on accurate object detection, a crucial component for decision sub-systems, as emphasized in [3]. While cameras play a crucial role in object detection scenarios in autonomous driving, they are complemented by signals from radar and LiDAR to enhance the safety of decision-making in autonomous driving [4]. The rapid evolution of modern object detection techniques has been driven by the advent of deep neural networks (DNN), particularly convolutional neural networks (CNN) and Autoencoders. Deep learning (DL) object detectors, as described in [5], employ supervised or semi-supervised learning, where the image data is split into train and test sets at first. The model learns from the training images and is evaluated later on test set images using performance metrics like mean average precision (mAP). The efficacy of the training process significantly impacts the quality of the resulting model and, consequently, the entire AD system.

In the process of training the model, data splitting is a critical step, determining whether the model is trained on data representative of the population and if the degree of similarity between data points accurately reflects the population. In the context of image data, two images may appear different but represent the same place, time, or situation. This type of information leak needs careful consideration when splitting the data. Researchers have explored various image similarity-based data splitting techniques to ensure that the training and test sets contain representative and diverse samples of the captured scenes. These data-splitting techniques take into account the similarities and differences between images, allowing for a balanced distribution of different scenarios and variations in lighting conditions, weather conditions, and other environmental factors and driving conditions. These data-splitting techniques aim to minimize the bias in the training and testing sets, ensuring that the models can generalize well to unseen scenarios and perform accurately in different real-world conditions. By leveraging image similarity-based data splitting, image perception systems can benefit from improved accuracy and robustness.

Existing approaches for measuring image similarity are either histogram-based (where pixel value distributions are captured) or structural similarity and feature-based approaches (where luminance, contrast, or different salient features like edges and corners are considered to measure similarity between two images). However, choosing this pixel-based or feature-based similarity measures to split image data may lead to cases where images from the same lighting, and weather conditions will appear in the same set (either train or test set). For better understanding, consider Fig. 1 where 5 images from different lighting conditions have been drawn; images 1, 2, and 3 represent dark light conditions, and images 4 and 5 come from bright (or daylight) conditions. When pixel-based similarity approaches are used to split them into train-test sets, chances are high to get images 1, 2, and 3 in one set, while images 4 and 5 will appear in the other set. In that way, the model will learn about only one type of lighting on the road (either dark or bright, depending on which set is being chosen as the train set). This

(a) Image 1 (15 vehicles, 2 vulnerable vehicles)

(b) Image 2 (28 vehicles, 1 vulnerable vehicle)

(c) Image 3 (3 vehicles, 14 pedestrians, 8 vulnerable vehicles)

(d) Image 4 (17 vehicles, 4 pedestrians, 9 vulnerable vehicles)

(e) Image 5 (13 vehicles, 2 pedestrians, 1 vulnerable vehicle)

Fig. 1. Sample Images in a dataset.

may lead to insufficient training of the model as well as poor performance during the testing phase. However, using the semantic information that is available with the image data (mentioned inside parentheses of the sub-figures title) as a similarity measure may result in a different combination of images for both sets. The results in that case may look like that images 3, 4, and 5 will appear in the same set, and images 1, and 2 will go into the other set. This solution represents a better mix of images of different lighting conditions, ensuring that the model will have enough exposure to the variety in the dataset during training.

To address this problem, this study investigates four semantic similarity measures through multiple computational experiments with the goal of exploring whether available semantic information improves the model's training process and later performance. The research question that is addressed in this study is:

RQ: *Which similarity measure for splitting image data leads to improved performance in the context of autonomous driving?*

The remainder of the paper is structured as follows: Sect. 2 includes information about existing works on and around this field(s) of interest. Section 3 explains the steps towards the experiment, including how the data preparation, feature vectors creation, and similarity calculation have been done, including how the experiment is done, and the platform specification followed by Sect. 4 where the findings of the experiment are summarized and shown. Finally, Sect. 5 discusses the findings and points out the key significance of the results, and Sect. 7 concludes the summary of the study and possible future directions.

2 Background and Related Work

Self-driving technologies have long been a significant focus in transportation. Recent advancements in this area, primarily attributed to Computer Vision (CV) technology, have marked notable progress. A key component of CV is object detection, aiding in the recognition of various road users such as vehicles, pedestrians, as well as traffic lights and signs. Object detection has emerged as a particularly formidable challenge within autonomous driving systems, primarily due to the complex nature of the real-world traffic environments [6]. Different weather, daylight, and road conditions are just some of the open-world scenarios that comprise the operational domain of autonomous driving [7]. The ability to detect objects regardless of image distortions or weather conditions is crucial for real-world applications of deep learning, but a range of standard object detection models suffers from severe performance loss of 30–60 % on distorted images [8].

To train an object detection model effectively, the data must be divided into two sets: one for training the model and the other for evaluating the model's performance. However, the process of data splitting is known to be a significant factor contributing to data leakage into test sets [9], emphasizing the need for careful handling. To prevent data leakage, it's crucial to establish a proper split, implement a late split, or apply pre-processing steps to the data before performing the split. An empirical investigation [10] examining data leakage resulting from improper splitting within the context of AI for IT operations (AIOPs) highlighted the substantial impact of selecting an appropriate split method over random splitting, which can significantly reduce the risk of data leakage. The study compared random splitting, time-based splitting, and baseline splitting strategies across varying train/validation ratios from 50%/50% to 90%/10%.

Furthermore, the true positive and false positive rates were also higher with random splitting (0.98% and 0.99%) compared to time-based splitting (0.64% and 0.7%), even with imbalanced datasets. Based on these findings, the authors concluded that time-based splitting was more suitable for evaluating AIOPs models, offering a lower risk of data leakage. However, it's worth noting that the study did not explore other splitting methods, such as similarity-based splitting. Additionally, while time-based splitting may be suitable for AIOPs data and regression tasks, its applicability to object detection tasks using image data, particularly within automotive perception systems, remains to be explored.

Image similarity could be an effective factor to be considered for splitting, where similar images will be grouped into either train or test sets. In that case, the similar images in one set will be identical to some extent to the images in the other set. The chosen image similarity measure would be the crucial factor in this process as the data will be split based on that. The existing image similarity measures can be divided mainly into two types: pixel-based measures and feature-based similarity measures. The pixel-based similarity measures are calculated using the distance between two image pixel values. Examples of pixel-based similarity measures are Euclidean distance, structural similarity index (SSiM), quasi-euclidean distance, etc. On the other hand, the feature-based similarity measures calculate similarity by extracting and comparing features of the images, such as edges and corners of the objects in the images. Moreover, a hybrid similarity measure called Histogram Feature Error Mean Measure (HFEMM) is introduced in [11] which combines both histogram similarity measure and feature similarity measure (FSIM). This new measure has been tested on different datasets and gave better performance than the other similarity measures, such as SSiM and FSIM. However, the proposed measure demonstrates outstanding performance when noise is introduced in the images but cannot guarantee the same performance on the images with low-lighting and foggy images, which is an obvious use-case in the context of Autonomous Driving (AD).

The work of Kotar et al. in [12] introduced a method to measure similarity based on intrinsic object properties that define object identity. The authors provided a benchmark dataset and proved that their combined deep feature learning approach is more effective in approximating similarity than other existing methods. Nevertheless, this similarity approach has not been tested on mixed environments with multiple objects of different classes present, which is the most common AD scenario.

This study introduces three new image similarity features based on different semantic information along with visual similarity feature extraction. In the end, the four similarity features were used to split an image dataset for AD.

3 Experiment Design

Each experiment consists of four main steps: 1) Data selection and 2) Data splitting, where the dataset is divided into train and test sets based on four different similarity measures. 3) Model training, where we utilized the YOLOv7x object detection model, a variant of YOLOv7 [13] known for its speed and accuracy, and it incorporates a trainable bag-of-freebies method to enhance 2D-object detection accuracy. 4) Model evaluation, where the trained model is assessed using the test dataset. The replication package of this study is made available[1].

YOLOv7x is one of the latest edition to the YOLO (You Only Look Once) model family, mostly known for its efficiency in object detection. It has been identified in a recent survey [14] as the method that surpasses other existing methods in both accuracy and speed by reducing large number of parameters and computations [13].

[1] https://figshare.com/s/305809154c0ade1c69c7.

3.1 Data Selection

The dataset used in this experiment is real in-use industry data that was selected and retrieved from the data pipeline of our partner company. The selected dataset consists of vehicular images captured using the front camera of eight different data collection vehicles. These data were collected, annotated and added to the pipeline throughout a year (from mid 2022 to mid 2023). The aim behind choosing a complete year timeline is to cover all seasonal changes in the road environment along with data on different weather and lighting conditions of the road, other road users, and surroundings as much as possible.

3.2 Data Preparation

The front camera images used in this study come from different data collection cars used in a vehicle OEM company (as mentioned in the previous subsection). The collected dataset contains 46,483 image frames along with their corresponding annotations. These annotations are objects or instances that belong to five classes: vehicle, pedestrian, vulnerable vehicle (e.g., wheelchair, stroller), mover (e.g., walkers, shopping trolleys), and animal (e.g., dog, moose, deer, etc.). Figure 2 shows the class distribution of the corresponding dataset with the total number of instances for each class.

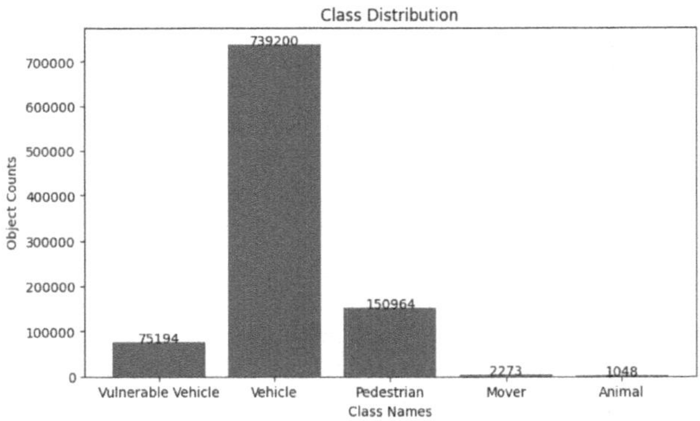

Fig. 2. Class distribution of the image data. The x-axis shows the 5 classes' names, and the y-axis shows the total objects of those classes present in the dataset.

3.3 Independent Variable - Treatments

The experiment contains four treatments, representing four splitting techniques based on different similarity measures applied. The treatments are prepared by calculating the designated similarity feature vectors, which are later used to split the dataset into train-test sets. Additionally, another treatment is introduced, representing a random split of 70-30 ratios in the train and test sets to be used as a baseline in the middle. To ensure a completely blind, unsupervised, and unbiased split of the dataset, k-means clustering algorithm was chosen. There are various reasons for choosing k-means for splitting tasks. One of the main reasons is its simplicity and efficiency [15], making it computationally feasible [16] even for large datasets [14]. Moreover, its effectiveness in handling high-dimensional data and scalability to accommodate a large number of data points [17] makes it a well-fit for this task. The following subsections discuss all the treatments and how they are obtained.

Treatment 0 - Random Split. This treatment represents the random splitting technique, which is one of the traditional and commonly used approaches to split data into train and test sets. The 70-30 split ratio is chosen for this treatment which means random 70% data is used as the training set and the rest 30% is put to test the model later. The reason for introducing the random split is to provide a baseline for further comparison of the results of image similarity-based splits.

Treatment 1 - Visual Similarity-Based Split. Visual similarity is calculated from the extracted visual feature values of the images using a pre-trained VGG16 model, which is extensively used for image feature extraction tasks in various fields of study [18]. The idea behind bringing visual similarity as a treatment for this particular experiment is to compare how the model's performance gets affected by putting the visually similar images together to train a model, and the test set contains the other part of the images that are visually different from the first group. The fact could be explained more easily from Fig. 1 where images 1, 2, and 3 look more similar to each other and hence used to train the image recognition model, which would be tested on images 4, and 5 that are almost visually identical compared to the first 3 images. This difficulty faced by the model in the testing phase might affect the overall detection performance of the model. Table 1 shows an illustration of how the extracted visual feature values look like. The VGG16 model was used to extract 4096 feature values per image. These values returned by the model are all decimal point values that represent different features of the images. The dimension of the visual feature vector is 46,483 (total no. of images) $\times$ 4096.

Table 1. An illustration of how the visual similarity features look like. Each image has 4096 visual feature values extracted by the pre-trained VGG16 model

Images	Value_0	Value_1	Value_2	...	Value_4095
Image 1	0.73	0.42	0.89	...	2.65
Image 2	0.97	0.88	0.47	...	1.60
...	...	...	...	...	...
Image 46483	–	–	–	...	–

Treatment 2 - Object Similarity-Based Split. To measure the object-based similarity of the images, a feature vector has been prepared with the object counts of different classes present in the images. Table 2 shows an example of how the object features look like. This feature vector dimension becomes 46,483 $\times$ 5, and it is used later on to calculate similarity among the image data and split into train-test sets.

Table 2. An illustration of how the object similarity features look like

Images	0 (Vehicle)	1 (Pedestrian)	2 (Vulnerable Vehicle)	3 (Mover)	4 (Animal)
Image 1	15	0	2	0	0
Image 2	28	0	1	0	0
...	...	...	...	...	...
Image 46483	–	–	–	–	–

Treatment 3 - MajorClass Similarity-Based Split. MajorClass features are extracted from the annotation files of the image data and consist of bounding-box (bbox) coordinates of the objects within the images in pixel values. According to the class distribution in Fig. 2, the highest number of objects belong to the "vehicle" class (almost 76.3%); hence, we named this class as the MajorClass of this dataset. The feature vector for this particular similarity measure contains the bbox values (i.e., center coordinates of the object, width, and height) and splitting is done based on the similarity scores calculated on this MajorClass feature vector accordingly. The analysis of the image annotations shows that 152 is the highest number of occurrences of the "vehicle" class ($152 \times 4 = 608$ bounding box values) in a single annotation file. So after padding 0 s to make the vector symmetric, the dimension of the feature vector becomes 46,483 $\times$ 608. Table 3 illustrates how the MajorClass feature vector looks like.

Table 3. An illustration of how the MajorClass similarity features look like.

Images	center_X (Vehicle1)	center_Y (Vehicle1)	Width (Vehicle1)	Height (Vehicle1)	... (Vehicle152)
Image 1	3723	1192	185	84	...
Image 2	1829	1194	384	340	...
...	...	...	...	...	...
Image 46483	–	–	–	–	–

Treatment 4 - AllClass Similarity-Based Split. The fourth similarity measure is the AllClass similarity and as the name says, the feature vector used to calculate the similarity contains the bbox values of all the existing objects in the images. The dataset has item(s) with the highest 182 objects in it which means the maximum length of a vector would be 182 × (4 values for each object bbox) = 728. Hence, after putting all the bounding-box values and padding additional zeros, the dimension of the feature vector becomes 46,483 × 728. The dataset has item(s) with the highest 182 objects in it which means the maximum length of a vector would be 182 × (4 values for each object) = 728. To make the vector symmetric, the remaining indices are filled with 0 s (zeros), as zero padding does not make any difference during similarity measurement between two feature vectors [19]. Hence, after putting all the bbox values and padding additional zeros, the dimension of the AllClass feature vector becomes 46,483 × 728. Table 4 unravels how the feature vector looks at the end.

All the similarity feature vectors was generated using the scripts provided with the replication package. The scripts' runtime are considerably fast (<1 min) however, it may vary depending on the number of images in the dataset.

Table 4. An illustration of how the AllClass similarity features look like.

Images	center_X (Instance1)	center_Y (Instance1)	Width (Instance1)	Height (Instance1)	... (Instance182)
Image 1	3723	1192	185	84	...
Image 2	1829	1194	384	340	...
...	...	...	...	...	...
Image 46483	–	–	–	–	–

3.4 Dependent Variables

The dependent variable in this study is the mean average precision (mAP), which serves as a benchmark for evaluating the effectiveness of various models trained on different data splits. Widely recognized in computer vision research [20], mAP is a standard metric for gauging the reliability of object detection models [21]. It is calculated as the mean of Average Precision (APs) across all classes, encapsulating the trade-off between precision and recall. While this study didn't explicitly consider metrics like false positives (FPs) and false negatives (FNs) separately, as they are inherent in precision and recall calculations, the primary focus remains on examining performance variations across different data splits used in training and evaluation. Introducing additional measures would complicate the comparison process due to increased complexity.

In this experiment, both the mean average precision (mAP) and F1-score were utilized for comparison. The yolov7x model automatically computes and generates both (mAP and F1-score) after each experiment, eliminating the need for manual calculations. This approach minimizes the potential for minor rounding and truncation errors, thereby establishing both measures as the most equitable measures to serve as the dependent variables for comparison.

3.5 Hypotheses

The null hypothesis for this study posits that the mean values of the mean average precision (mAP) across various treatments with different splits will be equal or remain unchanged for the test datasets; the hypothesis is given below.

$$\mu_{mAPt1_{\text{test}}} = \mu_{mAPt2_{\text{test}}} = \mu_{mAPt3_{\text{test}}} = \mu_{mAPt4_{\text{test}}} \tag{1}$$

And the hypothesis regarding the mean of F1-scores is:

$$\mu_{F1-scoret1_{\text{test}}} = \mu_{F1-scoret2_{\text{test}}} = \mu_{F1-scoret3_{\text{test}}} = \mu_{F1-scoret4_{\text{test}}} \tag{2}$$

This means the model performance in terms of both mAP and F1-score on the test sets resulting from the different similarity-based splits will remain the same or will not significantly differ from each other.

3.6 Pipeline

In this study, we employed a machine-learning pipeline centered around the pre-trained YOLOv7x model, which was originally trained on the MS COCO dataset. YOLOv7x is essentially an enhanced version of the YOLOv7 object detection model, delivering improved accuracy compared to the base model, as demonstrated in the chart found in [22]. The model receives image data along with object labels in a specific format, which includes training, validation, and test subsets. In each experiment, we substituted the standard train, validation, and test data with data corresponding to the specific treatments or splits we wanted to investigate. To assess the model's performance on either the validation or test data, we executed designated scripts and provided the necessary hyperparameters such as epochs and batch size.

3.7 Task

The primary objective of this research is to conduct 2D object detection in images using the YOLOv7 network [22]. However, the overarching goal is to investigate how different similarity-based data splits based on four different similarity measures impact the performance of the models. The image dataset contains five different class instances of vehicle, pedestrian, vulnerable vehicle, mover, and animal. To carry out the task, we employ YOLOv7x, which is a modified version of the YOLOv7 object detection model. The model will undergo training and evaluation for each treatment, where the data distribution in the training and test sets varies according to the specific splits.

3.8 Analysis Method

To examine the results of each treatment and determine whether the null hypothesis can be rejected, the Kruskal-Wallis test [23], a non-parametric statistical test, is employed. With one dependent variable across six treatments in this experiment and the inability to ensure normal distribution of values, the Kruskal-Wallis test is the most suitable method for analysing the variance of the dependent variable (mAP in this instance).

3.9 Experiment Setup

In our experiments, we adhered to the default hyperparameters (image size:640, learning rate:0.01, etc.) of YOLOv7x[2], as our study's primary focus was not on improving object detection accuracy but on investigating performance difference of ML models for different image similarity-based splitting. We conducted experiments for up to 100 epochs with a batch size of 16, a common practice for sufficiently training object detection models. Our analysis indicated that 100 epochs strike a balance between convergence, under-fitting (with 50 epochs), and over-fitting (with 500 epochs). Each experiment was repeated at least five times to avoid randomness and any bias in the results. The means of the dependent variables (mAP and F1-score) were reported for further statistical analysis in the next sections.

4 Results

This section shows the evaluation results of the four similarity-based splits introduced earlier. As the splits are done based on similarity, which means similar images are grouped together, and hence the similarity between train and test sets would be low for each of the splits. We have also introduced a random split with a train-test ratio of 70:30 where images were chosen randomly to put 70% in the train and 30% in the test set. After applying all five splitting, the pipeline model was repeatedly trained and evaluated for 5 times for each of the resulting train and test sets.

Table 5 shows the average performance scores resulting from different data splits applied. **Treatment 1 (visual similarity-based split)** has led to the second lowest performance in terms of both mAP and F1-score (0.296 and 0.32, respectively), which indicates visual similarity is not an optimal choice for splitting image data. When images are partitioned based on visually similar features, images with similar lighting properties are in the same set which leads the model to learn specific patterns of the surroundings, rather than learn to localize objects of the same classes. This is shown in the average precision (AP) scores of the top two classes (vehicle and pedestrian) in the dataset. The AP_vehicle is 0.601, which is the second lowest, and AP_pedestrian is 0.424, which is the lowest among the treatments. The object similarity-based split **(treatment 2)** results

[2] https://github.com/WongKinYiu/yolov7.

in the lowest overall mAP score of 0.292 and F1-score of 0.30 because only the object counts were taken as the similarity feature to split the dataset, which is very little information compared to the other similarity measures introduced in this study. However, the individual AP score of the vehicle class is 0.717 when the object similarity-based split is applied, which is the highest. This occurs due to the highest presence of this particular class instances in the dataset According to the class distribution in Fig. 2, a total of 7,39,200 object instances present in the dataset belong to the vehicle class, which is almost 76.3% of the total object counts. Because of this highness in numbers in the similarity feature vector, most of the images that contain a large number of vehicle objects are grouped, and the trained model was able to detect only this class quite accurately.

The third treatment, where the **MajorClass similarity** is used for splitting, leads to moderately higher performance of the model with 0.356 mAP and 0.44 F1-score. Even the individual class APs analogously follow the same order. This indicates that improvement of model performance could be possible by choosing a similarity measure with more intrinsic details for splitting the image dataset. In this case, the similarity features consist of more intrinsic features, which, besides improving performance, also helps to split the dataset more acceptably so that both the train and test sets have a good mixture of images with different environmental and lighting changes. The random 70-30 split leads to the second-highest performance of the object detection model with 0.390 mAP and 0.42 F1-score. Although random split causes higher detection performance of the model, it does not, however, guarantee that similar images belong to the same set (either train or test). When the images with high similarity are distributed over both train and test sets, the model often memorizes the image details rather than generalizing, which introduces the threat of data leakage occurrence [24].

Finally, the highest performance scores come from treatment 4 with the AllClass similarity-based split in action, which guarantees consistent performance increment by the addition of the highest possible intrinsic values in the similarity measuring process. This time the mAP score becomes 0.399 with a 0.44 F1-score which is approximately 0.05 and 0.08 higher compared to treatment 2 and 0.11 and 0.14 compared to the lowest results for the performance metrics respectively (Table 5). Recalling the definition of the AllClass similarity measure, it engages the bbox values of all existing class instances present in the images. The addition of such information helps to split the images in a proper manner where images of the same object properties are grouped, not necessarily the images that look alike visually.

Figure 3 depicts the train-test ratios of the image data when the four similarity measures were applied to split the dataset, along with the resulting performance scores when those similarity-based splits were employed. The blue and orange bars show that the train-test ratios for each of the splits were more or less similar. However, the performance scores highly varied based on which similarity measure was used to split the data. The scores can still be considered as low since these are obtained from evaluating a model which was trained for

Table 5. Summary of the mAP and F1-score for different similarity-based splits along with AP scores for "Vehicle" and "Pedestrian") classes.

Split-type	AP_Vehicle	AP_Pedestrian	mAP	F1-score
Object similarity-based	**0.717**	0.362	0.292	0.30
Visual similarity-based	0.601	0.424	0.296	0.32
MajorClass similarity-based	0.694	0.545	0.356	0.36
Random	0.696	0.518	0.390	0.42
AllClass similarity-based	0.704	**0.595**	**0.399**	**0.44**

100 epochs only but it can obviously be enhanced with an increased number of training epochs. This results only give the notion of how choosing similarity measure for data splitting may affect the evaluation performance.

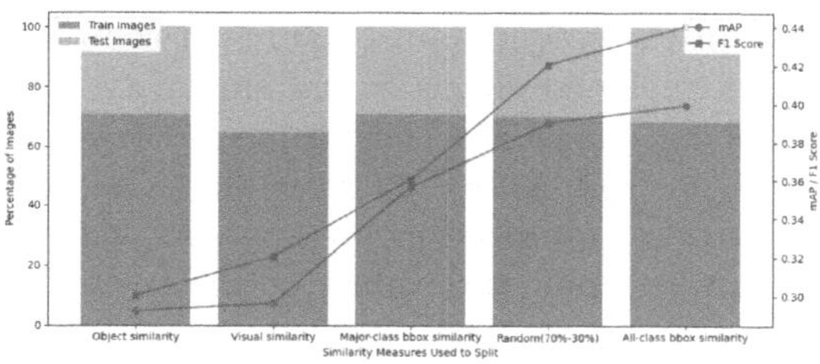

Fig. 3. Train-test ratio with performance scores based on different splits. (Color figure online)

A Kruskal-Wallis test on the performance scores (for both mAP and F1-score) has been conducted with a confidence level of 99% to see whether the obtained performance resulting from different similarity-based splitting strategies being applied significantly varies or not. The p-values stated in Table 6 are less than the alpha (0.01) for both the mAP and F1-scores, verifying that the null hypotheses can be rejected, which means the results are significantly different.

Table 6. Summary of the P-values of the statistical tests.

Kruskal-Wallis test	P-values
mAP	$0.00008 < 0.01$
F1-score	$0.00008 < 0.01$

5 Discussion

This study set off to find a similarity measure that helps to improve model performance when used for splitting data. The findings exhibit that the AllClass similarity-based split leads to the highest performance scores (both mAP and F1-score) of the object detection model. It indicates that when all the intrinsic information available is exposed and used during similarity measuring, the performance of the model becomes the best. In this case, the mAP scores increase by around 37%, and the F1-score hikes largely by 47% compared to the object similarity-based split. Moreover, this performance improvement is still around 12% higher in mAP and 22% in F1-score compared to the results consequent from the MajorClass similarity-based split. As the AllClass similarity measure utilizes the intrinsic features of all available objects to compare images, the highness in mixing images from different surroundings was possible in the train-test sets, which helped significantly improve the detection performance.

The object similarity-based split results in the lowest performance for the three metrics considered in this study, except for one of the classes– the "Vehicle" class. This exception occurs due to the biases by the high proportion presence (76.3%) of the "Vehicle" objects in the class distribution shown in Fig. 2. The visual similarity-based split, which considered the similarity of the visual features in the images, results in the second-lowest figures of the performance metrics. Essentially, this proves that choosing a visual similarity measure to split the image dataset is not an optimal choice, at least not in the context of AD and the object detection task. The result caused by the MajorClass similarity-based split is relatively higher than the two mentioned earlier. As MajorClass similarity is measured based on the bounding-box values of the "Vehicle" objects present in the images, it helps to compare images more in a semantic manner rather than visually. This helps to group images from various road environments and weather conditions that are similar in terms of present "Vehicle" objects and their properties.

Consider again the sample images exemplified in Fig. 1 to establish the consequences of choosing different similarity measures for separating train and test sets. The outcome of a visual similarity-based split would be the separation of all relatively dark images (Image 1a, 1b, and 1c) in the train set and the remaining bright images 1d, 1e in the test set. In this case, the train images do not really represent different lighting scenarios existing in the dataset which affects the model performance in the end when tested on the different lighting images. Even when object similarity is chosen, the resulting split will put images 1c, 1d, and 1e in the same set due to the similarity in terms of object counts which also not optimal as the remaining both test set images (1a, 1b) are dark light images. However, the AllClass similarity-based split has a marginally acceptable variation in the train-test set images where images 1a, 1c, and 1e are the member of the train set and images 1b and 1d belongs to test set. This is reasonably a balanced partitioning of the images where both train and test sets have representatives of both dark and bright images. This will help the model learn the object properties instead of learning common patterns in the backgrounds, which makes the model more generalizable and robust.

This is just a simplified example of the environmental differences in the road conditions. However, more environmental varieties such as rain, fog, snow and other scenario varieties like mountains, forests, etc., might also introduce additional complexities in the perceived driving environment for the automotive perception system. Recognizing the objects regardless of the lighting or weather conditions is extremely important, particularly in the AD scenario where a simple misclassification may cause lives. The introduced intrinsic information-based similarity features are capable of producing a balanced split of data by putting images from all scenarios into both train and test sets. Among them, the All-Class similarity measure seems the most fruitful one in significantly improving detection performance when used for splitting image data.

6 Validity Evaluation

We utilize the framework outlined by Wohlin et al. [25] to address four categories of validity threats: conclusion, internal, construct, and external.

Conclusion Validity: The use of mAP and F1-score as the dependent variables in this study may not always ensure reliability. Variations in class occurrences across different treatments could lead to different APs for individual classes, potentially impacting mAP scores. Future efforts aim to address this by ensuring a more balanced class distribution across individual splits. As parameters like class or instance counts do not consistently control splits, variations in class distribution among splits may affect performance.

Internal Validity: Training the object detection model for 100 epochs across all treatments may introduce a maturation threat due to differences in data points. This was mitigated by extending training to 500 epochs for most treatments, with marginal improvements observed in performance measures.

Construct Validity: The experiment focused solely on object detection, potentially introducing mono-operation bias threats. Future experiments will explore other operations, such as image segmentation, to examine the impact of similarity measures for image data splitting.

External Validity: The use of only the yolov7x object detection model could pose an external threat. However, the literature supports yolov7x as an appropriate choice due to its high performance and speed. Class imbalance in the dataset may impact external validity. Although achieving perfect balance in image recognition datasets is challenging, future experiments with less imbalanced datasets could enhance generalizability. Interaction of History and Treatment: External validity threats arise from using data from a single automotive OEM dataset. Including additional datasets is integral to ongoing work.

7 Conclusion and Future Work

This study focused on four different similarity-based splits and the performance of an object detection model when those data splits are applied. The idea was to group the image data based on four different similarity measures to create the train and test dataset so that both sets have a minimal similarity or higher dissimilarity. The final results were evaluated based on the highest values of the performance metrics (mAP and F1-score) as the data were split to ensure minimal similarity between the train and test sets with a better distribution of different weather and lighting images which will help to make a more robust model. The lowest performance was shown while the object similarity-based split was applied, the similarity measure that considers the fewest semantic information as similarity features. The model performance increases by a great margin (around 12–37% mAP and 22–47% F1-score) when more intrinsic information about the objects, such as object counts, their size, and localization information, are considered as the similarity features and used to split the data accordingly. According to the statistical test results, the difference in performances for these four similarity-based splits is significant. The highest model performance is demonstrated when AllClass similarity was used to split the data and this similarity feature also takes the highest number of intrinsics about the images as input to measure similarity. This rise in performance proves that the model was able to learn to localize objects better during testing because of getting an exposal of images from varied environmental and lighting conditions.

In the future, other image similarity features could be investigated, which consider not only visual features but also a mixture of visual and other additional semantic features of the images such as object occlusion, angle of view etc. Finding a similarity threshold that ensures enough diversity of the images in both train and test sets could also be a magnificent contribution to the computer vision research field. Nonetheless, the model's robustness could also be examined by providing out-of-distribution data besides applying the appropriate similarity measure for splitting the data.

References

1. Kiran, B.R., et al.: Deep reinforcement learning for autonomous driving: a survey. IEEE Trans. Intell. Transp. Syst. **23**(6), 4909–4926 (2021)
2. Jhung, J., Kim, S.: Behind-the-scenes (BTS): wiper-occlusion canceling for advanced driver assistance systems in adverse rain environments. Sensors **21**(23), 8081 (2021)
3. Rashed, H., et al.: Generalized object detection on fisheye cameras for autonomous driving: dataset, representations and baseline. In: Proceedings of the IEEE/CVF Winter Conference on Applications of Computer Vision, pp. 2272–2280 (2021)
4. Gupta, A., Anpalagan, A., Guan, L., Khwaja, A.S.: Deep learning for object detection and scene perception in self-driving cars: survey, challenges, and open issues. Array **10**, 100057 (2021)
5. Redmon, J., Divvala, S., Girshick, R., Farhadi, A.: You only look once: unified, real-time object detection. In: Proceedings of the IEEE Conference on Computer Vision and Pattern Recognition, pp. 779–788 (2016)
6. Boukerche, A., Hou, Z.: Object detection using deep learning methods in traffic scenarios. ACM Comput. Surv. (CSUR) **54**(2), 1–35 (2021)
7. Adam, G., et al.: Robustness and deployability of deep object detectors in autonomous driving. In: 2019 IEEE Intelligent Transportation Systems Conference (ITSC), pp. 4128–4133. IEEE (2019)

8. Michaelis, C., et al.: Benchmarking robustness in object detection: autonomous driving when winter is coming. arXiv preprint arXiv:1907.07484 (2019)
9. Wen, J., et al.: Convolutional neural networks for classification of Alzheimer's disease: overview and reproducible evaluation. Med. Image Anal. **63**, 101694 (2020)
10. Lyu, Y., Li, H., Sayagh, M., Jiang, Z.M., Hassan, A.E.: An empirical study of the impact of data splitting decisions on the performance of AIOps solutions. ACM Trans. Softw. Eng. Methodol. (TOSEM) **30**(4), 1–38 (2021)
11. Hamza, N.R., Dihin, R.A., Abdulameer, M.H.: A hybrid image similarity measure based on a new combination of different similarity techniques. Int. J. Electr. Comput. Eng. **10**(2), 1814–1822 (2020)
12. Kotar, K., Tian, S., Yu, H.-X., Yamins, D., Wu, J.: Are these the same apple? Comparing images based on object intrinsics. In: Advances in Neural Information Processing Systems, vol. 36 (2024)
13. Wang, C.-Y., Bochkovskiy, A., Liao, H.-Y.M.: YOLOv7: trainable bag-of-freebies sets new state-of-the-art for real-time object detectors. In: Proceedings of the IEEE/CVF Conference on Computer Vision and Pattern Recognition, pp. 7464–7475 (2023)
14. Wang, S., Sun, Y., Bao, Z.: On the efficiency of k-means clustering: evaluation, optimization, and algorithm selection. arXiv preprint arXiv:2010.06654 (2020)
15. Ikotun, A.M., Ezugwu, A.E., Abualigah, L., Abuhaija, B., Heming, J.: K-means clustering algorithms: a comprehensive review, variants analysis, and advances in the era of big data. Inf. Sci. (2022)
16. Awad, F.H., Hamad, M.M., Alzubaidi, L.: Robust classification and detection of big medical data using advanced parallel k-means clustering, yolov4, and logistic regression. Life **13**(3), 691 (2023)
17. Tufail, S., Riggs, H., Tariq, M., Sarwat, A.I.: Advancements and challenges in machine learning: a comprehensive review of models, libraries, applications, and algorithms. Electronics **12**(8), 1789 (2023)
18. Omiotek, Z., Kotyra, A.: Flame image processing and classification using a pre-trained VGG16 model in combustion diagnosis. Sensors **21**(2), 500 (2021)
19. Hashemi, M.: Enlarging smaller images before inputting into convolutional neural network: zero-padding vs. interpolation. J. Big Data **6**(1), 1–13 (2019)
20. Kosuge, A., Suehiro, S., Hamada, M., Kuroda, T.: mmWave-YOLO: a mmWave imaging radar-based real-time multiclass object recognition system for ADAS applications. IEEE Trans. Instrum. Meas. **71**, 1–10 (2022)
21. Liu, L., Ouyang, W., Wang, X., Fieguth, P., Chen, J., Liu, X., Pietikäinen, M.: Deep learning for generic object detection: a survey. Int. J. Comput. Vision **128**, 261–318 (2020)
22. Wang, C.-Y., Bochkovskiy, A., Liao, H.-Y.M.: YOLOv7: trainable bag-of-freebies sets new state-of-the-art for real-time object detectors. arXiv preprint arXiv:2207.02696 (2022)
23. McKight, P.E., Najab, J.: Kruskal-Wallis test. Corsini Encycl. Psychol. 1 (2010)
24. Ma, X., Ouyang, W., Simonelli, A., Ricci, E.: 3D object detection from images for autonomous driving: a survey. IEEE Trans. Pattern Anal. Mach. Intell. (2023)
25. Wohlin, C., Runeson, P., Höst, M., Ohlsson, M.C., Regnell, B., Wesslén, A.: Experimentation in Software Engineering. Springer, Heidelberg (2012). https://doi.org/10.1007/978-3-642-29044-2

A Meta-model for Documenting Conversational Requirements in Chatbots

Larissa Pereira Gonçalves[1(✉)], Edna Dias Canedo[1], and Gleison Santos[2]

[1] University of Brasilia (UnB), Brasilia, DF, Brazil
larissa.goncalves@redes.unb.br, ednacanedo@unb.br
[2] Universidade Federal do Estado do Rio de Janeiro (UNIRIO), Rio de Janeiro, RJ, Brazil
gleison.santos@uniriotec.br

Abstract. Context: Chatbots emerged in the decade of 60 and are currently a popular type of application that provides the experience of talking to a human-like robot. However, the similarity of their behaviour to a human is also what makes the elicitation and documentation of conversational-related requirements a hard task, due to the subjective nature of conversations. Currently there are no standards or guidelines to register and test subjective requirements, present in human conversations. **Methods:** We proposed a metamodel for documentation of conversational requirements and conducted the validation through a 2-step questionnaire. We then analysed the feedback received and applied improvements in the model instances. **Results:** Based on metamodel we propose the conversational integrated map, an artifact that correlates the subjective requirements with their associated KPIs. Validation was conducted through a simulation with 4 practitioners in a 2-step questionnaire. Artifact format choice revealed a preference for mainly textual and table models. Scalability and necessary time to complete were points of divergence between answers. **Conclusion:** Proposed artifact was well accepted and could provide pre-made models available for edition for ease of use. Future steps of this study include the elaboration of a guide of best practices on chatbot documentation.

Keywords: Chatbots · Conversational agents · Specification · Conversational requirements · Conversational integrated map

1 Introduction

In the decade of 60 s chatbots emerged in university labs to simulate psychologists - such as ELISA [23] - or specific psychological behaviours (as Parry [7]). The presence of human aspects such as the flow rate of the conversation, proactivity and personality maintenance through answers were object of interest since chatbots' beginning. They are expected to deliver a good user experience using only a conversation channel, differently from other softwares [19, 21] which rely heavier on visual elements [5].

A. Bertolino et al. (Eds.): QUATIC 2024, CCIS 2178, pp. 68–82, 2024.
https://doi.org/10.1007/978-3-031-70245-7_5

Despite their use and increasing complexity, error correction can be challenging for chatbots (specially AI-based), because they are prone to errors like misunderstandings or unpolite/inappropriate responses [11]. The conversational nature of chatbots presents unique challenges to designers, as their development differs significantly from other software and necessitates exploring new practices within the context of human-AI interaction and their impact on user experience [21]. Some approaches include using data-driven feedback loops, reinforcement learning and supervised learning [11]. Other concerns can be ethical considerations, bias in training data and privacy of user data [2].

Due to the level of complexity in correcting conversational mistakes or patterns [11], requirements phase is important to maintain consistency along development [17]. When fixing bugs and implementing improvements, requirements' documentation provides a starting point for identifying deviations from the desired behavior and planning corrections.

As conversational assistants and natural language interfaces proliferate, the demand for a precise understanding of quality software requirements for chatbots becomes increasingly critical. Silva and Canedo [20] have examined a dataset of conversational requirements from various agile chatbot development projects, identifying meaningful patterns in the language and structure used. The results emphasized the importance of structured documentation, conversation flow, and user interaction in chatbot development. The most desired quality attributes were capability, naturalness, straightforwardness, and clarity. Additionally, there was a strong emphasis on feature development and meeting acceptance criteria. Furthermore, the study highlighted the iterative nature of chatbot development, evidenced by frequent verbs related to improvement or refactoring. The roles of documentation and testing in ensuring chatbot quality and effectiveness were also noted.

Those subjective requirements which chatbots must meet are usually documented in adapted versions of current software documentation artifacts [10,19]. There are few new artifacts - such as conversational flows and decision trees - for chatbot's requirements documentation, at least in literature [10].

Lack of specific artifacts for chatbots is followed by difficulty of testing conversational requirements, due to their subjective nature [10,19]. Current artifacts do not preview or emphasize how to measure a subjective requirement [10], or how it should be implemented or tested. The absence of metrics or standards can induce biased validation.

Therefore, the objectives of this study are the proposal and validation of a software requirements specification (SRS) metamodel and model instances which addresses subjective requirements. The main contributions of this paper can be highlighted as the proposition of a new meta-model for chatbots' SRS for subjective and conversational requirements, and its validation with software practitioners through a 2-step survey. Preliminary results show the participants considered the proposed model easy to learn and use.

The paper is organized as it follows: Related works and background are presented in Sect. 2. Section 3 describes the study settings, process of metamodel proposal and validation strategy. The results of validation are shown in Sect. 4. Section 5 discusses the findings of this study and Sect. 6 describes the limitations of our study and possible threats to validity. Lastly, Sect. 7 presents our conclusions on the study.

2 Background and Related Work

As chatbot requirements differ significantly from other applications, the need to adapt or create new artifacts emerged. Castle-Green et al. [6] highlighted the format of decision trees to specify chatbot requirements, after creating workflows or stories to map the interaction steps.

In a later year, Borsting and Hesenius [3] proposed an adaptation of the "Interaction Room" method for gathering and documenting requirements in chatbots. The original method brings members from different areas to find solutions together. The findings were to be written on time by the moderator and the documents were disclosed and shared with all participants in the end. After this round, the requirements were registered into a divided Canvas document of intention, dialogue, and entities [3].

There is a considerable amount of literature data for the creation of chatbots to elicit and document software requirements [4,9,12,16,19,21], but the other way around - human elicitation and documentation to create and upgrade chatbots' applications – is not true so far. Schon et al. [18] conducted a broad systematic literature review on agile artifacts. They reported User Stories as being the most common artifact used in agile software development (ASD), followed by Prototypes, Use cases, Scenarios, and Story cards. User Stories are the most used artifact, however lack suitability to document non-functional requirements, and when it is needed to do so, they must be divided into smaller contexts or be complemented by other items such as acceptance criteria [18]. Use cases, however, showed to be more suited to address non-functional requirements since they can be highly adaptable [15].

Amna and Poels [1] focused specifically on user stories and identified research gaps in focused literature reviews, role that user stories play in human cognition and interaction, solutions for ambiguity issues early in projects, and validation and evaluation of proposed solutions. The authors found it difficult to retrieve literature studies that were devoted to research on user stories, even though this artifact is the most used in ASD.

Silva and Canedo [19] have conducted a survey with practitioners and found that they mostly adapt existing artifacts or use the ones available in chatbot's generation platforms. They also addressed several challenges in eliciting or documenting chatbots' requirements, such as distance from stakeholders' needs, poorly documented requirements, business management issues, and lack of specific tools for requirements engineering. In their study, conversational flows and user stories appear as the most common documentation techniques by the respondents [19].

To our knowledge, there are no works addressing specifically documentation artifacts related to chatbots' conversational requirements. However, there are studies approaching frameworks, techniques, challenges, and proposals for artifacts' templates in a broader scope such as user stories or use cases.

3 Study Settings

In order to specify requirements for a specific case, the metamodel starts with a situation, when an user generally starts the interaction and expects an answer from the chatbot. The answer formation is expected to comply with the requirements proposed (mainly conversational requirements) and their metrics of evaluation, as shown in Fig. 1.

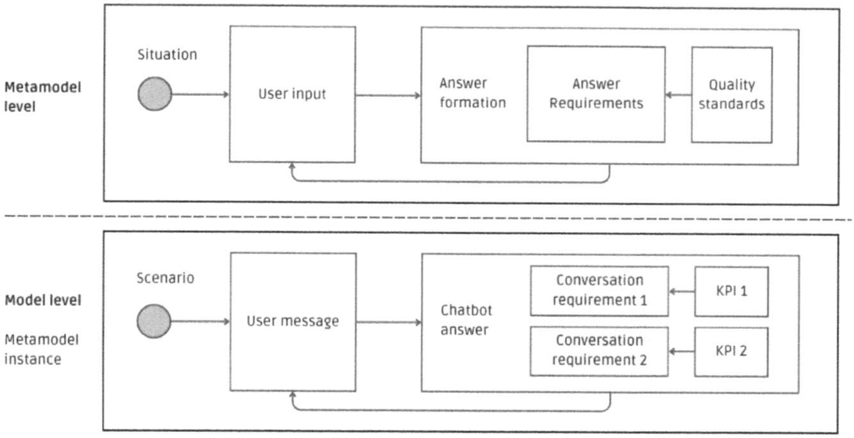

Fig. 1. Metamodel and model instance representation.

Each quality standard is related to a single requirement, and one given answer can have more than one associated requirement, which depends of the context. One requirement can also have more than one KPI. The model is expected to be created during requirements elicitation phase and reused during software development.

The conversational-related requirements and their associated metrics (KPIs) can be tested and evaluated throughout chatbot life cycle by software team, as represented in Fig. 2. We further use this metamodel to propose a model instance called conversational integrated map.

3.1 Conversational Integrated Map Proposal

The premises to build the derived model were the following: 1) it does not intend to replace all existing artifacts – the goal is to be a robust artifact that reduces the need for multiple documents; 2) it must be adaptable to different formats, showing the same important information regardless of the visualization (table,

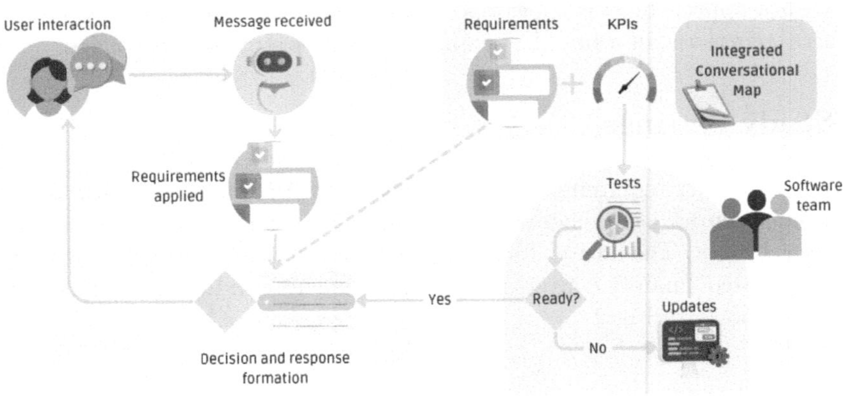

Fig. 2. Proposed use of model.

prototype, conversational flow, UML diagram, mind map); 3) it must be flexible, according to the practitioners' needs; 4) it must promote connection points between requirements and conversational elements; 5) It should be able to represent visual appearance; 6) It should provide a place to describe requirements; and 7) It has to show a sequence of interactions between the chatbot and the user.

To address the premises 2, 3, 4, 6, and 7 above, we defined the parts that the model should contain. They include a title, an epic (when this scenario is part of a bigger situation), a case description, a sequence of turns, and the content of messages between the chatbot and the user, along with the description of requirements attached to each message (Fig. 1). Additionally, we decided to add an optional field for KPIs [8] (or acceptance criteria), linked to each requirement, due to the common subjectivity of conversational requirements [19]. The model template can be adapted in a table format (supplementary data), prototype format, and diagram format, as shown in Figs. 3 and 4.

Table representation can be done in any software that manipulates sheets or text, being the most accessible presentation of artifacts. In this representation, however, the provision of the visual appearance is less addressed, therefore the visual fidelity is low. However, tables offer the additional capacity of the world search inside documents and filtering and are also easier to scale if used for bigger scenarios.

We used Draw.io tool for diagram representation. However, it can be done in any software with UML notations. The requirements and KPIs were adapted from UML class representations. The messages were adapted from UML objects. However, simple geometrical forms can be used to compose the diagram, regardless of notation. Diagram representation is more versatile than the table and can be adapted and incremented with other resources, such as photos or emojis. It also gives a increased sense of visual appearance than the tables. Address of

Table 1. Conversational artifact meta-model composition.

Component	Type	Description
Title	Mandatory	Presents the specific situation to be specified
Epic	Optional	If the scenario is part of a larger situation, it addresses the father scenario
Scenario Description	Mandatory	Describe a summary of the situation presented. Can contain information that the practitioner finds important, such as preconditions
Sequence Number	Optional	Shows the timeline of interaction and change in chatbot and user turns. It's recommended if needed to cite a previous message
Chatbot Message	Mandatory	Shows the chatbot's response or interaction
User Message	Mandatory	Shows the user's response or interaction
Requirement	Mandatory	Explanation of the requirement
KPI or Acceptance Criteria	Optional	Explanation of how the requirement is considered attended
User annotation	Mandatory	Highlights of user response

requirements can be done by highlighting the phrases with requirement assigned color, as shown in Fig. 3.

For the prototype representation, Figma tool was used. The creation process was composed of choosing a device and representing a conversation as a user would see it. Each requirement receives a color and is highlighted as it appears on the interaction. Prototype representation addresses visual appearance and usability requirements directly, and can also show dynamic interactions. The paid version also allows audiovisual resources such as videos or audio, which can be a more complete option if the chatbot is speech-based, or requires a video interaction. In general, audiovisual resources are rarely represented in software documentation [10].

Table 2. Comparison between proposed conversational integrated map and popular artifacts for chatbots' documentation.

Artifact	Visual Appearance	Requirements Description	Interaction Sequence	Link of Requirements and Elements
Conversational Integrated Map	Yes	Yes	Yes	Yes
Conversational Flow	No	No	Yes	No
Decision Tree	No	No	Yes	No
Scenario	No	No	Yes	No
Prototype	Yes	No	Yes	No
UML Diagram	No	No	Yes	No
Requirements Table	No	Yes	No	No

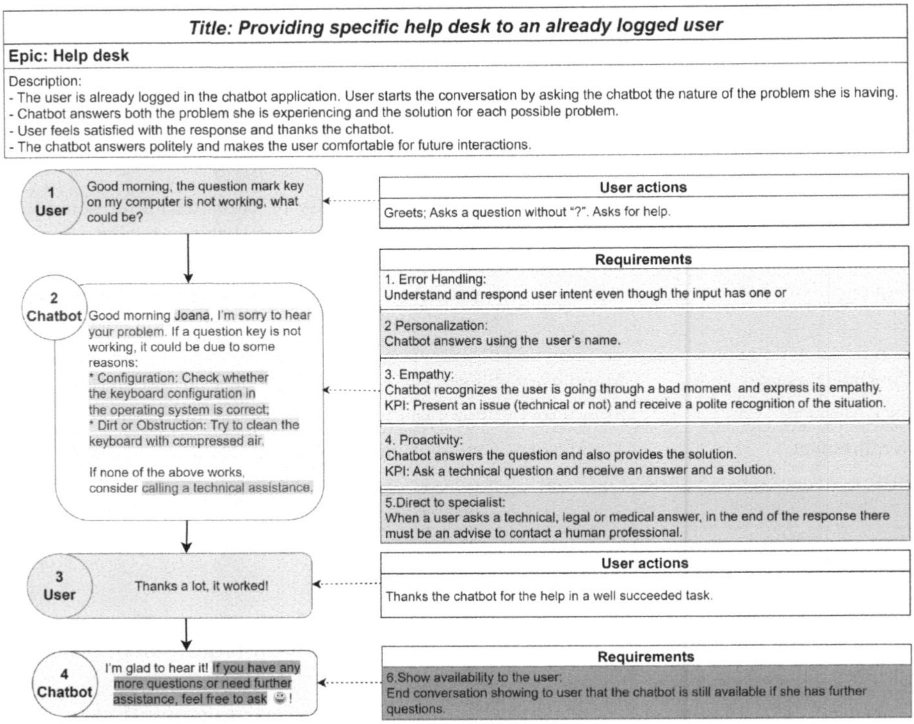

Fig. 3. Representation of the integrated conversational map in UML diagram.

Validation was carried out with practitioners experienced in analyzing chatbot requirements, during two simulation phases. The first phase consisted of presenting an example conversational flow, in which practitioners had to specify requirements without a defined documentation format. In the second phase, the integrated Conversational Map is presented, and practitioners are invited to use it to document requirements.

An example artifact, as well as instructions for using the Integrated Conversational Map, were made available to practitioners with theoretical and/or empirical experience in the areas of software testing and development. After reading the artifact and instructions, the practitioners simulated the specification and at the end responded to a survey about the artifact.

For the planning of the research, its execution and analysis of the responses, the guideline proposed by Pfleeger and Kitchenham [13] was used. The online questionnaire was developed using the free Google Forms software and disseminated organically on social networks and among practitioners in the field.

For the first phase, participants were invited to provide their email addresses, only so that we could contact them again at another time to request participation in the second phase of the research. Only participants who agreed to participate voluntarily, and agreed to the use of their data anonymously for publications

Fig. 4. Representation of the integrated conversational map in prototype format.

were taken into consideration for generating and analyzing results. Furthermore, the online survey allowed the participant to withdraw at any time, without any discomfort as the process does not require supervision. Both forms were available from March 18th to June 15th of 2024 (Table 3).

Participants received an example conversational flow and were invited to create documentation of conversational requirements based on the flow received, without a defined template. After preparing a proposal for documentation of requirements, another form was sent with access to instructions for using the Integrated Conversational Map and three templates (table, diagram and prototype), being able to choose one of their preference to continue.

Upon receiving access to the instructions and templates, practitioners were invited again to carry out the requirements documentation, using the proposed template. Finally, when delivering the completed requirements documentation, questions were asked about the perception of the artifact's use. The two phases of the questionnaire presented below, were expected to take between 15 and 20 min to complete (Table 3).

Phase 1 – Free Documentation: 1) I carry out or have carried out requirements analysis for chatbots; 2) How long have you worked or have been working in the area of requirements analysis? 3) In this activity, you will have access to a

Table 3. Questionnaire description

Phase	ID	Question
Questionnaire 1	Q1	I declare that I have been verbally informed and clarified about this document, understanding all the terms set out above, and that I voluntarily accept to participate in this study.
	Q2	I perform or have performed requirements analysis for chatbots
	Q3	Full name
	Q4	Email (required to contact for phase 2)
	Q5	How long have you worked or are you working in the area of requirements analysis?
	Q6	Submit your requirements specification here
	Q7	By submitting this form, I agree to be contacted for the second stage of the survey.
Questionnaire 2	Q1	I declare that I have been verbally informed and clarified about this document, understanding all the terms set out above, and that I voluntarily accept to participate in this study.
	Q2	Full name
	Q3	Submit your requirements specification here using the Integrated Conversational Map
	Q4	About requirements documentation: 1. 1. The model proposed in phase 2 was easy to use 2. The model I had proposed was easier to use 3. The model proposed in phase 2 is scalable 4. The proposed model is time consuming to document 5. I would use the model again 6. The proposed model is easy to learn 7. I am satisfied with the model proposed in phase 2
	Q5	Thank you for completing our form. This is a space for additional observations, suggestions and/or critics, if you have any.

Table 4. Description of all participants.

ID	Chatbot requirements experience?	Experience time
P1	No	–
P2	Yes	More than 5 years
P3	Yes	More than 5 years
P4	Yes	Up to 1 year
P5	Yes	1 to 3 years
P6	Yes	Up to 1 year
P7	Yes	Up to 1 year
P8	No	–
P9	Yes	1 to 3 years

conversational flow of a hypothetical conversation situation between a user and a chatbot. We ask you to read the conversation, and specify the requirements that you observed during the interaction, or perceive that they are important for the chatbot. This specification must be made in a separate document. Afterwards, you must send the document containing the specifications, here on this same form.

Phase 2– Documentation with Integrated Conversational Map and Participant Feedback: 2) In this activity, you will have access to the same conversational flow as in the previous phase, which represents a hypothetical conversation situation between a user and a chatbot. We ask that you read the document above again and specify the requirements you observed in the interaction. This specification must be made in a document called Integrated Conversational Map, with one of the models available below; and 2) To compare users' experience in carrying out the specification without a model and the specification with the Integrated Conversational Map, questions were applied in the format of the Likert [14] scale: 1) The model proposed in phase 2 was easy to use; 2) The model I had proposed was easier to use; 3) The model proposed in phase 2 is scalable; 4) The proposed model is time-consuming to document; 5) I would use the model again; 6) The proposed model is easy to learn; and 7) I am satisfied with the model proposed in Phase 2.

4 Conversational Artifact Model Validation Results

Phase 1 of the survey had 9 answers so far. 2 of the 9 practitioners in phase one declared they did not possess experience with requirements analysis for chatbots, as shown in Table 4. At the end of survey 1, all participants agreed to be on phase 2. As they were carried out on separated moments to avoid memory bias from practitioners, not every participant which answered phase 1 answered phase 2, resulting in 4 answers.

Regarding format choice of the users, in phase 1, 4 practitioners wrote requirements specification in plain text, using topics to organize the text. 1 of the participants wrote user stories for specification, another documented the requirements in a use case format, and one used topics and diagrams for documentation. On phase 2, 2 practitioners used the table model and 1 practitioner used prototype model to document the requirements.

Figure 5 shows participants' answers to each question of the second phase of the survey. A higher agreement on questions 1, 3, 5, 6 and 7 shows satisfaction with the meta-model, since the affirmations are positive. Sentences 2 and 4 are negative, and therefore, when a user agrees, means that this is a point for investigation and improvement.

The highest satisfaction is seen on items 1 and 6, followed by 5 and 7. All answers were positive for items 1, 5, 6 and 7. Item 1 addresses if the model is perceived as easy to use. Item 2 compares the model proposed with the format the participant previously chose for chatbot requirement documentation, which 3 participants find the model easier to use (Fig. 5).

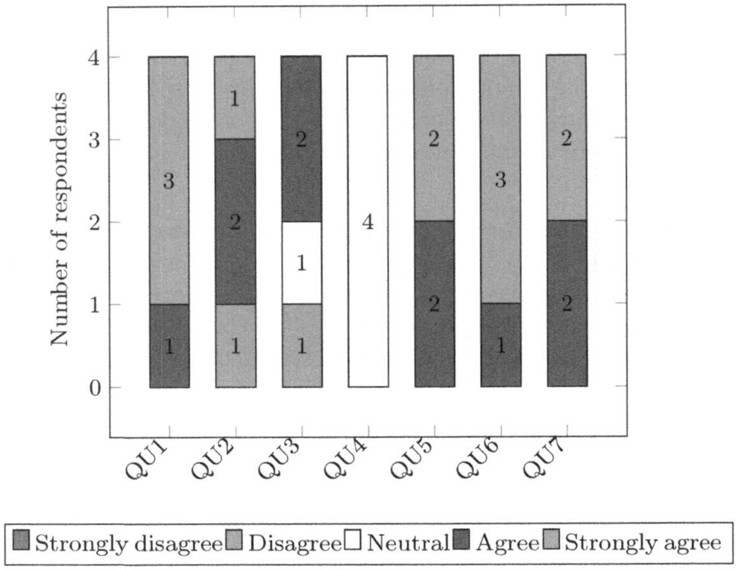

Fig. 5. Responses by question.

Item 3 addresses the scalability of the model, and received mixed answers. Item 4 is a point for investigation, because all answers were neutral. This specific item compares the time required to document requirements with the model and without the model. From the results, it can be inferred that there practitioners do not perceive much difference. Item 5 asks the participant if they would use the model again. All answers of item 5 were positive. Items 6 and 7 received also only positive answers, and are related to ease of learning and satisfaction with the artifact (Fig. 5).

5 Discussion

5.1 Conversational Integrated Map

The proposed model comprises the main features from key artifacts. Title and epic come from user stories, which are popular documentation artifacts for other types of software. They help to narrow large and unspecific requests, especially subjective non-functional requirements. The description below is derived from scenarios and helps to understand the general picture of the situation. It can be used as a reference and a first point of communication between stakeholders and the development team.

The conversational turns are required to illustrate directly how the interaction should be in practice and can serve as a reference in the test phase. Associated with conversational turns, the associated requirements are the main contribution of this model (Table 2), since current artifacts do not directly address this link.

Requirements can present or not a KPI, as it is an optional field (Table 1). However, we recommend that each requirement has one or more KPIs. In user stories, they would behave as acceptance criteria. Our KPI proposal is similar to Nguyen et al. [15] work, which adapted used cases for non-functional requirements [15]. The main reason for this proposal briefly explained above, is to enhance the importance of established measures of quality for subjective requirements, as they pose a challenge on testing and success or failure are difficult to address [19,21,22].

Our meta-model currently does not include a specific field to show architectural components or entities such as intents and entities. They were not included intentionally because the meta-model is designed to be a user-friendly document and enhance collaboration between stakeholders, and development and testing teams. However, this meta-model should be evaluated by practitioners to address if it is adherent to its purpose or if the features should be changed.

Another improvement that can be implemented in future works is the hierarchical division of scenarios inside epics and bigger contexts, similar to the visualization of ontology, mind maps, or decision tree visualizations, enhancing dynamic organization. The meta-model can be included in automated libraries in order to be accessible worldwide. Even the generation of one visualization can automatically generate the others. There is also the possibility of using AI and machine learning to predict the most common requirements for the project and make a previous suggestion based on the previous documentation.

6 Limitations and Threats to Validity

One important limitation to highlight is the potential discrepancy between the descriptions and discussions found in academic literature and actual practices in the development and implementation of chatbots. Literature may not fully capture the complexities and challenges faced by practitioners in the field, which suggests the need to complement bibliographic studies with empirical investigations.

We also conducted the validation of the model with 4 practitioners which had contact with chatbots requirement during software development. The division of questionnaires in 2 phases and the restrictions proposed prevented a bigger number of participants.

6.1 Proposed Meta-model

The meta-model proposed in this work was based on previous research but still poses some challenges. First, some variations of representation tend to emphasize or not some specific fields in the model. For example, in the Table, the message sender (user or chatbot) is not as visible as in the diagram or prototype visualization. The second point is that this model is recommended for short scenarios and conversations. Longer interactions with such an amount of information can bring a high cognitive load when visualizing. Some other actions can be done to overcome this issue, such as including an option to hide the excess of information when wanted.

An important note is that the meta-model should be evaluated among practitioners involved in the creation and development of chatbot projects, in order to access if the proposed solution meets the needs of software practitioners. It should also be evaluated if the documentation is understandable by stakeholders [18] and if it can be used as official documentation for chatbot development. Another concern is that the creation process can be really manual since there is the need to highlight specific points inside the conversation and present them outside. To overcome this obstacle, the creation and implementation of a plugin to prototype tools could connect in the prototyping platform and facilitate annotations inclusion and change.

6.2 Survey

The internal validity of this work is primarily threatened by the online-based and unsupervised nature of our survey. We lacked control over the participants while they were answering, although we made our contact information available in case they had any questions. On the positive side, the unsupervised environment meant participants were not pressured to respond and could quit at any time if they were not committed, which leads us to believe that those who completed the survey provided meaningful responses. The external validity is threatened by the fact that our survey included only Brazilian practitioners, limiting the generalizability of our findings. Although our sample size is small, it is worth noting that there are several other studies in the literature that also surveyed a small number of participants.

7 Conclusions

The conversational integrated map presented here is a flexible meta-model designed to address conversational requirements along user and chatbot interactions. It allows the direct link between the conversation itself, requirements, and KPIs that should be tested. Overall evaluation of integrated conversational map by participants was positive towards the model. It was considered easy to use, easy to learn and all participants that simulated documentation with the model would use it again (Fig. 5). However, future studies should investigate if this model and existing artifacts are enough to address all complex aspects of chatbots' specific conversational requirements or require further adaptation. Another remaining question would be the prioritization and testing of subjective requirements, an additional challenge posed by chatbot applications.

Next steps of this work should be to promote a guide for artifact utilization, publish models on internet and improve its ease of use, automation and scalability. Also, future studies should investigate how to design tests and metrics for subjective requirements.

References

1. Amna, A.R., Poels, G.: Systematic literature mapping of user story research. IEEE Access **10**, 51723–51746 (2022). https://doi.org/10.1109/ACCESS.2022.3173745
2. Belen Saglam, R., Nurse, J.R.C., Hodges, D.: Privacy concerns in chatbot interactions: when to trust and when to worry. In: Stephanidis, C., Antona, M., Ntoa, S. (eds.) HCII 2021. CCIS, vol. 1420, pp. 391–399. Springer, Cham (2021). https://doi.org/10.1007/978-3-030-78642-7_53
3. Börsting, I., Hesenius, M.: Towards a systematic approach for chatbot development in digital work environments. Digit. Supply Chains Hum. Factor 79–94 (2021)
4. Çalışkan, E.B.: Briefing with artificial intelligence for requirement elicitation: three cases with ChatGPT for exploration of possibilities. Architectus **75**(3) (2023)
5. Cameron, G., et al.: Back to the future: lessons from knowledge engineering methodologies for chatbot design and development. In: British HCI Conference 2018. BCS Learning & Development Ltd. (2018)
6. Castle-Green, T., Reeves, S., Fischer, J.E., Koleva, B.: Decision trees as sociotechnical objects in chatbot design. In: Torres, M.I., Schlögl, S., Clark, L., Porcheron, M. (eds.) Proceedings of the 2nd Conference on Conversational User Interfaces, CUI 2020, Bilbao, Spain, 22–24 July 2020, pp. 27:1–27:3. ACM (2020). https://doi.org/10.1145/3405755.3406133
7. Colby, K.M.: Artificial Paranoia: A Computer Simulation of Paranoid Processes. Pergamon Press (1975)
8. Dragicevic, S., Celar, S., Novak, L.: Use of method for elicitation, documentation, and validation of software user requirements (MEDoV) in agile software development projects. In: Al-Dabass, D., Ameti, V., Skenderi, F., Halili, F. (eds.) Sixth International Conference on Computational Intelligence, Communication Systems and Networks, CICSyN 2014, Tetova, Macedonia, 27–29 May 2014, pp. 65–70. IEEE (2014). https://doi.org/10.1109/CICSYN.2014.27
9. Dwitama, F., Rusli, A.: User stories collection via interactive chatbot to support requirements gathering. TELKOMNIKA (Telecommun. Comput. Electron. Control) **18**(2), 890 (2020). https://doi.org/10.12928/telkomnika.v18i2.14866
10. Gonçalves, L., Canedo, E.D., Silva, G.: Documentation artifacts for conversation-related requirements specification in chatbots: a systematic review and a meta-model proposal. In: da Silva, L.F., Portugal, R.L.Q. (eds.) Anais do WER24 - Workshop em Engenharia de Requisitos, Buenos Aires, Argentina, 7–9 August 2024. LFS (Universidad de Belgrano, Argentina) (2024)
11. Izadi, S., Forouzanfar, M.: Error correction and adaptation in conversational AI: a review of techniques and applications in chatbots. AI **5**(2), 803–841 (2024). https://doi.org/10.3390/ai5020041, https://www.mdpi.com/2673-2688/5/2/41
12. Johari, N.M., Nohuddin, P.N.E., Baharin, A.H.A., Yakob, N.A., Ebadi, M.J.: Features requirement elicitation process for designing a chatbot application. IET Netw. (2022). https://doi.org/10.1049/ntw2.12071
13. Kitchenham, B.A., Pfleeger, S.L.: Principles of survey research: part 3: constructing a survey instrument. SIGSOFT Softw. Eng. Notes **27**(2), 20–24 (2002). https://doi.org/10.1145/511152.511155
14. Nemoto, T., Beglar, D.: Likert-scale questionnaires. In: JALT 2013 Conference Proceedings. pp. 1–8 (2014)
15. Nguyen, Q.L.: Non-functional requirements analysis modeling for software product lines. In: ICSE Workshop on Modeling in Software Engineering, MiSE 2009, Vancouver, BC, Canada, 17–18 May 2009, pp. 56–61. IEEE Computer Society (2009). https://doi.org/10.1109/MISE.2009.5069898

16. Rajender Kumar Surana, C.S., Shriya, Gupta, D.B., Shankar, S.P.: Intelligent chatbot for requirements elicitation and classification. In: 2019 4th International Conference on Recent Trends on Electronics, Information, Communication & Technology (RTEICT), pp. 866–870 (2019). https://doi.org/10.1109/RTEICT46194.2019.9016907
17. Rasheed, A., Zafar, B., Shehryar, T., Aslam, N.A., Sajid, M., Ali, N., Dar, S.H., Khalid, S.: Requirement engineering challenges in agile software development. Math. Probl. Eng. **2021**(1), 6696695 (2021). https://doi.org/10.1155/2021/6696695
18. Schon, E., Thomaschewski, J., Escalona, M.J.: Agile requirements engineering: a systematic literature review. Comput. Stand. Interfaces **49**, 79–91 (2017). https://doi.org/10.1016/J.CSI.2016.08.011
19. Silva, G.R.S., Canedo, E.D.: Requirements engineering challenges and techniques in building chatbots. In: Rocha, A.P., Steels, L., van den Herik, H.J. (eds.) Proceedings of the 14th International Conference on Agents and Artificial Intelligence, ICAART 2022, Volume 1, Online Streaming, 3–5 February 2022, pp. 180–187. SCITEPRESS (2022). https://doi.org/10.5220/0010801800003116
20. Silva, G.R.S., Canedo, E.D.: Unveiling quality in chatbot conversations: quantitative analysis of chatbot requirements. In: Canedo, E.D., et al. (eds.) Proceedings of the XXII Brazilian Symposium on Software Quality, SBQS 2023, Brasilia, Brazil, 7–10 November 2023, pp. 148–157. ACM (2023). doi:https://doi.org/10.1145/3629479.3629481
21. Silva, G.R.S., Canedo, E.D.: Towards user-centric guidelines for chatbot conversational design. Int. J. Hum. Comput. Interact. **40**(2), 98–120 (2024). https://doi.org/10.1080/10447318.2022.2118244
22. Silva, G.R.S., Rodrigues, G.N., Canedo, E.D.: A modeling strategy for the verification of context-oriented chatbot conversational flows via model checking. J. Univers. Comput. Sci. **29**(7), 805–835 (2023). https://doi.org/10.3897/JUCS.91311
23. Weizenbaum, J.: ELIZA - a computer program for the study of natural language communication between man and machine (reprint). Commun. ACM **26**(1), 23–28 (1983). https://doi.org/10.1145/357980.357991

Do Modern Systems Require New Quality Dimensions?

Martina De Sanctis(✉), Paola Inverardi, and Patrizio Pelliccione

Gran Sasso Science Institute, 67100 L'Aquila, Italy
{martina.sanctis,paola.inverardi,patrizio.pelliccione}@gssi.it

Abstract. The digital society is characterised by a continuous presence of digital systems being pure software systems or cyber-physical systems, which help and support humans in their life activities. Humans can be passive or active, the interaction can be implicit or explicit, and they can be more or less conscious of the presence of digital systems. However, the impact of the digital systems on social, economic, and political spheres is clear and risky. This is also testified by, e.g., the recent AI Act of the European Community. In this paper, we analyse whether modern systems require a new understanding of quality and, consequently, new quality dimensions. We challenge the ISO/IEC 25010 quality standard with new emerging stakeholders needs, and we pave the way for a reconsideration of the standard and the traditional understanding of quality to include and consider also these new emerging needs.

Keywords: Quality Definition · Quality Standard · Modern Systems · Stakeholders Needs

1 Introduction

Nowadays, we continuously interact with or are affected by software systems, e.g., by using a mobile device, in our smart homes, or from on board of a (autonomous) transportation means, but also when using a banking system, asking for a loan, or competing for a work position. The widespread diffusion of AI technologies has an increasing impact on the social, economic, and political spheres. Automatizing services and processes inevitably impacts humans, being them active or passive in the explicit or implicit interaction with systems. This puts at danger humans autonomy, privacy, and impacts on our social and human values.

Traditionally, we are used to care for the quality of systems in terms of the "correctness" of their behaviour and their non-functional aspects, such as performance, reliability, availability, maintainability, usability, etc. This is, for instance, the main focus of the ISO/IEC 25010:2023 [8] quality standard. The rhetorical question in the title suggests that when dealing with modern systems, which are pervasive, autonomous and adaptive, integrated with our life, and impactful on our society, this traditional view of quality is not enough. This becomes even more evident in instances of accidents caused by human-machine

A. Bertolino et al. (Eds.): QUATIC 2024, CCIS 2178, pp. 83–90, 2024.
https://doi.org/10.1007/978-3-031-70245-7_6

systems, such as autonomous driving cars that, however, still necessitate human supervision. AI technologies are key enablers for most, but not all, of these systems thus drawing attention to qualities such as explainability, transparency, accountability. This evidence justifies the common, and abused, use of referring to these systems as AI systems.

The European Union (EU) is seriously confronting the dangers represented by unauthorised disclosure and mining of personal data, but there is a less evident but more serious risk which attains the core of the fundamental rights of the citizens. Worries about the growing of the data economy and the increasing presence of AI fuelled autonomous systems have shown that privacy concerns are insufficient: ethics and the human dignity are at stake [5,6]. "Accept/not accept" options do not satisfy our freedom of choice; and what about our individual preferences and moral views? As a matter of fact, individuals are unprotected and powerless in their interaction with the digital world. In a digital society where the relationship between citizens and machines is uneven, moral values such as individuality and responsibility are at risk. There is a general consensus about this, but legislation follows and does not prevent the problem, and it is debatable that the regulatory approach of the GDPR is effectively protecting the users. The only active approach is in the research on AI and responsible computing [6], where systems/software developers and companies should apply ethical codes and follow guidelines for the development of trustworthy systems in order to achieve transparency and accountability of decisions [4–6]. The recent *AI Act* released by the European Union is the first law to regulate the use of AI in Europe [12]. It provides a framework that delineates different requirements and obligations for both the use and provision of AI systems within the EU. It classifies AI systems based on risk for humans and society in four categories, and regulates if and how AI-based systems can be produced, used or deployed.

In this exploratory paper, we try to understand to what extent the traditional understanding of quality requires a reconsideration in order to be adequate to the modern software systems we use nowadays. We believe that needs of stakeholders have been changed and, consequently, the understanding of quality should change. To make this investigation, we first identify what are the emergent needs of stakeholders of modern systems. Then, we analyse whether the current version of the ISO/IEC 25010:2023 quality standard successfully covers these needs. We hope that this exploratory paper will contribute to reconsider the quality standard, as well as the traditional understanding of quality, to include and consider also new emerging needs.

2 Limitations of the Traditional Definition of Quality

ISO/IEC 25010:2023 [8] is the latest version of the standard that defines a model for software product quality. The standard is part of the ISO/IEC 25000 series, which covers various aspects of software engineering and quality management and has the goal of creating a framework for the evaluation of software product quality. The quality model determines which quality characteristics will be taken into account when evaluating the properties of a software product [8]. It defines eight main quality characteristics, both functional and non-functional, which include functional suitability, performance efficiency, compatibility, interaction capability, reliability, security, maintainability, flexibility, and safety. Within each quality characteristic, the ISO/IEC 25010:2023 standard provides a detailed set of sub-characteristics that further describe the specific aspects of software quality. For instance, safety includes sub-characteristics such as operational constraint, risk identification, fail safe, hazard warning, safe integration. For further details, we refer to the standard at [8]. The standard highlights the importance of considering quality throughout the software development life-cycle, from the definition of requirements to deployment and maintenance. It mainly targets software developers and engineers with the aim of helping software products to meet the expectations and requirements of customers.

However, this quality standard and the traditional understanding of quality seem to be not able to grasp the stakeholders' needs of modern systems, which often include AI components and expose various levels of automation. Moreover, digital systems are increasingly required to cooperate and collaborate with humans and, therefore, they are required to satisfy human and social values [14]. It is important to highlight that we are not suggesting to add a new definition of quality, but instead, we observe that the stakeholders' needs changed and will change in the near future. In fact, according to the ISO/IEC 25010:2023 standard, quality is defined as:

> "the degree to which the system satisfies the stated and implied needs of its various stakeholders, and thus provides value" [8].

This definition refers to stated and implied needs of the stakeholders, and consequently, if they change and evolve, the characteristics of quality are required to change and adapt to the new needs. Thus, *what are the stated and implied needs of the stakeholders of modern systems?* To answer this question, in the following we review four institutional bodies guidelines and four recent literature that clearly categorize new emerging stakeholders' needs.

Starting in 2019, the High-Level Expert Group on AI presented Ethics Guidelines for Trustworthy AI [5]. According to these guidelines trustworthy AI should be lawful, ethical, and robust. They state 7 key requirements for trustworthy AI systems, spanning from human agency and oversight, to accountability, passing through diversity, non-discrimination and fairness, to mention a few.

The Organization for Economic Cooperation and Development (OECD) identified five value-based principles [13] that should drive the various countries AI ecosystems in developing systems that are trustworthy and respectful of human rights and societal values like inclusive growth, sustainable development and well-being, as well as transparency and explainability.

The UNESCO recommendation on the ethics of AI [16] is built around four core values, namely human rights and human dignity, living in peaceful, ensuring diversity and inclusiveness, and environment and ecosystem flourishing. These values drive the development of ten core principles that form the foundation of a human-rights centred approach to AI systems.

The AI Bill of Rights [17] provides five driving principles and associated practices for the development of automated systems in the AI era that are respectful of democratic values, human rights, civil liberties and privacy.

In the research realm, Li et al. [9] present a holistic and clear set of 17 quality attributes of trustworthy AI systems. These attributes were retrieved from seven existing normative documents and four secondary studies, including international standards, draft acts, and technical report. The authors also identified similarities and differences in the analysed studies, which reveal still a lack of clarity about how these quality attributes contribute to the trustworthiness of AI systems. However, their relevance is evident also from other contributions (e.g., [2,3,7]). Interestingly, the analysed documents and studies (with a major contribution coming from the "Ethics Guidelines for Trustworthy AI" [5]) suggest that trustworthy AI systems should meet four basic principles: the principle of *respect for human autonomy*, principle of *prevention of harm*, principle of *fairness*, principle of *explicability*.

Lu et al. identified a roadmap [11] and best practices [10] for responsible AI systems aiming at ensuring the responsible development and operation of such systems. As emerged in the AI era, also ethical aspects must be considered to achieve trustworthy AI systems. In [11], the authors defined a roadmap about software engineering methods on how to develop responsible AI systems, including requirements engineering, systems design and operation. In [10] the authors present best practices for responsible AI, by means of a pattern-oriented approach. In their Responsible AI Pattern Catalogue[1], patterns are organized in: (1) Governance patterns, for establishing multi-level governance for responsible AI; (2) Process patterns, for setting up trustworthy development processes; and (3) Product patterns, for building responsible-AI-by-design into AI systems, which include fairness, privacy, and explainability, each organized in further sub-characteristics. For example, within the fairness patterns there is the *discrimination mitigator* summarised as follows: "discrimination mitigation algorithms are used to address unwanted bias throughout the entire lifecycle of AI systems"[2] In the same book, the authors also discuss different case studies to help organizations apply the defined generic patterns for all the AI ethics principles in different contexts. One of the reported case studies concerns a risk-based responsible AI approach adopted by Telstra, Australia's largest telecommunications company. Telstra created a Responsible AI Policy of several principles that clearly state what is expected when dealing with AI systems. To drive compliance with the Responsible AI Policy, they used risk assessment dimensions including human impact and fairness, assessing the effect that the company's use cases can have on their customers and other stakeholders, especially groups less able to defend their rights or particularly vulnerable [10].

In their recent work, Baldassarre et al. [1] tackle the problem of ensuring a responsible design and development of AI systems throughout their entire

[1] https://research.csiro.au/ss/science/projects/responsible-ai-pattern-catalogue/.

[2] It can be consulted in its entirety at: https://research.csiro.au/ss/science/projects/responsible-ai-pattern-catalogue/discrimination-mitigation/.

life-cycle. They highlight that despite several AI ethics principles and guidelines exist, these are too high-level to concretely affect the implementation of systems. To overcome this gap, the authors present a novel holistic framework for trustworthy AI, namely POLARIS, that aims to provide actionable guidelines and tools to support different types of stakeholders throughout the entire software development life-cycle. It is worth to mention that POLARIS has been built on top of the knowledge emerged after a review of the state of practice about trustworthy AI frameworks proposed by industry, academia, and other institutions, as well as a survey with AI practitioners. POLARIS focuses on four foundational pillars of trustworthy AI, namely privacy, security, fairness, and explainability and has been applied to an industrial case study for validation purposes[3]

Overall, several principles and stakeholders' needs arise from both researchers and practitioners realms, besides of the most traditional technical robustness and safety [5], prevention of harm [9], and security [1], which are already included in the standard. We outline them in Table 1 according to their sources.

Table 1. Stakeholders needs emerged from the analysed literature.

Name	Sources
Societal and environmental well-being	[5,13,16]
Accountability	[5,13,16]
Privacy and data governance	[1,5,10,16,17]
Human agency and oversight, human autonomy	[5,9,16,17]
Transparency	[5,13,16]
Explicability, Explainability	[1,9,10,13,16,17]
Diversity, non-discrimination and fairness	[1,5,9,10,13,16,17]

3 Analysis of the Quality Standards with Respect to Quality Needs

In this section we aim at analysing the quality standard with respect to quality needs. This analysis is based on the needs of stakeholders of modern systems, which are highlighted in Sect. 2. These enabled us to make the following observations on the quality standard [8]:

- *Societal and environmental well-being* indicates that these systems impact the society at whole, human beings and environment. They must therefore be evaluated with respect to the benefits they may provide to the society and their sustainability [5,13,16]. However, it is not included in the standard, which only mention user engagement, inclusivity and user assistance under the interaction capability characteristic. According to [5], this need should consider:

[3] Additional details on the framework can be found at: https://github.com/dom976/POLARIS_framework/tree/main.

  - *Sustainable and environmental friendliness* of AI systems.
  - *Social and societal impact* of AI systems, which should be carefully considered.
  - *Society and democracy*, considering that this specific aspect can be highly influenced by AI systems.
- *Accountability* refers to the possibility to determinate responsibilities for the systems' behavior and its outcome [5,13,16]. The standard [8] lists accountability as a sub-characteristic under security. We argue that accountability should also be relevant for the prevention of harm as well as safety. Besides, it can play a role also under societal and environmental well-being. Thus, it should be considered as a first order quality. Based on [5], accountability should include:
  - *Auditability*, which entails the enablement of the assessment of algorithms, data and design processes [5]. The guidelines further suggest that while it is not mandatory for business models to be transparent, the availability of evaluation reports contributes to the trustworthiness of the systems.
  - *Minimisation and reporting of negative impacts* refers to identifying, assessing, documenting and minimising the potentially negative impacts of AI systems [5].
  - *Tradeoffs* referring to the implementation of the requirements above.
  - *Redress* in case of the occurrence of adverse impact [5]. It also represent an important feature to ensure trust.

  All these accountability requirements, pose particular attention to vulnerable persons or groups.
- *Privacy* is not mentioned in the standard. To the contrary, as also evident from Table 1, it plays a central role among the needs of stakeholders of modern systems.
- With respect to *data governance*, based on [10] the standard should further consider:
  - *Accuracy, completeness, consistency, validity, timeliness, uniqueness* of the undertaken data quality measurements, to mitigate the bias in real-world data [10].
  - *Security and privacy*, specifically concerning the control about how data (especially personal data) is being collected, stored, modified, used, and exchanged between different parties [10].
  - *Access to data*.
- *Human agency and oversight* copes with the need to have the human in control [5,9,16,17]. We argue that this can be included under, and strengthen the content of, the interaction capability.
- *Transparency* refers to data, system, and AI business models [5,13,16]. According to [5], it includes:
  - *Explainability*, concerning the ability to explain both the technical processes of an AI system and the related human decisions (e.g. application areas of a system).
  - *Traceability* of the data sets and the processes that yield the AI system's decision.

  - *Communication*, intended as the humans right to know that they are interacting with a system.
- *Diversity, non-discrimination and Fairness* are recurrent in all the analysed works [1,5,9,10,13,16,17]. As described in [5], it should include:
  - *Avoidance of unfair bias* in data sets used by AI systems.
  - *Accessibility and universal/inclusive design*, to ensure the user-centricity of systems and their easy-of-use by any group of people, regardless of their age, gender, abilities.
  - *Stakeholders participation* throughout the entire systems life cycle.

From our analysis several aspects emerge. The ISO/IEC 25010:2023 [8] standard includes many relevant quality characteristics and sub-characteristics for the evaluation of software product quality. Despite they represent a solid foundation, recent years have seen the emergence of responsible computing, the need for engineering value-based ecosystems [14,15], and new legislation and policies concerning AI governance (e.g., the AI Act, the first law to regulate the use of AI in Europe [12]). These developments highlight the need for additional qualities that software products should exhibit to meet the expectations of modern systems. This is evident from the efforts of researchers and practitioners who have contributed to quality attributes for trustworthy AI [9], responsible AI [10,11], and actionable guidelines and tools to support different stakeholders throughout the entire software development life-cycle of trustworthy AI systems [1].

4 Conclusions and Future Work

In this paper we have challenged the present notion of quality for software systems in face of the development and widespread use of AI-enabled autonomous systems. We have outlined the urgency to rethink the notion of quality to be able to encompass the emergent needs of the digital society to deal with trustworthy systems that ethically collaborate with human beings. Future work requires a deeper and more exhaustive analysis of the threats and implications for the society of modern AI software systems that may exhibit different level of quality. The European AI act suggests a risk-based metric that may not be the right way to address the quality issue of these kind of systems in a comprehensive way.

References

1. Baldassarre, M.T., Gigante, D., Kalinowski, M., Ragone, A.: POLARIS: a framework to guide the development of trustworthy AI systems. In: Proceedings of the 3rd International Conference on AI Engineering: Software Engineering for AI, CAIN 2024. IEEE/ACM (2024, to appear)
2. Boltz, N., Yaman, S.G., Inverardi, P., de Lemos, R., Van Landuyt, D., Zisman, A.: Human empowerment in self-adaptive socio-technical systems. In: 19th International Conference on Software Engineering for Adaptive and Self-Managing Systems (SEAMS@ICSE) 2024 (2024, to appear)

3. Di Ruscio, D., Inverardi, P., Migliarini, P., Nguyen, P.T.: Leveraging privacy profiles to empower users in the digital society. Autom. Softw. Eng. **31**(1), 16 (2024). https://doi.org/10.1007/S10515-024-00415-2
4. European Commission: White paper on artificial intelligence (2020). https://ec.europa.eu/info/sites/info/files/commission-white-paper-artificial-intelligence-feb2020_en.pdf
5. High-Level Expert Group on AI: Ethics guidelines for trustworthy AI (2019). https://digital-strategy.ec.europa.eu/en/library/ethics-guidelines-trustworthy-ai. Accessed 31 Jan 2024
6. Inverardi, P.: The European perspective on responsible computing. Commun. ACM **62**(4), 64 (2019). https://doi.org/10.1145/3311783
7. Inverardi, P., Migliarini, P., Palmiero, M.: Systematic review on privacy categorisation. Comput. Sci. Rev. **49**, 100574 (2023). https://doi.org/10.1016/J.COSREV.2023.100574
8. ISO25000: ISO/IEC 25010 - system and software quality models (2023). https://iso25000.com/index.php/en/iso-25000-standards/iso-25010
9. Li, G., Liu, B., Zhang, H.: Quality attributes of trustworthy artificial intelligence in normative documents and secondary studies: a preliminary review. Computer **56**(04), 28–37 (2023). https://doi.org/10.1109/MC.2023.3240730
10. Lu, Q., Zhu, L., Whittle, J., Xu, X.: Responsible AI: Best Practices for Creating Trustworthy AI Systems. Pearson (2023). https://books.google.it/books?id=yFelzwEACAAJ
11. Lu, Q., Zhu, L., Xu, X., Whittle, J., Xing, Z.: Towards a roadmap on software engineering for responsible AI. In: Crnkovic, I. (ed.) Proceedings of the 1st International Conference on AI Engineering: Software Engineering for AI, CAIN 2022, Pittsburgh, Pennsylvania, 16–17 May 2022, pp. 101–112. ACM (2022). https://doi.org/10.1145/3522664.3528607
12. Madiega, T.A.,: Artificial intelligence act (2024). https://www.europarl.europa.eu/RegData/etudes/BRIE/2021/698792/EPRS_BRI(2021)698792_EN.pdf
13. OECD.AI Policy Observatory: OECD AI Principles overview (2019). https://oecd.ai/en/ai-principles. Accessed May 2024
14. Pelliccione, P., Buhnova, B., Gottschalk, S., Weber, I., Engels, G.: Architecting and engineering value-based ecosystems. In: Pelliccione, P., Kazman, R., Weber, I., Liu, A. (eds.) Software Architecture, pp. 41–68. Springer, Cham (2023). https://doi.org/10.1007/978-3-031-36847-9_3
15. Shahin, M., et al.: Operationalizing human values in software engineering: a survey. IEEE Access **10**, 75269–75295 (2022). https://doi.org/10.1109/ACCESS.2022.3190975
16. UNESCO: Recommendation on the ethics of artificial intelligence (2022). https://www.unesco.org/en/artificial-intelligence/recommendation-ethics
17. United States Government: Blueprint for an AI Bill of Rights Making Automated Systems Work for the American People (2022). https://www.whitehouse.gov/wp-content/uploads/2022/10/Blueprint-for-an-AI-Bill-of-Rights.pdf

Various shades of Software Testing

Mutation Testing of Smart Contracts As a Service

Morena Barboni[1(✉)], Andrea Morichetta[1], Andrea Polini[1], Sebastian Banescu[2], and Edward Zulkoski[2]

[1] University of Camerino, Camerino, Italy
{morena.barboni,andrea.morichetta,andrea.polini}@unicam.it
[2] Quantstamp, San Francisco, USA
{sebi,ed}@quantstamp.com

Abstract. Smart contracts are self-executing programs that operate on a blockchain. Due to their complex and specialized nature, smart contracts often undergo auditing by independent parties before deployment to production. One promising method to enhance the reliability of smart contracts is mutation testing, a powerful albeit time-consuming test adequacy assessment technique. This paper proposes a framework to streamline and parallelize the mutation testing process, making it more practical and accessible for auditors. Simulations conducted on real-world Solidity projects show that the implemented service can significantly reduce the computational time needed for a local, sequential mutation testing run.

Keywords: Parallel Mutation Testing · Smart Contract · Ethereum Blockchain · Auditing

1 Introduction

Blockchain is a revolutionary technology that has transformed transaction processes, offering unprecedented levels of security and transparency. At the heart of this revolution are **Smart Contracts**: self-executing agreements that operate on the blockchain. The immutable nature of smart contracts calls for thorough testing before deployment, as any vulnerabilities can lead to significant financial losses and erode trust in the underlying implementation [7,27,28]. To support the development of robust blockchain-based applications, recent literature has introduced numerous techniques, tools, and approaches [26]. Despite these advancements, the complex and specialized nature of smart contract security made developers seek the expertise of independent auditors for comprehensive testing and security assessments [12,21]. The **auditing** process is crucial for identifying and mitigating unforeseen vulnerabilities, errors, and potential malicious exploits that could compromise distributed applications [3]. One technique that can prove particularly valuable for auditors is **mutation testing** [6]. This technique evaluates the effectiveness of software tests based on their capabilities of detecting changes, or mutations, that are injected into the source code of a program. Although promising, the practical application of mutation testing

A. Bertolino et al. (Eds.): QUATIC 2024, CCIS 2178, pp. 93–109, 2024.
https://doi.org/10.1007/978-3-031-70245-7_7

is challenged by the substantial time investment required to run the test suite on each mutated program [8] and to manually examine every undetected mutation. Thus, balancing thorough testing with project timelines becomes a critical consideration for auditors and developers alike.

In this paper, we present a **framework** designed to **speed-up** and **streamline mutation testing** of smart contracts. Our goal is to lower entry barriers for auditors and encourage the adoption of thorough mutant analysis. The proposed framework relies on a remote service to distribute mutation testing task across parallel Docker containers, significantly reducing the time and resources required. We empirically evaluate five distinct work distribution strategies, comparing their performance and scalability on three open source Solidity projects. Then, we provide guidelines to help choose the optimal mutant distribution strategy, considering project-specific characteristics and potential resource constraints. The conducted simulations reveal that the most efficient strategy can, on average, reduce the computational time needed for a local, sequential mutation testing run by 70%.

The rest of this paper is structured as follows: Sect. 2 introduces blockchain technology, smart contract auditing fundamentals, and SuMo a mutation testing tool for the Solidity language. Section 3 presents the objectives of this work, providing a deeper understanding of the context in which SuMo operates. The framework we propose is detailed in Sect. 4, while Sect. 5 discusses its validation through simulations on real-world projects. Section 6 presents related work in the field of blockchain and mutation testing. Lastly Sect. 7 summarizes our findings and explores directions for future research.

2 Background

Mutation Testing. First proposed by Richard Lipton in 1971 [4], mutation testing aims to improve test suites by introducing small changes (mutations) to a program and evaluating whether the test suite can detect these changes. Despite its initial perception as costly and unconventional, mutation testing has become more prominent in the industry [10,22] due to advancements in cost-reduction techniques [25] and its potential to uncover bugs and improve knowledge about the code under test [6,23,24]. Key concepts in mutation testing that we will refer in the rest of this paper are: 1) **Mutant:** A minimal alteration in a portion of the source code that simulates a common programming error; 2) **Mutation Operators:** A set of rules that guide how code is altered to create mutants; 3) **Mutation Score (MS):** The adequacy value of the test suite, measured as the ratio of mutants it was able to detect (or **kill**).

SuMo. SuMo[1] is a mutation testing tool for Solidity, the main language for programming smart contracts on the Ethereum blockchain. SuMo includes a suite of mutation operators that simulate a wide variety of traditional and Solidity-specific faults [8]. SuMo undergoes a continuous refinement with respect to the

[1] SuMo repository: https://github.com/MorenaBarboni/SuMo-SOlidity-MUtator.

operators it offers [6]. However, being a stand-alone module [2], it requires local execution by users. Addressing time constraints and providing practical mutant analysis features are key areas of improvement to ensure that mutation testing continues to be a valuable technique in the blockchain domain.

Smart Contract Auditing. Smart contracts automate agreements on the blockchain, executing actions when predefined conditions are met. Once deployed, the smart contract code cannot be modified, making pre-deployment testing essential to ensure they are free from vulnerabilities or flaws [7,27,28]. Due to the unique nature of smart contracts, developers started relying on third-party auditing companies [12,21] or dedicated auditing platforms (e.g. Code4rena [1]). The typical **auditing process** involves a thorough **inspection** of the smart contract's source code, comprehensive testing, and meticulous security verification to identify and mitigate any vulnerabilities [3]. Once inspection is complete, the auditing team prepares a detailed report that recommends corrective actions for the project team to implement. When possible, a follow-up audit is also conducted to verify that all potential issues have been resolved. However, this thorough and expensive process can delay project release. To allow adequate time for mutant analysis without further extending the auditing time-frame, it is crucial to lower entry barriers and speed-up the execution of mutation testing.

3 Objectives

This work aims to make mutation testing a valuable addition to the smart contract auditing toolkit. The identified challenges and objectives are:

1) Streamlining Mutation Analysis. Our main goal is to provide a cohesive framework that enables auditors to conduct mutation testing on smart contract projects efficiently. This involves initiating mutation testing on a Solidity project, retrieving results, and analyzing mutants in a practical way. To tackle this challenge, we enhance the stand-alone SuMo tool with two key components: 1) a companion Visual Studio Code extension, and 2) a service that can be hosted on a remote node. The VSCode extension includes features that simplify the execution of mutation testing jobs and the inspection of results, all within the same working environment. The service permits to keep track of the remote mutation testing jobs run on each project under test. This also allows auditors to monitor the Mutation Score's evolution over successive project revisions and evaluate the effectiveness of test improvements made by developers.

2) Reducing Time Costs. Auditing is a thorough, complex process that can delay the release of a project. *Mutation testing*, by its nature, is a time consuming technique that can further extend the auditing time-frame. This stems not only from the duration of the testing process itself, but also from the substantial effort auditors must invest in examining live mutants. Still, the ability of this technique to rigorously evaluate and improve the effectiveness of a test suite

[2] SuMo npm module: https://www.npmjs.com/package/@morenabarboni/sumo.

can be invaluable. Our recent study [6] in collaboration with *Quantstamp*, a leader blockchain security company, showed that mutation testing can play an important role during manual code inspection. Analyzing live mutants can not only lead to test improvements, but also increase code knowledge and disclose issues in the contracts under test. Thus, live mutants should be presented to the auditors quickly, before the code review phase is complete. By providing SuMo as a service, we allow auditors to run parallel mutation testing tasks in the cloud, offering scalability and reducing execution time.

4 SuMo as a Service

In the design of our mutation testing framework, we recognized the need for a solution that offered efficiency, scalability and ease-of-use for auditors. One effective technique to speed-up mutation testing is parallel mutant execution [25]. Modern mutation analysis tools like PiT [2] typically support local parallelization to improve the efficiency of the testing process. However, a local approach is limited by the computational power and memory of a single machine. Additionally, it can introduce reliability issues due to the lack of isolation between parallel testing tasks, potentially leading to failures and inconsistent results. This is an important consideration for Solidity projects, where testing contracts typically involves setting up a test network that simulates the blockchain environment.

To address the limitations of local parallelization, several works explored distributing mutation testing executions across multiple nodes [11,18], such as Amazon EC2 instances [19]. While cloud services like EC2 offer scalable access to computational resources, they also incur higher costs based on time and resource consumption. Moreover, they require careful planning to ensure data security and compliance, especially when handling sensitive codebases.

In this work, we propose a framework that leverages Docker containers to parallelize mutant execution tasks. This approach offers portability, robustness, and good scalability. Indeed, each container operates in isolation, ensuring that testing environments do not interfere with each other. Docker containers can be created and shut down in seconds, which is ideal for mutation testing where many relatively short-lived environments must be spawned to run testing tasks. Furthermore, mutation testing can be run on any node equipped with Docker, scaling the number of parallel containers based on the workload and available infrastructure. The proposed framework consists of three main components:

1) The ***SuMo Tool*** retains the core functionality described in our previous work [8], requiring the user to install it as an npm module within a Solidity project. SuMo permits to select specific mutation operators, visualize available mutations for a project, and start mutation testing. At the end of an execution, it generates a detailed report that tracks the Mutation Score across subsequent project revisions, allowing auditors to monitor test quality during the fix review.

*2) The **SuMo Service*** is a complementary solution that can be deployed on a host to handle remote, parallel mutation testing jobs. This offers auditors the flexibility to run mutation testing either locally or in the cloud.
*3) The **SuMo VSCode Extension*** to provide a cohesive user experience, we implemented a companion Visual Studio Code extension for SuMo. This extension simplifies the configuration of mutation testing for projects and the inspection of live mutants. In particular, it allows auditors to easily adjust their testing preferences (e.g.: the mutation operators to be used or the contracts to be blacklisted) and start a remote - or a local - mutation testing run. As illustrated in Fig. 1, the extension features a dedicated panel for connecting to the SuMo service hosted at a specific address and port. Once mutation testing starts, it is possible to monitor the execution progress by selecting a preferred level of log granularity—from simple error logs to detailed container-level information. Thus, auditors can upload the project under test, run SuMo, and receive the results within the same VSCode workspace. Similar to tools like *coverage-gutters*[3], the extension displays mutation results directly on the Solidity code, making it easier for auditors to review mutations and understand their potential impact.

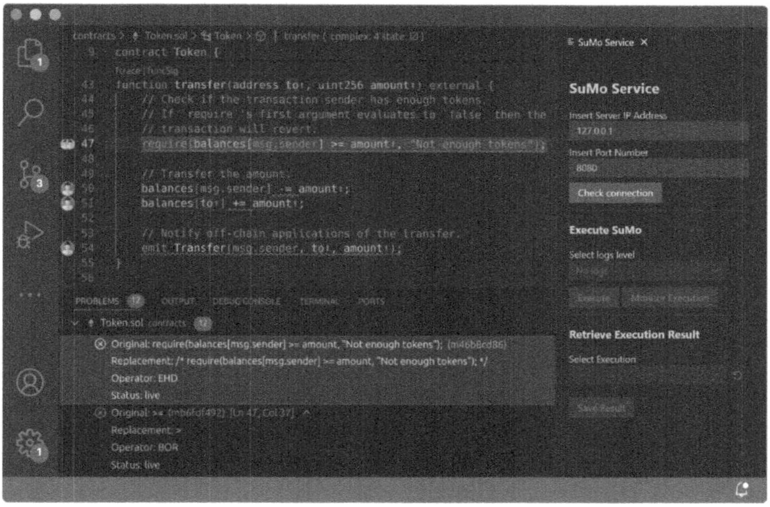

Fig. 1. SuMo VSCode extension: service configuration and mutant visualization features

Since the implementation of the SuMo mutation testing tool was extensively described in our previous work [8], in the following we only focus on the SuMo service, presenting the design and architectural considerations behind its development. In particular, Sect. 4.1 describes the high-level architecture of the

[3] vscode-coverage-gutters:https://github.com/ryanluker/vscode-coverage-gutters.

service while Sect. 4.2 presents the complete workflow of a remote mutation testing job. Lastly, Sect. 4.3 introduces the custom Docker executors we implemented to parallelize mutant execution.

4.1 SuMo Service High-Level Architecture

The SuMo service is a Spring application that leverages Java's robust support for multithreading to ensure scalability and efficient handling of concurrent requests. As introduced above, clients can interact with the service through the SuMo VSCode extension. In particular, they can upload the Solidity Project Under Test (PUT) and the relative SuMo configuration to the service, which will start the testing process. Specifically, we define:

1. A **Mutation Testing Job**: the execution of a **complete** mutation testing run on a PUT. A mutation testing job can be split into parallel mutation testing tasks executed within individual Docker containers;
2. A **Mutation Testing Task**: the execution of a **partial** mutation testing run on a PUT, wherein only a subset of the generated mutants are tested within a Docker container.

The SuMo service can run parallel mutation testing tasks on the same PUT, and concurrent jobs over different PUTs. This logic is handled by two core components (See Fig. 2):

1. The **Mutation Service** receives the PUT and prepares it for a mutation testing job. In particular, it defines and allocates parallel execution tasks through the Docker Service.
2. The **Docker Service** starts and manages the execution of mutation testing tasks within parallel Docker containers run on the same host. Each container hosts a copy of the PUT and its dependencies, including SuMo.

The *Docker Service* manages the workload distribution and the execution of containers by creating an **Executor** in charge of running SuMo on the PUT. Docker executors are a concept commonly associated with CI/CD pipelines, where they refer to the agents or workers responsible for running individual pipeline jobs within containers. Similarly, we utilize Docker executors for managing mutation testing tasks and jobs. The SuMo service currently provides five custom executors, although only one can be utilized at a time: the Operator Executor (OE), Smart Combined Operator Executor (SCOE), Smart Combined Mutants Executor (SCME), Dockerized Combined Operators Executor (DCOE), and Dockerized Combined Mutants Executor (DCME). All the executors can create, start, stop, and manage containers through the Docker Client. However, the defined *Executor interface* allows the SuMo service to be integrated with different containerization technologies. The characteristics of each executor are presented in detail in Sect. 4.3.

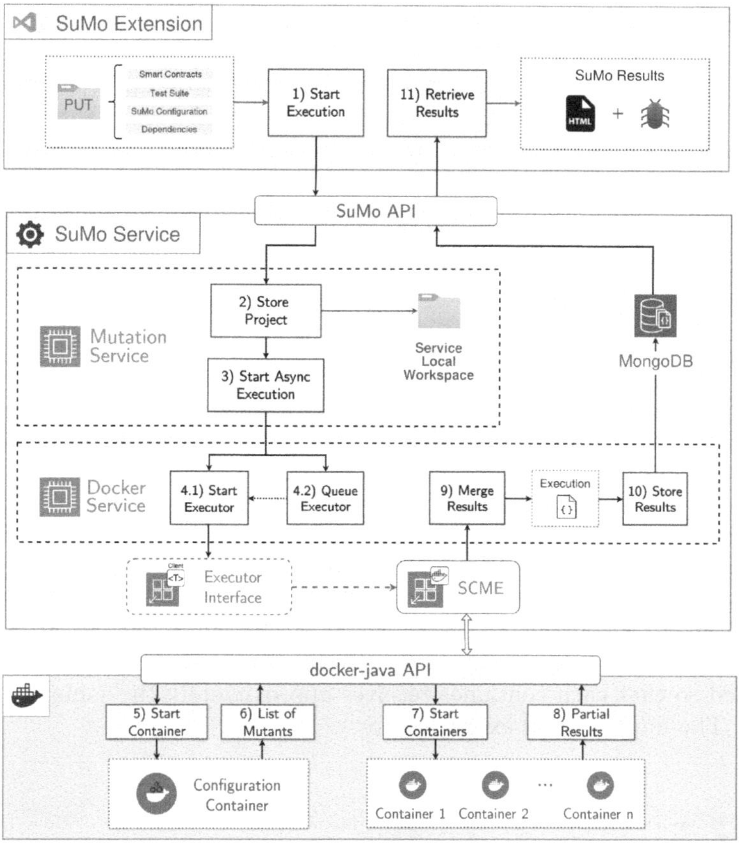

Fig. 2. SuMo Service Architecture and Workflow

4.2 Mutation Testing Workflow

This Section describes the step-by-step workflow of a remote mutation testing job executed through the SuMo service, as depicted in Fig. 2. The process begins when a user uploads the Solidity Project Under Test (PUT) from their VSCode workspace to the SuMo service ①. When the *Mutation Service* receives the PUT, it unpacks it in a workspace directory ②. Then, it activates the *Docker Service* ③, which is responsible for creating the specific executor chosen by the user. The *Docker Service* checks if the host's available resources are sufficient to run SuMo on the PUT. If resources are insufficient the task is queued (4.2), otherwise mutation testing can start (4.1). For instance, in the workflow depicted in Fig. 2, the selected executor is the *Smart Combined Mutant Executor* (SCME). This executor first creates a *Configuration Container* ⑤ where preliminary operations are performed. These operations include installing the PUT's dependencies, enabling the user-selected mutation operators, and computing the list of mutants generated by SuMo for the PUT. This list is then returned to the executor ⑥, which evenly distributes the mutants across a user-selected number of containers n. At this point, the executor can start n mutation testing tasks by running each container in parallel ⑦. Upon completion of a mutation testing task, the respective container sends its partial results back to the executor ⑧. The executor then relays these results to the *Docker Service*, which merges them into a single *Execution* object ⑨. This object is subsequently stored in the database ⑩. Once all the containers have terminated, the user can retrieve, save and visualize ⑪ the complete mutation testing results locally, using the built-in feature of the SuMo VSCode extension.

4.3 Mutation Testing Executors

The Executor package of the SuMo service hosts the *Docker Client* responsible for building images, starting-up and tearing-down containers. This component currently includes five custom executors for running mutation testing tasks on a given project, each employing a distinct logic for container creation and workload distribution. Considering that mutation testing is not conducted over multiple nodes with heterogeneous hardware, we employ static distribution algorithms such as the one originally proposed by Offut et al. [20]. Such algorithms minimize overhead by splitting the workload (i.e., the mutants to be tested) only once, before starting the mutation testing process [11]. The workload is then distributed so that each container receives approximately the same quantity of mutants. The implemented executors are:

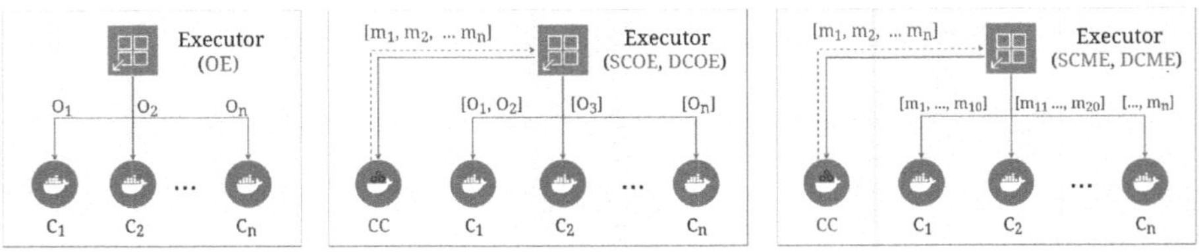

Fig. 3. Workload distribution strategies for each executor

OE - Operators Executor: The OE implements a baseline parallelization solution that assigns a single mutation operator to each container. As illustrated in Fig. 3, OE creates a preset number n of parallel containers $C_1, ..., C_n$ from a shared Docker image, so that each container holds a copy of the PUT. When a given container C_i is started, it installs all necessary PUT dependencies and enables a single SuMo mutation operator O_i. Once all the mutants generated by O_i have been tested, C_i is terminated and a new container is spawned in its place. This process continues until all the mutation operators enabled by the user have been run on the PUT.

SCOE - Smart Combined Operators Executor: The SCOE differs from OE in that it first computes the list of mutants $m_1, ..., m_n$ generated by SuMo for the PUT through a *Configuration Container CC*. SCOE then distributes the mutation operators $O_1, ..., O_n$ over a fixed number of containers $C_1, ..., C_n$, commensurate with the amount of mutants they generated. Although this does not guarantee that each container receives the exact same number of mutants, it approximates an equitable distribution by aligning the output of each operator.

SCME - Smart Combined Mutants Executor: The SCME works on analogous principles as the SCOE. However, instead of creating execution tasks by distributing operators, it directly allocates the generated mutants $m_1, ..., m_n$ to the spawned containers. This approach optimizes workload distribution, as the quantity of mutants per container remains nearly uniform.

DCOE - Dockerized Combined Operators Executor: The DCOE distributes mutation operators over a preset number of parallel containers just like SCOE. However, it uses a custom Dockerfile to build a Docker image tailored to the PUT's requirements. This approach speeds-up initial setup operations because each newly spawned container already includes all dependencies needed for running SuMo on the PUT. Furthermore, Docker caches the image after the first build, speeding up subsequent mutation testing jobs on the same project.

DCME - Dockerized Combined Mutants Executor: The DCME distributes the mutants evenly over a fixed number of containers like SCME, while employing the same custom image creation strategy as DCOE.

5 Validation

In the next, we discuss the experimental setup (Sect. 5.1), and the results of the simulations we performed to evaluate the proposed framework (Sect. 5.2). The validation centers around the diverse executors offered by the SuMo service and their impact on performance. The objective is to gain insights into how different parallelization modes may help reduce the time needed for mutation testing within real-world software projects (Sect. 5.3).

5.1 Methodology

To evaluate the SuMo service we ran simulations on three real-world Solidity projects with different scales and complexities. All the subjects, with the exception of the *MetaCoin* boilerplate, were selected from Code4Rena, as it provides realistic examples of contracts submitted by developers for a security audit:

- **MetaCoin**[4] is a compact template for token development;
- **ENS**[5] is a decentralized naming service to resolve a wide array of resources;
- **VTVL**[6] is a token management platform for founders of Web3-based projects.

[4] MetaCoin repository: https://github.com/truffle-box/metacoin-box.
[5] ENS repository: https://github.com/code-423n4/2023-10-ens.
[6] VTVL repository: https://github.com/code-423n4/2022-09-vtvl.

In particular, for each project we performed the following steps:

1. **Local Execution:** First, we ran the stand-alone SuMo package on the project to establish a performance baseline;
2. **Service Execution:** Then, we executed five independent mutation testing runs on the project, one for each executor implemented in the service: OE, SCOE, SCME and DCOE and DCME. For this experiment, we fixed the maximum number of parallel containers spawned by each executor to 6. However, we ran additional simulations for the SCME and DCME executors, with variations in the number of parallel containers, to evaluate how the service performance responds to specific changes.

All simulations were performed on a Ubuntu Server 22 LTS machine with 8 cores, 16 threads and 16 GB of RAM.

5.2 Simulations Results

This Section compares the performance of the stand-alone SuMo tool against the SuMo service. Table 1 reports the total time required to complete a local mutation testing run on each project, and the average time needed to test a single mutant (Avg. TPM). It also shows the number of generated (#G), killed (#K) and live (#L) mutants, together with the achieved Mutation Score (MS). As can be seen, it took only 7 min to evaluate a simple boilerplate like MetaCoin. Instead, for a complex project with a large test suite like ENS, where SuMo produced over 3k mutants, the process required about 29 h. Table 2 compares the performance of SuMo when executed locally and remotely, considering the different executors offered by the service: OE, SCOE, SCME, DCOE and DCME. For the latter, the Table details the time allocation for individual activities: 1) Extract Project, 2) Distribute Mutants, 3) Build Image and 4) Run SuMo. In the following we discuss the overhead introduced by each executor when performing preliminary operations, and their impact on the mutation testing time.

Table 1. Results for the local SuMo execution

Project	$\#G$	$\#L$	$\#K$	$MS(\%)$	$Time$	$Avg.TPM(s)$
MetaCoin	28	12	15	55.6	00:07:07	15.1
VTVL	336	131	191	59.1	01:08:33	12.2
ENS	3294	122	183	59.9	29:42:22	27.9

Overhead Time. While running SuMo is the most time-consuming activity of a mutation testing job, the service can introduce additional overhead while preparing the PUT for execution. Figure 4 compares the time required by each executor to perform these preliminary operations:

1. **Extract Project:** This task involves unpacking the PUT into the service's *workspace* directory. The time required for the project extraction phase is negligible across all projects and executors.

Table 2. Results for the SuMo service execution

Project	Task	Executor Type					
		Local	OE	SCOE	SCME	DCOE	DCME
MetaCoin	1) Extract Project	–	00:00:01	00:00:01	00:00:01	00:00:01	00:00:01
	2) Distribute Mut.	–	00:00:01	00:01:49	00:01:39	00:00:04	00:00:03
	3) Build Image	–	00:00:00	00:00:00	00:00:00	00:02:02	00:02:00
	4) Run SuMo	00:07:07	00:37:00	00:06:30	00:06:43	00:02:10	00:01:45
	TOT	00:07:07	00:37:02	00:08:20	00:08:23	00:04:17	00:03:49
VTVL	1) Extract Project	–	00:00:01	00:00:01	00:00:01	00:00:01	00:00:01
	2) Distribute Mut.	–	00:00:00	00:01:08	00:01:26	00:00:04	00:00:03
	3) Build Image	–	00:00:00	00:00:00	00:00:00	00:02:10	00:02:09
	4) Run SuMo	01:08:33	00:42:15	00:37:16	00:16:06	00:34:56	00:12:03
	TOT	01:08:33	00:42:16	00:38:25	00:17:33	00:37:11	00:14:16
ENS	1) Extract Project	–	00:00:02	00:00:02	00:00:02	00:00:03	00:00:02
	2) Distribute Mut.	–	00:00:00	00:01:32	00:01:40	00:00:12	00:00:13
	3) Build Image	–	00:00:00	00:00:00	00:00:00	00:02:17	00:02:08
	4) Run SuMo	29:42:22	11:06:42	11:31:41	07:34:26	11:49:27	07:58:53
	TOT	29:42:22	11:06:44	11:33:15	07:36:08	11:49:59	08:01:16

2. **Distribute Mutants:** This task involves the creation and execution of the *Configuration Container*. As explained in Sect. 4.2, this component builds the list of mutants that will then be distributed to the parallel containers according to the specific strategy implemented by a given executor. Thus, this step is not applicable to OE, which simply enables a single operator per container. As shown in Fig. 4, SCOE and SCME take considerably longer to complete this task than DCOE and DCME. This is because the former must install the project dependencies during this step, while the latter install dependencies while building the Docker image.

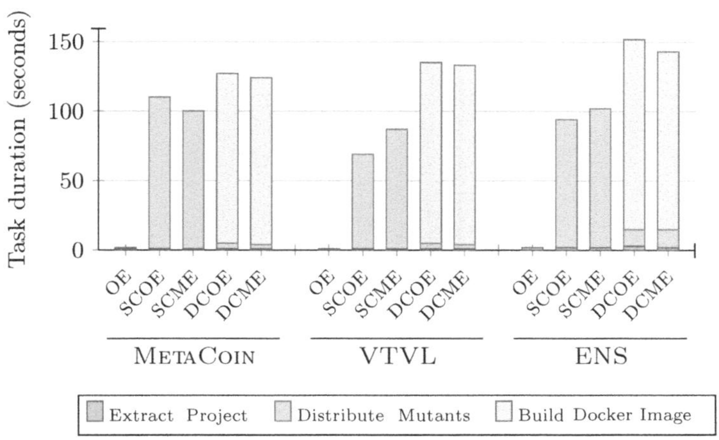

Fig. 4. Execution overhead of different Executors across projects

3. **Build Docker Image:** This task involves building a custom Docker image from a Dockerfile tailored to the PUT's requirements and installing its dependencies. Therefore, it is only applicable for the Dockerized executors, DCOE and DCME. It is important to note that the image must only be built once. Subsequent container creations do not necessitate image rebuilding, optimizing the execution workflow for DCME and DCOE.

SuMo Execution Time. The time required to run mutation testing varies significantly across executors, with the Operators Executor (OE) taking the longest, and the Smart and Dockerized Combined Mutant Executor (SCME and DCME) showing significant efficiency (See Fig. 5).

The **Operators Executor** (OE) proved to be rather inefficient due to its uneven distribution of mutants and repeated dependency installation process. This is evident in the MetaCoin project project, where the long time required for dependency installation negated the advantages of parallelism. In fact, the parallel execution took about five times longer than the local one.

The **Smart Combined Operators Executor** (SCOE) and **Dockerized Combined Operators Executor** (DCOE) increased efficiency by merging operators and distributing them across containers. However, they both showed limitations when handling larger projects. Indeed, it is not possible to optimally balance the distribution of mutants between containers using an operator-based grouping, making parallelization less efficient.

The effectiveness of the **Smart Combined Mutant Executor** (SCME) and **Dockerized Combined Mutant Executor** (DCME) lies in their capacity to evenly distribute mutants across Docker containers, contributing to a more efficient and balanced execution process. As Fig. 5 shows, DCME outperformed SCME in most scenarios, **reducing the time** needed to run mutation testing **by 70%** with respect to the local SuMo execution (−57% for MetaCoin, −79.4% for VTVL and −73% for ENS). The SCME also achieved good time

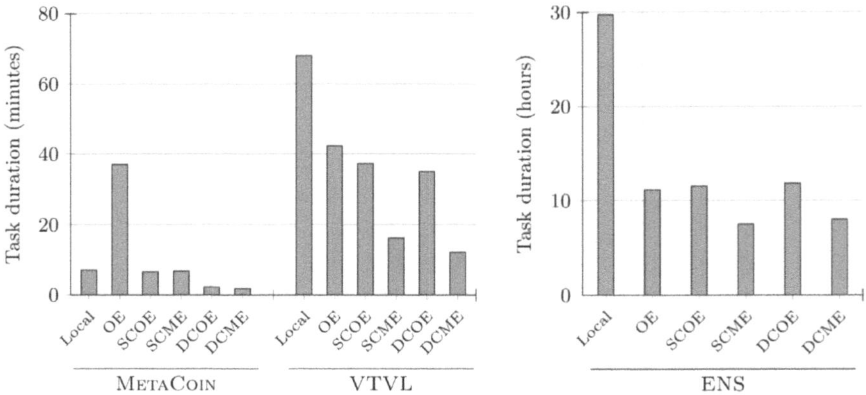

Fig. 5. Time required to run SuMo on the PUT using different executors

savings (−74.5% for VTVL and −74.5% for ENS), but it under-performed in smaller scale projects, to the point of increasing the execution time for METACOIN (+17.1%) with respect to the local run. These two executors employ the same mutant distribution strategy, but they differ in their set-up processes and in the preparation of the containers for testing. DCME only needs to build the custom Docker image and install the project dependencies once, thus shortening the overhead time for subsequent mutation testing tasks. Instead, SCME uses a pre-built image, but is slowed down by the necessity to re-install all the dependencies every time a container is spawned to run SUMO on the PUT. This makes SCME less efficient in case of projects with a lengthier dependency installation such as METACOIN and VTVL.

Table 3 compares the mutation testing duration of the two best executors, SCME and DCME, under various degrees of parallelism: 4, 6 and 8 Docker containers. While increasing the number of containers from 4 to 6 generally reduced testing time, further increasing the count to 8 did not yield proportional improvements, and even slightly extended the job duration for most projects. This plateau can be attributed to the limitations of the hardware used for running the simulation, but in any case a higher degree of parallelism may not always lead to performance improvements. To make the mutation testing process efficient and scalable, it is important to introduce a dynamic allocation strategy that adjusts the number of containers based on available resources and workload demands.

Table 3. Time required to complete a mutation testing job using the SCME and DCME executors with 4, 6 and 8 parallel containers

Project	SCME			DCME		
	4-Cont.	6-Cont.	8-Cont.	4-Cont.	6-Cont.	8-Cont.
METACOIN	00:07:02	00:08:23	00:10:05	00:04:14	00:03:49	00:04:13
VTVL	00:20:41	00:17:33	00:17:44	00:18:06	00:14:16	00:12:40
ENS	08:58:20	07:36:08	07:57:34	09:21:21	08:01:16	08:14:36

5.3 Optimal Executors for Mutation Testing

The choice of the most suitable executor for mutation testing must be guided by project-specific considerations. These include the size and complexity of the project, the time required for dependency installation, and the availability of resources. The two top-performing executors in this context are Smart Combined Mutants Executor (SCME) and Dockerized Combined Mutants Executor (DCME). Both efficiently distribute mutants across Docker containers, making them a valid solution for large-scale projects that would normally result in long, expensive mutation testing runs. Notably, DCME has demonstrated a significant reduction in time consumption compared to local execution (−70%), closely followed by SCME. However, both executors can be particularly suitable in specific situations.

The **Smart Combined Mutant Executor** (SCME) utilizes a pre-built, optimized Docker image, which helps to conserve disk space, reduce build time and minimize resource usage. Its lightweight nature makes SCME especially suitable in scenarios with limited resources, such as constrained CPU or memory. However, in the METACOIN project, lengthy dependency installations canceled out the advantages of parallelism, resulting in longer testing times compared to local, sequential execution. On the other hand, the **Dockerized Combined Mutant Executor** (DCME) leverages Docker's image management and dependency caching, significantly reducing the overhead of repeated dependency installations. This makes DCME particularly effective for projects with extensive dependency requirements. At the same time, building a custom Docker image may require significant resources, such as disk space and CPU, especially for large or complex applications.

Ultimately, the time savings achieved by SCME and DCME are very similar for projects that generate large amounts of mutants. Understanding the strengths of each executor can guide developers to make informed decisions that best align with the project's characteristics and available resources.

6 Related Work

While there is a substantial body of research in mutation analysis for smart contracts [5,8,9,13–15,17], no previous studies have proposed a comprehensive framework to streamline mutation testing for auditing activities. Over the past decade, various studies have focused on speeding up sequential mutation analysis, exploring techniques such as selective mutation, evolutionary algorithms, and higher-order mutation [25]. In the domain of smart contracts, *ContractMut* [14] implemented a manageable set of mutation operators, using selective mutation techniques to limit the number of generated mutants. The *Vertigo* tool [15], used mutant sampling technique to reduce the number of mutants to be run against the test suite. Instead, the *ReSuMo* [9] framework leveraged the outcomes from previous program revisions to incrementally update mutation testing results, thereby accelerating the mutation testing process for evolving projects.

Parallel processing has also played a significant role in advancing mutation analysis. Historically, the concept of parallelizing mutation analysis locally has been recognized since the early 1990s [20]. Reales and Polo [18] later demonstrated that executing mutants in parallel can significantly reduce testing time, with the reduction scaling with the number of nodes employed. Li et al.'s work [16] extended this approach to Ruby programs utilizing cloud infrastructure for parallel execution. Closer to our proposal, Merkel and Georgeson [19] proposed a cloud-based distributed mutation testing system for Java programs, which addresses performance limitations by distributing tasks across Amazon EC2 computing nodes. Their system optimizes the distribution of mutation tasks by allocating equal-sized batches of mutants to each worker node, proving this approach to be most effective for workload distribution. More recent work by Canizares et al. [11] improved the performance of mutation testing for large-scale systems by parallelizing mutant compilation and equivalent mutants detection, and proposing an advanced load distribution algorithm.

7 Conclusions and Future Work

This work presented a framework designed to seamlessly integrate mutation testing into the smart contract auditing process. The framework simplifies mutation analysis and enables the execution of remote mutation testing jobs, allowing auditors to quickly retrieve results and allocate more time to the inspection of live mutants. By leveraging parallel processing of testing tasks across Docker containers, the system delivers mutation testing results in acceptable time-frames, making it viable even for large projects. We evaluated five different strategies for distributing work and, based on performance assessments, we provided guidelines for choosing the optimal configuration. Our findings reveal that the most efficient mutant distribution strategy can reduce the duration of traditional, sequential mutation testing by up to 70%.

Future work should focus on several key areas. Firstly, the framework should be evaluated on a broader spectrum of real-world projects to better asses its efficacy under different conditions. To ensure optimal resource usage, future enhancements should introduce the orchestration of mutation testing jobs across multiple nodes and dynamically adapt the size of the container pool to meet project-specific requirements and available infrastructure. Inspired by practices in industrial settings, such as Google's use of developer feedback [22], we also plan to expand the implemented service to track the auditor's feedback on the productivity of live mutants. This information will help to develop heuristics for prioritizing interesting mutants for analysis, reducing the cognitive burden placed on auditors.

Acknowledgments. This work has been supported by Quantstamp. We would like to thank Damiano Cacchiarelli and Roberto Cesetti for their valuable feedback.

References

1. Code4rena—code4rena.com. https://code4rena.com/
2. PIT Mutation Testing—pitest.org. https://pitest.org/
3. What is a Smart Contract Audit?—quantstamp.com. https://quantstamp.com/blog/what-is-a-smart-contract-audit
4. Acree, A.T., DeMillo, R.A., Budd, T., Lipton, R.J., Sayward, F.G.: Mutation analysis. School of Information and Computer Science, Georgia Institute of Technology (1979)
5. Andesta, E., Faghih, F., Fooladgar, M.: Testing smart contracts gets smarter. In: Proceedings of the ICCKE, pp. 405–412. IEEE (2020)
6. Banescu, S., Barboni, M., Morichetta, A., Polini, A., Zulkoski, E.: Enhanced mutation testing of smart contracts in support of code inspection. In: Proceedings of the ICBC, pp. 558–566. IEEE (2024)

7. Barboni, M., Morichetta, A., Polini, A.: Smart contract testing: challenges and opportunities. In: Proceedings of the WETSEB@ICSE, pp. 21–24. ACM (2022)
8. Barboni, M., Morichetta, A., Polini, A.: SuMo: a mutation testing approach and tool for the ethereum blockchain. J. Syst. Softw. **193**, 111445 (2022)
9. Barboni, M., Morichetta, A., Polini, A., Casoni, F.: ReSuMo: a regression strategy and tool for mutation testing of solidity smart contracts. Software Qual. J. **32**(1), 225–253 (2024)
10. Beller, M., et aal.: What it would take to use mutation testing in industry - a study at Facebook. In: Proceedings of the ICSE (SEIP), pp. 268–277. IEEE (2021)
11. Cañizares, P.C., Núñez, A., Filgueira, R., de Lara, J.: Parallel mutation testing for large scale systems. Clust. Comput. **27**(2), 2071–2097 (2024)
12. Chaliasos, S., et al.: Smart contract and DeFi security tools: do they meet the needs of practitioners? In: Proceedings of the ICSE, pp. 60:1–60:13. ACM (2024)
13. Chapman, P., Xu, D., Deng, L., Xiong, Y.: Deviant: a mutation testing tool for solidity smart contracts. In: Proceedings of the Blockchain, pp. 319–324. IEEE (2019)
14. Hartel, P., Schumi, R.: Mutation testing of smart contracts at scale. In: Ahrendt, W., Wehrheim, H. (eds.) TAP 2020. LNCS, vol. 12165, pp. 23–42. Springer, Cham (2020). https://doi.org/10.1007/978-3-030-50995-8_2
15. Honig, J.J., Everts, M.H., Huisman, M.: Practical mutation testing for smart contracts. In: Pérez-Solà, C., Navarro-Arribas, G., Biryukov, A., Garcia-Alfaro, J. (eds.) DPM/CBT -2019. LNCS, vol. 11737, pp. 289–303. Springer, Cham (2019). https://doi.org/10.1007/978-3-030-31500-9_19
16. Li, N., West, M., Escalona, A., Durelli, V.H.S.: Mutation testing in practice using ruby. In: Proceedings of the ICST, pp. 1–6. IEEE Computer Society (2015)
17. Li, Z., Wu, H., Xu, J., Wang, X., Zhang, L., Chen, Z.: MuSC: a tool for mutation testing of ethereum smart contract. In: Proceedings of the ASE, pp. 1198–1201. IEEE (2019)
18. Mateo, P.R., Usaola, M.P.: Parallel mutation testing. Softw. Test. Verif. Reliab. **23**(4), 315–350 (2013)
19. Merkel, R.G., Georgeson, J.: Cloud-based distributed mutation analysis. CoRR abs/1601.07157 (2016). http://arxiv.org/abs/1601.07157
20. Offutt, A.J., Pargas, R.P., Fichter, S.V., Khambekar, P.K.: Mutation testing of software using MIMD computer. In: Proceedings of the ICPP, pp. 257–266. CRC Press (1992)
21. Palechor, L., Bezemer, C.: How are solidity smart contracts tested in open source projects? An exploratory study. In: Proceedings of the AST, pp. 165–169. ACM/IEEE (2022)
22. Petrovic, G., Ivankovic, M., Fraser, G., Just, R.: Practical mutation testing at scale: a view from google. IEEE Trans. Softw. Eng. **48**(10), 3900–3912 (2022)
23. Petrovic, G., Ivankovic, M., Fraser, G., Just, R.: Please fix this mutant: how do developers resolve mutants surfaced during code review? In: Proceedings of the SEIP@ICSE, pp. 150–161. IEEE (2023)
24. Petrovic, G., Ivankovic, M., Kurtz, B., Ammann, P., Just, R.: An industrial application of mutation testing: lessons, challenges, and research directions. In: Proceedings of the ICST Workshops, pp. 47–53. IEEE Computer Society (2018)
25. Pizzoleto, A.V., Ferrari, F.C., Offutt, J., Fernandes, L., Ribeiro, M.: A systematic literature review of techniques and metrics to reduce the cost of mutation testing. J. Syst. Softw. **157** (2019)

26. Vacca, A., Di Sorbo, A., Visaggio, C.A., Canfora, G.: A systematic literature review of blockchain and smart contract development: techniques, tools, and open challenges. J. Syst. Softw. **174**, 110891 (2021)
27. Wan, Z., Xia, X., Lo, D., Chen, J., Luo, X., Yang, X.: Smart contract security: a practitioners' perspective. In: Proceedings of the ICSE, pp. 1410–1422. IEEE (2021)
28. Zou, W., et al.: Smart contract development: challenges and opportunities. IEEE Trans. Softw. Eng. **47**(10), 2084–2106 (2021)

Conceptualization of Multi-user Collaborative GUI-Testing for Web Applications

Riccardo Coppola(✉), Tommaso Fulcini, and Marco Torchiano

Politecnico di Torino, Turin, Italy
{Riccardo.Coppola,Tommaso.Fulcini,Marco.Torchiano}@polito.it

Abstract. System testing through the Graphical User Interface (GUI testing) is often overlooked in real-world software projects. The mechanics proper of Gamification are often adopted to increase the motivation and engagement of testers in such scenarios. There is however little evidence in the literature about collaborative – rather than competitive – Gamification mechanics for software testing. In this manuscript, we describe a prototype for a collaborative GUI-testing prototype for web applications based on micro-tasks, of which we perform a small-scale preliminary evaluation. We find that the use of a microtask-based collaboration environment incentivizes depth-first testing of web applications and increases local coverage. We also collected positive experience reports from practitioners about the practice.

Keywords: GUI Testing · Crowdsourcing · Web Testing · Software Testing

1 Introduction

The creation of automated software test suites is a fundamental practice in Software Engineering, but is often seen as a tedious and time-consuming activity and is therefore neglected by developers. However, there are several testing activities that are crucial for modern-day software. For web applications, it is crucial to perform System testing through the Graphical User Interface (GUI) of the applications, to ensure that the use cases and scenarios of the application are correctly carried out and that the user can obtain the desired results by interacting with the application in the browser. Evidence in the software engineering literature highlights that there is a general preference in development teams towards manual testing of the interfaces, instead of adopting specific tooling and structured testing methodologies [17].

To increase the motivation and engagement of testers, one solution that has been many times used in literature is Gamification. Gamification consists of the use of elements, philosophies and mechanics that are typical of game design in non-playful contexts. The assumption behind the adoption of such practice is

A. Bertolino et al. (Eds.): QUATIC 2024, CCIS 2178, pp. 110–125, 2024.
https://doi.org/10.1007/978-3-031-70245-7_8

that – with the use of Gamified mechanics – testers may perceive the testing process as more entertaining and engaging, increasing the number of generated test cases and as a consequence ensuring a higher quality for the applications [2].

Gamification has an inherent social aspect since the results and achievements of the practitioners are typically compared with those of others, to provide motivation and incentive best practices. While this competitive aspect of gamification has been deeply investigated, there is very little evidence in the literature about the collaborative uses of gamification [10].

The objective of this work is to extend an existing gamified web application testing tool with elements of collaborative gamification and crowdsourcing, with the final objective of using the collective efforts of a multiplicity of collaborating peers to obtain better results in a web application testing activity. To the best of our knowledge, this is the first practical approach that subdivides a complex test case to enable crowdsourcing in visual GUI testing, instead of simply providing complex test cases to the crowd.

The remainder of the manuscript is organized as follows: in Sect. 2, we provide background information about GUI testing, Gamification, and Crowdsourcing; in Sect. 3, we illustrate our assumption about collaboration in GUI testing for web applications and describe the prototype framework we used; in Sect. 4, we report the results of a small-scale preliminary evaluation of the tool; in Sect. 5, we provide a conclusion to this investigation and describe future directions for our work.

2 Background and Related Work

2.1 GUI Testing

GUI testing is the activity of verifying the functional correctness of a software product by interacting with its Graphical User Interface. GUI testing is typically based on the interaction with individual atomic elements of the user interfaces (called *web elements* or *widgets*) and the verification of their properties after *sequences* of interaction are executed.

GUI testing techniques, activities and tools can be classified in different ways. One first classification, proposed by Alégroth et al., organizes them according to the way the widgets on the screen are identified and the used properties for functional verification [1]: first-generation (or coordinate-based) GUI testing techniques, now mostly abandoned, identify elements on the screen by using their exact x and y coordinates on screen; second-generation (or property-based) use textual properties of the GUI-description (typically the DOM model for web applications); third-generation (or visual) use graphic clues and computer vision techniques to identify and verify widgets through their exact visual appearance.

Linares-Vasquez et al. propose another classification based on the way the test sequences are created against the widgets in the GUI [12]: script-based testing techniques take advantage of custom scripting languages to code repeatable test sequences; capture and replay techniques collect the inputs of a human user with the GUI to generate replayable sequences; model-based testing techniques use (or generate) a model of the GUI (e.g. a finite state machine or a directed graph) to automatically generate test sequences to obtain maximum model coverage; automated input generation techniques use specific criteria (from pure random to search-based) to select widgets to interact within the GUI.

A recently introduced technique for GUI testing is that of Augmented Testing, which was presented by Nass et al. to address the challenges of frequent and costly maintenance of test scripts, and the difficulty of obtaining high screen and widget coverage with traditional Capture and Replay tools [14]. The technique involves an additional interface overlaid on that of the System Under Test, providing the user with test suggestions and data, highlighting important areas, or offering other forms of support, while also allowing observation and recording of inputs. The Augmented GUI is the only interface presented to the tester, and interaction occurs solely through it. A driver translates the received inputs to the SUT's GUI. Possible inputs include checks, issues, and augmented actions, which are saved in a model and then replayed on the SUT's interface. The tool Scout was proposed to demonstrate the benefits of augmented testing and is specific to web applications [14]. Scout is a Capture and Replay tool for Augmented Testing characterized by a closed-source core that implements the logic of the state model but with other functionalities left to ad hoc plugins, including the *SeleniumPlugin* that links Scout with the target web page under testing. In Scout, the model in which the tester's interactions are saved is represented as a weighted graph, where each node represents a state of the application. Each state includes all dependencies such as internal memory, saved data, and external applications at a given moment. Nodes are interconnected by actions, which are the tester's actions, such as mouse clicks or keyboard inputs.

2.2 Gamification in Software Engineering

Gamification is a strategic attempt to improve systems, services, organizations, and activities to motivate and engage users. A comprehensive definition of Gamification is provided by Deterding, as "the use of game design elements for games in non-game contexts" [8]. This differs from the concept of *serious games*, which refers to actual games with typically educational purposes. Gamification aims to enhance non-gaming activities by increasing user productivity, facilitating learning and knowledge retention, improving the usability of provided tools, and many other benefits [11].

Several frameworks have been provided to characterize efforts in gamification. A popular framework is the Octalysis, defined by Yu-Kai Chou [18]. The Octalysis framework identifies 8 core drives for gamification, and defines a set of game mechanics for each drive: (i) Epic Meaning and Calling, i.e. the desire to participate in something greater than just the activity which is gamified; (ii) Development and Accomplishment, i.e. game elements associated with progress, such as points, badges, and rankings indicating progress; (iii) Empowerment of Creativity and Feedback, i.e., challenges where users must express their creativity to overcome them, receiving immediate feedback on their actions; (iv) Ownership and Possession:, i.e. possess of something tangible inside gamified enviromments;

(v) Social Pressure and Relatedness, i.e. the introduction of social concepts like collaboration and competition; (vi) Scarcity and Impatience, i.e. fostering specific gamified aspects by making them appear scarce in the gamified context; (vii) Unpredictability and Curiosity, i.e. fostering gamified aspects by making them ever-evolving and unpredictable; (viii) Loss and Avoidance, i.e., the possibility of something negative happening, such as losing something that has been built over time, driving people to continue their actions.

Over the years, there have been numerous attempts to apply gamification in Software Engineering education, to increase engagement, enhance performance and engagement, and incentivise best practices taught in courses [2].

Several works in Software Engineering literature have applied Gamification to the practice of software testing [10]. A prominent example of gamification in testing is Code Defenders, developed by Rojas and Fraser [16]. This tool is specific to mutation testing, which involves creating slightly modified versions of the same program called mutants. Parizi et al. implemented GamiTracify, to encourage developers to trace all artifacts involved in specific test cases during test case writing and provides incentives for doing so [15]. Coppola et al. applied a framework of gamified mechanics to GUI testing of web applications, proving that gamification has a tangible effect on the obtained coverage of generated test sequences [7].

2.3 Crowdsourcing in Software Engineering

Crowdsourcing is defined as the collective execution of a given activity, tailored to involve groups of participants. The use of crowdsourcing brings many advantages like lower costs, speed in conducting tasks, flexibility and scalability of the jobs. Crowdsourcing can be classified as *explicit*, where the users collaborate to complete specific and well-defined tasks, and *implicit*, where the users solve problems as a collateral effect of other activities that they are performing.

Testing with the aid of crowdsourcing has the advantage of being able to utilize ordinary users without specific experience to perform testing tasks. In the study by Mao et al., several examples of crowdsourcing applications are presented [13]. These activities include functionality testing, performance testing, GUI testing, automatic test case generation, and the oracle problem. Functional testing is a significant portion of the time dedicated to testing in the software development cycle and can be quite expensive. This type of testing, with the assistance of crowdsourcing, has demonstrated the ability to uncover potential issues as effectively as employing experts. The advantages of using crowdsourcing are reflected in monetary terms, product delivery speed, and accessibility to this practice.

Chen et al. proposed a tool to increase testing coverage, assisting the users by showing information on navigation paths that have been already performed by other testers [5].

Wang et al. developed an approach named SETU (ScrEenshots and TextUal description) [19]. The approach allows crowd testers to characterize screenshots of test sequences with image features and textual descriptions, whilst creating a hierarchical algorithm to detect duplicate information between different sessions.

3 Methodology

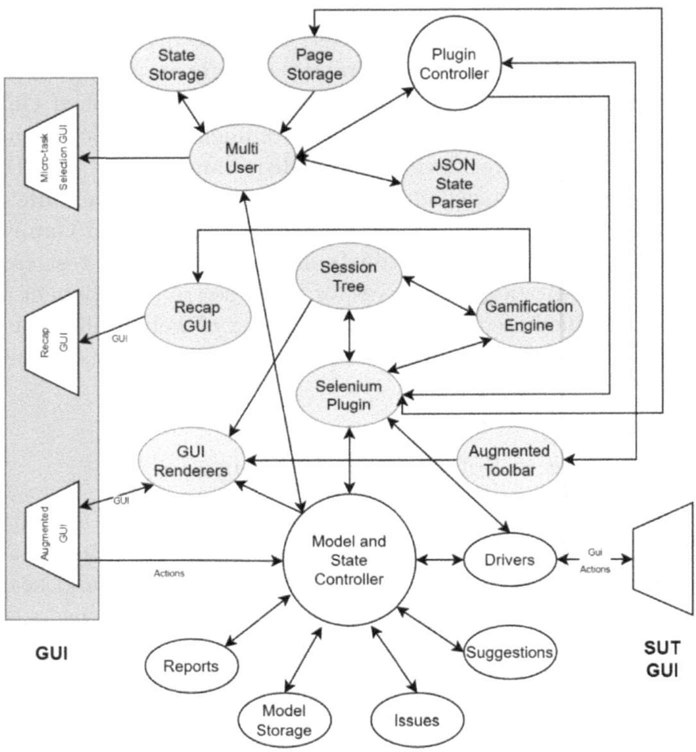

Fig. 1. The Scout tool with the Gamification and Crowdsourcing plugins

The objective of this work has been to create a prototype framework for the application of Gamification and Crowdsourcing for GUI-testing of web applications.

To that extent, we have selected the Scout tool, developed by Nass et al. [14], implementing an Augmented Testing methodology for web applications. The tool has been selected because of its high modularity and the possibility of adding new features through the development of plugins.

We have built upon a previous study by Cacciotto et al. [4], which introduced Gamification elements in the tool. A high-level depiction of the architecture is reported in Fig. 1. In the figure, the base modules of the Scout tool are reported in white. Among them, the state model is in charge of describing all the states of the SUT that were traversed during a user's testing sessions. The model is implemented as a weighted graph in which each node represents an application state, and the arcs are the tester's actions determining a state change. The *Augmented GUI* is the only interface the tester is using and acts as a proxy between the tester and the SUT. The Augmented GUI enriches the GUI of the SUT with suggestions and results of checks on the widgets and acts as a proxy to collect all the testers' inputs.

The components for the Gamification module are highlighted in orange (the plugins already present in Scout that were enhanced) and in green (those introduced ex-novo for gamification aspects). The Selenium plugin is in charge of obtaining information about the widget hierarchy of the current screen from the DOM model of the web application. The Gamification Engine is in charge of assigning a score to each tester according to the exploration activity, the reached coverage in the test session, and other parameters like the average speed for the execution of interactions (the interested reader can refer to the original work by Cacciotto et al. for details on the score computation [4]). The Session Tree component generates a simplified exploration graph that does not create a new state for each interaction with the GUI but instead performs a 1-to-1 mapping between pages of the web applications and states in the graph.

The components in blue in the diagram are those composing the Crowdsourcing plugin. The main components of the Crowdsourcing plugin are the Multi-User module and the JSON State Parser, which are in charge of loading the shared state, creating the micro-tasks, and resolving conflicts in merging the activities performed by different users. The ways these operations are performed are described in detail in the following subsections.

3.1 State Representation

For the purpose of this study, we adopted a state representation, which is a simplified version of the one used by the original Scout tool. In our crowdsourced plugin, we use a state representation where two states are considered coincident if they are web pages with the same URL. This state representation is a limitation for Single Page Applications (SPA) which would require a finer definition of the states to allow the creation of multiple states during the navigation on the same page.

All the testers that are performing activities on the same page share a state model, with information on the widgets that have been interacted with to transition from one state to the other. Each widget interaction and page keeps information about the tester who performed the first interaction with or within it, who modified it or cancelled it from the test sequence.

The model of the collaborative testing session is represented in a human-readable JSON file. An example of a JSON file for web application exploration is reported as an online appendix[1].

[1] https://doi.org/10.6084/m9.figshare.25705425.

3.2 Integration of Sessions by Multiple Users

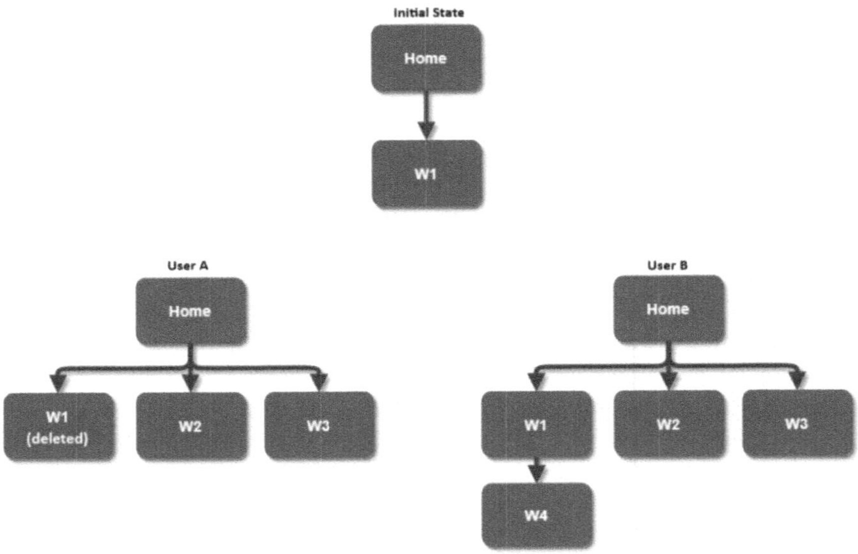

Fig. 2. A collaborative session scenario

One of the main requirements for a crowdsourced platform is the integration of the efforts performed by multiple users. In our context, each testing session contains interactions with widgets, that are stored with the information about the new widget status. When dealing with their test sequences, we can identify three different operations made by the users:

- *Addition* of an interaction with a widget, with the consequent modification of the state, or transition to a new state (i.e., page) in the web application;
- *Modification* of the interaction performed with a widget;
- *Deletion* of the interaction with a widget. This operation deletes all the next states that were initially explored in the test sequence.

When multiple users use the Scout tool to interact with the same application, it is necessary to perform a merge of the interactions that were performed. In case of conflicts, the rules are described in Table 1. This set of rules has been defined in the conceptualization of multi-user testing performed by Bauer and Alégroth [3].

As an example of how the merge is implemented, we report two example test sequences performed by two users (Fig. 2). The users have performed, starting from the application's home page, some interactions with the widgets (w1, w2, and w3 for convenience) leading to separate states of the application. At the

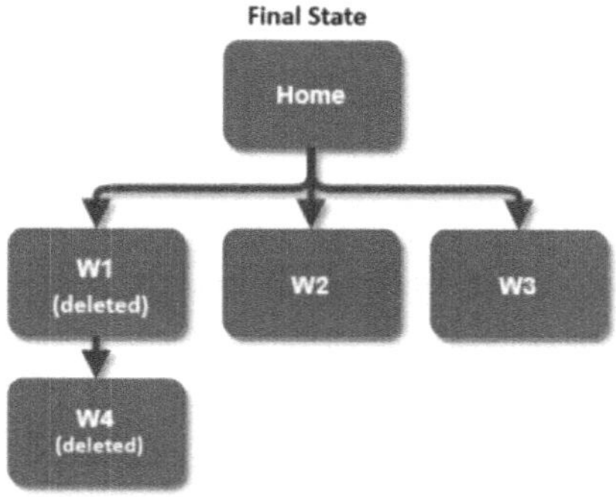

Fig. 3. Result of the collaborative session scenario

Table 1. Merge strategy depending on operations performed by users

User A	User B	Integration strategy
Add	Add	If the two additions are on the same widgets, a single status change is added to the exploration tree. Otherwise, both states are added to the exploration tree
Add	Modify	Both actions are added to the state tree. The add creates a transition to a new state, and the modification is reported in the state tree
Add	Delete	The delete is privileged. The state and all the other ones in the exploration tree are marked as cancelled
Delete	Modify	The delete is privileged. The state and all the other ones in the exploration tree are marked as cancelled
Modify	Modify	The most recent modifications by the users are kept

end of the session user A marks the interaction with widget w1 as eliminated. B performs the same interactions with widgets w1, w2 and w3, and performs an additional interaction with widget w4 in the state after w1. The merge of the explorations performed by the two users is reported in Fig. 3. With the adopted strategy, the merged exploration contains both the operations on w2 and w3 with no conflicts and both the interactions with w1 and w4 will be considered as cancelled.

The developed prototype currently handles updates to the state flow graph by synchronizing with the master graph stored in the server only at the end of each session. We acknowledge that based on the size of the difference between the resulting graph and the source graph, different update approaches may be needed instead (e.g., synchronization at the creation of each graph node, mutual synchronization between concurrent processes, etc.).

3.3 Generation of Microtasks

In addition to the possibility of merging multiple test sequences performed by users, the tool creates *micro tasks* for the users to perform in their testing session. A microtask is an atomic activity that has to be performed by the user, and it is a common decomposition used in crowdsourced processes. By definition, a microtask can be performed with limited resources and require little time to be completed. The users completing a microtask receive immediate feedback about their job. This immediate feedback can lead to an increased motivation for the user, who can immediately understand the purpose of his actions.

In the case of web application tasting, we identify a micro task as any step in a full use case/user scenario with the application. In the context of our prototype tool, we defined micro tasks as requests for the users to increase the widget coverage (i.e., maximize the number of interactions) within a single web page of the software under test. Before the execution of every test session, the tool selects a set of web pages that still have a low widget coverage and creates a list of micro tasks that can be selected by the user (see Fig. ??). Each microtask asks the user to explore the application in proximity to a given state (or page) of the application, instead of traversing the application in more depth. Therefore, this type of microtask privileges an in-depth exploration of the pages instead of increasing the breadth of the generated test sequences.

3.4 Evaluation of the Gamification Aspects of the Prototype

To evaluate the gamification aspects of the prototype, we use the Octalysis gamification framework theorized by Yu-Kai Chou [18].

The starting gamified tool on the basis of which the crowdsourcing logic was added and the rationale behind its design and development is left to the interested reader who can find it in [6,9]. The main gamification aspects covered by the tool are the following:

- **Accomplishment:** game elements concerning progress, skill-building, and overcoming challenges. This Core Drive often focuses on points, badges, and leaderboards.
- **Empowerment:** game elements enabling the user's need to express their creativity, see results, receive feedback, and respond.
- **Social Influence:** this aspect includes social elements such as mentorship, acceptance, companionship, competition, and envy. It also includes the drive to draw closer to relatable people, places, or events.
- **Scarcity:** game elements related to poor goods availability or appointment dynamics creating the need of wanting something because you can't have it right away: this motivates people to think about it all day long.
- **Epic Meaning:** game elements aiming to make players feel they're doing something greater than themselves or to be "chosen" to do something for a greater entity.

A graphical evaluation of the gamification elements introduced is reported in the Octalysis graph in Fig. 4.

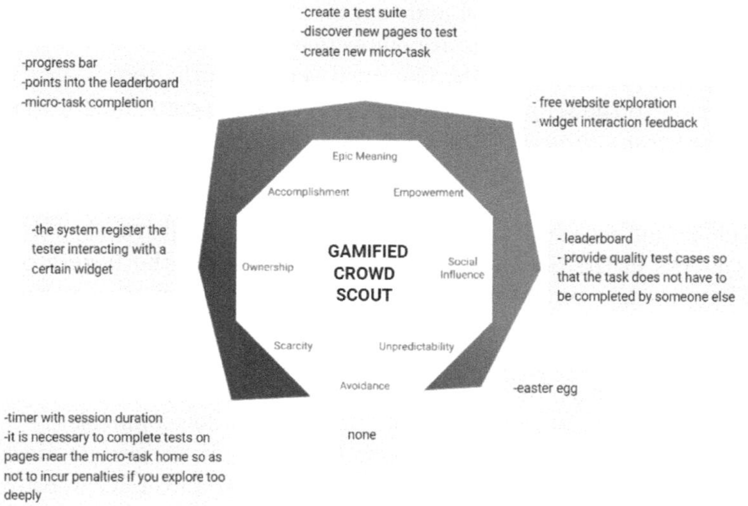

Fig. 4. Octalysis Evaluation for our gamified and crowdsourced tool

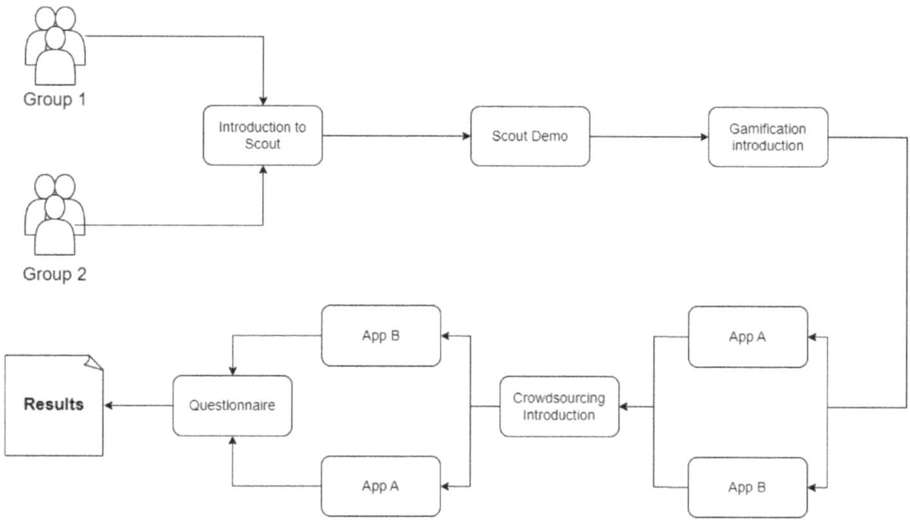

Fig. 5. Phases of the evaluation process

4 Preliminary Evaluation

To evaluate the benefits introduced by crowdsourcing to the web application testing activities conducted with the Scout tool, we set up a small preliminary experimental evaluation with a sample of testers. The phases of the preliminary evaluation – graphically described in Fig. 5 – are the following:

1. Introduction to the Scout tool and tool demo, followed by an introduction to the Gamification aspects that are embedded in the tool;
2. Creation of test suites with the Gamified version of the tool;
3. Introduction to the Crowdsourcing aspects that are embedded in the tool;
4. Creation of test suites with the Crowdsourced versions of the tool;
5. Questionnaire about the user experience provided by the tool.

For the preliminary evaluation, we recruited a sample of six testers from among students in the Software Engineering course. All the testers conducted Master's studies in Computer Engineering and had previous experience with programming languages. Four respondents (66%) had previous experience with web application testing. Only two respondents (33%) had previous experience with gamified platforms for software development; no respondent had previous experience with crowdsourced platforms for software development.

The groups executed test sequences on two different websites: a marketplace web application (application A)[2], and an institutional university website (application B)[3]).

Both the applications were provided with an initial test session, to simulate the existence of collaborators that already performed testing operations before the current participant in the experiment.

As can be seen in the experiment design, the respondents were divided into two groups in which the applications were tested in different orders, to reduce any learning effect of the application on the result.

All the experimental sessions were executed on the same device to avoid configuration and timing issues related to the use of the respondents' machine.

4.1 Exploration and Coverage

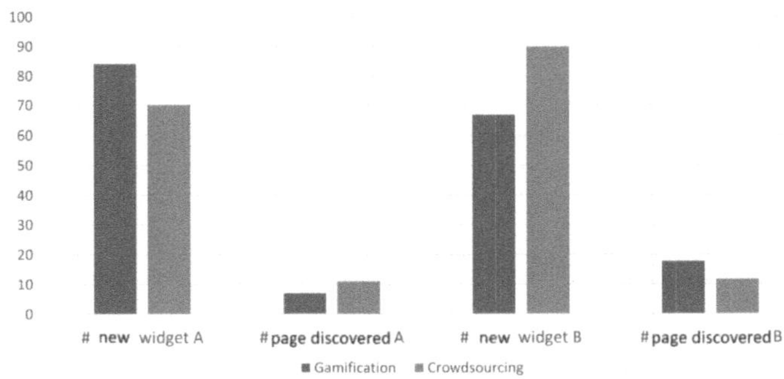

Fig. 6. Results for new widgets and new pages interacted

[2] http://magi-giovanni-funghi-e-tartufi.webnode.it/.
[3] http://www.polito.it.

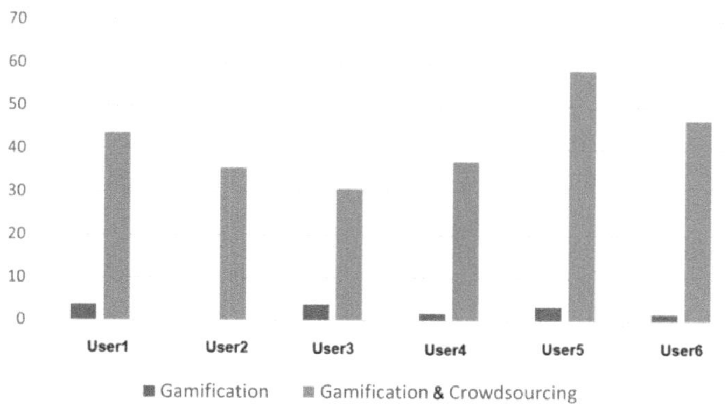

Fig. 7. Increase in local widget coverage with active crowdsourcing plugin

The first dimension that we inspected was the test exploration and coverage of the application under test that was obtained in the executed test sessions.

In Fig. 6 we report the comparison of the total number of new widgets and new pages found by the six test suites with gamification or with crowdsourcing. We notice a decrease in the number of widgets discovered for site A (−15%) and an increase in the number of widgets discovered for site B (+32%). The users discovered more pages for site A (+57%) and less for site B (-30%). Based on these figures, we can argue that the number of widgets and page coverage obtained does not depend on the type of tool used but is instead dependent on the specific software under test.

In Fig. 7 we report the increase in *Local Coverage* that was obtained by each user in the two sessions of the experiment. The concept of local coverage was defined for the purpose of this experiment as *the average widget coverage on the specific page that acts as the starting point for the test case.* We can notice that in all the test sessions that were conducted without the crowdsourcing tool, there was little to no increase in local coverage. On the other hand, there was a significant increase in the local coverage obtained with the tool implementing crowdsourcing mechanisms. This result suggests that the use of micro-tasks made the users very focused on obtaining the highest possible coverage on the web page where the test session was starting, therefore privileging a depth-first rather than a breadth-first (i.e., more explorative of other undiscovered web pages) approach to testing.

4.2 User Experience

Table 2. Post-experiment questionnaire

ID	Question	Type
q1	Have you understood all the features of Scout and how to use it?	Likert
q2	Have you understood the microtask concept and its finality?	Likert
q3	Did you find the screen for microtask selection comprehensible?	Likert
q4	Do you find the addition of micro tasks useful?	Likert
q5	Knowing that there is a bonus in the score if you are focusing on the microtask made you focus more on the starting page?	Likert
q6	Knowing that your work will be continued by other people made you more motivated?	Likert
q7	Do you prefer the version with crowdsourcing rather than the standard version of the gamified tool?	Likert
q8	Do you think that the tool could be easily integrated into an existing test team in a real-world scenario?	Likert
q9	What are in your opinion the main drawbacks of the prototype?	Open question
q10	Do you have suggestions to improve the prototype?	Open question

At the end of the experimental sessions, we administered a short questionnaire with five-level Likert questions to the respondents, reported in Table 2.

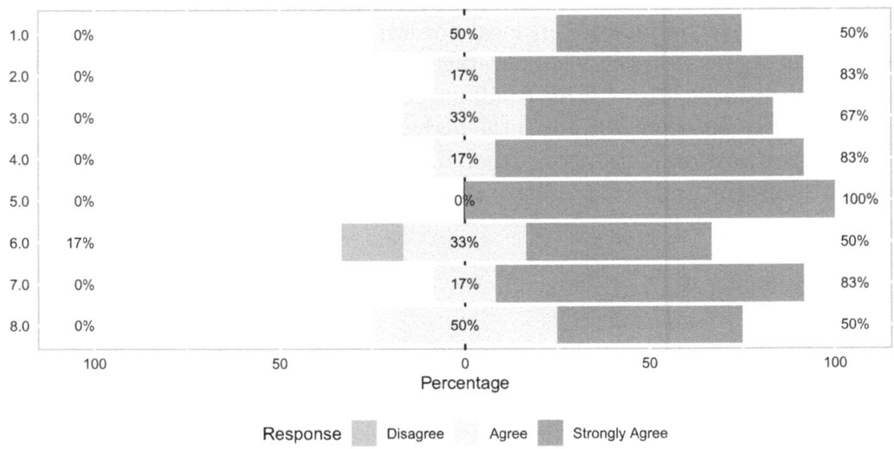

Fig. 8. Distribution of the answer to q1–q8

In Fig. 8 it can be seen the distribution of the answers to the questionnaire. The distribution suggests an overall appreciation of the tool between all the respondents. Mixed answers were received for question 6, with a disagreement among the respondents. This aspect is worth investigating in future research efforts since the motivation induced by the collaboration is the foundation for any framework implementing explicit crowdsourcing.

The open-ended questions of the questionnaire received mostly technical responses. Regarding question q9, three respondents reported no problems. Two respondents identified slow page loading as a significant issue, leading to confusion about whether Scout was loading a new page or if they could already begin interacting with the one displayed. Finally, a respondent indicated issues in the visualization of the gamified mechanics.

The new plugin places great emphasis on testing with high coverage on pages near the root of the microtask. One participant suggested adding a pop-up notification when a page reaches 100% coverage and including a numerical indication of the number of tested widgets compared to the total, as they did not find the already present progress bar sufficient. During testing with the multi-user version, all participants frequently interacted with the Augmented Toolbar to use the "Go Micro Task Home" button and increase local coverage on the starting page. A common proposal by respondents is to add keyboard shortcuts to expedite this action and eliminate the time spent interacting with the toolbar.

5 Conclusion and Future Work

In this paper, we described a prototype tool to integrate collaborative and crowdsourcing-based aspects into a Gamified web application GUI testing tool. We implemented a proof-of-concept of the tool as an extension of an existing Augmented testing tool, Scout, and we performed a preliminary evaluation with graduated Master's students, that highlighted the capability of microtask-based collaborative gamification of increasing the focus of the testers on performing depth-first test sequence creation.

Our immediate future work includes an empirical evaluation of the framework with a statistically significant sample of respondents and a focus on the quality of the generated test cases. Another extension of the present work is the creation of microtasks based on use cases (or portions of them) in order to incentivise the conduction of test sequences near the main functionalities of the app instead of focusing on a single screen at a time.

Acknowledgement. This study was carried out within the "EndGame - Improving End-to-End Testing of Web and Mobile Apps through Gamification" project (2022PCCMLF) - funded by European Union - Next Generation EU within the PRIN 2022 program (D.D.104 - 02/02/2022 Ministero dell'Università e della Ricerca). This manuscript reflects only the authors' views and opinions and the Ministry cannot be considered responsible for them.

References

1. Alégroth, E., Gao, Z., Oliveira, R., Memon, A.: Conceptualization and evaluation of component-based testing unified with visual GUI testing: an empirical study. In: 2015 IEEE 8th International Conference on Software Testing, Verification and Validation (ICST), pp. 1–10. IEEE (2015)
2. Alhammad, M.M., Moreno, A.M.: Gamification in software engineering education: a systematic mapping. J. Syst. Softw. **141**, 131–150 (2018)
3. Bauer, A., Alégroth, E.: We tried and failed: an experience report on a collaborative workflow for GUI-based testing. In: 2023 IEEE International Conference on Software Testing, Verification and Validation Workshops (ICSTW), pp. 1–9. IEEE (2023)
4. Cacciotto, F., Fulcini, T., Coppola, R., Ardito, L.: A metric framework for the gamification of web and mobile GUI testing. In: 2021 IEEE International Conference on Software Testing, Verification and Validation Workshops (ICSTW), pp. 126–129. IEEE (2021)
5. Chen, Y., Pandey, M., Song, J.Y., Lasecki, W.S., Oney, S.: Improving crowd-supported GUI testing with structural guidance. In: Proceedings of the 2020 CHI Conference on Human Factors in Computing Systems, pp. 1–13 (2020)
6. Coppola, R., Ardito, L., Fulcini, T., Garaccione, G., Torchiano, M., Morisio, M.: A framework for the gamification of GUI testing. In: Cooper, K.M.L., Bucchiarone, A. (eds.) Software Engineering for Games in Serious Contexts, pp. 215–242. Springer, Cham (2023). https://doi.org/10.1007/978-3-031-33338-5_10
7. Coppola, R., Fulcini, T., Ardito, L., Torchiano, M., Alègroth, E.: On effectiveness and efficiency of gamified exploratory GUI testing. IEEE Trans. Softw. Eng. (2023)
8. Deterding, S., Dixon, D., Khaled, R., Nacke, L.: From game design elements to gamefulness: defining gamification. In: Proceedings of the 15th International Academic MindTrek Conference: Envisioning Future Media Environments, pp. 9–15 (2011)
9. Fulcini, T., Ardito, L.: Gamified exploratory GUI testing of web applications: a preliminary evaluation. In: 2022 IEEE International Conference on Software Testing, Verification and Validation Workshops (ICSTW), pp. 215–222 (2022). https://doi.org/10.1109/ICSTW55395.2022.00045
10. Fulcini, T., Coppola, R., Ardito, L., Torchiano, M.: A review on tools, mechanics, benefits, and challenges of gamified software testing. ACM Comput. Surv. **55**(14s), 1–37 (2023)
11. Hamari, J., Koivisto, J.: Social motivations to use gamification: an empirical study of gamifying exercise. In: ECIS, vol. 105, pp. 18–19 (2013)
12. Linares-Vásquez, M., Moran, K., Poshyvanyk, D.: Continuous, evolutionary and large-scale: a new perspective for automated mobile app testing. In: 2017 IEEE International Conference on Software Maintenance and Evolution (ICSME), pp. 399–410. IEEE (2017)
13. Mao, K., Harman, M., Jia, Y.: Crowd intelligence enhances automated mobile testing. In: 2017 32nd IEEE/ACM International Conference on Automated Software Engineering (ASE), pp. 16–26. IEEE (2017)
14. Nass, M., Alégroth, E., Feldt, R.: Augmented testing: industry feedback to shape a new testing technology. In: 2019 IEEE International Conference on Software Testing, Verification and Validation Workshops (ICSTW), pp. 176–183. IEEE (2019)

15. Parizi, R.M.: On the gamification of human-centric traceability tasks in software testing and coding. In: 2016 IEEE 14th International Conference on Software Engineering Research, Management and Applications (SERA), pp. 193–200. IEEE (2016)
16. Rojas, J.M., Fraser, G.: Code defenders: a mutation testing game. In: 2016 IEEE Ninth International Conference on Software Testing, Verification and Validation Workshops (ICSTW), pp. 162–167. IEEE (2016)
17. Straubinger, P., Fraser, G.: A survey on what developers think about testing. In: 2023 IEEE 34th International Symposium on Software Reliability Engineering (ISSRE), pp. 80–90. IEEE (2023). https://ieeexplore.ieee.org/abstract/document/10301252/
18. Teixes, F.: Yu-kai chou (2016). actionable gamification: beyond points, badges and leaderboards. octalysis media: Fremont. ca. RIO: Revista Internacional de Organizaciones (18), 137–144 (2017)
19. Wang, J., Li, M., Wang, S., Menzies, T., Wang, Q.: Images don' lie: duplicate crowdtesting reports detection with screenshot information. Inf. Softw. Technol. **110**, 139–155 (2019)

Towards Generating Executable Metamorphic Relations Using Large Language Models

Seung Yeob Shin[1(✉)], Fabrizio Pastore[1], Domenico Bianculli[1], and Alexandra Baicoianu[2]

[1] SnT Centre, University of Luxembourg, Luxembourg, Luxembourg
{seungyeob.shin,fabrizio.pastore,domenico.bianculli}@uni.lu
[2] Siemens Industry Software, Braşov, Romania
alexandra.baicoianu@siemens.com

Abstract. Metamorphic testing (MT) has proven to be a successful solution to automating testing and addressing the oracle problem. However, it entails manually deriving metamorphic relations (MRs) and converting them into an executable form; these steps are time-consuming and may prevent the adoption of MT. In this paper, we propose an approach for automatically deriving executable MRs (EMRs) from requirements using large language models (LLMs). Instead of merely asking the LLM to produce EMRs, our approach relies on a few-shot prompting strategy to instruct the LLM to perform activities in the MT process, by providing requirements and API specifications, as one would do with software engineers. To assess the feasibility of our approach, we conducted a questionnaire-based survey in collaboration with Siemens Industry Software, a worldwide leader in providing industry software and services, focusing on four of their software applications. Additionally, we evaluated the accuracy of the generated EMRs for a Web application. The outcomes of our study are highly promising, as they demonstrate the capability of our approach to generate MRs and EMRs that are both comprehensible and pertinent for testing purposes.

Keywords: metamorphic testing · large language model · LLM · executable metamorphic relations

1 Introduction

In many sectors, software is typically verified with executable test cases that, at a high level, consist of a set of inputs provided to the software under test (SUT) and a set of test assertions verifying that the SUT outputs match the expected results. However, defining executable test cases is expensive because of the many intellectual activities involved. This cost limits the number of test cases that can be implemented. Moreover, software faults are often subtle and triggered by a narrow portion of the input domain. Therefore, they are detected only after exercising the SUT with a large set of test inputs.

A. Bertolino et al. (Eds.): QUATIC 2024, CCIS 2178, pp. 126–141, 2024.
https://doi.org/10.1007/978-3-031-70245-7_9

Although several tools for the automated generation of test inputs have been developed [9,10], they can only identify crashes or regressions faults, because they lack the capability of determining what the expected output for the software should be. Further, manually specifying test assertions for thousands of automatically generated test inputs is practically infeasible. The impossibility to programmatically derive expected outputs is known as the *oracle problem* [3].

Metamorphic testing (MT) has recently gained success as a solution to address the oracle problem in many contexts [6]. MT relies on the concept of metamorphic relations (MRs), which describe the relationships between input transformations and expected output changes, serving as oracles in software testing. Briefly, to perform MT on the SUT, engineers first need to derive MRs from the SUT's requirements and then convert the derived MRs into an executable form to determine the test outcome. These steps require substantial manual effort, which increases the MT cost and may prevent its adoption.

Many MT approaches have been developed to test various SUTs, including search engines [26], Web applications [5], and embedded systems [1]. These methods, however, require significant manual efforts to define MRs, which limits their scalability, particularly in cases where SUT executions are lengthy and expensive. A few recent studies [12,25] have investigated using Large Language Models (LLMs) to automate MR derivation directly from LLM knowledge bases. However, they currently only work with SUTs known during LLM training and are not effectively applicable to test new, unseen systems. In addition, to the best of our knowledge, there is no existing work that aims at automating the conversion of MRs into an executable form, hereafter referred to as EMRs (Executable MRs), which is an essential step to fully automate the MT process.

Contribution. In this paper, we propose an approach for automatically deriving EMRs from the SUT's requirements using LLMs. Differently from existing work, our approach does not merely involve querying an LLM for MRs based solely on the LLM knowledge base. Instead, we rely on prompt engineering practices to teach the LLM both (1) the specifications of the SUT, which are necessary to derive MRs, and (2) the DSL to use for EMRs, which is necessary to enable MR execution.

We evaluated the feasibility of our approach through two experiments: (1) by conducting a questionnaire-based survey in collaboration with Siemens Industry Software, a worldwide leader in providing software and services across industry domains (hereafter, SISW), involving four of their software applications, and (2) by assessing the correctness of the generated EMRs for a Web application.

In our experiments, we used OpenAI GPT-3.5 and GPT-4 [15] as LLM, accessed (to provide prompts and generate responses for deriving MRs and subsequently converting them into EMRs) through the web interface of ChatGPT [14]. When converting MRs into EMRs, we instructed the LLM to use SMRL [13] as a domain-specific language (DSL) for specifying MRs in an executable form. The results are promising, indicating that the generated MRs and EMRs are understandable and relevant for testing, and that the EMRs were correctly converted from their corresponding MRs.

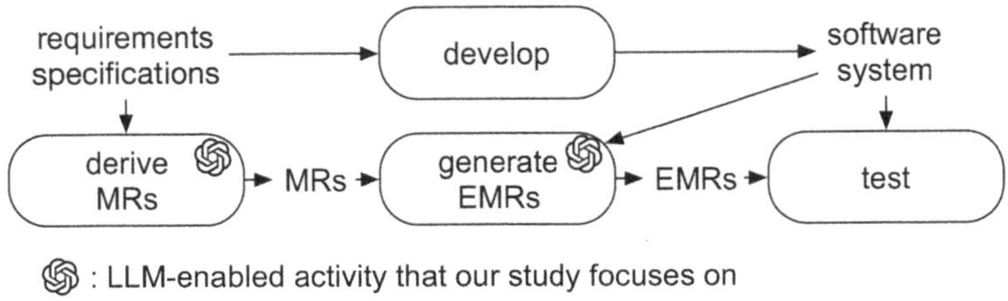

Fig. 1. Our approach for generating EMRs using LLMs

Organization. The remainder of this paper is structured as follows: Sect. 2 describes our approach. Sections 3 and 4, respectively, present our experiment design and results. Sections 5 discusses threats to the validity and research opportunities. Section 6 surveys related work. Section 7 concludes the paper.

2 Approach

This section describes our approach to automatically deriving EMRs from the requirements of the SUT. Specifically, our approach relies on an LLM to automate the MT process, particularly by leveraging the LLM's capabilities in understanding and processing natural language documents, identifying relevant information, and synthesizing that information into structured forms (i.e., MRs and EMRs) useful for software testing.

2.1 Overview

Our approach, shown in Fig. 1, advances the MT process by introducing two automated activities: "derive MRs" and "generate EMRs". The "derive MRs" activity takes as input requirements specifications (in the form of specification documents) and outputs (MRs in natural language). Unlike existing work that queries an LLM for MRs based on the LLM built-in knowledge, we provide SUT specification documents to the LLM. This enables our approach to derive SUT-specific MRs, which would otherwise be unattainable because the LLM lacks awareness of the specific software properties that need to be considered. The "generate EMRs" activity takes as input MRs and the SUT (depicted as "software system" in Fig. 1). It outputs EMRs, which are executable programs used to verify that the SUT satisfies the properties captured by the MR. In the following subsections, we further describe these activities, focusing on their implementation as adopted in our preliminary experiments (see Sect. 3).

2.2 Deriving Metamorphic Relations

We aim at automatically deriving MRs from the provided requirements specification documents. To this end, our approach relies on ChatGPT and develops

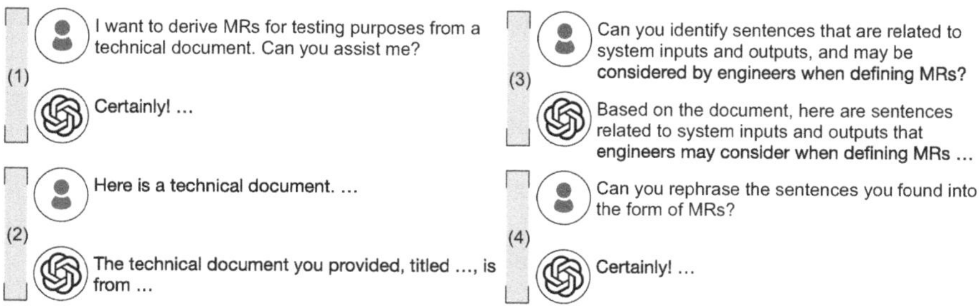

Fig. 2. Prompts to derive MRs from the SUT's requirements, grouped by phases in the conversation: (1) setting the context, (2) providing requirements specification document(s), (3) identifying relevant sentences, and (4) rewriting these sentences into MRs

a prompt sequence for automation. Since deriving MRs from requirements is a complex task, when using ChatGPT for this purpose, we break the task down into simpler, decomposed steps[1].

Figure 2 shows the prompts that derive MRs from the requirements of the SUT. We have omitted some parts of the text, indicated by "...", to focus on the essential prompts of our work. Note that the complete prompts are available online [17]. As shown in Fig. 2 (1), our prompt sequence begins by setting the context, i.e., deriving MRs, to guide ChatGPT for the following interactions. The remaining sequence, which decomposes the task of deriving MRs, consists of prompts directing ChatGPT to perform simpler steps, as described below. First, our approach instructs ChatGPT to read a requirements document in order for ChatGPT to access the requirements needed for defining MRs for the SUT (see Fig. 2 (2)); in response, ChatGPT provides a short summary of it. Second, given the requirements document, ChatGPT is directed to find sentences that are specifically related to the SUT's inputs and outputs, as well as those that engineers may consider when defining MRs (Fig. 2 (3)). This step is important because MRs fundamentally describe how outputs should be changed in response to specific changes in inputs. The last step then asks ChatGPT to write MRs based on the identified relevant sentences (Fig. 2 (4)).

For example, consider a scenario where our approach is used to derive MRs from the requirements document of an online shopping system that includes a `searchItem` function. After setting the context and reading the requirements document, ChatGPT could identify requirement R1 in Table 1, which concerns the advanced search options in the `searchItem` function. Given requirement R1, ChatGPT then proceeds to define an MR, referred to as MR1 in the table. MR1 specifies the relationship between the outputs of an initial search query and those of a subsequent query where additional filters are applied.

[1] We note that when we passed a single, monolithic query to ChatGPT for deriving MRs, it was unable to derive meaningful MRs.

Table 1. An example requirement for an online shopping system and an MR derived from this requirement.

R1	The system should provide advanced search options to allow users to refine their searches based on specific attributes such as price range, category, brand, customer ratings, and availability
MR1	For a given search query, applying additional filters (e.g., narrowing down by category or price range) should reduce the number of search results or refine them to match the filters more closely

2.3 Generating Executable Metamorphic Relations

We ask ChatGPT to convert MRs written in natural language into EMRs specified using SMRL [13], a DSL developed for specifying EMRs. SMRL provides MR-specific language constructs, which are built on Java, to specify EMRs. Table 2 presents a subset of SMRL constructs. The construct `Input(int i)` refers to the i-th sequence of actions performed by a user with the SUT. The construct `Output(int i)` refers to the sequence of outputs produced by the SUT in response to `Input(i)`. The construct `CREATE(Object y, Object x)` defines `y` as a copy of `x` and satisfies `y = x`. The last three rows in the table capture Boolean expressions corresponding to implication (`IMPLIES()`), negation (`NOT()`), and disjunction (`OR()`). Using these constructs, engineers can specify EMRs in terms of inputs, input transformations, outputs, output changes, and logical expressions to define the expected relations among them. In addition, SMRL is already integrated into the MST-wi framework [5], which generates executable Java code from specified EMRs to automatically perform MT.

Figure 3 depicts a sequence of prompts that converts MRs into EMRs, selectively omitting text using "..." for a clearer exposition. Our approach involves instructing ChatGPT to understand SMRL and to use SMRL for converting MRs into EMRs. Specifically, as shown in Fig. 3 (1), when using ChatGPT, we first set the context by indicating that the subsequent interactions will aim at converting MRs into EMRs. We then provide ChatGPT with the notations for the SMRL constructs (see Table 2), enabling it to use the SMRL constructs when converting MRs into EMRs (Fig. 3 (2)). To transform MRs into EMRs in a consistent form, we provide ChatGPT with an EMR template (Fig. 3 (3)). Subsequently, we apply the few-shot learning strategy [21] to instruct ChatGPT to understand SMRL, by providing three pairs of MR and corresponding EMR

Table 2. A subset of the SMRL constructs.

Construct	Description
`Input(int i)`	returns the i-th input sequence
`Output(int i)`	returns the sequence of outputs generate by Input(i)
`CREATE(Object y,Object x)`	creates y as a copy of x
`IMPLIES(boolean x,boolean y)`	is equivalent to the Java expression `!x || y`
`NOT(boolean x)`	is equivalent to the Java expression `!x`
`OR(boolean x,boolean y)`	is equivalent to the Java expression `x || y`

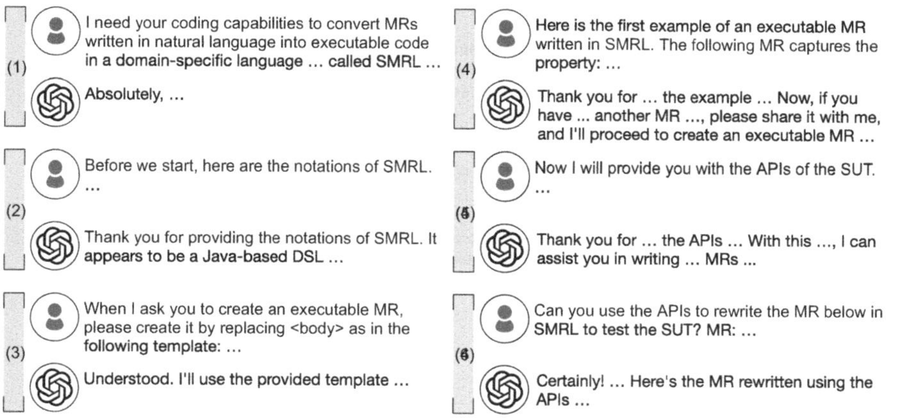

Fig. 3. Prompts to convert MRs into EMRs, grouped by phases in the conversation: (1) setting the context, (2) learning the syntax of SMRL, (3) instructing the output format, (4) few-shot learning of SMRL, (5) learning the SUT's APIs, and (6) transforming MRs into EMRs

from prior work [5] (Fig. 3 (4)). The few-shot learning strategy is suitable in our study context, as SMRL is a state-of-the-art DSL with a limited number of examples available, and it is built on Java, which ChatGPT already knows. In addition, we further instruct ChatGPT to understand the SUT's APIs by providing the documentation and signature of the API methods (Fig. 3 (5)). For example, to test the Web application described in prior work [5], which includes 38 APIs, we need to provide ChatGPT with the details of these APIs. Last, we then ask ChatGPT to transform MRs into EMRs using SMRL and to invoke the APIs in the EMRs for testing the SUT (Fig. 3 (6)).

Figure 4 shows an EMR generated by our approach, corresponding to the MR described in Table 1. This EMR specifies that adding filters to a search query should either reduce the number of results or refine them to better match the filter criteria. Below, we provide the comments generated by ChatGPT to explain the EMR statements; each corresponds to one annotation //(#) in Fig. 4.

(1) & (2): Iterate over all actions within the input sequence to identify search actions. (3): Retrieve the original search results before any additional filters are applied. (4): Iterate over possible filter types (e.g., categories, price ranges) that can be applied to the search. (5): Create a new input sequence where a specific filter is applied to the identified search action. (6): Ensure the new input sequence (`Input(2)`) is properly created with the applied filter. (7): Check that the same filter hasn't already been applied to the search action to avoid redundant checks. (8): Verify that applying the filter results in fewer search results compared to the original, indicating a refinement of the search output. (9): Alternatively, check that the results are more relevant to the applied filter, even if the number of results does not decrease. This could involve comparing the characteristics of the search results against the filter criteria to ensure they match more closely.

```
MR {{
for (Action searchAction : Input(1).actions()) { //(1)
  if (!isSearchAction(searchAction)) continue; //(2)
  var originalResults = Output(Input(1), searchAction.getPosition()); //(3)
  for (var filterType : getFilterTypes()) { //(4)
    var filteredInput = applyFilter(Input(1),searchAction.getPosition(),filterType);//(5)
    IMPLIES(
    CREATE(Input(2), filteredInput) && //(6)
    notSameFilterApplied(searchAction, filterType), //(7)
    OR(
    fewerResults(Output(Input(2), searchAction.getPosition()), originalResults), //(8)
    moreRelevantResults(Output(Input(2), searchAction.getPosition()), originalResults,
         filterType) //(9)
    )
    );//end-IMPLIES
  }//end-for
}//end-for
}}//end-MR
```

Fig. 4. An EMR generated by ChatGPT based on the MR presented in Table 1

We note that we did not provide ChatGPT with the API details of the online shopping system. Hence, ChatGPT autonomously created some function invocations, such as `applyFilter()` and `notSameFilterApplied()`, to implement the EMR using SMRL. This capability of ChatGPT is desirable in test-driven development practices as it helps engineers identify which APIs are needed to test the SUT at early development stages.

3 Experiment Design

To assess the feasibility of our approach, we have carried out two experiments, namely EXP1 and EXP2. EXP1 aims at collecting feedback from practitioners. EXP2 aims at evaluating the correctness of generated EMRs.

EXP1 - SISW Applications. To assess whether our approach can practically help software practitioners, it is important to collect and analyze their perceptions on our work. In collaboration with SISW, we have conducted a questionnaire-based survey to gather their feedback on the MRs and EMRs obtained by applying our approach to their software applications. Due to confidentiality reasons, SISW was not able to share the requirements and the APIs of their applications; instead, SISW selected four non-confidential technical documents based on their interests. These documents describe their applications (modelling and simulation) for marine design [19], wind turbine [18], aircraft propulsion [20], and aero-acoustics [4]. They provided us with these documents (83 pages in total) as requirements specifications. As remarked above, in absence of appropriate APIs, ChatGPT suggests invoking functions that should be implemented to automate the execution of the MR. Further, despite the lack of APIs, considering the preliminary nature of this work, these subjects still enable us to gather feedback from practitioners on how well ChatGPT can generate EMRs.

In EXP1, we relied on GPT-4 because, at the time we designed our experiments (January 2024), it was the only available top-5 leaderboard LLM capable of processing PDF documents[2]. Note that our questionnaire-based survey study does not enforce practitioners to respond to all questions. We adopted this survey strategy to obtain higher quality responses to the questions that practitioners feel confident in answering, since the participating practitioners have varying levels of expertise across the four applications developed by SISW.

The questionnaire for MRs (resp. EMRs) contains three statements for each MR (resp. EMR). It requests practitioners to indicate their level of agreement with the statements on a Likert scale (i.e., strongly agree, agree, neutral, disagree, and strongly disagree). We designed the statements in our questionnaire-based survey, drawing inspiration from Rogers' theory of innovation diffusion [16]. In this theory, the following five characteristics, based on practitioners' perceptions, are introduced for their impact on the adoption of innovative solutions:

Complexity: Reflecting the extent to which an innovation is perceived as challenging to understand or implement.
Compatibility: Referring to the extent to which an innovation aligns with practitioners' existing values, experiences, and needs.
Trialability: Indicating the extent to which an innovation can be tried on a limited scale or adopted incrementally.
Observability: Pertaining to the visibility of the results of an innovation to others.
Relative advantage: Describing the perception of an innovation's superiority compared to what is currently used.

Out of these five characteristics, our focus is on the first three: complexity, compatibility, and trialability. Note that the last two characteristics remain unaddressed in our survey, as our approach is still preliminary and has not yet been deployed in practice.

The questionnaire on MRs, available online [17], includes, for each MR, a form showing the generated MR (e.g., see Table 1) and three assessment statements (S1, S2, and S3) described in Table 3. These forms are grouped by application, and for each application, the questionnaire invites practitioners to provide open feedback. Statement S1 in Table 3 is about complexity; it assesses the degree to which a derived MR is understandable. Statement S2 relates to compatibility; it assesses the degree to which a derived MR aligns with practitioners' perceptions as a property to be considered in testing the SUT. Statement S3 concerns triability; it examines how helpful a derived MR is as an instrument for defining test cases (i.e., input and expected output pairs).

The questionnaire on EMRs, available online [17], first introduces SMRL by explaining its constructs, providing three examples of EMRs written in SMRL, and a link to the SMRL paper [5]. The questionnaire then, for each MR, provides a form with an MR (e.g., see Table 1), an EMR (e.g., see Fig. 4), and three statements ($S1^E$, $S2^E$, and $S3^E$, listed in Table 4). These forms are grouped by each SISW application. For each application group, the questionnaire includes

[2] https://lmsys.org/blog/2023-12-07-leaderboard/.

Table 3. Statements (S1, S2, and S3) for collecting feedback on MRs

S1	The MR is easy to understand. ☐ strongly agree ☐ agree ☐ neutral ☐ disagree ☐ strongly disagree
S2	The MR captures a property that needs to be considered when testing the application. ☐ strongly agree ☐ agree ☐ neutral ☐ disagree ☐ strongly disagree
S3	The MR helps identify the expected outputs for given inputs. ☐ strongly agree ☐ agree ☐ neutral ☐ disagree ☐ strongly disagree

an open question to collect additional feedback. Statement $S1^E$ in Table 4 is about complexity, assessing the extent to which an EMR is understandable. Statement $S2^E$ relates to compatibility, evaluating the degree to which an EMR aligns with its corresponding MR. Statement $S3^E$ concerns triability, examining the feasibility of implementing the functions invoked in an EMR.

Our approach derived 50 MRs and their corresponding EMRs from the four documents. Of these MRs, SISW independently assigned two practitioners to evaluate the 14 MRs derived for the aero-acoustics application, while one was assigned to 36 MRs for the remaining three applications, totaling 64 MRs analyzed. For the EMRs, one practitioner was assigned to all the applications. Note that these assignments were independently decided by SISW.

EXP2 - Web Application. EXP2 evaluates the correctness of the EMRs generated by our approach. Recall that EXP1 studies EMRs that are incomplete with regard to invoking the SUTs' APIs. Therefore, EXP2 employs a different application, for which we have its API specifications. EXP2 uses the experiment dataset provided by the prior work on MST-wi [5], containing both the APIs enabling the testing of a Web application (hereafter, SUT) and MRs that are designed to detect security vulnerabilities. Specifically, in EXP2, we randomly selected ten MRs among the ones published online *after the cutoff date* of GPT-3.5 (in EXP2, we relied on GPT-3.5 for this reason). Given the ten MRs and the SUT's APIs, we applied our approach to produce ten corresponding EMRs.

To assess the correctness of the ten generated EMRs, we inspected and annotated each line of the EMRs with one of the 13 labels described in Table 5. In

Table 4. Statements ($S1^E$, $S2^E$, and $S3^E$) for collecting feedback on EMRs

$S1^E$	The EMR is easy to understand. ☐ strongly agree ☐ agree ☐ neutral ☐ disagree ☐ strongly disagree
$S2^E$	The EMR is consistent with the corresponding MR. ☐ strongly agree ☐ agree ☐ neutral ☐ disagree ☐ strongly disagree
$S3^E$	It is feasible to implement all the functions used in the EMR. ☐ strongly agree ☐ agree ☐ neutral ☐ disagree ☐ strongly disagree

Table 5. Annotation labels used in EXP2

Label	Type	Description
CLC	Simple	The statement contains a correct language construct
C	Complex	The statement is correct
AI	Complex	The statement does not perform exactly what the original MR does, but it is a valid alternative implementation
WLC	Simple	The statement misuses a language construct
WS	Complex	The statement is wrong; it misses some required actions, performs the wrong operation, and the explanation does not reflect what is requested in the MR text
WI	Complex	The statement does not correctly implement what is suggested in the explanation
IE	Complex	The statement invokes an API function invented by ChatGPT, even if an adequate one exists
INE	Complex	The statement invokes an API function invented by ChatGPT because an adequate one does not exist
ITE	Complex	The statement invokes an API function invented by ChatGPT but delegates too much logic to it
ES	Complex	The statement invokes an existing and appropriate API function but swaps parameters
ENO	Complex	The statement invokes an existing and appropriate API function but not in an object-oriented manner
WAU	Complex	The statement misuses valid APIs
MISS	Complex	The statement misses an instruction required to implement what is reported in the explanation

the annotation process, we considered both the EMRs and their explanations (i.e., comments on the EMRs) generated by our approach. Note that each EMR statement is associated with an explanation in natural language produced by ChatGPT. Our labels distinguish between *complex* and *simple* statements. Simple statements are the ones including only one language construct (e.g., `IMPLIES`, `NOT`, `OR`). Complex statements include at least one method invocation. Further, our labels are classified into two groups: *correct* and *incorrect*. The former contains three labels (i.e., C, CLC, and AI in Table 5) indicating, respectively, whether a statement in an EMR implements part of the corresponding MR exactly, uses SMRL constructs correctly, or implements valid alternatives. The latter includes the remaining ten labels, each indicating a different type of issue, such as "incorrect use of SMRL constructs" and "misuse of the SUT's APIs". For example, in Fig. 4, the statement `if (!isSearchAction(searchAction)) continue;` on line 3 is annotated with the INE label, indicating that ChatGPT invented `isSearchAction()` and the EMR invokes it because an adequate API of the SUT was not provided to ChatGPT when generating the EMR from the MR described in Table 1.

4 Experiment Results

EXP1. Table 6 shows the results of EXP1, focusing on the combined number of responses (i.e., Likert ratings) for each statement across the 64 MRs reviewed by the three practitioners at SISW. From the results of statement S1, we found that in 49 out of the 64 MRs (77%), the practitioners were able to understand the proposed MRs and expressed positive feedback, i.e., "strongly agree" or "agree". In 12 MRs, the practitioners were neutral, and in the remaining 3 MRs, they disagreed with statement S1. Regarding statement S2, the practitioners agreed that the MRs capture properties that need to be considered when testing the SUT for 41 out of the 64 MRs (64%). In 10 MRs, the practitioners were neutral; in the remaining 13 MRs, the practitioners disagreed or strongly disagreed with statement S2. In contrast to these results, which are more positive, the responses to statement S3 showed mixed ratings. This statement indicates whether the presented MR helps identify the expected outputs for given inputs. In 18 MRs, the practitioners agreed; in 19 MRs, they were neutral; and in the remaining 27, they disagreed or strongly disagreed.

Regarding the non-positive responses to statement S3, we identified possible reasons from the practitioners' qualitative feedback. In particular, one practitioner, who provided 11 ratings as "disagree" and one as "strongly disagree" to the statement, stated that while most of the MRs are correct and useful for reminding someone what to test, they are too generic to aid in deriving appropriate testing. This aligns with feedback from another practitioner at SISW who, despite not assessing the MRs, collected and reviewed the responses to the MRs questionnaire. The practitioner provided a possible reason for some of the MRs being very generic, stating that it could be attributed to the nature of the documents provided by SISW.

Regarding the survey results for the 50 EMRs in EXP1, one practitioner provided consistent responses across all EMRs, stating they perceived that the EMRs *were clean and understandable* and *consistent with their corresponding MRs*. However, the practitioner deemed that not all functions used in the EMRs were feasible to be implemented. Regarding the last opinion, the practitioner noted that the functions in the EMRs, generated by ChatGPT, were specific to each EMR. Therefore, there is little opportunity for reusing these functions

Table 6. Responses to the MRs survey, for each statement (S1, S2, S3) in Table 3

	strongly agree	agree	neutral	disagree	strongly disagree
S1	3	46	12	3	0
S2	0	41	10	12	1
S3	0	18	19	24	3

across different EMRs, meaning the effort required for implementation would be significant. In addition, the specific constraints of the testing environment for their applications may pose challenges in using the exposed APIs to implement functions in the EMRs. Even though EXP1 generated incomplete EMRs with regard to using the SUT's APIs, as discussed above, this finding suggests that the characteristics of the SUT, such as its APIs, should be considered when further elaborating our approach to deriving EMRs.

The results for EXP1 indicate that our approach generates MRs and EMRs that practitioners deem to be understandable and relevant for testing.

EXP2. In EXP2, we annotated each line of the ten EMRs, which were converted from the corresponding ten MRs studied in prior work [5]. These EMRs have a minimum of 10 statements, a mean of 13.6 statements, and a maximum of 20 statements, totaling 136 statements.

Table 7 shows the results of EXP2 annotations using the labels defined in Table 5. Out of the 136 statements in the EMR code, the majority (107 statements, 78.6%) were classified as correctly converted. Specifically, 52 of the 107 statements are complex, and correctly and exactly implement part of the corresponding MRs, as shown by column C in Table 7. 54 of the 107 statements are simple, and correctly use SMRL constructs (column CLC). The remaining complex statement is valid and correct with respect to the corresponding MR (column AI). As for the 30 statements that were deemed incorrect, they can be further categorized as follows:

- 16 statements incorrectly use APIs (labeled with IE, INE, ITE, ES, and ENO). For example, five ITE cases introduce the method `isAuthorized` to check if a user is authorized to perform an action, instead of verifying that the outputs obtained by the source and the follow-up inputs differ.
- 10 statements incorrectly use SMRL constructs (column WLC). They are all related to the LLM "forgetting" how to use the construct `IMPLIES`; indeed, instead of separating the right-hand side of the implication with a comma (see end of Line 9 in Fig. 4), it uses an `&`. They can be easily fixed manually.
- Three statements are wrong (column WS); for example, the generated MR checks if the returned page is an error page instead of the opposite.
- Three statements miss implementing what is described in the corresponding explanations (column MISS); specifically, they do not compare the outputs of the source and the follow-up inputs. Further, these three statements had

Table 7. Distribution of annotation labels (from Table 5) for the 10 EMRs obtained from EXP2

C	CLC	AI	WS	WI	IE	INE	ITE	ES	ENO	WAU	WLC	MISS
52	54	1	3	0	3	1	9	1	2	0	10	3
38.2%	39.7%	0.7%	2.2%	0.0%	0.7%	0.0%	6.6%	0.7%	1.5%	0.0%	7.4%	2.2%

been annotated also with another label because, in addition to miss some instructions, they contained an incorrect implementation (i.e., ENO and WS), which is the reason why our labels sum up to 139 instead of 136.

The results for EXP2 indicate that the generated EMRs are largely correct with respect to their MRs.

5 Threats to Validity and Research Opportunities

Even though the experiment results are promising, we recognize that our work is in its preliminary stages, and there are some potential threats to its validity. In this section, we discuss these concerns, focusing on those that lead to challenging yet important directions for future research.

Prompt Engineering. Our prompts are designed by decomposing the processes of deriving MRs from requirements and transforming MRs into EMRs into smaller, simpler steps. Despite these decomposed steps aligning with those that engineers would conduct manually, when using LLMs there might be better sequences of prompts that could improve the accuracy and relevance of the automatically generated MRs and EMRs. Further research is necessary to refine and compare the prompts, ensuring that they efficiently guide LLMs in producing effective MRs and EMRs.

Assessing MRs and EMRs. We evaluated the MRs and EMRs generated by our approach using the questionnaire-base survey and annotation studies, which rely on the quality of human assessments. Hence, such assessments are naturally biased by the participating personnel in the study. To minimize any threat to construct validity (i.e., researcher expectations affecting human subjects' assessment), our industrial partner, SISW, invited four practitioners with different backgrounds for the questionnaire-based survey study. For the annotation study, the second author, who is familiar with SMRL, annotated the EMRs to ensure that the annotations are accurate. Although our choice may introduce a construct validity threat, the availability of experimental data enables other researchers to further investigate our findings.

As part of our future work, to better address face validity (i.e., the selection of appropriate reflective indicators), we aim to leverage recent studies on the assessment of code generation models [8] and select additional quantitative metrics to measure the degree to which MRs and EMRs are accurate and relevant to the SUT. Such metrics are desirable not only for objective assessment but also for automating the MT process; indeed, such metrics might be used as reward to improve LLMs results.

Human Expertise. In our work, we leveraged human expertise to select technical documents and assess the outputs, i.e., MRs and EMRs. Since our approach does not involve humans-in-the-loop (e.g., the textual MRs generated by the LLM for EXP1 are not rewritten by humans before generating EMRs), the quality of outputs highly depends on the quality of inputs. To mitigate any bias originated from the input documents (construct validity), SISW selected four technical documents independently from the authors who developed the approach.

In the future, even if we aim to automate the MT process, incorporating humans in the loop could be used to refine and validate the inputs and the intermediate outputs, to efficiently and effectively guide our approach to produce more accurate and relevant MRs and EMRs. Therefore, future research should explore methods to effectively incorporate human expertise into an AI-based MT process, balancing automation with human interventions.

External Validity. To mitigate generalizability threats, for EXP1, we considered specifications of industrial modelling and simulation software for four different applications domains (marine design, wind turbine, air-craft propulsion, and aero-acoustics). Although such software may differ from other types of software systems (e.g., content management software), it is of high complexity and adopted in many industrial sectors including automotive and space. Further, for EXP2, we focused on MRs that demonstrated effective for content management (e.g., Joomla [11]) and Web-based automation software (e.g., Jenkins [7]), thus complementing the choice made for EXP1.

6 Related Work

Many MT approaches have been developed for testing various SUTs, such as search engines [26], Web applications [5], and embedded systems [1], accounting for the requirements specific to these SUTs. However, these approaches heavily rely on manual efforts to elicit MRs, inherently limiting the applicability of MT. To reduce the cost of defining MRs, researchers have proposed relying on meta-heuristic search [23,24] and genetic programming [2] to automatically derive MRs from execution data. Although promising, such approaches require several executions of the SUT, which makes them suitable for small programs, but may not scale for large software where executions may take several minutes and a lot of outputs are produced.

Recently, a few studies [12,25] have proposed the use of LLMs to automatically derive MRs from the knowledge base of LLMs. However, these studies are limited to deriving MRs for SUTs already known in the adopted LLMs. In other words, there are no studies demonstrating the applicability of LLMs to derive MRs that account for the requirements specific to an SUT that was unseen during the LLM training phases. Considering that, in industrial contexts, software testing activities often target new products implementing requirements different from those implemented by existing systems, LLM-based approaches for the automated generation of MRs should be capable of handling unseen requirements. This capability is what we presented in this paper.

Additionally, we note that, to the best of our knowledge, there is no work that automates the conversion of MRs into an executable form, which is required to fully automate the MT process. Chaleshtari et al. [5] proposed the adoption of a DSL to automate the execution of MRs; however, DSL-based MRs may have limited readability, contrary to MRs in natural language.

In summary, there is no solution in the literature that aims at fully automating the MT process, involving the derivation of MRs from SUT-specific requirements and the generation of EMRs, for the automated determination of test results in MT. An alternative is the automated generation of test cases—including oracles—using LLMs, which is under active development [22]. However, since LLM-generated code may still require human validation, we believe that validating EMRs is more cost-effective than validating test cases. Indeed, a single validated EMR enables exercising the SUT with multiple inputs, which might otherwise be exercised by different test cases, each needing validation.

7 Conclusion and Future Work

In this paper, we have introduced our approach for automatically deriving EMRs from requirements using LLMs. In our preliminary experiments, we applied our approach to four applications of our industry partner (SISW) and conducted a questionnaire-based survey study to collect opinions from SISW practitioners. In addition, we evaluated the correctness of the EMRs generated by our approach, by applying it to a Web application. The feedback from practitioners at SISW confirmed that our work is a promising direction for automating the derivation of MRs and EMRs from requirements. Furthermore, our annotation results indicate that our approach has strong potential for correctly generating EMRs from MRs. However, our results also reveal that the derived MRs need to be more specific to the SUTs, and the derived EMRs could be further improved with regard to the use of DSL constructs and APIs, which necessitate further research.

In our future work, we plan to explore several key areas related to our current research. A primary focus will be on automating prompt engineering to facilitate the generation of prompts for deriving MRs from requirements and their subsequent conversion into EMRs. Recognizing the significance of input quality, particularly in requirements, another important area will involve developing methods to assist engineers in providing high-quality inputs. Integrating human expertise, or "human in the loop", will also be an important aspect of our research, aiming to further enhance the accuracy and relevance of the generated MRs and EMRs.

Data Availability. Our experiment package with prompts, MRs, EMRs, and questionnaires is available online [17].

References

1. Ayerdi, J., Segura, S., Arrieta, A., Sagardui, G., Arratibel, M.: QoS-aware metamorphic testing: an elevation case study. In: ISSRE, pp. 104–114 (2020)
2. Ayerdi, J., Terragni, V., Arrieta, A., Tonella, P., Sagardui, G., Arratibel, M.: Generating metamorphic relations for cyber-physical systems with genetic programming: an industrial case study. In: ESEC/FSE, pp. 1264–1274 (2021)

3. Barr, E.T., Harman, M., McMinn, P., Shahbaz, M., Yoo, S.: The oracle problem in software testing: a survey. IEEE TSE **41**(5), 507–525 (2015)
4. Bériot, H., Gabard, G., Hamiche, K., Williamschen, M.: High-order unstructured methods for computational aero-acoustics. Progress in simulation, control and reduction of ventilation noise, Publisher (2015)
5. Chaleshtari, N.B., Pastore, F., Goknil, A., Briand, L.C.: Metamorphic testing for web system security. IEEE TSE **49**(6), 3430–3471 (2023)
6. Chen, T.Y., et al.: Metamorphic testing: a review of challanges and opportunities. ACM Comput. Surv. **51**(1) (2018)
7. Eclipse Foundation: Jenkins ci/cd server (2018). https://jenkins.io/
8. Evtikhiev, M., Bogomolov, E., Sokolov, Y., Bryksin, T.: Out of the bleu: how should we assess quality of the code generation models? J. Syst. Softw. **203**(C) (2023)
9. Fioraldi, A., Maier, D.C., Eißfeldt, H., Heuse, M.: AFL++: combining incremental steps of fuzzing research. In: WOOT, pp. 1–12 (2020)
10. Fraser, G., Arcuri, A.: EvoSuite: automatic test suite generation for object-oriented software. In: ESEC/FSE, pp. 416–419 (2011)
11. Joomla: Joomla (2018). https://www.joomla.org/
12. Luu, Q.H., Liu, H., Chen, T.Y.: Can ChatGPT advance software testing intelligence? An experience report on metamorphic testing (2023)
13. Mai, P.X., Pastore, F., Goknil, A., Briand, L.: Metamorphic security testing for web systems. In: ICST, pp. 186–197 (2020)
14. Open AI: Chatgpt. https://openai.com/blog/chatgpt
15. OpenAI: GPT-4 Technical report (2023). CoRR **abs/2303.08774**
16. Rogers, E.M., Singhal, A., Quinlan, M.M.: Diffusion of innovations. In: An Integrated Approach to Communication Theory and Research, pp. 432–448. Routledge (2014)
17. Shin, S.Y., Pastore, F., Bianculli, D., Baicoianu, A.: Replication package. https://doi.org/10.6084/m9.figshare.25046276.v1
18. Siemens: Improving wind turbine gearbox simulation (2021). https://resources.sw.siemens.com/en-US/white-paper-full-scale-cfd. Accessed 2024
19. Siemens: Full-scale simulation for marine design (2023). https://resources.sw.siemens.com/en-US/white-paper-full-scale-cfd. Accessed 2024
20. Siemens: Leveraging preliminary design and simulation to drive next-generation propulsion systems (2023). https://view.highspot.com/viewer/65a7c309c5926b7b3e0192c6. Accessed 2024
21. Song, Y., Wang, T., Cai, P., Mondal, S.K., Sahoo, J.P.: A comprehensive survey of few-shot learning: evolution, applications, challenges, and opportunities. ACM Comput. Surv. **55**(13s) (2023)
22. Wang, J., Huang, Y., Chen, C., Liu, Z., Wang, S., Wang, Q.: Software testing with large language models: survey, landscape, and vision (2024)
23. Zacchia Lun, Y., D'Innocenzo, A., Smarra, F., Malavolta, I., Domenica Di Benedetto, M.: State of the art of cyber-physical systems security: an automatic control perspective. JSS **149**, 174–216 (2019)
24. Zhang, J., et al.: Search-based inference of polynomial metamorphic relations. In: ASE, pp. 701–712 (2014)
25. Zhang, Y., Towey, D., Pike, M.: Automated metamorphic-relation generation with ChatGPT: an experience report. In: COMPSAC, pp. 1780–1785 (2023)
26. Zhou, Z.Q., Xiang, S., Chen, T.Y.: Metamorphic testing for software quality assessment: a study of search engines. IEEE TSE **42**(3), 260–280 (2016)

Exploring Browser Automation: A Comparative Study of Selenium, Cypress, Puppeteer, and Playwright

Boni García[1(✉)], Jose M. del Alamo[2], Maurizio Leotta[3], and Filippo Ricca[3]

[1] Universidad Carlos III de Madrid, Leganés, Spain
boni.garcia@uc3m.es

[2] Universidad Politécnica de Madrid, Madrid, Spain
jm.delalamo@upm.es

[3] Università di Genova, Genoa, Italy
{maurizio.leotta,filippo.ricca}@unige.it

Abstract. Browser automation refers to the use of specific software to perform user tasks (such as navigation among web pages, interaction with forms, etc.) automatically in a web browser. It is commonly performed programmatically for automated testing of various types of applications, web-based, cloud-based, or composed of multiple microservices, although other uses are possible (e.g., web scraping or automating repetitive tasks). For many years, Selenium has been considered the de-facto tool for browser automation. However, recently, we have witnessed the advent of alternative tools, such as Cypress, Puppeteer, or Playwright. This paper gives a comparative high-level overview and presents their architecture and key features. We expect this information will assist researchers and practitioners in making well-informed decisions regarding the browser automation tool that merits their attention.

Keywords: Browser Automation · Free and Open Source Software · End-to-End Testing · Software Tools

1 Introduction

Selenium has been the reference for browser automation for the last two decades. Nowadays, it is widely used to develop automated end-to-end tests for web applications, including cloud-based ones, and supports a multi-million dollar industry [7]. Selenium proves invaluable in testing web-based applications, including those hosted on cloud platforms. Regardless of the hosting environment, if the application is accessible via a web browser, Selenium adeptly interacts with its elements, emulates user actions, and validates expected behaviors. Moreover, it extends its utility beyond traditional web applications, offering robust testing capabilities for applications built with various microservices [8,9].

A. Bertolino et al. (Eds.): QUATIC 2024, CCIS 2178, pp. 142–149, 2024.
https://doi.org/10.1007/978-3-031-70245-7_10

Nevertheless, Selenium is not a testing framework itself. Selenium is defined as a general purpose browser automation library, primarily used for automated web testing [2]. For this reason, problems related to end-to-end testing with Selenium, such as synchronization, brittleness, or flakiness, have been reported [5]. Thus, different alternatives in browser automation have emerged in the last few years. Some of these tools have been conceived as a comprehensive end-to-end testing framework, promising to overcome the limitations of Selenium and provide a seamless experience for automated testing. This diversity of tools indicates the increasing demand for advanced browser automation solutions. Nevertheless, practitioners usually need guidance regarding what tool to choose. This article aims to help these developers and testers by comparing four of the most popular open source browser automation frameworks nowadays: Selenium, Cypress, Puppeteer, and Playwright.

Section 2 introduced the selected tools under study. Then, Sect. 3 provides a high-level description of the architecture of each tool, and Sect. 4 compares their main features. Section 5 discusses the major differences. Finally, Sect. 6 summarizes the main findings of this piece of research and provides some hints about the future perspectives in browser automation.

2 Tools Under Study

The number of available tools devoted to browser automation tools is increasingly high. To our knowledge, no scientific literature exists to explain the current state of the art in browser automation. However, we can find grey literature that gathers and maintains a comprehensive body of knowledge in the browser automation space. One example is "Awesome Browser Automation[1]," an open GitHub repository that provides a curated list of browser automation tool and resources. As can be seen in this list, practitioners can use a wide range of tooling for browser automation. Therefore, to narrow down the considered tools in this paper, we focus on popular Free and Open Source Software (FOSS) tools that provide an API to develop scripts that control browsers programmatically. This way, the remainder of this article analyses the following:

- **Selenium**[2] is a suite of open source tools (Apache 2.0 license) used to automate web browsers. The heart of the Selenium project is Selenium WebDriver (often called simply Selenium), a library that allows controlling web browsers programmatically using different languages, officially supported in Java, JavaScript, Python, Ruby, and .Net.
- **Cypress**[3] is a JavaScript end-to-end automated testing framework created in 2014 to provide a seamless experience for web testing.

[1] https://github.com/angrykoala/awesome-browser-automation.
[2] https://www.selenium.dev/.
[3] https://www.cypress.io/.

- **Puppeteer**[4] is an open source (MIT license) Node.js library that provides a high-level API to control Chromium-based browsers (although there is experimental Firefox support). Puppeteer has been maintained by the Chrome DevTools team at Google since 2017.
- **Playwright**[5] is an open source framework (Apache 2.0 license) for web testing and automation, maintained since 2020, when the original team behind Puppeteer moved from Google to Microsoft. Playwright originally started as a Node.js library. Currently, in addition to JavaScript and Typescript, it supports other programming languages, namely Python, Java, and .Net.

3 Architecture

3.1 Selenium

Selenium was initially launched in 2004. This early version of Selenium used JavaScript to support browser automation. Nevertheless, due to the limitations of JavaScript to automate some actions (e.g., popup dialog handling), the architecture of Selenium was renewed entirely into Selenium 2+ (rebranded since then as Selenium WebDriver). As of this version, Selenium uses the native capabilities of each browser to support automation. For this reason, as illustrated in Fig. 1, a script using the Selenium API requires an intermediate component called driver. Each major browser vendor provides each specific driver (e.g., chromedriver for Chrome or geckodriver for Firefox). Each driver receives incoming messages from the Selenium scripts using a standard protocol called W3C WebDriver[6], based on JSON messages over HTTP. The driver translates each W3C WebDriver message to some native command the browser can execute. The management (i.e., download, setup, and maintenance) of these drivers was cumbersome for Selenium users [3]. For this reason, the Selenium project introduced Selenium Manager[7] as a built-in tool for automated driver management in 2022.

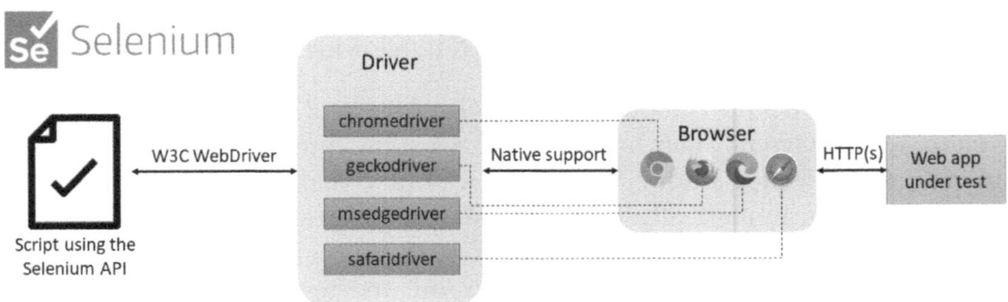

Fig. 1. Selenium Architecture

[4] https://pptr.dev/.
[5] https://playwright.dev/.
[6] https://www.w3.org/TR/webdriver/.
[7] https://www.selenium.dev/documentation/selenium_manager/.

3.2 Cypress

As illustrated in Fig. 2, the Cypress architecture consists of a Node.js process plus a tool called Test Runner executed in a browser. The Test Runner is an interactive web application that embeds the current test script to be executed (based on Mocha, a JavaScript unit testing framework [1]) plus the web application under test as two iframes. This way, the test and the client-side portion of the web application under test run in the same browser tab (i.e., in the same JavaScript loop). The Node.js process communicates with the Test Runner using a WebSocket to track the test execution. Cypress also operates at the network layer by intercepting the HTTP(S) traffic with the server-side portion of the web application under test. Lastly, Cypress provides a plugin mechanism to modify or extend its internal behavior. Cypress supports Chromium-based browsers (including Chrome and Edge) and Firefox. Moreover, it provides experimental support to WebKit (i.e., the web browser engine used by Safari). The Cypress Test Runner is open source (MIT license). Besides, the company behind Cypress also provides commercial support for advanced features, such as the Cypress Dashboard, a cloud-managed web application for tracking Cypress tests.

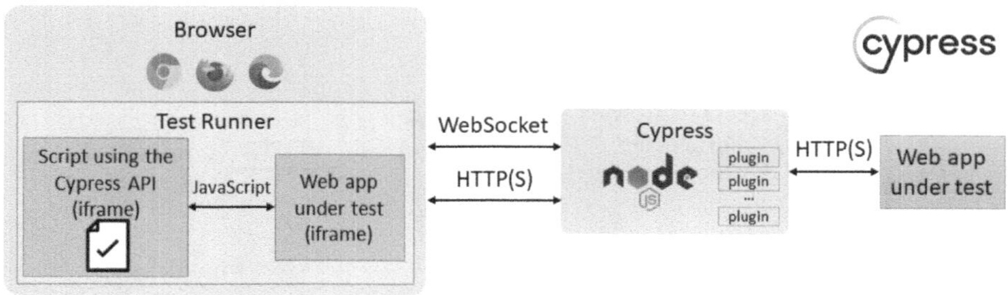

Fig. 2. Cypress Architecture

3.3 Puppeteer

Puppeteer uses the Chrome DevTools Protocol[8] (CDP) to send JSON-RPC messages for inspecting, debugging, and profiling Chromium-based browsers. When installed, Puppeteer automatically downloads and uses a browser called "Chrome for Testing[9]", which is a minimal Chromium release specifically maintained to address the testing use case and guaranteed to work with. Moreover, other Chromium-based browsers, such as Chrome or Edge, can be driven by Puppeteer. As depicted in Fig. 3, a script using the Puppeteer API (written in JavaScript or TypeScript) sends CDP messages to the browser, which interacts via HTTP(S) with the web application under test accordingly.

[8] https://chromedevtools.github.io/devtools-protocol/.
[9] https://googlechromelabs.github.io/chrome-for-testing/.

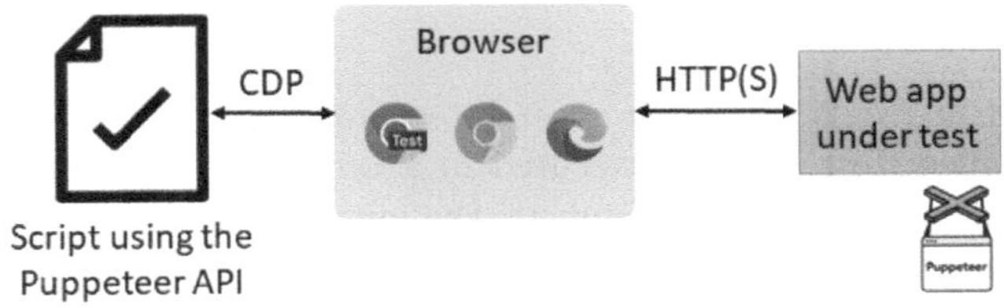

Fig. 3. Puppeteer Architecture

3.4 Playwright

As illustrated in Fig. 4, Playwright supports three types of web engines: Chromium, Firefox, and WebKit. Playwright allows control of patched versions of these browsers but not actual releases. Therefore, the Playwright team maintains patched versions of these browsers, exposing the necessary capabilities to enable automation through an event-driven architecture that allows access to different internal browser processes (e.g., the render, network, browser, or service worker). Playwright automatically downloads these patched releases locally, making them available for scripts seamlessly.

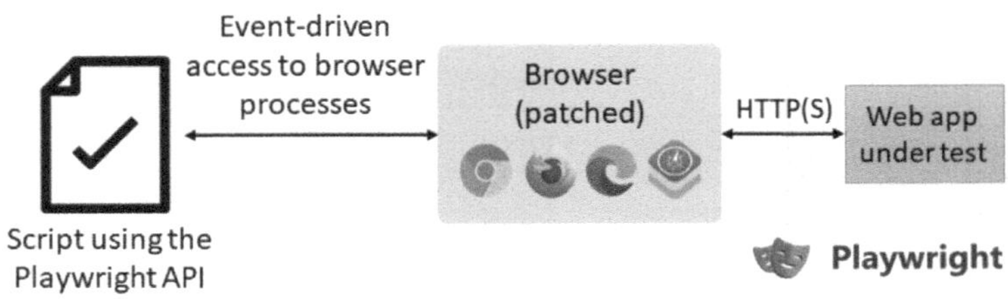

Fig. 4. Playwright Architecture

4 Features

To identify a comprehensive list of features provided by the tools under study, first, we reviewed the existing literature (e.g., [2,6]). Then, we analyzed the official documentation of each tool to match and complement the identified features. As a result, we discovered that most of the common features for browser automation, such as element location, impersonating mouse and keyboard actions, handling cookies, or making screenshots, are available in each tool under study. Nevertheless, as summarized in Table 1, there are relevant differences.

The central proposition of Selenium is being built on standards to provide a single API that works across all major browsers. This way, it is the only tool that allows comprehensive multilanguage and cross-browser support. Then, a key feature of Cypress is the auto-waiting when locating web elements. This feature is achieved by executing the Cypress test script in the browser simultaneously

Table 1. Feature differences of Selenium, Cypress, Puppeteer, and Playwright (✓ = supported, ✗ = not supported, P = partial support)

Feature	Selenium	Cypress	Puppeteer	Playwright
Multilanguage	✓	✗	✗	✓
Cross-browser	✓	P	P	P
Automatic waiting	✗	✓	✗	✗
Tabs handling	✓	✗	✓	✓
Frames and iframes	✓	P	✓	✓
Console log gathering	P	✗	✓	✓
Session recording	✗	✓	✓	✓
Assertions	✗	✓	✗	✓
Live reload	✗	✓	✗	✗
Test retries	✗	✓	✗	✗
Visual testing	✗	P	✗	✓
Component testing	✗	✓	✗	P
REST API testing	✗	✓	✗	✓

with the application under test. That solution can be effective for most use cases, although certain operations cannot be automated with JavaScript (e.g., handling tabs [6]). Finally, Puppeteer and Playwright aim to pioneer browser automation by providing advanced features using non-standard mechanisms. This approach enables most of the common use cases but is not cross-browser.

A feature showcasing the differences between the tools under study is console log gathering, i.e., the ability to get the information written in the console browser (e.g., debug information or JavaScript error traces) by the application under test. This feature is not available in the W3C WebDriver specification. Nevertheless, chromedriver has done a custom implementation for that [4]. Then, Cypress is not able to provide this feature through JavaScript. Finally, Puppeteer and Playwright provide this feature using non-standard mechanisms.

Another relevant difference is that Selenium and Puppeteer are not testing frameworks but general-purpose browser automation libraries. Therefore, additional tooling (e.g., unit testing frameworks) is required to conduct complete end-to-end tests with these libraries. On the other hand, Cypress and Playwright have been conceived as testing frameworks. Therefore, they incorporate built-in high-level features like test assertions, component testing, or REST API testing. The latter feature is especially appealing for testing web services, for instance, in cloud and microservices-based apps.

5 Discussion

Contrary to popular belief, Selenium is not a testing framework but a browser automation library. This fact has relevant implications for using Selenium as the foundation tool for automated end-to-end testing. First, the calls to the Selenium API are usually embedded into a unit testing framework (e.g., JUnit) to create actual test scripts. Second, and more importantly, high-level features for automated testing, such as auto-waiting for locating web elements, session recording, or visual testing capabilities, are not part of Selenium. On the other hand, modern browser automation tools such as Cypress and Playwright have been created as testing frameworks. For this reason, these tools do provide specific features for testing purposes. Practitioners find these characteristics appealing, but implementing them comes at a cost.

Cypress uses JavaScript to automate the browsers. This approach was already used in the early versions of Selenium (what we call today "Selenium 1"). Nevertheless, the Selenium project abandoned this approach due to JavaScript's underlying limitations in automating some browser actions. Consequently, one potential weakness of Cypress is its restriction to JavaScript instead of automation standards such as W3C WebDriver.

Then, Puppeteer and Playwright aim to provide advanced features for browser automation and end-to-end testing. However, these features are built on top of non-standard mechanisms. First, Puppeteer relies on CDP, primarily available on Chromium-based browsers. The limitation of this approach is the cross-browser support (e.g., Firefox implements only a subset of CDP). Second, Playwright uses patched browser versions of Chromium, Firefox, and WebKit rather than actual releases. This fact is a limitation since, ideally, automated end-to-end testing should be carried out using the same browser releases that end-users use.

6 Conclusions and Future Perspectives

Comparing Selenium, Cypress, Puppeteer, and Playwright is not straightforward since their natures are different. Although all of them allow automation browsers, Cypress and Playwright incorporate high-level features for end-to-end testing. This way, all these tools have strengths and limitations. Selenium is a mature project wholly based on standards, but it does not provide specific testing features. Cypress uses JavaScript to execute a test in the browser simultaneously with the application under test, providing fast execution and automatic waiting, but some features are not possible (e.g., tab handling). Puppeteer provides comprehensive automation capabilities due to direct communication with the browser using CDP, which is mainly available in Chromium-based browsers. Finally, Playwright provides a comprehensive programming model for automated tests, but rather than actual browsers, it uses patched browser releases.

The W3C WebDriver BiDirectional (BiDi)[10] aims to be the future of browser automation. BiDi is the evolution of W3C WebDriver and is a work-in-progress open standard that will provide advanced features for browser automation. It is being designed with the lessons learned from W3C WebDriver (i.e., cross-browser support) and CDP (e.g., fast bidirectional communication). BiDi is a joint effort

[10] https://w3c.github.io/webdriver-bidi/.

of browser vendors (Chrome, Edge, Firefox, Safari), open source automation projects (e.g., Selenium), and companies offering browser automation services (e.g., Sauce Labs). This protocol will probably change the supported features and the popularity of browser automation tools: those who manage to quickly and successfully integrate this protocol will likely capture a significant portion of the market. At the time of this writing, Selenium and Puppeteer have already included initial support for WebDriver BiDi. The Playwright team has declared not to support BiDi until all major browsers support it.

Acknowledgments. This work has been partially supported by the "Generation of Reliable Synthetic Health Data for Federated Learning in Secure Data Spaces" Research Project (PID2022-141045OB-C43 (AEI/ERDF, EU)) funded by MCIN/AEI/ 10.13039/501100011033 and by "ERDF A way of making Europe" by "the European Union", and by the MCIN/AEI/ 10.13039/501100011033 through the H2O Learn Research Project (PID2020-112584RB-C31). This work was also partially supported by the "EndGame - Improving End-to-End Testing of Web and Mobile Apps through Gamification" project (2022PCCMLF) - funded by the Ministero dellUniversità e della Ricerca - within the PRIN 2022 program (D.D.104 - 02/02/2022).

References

1. Fard, A.M., Mesbah, A.: JavaScript: the (un) covered parts. In: 2017 IEEE International Conference on Software Testing, Verification and Validation (ICST), pp. 230–240. IEEE (2017)
2. García, B.: Hands-On Selenium WebDriver with Java. O'Reilly Media, Inc., Sebastopol (2022)
3. García, B., Munoz-Organero, M., Alario-Hoyos, C., Kloos, C.D.: Automated driver management for Selenium WebDriver. Empir. Softw. Eng. **26**(5), 107 (2021). https://doi.org/10.1007/s10664-021-09975-3
4. García, B., Ricca, F., del Alamo, J.M., Leotta, M.: Enhancing web applications observability through instrumented automated browsers. J. Syst. Softw. **203**, 111723 (2023). https://doi.org/10.1016/j.jss.2023.111723
5. Leotta, M., García, B., Ricca, F., Whitehead, J.: Challenges of end-to-end testing with selenium WebDriver and how to face them: a survey. In: The 16th IEEE Conference on Software Testing, Verification and Validation (ICST), pp. 339–350 (2023). https://doi.org/10.1109/ICST57152.2023.00039
6. Mwaura, W.: End-to-End Web Testing with Cypress: Explore Techniques for Automated Frontend Web Testing with Cypress and JavaScript. Packt Publishing Ltd., Birmingham (2021)
7. Niranjanamurthy, M., Navale, S., Jagannatha, S., Chakraborty, S.: Functional software testing for web applications in the context of industry. J. Comput. Theor. Nanosci. **15**(11–12), 3398–3404 (2018)
8. Sotomayor, J.P., Allala, S.C., Santiago, D., King, T.M., Clarke, P.J.: Comparison of open-source runtime testing tools for microservices. Softw. Qual. J. **31**(1), 55–87 (2022). https://doi.org/10.1007/s11219-022-09583-4
9. Waseem, M., Liang, P., Shahin, M., Di Salle, A., Márquez, G.: Design, monitoring, and testing of microservices systems: the practitioners perspective. J. Syst. Softw. **182**, 111061 (2021). https://doi.org/10.1016/j.jss.2021.111061

Improving Model-Based Testing Through Interactive Validation, Evaluation and Reconstruction of Test Cases

Oleksandr Kolchyn(✉) and Stepan Potiyenko

V.M. Glushkov Institute of Cybernetics NAS of Ukraine, Kyiv, Ukraine
kolchin_av@yahoo.com

Abstract. Automatic test case generation is a popular software testing strategy. However, many reports show shortage of such test cases in poor quality and doubtable efficiency. In order to alleviate these problems and to make test cases trustable, we propose an interactive post-processing method which allows (1) analyzing the path that is examined by the test case, (2) making safe changes to the path which will eliminate the shortcomings while leaving the coverage targets of the test case unharmed. The method is based on visualization of the path along the control flow graph of the model with additional information about factual evaluation history of all variables and possible alternative variants of behavior. The method reduces the time spent on researching the results of test generation and editing the obtained test cases, and its use has a positive effect on the quality and efficiency of the test suite.

Keywords: Model-based testing · tests quality · debugging · maintenance

1 Introduction

Formal models are actively used for prototyping and can also be considered as abstract realizations of requirements in the development of safety-critical systems. The development of formal model checking methods allows automating not only the verification of properties, but also the creation of test scenarios that can be used as a basis for validating future implementations.

For large systems with complex behavioral logic, automated test generation can significantly reduce labor intensity and project implementation time and also increase test coverage. However, such automation is desirable only if the quality of the resulting tests is sufficiently high. The problem lies in the substantial shortcomings of the results: generation algorithms are mainly focused on achieving a required coverage of a certain structural criterion, and the sequence of test events is determined by the order of the alternatives enumeration performed by the model behavior traversal algorithm, rather than their cause-and-effect relationship. Therefore, testing scenarios often have no semantic content and are terminated without reaching a logical completion (the performed calculation did not produce an observable effect that could be verified), and, as a result,

A. Bertolino et al. (Eds.): QUATIC 2024, CCIS 2178, pp. 150–158, 2024.
https://doi.org/10.1007/978-3-031-70245-7_11

are ineffective in terms of error detection. Automatically generated test cases require manual support to determine the conditions for successful passing, as well as for further updating due to changes in the product code. Many works emphasize that poorly written tests have a negative effect on their maintenance. The decision to include a particular test case in the project test suite must be made by an engineer. Therefore, cost-effective validation of test generation results is needed. Often, the identified problems can be solved by small changes in a test case, but this requires consistent computations in accordance with the updates. And such computations can be difficult to perform manually, but can be easily automated. Such automation is the goal of the proposed methods. In this paper, we will show typical problems of generated test cases that we have encountered in practice [1, 2] and describe the developed methods of debugging test scenarios, assessing their significance, and also their safe editing.

2 Challenges of Creating a Test Suite and Motivational Examples

The set of all behaviors of a software system can be excessively large, and in the presence of loops, even infinite. Therefore, in practice, a test suite should provide a certain coverage [3]. Coverage criteria help determine whether the test suite covers a large enough subset of the state space to trust the software system. Often, the completeness of test coverage is assessed by the number of executed code statements, as well as branches, paths, reaching the boundary values of functions, fulfilling conditions in expressions, etc. Many studies have been devoted to comparing the efficiency and standardization of different types of coverage. For example, the Modified Condition/Decision Coverage (MC/DC) criterion is used in the DO-178B and DO-178C certification of airborne systems, and is also part of the requirements for the ISO 26262 Road Vehicle Functional Safety standard.

But the issue of the ability of such tests to detect errors remains controversial [1, 3, 5]. Traditional approaches to test suite development are mainly focused on achieving a higher level of coverage as the main goal. This strategy often results in tests achieving their coverage elements in convoluted ways. Many empirical studies [3, 5–7] show that the level of structural coverage is not a good indicator of the efficiency of automatically generated tests by itself and should not be used as the main indicator of quality. There are reports (e.g. [6, 7]) that suggest that providing structural coverage as a goal for test generation is generally a misguided strategy: such metrics are designed to measure the incompletes of coverage of an existing test suite and localize uncovered areas, and do not necessarily lead to satisfactory results when used in the opposite role as specifications for test generation.

Below are typical cases we encountered [1] when using test generation methods.

Example 1: Problem: early termination (Fig. 1). The test scenario that follows the path $\{1, 2, 3, 6, 7\}$ calculates certain value (the call of the compute() function is in line 3), but then causes the system to stop due to an unrelated exception (in an effort to be "short"). The test suite may no longer contain a call of the compute() function because it has "already been covered" and as a result, the value of res does not become part of the observed output. This early termination is often caused by a breadth-first search (BFS) strategy and leads to poor fault detection ability. For example, experiments conducted in

[6] show that randomly generated tests detected more mutants than tests with MC/DC and branch coverage obtained by BFS.

Example 2: Problem: the scenario is too long and runs through unrelated functionality. Tests created using depth-first search (DFS) are usually confusing and contain execution of lines/functions that are not related to the main purpose of the test, and suffer from a high level of test overlap and uneven coverage. This is due to the nature of the DFS traversal strategy and leads to two main problems: very unbalanced testing of the model's behavior [8] and complex test maintenance (unnecessary resource consumption; a small change in the source model can affect a large part of the test suite). Figure 2 shows the code where the test scenario $\{1, 2, 3, 4, 5, 6, 8, 9, \ldots\}$ was generated to cover the call of the stmt1() function. The problem of the scenario is that passes through the five-minute wait (line 4), although such time consumption could be avoided by the appropriate path $\{1, 2, 6, 7, 8, 9, \ldots\}$. Moreover, the $\{1, 2, 3, 4, 5\}$ prefix was also used to cover subsequent lines of code, i.e., stmt2() calls, etc., and only one test case (covering line 7) avoided this wait.

```
1.  in(x);
2.  if( x == 1 )
3.     res := compute();
4.  else
5.     res := -1;
6.  if(exception)
7.     return -1;
8.  print res;
    ...
9.  return 1;
```

Fig. 1. Lost calculation

```
1.   in(x);
2.   if( !access granted ) {
3.     while(!access granted)
4.       wait(5 min);
5.     allocate1();
6.   }else
7.     allocate2();
8.   if(x == 1)
9.     stmt1();
10.  if(x == 2)
11.    stmt2();
```

Fig. 2. Unnecessary resource consumption

Such cases occur quite often. To prevent these shortcomings, various generation methods are developed: special heuristics are integrated and more thorough coverage criteria are applied [1, 2, 9]. Although such measures can improve the results (e.g., data flow coverage helps to solve problems with the absence of an observed effect), it is still desirable to use automation as a "calculator" and "advisor" rather than to completely replace a human [10], especially at the stage of validation and integration of tests into the project's test suite.

In this paper, we will not consider approaches of test scenarios generation, but rather focus on the problem of their debugging and improving. Getting trustworthy tests requires a lot of work. One has to manually examine the behavior according to the input data and (1) check that there is no error or excessive abstraction, (2) ensure that the test makes sense, as often in the pursuit of coverage tests turn out to be meaningless, and also (3) look for the possibility of a small change in the test to significantly improve its quality characteristics [8, 9, 11, 12].

3 Objective Evaluation of the Test Scenario and Its Explanation

First, it is necessary to evaluate the original test case and get information about it that is important to the project. For example, what was the examined objective? What was its main purpose? What requirements does it verify? It is often useful to create some kind of traceability matrix between the requirements for the system, its implementation, and the tests that verify the requirements. This allows tracking the coverage of the requirements and helps to create goal-oriented tests. Information about auxiliary merits such as error detection, resource consumption, data coherence and consistency, and evenness of coverage is also useful [1, 8].

Evaluation of Coverage. First, for the entire test suite, we will create a table of correspondence for the coverage elements. For example, for a simple criterion of covering lines of code, we will match each test with a set of line numbers it executes, or, if this test is built to test the fulfillment of a certain requirement that was expressed using a temporal logic formula, the corresponding requirement (or formula). This will make it possible to track the evenness of coverage and will be a hint to possible changes in the test. Also, additional information is retrieved about the coverage of boundary cases (in predicates of conditions, indexing of arrays, etc.). Particular attention will be paid to the coverage elements that are examined in only one test.

Assessment of the Ability to Detect Defects. For this purpose the mutation approach is used. For each test case, the model mutations that this test case can detect will be identified. There is no need to generate set of separate models with mutations, instead, a global set of all typical model mutations will be automatically constructed in advance, after which the corresponding subset of killed mutants can be determined for each individual test scenario. For example, if an assignment statement in a test scenario results in a variable taking on a new value and reaches the corresponding observable output, then this means that a "missed assignment" mutation has been detected. Mutations in the preconditions are handled in a similar way: if a mutation makes a certain condition in the test scenario unsatisfiable, then such a mutation will be considered detected (the test will fail on it). As a result, a quantitative and qualitative assessment of the "defect detection ability" for each test case will be automatically obtained.

Assessment of Resource Consumption. In real-world systems, it is often necessary to take into account labor intensity of creating an appropriate test environment and the resources required to successfully complete the test. For example, it would be irrational to test the operation of an indicator while requiring many minutes of waiting for data to be displayed or for the vehicle to reach its maximum speed. This assessment should result in the identification of critical resources and where they are consumed.

Assessment of Data Cohesion. Among the most typical drawbacks of automatically generated tests is the weak data cohesion within the test scenario [1, 2, 8, 9]. Situations when some values are calculated but not used affects the readability of the test, the comprehension of its behavior, and the level of redundancy. In this regard, we propose to take into account the coverage of the data flow (both individual definition-usage pairs and certain chains of computations). In this case, a higher number of covered def-use pairs (or chains) will correspond to a higher coherence, and each case of 'unused assignment', on the contrary, will reduce this score. The estimates can be refined by selecting special points of interest and considering the data cohesion selectively.

Assessment of Test Overlap. An overlap score may not actually be a direct indication of a flaw in the test suite. Unevenness is often neglected, for example, in favor of reducing resource consumption, i.e., some area is frequently encountered because it bypasses resource-intensive paths irrelevant to the test goal. However, evenness of coverage is a desirable property [1, 8], which can be evaluated by simply collecting statistics on the coverage of lines across the entire test suite.

Explanation of Computation Histories in the Test Scenario. To investigate the computation history of a certain variable (with reference to the control flow), an SSA (Static Single Assignment) form of the model is primary built, based on which the dependencies of the data and control flow are analyzed using classical methods [13]. The explanation also includes reasons of unsatisfiability [14] for each condition adjacent to the scenario path. It should also be noted that the semantics of symbolic execution can specify constraints on a variable in a precondition, and in case of the equivalence (or inequality) classes encountered, a variable can acquire its value even without being contextually included in the precondition. For example, after the precondition (a==b), the variable b will get value 0 after the next execution of the condition (a==0). Such explanation process is similar to an advanced debugging mode, in which it is possible to move not only forward but also analyze causal relationships backwards, with hints on where the actual and potential changes in the values of the model variables are. Let us consider the example model shown in Fig. 3. It shows the model control flow graph with a highlighted path corresponding to the selected test scenario. The history of computations of the variable b will be described by the sequence {input b; a=b; b=0; b:=1; output b} including appropriate references to the locations of control flow graph.

Working with Loops. Since the scenario path has a certain limited length, it is possible to distinguish all executed iterations of loops as separate sections. So, it is possible to "collapse" all iterations into one (which will look like the corresponding part of the control flow graph), or "expand" certain individual iterations for their detailed study [14], for example, it is possible to separate the last iteration to analyze the exit condition in more detail.

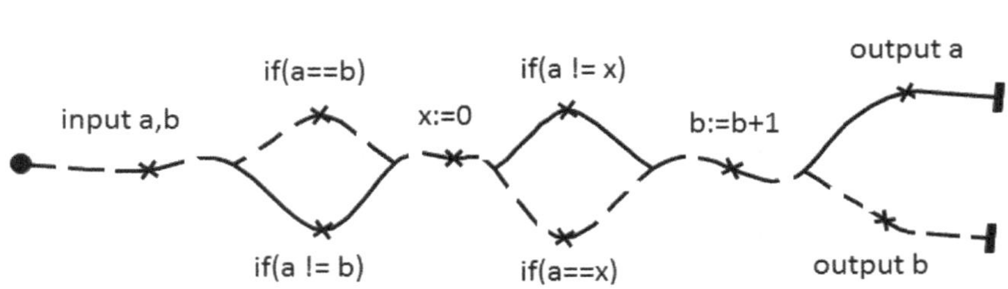

Fig. 3. Model control flow with a highlighted (dashed) test scenario path

4 Subjective Validation of the Test Scenario

The essence of this stage is visual control over the path of the test scenario, i.e., the sequence of operators (conditions, rules, actions) of the model. Particular attention should be paid to the unique coverage, i.e. those elements (requirements or properties) of the model that will be tested only in this scenario among the entire test suite. Such control is subjective [12] and is performed "manually" (the level of clarity, meaningfulness, readability [15] is determined), however the check for compliance with certain characteristics can be automated, for example, whether the effects of coverage become observable (reach the output signals). For reasons of brevity in visualizing the scenario, the "observables only" mode is useful, in which hammock folding of sections that do not include input-output signals is used. The analysis of the influence and dependence of individual statements is automated by building the appropriate slices (forward or backward). The number of scenario statements that do not belong to either the backward slice or the pre-dominator tree may be a signature of unnecessary actions in the test scenario with respect to the coverage of the selected point of interest. As a result, a certain quantitative assessment of the test can be made and areas that need editing can be located. If the score is unsatisfactory or if there are many areas for changes, then such a test can be omitted from the test suite, while information about the test objectives and the coverage elements achieved in it should be saved for further processing (or for restarting the generation).

5 Reconstruction of the Test Scenario

This section describes the methods for editing a test scenario. The need to make changes may be invoked due to shortcomings identified at previous stages, or changes in the source model during the project maintenance. In case of fully "manual" editing, there are problems in synchronizing related changes that need to be detected and computed anew, and also in updating information on related coverage elements. To solve these problems, an interactive trace constructor has been developed [16]. Its purpose is an automatic computations of the values of model variables throughout the history of the scenario and collection of information about the resulting coverage. Let us consider example of its work.

First, it's useful to fix the areas of the test scenario that should not be changed (due to unique coverage or other reasons). For them, we will build a combination of backward slices. As a result, we get an even larger number of "fixed" scenario statements that cannot be changed. But the rest of them can be edited without affecting important coverage. It is assumed that the sections that need to be replaced have already been identified, and then the feasibility of the corresponding alternatives, i.e. the fulfillment of other conditions on the branches, needs to be assessed. The fulfillment of all the conditions located on the branches adjacent to the selected scenario can be computed in the process of interactive work, as their set is limited with the length of the selected scenario. Next, the user will edit the scenario by selecting an admissible alternative (whose condition is marked as "enabled"). In this case, the scenario path will be divided into a prefix part (before the change) and a suffix part (the change itself and after it). The prefix part remains unchanged, and the suffix part will be automatically updated according to the impact of the changed condition. It should be noted that this change cannot be included in the "fixed" parts.

The situation in which changes are required to areas that belong to the backward slice is more complex and requires more user involvement. In the most difficult case, the user will accompany the selection of alternatives at branches along the entire path of the test scenario.

Example in Fig. 4 shows the updated path (dashed line) which avoids redundant (with respect to coverage of stmt2) wait discussed in Example 2. The change is possible because both (if and else) conditions on the first branching are enabled due to non-deterministic value of "access" parameter.

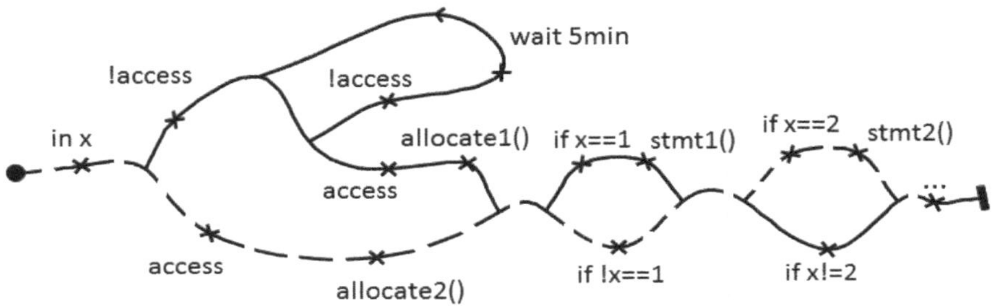

Fig. 4. Changed test scenario path (dashed)

During the evolution of the project, changes may require a corresponding update of the test suite. Even small changes raise the issue of synchronizing the computations affected by these changes in the existing test suite. With a simple approach, the whole test suite shall be re-generated on the updated model. However, there is a high risk of getting completely different test scenarios, because they are determined by the order of traversal of the model's behavior graph, and therefore, changing the alternative at the beginning of the unfolding can significantly affect the entire subsequent search. As a result, the entire stage of test suite validation and test environment creation will have to be repeated, which is an unreasonably time-consuming process. Therefore, the task of checking the suitability of previous tests is relevant. To do this, we will check the passage of the previous test scenario against the new model and point out each conflict that will be encountered for further resolution under the user's guidance.

6 Conclusions

The paper is devoted to automating the creation of tests and increasing their quality and efficiency. A method of interactive debugging of test scenarios and their validation is proposed. The role of the user in deciding whether to add a test case to the project test suite and make changes to it remains crucial, but to reduce labor intensity, the following processes are automated: evaluation of test scenarios according to certain objective characteristics (level of coverage, ability to detect defects, data cohesion, etc.); highlighting of possible alternatives for making corrections; consistent updating of computations for the corresponding corrections.

Unlike existing simulation methods (e.g. [17]), the proposed method not only informs about the values of variables, but also explores the history of their computations and additionally provides information about admissible alternatives and helps answer the questions like "why?" and "what if?".

A prototype was developed based on the proposed method. Its use in several pilot projects (in particular, for the modernization of legacy systems) allowed to prevent the loss of test suite generation results (the output of the test generator had problems similar to those described in examples 1 and 2) due to the ease of identifying coverage targets and the efficiency of editing scenarios. We believe that the described method can be a useful complement to various model-based test generation approaches.

References

1. Kolchin, A., Potiyenko, S., Weigert, T. Challenges for automated, model-based test scenario generation. In: Damaševičius, R., Vasiljevienė, G. (eds.) Information and Software Technologies, ICIST 2019. CCIS, vol. 1078, pp. 182–194. Springer, Cham (2019). https://doi.org/10.1007/978-3-030-30275-7_15
2. Kolchin, A., Potiyenko, S.: Extending data flow coverage to test constraint refinements. In: ter Beek, M.H., Monahan, R. (eds.) IFM 2022. LNCS, vol. 13274, pp. 313–321. Springer, Cham (2022). https://doi.org/10.1007/978-3-031-07727-2_17
3. Rushby, J.: Automated test generation and verified software. In: Meyer, B., Woodcock, J. (eds.) VSTTE 2005. LNCS, vol. 4171, pp. 161–172. Springer, Heidelberg (2008). https://doi.org/10.1007/978-3-540-69149-5_18
4. Dssouli, R., et al.: Testing the control-flow, data-flow, and time aspects of communication systems: a survey. Adv. Comput. **107**, 95–155 (2017)
5. Inozemtseva, L., Holmes, R.: Coverage is not strongly correlated with test suite effectiveness. In: Proceedings of the 36th International Conference on Software Engineering, pp. 435–445 (2014)
6. Gay, G., Staats, M., Whalen, M., Heimdahl, M.: The risks of coverage-directed test case generation. IEEE Trans. Softw. Eng. **41**, 803–819 (2015)
7. Staats, M., Gay, G., Whalen, M., Heimdahl, M.: On the danger of coverage directed test case generation. In: de Lara, J., Zisman, A. (eds.) FASE 2012. LNCS, vol. 7212, pp. 409–424. Springer, Heidelberg (2012). https://doi.org/10.1007/978-3-642-28872-2_28
8. Palomba, F., et al.: Automatic test case generation: what if test code quality matters? In: Proceedings of the 25th International Symposium on Software Testing and Analysis, pp. 130–141 (2016)
9. Meng, Y., Gay, G., Whalen, M.: Ensuring the observability of structural test obligations. IEEE Trans. Softw. Eng. **46**(7), 748–772 (2018)
10. Pérez, F., Font, J., Arcega, L., Cetina, C.: Empowering the human as the fitness function in search-based model-driven engineering. IEEE Trans. Softw. Eng. **48**(11), 4553–4568 (2022)
11. Ceccato, M., et al.: Do automatically generated test cases make debugging easier? An experimental assessment of debugging effectiveness and efficiency. ACM Trans. Softw. Eng. Methodol. **25**(1), 1–38 (2015). https://doi.org/10.1145/2768829
12. Lucrédio, D., Vincenzi, A., Almeida, E., Ahmed, I.: Test case quality: an empirical study on belief and evidence. arXiv:2307.06410 (2023)

13. Rastello, F., Tichadou, F.: SSA-Based Compiler Design, p. 382. Springer, Cham (2022). https://doi.org/10.1007/978-3-030-80515-9
14. Kolchin, A.V.: An automatic method for the dynamic construction of abstractions of states of a formal model. Cybern. Syst. Anal. **46**(4), 583–601 (2010). https://doi.org/10.1007/s10559-010-9235-9
15. Winkler, D., Urbanke, P., Ramler, R.: What do we know about readability of test code? - A systematic mapping study. In: IEEE International Conference on Software Analysis, Evolution and Reengineering (SANER), Honolulu, HI, USA, pp. 1167–1174 (2022)
16. Kolchin, A.: Interactive method for cumulative analysis of software formal models behavior. In: Proceeding of the 11th International Conference on Programming UkrPROG 2018, vol. 2139, pp. 115–123. CEUR-WS (2018)
17. Vu, F., Leuschel, M.: Validation of formal models by interactive simulation. In: Glässer, U., Creissac Campos, J., Méry, D., Palanque, P. (eds.) ABZ 2023. LNCS, vol. 14010, pp. 59–69. Springer, Cham (2023). https://doi.org/10.1007/978-3-031-33163-3_5

Energy Efficiency and Self-Adaptation

A Controlled Experiment on the Energy Efficiency of the Source Code Generated by Code Llama

Vlad-Andrei Cursaru, Laura Duits, Joel Milligan, Damla Ural, Berta Rodriguez Sanchez, Vincenzo Stoico(✉), and Ivano Malavolta

Department of Computer Science, Vrije Universiteit Amsterdam, Amsterdam, The Netherlands
{v.cursaru,v.stoico,i.malavolta}@vu.nl,
{l.b.m.duits,j.a.milligan,d.ural,b.rodriguezsanchez}@student.vu.nl

Abstract. *Context.* Large Language Models (LLMs) are now crucial for developers to increase productivity and reduce software development time and cost. Code Llama, an LLM from Meta, is one of the most recent LLM tools. However, currently there is no objective assessment of the energy efficiency of the source code generated by Code Llama.

Goal. In this paper, we present an empirical study that assesses the energy efficiency of the source code generated by Code Llama with respect to human-written source code.

Method. We design an experiment involving three human-written programming problems implemented in C++, JavaScript, and Python. We ask Code Llama to generate the code of the problems using different prompts and temperatures, which sets the predictability of the output of an LLM. Therefore, we execute both implementations and profile their energy efficiency.

Results. Our study shows that the energy efficiency of the code generated by Code Llama varies according to the chosen programming language and code characteristics. Human implementations tend to be more energy efficient overall, with generated JavaScript code outperforming its human counterpart. In addition, explicitly asking Code Llama to generate energy-efficient code results in an equal or worse energy efficiency, and using different temperatures does not seem to affect the energy efficiency of generated code.

Conclusions. According to our results, code generated using Code Llama does not guarantee energy efficiency, even when prompted to do so. Therefore, software developers should evaluate the energy efficiency of generated code before integrating it into the software system under development.

Keywords: Green Software · Large Language Model · Code Llama · Energy Consumption

A. Bertolino et al. (Eds.): QUATIC 2024, CCIS 2178, pp. 161–176, 2024.
https://doi.org/10.1007/978-3-031-70245-7_12

1 Introduction

The usage of AI tools in the development process has increased rapidly over the last few years. The annual developer survey of 2023 conducted by Stack Overflow [21] found that, amongst 90,000 developers and technologists, 44% are already using these AI tools. The majority of developers using AI tools (*i.e.,* 83%) indicate to use these tools to generate code [21]. *Large Language Models (LLMs)* are a specific category of generative AI tool that can assist developers write code. GitHub Copilot[1] is an LLM that generates code snippets based on the context provided by the user (*e.g.,* surrounding code and comments). Similarly, OpenAI's ChatGPT[2] is able to translate natural language to code. On August 24, 2023, Meta AI released its own LLM: Code Llama. Code Llama is a code-specific variant of the general-purpose Llama 2 model[3]. The training phase of LLaMA and Code LLaMA already produced about 1,015 tons of carbon emission (tCO2eq) [19] and 63.5 tCO2eq [17], respectively. The developers of LLaMA hope that releasing the models will reduce greenhouse gas emissions in the future because, due to their small size, they can run on less powerful hardware (*e.g.,* a single GPU), and, at the same time, there is no need to retrain them [19]. Nevertheless, the solutions generated by the LLaMA models may be energy-greedy and compromise the overall software quality, if integrated [15]. To the best of our knowledge, there is an existing research gap when it comes to the energy efficiency of code generated by Code Llama. The **goal** of this paper is to assess the *energy efficiency* of the source code generated using Code Llama. We design and execute an empirical study to answer three research questions:

RQ1: *How does the energy efficiency of the generated code compare against human implementations?* We select three programming problems implemented in three programming languages: C++, JavaScript, and Python. Afterwards, we ask Code Llama to generate a solution (*i.e.,* the source code) to the three problems in each language. Both the human-written and generated solutions are executed on a Raspberry Pi.

RQ2: *Can Code Llama improve the energy efficiency of code with prompting?* As shown in literature [8,9], other LLMs have proven able to resolve security vulnerabilities, repair bugs, and improve their code style if prompted to do so. Similarly, this question investigates whether Code Llama can refactor programs to improve their energy efficiency when prompted.

RQ3: *How does energy efficiency differ between different solutions generated from the same prompt?* With this research question, we evaluate the temperature, which is a parameter of the prompt that regulates the ability of the model to generate creative and novel outputs (*i.e.,* the randomness) [2,17]. Therefore, we consider the difference in energy efficiency of code variations generated from the same prompt at different levels of temperature.

---

[1] https://github.com/features/copilot/.
[2] https://chat.openai.com.
[3] https://www.llama2.ai/.

This work represents *the first empirical evaluation of the energy efficiency of code generated by Code Llama*. The **results** of our study show that the programming language and code characteristics have a significant influence on the energy efficiency of generated code. In addition, the considered human implementation counterpart resulted in more energy efficiency overall, with generated JavaScript code outperforming the corresponding human code. Moreover, explicitly asking Code Llama to generate energy-efficient code results in an equal or worse energy efficiency, as well as using different temperatures seems not to affect the energy efficiency of the generated code. In summary, the main **contributions** of this paper are: (i) an *empirical assessment* of the energy efficiency of source code generated by Code Llama against human-written source code, (ii) an in-depth *discussion* of the implications of obtained results, and (iii) the *replication package* of the study including the prompts used to generate the code, the implementations of the programming problems, and the scripts for orchestrating the experiments, as well as raw data, and data analysis scripts [1].

2 Experiment Planning

2.1 Subjects Selection

To evaluate the energy efficiency of code generated by Code Llama, we select three programming problems and compared the solutions to the problems generated by Code Llama against the corresponding human implementation. We use three simple programming problems, as Code Llama, at the time of writing, has been shown more likely to generate correct code for simple problems. Roziere et al. [17] demonstrate that Code Llama generates correctly more than half of the HumanEval benchmark [4], which mostly includes simple problems, such as generating pseudo-random integers, converting an integer to its Roman numeral equivalent, and replacing all the spaces of a string with underscores. In addition, as reported by Rasnayaka et al. [16], LLMs can be particularly useful for creating *basic* design patterns, data structures, and algorithms.

We select the problems according to three characteristics that can impact software energy usage: CPU-bound, memory-bound, and I/O-bound. Diversifying the characteristics of subjects can help identify those aspects that could potentially influence energy consumption and optimize them before execution. In addition, Code Llama might only know optimizations for specific characteristics, e.g., loop unrolling for CPU-bound implementations. Problems that are CPU-bound are heavily energy-consuming as they require the CPU to work harder over a longer period of time [7]. One example of such a problem is Closest Numbers (CN), which determines the pairs with the smallest absolute difference. The solution considered for CN involves iterating over a list of numbers and, in every step, calculating the absolute difference of a different pair in the list. This task is time-consuming, especially if the initial list is unsorted. We picked one of the implementations of CN provided by HackerRank[4].

[4] https://www.hackerrank.com/challenges/closest-numbers/problem.

Our set of subjects includes Two Sum (TS), which requires the program to find the two elements in a given array of size n that make the sum $(x + y) == k$ for a given number k. TS is CPU-bound and it complexity depends on the implementation. The human implementation of TS is taken from LeetCode[5]. As third problem, we chose a typical memory- and I/O-bound problem referred, in this paper, as String Replacement (SR). SR executes three steps: (i) reading the content of a file, (ii) searching for a given string, and (iii) replacing it with a new one. The computational complexity of SR depends on the size of the input file. As for the other problems, we found the human implementation of SR, in Python and JavaScript, on gray literature[6],[7]. Whereas, the C++ version was implemented by master's degree students in computer science.

2.2 Experiment Design

All our research questions investigate aspects impacting the energy consumption per execution, which is measured in millijoules (mJ), of a specific problem implementation. Our independent variables include implementation-specific characteristics and variables influencing the code generation process. We vary the *source code* of the considered problems, which can be generated or human-written. Further, we analyze the same problem written in three *programming languages*: C++, JavaScript, and Python. In fact, a model might be more adept at generating energy efficient code for a specific language because of how it has been trained. Therefore, we vary the language. These languages are chosen according to the results of Pereira et al. [14] and exhibit different energy efficiency: high, medium, and low, respectively. Moreover, these languages are among the most popular ones[8].

For RQ2 and RQ3, we analyze factors related to the code generation process. These factors include the *prompt* provided to Code Llama and the *temperature* used. We use a prompt to generate the code for each problem (*i.e.*, TS, CN, and SR) and another one to get the energy-optimized version. For example, assuming we want to generate a program that prints the string `''Hello World!''` in Python and its energy-optimized version. Therefore, we supply Code Llama with the prompt: "Write a program that prints *'Hello World!'* in Python" and its energy-optimized version: "Write a program that prints 'Hello World!' in Python. Make the code as energy-efficient as possible". We evaluate three different temperature values: 0.6, 0.8, and 1.0, representing low to high randomness. This study is designed as *multiple factor, multiple treatment* (MF-MT) since it involves four different factors and multiple treatments for each factor. The above-described independent variables correspond to the factors in our experiment. The experiment follows a *full-coverage factorial design* to ensure that we

---

[5] https://leetcode.com/problems/two-sum/solutions/4082514/98-21-hashmap-time-complexity-1-line-code/.

[6] https://www.geeksforgeeks.org/how-to-search-and-replace-text-in-a-file-in-python/.

[7] https://attacomsian.com/blog/nodejs-replace-string-in-file.

[8] According to the TIOBE index of October 2023.

cover every combination of each factor. Thus, the total number of trials is equal to 3 programming languages × 3 temperatures × 2 prompts × 3 algorithms. We used Mann-Whitney test to compare independent samples collected to answer RQ1 and RQ2, namely varying source code and prompt, and Kruskal-Wallis test to assess statistical significance of changing the temperature level (RQ3).

3 Experiment Execution

We execute all the implementations of the programming problems on a Raspberry Pi, whereas we generate the code and, therefore, deploy Code Llama on a personal computer (PC) (*i.e.,* the orchestrator).

The energy consumption of the Raspberry Pi is monitored using a Monsoon Power Monitor [12]. The Monsoon Power Monitor is a physical power meter that measures the energy requested by the Raspberry Pi at a given frequency.

The three devices are connected through USB 2.0 cables. Figure 1 shows the experimental setting used in this study. We decided to use a PC for code generation since it greatly outperforms the Raspberry Pi, speeding up the process. Instead, we use a Raspberry Pi for the energy measures due to its simpler architecture, which allows for a more controllable testbed. For example, due to the absence of a GPU on the Raspberry Pi, we did not consider any GPU-related optimizations for this experiment (this is left for future work).

The orchestrator includes a Ryzen 5 7600X processor, 32 GB of DDR5 RAM running at 5600 MHz, and an RTX 3060 12 GB GPU. The code is generated using the *CodeLlama-7b-instruct* model [11], running on Ubuntu 22.04 WSL. We select the version with 7 billion parameters due to the limited computational resources of the orchestrator. In addition, we chose the instruct model as it is optimized for natural language processing for code generation [17]. Indeed, more powerful LLMs require more computation resources, such as multiple GPUs [22]. The orchestrator machine runs Experiment Runner [18], which is a framework that facilitates setting up an experiment including pre-experiment actions, number of trials, and start/stop conditions for energy measures. The orchestrator issues commands to the Raspberry Pi via HTTP on a local network and gathers energy measures collected by the Monsoon Power Monitor via USB.

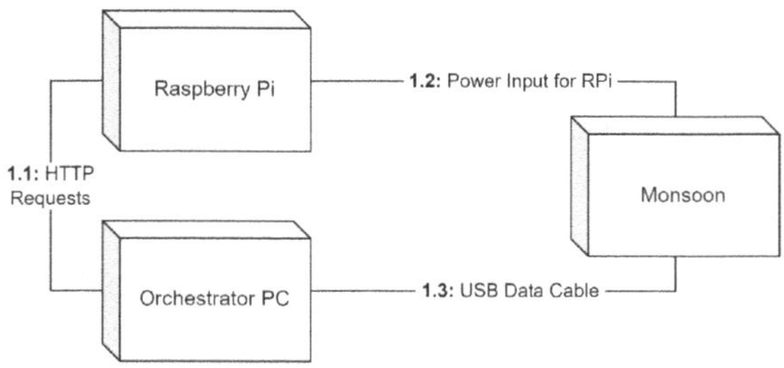

Fig. 1. Experimental Setting

Before the execution of the experiment, we install on the Raspberry Pi all the tools and libraries required to run all the implementations of each programming problem. We use C++ `20`, Python `3.92`, Javascript `18.18.2`. We compile the C++ code directly on the Raspberry Pi before the execution phase to avoid compatibility issues with the operating system and libraries on the Raspberry Pi. We generate a total of 54 programs using the `src/instruction-runner.py` script available in the replication package [1]. Code is generated in separate runs according to the considered treatments. The prompts used to generate the solutions for the programming problems can be found in the `study_prompts.txt` file of the replication package [1]. Each implementation is executed using a single input leading to the worst case execution scenario of the problem. In such a way, we consider the case that could potentially consume more energy. The output of each program execution is checked manually to assess the correctness of the code. The experiment is started by Experiment Runner, which configures the Monsoon Power Monitor, starts/stops recordings, executes the source code under analysis, and stores energy measures in a CSV file. These steps are repeated for all combinations of languages, algorithms, temperatures, and executions resulting in $3 \cdot 3 \cdot 3 \cdot 30 = 810$ CSV files for Code Llama-generated code, and $3 \cdot 3 \cdot 30 = 270$ CSVs for the human code. Therefore, these files are parsed and averaged to obtain the mean energy efficiency for the combinations of the aforementioned factors. To answer RQ2, we investigate whether Code Llama can enhance the energy efficiency of its responses when specifically prompted to produce energy-efficient source code. Thus, we append to the prompts the sentence: *"Make the code as energy-efficient as possible"* to explicitly request Code Llama to generate an energy-efficient version of the source code. After restructuring the prompts, we re-run the experiment. This resulted in 810 additional runs. After collecting the new energy measures, we compare them with the results obtained from executing the code generated using the first version of the prompts. We include a 1-second cooling down period between each run to mitigate the influence that the execution of a run might have on the following one. In addition, we use the Monsoon Power Monitor to retrieve 5000 measurements per run and increase the accuracy of observed energy consumption values. The data collection process took a total of *36 h*.

4 Results

This section reports results aimed at answering the research questions outlined in Sect. 1. Table 1 and Table 2 presents the overall results for generated and human code, respectively. Therefore, the energy consumption values measured varying problems, prompts, programming languages, and temperatures.

4.1 RQ1: How Does the Energy Efficiency of the Generated Code Compare Against Human Implementations?

Figure 2a compares energy consumption between generated and human code across different programming languages. As the energy consumption dataset

Table 1. Descriptive statistics of the energy consumption (mJ) of Code Llama-generated code.

Closest Numbers																		
Prompt	Basic									Efficient								
Lang.	**C++**			**JS**			**Py**			**C++**			**JS**			**Py**		
Temp	0.6	0.8	1.0	0.6	0.8	1.0	0.6	0.8	1.0	0.6	0.8	1.0	0.6	0.8	1.0	0.6	0.8	1.0
Mean	6.0	5.9	5.9	1.3	1.3	1.4	229.7	232.1	227.9	4.0	6.3	6.3	3.4	3.4	3.4	237.3	232.6	230.0
SD	0.5	0.2	0.2	0.1	0.1	0.5	13.0	13.1	7.9	0.8	0.1	0.1	0.1	0.3	0.2	43.9	17.0	10.9
Min	5.6	5.6	5.6	1.2	1.2	1.2	214.8	216.2	216.7	3.6	6.1	6.1	3.2	3.1	3.2	215.0	211.8	214.8
Med	5.8	5.8	5.9	1.3	1.3	1.3	225.9	229.2	227. 2	3.8	6.3	6.3	3.4	3.3	3.4	230.1	230.3	229.5
Max	7.7	6.2	6.3	1.8	1.6	4.1	270.2	287.7	248.3	6.8	6.8	6.5	3.7	4.8	3.9	461.0	305.4	268.4
CV	8.2	2.7	2.9	11.4	8.9	38.0	5.7	5.7	3.5	18.9	2.1	1.5	3.5	8.6	5.0	18.5	7.3	4.8
Two Sum																		
Prompt	Basic									Efficient								
Lang.	**C++**			**JS**			**Py**			**C++**			**JS**			**Py**		
Temp.	0.6	0.8	1.0	0.6	0.8	1.0	0.6	0.8	1.0	0.6	0.8	1.0	0.6	0.8	1.0	0.6	0.8	1.0
Mean	41.4	35.6	35.7	1.2	1.2	1.1	367.5	401.6	397.8	0.1	0.2	0.2	1.3	1.3	1.3	432.3	434.2	435.4
SD	0.6	13.1	13.1	0.6	0.4	0.4	133.8	64.1	63.0	0.0	0.1	0.1	0.1	0.1	0.2	9.3	10.1	34.6
Min	40.4	0.13	0.13	0.1	0.1	0.1	0.1	283.2	283.7	0.1	0.1	0.1	1.1	1.1	1.1	423.3	424.3	423.6
Med.	41.4	41.5	41.7	1.2	1.2	1.2	426.5	427.8	427.0	0.1	0.1	0.1	1.2	1.2	1.2	429.0	430.6	427.8
Max	43.2	43.6	43.5	3.5	1.5	1.6	451.1	476.7	472.6	0.3	0.6	0.6	1.7	1.6	1.7	462.2	460.3	615.7
CV	1.4	36.8	36.7	47.3	31.8	32.0	36.4	16.0	15.8	25.6	58.8	57.1	11.6	10.3	12.0	2.1	2.3	7.9
String Replacement																		
Prompt	Basic									Efficient								
Lang.	**C++**			**JS**			**Py**			**C++**			**JS**			**Py**		
Temp.	0.6	0.8	1.0	0.6	0.8	1.0	0.6	0.8	1.0	0.6	0.8	1.0	0.6	0.8	1.0	0.6	0.8	1.0
Mean	8.3	7.7	7.7	12.6	12.7	12.6	14.3	12.0	11.9	7.7	7.7	7.7	12.6	12.6	12.6	20.2	20.1	34.3
SD	2.7	0.1	0.2	0.2	0.4	0.3	1.7	0.3	0.2	0.1	0.2	0.1	0.3	0.2	0.4	1.9	1.3	0.5
Min	7.5	7.5	7.5	12.2	12.0	12.0	13.5	11.6	11.6	7.5	7.5	7.5	11.9	12.0	12.0	19.6	19.7	33.8
Med.	7.7	7.7	7.7	12.6	12.6	12.6	14.0	11.9	11.9	7.7	7.7	7.6	12.6	12.6	12.6	19.9	19.9	34.2
Max	22.0	8.0	8.1	13.0	12.8	13.7	23.2	13.3	12.4	8.0	8.1	7.9	13.1	13.0	14.1	30.0	26.8	36.1
CV	32.1	1.7	2.1	1.4	2.9	2.4	11.9	2.5	1.5	1.2	2.0	1.5	2.1	1.7	3.0	9.2	6.3	1.3

Legend - Py: Python, JS: Javascript, Lang: Language, Temp.: Temperature, SD: Standard Deviation, CV: Coefficient of Variation, Med: Median

Table 2. Descriptive statistics of the energy consumption (mJ) for the human implementations.

Alg.	CN			TS			SR		
Lang.	**C++**	**JS**	**Py**	**C++**	**JS**	**Py**	**C++**	**JS**	**Py**
Mean	0.2	1.6	0.4	0.4	1.5	0.7	8.0	13.8	11.9
SD	0.11	0.10	0.04	0.04	0.13	0.05	0.22	0.29	0.49
Min	0.13	1.47	0.39	0.38	1.36	0.67	7.83	13.06	11.30
Med	0.15	1.56	0.41	0.42	1.50	0.76	8.00	13.80	11.85
Max	0.60	1.90	0.62	0.52	1.86	0.95	9.07	14.48	13.63
CV	60.8	6.2	10.4	9.1	8.6	7.3	2.7	2.1	4.1

Legend - Py: Python, JS: Javascript, Lang: Language, SD: Standard Deviation, CV: Coefficient of Variation, Med: Median

Table 3. Energy consumption difference between initial and optimized generated code.

Lang.	**Δ CN**	**Δ TS**	**Δ SR**
C++	-0.374	-37.408	-0.2
JS	2.043	0.095	-0.013
Py	3.381	45.019	12.154

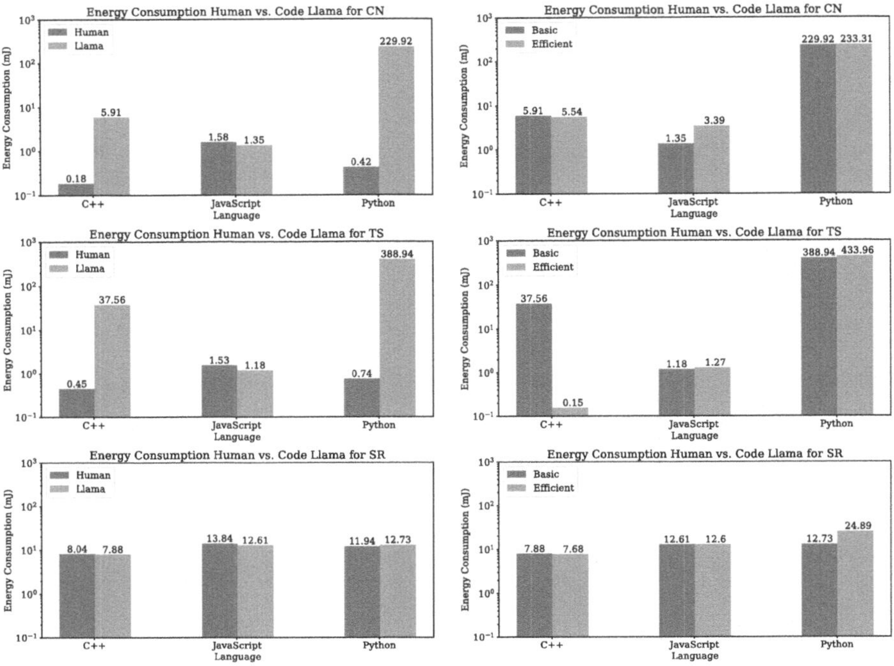

(a) Average energy consumption of human and generated code (in log scale).

(b) Average energy consumption of code generated using basic and energy-efficient prompts (in log scale).

Fig. 2. Comparison of energy consumed by human-written versus generated code

presents a wide range of values, the y-axis in Fig. 2 is logarithmically scaled. To answer RQ1, we analyze the measurements obtained from executing the implementations generated while varying temperatures. Implementations generated using energy-optimized prompts are excluded for this analysis. In our experiment, Code Llama produced more energy efficient JavaScript code. Indeed, the generated JavaScript code consumed less energy than its human counterpart for CN, TS, and SR. As can be seen in Table 1 and Table 2, the difference between the energy consumption of the human implementation in Javascript of the three problems is similar compared with the generated one in the basic case. The C++ and Python human implementations for CN and TS are more energy-efficient than the generated ones. There is no significant difference in energy consumption between different SR implementations. As opposed to CN and TS, the generated code outperformed the human code for C++ and JavaScript. On the contrary, the human implementation in Python proved to be more energy efficient. Table 1 and Table 2 show a significant difference in the energy efficiency of the human-written code compared to the generated one. This difference is prominent, especially for the Python implementations of TS, namely 0.7 mJ spent by the human implementation versus the 401.6 mJ spent by the generated counterpart. Overall, the results of RQ1 indicate that the code generated by Code Llama tends to consume more energy with respect to the corresponding human implementation. However, the JavaScript implementations of the three problems generated by Code Llama turned out to be more energy-efficient.

We applied the Mann-Whitney non-parametric test to compare two independent samples, which, in this case, are the energy consumption data from the human-written code and Code Llama-generated code. The p-values suggest that, for the problems and programming languages considered in this study, we can reject the null hypothesis. Thus, there is one group (*i.e.*, human-written or generated code) that has higher energy consumption values. Since we can reject the null hypothesis, we compute the effect size estimation with Cliff's delta [10]. The Cliff's delta estimates are all close to 1 or -1. Therefore, there is a large effect size between generated code and human-written code.

4.2 RQ2: Can Code Llama Improve the Energy Efficiency of Code with Prompting?

To answer RQ2, we compared the energy consumption of the implementations generated with the initial prompt to those resulting from asking Code Llama an energy-efficient version of a problem implementation. As described in Sect. 3, we added the sentence: "Make the code as energy-efficient as possible" to ask Code Llama an energy-efficient version of the problems. Table 3 shows that the prompt has little impact on the implementation of CN. The maximum difference is obtained for Python (*i.e.*, 3.381 mJ). Figure 2b shows more detailed results. Indeed, it shows that in *most of the cases* the energy-optimized generated code *consumes similar amount of energy as the original code*. The results show that Code Llama is successful in generating energy-optimized code for the C++ implementations of CN and TS. In the latter, the difference is significant as can be seen in Table 1. However, since this is a single case this result could be accidental. In the other cases, the energy consumption variation is not significant. Overall the energy-efficient version of Python and JavaScript code results in a worse energy consumption.

The Mann-Whitney non-parametric test is applied to compare independent samples consisting of the energy consumption data for the original and the energy-optimized generated code. The p-values show that in some cases, such as for the TS prompt in JavaScript, there is not enough evidence to reject the null hypothesis. On the other hand, there are also cases, such as the CN prompt in JavaScript, where the null hypothesis can be rejected, which suggests that either the original or the improved version of the code had higher values for energy consumption. In this case, we do not compute the effect size estimation because there are instances where we could not reject the null hypothesis.

4.3 RQ3: How Does Energy Efficiency Differ Between Different Solutions Generated from the Same Prompt?

We observe that the temperature does not have a significant effect on the energy consumption. Specifically, for CN, we observe that having different temperatures does not change the energy consumption significantly. The results for TS show that there is not a significant difference for JavaScript and Python. However, we observe that the energy consumption at 0.6 temperature for C++ is slightly higher compared to the other two temperatures. For SR, Python performed slightly worse at 0.6 than the other temperatures, while JavaScript and C++ exhibit similar values. All the values are provided by Table 1.

We applied the Kruskal-Wallis non-parametric test. It determines whether there are statistically significant differences between the energy consumption at different temperature values: 0.6, 0.8, and 1.0. Only the SR prompt in Python led to enough evidence to reject the null hypothesis. For all other cases, the p-values prove that there is not enough evidence to reject the null hypothesis. We do not compute the effect size estimation because, in most cases, we could not reject the null hypothesis. The p-values of the Kruskal-Wallis test, as well as those resulting from the statistical tests discussed for the RQ1 and RQ2, can be found in the replication package in the R Data Analysis/p_values.txt file [1].

5 Discussion

5.1 Reflections on the Obtained Results

To provide for a meaningful interpretation of the data, we analyse the results presented in Sect. 4 according to our three pairs of hypotheses. The first research question (*RQ1*) focuses on the comparison between code generated by Code Llama, and human implementations. While there appears to be a significant difference between the energy efficiency of code generated by Code Llama and the code implementations provided by humans, *neither consistently outperforms the other.* Moreover, we reported similar findings for *RQ2*: when comparing the energy consumption difference between the initial Code Llama implementation and the explicitly requested energy-efficient solution, Code Llama's ability to effectively generate efficient code varies on a case-by-case basis, depending on the language and algorithm, as well as the used prompt. *We speculate that this could be attributed to the quality and quantity of code examples for each language present in the model training data.* The model is trained "predominantly on a near-deduplicated dataset of publicly available code" [17], including questions and answers from forums. Such public code repositories are unlikely to enforce strict quality requirements on the code being shared, which we believe is likely to affect the outputs of the model as well.

Code Llama provides the possibility of adjusting the temperature of the models. However, from the results of *RQ3*, it appears that this only affects the solutions generated for the SR problem in Python. More specifically, the solution generated by a temperature of 0.6 deviates from the other two. A lower temperature affects the predictability of the solution generated by the model. With lower temperature values, the model tends to select more probable tokens more often. Therefore, this result indicates that the SR prompt may be misleading the model. The prompt explicitly states "consider that the files can be too large to fit in memory", which might be too specific, thus resulting in an inefficient implementation of the problem. In general, the Python solutions resulted in higher energy consumption. This is in line with the results from Pereira *et al.* [14], who ranked Python as one of the most energy-consuming languages. Nevertheless, there is a significant difference between the energy efficiency of solutions generated by Code Llama versus the solutions provided by humans. Therefore, the energy consumption cannot be fully attributed to the programming language, but also partially to the model. Meta also provides a version of Code Llama specifically for Python, which could potentially result in more energy-efficient solutions. This is an avenue for further research.

Figure 2a shows that the JavaScript code generated by Code Llama is more efficient for all the problems considered. This may depend on how Code Llama was trained, which may be more informed about specific types of languages and coding style. Indeed, the problems utilised in this study are either CPU-bound, I/O-bound and memory-bound. These characteristics can influence the results as the energy efficiency depends on the coding style, and therefore how the hardware is used by the software. For example, devices with less efficient CPUs will be affected more strongly by an inefficient CPU-bound workload. Similarly, slower memory may increase the runtime of the program in memory-intensive benchmarks and, as such, the overall power consumption. Furthermore, the results in Table 3 *show that explicitly asking Code Llama to generate energy-efficient code does not bring any optimization in the generated code.* Code Llama generates code that implements the desired functionality, but, considering our results, it does not appear to be able to generate energy-efficient code or optimize the energy consumption of the code it generates. In some cases, generated code is even worse than human-written code. **Further experiments are needed to clarify this aspect.**

5.2 Implications for Developers and Organizations

According to the results of our experiment, **it is important that developers are aware that the source code generated by Code LLaMA might not be as energy-efficient as human-generated source code**. While the models can generate correct code, this research shows that the energy efficiency of the resulting programs is inconsistent across different languages and tasks. As such, taking the generated code at face value may provide sub-optimal results. We would like to stress that we are not suggesting avoiding using LLMs altogether for development purposes. Nevertheless, **we urge developers to adopt a critical mindset regarding the efficiency of LLM-generated source code and its potential runtime impact**, encompassing not only energy efficiency but also other quality attributes such as performance, security, and reliability. In software projects where energy efficiency is of prime importance, LLM-generated source code can be used as a starting point for carrying out a programming task in an initial prototypical phase of the software product being realized; such source code can then be optimized via further iterations, at best after an empirical assessment of its energy efficiency.

Given the widespread traction that LLMs are gaining as tools for supporting development activities [21], we invite LLMs maintainers to promote energy efficiency as a first-class feature to be considered during the training phases of their LLMs. The European Union is actively working towards promoting and adopting measures towards achieving climate-neutral datacenters and communication networks and services by 2030, with an explicit mention of including "software-related efforts such as intelligent energy-saving functions", in addition to the various improvements at the hardware and infrastructural levels [3]. By prioritizing energy efficiency as a fundamental aspect in their reasoning processes when recommending source code to developers, LLMs can significantly contribute to turning this strategic vision into reality.

6 Threats to Validity

The aim of our study was to investigate the energy efficiency of Code Llama-generated code. In this section, we present the threats to validity that our study poses, divided into the four categories as defined by Cook and Campbell [5].

Internal Validity: to ensure more accurate energy consumption results, 5000 measurements were taken per second, and the mean of 30 runs was used to mitigate data fluctuations. A Monsoon Power Monitor was used to measure power usage, and running the code on a Raspberry Pi helped mitigate background process interference. However, consecutive runs and temperature accumulation could still affect the results, so a 1-second cooldown period was implemented. However, the duration of the cooldown period could not be enough to cool the Raspberry Pi and, therefore, it poses a threat to internal validity. In addition, the selection of the implementation of the human-written code can be a threat to internal validity as it could result in optimized code. Despite this threat, Code Llama was able to generate more efficient code in some cases.

External Validity: the characteristics of the chosen programming problems pose a threat to external validity. Indeed, each problem can be implemented with specific characteristics in mind, such as readability or modularity, and that can influence energy efficiency. We mitigated this threat by choosing simple problems and by choosing human-written implementations that can be written by novice software developers. This choice is made to increase the probability of considering code with similar characteristics and obtaining the correct code from Code Llama. In addition, we evaluate code written in only three programming languages. The specific languages were selected based on their energy efficiency level and popularity. While the respective languages represent the high, middle, and low energy-efficient languages as found by [14], the popularity factor limits the generalisability of the findings. There is more data available on these popular languages in comparison to lesser-known languages such as TypeScript[9]. Due to this imbalance of data, the Code Llama models will be limited in the solutions it could provide for those so-called "unpopular" languages, making our results non-representative for this group. Nevertheless, we argue that popularity is still a good factor for selecting languages as these popular languages are widely used by all kinds of software developers.

Construction Validity: the input of the programming problems is a variable that can affect the results. This study considers only one input corresponding to the one leading to the worst-case execution scenario. Since this study only considers one input per problem, there is a threat to construct validity. For a complete comparison, there is a need to consider multiple inputs that could trigger different execution flows and thus different energy and performance values.

Conclusion Validity: we execute 30 runs to ensure a sufficient sample size. Nevertheless, due to the non-normal distribution of some of the data samples, it was not possible to use the *t-test* for RQ1 and RQ2 nor the *ANOVA* test for RQ3. Therefore, we chose the *Mann-Whitney* for the former and the *Kruskall-Wallis* test for the latter instead. The results show that the energy efficiency of Code Llama-generated code is heavily influenced by the specific programming languages utilised, as well the specific problem characteristics. While the p-values all indicate rejection of the null hypothesis of RQ1, the results for the statistical tests conducted for RQ2 and RQ3 are conflicting. Therefore, the conclusions with respect to these research questions are more specific to the individual cases and thus pose a threat to conclusion validity. However, these results provide important insights into the influence of the programming language and prompt on the energy efficiency of code generated by Code Llama.

7 Related Work

Several studies have analysed AI-generated code, investigating security [8,13], correctness [9], code quality [9], runtime performance [6], among others. The investigation conducted by Vartziotis *et al.* [20] focuses on quantifying the quality of code generated by Open AI's ChatGPT, GitHub CoPilot, and Amazon CodeWhisperer. The authors introduce a multi-property metric called Green Capacity (GC) that expresses the eventual improvements in code quality. The GC considers the improvement in energy efficiency, runtime, memory usage, and floating-point operations (FLOPs). The experiment involves six programming problems implemented in Python and taken from LeetCode. The goal of Vartziotis *et al.* aligns with the objective of this work, we consider CodeLlama as LLM and problems implemented in different programming languages, namely Python, Javascript, and C++. To the best of our knowledge, *there are no works targeting the energy consumption of code generated by Code Llama.* This section presents an overview of the works analyzing code generated by LLMs.

[9] According to the Tiobe list of languages.

Khoury *et al.* [8] conducted an experiment to evaluate the security of programs generated by ChatGPT.The experiment involved ChatGPT generating 21 programs in five different programming languages, followed by an evaluation of the resulting code. The findings suggest that ChatGPT is able to identify potential vulnerabilities if prompted, but often provides insecure code. The research conducted by Pearce *et al.* [13] is related to Khoury *et al.* as both assess the security of code generated by GitHub Copilot. Pearce et al. established 89 scenarios based on the CWE list and 3 programming languages: Python, C, and Verilog, resulting in 1,689 programs. The vulnerability of the generated code was assessed using CodeQL and manual inspection, revealing that 41% of the programs completed by Copilot were deemed vulnerable. Similarly, like Pearce et al. and Khoury *et al.*, this research also considers multiple code options, provided by Llama, but focuses on analyzing the energy efficiency instead of vulnerabilities.

Liu *et al.* [9] investigate the quality of the code produced by ChatGPT, with regards to both its code generation performance, in terms of functional correctness, and the quality of the generated code. They achieve this by prompting ChatGPT3.5-March23 to generate solutions to 2,033 LeetCode questions, in both Python and Java. The authors found that 66% of the Python solutions and 69% of the Java solutions were functionally correct following the first prompt. However, the authors noted that the model performance dropped nearly five-fold on problems released after the dataset was collected, hinting at the fact that some of the prior questions might have been contained within the training set, offering the model an advantage. In terms of quality, 53% of the Java programs and 35% of the Python programs contained code style issues, code smells, or similar bad practices. An additional finding is that the model was able to resolve between 20% and 60% of issues itself when asked to do so. This work differs from this paper in two main aspects. Firstly, LLaMA is used in place of ChatGPT for code generation. Secondly, while [9] investigates the correctness of the programs and the overall quality of the code, the present paper investigates the energy efficiency of the resulting algorithms.

Erhabor *et al.* [6] evaluate Github Copilot in terms of runtime performance. It presents a user study involving 32 participants who were tasked with solving two C++ programming problems, one with the assistance of Copilot and the other without it. The results indicate that using Copilot may lead to significantly slower runtime performance. This related paper also highlights the potential trade-off between using Copilot for code generation, which may improve developers' productivity but has limitations when it comes to runtime performance. While [6] primarily focuses on runtime performance, this study examines the impact of LLaMA's generated code on energy efficiency.

8 Conclusions

This work presents the first investigation of the energy efficiency of Code Llama-generated code. We compared the energy efficiency of generated code against the corresponding human-written implementation. We evaluated three programming problems considering their implementation in C++, Python, and Javascript. In addition, we considered variations of the prompts used to generate the code. We explicitly asked Code Llama to generate energy-efficient code and regulate the temperature, namely the randomness of the output generated by Code Llama. We did not find a clear-cut answer to comparing generated code versus human-written code. In most cases, the one written by humans was more energy efficient. In addition, we noticed that, in our case, explicitly asking for an energy-efficient version of the implementation does not affect the energy efficiency of the generated code.

Our contribution to the field of energy measurement of AI-generated code consists of an *initial* analysis of Code Llama-generated code. This study could be further improved with a larger set of data; *i.e.,* more algorithms ran in additional languages which we were not able to include in this paper and more inputs to further stress the considered algorithms. Furthermore, as mentioned before, this paper has been limited by only being able to run the smallest 7B model of Code Llama [11]. Given more resources, the research would be further improved by generating code with the other available models, such as the larger instruction-based models, the code-completion models, or the Python-specific models. Finally, a deeper investigation of the prompt is needed. The prompts can include more details, such as developer experience and hardware specification, to improve the energy efficiency of generated code as well as more parameters, *e.g.,* top-k and top-p.

Acknowledgements. This project has received funding from the European COST program under the action identifier CA19135 (CERCIRAS).

References

1. Replication package of this study. https://github.com/S2-group/quatic-2024-code-llama-energy-gen-code-rep-pkg
2. Amazon: Code llama code generation models from meta are now available via amazon sagemaker jumpstart (2023). https://aws.amazon.com/blogs/machine-learning/code-llama-code-generation-models-from-meta-are-now-available-via-amazon-sagemaker-jumpstart/
3. Bilsen, V., et al.: Study on greening cloud computing and electronic communications services and networks (2022)
4. Chen, M., et al.: Evaluating large language models trained on code (2021). https://arxiv.org/abs/2107.03374
5. Cook, T., Campbell, D.: Quasi-experimentation: Design & Analysis Issues for Field Settings. Houghton Mifflin, Boston (1979)
6. Erhabor, D., Udayashankar, S., Nagappan, M., Al-Kiswany, S.: Measuring the runtime performance of code produced with github copilot (2023). https://arxiv.org/abs/2305.06439
7. Etinski, M., Corbalán, J., Labarta, J., Valero, M.: Understanding the future of energy-performance trade-off via DVFS in HPC environments. J. Parallel Distrib. Comput. **72**(4), 579–590 (2012)

8. Khoury, R., Avila, A.R., Brunelle, J., Camara, B.M.: How secure is code generated by chatgpt? In: 2023 IEEE International Conference on Systems, Man, and Cybernetics (SMC), pp. 2445–2451. IEEE (2023)
9. Liu, Y., et al.: Refining ChatGPT-generated code: characterizing and mitigating code quality issues. ACM Trans. Softw. Eng. Methodol. (2023)
10. Macbeth, G., Razumiejczyk, E., Ledesma, R.D.: Cliff's delta calculator: a non-parametric effect size program for two groups of observations. Universitas Psychologica **10**(2), 545–555 (2011)
11. Meta: Code Llama GitHub Repository (2024). https://github.com/meta-llama/codellama/tree/main
12. Monsoon Solutions: Monsoon power monitor. https://www.msoon.com/. Accessed 26 Sept 2021
13. Pearce, H., Ahmad, B., Tan, B., Dolan-Gavitt, B., Karri, R.: Asleep at the keyboard? assessing the security of github copilot's code contributions. In: 2022 IEEE Symposium on Security and Privacy (SP), pp. 754–768. IEEE (2022)
14. Pereira, R., et al.: Energy efficiency across programming languages: how do energy, time, and memory relate? In: Proceedings of the 10th ACM SIGPLAN International Conference on Software Language Engineering, pp. 256–267 (2017)
15. Perry, N., Srivastava, M., Kumar, D., Boneh, D.: Do users write more insecure code with AI assistants? In: Proceedings of the 2023 ACM SIGSAC Conference on Computer and Communications Security, pp. 2785–2799 (2023)
16. Rasnayaka, S., Wang, G., Shariffdeen, R., Iyer, G.N.: An empirical study on usage and perceptions of LLMs in a software engineering project (2024). https://arxiv.org/abs/2401.16186
17. Roziere, B., et al.: Code llama: open foundation models for code (2023). https://arxiv.org/abs/2401.16186
18. Software and Sustainability Group, Vrije Universiteit Amsterdam: Experiment Runner: a Framework to automatically execute measurement-based experiments on any platform (2023). https://github.com/S2-group/experiment-runner
19. Touvron, H., et al.: Llama: open and efficient foundation language models (2023). https://arxiv.org/abs/2302.13971
20. Vartziotis, T., et al.: Learn to code sustainably: an empirical study on LLM-based green code generation (2024). https://arxiv.org/abs/2403.03344
21. Yepis, E.: Hype or not? AI's benefits for developers explored in the 2023 developer survey (2023). https://stackoverflow.blog/2023/06/14/hype-or-not-developers-have-something-to-say-about-ai/
22. Zhang, S., et al.: Opt: open pre-trained transformer language models (2022). https://arxiv.org/abs/2205.01068

Electron vs. Web: A Comparative Analysis of Energy and Performance in Communication Apps

Jonathan Thangadurai[1], Priyeta Saha[1], Korawit Rupanya[1], Rosheen Naeem[1], Alejandro Enriquez[1], Gian Luca Scoccia[2], Matias Martinez[3], and Ivano Malavolta[1(✉)]

[1] Vrije Universiteit Amsterdam, Amsterdam, The Netherlands
{j.t.selvaraj,p.saha,k.rupanya,r.naeem, a.s.enriquez.mancheno}@student.vu.nl, i.malavolta@vu.nl
[2] Gran Sasso Science Institute, L'Aquila, Italy
gianluca.scoccia@gssi.it
[3] Universitat Politècnica de Catalunya, Barcelona, Spain
matias.martinez@upc.edu

Abstract. Nowadays, remote communication and collaboration apps are indispensable tools for working and recreation. Typically, they can be accessed either via a Web browser or by installing a desktop application. The desktop versions of the most popular communication apps are implemented using a framework called Electron. The primary objective of this research is to critically assess Electron-based communication apps against their Web-based equivalents, to quantify aspects related to energy efficiency and computational demands. An exhaustive multifactor and multi-treatment experimental design was employed. This structure encompasses unique scenarios that account for platform types, modes of interaction, and interaction durations. The experiment demonstrates that there are differences, with varying effect sizes, in energy consumption and performance between Electron- and Web-based apps. While Electron-based apps exhibit higher CPU utilization and in some cases slightly higher network usage, their Web-based counterparts tend to consume more energy and memory under various configurations.

Keywords: Energy consumption · Web browser · Empirical study

1 Introduction

In today's digitally connected environment, technology communication platforms like Skype[1], Discord[2], and Slack[3] have become indispensable tools for remote work, educational institutions, and organizations. The ubiquity of these communication platforms, used daily by millions of users, makes it crucial to examine

[1] https://www.skype.com/en/.
[2] https://discord.com/.
[3] https://slack.com/.

A. Bertolino et al. (Eds.): QUATIC 2024, CCIS 2178, pp. 177–193, 2024.
https://doi.org/10.1007/978-3-031-70245-7_13

their energy consumption profiles. Given that small improvements in energy efficiency can significantly reduce global energy demand, the absence of comprehensive research comparing these platforms is conspicuous.

All of these mentioned applications are available to the user in two versions: as a *web* application and as a *desktop* application. *Web* apps operate within web browsers and are accessible over the Internet, offering a degree of platform agnosticism. They prioritize ease of use and accessibility, though they may lack full access to native system resources [15]. *Desktop* applications, being directly installed onto a user's computer, often leverage native APIs and system resources efficiently, offering more responsive and feature-rich experiences [15].

The mentioned communication apps all implement their desktop applications using `Electron`[4], an open-source framework that enables the development of cross-platform desktop apps using web technologies. Electron offers a unified runtime environment by leveraging the capabilities of Chromium and Node.js, allowing access to native system APIs via JavaScript code. This approach maintains the flexibility and familiarity of web development environments, offering a seamless transition for developers accustomed to web technologies.

The primary goal of this research is to rigorously evaluate Electron-based desktop applications, namely Skype, Discord, and Slack, against their web-based equivalents, aiming to quantify metrics related to energy efficiency and computational demands. Our study employs energy profiling tools to quantitatively measure the energy consumption of selected Electron-based desktop applications and their web-based counterparts. This approach systematically evaluates their performance under various scenarios, providing a data-driven analysis of key considerations for energy efficiency. The results of our experiment show that Electron applications tended to be more energy efficient than their Web counterparts, and exhibited lower memory consumption and network usage.

This research bridges the gap between software and Green IT, offering empirical insights into an under-researched domain. It focuses especially on empowering end-users with the data they need to make energy-efficient choices on their online communication platforms. Also, it offers valuable insights that could steer software companies and regulations toward more energy-efficient designs.

The paper is organized as follows. Section 2 reviews the existing literature. Section 3 defines our experiment. Section 4 presents the experiment planning, Sect. 5 its execution. Section 6 presents the results while Sect. 7 discusses them. Section 8 details the threats to validity. Section 9 closes the paper.

2 Related Work

Several studies have investigated the sustainability of videoconferencing platforms [2,14,19]. Bieringa et al. explored the resource usage of video conferencing platforms such as Zoom and Microsoft Teams [2]. They employ empirical methods to conclude that Zoom's desktop app surpasses its web counterpart in

[4] https://www.electronjs.org/.

resource utilization. However, their work does not focus on the energy efficiency or underlying technology frameworks of these platforms. Wattenbach et al. conducted a comprehensive exploration into the energy consumption patterns of Android video conferencing apps [19]. The examination of how different features and settings impact energy consumption offers critical insights for developers striving to optimize energy efficiency in various environments, while emphasizing the need of considering feature-specific energy consumption. Ong et al. offered a comprehensive perspective by contrasting the energy and carbon footprints of videoconferencing with those of physical meetings [14]. They noted that virtual meetings consume substantially less energy. However, their research does not dissect the technology stacks of different platforms as we do.

In the literature, multiple studies have focused on cross-platform web apps [12, 15, 16]. Scoccia et al. [15, 16] studied the advantages and disadvantages of desktop web app frameworks. While they touch upon performance and energy considerations, their primary focus is on platform compatibility and bugs. Their research reveals methodological complexities in studying desktop applications but leaves a significant gap in empirical data related to energy efficiency, a gap our study is designed to fill. In the context of addressing fragmentation in app development due to various operating platforms, the study by Malavolta et al. provides invaluable insights [12]. The study highlights the extensive use of code reuse and the similarity in user-perceived value between hybrid and native apps, offering parallels to desktop web app development strategies.

In summary, existing research, while extensive, is centered on specific platforms or general energy considerations. A comparative study between Electron-based and Web-based platforms in the context of energy efficiency remains absent. Our research fills this void by conducting an empirical study, having similarities in methodological approach to the works cited but unique in its focus.

3 Experiment Definition

The Goal-Question-Metric (GQM) framework serves as the backbone of our research strategy. By defining specific goals, refining these into concrete questions, and then measuring them using well-defined metrics, the GQM model offers a robust methodological foundation [4]. The GQM of our study is in Fig. 1.

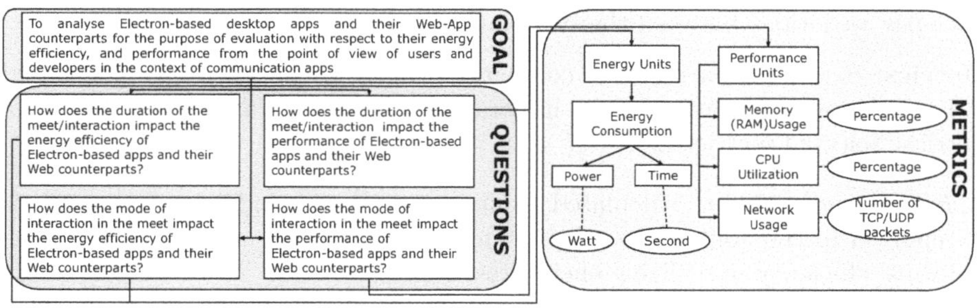

Fig. 1. Visual representation of GQM.

Goal: The goal of this experiment is *"To analyse Electron-based desktop apps and their Web counterparts for the purpose of evaluation with respect to their energy efficiency, and performance from the point of view of users and developers in the context of communication apps"*.

Research Questions: To systematically explore the distinctions between Electron-based apps and their Web counterparts, we have categorized our research questions into two principal domains: Energy Efficiency and Performance. This split allows for a focused investigation into each aspect separately.

[RQ1]. *What is the difference in energy efficiency between Electron-based apps and their Web counterparts?*

[RQ1.1]. *How does the duration of the interaction impact the energy efficiency of Electron-based apps and their Web counterparts?*

Rationale: Exploring how the duration of interaction in an online meeting affects energy efficiency yields insight into the way extended usage influences the energy consumption patterns of both platforms. This allows for a detailed analysis of sustainability over time.

[RQ1.2]. *How does the mode of interaction in the meeting impact the energy efficiency of Electron-based apps and their Web counterparts?*

Rationale: Different modes of interaction, such as audio-only (A), audio and video (V), audio and screen sharing (AS), video and screen sharing (VS), can have varying energy requirements. This exploration helps in understanding the energy disparities under diverse interaction modes.

[RQ2]. *How does the performance of Electron-based apps compare to that of their Web counterparts?*

[RQ2.1]. *How does the duration of the interaction impact the performance of Electron-based apps and their Web counterparts?*

[RQ2.2]. *How does the mode of interaction in the meeting impact the performance of Electron-based apps and their Web counterparts?*

Rationale: Just as the duration and mode of interaction can influence energy efficiency, they also play a pivotal role in determining performance dynamics. Evaluating these factors will help discern resource utilization and operational efficiency variations between the two platforms in diverse scenarios.

Metrics: to conduct a rigorous comparative analysis between Electron-based and web-based applications, it is imperative to establish a well-defined set of metrics. Selected metrics are:

- *Energy consumption:* calculated from power (Watt) and time (seconds), is reported in the Joules unit. It provides a fundamental measure of the platforms' efficiency in utilizing energy resources.
- *Memory usage:* measured in percentage (%), its examination offers valuable information about the applications' memory management efficiency.

- *CPU utilization:* measured in percentage (%), provides a crucial perspective on how efficiently each type of application utilizes processing resources.
- *Network usage:* measured in terms of the number of TCP/UDP packets sent and received, sheds light on how efficiently data is transfered.

4 Experiment Planning

The full replication package of this study is publicly available [18].

Subjects Selection: our study focuses on contrasting Electron and Web apps, aiming to delve into energy and performance disparities. The selected subjects for this empirical examination are online communication platforms, particularly Skype, Discord, and Slack. Their choice is based on multiple criteria:

i) *Presence of both versions:* each subject possesses both an Electron and a Web-based client, allowing for a direct and balanced comparison.
ii) *Usage:* Discord reports over 150 million monthly active users[5], while Slack has 10 million daily active users[6]. Skype's longstanding market presence suggests a comparably extensive user base. These statistics ensure that our study's outcomes reflect the experiences of a broad user spectrum.
iii) *Multi-functionality:* The selected platforms extend beyond text messaging capabilities, incorporating diverse modes of interaction. By focusing on platforms that offer a spectrum of interaction modes and durations, we seek to understand the dynamics of energy and performance in real-world scenarios.

Experimental Variables: Variables are described in the following.

Independent Variables:

i) *Platform type:* The classification of the platform, i.e., Electron-based or Web app. This variable is central for addressing both RQ1 and RQ2.
ii) *Mode of interaction:* the interaction types offered by the platforms: *Audio-only interaction (A)*, *Video interaction (V)*, *Audio with screen sharing interaction (AS)*, and *Video with screen sharing interaction (VS)*. Examining these diverse interaction modes, we can gain a better understanding of the inherent complexities and their influence on the overall resource utilization.
iii) *Duration of interaction:* interaction durations are set at 2 and 8 min to represent short and extended meetings, respectively. These durations have been selected to vary meeting duration, while still limiting the total duration of an experiment run, to allow for a manageable experiment execution.

Dependent Variables: Each metric described in Sect. 3 is actually a dependent variable, totaling four distinct dependent variables: Energy Consumption, Memory Usage, Network Usage, and CPU Utilization.

[5] https://discord.com/company.
[6] https://bit.ly/4cVPjIk.

Control Variables:

i) Operating system and hardware configuration: a consistent operating system and hardware configuration are maintained throughout the experiments.
ii) Browser environment: a single version of a Web browser is used for running the Web apps to ensure uniformity in browser performance and features.
iii) Network conditions To the extent possible, network conditions are kept consistent. For that, we use the same WiFi network throughout the experiment, keep the distance between the router and laptop constant, and make sure that the laptop was the only device connected to the network.

Experimental Hypotheses: The comparative analysis pivots on quantitative assessments, evaluating the differential impacts of these apps on critical dependent variables—energy consumption, CPU usage, memory usage, and network usage. We denote with μ the empirical mean value derived post-experiment, representing the collective measured usage of the dependent variables.

The study employs a multi-layered approach in hypothesis formulation. We begin with a central hypothesis that subsequently unravels into nuanced sub-hypotheses. This approach ensures a multi-dimensional analysis, addressing each research question in-depth and allowing an exhaustive exploration of diverse scenarios and independent variables.

Energy Efficiency: For energy efficiency, we aim to discern whether differences exist in energy consumption between Electron-based apps and their Web counterparts across different durations and modes of interaction.

Null Hypothesis ($H1_0$): For every time duration $t \epsilon$ {2 m, 8 m} and mode of interaction $m \epsilon$ {A, V, AS, VS}, the mean energy consumption μ of Electron-based apps and Web apps do not significantly differ.

Alternative Hypothesis ($H1_a$): There exists at least one combination of duration and mode of interaction where the mean energy consumption of Electron-based apps and Web apps significantly differ.

$$H1_0: \mu_{Web}^{en,t,m} = \mu_{Electron}^{en,t,m} \begin{array}{l} \forall t \in \{2m,8m\}, \\ \forall m \in \{A,V,AS,VS\} \end{array} \quad H1_a: \mu_{Web}^{en,t,m} \neq \mu_{Electron}^{en,t,m} \begin{array}{l} \exists t \in \{2m,8m\}, \\ \exists m \in \{A,V,AS,VS\} \end{array}$$

Performance: similarly, for exploring performance disparities, we are interested in comparing resource utilization and responsiveness between Electron-based apps and Web apps under different durations and modes of interaction.

Null Hypothesis ($H2_0$): For every duration $t \epsilon$ {2 m, 8 m}, mode of interaction $m \epsilon$ {A, V, AS, VS}, the mean performance (CPU, memory, network usage) denoted by μ of Electron-based apps and Web apps do not significantly differ.

Alternative Hypothesis ($H2_a$): There exists at least one combination of duration and mode of interaction where the mean performance of Electron-based apps and Web apps significantly differ.

$$H2_0 \colon \mu_{Web}^{x,t,m} = \mu_{Electron}^{x,t,m} \begin{array}{l} \forall x \in \{cpu, mem, net\}, \\ \forall t \in \{2m, 8m\}, \\ \forall m \in \{A, V, AS, VS\} \end{array} \quad H2_a \colon \mu_{Web}^{x,t,m} \neq \mu_{Electron}^{x,t,m} \begin{array}{l} \exists x \in \{cpu, mem, net\}, \\ \exists t \in \{2m, 8m\}, \\ \exists m \in \{A, V, AS, VS\} \end{array}$$

Experiment Design: In our experiment, a pairwise multi-factor and multi-treatment (MF-MT) approach has been adopted, aligning with the predetermined three independent variables and their corresponding treatments.

The first factor examined is the *diversity of platforms*, namely Electron-based and Web apps. This consideration stems from the inquiries posited in research questions RQ1 and RQ2 and will be investigated through a one-factor, two-treatment (1F-2T) design for each application considered.

The second factor is *modes of interaction*, emerging from Sub-RQ1.1 and Sub-RQ2.1. A multi-treatment design methodology will be employed to explore the varying interaction modes, such as A, V, AS, and VS and a combination of audio, video, and screen sharing. Instead of studying all combinations simultaneously, we have decided on pairwise comparisons to discern effects more clearly. This means for each duration (2 or 8 min), every mode of interaction will be compared between Electron-based and Web apps for each application.

The third factor is *duration of interaction*. It is divided into two levels: short (2 min) and extended (8 min) durations. It is associated with Sub-RQ1.2 and Sub-RQ2.2. Each level will be applied across all application subjects.

The experiment aims to highlight variations in energy consumption and performance, evaluated using the mentioned metrics. For that, it conducts a series of pairwise tests, resulting in specific comparisons, e.g., <Skype desktop, A mode, 2m> vs. <Skype web, A mode, 2m>. The experiment involves conducting individual trials for all three applications in both their Electron- and Web-based versions. The empirical data gathered serves as the foundation for our analysis, providing quantifiable measures to validate or refute the postulated hypotheses.

Data Analysis: the first step in our analysis process is a preliminary data exploration. Here, the collected data undergo a qualitative assessment using descriptive statistics and visualization tools. This step provides preliminary insights, aiding in understanding variances and distributions in measurements.

Given our research design, where we have multiple pairwise comparisons for each mode of interaction and duration, the primary analysis involves conducting pairwise tests. If the data meet the assumptions of normality and equal variance, the t-test [3] is applied. However, if these assumptions are not met, we resort to the Mann-Whitney U test [7]. To verify normality, we use the Shapiro-Wilk test [17], complemented by Q-Q plots [8]. Should the data exhibit normality, we further assess the homogeneity of variances using Levene's test [5]. Considering the number of pairwise tests we intend to perform, it is imperative to address the possibility of Type I errors. Hence, we employ the Benjamini-Hochberg correction [1] to maintain a more stringent control over false positives.

When discerning significant differences, effect size estimation is crucial. For normally distributed data, we use Cohen's d [9] to provide a measure of the difference's magnitude. In instances of non-normality, Cliff's delta [11] will be our go-to metric. In the interpretation of effect sizes, Cohen's d values will be categorized into 'small' (0.2), 'medium' (0.5), and 'large' (0.8) effect sizes, following Cohen's standard conventions [6]. Similarly, for Cliff's delta, we will consider values near 0 as indicative of a negligible effect, values closer to 0.147, 0.33, and 0.474 as small, medium, and large effects, respectively.

5 Experiment Execution

Experiment Setup: To conduct the experiment, we utilize a laptop with an Intel i7-11370H @ 3.30 GHz CPU (CPU scaling enabled), an NVIDIA GeForce RTX 3050ti GPU, 4 GB GDDR6 RAM, a 512 GB PCIe NVMe M.2 SSD disk, and a virtual Web Camera (30 FPS, 1280×720 resolution), running Ubuntu 22.04.2.

We built a Bash script that automatizes the execution of video conferences. First, the Bash script initiates a meeting between two participants and sets the initial values for microphone, camera, and screen sharing, according to each execution's needs. For each meeting tool, the script launches meetings in both the Electron desktop and Web browser versions. For the desktop version, we selected the most recent releases at the time this experiment has been executed (October 2023), i.e., Skype (version 8.104.0.207), Slack (4.34.120), and Discord (6.2.0-33-Generic). For the Web version, the latest version is automatically provided from the servers, accessed through the Google Chrome browser (117.0.5938.92).

Second, the script initializes the predetermined input streams (audio, video, and/or screen sharing according to the execution's needs). To ensure uniform data inputs, all experimental runs receive the same video and audio inputs, with the same video/audio quality across all experiment runs and applications. We use a virtual camera, equipped with a predetermined video, and the microphone is synchronized with the predetermined audio. The same audio/video sharing settings were used across all experiments. By maintaining a consistent hardware and procedural environment, we aim to construct a well-defined and controlled experimental setup, crucial for obtaining reliable and valid results.

Third, the script invokes the measurement tools for the metrics of Sect. 3:

- *PowerJoular (version 0.6.2)* [13]: a command-line tool for real-time monitoring of power consumption in CPU, GPU, and processes on GNU/Linux systems with low overhead. We choose this tool to capture, one sample per second, both *energy consumption* and *CPU utilization*.
- *ps (procps-ng version 3.3.17): ps*[7] is a Linux command line tool used for retrieving process information. We adopt it to measure *memory usage*. This command outputs data for a single point in time, so we execute it repeatedly with a one-second interval to measure memory usage during the meeting.

[7] https://bit.ly/3Vkzm6G.

- *TShark (version 4.0.10): TShark*[8] is a command-line version of Wireshark , a network analyzer application. It measures the number of TCP/UDP packets sent and received by intercepting and analyzing network traffic at the packet level. We use it to measure *network usage* during the experiment.

In our measurements, observed CPU utilization refers to the combined usage of all 4 physical cores, given that hyper-threading is enabled. Similarly, memory utilization is calculated as the process' Resident Set Size (RSS) divided by the total device RAM. This metric specifically measures the physical memory used by the process we are analyzing. Swap space was not considered.

Experiment Execution Plan: we structure the execution of our experiment as a series of independent runs. Each run represents a unique combination of treatments, specifically a platform type (Electron-based apps or Web apps), an interaction mode (A, V, AS, or VS), and the interaction duration (2 or 8 min). Each distinct combination is executed eight times on each of our selected subjects to mitigate statistical anomalies and improve the reliability of the data. We introduce a standardized interval of two minutes between each run to counterbalance potential external variables affecting the measurements, such as CPU heating. In addition, treatments are administered in random order to avoid bias and to ensure an unbiased representation of each treatment combination.

6 Results

Data Preparation: after collecting the data, we evaluate its quality to ensure reliability in subsequent analysis. First, we did not find missing values. Second, using Tukey's Fences approach [10], we detected 23 outliers in memory usage values and 20 in network usage values for Web applications, and 14 outliers in the network usage values for the Electron apps. These outliers were capped at the lower and upper bounds to minimize their impact on further analysis.

Data Exploration: we use violin plots to visualize the distribution of metrics for Electron and Web applications. For Web (Electron) apps engaged in 2 min meetings we observed median values of 10.223J (10.216J), 14.33% (15.94%) CPU utilization, 2.899% (2.019%) memory utilization, and 14,204 (19,561) exchanged network packets. Regarding 8 min meetings, for Web (Electron) apps we observed median values of 41.17J (40.98J), 14.03% (15.91%) CPU utilization, 2.897% (2.02%) memory utilization, and 45,563 (71,413) exchanged network packets. Other statistics (min, quartiles, median) can be found in our appendix.

Energy Consumption: From the collected statistics, there is a minimal difference between the mean energy consumed by the two platforms (2 m: 10.223J for Web vs. 10.216J for Electron; 8 m: respectively 41.17J and 40.98J). Figures 2a and 2b show the distributions of energy consumption from the execution of the Electron and Web apps for meetings lasting 2 and 8 min, respectively. For both durations,

[8] https://bit.ly/4emv1bP.

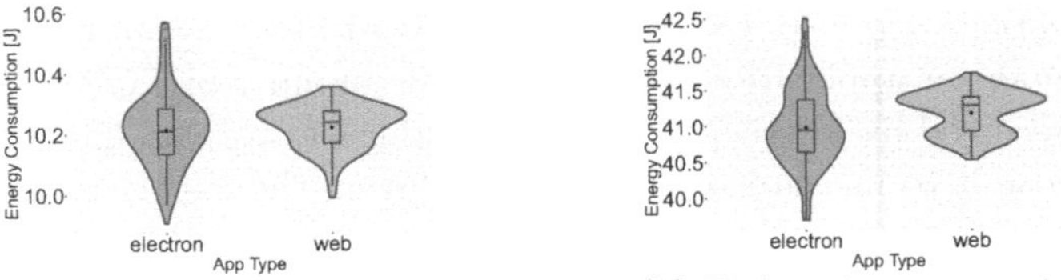

(a) Two minutes meeting (b) Eight minutes meeting

Fig. 2. Distributions of energy consumption.

(a) Two minutes meeting (b) Eight minutes meeting

Fig. 3. Distributions of CPU usage.

we observe that Electron-based apps exhibit a wide distribution in energy usage, hinting at a considerable variability among subjects. In contrast, the Web-based apps show a narrower distribution, suggesting a more consistent energy consumption pattern. Furthermore, Electron apps have a slightly lower median energy consumption. In conclusion, Web and Electron applications exhibit comparable energy consumption at the 2-min duration, with a slight increase in the former's consumption by the 8-min mark.

CPU Usage: Web applications at both durations have means of 14.33% and 14.03% respectively, while Electron apps demonstrated means of 15.94% for the 2-min duration and 15.91% for the 8-min duration. Thus, Web apps use, as mean, less CPU than Electron ones. Let us observe the distributions of CPU usage in Figs. 3a, 3b. Electron applications exhibited greater variability. Web applications, however, consistently lean towards a narrower distribution. Their more tapered pattern implies that Web apps generally maintain a steadier CPU utilization, with their median CPU usage being marginally lower than Electron's

(a) Two minutes meeting (b) Eight minutes meeting

Fig. 4. Distributions of memory usage.

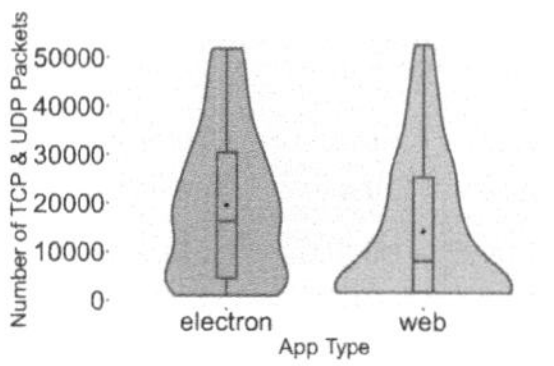

(a) Two minutes meeting

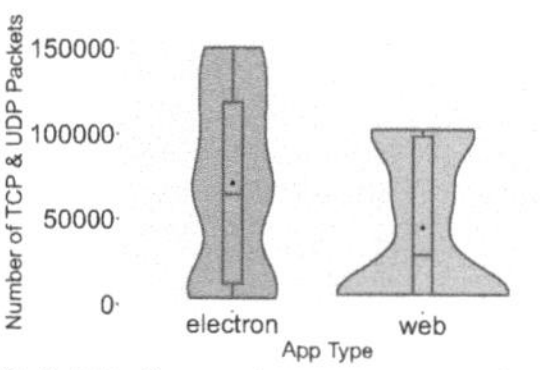

(b) Eight minutes meeting

Fig. 5. Distributions of Network usage.

at both the 2-min and 8-min mark. In conclusion, Electron apps tend to utilize more CPU than Web apps, especially in the early 2-min mark.

Memory Usage: Web applications have means of 2.899% and 2.897% for the 2-min and 8-min durations, respectively. Electron's mean memory usage for the same durations was 2.033% and 2.019%. Thus, on average, Web apps tend to use more memory than Electron apps. Figures 4a, 4b show the distributions. First, we observe that Web-based executions consumes a higher % of memory than Electron apps. The reason could be the memory overhead added by the Web browser. Second, we note that the distributions do not change w.r.t. the meeting duration. Third, the distributions have different shapes. Electron apps display a fairly uniform distribution across the range. Conversely, Web apps demonstrate a more intricate pattern with a broader spread near the median, denoting a dense cluster of apps with comparable memory usage. In conclusion, Web apps demand more memory than Electron across both durations.

Network Usage: Web applications have a mean of 14,204 packets at 2 min of network usage, which increased to 45,563 at 8 min. In contrast, Electron apps began with a mean of 19,561 at 2 min, escalated to 71,413 by the 8-min mark. Hence, on average, Electron apps use the network more than the Web apps. Figures 5a, 5b show the distribution of network usage. We observe that the median network usage for Web applications is lower compared to Electron applications at both 2 m and 8 m. The lower quartiles from the Web apps are much shorter (and tails of these distributions are fatter) than those from the Electron's distribution. For 8 min meetings, Electron apps exhibit a broader distribution. In contrast, Web apps have a narrower distribution, leaning towards lower packet counts. In conclusion, Electron's network usage surpasses Web applications by the 8-min mark, indicating more prolonged data interactions.

Hypotheses Testing: We assess the normality of the data as described in Sect. 4. As the Quantile-Quantile (QQ) analysis and Shapiro-Wilk test indicated non-normality of some of our distribution, we prompt our choice of the non-parametric Mann Whitney U test for our analyses. Table 1 shows the results of the tests for the aggregated modes of interaction. In the appendix, we present a complete table with the result of the test done on each trial.

Energy: Upon examining the two first rows from Table 1, we observe that the energy metric at 8 min exhibits significant differences between the energy

Table 1. Result Interpretation - Aggregated Modes of Interaction.

Metric	Time	Mann Whitney P	Corrected P	Significance	Cliff's Delta	Effect Size	Interpretation
ENERGY	2 m	3.97×10^{-01}	3.97×10^{-01}	Not Significant	−0.0707	Small	Electron ≈ Web
ENERGY	8 m	2.95×10^{-03}	3.93×10^{-03}	**Significant**	−0.2484	Medium	Web > Electron
CPU	2 m	1.05×10^{-2}	1.21×10^{-02}	**Significant**	0.2137	Medium	Electron ≠ Web
CPU	8 m	4.017×10^{-04}	1.07×10^{-03}	**Significant**	0.29583	Medium	Electron ≠ Web
MEM	2 m	5.02×10^{-33}	2.08×10^{-32}	**H. Significant**	−1	Large	Web≫Electron
MEM	8 m	5.208×10^{-33}	2.08×10^{-32}	**H. Significant**	−1	Large	Web≫Electron
NETWORK	2 m	1.72×10^{-03}	2.76×10^{-03}	**Significant**	0.2619	Medium	Electron ≠ Web
NETWORK	8 m	9.99×10^{-04}	1.998×10^{-03}	**Significant**	0.2748	Medium	Electron ≠ Web

Table 2. Significance of statistical tests (Significance: *s* = significant; *ns* = not significant; *hs* = highly significant. Effect size: *se* = small; *me* = medium; *le* = large.)

	A (Audio)				V (Video)				AS (A+Sharing)				VS (V+Sharing)			
	2 m		8 m		2 m		8 m		2 m		8 m		2 m		8 m	
	Sig	ESI	Sig	ESI	Sig	ESI	Sig	ESI	Sig	ESI	Sig	ESI	Sig	ESI	Sig	ESI
Energy	s	**le**	**hs**	**le**	ns	se	**hs**	**le**	ns	se	**hs**	**le**	ns	se	**hs**	**le**
CPU	s	**le**	s	**le**	s	**le**	s	**le**	s	**le**	s	**le**	s	**le**	s	**le**
Memory	**hs**	**le**	**hs**	**le**	**hs**	**le**	**hs**	**le**	**hs**	**le**	**hs**	**le**	**hs**	**le**	**hs**	**le**
Network	ns	se	s	**le**	ns	me	ns	me	ns	me	s	**le**	ns	**le**	ns	se

consumption of Electron and Web applications. In contrast, the energy metric at the 2-min duration lacks statistical significance.

Now we focus on the impact on the interaction mode on the energy (RQ1.2). Table 2 showcases that at the 2 min mark, the energy metrics for V, AS, and VS are not significant. In contrast, the A mode at 2 min and all modes at 8 min exhibit significant differences. These findings lead us a conclusion: time duration markedly influences the differences in energy metrics between Electron and Web apps. Given our observed significant differences across various combinations, we reject the null hypothesis $H1_0$, underscoring the pronounced effect of time duration and interaction mode on energy consumption.

Performance: Turning our focus to the performance metrics (CPU, Memory, and Network usage), our analyses uncover statistically significant differences in both the aggregated modes of interaction (Table 1) as well as individual modes of interaction (Table 2) across both tested durations, with the sole exception of network usage for which a non-significant difference was observed. Given these findings, and considering significant or highly significant results for the performance metrics, we reject the null hypothesis $H2_0$. This suggests that there's a distinguishable difference in the mean performance between Electron-based and Web apps across the specified combinations of duration and mode of interaction.

As a complement to our statistical analyses, we assess the magnitude of the observed differences using the Cliff's Delta effect size statistic. Cliff's Delta has been applied with Web Apps as the first group while testing Aggregated Modes of Interaction (as in Table 1) and with Electron Apps as the first group while testing multiple pairwise comparisons with differing mode and duration.

7 Discussion

7.1 Answer to the Research Questions

RQ1.1: *How does the duration of interaction impact the energy efficiency of Electron-based apps compared to their Web-based counterparts?*

Upon aggregating all modes of interaction, it becomes evident that for shorter meetings the differences in energy consumption between platforms are minimal. The effect size in this context is small, suggesting that for 2-min durations, the energy utilization patterns of Electron apps closely resemble those of Web apps when considering an aggregated combination of all interaction modes (A, V, AS, and VS). For longer meetings, the energy data highlights more pronounced disparities, with a medium effect size, thus suggesting a clearer distinction in energy consumption patterns between the two app types.

RQ1.2: *How does the mode of interaction in the meeting impact the energy efficiency of Electron-based apps and their Web counterparts?*

For a duration of 2 min, Web apps tend to consume more energy than Electron apps when employing an A (*Audio-only*) mode of interaction. Conversely, for other modes, Electron and Web apps displayed similar energy consumption metrics. Observing 8-min duration meetings, Web applications consistently drew more energy than Electron-based apps across all interaction modes.

The apparent discrepancies between the conclusions drawn from RQ1.1 and RQ1.2 can be traced back to the data analysis methodology. In RQ1.1, using aggregate data offers a broad overview, potentially overshadowing tendencies inherent in individual interaction modes. RQ1.2, with its mode-specific analysis, provides nuanced insights, emphasizing the unique energy dynamics associated with each interaction mode. Hence, Electron may outshine Web apps in particular contexts, while the two closely align when considering all interaction types.

RQ2.1: *How does the duration of interaction impact the performance of Electron-based apps compared to their Web-based counterparts?*

For the CPU metric, at a duration of 2 min, the results reveal minimal performance differences, with a medium effect size, suggesting a similar performance pattern between the two app types. However, for 8 min duration, the disparity becomes more discernible. Again, with medium effect size, the data implies a notable difference in CPU performance, with the Web apps being more efficient.

Moving on to the memory utilization, at both 2 and 8 min durations, the findings are highly significant, indicating a substantial difference in memory consumption patterns. With a large effect size in both cases, it is clear that Web-based apps consume more memory than their Electron-based counterparts.

Lastly, for the network usage, at the 2-min mark, there is a noticeable difference in Electron and Web apps, with a medium effect size, which conveys that web apps consume lesser network resources. This trend continues for 8-min durations, suggesting a performance gap between the two types of apps.

In conclusion, the duration of interaction does play a role in delineating the performance disparities between Electron- and Web-based apps. While both app types might showcase comparable CPU performances in shorter durations, differences become more pronounced for longer interactions. In terms of memory and network usage, Electron apps tend to consume more resources.

RQ2.2: *How does the mode of interaction in the meeting impact the performance of Electron-based apps and their Web counterparts?*

At a granular level, Electron applications often exhibited higher CPU utilization, especially in VS mode. Conversely, Web apps consistently consumed more memory. Additionally, network consumption at a granular level does not provide a significant difference across the different modes of interaction.

7.2 Additional Considerations

Energy Consumed vs CPU Utilization: Despite higher CPU utilization, Electron apps exhibited comparable or even lower energy consumption than Web apps. Although they engage the CPU more actively, especially in complex modes such as video and screen sharing, Electron apps perform these tasks more efficiently. We speculate that this efficiency stems from their ability to directly interact with the system's hardware and make optimized use of system APIs.

Memory Consumption: Web applications consistently displayed greater memory consumption. This could be attributed to the inherent characteristics of the browser's memory management system, which may not rival the more application-specific memory management found in Electron apps. Electron's official documentation acknowledges the significance of optimizations, underscoring the potential for performance tuning that may lead to more efficient memory use.

Network Usage: Our findings indicate that network consumption was similar for both Electron and Web apps, and in some scenarios, Web apps even consumed less network resources. This could be attributed to various factors, including the efficiency of data transfer protocols employed by Web apps, and their potential for better optimization of network requests within the browser environment.

Choice of Communication App: In our study, we did not investigate which of the tested apps is more energy efficient and what is the potential energy saving that might be achieved by changing communication app. Indeed, such change a might not always be possible, due to organizational constraints and other external factors. In these scenarios, energy-aware users can take advantage of our study to choose the more energy-efficient version of the employed application.

Implications for End Users: From the user perspective, the choice between Electron and Web-based applications needs careful consideration based on the nature and duration of the intended use. For shorter interactions, both energy consumption and performance differences were marginal. Hence, users might prioritize other factors, such as ease of use. However, for prolonged interactions, there are evident trade-offs. Users prioritizing energy conservation might lean towards Electron applications due to their apparent energy and memory efficiency. However, they should also be aware of the potentially increased CPU utilization, especially in demanding scenarios such as video/screen sharing. In essence, the optimal choice depends on the specific context and the tasks to perform.

8 Threats to Validity

Internal Validity. Our study is potentially sensitive to historical factors, with the device's temperature being a prime concern. To mitigate this threat, we introduced intervals of 2 min of sleep between each application run. Given the nature of pairwise testing and the increased number of tests, there's a possibility for heightened variance. To address this, we aggregated the different modes of interaction while answering our research questions regarding the impact of interaction duration on energy efficiency and performance for the two durations. Moreover, during the experiment, garbage collection could have impacted measured CPU utilization and power consumption. Multiple runs of each experiment trial were executed to mitigate this threat.

External Validity. The selected subjects cover a vast user demographic, thereby enhancing the general applicability of our findings. However, it is important to note that our study focuses specifically on communication apps. This limits the generalizability of our outcomes. Device specificity, choice of browsers, or configurations can also potentially narrow the applicability of our results. To mitigate this, we deployed devices that reflect average user settings. Additionally, factors like Internet bandwidth and concurrent background processes can introduce inconsistencies. We addressed these variables by maintaining a consistent Internet connection and minimizing non-essential tasks during testing.

Construct Validity. Our experimental design, metrics, influential factors, and tools are described accurately. By articulating clear hypotheses and scenarios, we aspire to bring forth a clear view of our research questions and derived findings. Although our study spans a variety of dependent variables, the tools chosen for measurements could have innate biases. The decision to aggregate certain data points might introduce a risk of oversimplifying complex interactions between variables. To mitigate this threat, we ensured our tools have undergone peer review or have found acceptance in earlier research endeavors.

Conclusion Validity. To augment the validity of our outcomes, we diversified our data collection strategies, deploying different treatment combinations across the three chosen applications. Before proceeding with our statistical interpretations, we inspect our data for any violated assumptions. This step ensures that our statistical tests align perfectly with the nature of our dataset. Given the large number of tests we conducted, there's a potential inflation of Type I error rates, which we address using appropriate multiple comparison corrections. Furthermore, we designed treatments that reflect real-world app usage. Nonetheless, we did not consider usage patterns that involve the use of multiple communication apps in a single browser instance, by loading them into distinct browser tabs.

9 Conclusions

We systematically examined the energy and performance metrics of Electron- vs. Web-based applications. The findings indicate negligible differences in shorter interactions, while extended durations uncovered significant discrepancies in energy and performance efficiency. For further research, one potential direction is to evaluate the prolonged use of these applications that may reveal insights into hardware longevity and associated factors like battery degradation. Analogously, another direction could be focusing on variations in energy consumption during the meeting duration, as they could help in identifying factors that result in a large energy expenditure (e.g., handshake costs). Another avenue is the assessment of security and privacy aspects. Given the increasing concerns about data security, a comparative study focusing on vulnerability, data handling practices, and privacy in Electron and Web applications would be highly relevant.

References

1. Benjamini, Y., Hochberg, Y.: Controlling the false discovery rate: a practical and powerful approach to multiple testing. J. R. Stat. Soc. Ser. B (Methodol.) **57**(1), 289–300 (1995)
2. Bieringa, R., Radhakrishnan, A., Singh, T., Vos, S., Donkervliet, J., Iosup, A.: An empirical evaluation of the performance of video conferencing systems. In: Companion of the ACM/SPEC International Conference on Performance Engineering. ACM (2021)
3. Boslaugh, S.: Statistics in a Nutshell: A Desktop Quick Reference. O'Reilly Media Inc., Sebastopol (2012)
4. Caldiera, V.R.B.G., Rombach, H.D.: The goal question metric approach. Encycl. Softw. Eng. 528–532 (1994)
5. Carroll, R.J., Schneider, H.: A note on levene's tests for equality of variances. Stat. Probab. Lett. **3**(4), 191–194 (1985)
6. Cohen, J.: Statistical Power Analysis for the Behavioral Sciences. Academic press, Cambridge (2013)
7. Fay, M.P., Proschan, M.A.: Wilcoxon-mann-whitney or t-test? on assumptions for hypothesis tests and multiple interpretations of decision rules. Stat. Surv. **4** (2010)
8. Ghasemi, A., Zahediasl, S.: Normality tests for statistical analysis: a guide for non-statisticians. Int. J. Endocrinol. Metab. **10**(2), 486–489 (2012)
9. Hedges, L.V., Olkin, I.: Statistical Methods for Meta-analysis. Academic press, Cambridge (2014)
10. Hubert, M., Van der Veeken, S.: Outlier detection for skewed data. J. Chemometr. J. Chemometr. Soc. **22**(3–4), 235–246 (2008)

11. Macbeth, G., Razumiejczyk, E., Ledesma, R.D.: Cliff's delta calculator: a non-parametric effect size program for two groups of observations. Universitas Psychologica **10**(2), 545–555 (2011)
12. Malavolta, I., Ruberto, S., Soru, T., Terragni, V.: Hybrid mobile apps in the google play store: an exploratory investigation. In: 2015 2nd ACM International Conference on Mobile Software Engineering and Systems, pp. 56–59 (2015)
13. Noureddine, A.: Powerjoular and joularjx: multi-platform software power monitoring tools. In: 18th International Conference on Intelligent Environments (IE2022) (2022)
14. Ong, D., Moors, T., Sivaraman, V.: Comparison of the energy, carbon and time costs of videoconferencing and in-person meetings. Comput. Commun. **50**, 86–94 (2014)
15. Scoccia, G.L., Autili, M.: Web frameworks for desktop apps: an exploratory study. In: Proceedings of the 14th ACM / IEEE International Symposium on Empirical Software Engineering and Measurement (ESEM). ACM (2020)
16. Scoccia, G.L., Migliarini, P., Autili, M.: Challenges in developing desktop web apps: a study of stack overflow and github. In: 2021 IEEE/ACM 18th International Conference on Mining Software Repositories (MSR), pp. 271–282 (2021)
17. Shapiro, S.S., Wilk, M.B.: An analysis of variance test for normality (complete samples). Biometrika **52**(3/4), 591 (1965)
18. Thangadurai, J., et al.: Replication package of this study (2024). https://github.com/S2-group/quatic-2024-electron-web-energy-perf-rep-pkg
19. Wattenbach, L., Aslan, B., Fiore, M.M., Ding, H., Verdecchia, R., Malavolta, I.: Do you have the energy for this meeting? an empirical study on the energy consumption of the google meet and zoom android apps. In: Proceedings of the 9th IEEE/ACM Int. Conf. on Mobile Software Engineering and Systems, pp. 6–16. MOBILESoft 2022, Association for Computing Machinery, New York, NY, USA (2022)

On the Energy Consumption of CPython

Rolf-Helge Pfeiffer(✉)

IT University of Copenhagen, Rued Langgaards Vej 7, 2300 Copenhagen, Denmark
ropf@itu.dk

Abstract. Interpreted programming languages, like Python, are amongst the most popular programming languages. This, combined with high developer efficiency leads to many web-application backends and web-services that are written in Python. While it is known that that interpreted languages like Python are way less energy efficient compared to compiled languages like C++, Rust, etc., little is known about the energy efficiency of various versions of Python interpreters. In this paper, we study via a controlled lab experiment the energy consumption of various versions of the Python interpreter CPython when running a server-side rendered web-application. Our results indicate that currently the most energy efficient version is CPython 3.12. Energy consumption of CPython 3.12 can drop by more than 8% compared to previous versions.

Keywords: Software engineering · Energy consumption · CPython

1 Introduction

Interpreted languages are amongst the most popular programming languages. Python is ranked to be the most popular programming language[1,2] in the early 2020s. The Python programming language is used in almost all domains of software development ranging from small scripts of "glue code", over scientific computing to development of web-applications.

Big corporations and projects use Python due to its ease of use and understandability which allows for short development times[3] [21,25]. For example, Airbnb created and relies on the Python-based workflow management platform Apache Airflow,[4] Google's YouTube is powered by Python [27], circa 20% of Facebook's infrastructure is written in Python,[5] Instagram is a Python application using the Django web-framework,[6] or circa 80% of Spotify's backend services are written in Python.[7] Since such big projects and in general evermore software is written

[1] https://www.tiobe.com/tiobe-index/.

[2] https://spectrum.ieee.org/the-top-programming-languages-2023.

[3] https://computerhistory.org/profile/guido-van-rossum/.

[4] https://airflow.apache.org/.

[5] https://engineering.fb.com/2016/05/27/production-engineering/python-in-production-engineering/.

[6] https://instagram-engineering.com/web-service-efficiency-at-instagram-with-python-4976d078e366.

[7] https://engineering.atspotify.com/2013/03/how-we-use-python-at-spotify/.

A. Bertolino et al. (Eds.): QUATIC 2024, CCIS 2178, pp. 194–209, 2024.
https://doi.org/10.1007/978-3-031-70245-7_14

in high-level interpreted languages like Python and since we as software engineers have to contribute to reducing the carbon footprint of our sector [1], software qualities like sustainability in the sense of energy efficiency become more important.

Usually, interpreted programming languages are slower than programming languages that are compiled to native code. Therefore, the authors of CPython started to focus on improving performance of the interpreter,[8] e.g., by introduction of Just-In-Time compilation, removal of the so-called global-interpreter lock,[9] etc. CPython is the open-source reference implementation of the Python[10] programming language originally implemented by Guido van Rossum, which is now maintained and improved by a team of developers.[11]

Besides being less performant, interpreted programming languages are reported to be of low energy efficiency, see e.g., [2,6,19,20]. But it seems that energy efficiency is of secondary interest for language designers and maintainers so far. For example, non of the current Python Enhancement Proposals (PEPs)[12] is about energy efficiency.

Additionally, it is unclear how current performance improvements of CPython[13] impact energy efficiency. Furthermore, there is little knowledge on how to assess energy efficiency of various versions of language interpreters like CPython.

In this paper, we investigate the energy consumption of various versions of CPython. Our research question is: *What is the energy consumption of different versions of the Python interpreter CPython?* To answer this question, we design and conduct a controlled lab experiment. Before executing our experiment, we assume that newer versions of Python are less energy efficient due to increasing language features and internal extensions. Our assumption is loosely inspired by "Wirth's law" [28] which states that *"software manages to outgrow hardware in size and sluggishnes"* [23].

To investigate our research question, we conduct a controlled lab experiment in which we measure energy consumption of a server running a web-application. Three clients execute long-running *scenarios* against the server, where a scenario is an automated sequence of actions that a potential user could perform, like requesting a page, registering a user, etc. The only variable in our experiment is the version of CPython running the application. The web-application, its dependencies, the operating system (FreeBSD), webserver (Gunicorn), etc. are all fixed to the same versions.

Contrary to our initial assumption, our results indicate that newer versions of CPython (versions CPython 3.11, 3.12, and 3.13) are not only more performant, they are also more energy efficient than previous versions. In particular, CPython

8 https://github.com/markshannon/faster-cpython/blob/master/plan.md.
9 https://peps.python.org/pep-0703/.
10 https://www.python.org/.
11 https://devguide.python.org/core-developers/developer-log/#developers.
12 https://peps.python.org/.
13 https://www.python.org/downloads/release/python-3110/.

3.12 appears to be currently the most energy efficient CPython interpreter. On average it consumes 8.41% less energy than the most energy consuming version 3.10. Consequently, software developers or maintainers can make their CPython-based products more sustainable plainly by updating to CPython 3.12.

Our contributions are:

- We present an experiment design to directly measure energy consumption of a server in a networked client-server architecture. Our design can serve as a blueprint for similar sustainability experiments.
- We demonstrate that recent versions of CPython are more energy efficient than older versions.
- We provide a complete replication kit with automated experiment together with this paper.[14]

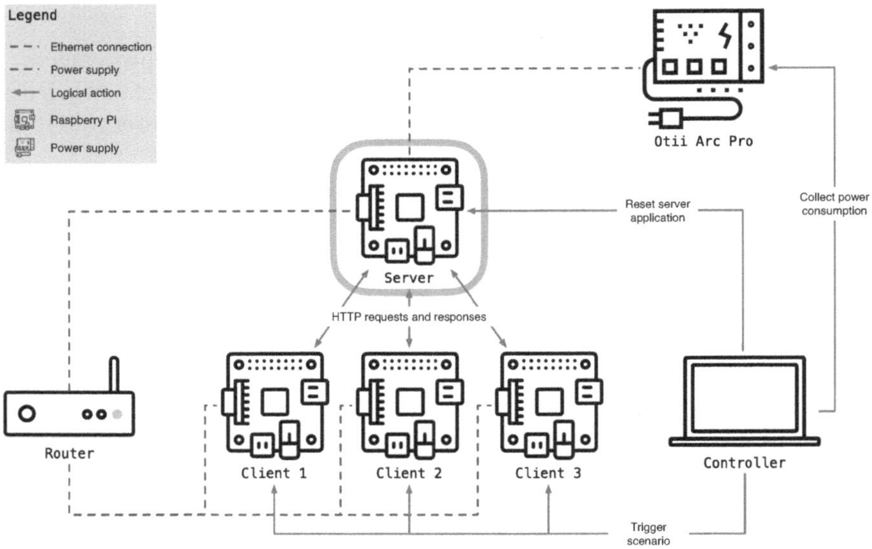

Fig. 1. Illustration of our experiment design. Highlighted in orange, is the webserver for which we study energy consumption.

[14] https://github.com/HelgeCPH/cpython_energy.

2 Experiment Design

In this section, we describe how we measure and evaluate the energy consumption of various versions of CPython in a controlled lab experiment.

Figure 1 illustrates our experiment setup with one webserver (center in Fig. 1) and three clients (bottom center in Fig. 1). The three clients and the webserver are all Raspberry Pis (Model B+ V1.2) that are connected via ethernet to a Wi-Fi router in a network. The webserver is powered by an Otii Arc Pro.[15] This is a power supply with integrated meter that allows to accurately profile and analyze voltage, current, power, etc. That is, we collect power draw of the server directly compared to indirect estimation of energy consumption, e.g., via Intel's Running Average Power Limit [7] or similar.

The power supply is connected to a computer which we call *controller* via USB (bottom right in Fig. 1). On that computer runs the Otii software suite[16] that allows us to collect measurement data about power draw, current, voltage, etc. Besides used as data collector, the *controller* orchestrates single runs of the experiment.

The webserver and clients are provisioned with FreeBSD 13.3. On the webserver, we install CPython 3.8, 3.9, 3.10, 3.11, 3.12, and 3.13. These are the versions of CPython for which measure energy consumption in our experiment. CPython 3.8, 3.9, 3.10, and 3.11 are installed via their respective packages with the `pkg` tool.[17] These contain pre-compiled distributions of the latest versions of the respective CPython interpreter for the ARM architecture of the Raspberry Pi. Since no pre-compiled packages exist yet for CPython 3.12 and 3.13, we install these via `pyenv`.[18]

Previous work on assessment of energy consumption of software often relies on exemplary implementations of certain algorithms, see e.g. [2,6,10,17,19,20,26]. However, we decide that we want to conduct our experiment in an environment that resembles more a realistic software product, similar to [6,9]. Therefore, the server will run a server-side rendered web-application called MiniTwit. It is a Twitter-like minimal micro-blogging web-application. The MiniTwit application is originally written in Python 2 by Armin Ronacher. It used to be an example application for his Python web-framework Flask.[19] Python 2 and 3 are incompatible versions of the programming language. Therefore, we update the original MiniTwit application to be compatible with Python 3 and contemporary versions of the Flask framework.

The MiniTwit Flask application is served via the WSGI HTTP server Gunicorn,[20] which is a Python application too. For this experiment, we do not serve

[15] https://www.qoitech.com/otii-arc-pro/.
[16] https://www.qoitech.com/software/.
[17] https://man.freebsd.org/cgi/man.cgi?query=pkg&sektion=8&format=html.
[18] https://github.com/pyenv/pyenv.
[19] https://github.com/pallets/flask/tree/1592c53a664c82d9badac81fa0104af226cce5a7/examples/minitwit.
[20] https://gunicorn.org/.

the MiniTwit web-application via a reverse proxy server like nginx[21] or the Apache HTTP Server[22] as likely done in a production setup. The main reason is that we want to prevent caching of responses, so that the effect of the Python interpreters on energy consumption is better represented.

Consequently, to be operational, the MiniTwit application requires Flask and Gunicorn to be installed on the server. Both of these are distributed as Python packages on the Python Packaging Index (PyPI).[23] We manually download the latest versions of these packages, together with their transitive dependencies, from PyPI. We do that so that we can vendor pinned versions of dependencies with our experiment setup to facilitate reproduction and replication. Note, a replication kit is provided online (see footnote 14). It contains complete descriptions on how to prepare the experiment computers, provisioner scripts for the server and clients, etc. To sum up, we make sure that the experiment variable in our experiment is the precise version of CPython running the web-application.

The technical setup described above, see Fig. 1, provides the environment for experiment execution. The experiment consists of so-called *scenarios*. In a scenario, a client performs a sequence of actions against the MiniTwit web-application on the server. These are actions like loading the application's front-page (which lists latest tweets), registering a new user, sending tweets, following other users, and requesting a user's private timeline (which displays only a selection of tweets). Figure 2b sketches such a scenario as UML sequence diagram. The exact scenario can be inspected in the replication kit.

Per version of CPython (3.8 to 3.13), we execute ten iterations of the same scenario in parallel from the three clients, as illustrated in Fig. 2a. That is, each of the three clients executes ten times the same scenario against the server. We execute ten iterations of the same scenario per version of CPython to minimize the effect of potentially running other processes on the multi-tasking operating system FreeBSD.

Note, before the ten parallel scenarios are executed for a version of CPython, the *controller* resets the server's web-application. That is, the database of users, their tweets, and their follower structure is reset to a predefined state so that the MiniTwit application operates in the completely same environment for each version of CPython. Once that step is completed, the *controller* starts the execution of the scenario on each of the three clients. We call the execution of a scenario in parallel over three clients an *experiment run*. Per experiment run, we record the power draw of the server (in Watt) with 10000 samples per seconds and the time it took to execute. That is, the reset of the web-application is not recorded in our measurements. Only the energy consumption of the body of the loop in Fig. 2a is recorded. All measurement data is stored automatically in CSV files, which are also distributed in our replication kit.

[21] https://nginx.org/.

[22] https://httpd.apache.org/.

[23] https://pypi.org/.

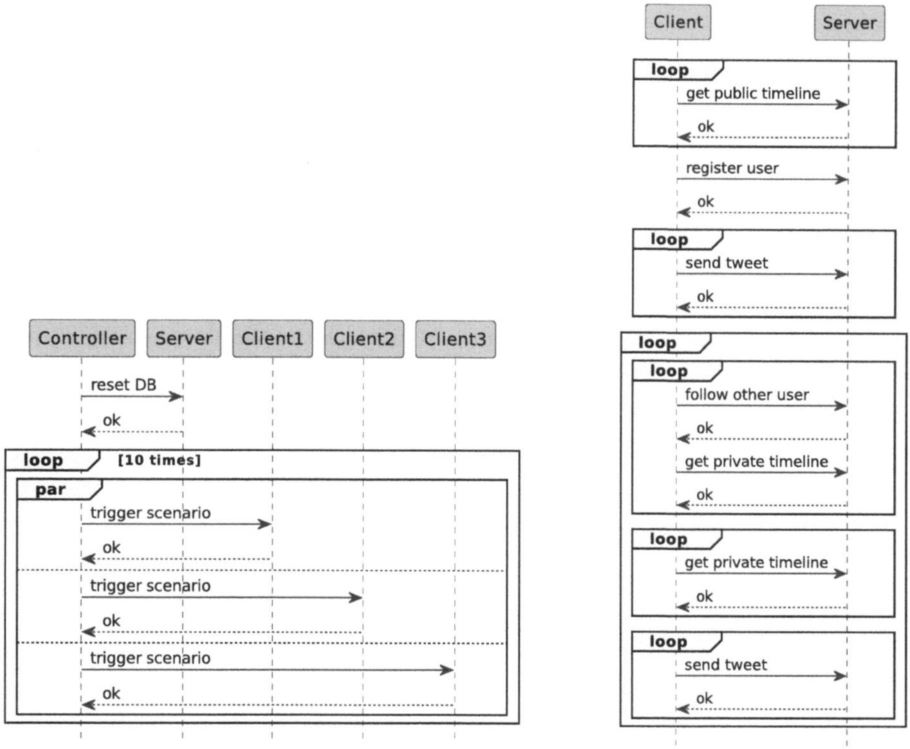

(a) Illustration of ten *experiment runs*, i.e., how the *controller* executes ten iterations of the experiment scenario in parallel across the three clients.

(b) Illustration of a single scenario that a client executes against the web-application on the server.

Fig. 2. Illustration of ten *experiment runs* (left) and a *scenario* (right).

The experiment runs per version of CPython are completely automated using the Otii Automation Toolbox.[24,25] After recording energy consumption of one version of CPython, we manually log to the server from the controller, stop the web-application, and switch to the next version of CPython.

---

[24] https://www.qoitech.com/docs/advanced/scripting-with-python.

[25] https://github.com/HelgeCPH/otii-tcp-client-python.

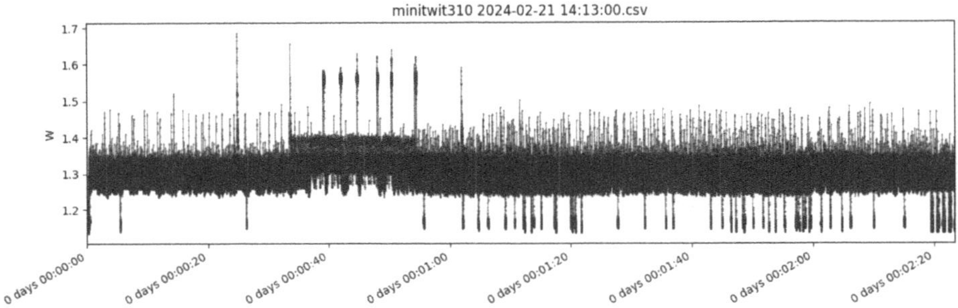

Fig. 3. Power draw of the first experiment run in which the MiniTwit web-application runs on CPython 3.10.

3 Results

The results of our measurements of the server's power draw for a single experiment run look as illustrated in Fig. 3. This plots the power draw of the first experiment run in which the MiniTwit web-application runs on CPython 3.10. It illustrates power draw over time with 10000 samples per second (x-axis). On the y-axis power draw in Watt (W) is plotted. It can be seen that this experiment run lasts for ca. $2\,min23\,s$. On average, the server's power draw is $\mu \approx 1.286$ W ($\sigma \approx 0.034$ and $q_2 \approx 1.282$ W). Minimum and maximum power draw are $q_0 \approx 1.133$ W and $q_4 \approx 1.685$ W respectively.

Note, for reporting we use the following notation: q_0 denotes the minimum, q_1 the 25th quartile, q_2 the median, q_3 the 75th quartile, q_4 the maximum, μ is the arithmetic mean (we use average and arithmetic mean synonymously), and the standard deviation is denoted by σ.

To facilitate statistical analysis and visual inspection, we compute the average power draw per experiment run and plot these in a box plot, see Fig. 4a. It shows that, CPython 3.11 has the highest power draw for all ten experiment runs ($q_0 = 1.286579$ W, $q_1 = 1.287268$ W, $q_2 = 1.287694$ W, $q_3 = 1.288286$ W, $q_4 = 1.288864$ W, $\mu = 1.287683$ W, $\sigma = 0.000770$) and CPython 3.13 the lowest power draw per experiment run ($q_0 = 1.283466$ W, $q_1 = 1.283782$ W, $q_2 = 1.284120$W, $q_3 = 1.284786$W, $q_4 = 1.285268$ W, $\mu = 1.284268$ W, $\sigma = 0.000667$). The other versions of CPython have power draws in between these respective maximum and minimum.

Note, the y-axis of Fig. 4a. It shows that differences between power draw of the various versions of CPython are small, in the range of milliWatts (mW). The difference between the highest and lowest power draw of all experiment runs is ca. 4.13 mW.

Besides power draw of the server, we record the runtimes per experiment run. Figure 4b illustrates these in seconds (s) per version of CPython. This box plot shows that, in general, runtimes for CPython 3.12 are the lowest ($q_0 \approx 127.84$ s, $q_1 \approx 128.39$ s, $q_2 \approx 128.89$ s, $q_3 \approx 129.75$ s, $q_4 \approx 131.25$ s, $\mu \approx 129.09$ s, $\sigma \approx 1.06$) and runtimes for CPython 3.10 are the highest ($q_0 \approx 139.63$ s, $q_1 \approx 140.11$ s,

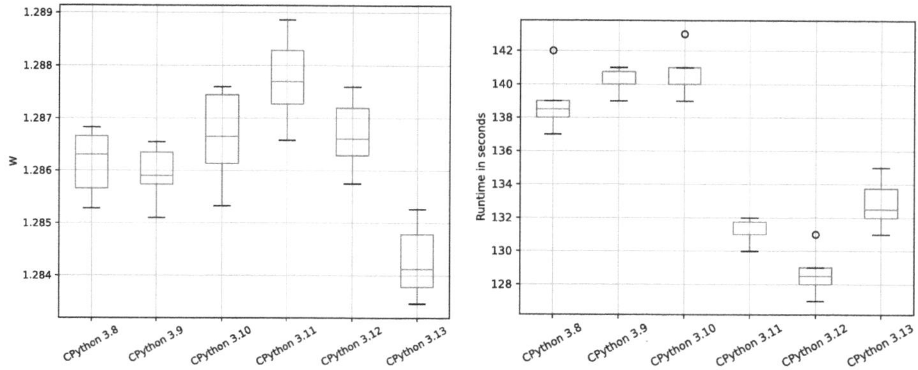

(a) Average power draw in Watt (W). (b) Runtimes in seconds.

Fig. 4. Power draw and runtimes of the experiment runs per version of CPython.

$q_2 \approx 140.68$ s, $q_3 \approx 141.61$ s, $q_4 \approx 143.48$ s, $\mu \approx 140.94$ s, $\sigma \approx 1.20$). That is, the difference between the fastest and slowest experiment run over all versions of CPython is ca. 15.64 s. All other runtimes are between these extremes.

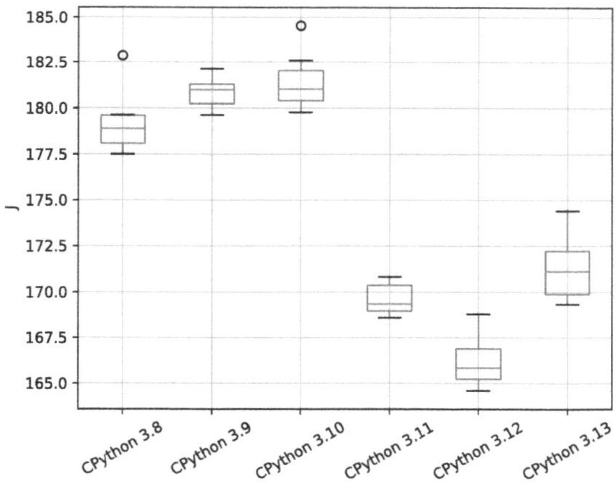

Fig. 5. Energy consumption in Joule (J) of all experiment runs per version of CPython.

Based on these measurements for power draw and runtimes, we compute energy consumptions of the experiment runs via $E_{nergy}[\mathrm{J}] = P_{ower}[\mathrm{W}] \times t_{ime}[\mathrm{s}]$. Figure 5 illustrates energy consumption of the experiment runs. It shows that CPython 3.10 consumes most energy ($q_0 \approx 179.77$ J, $q_1 \approx 180.40$ J, $q_2 \approx 181.03$ J, $q_3 \approx 182.04$ J, $q_4 \approx 184.54$ J, $\mu \approx 181.35$ J, $\sigma \approx 1.47$) and that CPython 3.12 consumes the least energy ($q_0 \approx 164.60$ J, $q_1 \approx 165.23$ J, $q_2 \approx 165.84$ J, $q_3 \approx 166.90$ J, $q_4 \approx 168.80$ J, $\mu \approx 166.10$ J, $\sigma \approx 1.30$). Energy consumption of CPython

Table 1. Descriptive statistics of energy consumption in Joule (J) rounded to two digits.

	CPython 3.8	CPython 3.9	CPython 3.10	CPython 3.11	CPython 3.12	CPython 3.13
min (q_0)	177.51 J	179.64 J	179.77 J	168.61 J	164.60 J	169.35 J
q_1	178.09 J	180.23 J	180.40 J	168.96 J	165.23 J	169.90 J
median (q_2)	178.90 J	180.98 J	181.03 J	169.34 J	165.84 J	171.14 J
q_3	179.60 J	181.29 J	182.04 J	170.37 J	166.90 J	172.23 J
max (q_4)	182.87 J	182.13 J	184.54 J	170.84 J	168.80 J	174.42 J
μ mean	179.12 J	180.84 J	181.35 J	169.58 J	166.10 J	171.21 J
σ	1.52	0.84	1.47	0.83	1.30	1.60

3.8 and 3.9 are all between ca. 177.51 J and ca. 184.54 J, whereas newer versions of CPython (3.11 to 3.13) generally consume less energy (between ca. 164.60 J and 174.42 J respectively). For completeness, Table 1 lists the descriptive statistics for the energy consumption of all versions of CPython.

Visual inspection of all experiment runs' energy consumptions (Fig. 5) in combination with the descriptive statistics in Table 1 show that CPython 3.10 and 3.12 have the biggest difference in energy consumption. In general, CPython 3.10 consumes the most and 3.12 consumes the least.

4 Analysis and Discussion

We conduct a Kruskal-Wallis test [11] to analyze if energy consumption differs significantly across versions of CPython. Unlike an ANOVA test, a Kruskal-Wallis test has fewer preconditions, such as, that our recorded energy consumptions come from a normally distributed population or that the standard deviations of the groups are all equal (homoscedasticity). Since we only conduct ten experiment runs per version of CPython, we have too few samples to test for these two preconditions. Visual inspection of the histograms of energy consumptions per version of CPython suggest they are not from a normal distribution. Therefore, we settle on a Kruskal-Wallis test, for which we formulate the following null and alternative hypotheses.

Null Hypothesis (H_0) There is no significant difference in energy consumption depending on the version of CPython. In other words, energy consumption of the server is more or less equal no matter which version of CPython is used to run the web-application.
Alternative Hypothesis (H_a) At least one of the group means differs significantly from at least one other group mean. That is, at least one version of CPython interpreter consumes considerably less or more energy than the others.

For our recorded energy consumptions, the Kruskal-Wallis H statistics is ≈ 53.07 (p-value $\approx 3.25 \times 10^{-10}$). Since the value of the H statistics is quite large and the p-value is below 0.05, we have to reject the null hypothesis and settle on the alternative hypothesis. That is, the energy consumption of at least one version of CPython is significantly different than the others. This result is supported by visual inspection of Fig. 5.

In general, one can observe a drop in energy consumption between CPython versions 3.8, 3.9, and 3.10 compared to CPython versions 3.11, 3.12, and 3.13, see Fig. 5. The biggest difference is between CPython 3.10 and 3.12. The median energy consumption of CPython 3.12 is $\approx 8.39\%$ lower than the one of CPython 3.10. The average energy consumption drops by $\approx 8.41\%$.

Remember, our initial assumption was that newer versions of Python are less energy-efficient. The results above (and as plotted in Fig. 5) suggest that this is generally not the case. To the contrary, newer versions of CPython are actually more energy efficient than older versions. If only considered for CPython 3.8 to 3.10, our initial assumption seems to be true as there is a continuous increase in energy consumption across these three versions of CPython. However, the more recent versions CPython 3.11, 3.12, and 3.13 consume all less energy than the previous versions in our experiment. Only the energy consumption of CPython 3.13 appears to increase again compared to the previous two versions. Notably, the maximum energy consumption of CPython 3.13 ($q_4 \approx 174.42$ J) is still circa 3.09 J lower than the minimal energy consumption of CPython 3.8 ($q_0 \approx 177.51$ J).

CPython 3.11 was the first in a series of releases in which the language developers focused on improving performance of the Python interpreter. The release notes state: *"The Faster CPython Project is already yielding some exciting results. Python 3.11 is up to 10–60% faster than Python 3.10. On average, we measured a 1.22× speedup on the standard benchmark suite."* (see footnote 13)

A performance improvement is visible in our experiment too, see Fig. 4b, though to a lower degree than stated by the language developers. On average, in our scenario, CPython 3.11 performs 6.56% faster than 3.10 and CPython 3.12 is 8.41% faster than 3.10.

Interestingly, the power draw of CPython 3.11 is the highest of all investigated versions of CPython, where CPython 3.12 is comparable to 3.10, and 3.13 sports the lowest. That is, it seems that the implemented performance improvements come at the cost of slightly higher power draw. However, the relative difference between the versions of CPython with highest and lowest power draw are marginal. The average power draw drops by only 0.26% between CPython 3.11 and 3.13 (q_2 drops ca. 0.28%).

Consequently, there is a sweet spot between performance optimizations and how they are implemented. In future, the Python language developers might face the situation, in which further performance improvements decrease energy efficiency in case power draw becomes more dominating. While some researchers describe that performance improvements suffice to decrease energy consumption, see e.g., Yuki et al. [29], others find that in certain cases power draw has an impact too, see e.g., Koedijk et al. [10]. Since the increases in power draw are comparably small, it seems however that a focus on performance optimizations is advisable for the Python project.

4.1 Threats to Validity

Conclusion Validity: Since we cannot conclusively test for normal distribution or homoscedasticity due to small sample size of energy consumptions, we can only conduct the less powerful Kruskal-Wallis test instead of the more powerful one-way ANOVA test. However, the results of Kruskal-Wallis test together with the plots that we provide in this paper, make us confident that the energy consumption of the various versions of CPython actually differ in a statistically significant way.

Internal Validity: To minimize the influence of other running processes, garbage collector runs, etc., we execute ten iterations of the same experiment per version of CPython. A higher number of experiment runs could increase the confidence in our results.

We chose to conduct our experiment on the FreeBSD operating system, since the amount of processes and daemons running in a default installation is quite small compared to modern Linux, MacOS, or Windows setups. Besides controlling the amount of running processes, one could opt to replicate our experiment on a unikernel operating system like Unikraft [12]. We are confident that our reported results are caused by the version of CPython and that similar patterns of energy consumption would occur in such a setup.

Construct Validity: At the time of setting up our experiment, FreeBSD does not have pre-compiled packages for CPython 3.12 and 3.13. We install them via `pyenv`. Thereby, CPython gets build from sources on the experiment server before installation. We install these two versions of CPython with `pyenv`'s defaults. We did not inspect how precisely the pre-compiled FreeBSD packages are built. There might be a risk that different optimization switches are used to build FreeBSD CPython packages compared to `pyenv`. In case `pyenv` optimizes more aggressively for performance, then our results might overemphasize the more favorable energy efficiency especially of CPython 3.12.

External Validity: We conduct our experiment only on one platform, the Raspberry Pi 1 Model B+ V1.2, which sports a single core Broadcom BCM2835 ARM 6 CPU. Currently, we do not know to which degree our results can be generalized to other or multi-core (ARM) processors.

5 Related Work

With the increased availability of mobile applications, researching the energy impact of various aspects of software became more relevant to larger parts of the software engineering community. On mobile devices, power hungry software is directly perceivable by end-users via quick battery drain. Consequently, researchers focused attention on energy impact of mobile applications on Android or iOS, see e.g., [3,4,8,14,16].

Olivera et al. [16] compare the energy consumption of applications using the three mobile application development frameworks Flutter, React Native, and

Ionic to native Java applications. They find that generally, Flutter imposes the least energy overhead. We believe that our work, can provide the backend counter part to Olivera et al.'s work. Even though possible,[26] CPython applications are rarely deployed to mobile platforms but more often as backend software to data centers in "the cloud". In such environments, software engineers *"rarely have requirements or goals about energy usage"* [15]. That might explain, why high-level interpreted languages like Python, have been of lower priority for the green software engineering community, which we attempt to change with this work.

In general, software engineers care about the energy impact of their code [15]. However, they lack knowledge and support on how to improve energy efficiency of their applications [15,18,22]. The results of our experiment yield an easy to apply high-level solution to increase energy efficiency of CPython applications by just executing them on the "right" version of the interpreter. This differentiates our work from previous work, see e.g., [3,4,13,14,24] which usually focuses on application-level modifications to improve energy efficiency. Our experiment is more coarse-grained. We consider the application a black-box and investigate the impact of the execution environment, the CPython interpreter. To the best of our knowledge, we report the first results of an experiment of such kind.

A common experiment design to investigate energy efficiency of software, is that a set of benchmarks (often the Computer Language Benchmark Game[27] or Rosetta Code[28]) which implement certain algorithms in various programming languages, are executed. Then energy consumption is measured indirectly via power profiling tools like Intel's Power Gadget,[29] Running Average Power Limit [7], Performance Counter Monitor,[30] PowerJoular,[31] or similar estimation tools.[32] Subsequently, programming languages are compared to each other with regards to energy consumption, see, e.g., [2,6,10,17,19,20,26]. In all of these experiments, only a single language version, i.e., interpreter or compiler is considered. Our experiment design differs in that we investigate only one case application, the MiniTwit web-application, where the experiment variable is the version of CPython, the language interpreter.

More rare are experiments that meter power draw or energy consumption directly via a physical power meter, see, e.g., [5,6,9]. Our experiment design is similar to these works. However, we conduct our direct measurements via the Otii Arc Pro, which we are not aware of as reported in similar experiments.

Kirkeby et al. [9] suggest to investigate energy consumption of the live software system, Edora A/S's Work Force Planner. Admittedly, our software is not a production grade system and our three clients are executing predefined scenarios. However, our case application (MiniTwit) is a complete web-application

[26] https://beeware.org/.
[27] https://benchmarksgame-team.pages.debian.net/benchmarksgame/index.html.
[28] https://rosettacode.org/wiki/Rosetta_Code.
[29] https://www.intel.com/content/www/us/en/developer/articles/tool/power-gadget.html.
[30] https://github.com/intel/pcm.
[31] https://github.com/joular/powerjoular.
[32] https://luiscruz.github.io/2021/07/20/measuring-energy.html.

that resembles more a production ready application than the more "artificial" benchmarks used in previous research [2,6,10,17,19,20,26].

Kwon et al. [14] investigate the effect of various distributed programming abstractions like sockets, remote-procedure calls, messages, etc. They experiment with a client-server setup with two separate computers. However, they only have a single client and they measure energy consumption indirectly on the server via the process-level power profiling tool pTopW for a single version of Java. Their experiment variable are the respective distributed programming abstractions.

We are not aware of any experiment that reports assessment of energy efficiency of multiple versions of the same programming language. Wagner et al.'s experiment [26] is most similar to ours in that they compare two web-assembly runtimes (Wasmer and Wasmtime) against each other. These runtimes could be compared to the versions of CPython in our experiment. Unlike in our results, the authors do not find a statistically significant difference in energy consumption when running the same programs on different web-assembly runtimes.

Currently, research results on the impact of runtime to energy efficiency are mixed. For example, Yuki et al. [29] confirm that programs that are optimized for performance are also more energy efficient. On the other hand, e.g., Koedijk et al. [10] identify certain cases where slower programs are more energy efficient compared to faster ones. The results of our experiment show that runtime has the most impact on energy consumption. However, our results also illustrate that runtime optimizations come at the cost of power draw. Future work has to identify the sweet-spot between these two.

6 Future Work

In this paper, we report the first of a planned series of experiments. We will extend this experiment by executing the Python Performance Benchmark Suite.[33] We want to investigate more thoroughly the relation between performance improvements and power draw. Additionally, we plan to conduct these measures not only on one model of the Raspberry Pi but on various newer models and other architectures too. The purpose is to increase confidence in that our results are generalizable over different versions of the ARM processor architecture and over other architectures like Intel/AMD x86.

In the farther future, we plan to substantially extend this work by implementing the same MiniTwit web-application in various programming languages and with different web-frameworks. Our goal is to create more nuanced and more directly applicable results that support practitioners in choosing the "right tool for the job" when implementing sustainable web-applications.

7 Conclusions

In this paper, we investigate the research question: *What is the energy consumption of different versions of the Python interpreter CPython?* Initially, we

[33] https://pyperformance.readthedocs.io/.

assume that more recent versions of Python are less energy efficient than older ones. To investigate our research question, we conduct a controlled lab experiment in which we determine the energy consumption of a webserver sporting various versions of CPython. Three clients execute parallel scenarios against a web-application running on a server. Contrary to our initial assumption, our results show that recent versions of CPython are actually more energy efficient than older versions. Currently, the most energy efficient, i.e., sustainable, version is CPython 3.12. Energy consumption of a web-application can drop by more than 8%, only by exchanging older versions of CPython with CPython 3.12.

Impact for Practitioners: For developers and maintainers, we recommend to switch to CPython 3.12 since our results indicate that it is currently the most energy efficient CPython interpreter. In our experiment, energy consumption drops by more than 8% compared to the most energy consuming CPython 3.10.

For the developers of CPython, our results indicate that the performance improvements that were implemented in recent versions of CPython are not only beneficial from a performance point of view, they also render CPython more sustainable compared to previous versions. We suggest to execute the Python Performance Benchmark Suite (see footnote 33) in a setup similar to ours to continuously monitor also energy efficiency of future CPython versions.

Impact for Researchers: Our work raises multiple questions for researchers to address. Unanswered by our current work, but relevant for future language improvements are questions like a) *Which implementation details cause a Python interpreter to draw more power or to become faster and thereby impact energy consumption?* or b) *What is the precise reason for that power draw increases for certain versions of CPython that are optimized for performance?* We hope that our work inspires other researchers to investigate such questions and thereby help to increase energy efficiency of the reference implementation of the currently most popular programming language.

References

1. Caballar, R.D.: We need to decarbonize software: the way we write software has unappreciated environmental impacts. IEEE Spectr. **61**(4), 26–31 (2024)
2. Couto, M., Pereira, R., Ribeiro, F., Rua, R., Saraiva, J.: Towards a green ranking for programming languages. In: Proceedings of the 21st Brazilian Symposium on Programming Languages, pp. 1–8 (2017)
3. Cruz, L., Abreu, R.: Performance-based guidelines for energy efficient mobile applications. In: 2017 IEEE/ACM 4th International Conference on Mobile Software Engineering and Systems (MOBILESoft), pp. 46–57. IEEE (2017)
4. Cruz, L., Abreu, R.: Catalog of energy patterns for mobile applications. Empir. Softw. Eng. **24**, 2209–2235 (2019)
5. Eder, K., et al.: ENTRA: whole-systems energy transparency. Microprocess. Microsyst. **47**, 278–286 (2016)

6. Georgiou, S., Kechagia, M., Spinellis, D.: Analyzing programming languages' energy consumption: an empirical study. In: Proceedings of the 21st Pan-Hellenic Conference on Informatics, pp. 1–6 (2017)
7. Khan, K.N., Hirki, M., Niemi, T., Nurminen, J.K., Ou, Z.: RAPL in action: experiences in using RAPL for power measurements. ACM Trans. Model. Perform. Eval. Comput. Syst. (TOMPECS) **3**(2), 1–26 (2018)
8. Kholmatova, Z.: Impact of programming languages on energy consumption for mobile devices. In: Proceedings of the 28th ACM Joint Meeting on European Software Engineering Conference and Symposium on the Foundations of Software Engineering, pp. 1693–1695 (2020)
9. Kirkeby, M.H., Gallagher, J.P., Thomsen, B.: An approach to estimating energy consumption of web-based it systems. In: CERCIRAS Workshop-01: Abstracts, p. 18 (2021)
10. Koedijk, L., Oprescu, A.: Finding significant differences in the energy consumption when comparing programming languages and programs. In: 2022 International Conference on ICT for Sustainability (ICT4S), pp. 1–12. IEEE (2022)
11. Kruskal, W.H., Wallis, W.A.: Use of ranks in one-criterion variance analysis. J. Am. Stat. Assoc. **47**(260), 583–621 (1952)
12. Kuenzer, S., et al.: Unikraft: fast, specialized unikernels the easy way. In: Proceedings of the Sixteenth European Conference on Computer Systems, pp. 376–394 (2021)
13. Kumar, M., Li, Y., Shi, W.: Energy consumption in java: an early experience. In: 2017 Eighth International Green and Sustainable Computing Conference (IGSC), pp. 1–8. IEEE (2017)
14. Kwon, Y.W., Tilevich, E.: The impact of distributed programming abstractions on application energy consumption. Inf. Softw. Technol. **55**(9), 1602–1613 (2013)
15. Manotas, I., et al.: An empirical study of practitioners' perspectives on green software engineering. In: Proceedings of the 38th International Conference on Software Engineering, pp. 237–248 (2016)
16. Oliveira, W., Moraes, B., Castor, F., Fernandes, J.P.: Analyzing the resource usage overhead of mobile app development frameworks. In: Proceedings of the 27th International Conference on Evaluation and Assessment in Software Engineering, pp. 152–161 (2023)
17. Oliveira, W., Oliveira, R., Castor, F.: A study on the energy consumption of android app development approaches. In: 2017 IEEE/ACM 14th International Conference on Mining Software Repositories (MSR), pp. 42–52. IEEE (2017)
18. Pang, C., Hindle, A., Adams, B., Hassan, A.E.: What do programmers know about software energy consumption? IEEE Softw. **33**(3), 83–89 (2015)
19. Pereira, R., et al.: Energy efficiency across programming languages: how do energy, time, and memory relate? In: Proceedings of the 10th ACM SIGPLAN International Conference on Software Language Engineering, pp. 256–267 (2017)
20. Pereira, R., et al.: Ranking programming languages by energy efficiency. Sci. Comput. Program. **205**, 102609 (2021)
21. Perez, F., Granger, B.E., Hunter, J.D.: Python: an ecosystem for scientific computing. Comput. Sci. Eng. **13**(2), 13–21 (2010)
22. Pinto, G., Castor, F., Liu, Y.D.: Mining questions about software energy consumption. In: Proceedings of the 11th Working Conference on Mining Software Repositories, pp. 22–31 (2014)
23. Reiser, M.: The Oberon system: user guide and programmer's manual, chap. Preface, p. v. ACM (1991)

24. Reya, N.F., Ahmed, A., Islam, T.: GreenPY: evaluating application-level energy efficiency in python for green computing. Ann. Emerg. Technol. Comput. (AETiC) **7**(3), 93–110 (2023)
25. Van Rossum, G., et al.: Computer programming for everybody. CNRI: Corporation for National Research Initiatives **1999** (1999)
26. Wagner, L., Mayer, M., Marino, A., Soldani Nezhad, A., Zwaan, H., Malavolta, I.: On the energy consumption and performance of webassembly binaries across programming languages and runtimes in IoT. In: Proceedings of the 27th International Conference on Evaluation and Assessment in Software Engineering, pp. 72–82 (2023)
27. Winters, T., Manshreck, T., Wright, H.: Software Engineering at Google: Lessons Learned from Programming Over Time, chap. 24, p. 507. O'Reilly Media, Sebastopol (2020)
28. Wirth, N.: A plea for lean software. Computer **28**(2), 64–68 (1995)
29. Yuki, T., Rajopadhye, S.: Folklore confirmed: compiling for speed = compiling for energy. In: Caşcaval, C., Montesinos, P. (eds.) LCPC 2013. LNCS, vol. 8664, pp. 169–184. Springer, Cham (2014). https://doi.org/10.1007/978-3-319-09967-5_10

Self-adaptation for Sustainable Software and Its Application in Current Approaches - An SLR

Claudia Raibulet[1(✉)] and Qiuyang Fu[2]

[1] University of Milano-Bicocca, DISCo, Viale Sarca 336, 20126 Milan, Italy
claudia.raibulet@unimib.it
[2] Vrije Universiteit Amsterdam, De Boelelaan 1111, Amsterdam, The Netherlands
http://www.disco.unimib.it

Abstract. The role of sustainable approaches has never been as important as it is today, especially with the rising concerns of climate change. Since software is everywhere, sustainability is a key aspect also for software systems. In recent years, the software engineering community is considering more and more the reduction of the overall energy consumption as a key goal for software systems during their execution. To address sustainability from the software engineering perspective, various approaches have been proposed, self-adaptation being one of them. Self-adaptation enables software to be context-aware and self-aware, hence, to change its functioning and performance based on the current execution conditions. From the sustainability point of view, self-adaptation ensures flexibility and efficiency in resource and energy management, for example based on current energy sources, energy consumers, tasks to be executed, and user expectations. In this research, we perform a systematic literature review (SLR) on (1) the use of self-adaptation for achieving sustainability, and (2) the existing approaches in various application domains. Identified studies show that self-adaptation is an effective approach to reach sustainability, mainly reflected in the key abilities of ensuring performance, efficient resource management, and adaptability.

Keywords: Sustainability · Sustainable software · Self-adaptation

1 Introduction

Sustainability is one of the most important global development objectives worldwide. Since software is used everywhere, sustainability is a key aspect also for software systems. The software engineering community is active in achieving sustainability of software systems, such as in the reduction of the overall energy consumption during their execution [5].

Sustainability has four main dimensions: technical, economical, social, and environmental [4]. Further dimensions may be considered, e.g., individual [2]. In this paper, we focus on the technical one: sustainable software aims to continue

A. Bertolino et al. (Eds.): QUATIC 2024, CCIS 2178, pp. 210–226, 2024.
https://doi.org/10.1007/978-3-031-70245-7_15

functioning effectively over a long period of time. To achieve this goal regarding the technical dimension, many quality attributes may be considered, including performance, energy consumption, maintenance, resource management, scalability, and more [12].

One of the available approaches to achieve sustainability for software systems is self-adaptation. Self-adaptation [8,17,24,27,28] enables software to cope with the highly dynamic execution environments. It makes software context-aware and self-aware, and therefore, changes its functioning and performance based on the current execution conditions. This is done in an autonomous way, by the software itself during its execution. From the sustainability point of view, self-adaptation ensures software flexibility over time as well as efficiency in the resources and energy management, for example based on current energy sources, energy consumers, tasks to be executed, and user requirements and expectations.

The goal of this study is to investigate the correlation between sustainability and self-adaptation since both of them have as main objective the "good health" of software. We aim to analyze how self-adaptation can contribute to the development of sustainable software. The focus of our study is to identify the available approaches to build sustainable software through self-adaptation and the quality attributes they address. We are also interested if the available approaches can be applied during the design of the software and/or during its execution. Furthermore, we are interested in the domain dependence of the identified approaches in order to understand their potential applicability and reusability in different application domains. As far as concerns our knowledge, no literature review on the correlation between sustainability and self-adaptation in general (domain independent) is available.

From the results of our study, it is expected to better comprehend the advantages of applying self-adaptation at both design-time and run-time, and have a clear understanding of how the implementations address sustainability as an explicit and primary objective. To accomplish these goals, the literature review follows the approach proposed by Kitchenham et al. [13]. An initial search has lead to the identification of 234 potential results, that have been further reduced to 12 primary studies. The study has been performed between December 2022 and December 2023.

The rest of the paper is organized as follows. Section 2 summarizes the related work. Section 3 describes the study design. The extracted data is analyzed in Sect. 4. Section 5 presents the results and answers research questions. Results are discussed in Sect. 6. Section 7 addresses the threats to validity. Conclusions and further work are summarized in Sect. 8.

2 Related Work

In this section, related studies on enabling technical sustainability through self-adaptation are mentioned.

Moghaddam et al. [21] study the existing approaches for energy efficiency using self-adaptive software and classify them into three major categories: Software Design Approaches (SDA), System Engineering Approaches (SEA),

SEA+SDA. The authors analyze the publication trends, application domains, and types of software systems for the identified results. Their analysis has shown that the SEA type of approaches has been dominating the research field, and the hybrid SEA+SDA are only occasionally discussed. Self-adaptation and energy efficiency are discussed in their review, and their research goals share some common interests with our study, i.e., to identify and evaluate sustainable (energy efficiency is a part of it) self-adaptive solutions.

Restrepo et al. [25] perform a mapping study on sustainable approaches for self-adaptive cyber-physical systems. Even though some of their research objectives are on hardware, their software point of view also provides valuable information. They present the system development life cycle (SDLC) to explain how systems are built in different stages. To address self-adaptation, they introduce the MAPE-K (Monitoring, Analysis, Planning, Execution on a common Knowledge base) feedback loop to demonstrate how the systems manage themselves to achieve their objectives. Detailed descriptions of how each stage of SDLC can address self-adaptation is provided. Sustainability is seen as a quality attribute in the development phase, and it is linked to adaptability, scalability, energy efficiency, modularity, and reusability.

Mistrik et al. [26] present a systematic literature review on the trade-off (among multiple quality attributes) managing in engineering self-adaptive software. They outline that to build sustainable software through self-adaptation, an optimal trade-off management is crucial to deal with uncertainties at runtime [26]. The quality attributes mentioned in the trade-off management are: adaptability, complexity, reliability, safety, flexibility, performance, energy efficiency.

Our study focuses on self-adaptive solutions that address sustainable and green software in general. It identifies the quality attributes addressed through self-adaptation that have an impact on sustainability. Further, it analyses the identified approaches based on their domain-dependency and on time (e.g., design time, runtime) when sustainability is addressed.

3 Study Design

This study investigates the correlations between sustainable software and self-adaptation and examines the quality attributes addressed by self-adaptation meaningful for sustainability. Further, it identifies the current approaches of building sustainable software through self-adaptive mechanisms. To formulate the research questions, the "Goal-Question-Metric" method [10] is applied.

Purpose: Identify the influence of self-adaptation on building sustainable software, as well as the approaches to achieve this goal.

Issue: With the emergence of climate change, building sustainable software is more important than ever. Software is expected to run in dynamic environments, which are not completely predictable at design time. Hence, software needs to be able to deal with unpredictable issues in constantly changing complex execution conditions. To enable software to adapt and update itself in dynamic environments, self-adaptation needs to be implemented to ensure its performance, and, hence, its sustainability.

Object: Self-adaptation and sustainability.

Viewpoint: Self-adaptation and sustainability share some common interests, including but not limited to: performance, optimization, efficiency, resource utilization and management, robustness. Therefore, self-adaptation represents an efficient approach to build sustainable software.

To achieve these goals, we formulate the following research questions:

RQ1: How can self-adaptation contribute to greener software regarding the technical dimension of sustainability?

By answering RQ1, the main correlations between self-adaptation and sustainability are identified. This contributes to the understanding of the motivation, use, and application of self-adaptation for greener software.

RQ2: For each primary study concerning self-adaptation for sustainable software, is it domain-dependent or independent? And when is sustainability addressed: at design time or at run time?

By answering RQ2, approaches to build sustainable software through self-adaptation are identified, as well as their application domains. We investigate whether available approaches in an application domain can be applied/reused also in other application domains. For each approach, we indicate when sustainability is addressed, at design and/or run time.

Initial Search: For the search of potentially meaningful scientific results, we extract the following keywords from our two RQ: **"self adapt*" AND (sustainab* OR green) AND software**. Different ways to describe "sustainability" and "self-adaptive" are included for searching. And because the focus is on software rather than hardware, *software* is added to the query as a constraint to filter false positive results.

The selected scientific databases are ACM Digital Library, IEEE Xplore, Science Direct, and Scopus. The query for Science Direct is slightly modified due to its syntax requirements. All types of research papers are included. After searching using the above query and selecting appropriate filters to rule out non-English and inaccessible literature, there are initially 234 (see Fig. 1) results.

Selection Criteria: By applying the following literature inclusion (IC) and exclusion (EX) criteria, we identified the relevant literature for this study.

- IC1- The study extensively addresses "self-adaptation" as a solution or goal to achieve.
- IC2- The study extensively addresses "sustainability", "green software", or "energy efficiency" as a significant quality attribute.
- IC3- The study introduces approaches or methods to achieve sustainable software through self-adaptation.
- IC4- The study is peer-reviewed. This criterion guarantees the quality of the selected literature.

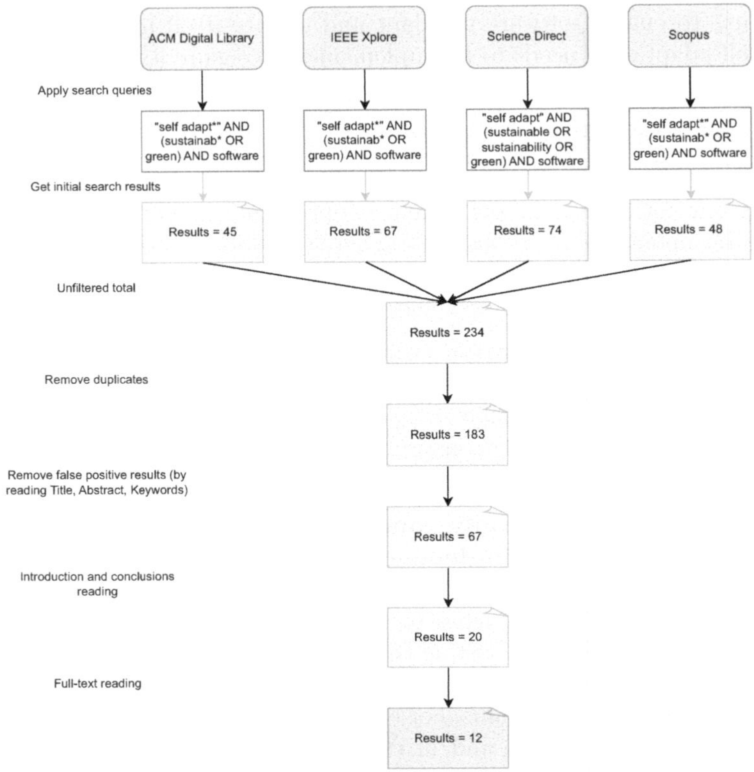

Fig. 1. Literature Selection

EX1- The study does not provide solutions for "self-adaptation".
EX2- The study does not take "sustainability" into account. For "sustainability", we ensure it is from a software point of view rather than hardware and others.
EX3- The study is not published in the field of software engineering/computer science and is not written in English.

Literature Selection Process: Figure 1 shows the steps of selecting relevant literature. Through the queries to the search engines, 234 studies have been identified. The removal of duplicates has lead to 183 unique results. We have examined the titles, abstracts, and keywords of the 183 results to identify the relevant papers and remove the false positive ones. The number of results has been reduced to 67. We have further read the Introduction and the Conclusion sections, to have a better overview of the papers. We have reduced the number of the results to 20. We have also applied snowballing to identify further potential primary studies. No additional studies have been identified. The last step consisted in reading the 20 papers. We have identified 12 primary studies.

Data Extraction: Table 1 presents the finalized list of the identified studies.

Table 1. Literature Identifiers

ID	Ref	Literature Title
Weyns 2023	[30]	Self-Adaptation in Industry: A Survey
Gerostathopoulos 2022	[9]	Expressing the Adaptation Intent as a Sustainability Goal
Fierro 2021	[7]	Self-Adapting Software for Cyberphysical Systems
Kumar 2020	[14]	DATESSO: Self-Adapting Service Composition with Debt-Aware Two Levels Constraint Reasoning
Moghaddam 2019	[19]	Self-adaptation for energy efficiency in software systems
Hidaka 2019	[11]	Design and Engineering of Adaptive Software Systems
Michanan 2017	[18]	GreenC5: An adaptive, energy-aware collection for green software development
Moghaddam 2017	[20]	A self-adaptive framework for enhancing energy efficiency in mobile applications
Bergen 2014	[3]	Towards software-adaptive green computing based on server power consumption
Macías-Escrivá 2013	[16]	Self-adaptive systems: A survey of current approaches, research challenges and applications
Perez-Palacin 2011	[22]	Enhancing a QoS-based self-adaptive framework with energy management capabilities
Dustdar 2010	[6]	A roadmap towards sustainable self-aware service systems

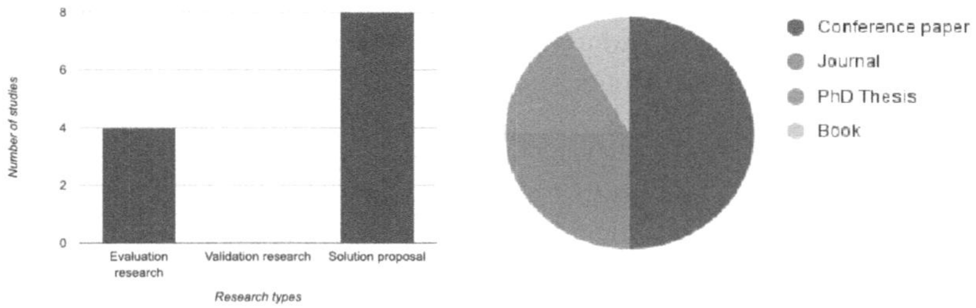

Fig. 2. Data Analysis: a) Research Types b) Publication Types

Study Replicability: The search process can be replicated by applying queries mentioned in Fig. 1, using the inclusion and exclusion criteria, and appropriate filter options in search engines. The data extraction Excel sheet that contains extracted data from primary studies can be found in a Drive folder[1].

4 Data Analysis

A first analysis of the identified studies is done based on their main goal: solution proposal, validation research, and evaluation research [23] (see Fig. 2). Solution proposals provide detailed descriptions on how to achieve implementation goals. They introduce new approaches. Validation researches verify the correctness of implementations and provide valuable feedback based on experiment results. Evaluation researches represent the studies that assess the quality of existing

[1] https://docs.google.com/spreadsheets/d/1K0TicPcOQXKZC-tdXH1N6C1fupPeB -qq/edit?usp=sharing\&ouid=104274783440284037753\&rtpof=true\&sd=true GoogleDrive.

methods. We observe that most of our primary studies represent solution proposals, while there is a lack in validation research.

Further, half of the studies are conference papers (see Fig. 2). A possible motivation for no workshop papers, may indicate the availability of a limited number of workshops on this topic. A limited number of journal papers may indicate the topic is still new, not mature yet. Finally, we note that the primary studies are published starting from 2010. We may suppose that studies on self-adaptation before 2010 rarely discuss sustainability as a key objective.

5 Results

In this section, the two RQs are answered by providing an overview on each primary study and extracting the quality attributes addressed through self-adaptation that have impact on sustainability. Further, for each primary study, we investigate if the approach is domain independent or domain dependent, and if sustainability is addressed at design time, at runtime, or both.

The primary studies are ordered based on their publication year, from the most recent to the less recent one.

5.1 RQ1

How can self-adaptation contribute to greener software regarding the technical dimension of sustainability?

[Weyns 2023] [30] evaluates the application of self-adaptation in industry, and reports that self-adaptation may improve resource/cost utility and energy savings over time, and reduce human handling errors [30]. Hence, sustainability is translated into efficient resource management and software quality maintenance (e.g., by automating administration tasks and avoiding human errors). It addresses the following quality attributes: availability, robustness, safety, resilience, complexity, energy efficiency, performance, and adaptability. This study is an extension of [29].

[Gerostathopoulos 2022] [9] proposes an approach that uses decision maps to make decisions on sustainability as a significant quality attribute while designing sustainable software through self-adaptation. The method guarantees that the "green concept" is addressed in every step of self-adaptation and therefore the final product is sustainable. The following quality attributes are indicated: stability, performance, energy efficiency, maintainability, and reliability.

[Fierro 2021] [7] exploits self-adaptation in cyber physical environments for understanding the execution context and consequentially for configuring properly the functionalities. It addresses various quality attributes including performance, energy efficiency, availability, maintainability, robustness, contriollability, reusability, resilience, and availability.

[Kumar 2020] [14] proposes a framework using the "technical debt" metaphor which aims to significantly decrease the accumulated debt over time, therefore increasing the accumulated benefits in the long term. The discussed quality attributes are: maintainability, performance, and energy efficiency.

[Moghaddam 2019] [19] stats that traditional software is not as energy efficient as the self-adaptive ones because it does not adapt to dynamic changes in the environments and, hence, does not allocate resources accordingly; these matters limit their performance. Through self-adaptation, software is not only capable of adapting changes, but also recovering from them. The quality attributes addressed are: stability, maintainability, energy efficiency, adaptability, availability, reliability, flexibility, performance, resilience, scalability, reusability, and resilience.

[Hidaka 2019] [11] outlines guidelines for the development of self-adaptive solutions based on the steps of the MAPE-K feedback loop. Further, it proposes an approach to handle models in self-adaptive systems. The main quality attributes considered are performance, controllability, and reliability.

[Michanan 2017] [18] introduces the "GreenC5" prototype, a software development approach using adaptation. It demonstrates that the GreenC5 data structure can be trained to enable self-awareness, thus providing the ability to classify, predict, and adapt for changes at run-time to achieve energy efficiency. The mentioned quality attributes are: performance, energy efficiency, reusability, maintainability, and flexibility.

[Moghaddam 2017] [20] proposes a self-adaptive framework to enhance energy efficiency for mobile applications, and stats that the framework would contribute to green software by introducing more efficient resource allocation methods. They address adaptability, performance, and energy efficiency.

[Bergen 2014] [3] evaluates the effects of self-adaptation on power consumption of a data center, and proposes an adaptive framework to achieve sustainability. They show that self-adaptive techniques improve job scheduling and resource provisioning, and reduce overall power consumption in clouds. The discussed quality attributes are: scalability, performance, energy efficiency, adaptability, and controllability.

[Macías-Escrivá 2013] [16] evaluates the consequences of applying self-adaptation techniques, and concludes that self-adaptive software tend to have better flexibility, resource utilization, energy efficiency, and robustness. These benefits strengthen the ability to deal with changes in dynamic environments. The quality attributes they mention are: dependability, robustness, adaptability, availability, flexibility, stability, performance, and reliability.

[Perez-Palacin 2011] [22] proposes a QoS-based self-adaptive framework that includes energy management capabilities as a core requirement. It concludes that self-adaptation can lead to less energy waste over time and it makes systems to only use the resources when necessary. The addressed quality attributes are: energy efficiency, adaptability, and performance.

[Dustdar 2010] [6] notices that in service systems, sustainability does not only address energy consumption, but all limited resources. If the self-adaptation level for services is high, services should consume less energy and better use

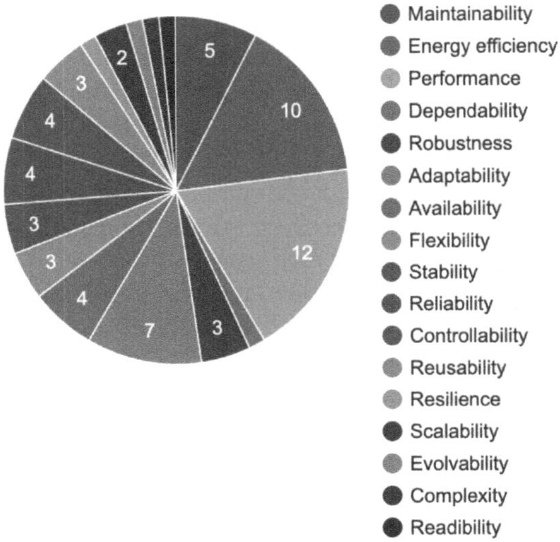

Fig. 3. Quality Attributes Addressed by Self-Adaptation Meaningful for Sustainability

Table 2. Main Objectives of Self-Adaptation and Their Link to Sustainability

Nr.	Objectives	Objectives common to sustainability
1	Improve overall performance	*
2	Increase reliability	*
3	Strengthen robustness	*
4	Minimize human interactions	
5	Increase usability	
6	Enhance safety through self-protecting	*
7	Improve resource management	*
8	Ensure maintainability	*
9	Enable scalability	*
10	Adaptation to dynamic environments	*

resources. The mentioned quality attributes are: adaptability, controllability, energy efficiency, reliability, performance, robustness, and availability.

Figure 3 shows the quality attributes mentioned in the primary studies that are addressed by self-adaptation and that are meaningful for the sustainability. It also indicates the number of times the quality attributes are discussed in the primary studies. Table 2 summarizes some of the well-known main objectives of self-adaptation in general [27,28]. We indicate which of these objectives are correlated to sustainability [1,15].

5.2 RQ2

For each primary study concerning self-adaptation for sustainable software, is it domain-dependent or independent? And when is sustainability addressed: at design time or at run time?

[Weyns 2023] [30] explains that self-adaptation is used at different levels of software in industry (i.e., domain-independent), and the most popular types of adaptation to reduce cost and improve performance efficiency are: auto-scaling, auto-configurations, and auto-tuning (i.e., *runtime*).

[Gerostathopoulos 2022] [9] proposes a software design strategy using decision maps to address self-adaptation and sustainability *at design time* in the engineering process (i.e., *domain independent*).

[Fierro 2021] [7] proposed two programming models for self-adaptive software: Stayed, and Interactive. Both use SPARQL to access the metadata model defining specific environments; implementations are conducted together with hardware engineering. This study builds self-adaptive software for cyber-physical systems (*domain-dependent*). Sustainability is discussed at *design-time.*

[Kumar 2020] [14] focuses on service oriented composition and provided a two level constraint (global and local) reasoning approach (i.e., *domain-dependent*). The approach has more effective utilization, less latency, while introducing "self" properties to enable them to be more sustainable. Sustainability is managed at both *design and run-time.*

[Moghaddam 2019] [19] proposes an approach for modeling energy-efficient software by exploiting self-adaptation (i.e., *domain-independent*). The approach includes architectural and infrastructural concepts, which provides an overall image of enabling self-adaptability in software. Sustainability is addressed both at *design and runtime.*

[Hidaka 2019] [11] provides generic implementation methods to build self-adaptive software, and describes a conceptual model of how to identify different components of an adaptive system (i.e., *domain-independent*). They state that a good practice of building such a system is to provide appropriate implementations for the five dimensions: identification, observation, representation, control, and adaptation mechanisms. Sustainability is addressed at *run-time.*

[Michanan 2017] [18] explains that on top of including sustainability into every phase of the software engineering process, they also apply adaptive green data structure to deal with dynamic workload. With machine learning, the green data structure can efficiently adapt for energy efficiency with low overhead. Due to the broad applications of green data structure, it can be potentially applied in many different areas with optimal performance (i.e., *domain independent*). Sustainability is addressed at both *design and run-time.*

[Moghaddam 2017] [20] categorizes the components of the framework using the MAPE model. The proposed solution introduces a "schedular" to use resources in mobile applications, and five related strategies: Baseline Strategy, Bunding Strategy, FIFO Strategy, Multipath Strategy, and Multi-interface Strategy. Together with the MAPE model, these strategies can be used accordingly for better mobile application production (i.e., *domain dependent*). The study addresses sustainability at *design-time.*

[Bergen 2014] [3] evaluates studies that explain the steps through which software can become more situation-aware and green-aware in dynamic conditions. They conclude that the main three steps are: improve the models of context, enable the resulting models to support variations in the context at run-time, and enhance monitoring techniques so they can adapt changes in the environments. Their study focuses on cloud-based software (i.e., *domain-dependent*), and sustainability is addressed at *run-time.*

[Macías-Escrivá 2013] [16] explores the approaches to build self-adaptive systems and classifies them into two categories. The top-down systems are usually centralized, and the central controllers or policies learn the behaviors in the environments, and adjust themselves accordingly. The bottom-up approaches operate without a central controller and are decentralized, i.e., the components adapt themselves separately. This study provides valuable information on designing self-adaptive software systems. The approaches they studied are *domain-independent*, and they addressed sustainability at *design-time.*

[Perez-Palacin 2011] [22] studies a three-layer architecture for self-adaptive systems named KM-3L. The layers (goal management, change management, component control) enable systems to adapt to changes and react in dynamic environments by learning the results from monitoring. Their study focuses on service-based software (i.e., *domain-dependent*), and addresses sustainability at both *design and run-time.*

[Dustdar 2010] [6] identifies 5 conceptual awareness levels in order to achieve optimal self-adaptation: event-awareness, situation-awareness, adaptability-awareness, goal-awareness, and future-awareness. Theses concepts are particularly useful for building self-adaptive service systems (i.e., *domain-dependent*) as developers are able to diagnose how much of self-adaptation has been put into the systems. Sustainability is addressed at *design-time.*

Figure 4 shows the numbers of studies that are domain-dependent or independent and the numbers of studies that address sustainability at design-time, or run-time, or both.

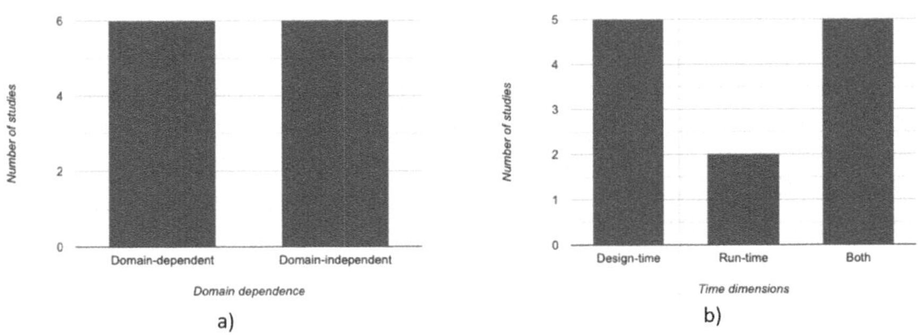

Fig. 4. Domain and Time Dependence

6 Discussion

RQ1: Discussion and Findings: Through our study we have identified the three most addressed quality attributes in building sustainable software through self-adaptation in the available approaches: *performance*, *energy efficiency*, and *adaptability* (see Fig. 3). This result confirms and outlines the correlation between self-adaptation and sustainability: these quality attributes are also among the most important objectives of self-adaptation in general (see Table 2), and all of them contribute to achieve sustainability. From the results analyzed in Sect. 5, it is safe to conclude that self-adaptation can contribute to greener software by ensuring that software continues to function optimally over time (i.e., performance) despite environmental changes and reducing the likelihood of failures and downtime (i.e., adaptability). Further, self-adaptation can also contribute to software sustainability by adjusting dynamically the resource usage according to the changing execution conditions, and therefore, leading to a more efficient resource management and reducing energy waste (i.e., energy efficiency).

Finding 1: Three main quality attributes for sustainable software are achieved through self-adaptation: (1) ensure software **performance** in any execution conditions and in any moment in time, (2) manage resources dynamically to achieve **energy efficiency**, and (3) be flexible to ensure **adaptability** to changes without human intervention.

RQ2: Discussion and Findings: The analysis in Sect. 5 shows that there are various approaches to build sustainable software using self-adaptive mechanisms. They can be discussed from different points of view. In this paper, we focused on two of them: domain dependence and time dependence.

The domain dependence dimension indicates if the available approaches can be applied to every software or they are specific to software for an application domain. The results show that the number of domain dependent and domain independent available approaches is equal (see Fig. 4). The domain dependent approaches are mostly build for cyber-physical systems, service-based software, mobile software, cloud-based software, or service systems.

Finding 2: Both **domain dependent** and **domain independent** approaches for achieving sustainability through self-adaptation are available.

We can discuss that approaches effective in one domain may not be suitable or effective in another, making it important to tailor self-adaptive software solutions to the specific needs of each domain. For example, self-adaptation approaches for cyber-physical systems (CPS) are designed to manage the complexity and uncertainty of CPS environments by adapting to changes in the environment, system behavior, and workload. These approaches often rely on sensing, decision-making, and actuation mechanisms to dynamically adjust system parameters to maintain desired levels of performance and reliability. However, self-adaptation approaches for CPS may not be directly applicable to cloud computing environments for several reasons. For example, CPS and cloud computing environments have different characteristics and requirements. CPS often involve physical processes that are tightly coupled with their computing and communication systems, whereas cloud computing environments may be more focused on software and virtualized resources. Or, cloud computing environments may have different requirements for reliability, performance, and scalability than CPS environments. For example, in a CPS environment, safety can often be the primary concern, whereas in a cloud computing environment, scalability and cost-effectiveness may be the key qualities.

Finding 3: Different domains may have unique requirements, constraints, and operating conditions, which can impact the effectiveness of specific approaches for building sustainable software through self-adaptation. Therefore, the design and implementation of sustainable self-adaptive software requires ***domain-specific knowledge***.

The time dependence dimension indicates if the available approaches focus on solutions applied at design time or at runtime. The results show that the number of design time and runtime approaches is equal (see Fig. 4). Additionally, there are two approaches considering both design time and runtime solutions. The design time solutions consider explicitly the sustainability goals, its requirements, and its impact on the design of a software. For example, software is designed to include monitoring and reasoning mechanisms, i.e., mechanisms common to self-adaptation. Therefore, they are of key importance during the entire lifecycle of a software. The runtime solutions come to extend and complement the design time ones, by applying the mechanisms dedicated to achieving sustainability during the software execution. For example, various self-adaptation strategies targeting sustainability can be used or learnt at runtime.

Finding 4: Sustainability is not implicitly achieved in any software. It should be addressed as an explicit requirement considered during the design and implemented through dedicated mechanisms. Further, since sustainability concerns the functioning of a software *over time*, it is achieved during the execution phase. Therefore, both **design time** and **runtime solutions** are needed for building sustainable software through self-adaptation.

7 Threats to Validity

This section discusses briefly the four main threats to validity widely mentioned in the software engineering field.

External Validity: To minimize the external influences, the quality of the databases is ensured by selecting the most reputed academic digital libraries for computer science and software engineering.

Internal Validity: RQs are defined to identify the relevant papers on sustainability and self-adaptation. In spite of our effort, the search queries may have limitations in not identifying all the variants of the searched keywords.

Construct Validity: The GQM method is applied for constructing the RQs. This ensures that the goals of the study are early defined. Every step of the study design is documented.

Conclusion Validity: The results of our study emerge from the analyzed data. The answers to the RQs reflect the content of the primary studies.

8 Conclusions and Further Work

This literature study focuses on the relationship between self-adaptation and sustainability with the objective to find potential links among them. *Self-adaptation and sustainability share some common goals.* On one hand, self-adaptation empowers software with "self" properties such as self-configuration, self-healing, self-optimizing, and self-protecting. Through these properties, software is able to optimize its resource usage, to ensure its performances, to detect faults and potential threats, and, hence, to adapt to uncertainties and changes in dynamic environments without (or with minimal) human interaction. This ensures and improves software performance. On the other hand, sustainability denotes the capacity of a software to endure and preserve its function and performances over time. Hence, sustainability is concerned with energy efficiency, scalability, maintainability, robustness, performance, among others.

Self-adaptation and sustainability have the common objective of ensuring the health, i.e., the appropriate and good functioning and performance of software systems in the dynamic contexts. Self-adaptation is focused on short time frames, while sustainability is focused on long time frames. Therefore, self-adaptation may be a promising mechanism to ensure sustainability.

This study has identified the quality attributes addressed by self-adaptation that have a significant impact on achieving sustainability. It has outlined the main objectives of self-adaptation that contribute to achieve sustainability.

Further, we have identified various different approaches that aim to use self-adaptation to build green software. They are domain-dependent or independent. And sustainability can be addressed both at design and run-time. The approaches that address sustainability at design-time illustrate ways to allow developers to "think green" and design greener architectures during development. The approaches that address sustainability at run-time provide explicit hints and guidelines on how to include the self properties and the key quality attributes that contribute to achieve sustainability using code. It is also worth noting that the domain-dependent approaches are designed for specific areas of application and may not work in other different domains. The requirements, constraints and operating conditions can be completely different and the domain-specific strategies, knowledge, and metrics are also not transferable to other domains.

A potential future research direction could be combining some of the existing domain-dependent approaches and develop a new hybrid solution that integrates their features. Another next step may include the mapping of sustainability goals on self-adaptive goals. Sustainability may be defined as a set of self-adaptation steps that should be achieved over time. Furthermore, there is a need of defining self-adaptation strategies that reflect sustainability goals and that are applied continuously over time.

References

1. Andrikopoulos, V., Boza, R., Perales, C., Lago, P.: Sustainability in software architecture: a systematic mapping study. In: Callicó, G.M., Hebig, R., Wortmann, A. (eds.) 48th Euromicro Conference on Software Engineering and Advanced Applications, pp. 426–433 (2022). https://doi.org/10.1109/SEAA56994.2022.00073
2. Becker, C., et al.: Sustainability design and software: The karlskrona manifesto. In: 37th International Conference on Software Engineering, pp. 467–476 (2015). https://doi.org/10.1109/ICSE.2015.179
3. Bergen, A., Desmarais, R., Ganti, S., Stege, U.: Towards software-adaptive green computing based on server power consumption. In: 3rd International Workshop on Green and Sustainable Software, pp. 9–16 (2014). https://doi.org/10.1145/2593743.2593745
4. Betz, S., Caporale, T.: Sustainable software system engineering. In: 4th International Conference on Big Data and Cloud Computing, pp. 612–619 (2014). https://doi.org/10.1109/BDCloud.2014.113
5. Calero, C., et al.: 5ws of green and sustainable software. Tsinghua Sci. Technol. **25**(3), 401–414 (2020). https://doi.org/10.26599/TST.2019.9010006
6. Dustdar, S., et al.: A roadmap towards sustainable self-aware service systems. In: ICSE Workshop on Software Engineering for Adaptive and Self-Managing Systems, pp. 10–19 (2010). https://doi.org/10.1145/1808984.1808986
7. Fierro, G.: Self-Adapting Software for Cyberphysical Systems. Ph.D. thesis, EECS Department, University of California, Berkeley (2021). http://www2.eecs.berkeley.edu/Pubs/TechRpts/2021/EECS-2021-159.html
8. Ganek, A.G., Corbi, T.A.: The dawning of the autonomic computing era. IBM Syst. J. **42**(1), 5–18 (2003). https://doi.org/10.1147/sj.421.0005
9. Gerostathopoulos, I., Raibulet, C., Lago, P.: Expressing the adaptation intent as a sustainability goal. In: International Conference on Software Engineering: New Ideas and Emerging Results, pp. 36–40 (2022). https://doi.org/10.1145/3510455.3512776
10. Gianluigi, V.R.B.G.: The goal question metric paradigm: The goal question metric approach. Encycl. Softw. Eng. **1**, 528–532 (1994)
11. Hidaka, S., et al.: Design and engineering of adaptive software systems, pp. 1–33 (2019). https://doi.org/10.1007/978-981-13-2185-6_1
12. Johann, T., Dick, M., Kern, E., Naumann, S.: Sustainable development, sustainable software, and sustainable software engineering: an integrated approach. In: 2011 International Symposium on Humanities, Science and Engineering Research, pp. 34–39 (2011). https://doi.org/10.1109/SHUSER.2011.6008495
13. Kitchenham, B., Pearl Brereton, O., Budgen, D., Turner, M., Bailey, J., Linkman, S.: Systematic literature reviews in software engineering - a systematic literature review. Inf. Softw. Technol. **51**(1), 7–15 (2009). https://doi.org/10.1016/j.infsof.2008.09.009

14. Kumar, S., Chen, T., Bahsoon, R., Buyya, R.: Datesso: self-adapting service composition with debt-aware two levels constraint reasoning. In: 15th International Symposium on Software Engineering for Adaptive and Self-Managing Systems, pp. 96–107 (2020). https://doi.org/10.1145/3387939.3391604
15. Lago, P., Greefhorst, D., Woods, E.: Architecting for sustainability. In: Wohlgemuth, V., Naumann, S., Arndt, H., Behrens, G., Höb, M. (eds.) 36th International Conference on Informatics for Environmental Protection. LNI, vol. P-328, pp. 199–210 (2022). https://dl.gi.de/20.500.12116/39397
16. Macías-Escrivá, F.D., Haber, R., del Toro, R., Hernandez, V.: Self-adaptive systems: a survey of current approaches, research challenges and applications. Expert Syst. Appl. **40**(18), 7267–7279 (2013). https://doi.org/10.1016/j.eswa.2013.07.033
17. Masciadri, L., Raibulet, C.: Frameworks for the development of adaptive systems: evaluation of their adaptability feature through software metrics. In: 4th International Conference on Software Engineering Advances, ICSEA 2009, pp. 309–312 (2009). https://doi.org/10.1109/ICSEA.2009.51
18. Michanan, J., Dewri, R., Rutherford, M.J.: Greenc5: an adaptive, energy-aware collection for green software development. Sustain. Comput. Inf. Syst. **13**, 42–60 (2017). https://doi.org/10.1016/j.suscom.2016.11.004
19. Moghaddam, A.: Self-adaptation for energy efficiency in software systems. Ph.D. thesis, University of Amsterdam (2019)
20. Moghaddam, F.A., Simaremare, M., Lago, P., Grosso, P.: A self-adaptive framework for enhancing energy efficiency in mobile applications. In: 2017 Sustainable Internet and ICT for Sustainability (SustainIT), pp. 1–3 (2017). https://doi.org/10.23919/SustainIT.2017.8379811
21. Moghaddam, F.A., Lago, P., Ban, I.C.: Self-adaptation approaches for energy efficiency: a systematic literature review. In: 6th International Workshop on Green and Sustainable Software, pp. 35–42 (2018). https://doi.org/10.1145/3194078.3194084
22. Perez-Palacin, D., Mirandola, R., Merseguer, J.: Enhancing a QoS-based self-adaptive framework with energy management capabilities. In: 7th International Conference on the Quality of Software Architectures and 2nd International Symposium on Architecting Critical Systems, pp. 165–170 (2011). https://doi.org/10.1145/2000259.2000287
23. Petersen, K., Feldt, R., Mujtaba, S., Mattsson, M.: Systematic mapping studies in software engineering. In: 12th International Conference on Evaluation and Assessment in Software Engineering, pp. 68–77 (2008)
24. Raibulet, C., Fontana, F.A., Carettoni, S.: A preliminary analysis of self-adaptive systems according to different issues. Software Qual. J. **28**(3), 1213–1243 (2020). https://doi.org/10.1007/s11219-020-09502-5
25. Restrepo, L., Aguilar, J., Toro, M., Suescún, E.: A sustainable-development approach for self-adaptive cyber-physical system's life cycle: a systematic mapping study. J. Syst. Softw. **180**, 111010 (2021). https://doi.org/10.1016/j.jss.2021.111010
26. Salama, M., Bahsoon, R., Bencomo, N.: Chapter 11 - managing trade-offs in self-adaptive software architectures: a systematic mapping study. In: Mistrik, I., Ali, N., Kazman, R., Grundy, J., Schmerl, B. (eds.) Managing Trade-Offs in Adaptable Software Architectures, pp. 249–297. Morgan Kaufmann, Boston (2017). https://doi.org/10.1016/B978-0-12-802855-1.00011-3
27. Salehie, M., Tahvildari, L.: Self-adaptive software: Landscape and research challenges. ACM Trans. Auton. Adapt. Syst. **4**(2), 14:1–14:42 (2009). https://doi.org/10.1145/1516533.1516538

28. Weyns, D.: An Introduction to Self-adaptive Systems: A Contemporary Software Engineering Perspective (2020)
29. Weyns, D., et al.: Preliminary results of a survey on the use of self-adaptation in industry. In: 17h Symposium on Software Engineering for Adaptive and Self-Managing Systems, pp. 70–76 (2022). https://doi.org/10.1145/3524844.3528077
30. Weyns, D., et al.: Self-adaptation in industry: a survey. ACM Trans. Auton. Adapt. Syst. **18**(2), 5:1–5:44 (2023). https://doi.org/10.1145/3589227

A New Metric of Adaptivity for Self-adaptive Systems

Giulio Masetti[1,2](✉), Silvano Chiaradonna[1], and Felicita Di Giandomenico[1]

[1] Istituto di Scienza e Tecnologia dell'Informazione, CNR, Pisa, Italy
106ohm@gmail.com, {silvano.chiaradonna, felicita.digiandomenico}@isti.cnr.it
[2] Istituto Comprensivo di Anghiari e Monterchi, Anghiari, Italy

Abstract. With focus on open-ended architectural adaptation, where individual components represent alternatives that can be added and removed dynamically at runtime, a new metric is proposed to provide insights on the effectiveness of architectural changes, such as the addition or removal of components. Specifically, the new metric allows to assess how much the system actually adapts to variations of the environment by properly applying a system reconfiguration. The approach is based on a statistical analysis of the system, which exploits the Bell inequality, conveniently adapted from the Quantum Mechanic theory. The formal definition of the new adaptability metric is presented, as well as an example of application in a simple case study.

Keywords: self-adaptive architectures · adaptivity metric · statistical analysis

1 Introduction and Related Work

Self-adaptive systems are able to change their structure and behavior at runtime according to the volatile environments in which they are executed in order to continue to meet their nonfunctional goals, such as their lifespan, resource use, operating costs and response latency. They are typically realized via feedback loops that continuously monitor their environment and state, and apply changes to the system [8,9]. In recent years the interest of the community in adaptivity evaluation methodologies and frameworks is increasing [10,11].

In this short paper we consider architecture-based self-adaptive systems, and the focus is on open-ended architectural adaptation, where individual components represent alternatives that can be added and removed dynamically at runtime [8]. In this context, quality metrics [14] such as average response latency and average utility value (that combines latency, revenue and cost) are typically used to select the most suitable architectural configuration (composition) with respect to the current workload pattern (environment) and to the adaptation goal. Moreover, adaptivity metrics are used to evaluate the quality of the adaptation from a local

A. Bertolino et al. (Eds.): QUATIC 2024, CCIS 2178, pp. 227–234, 2024.
https://doi.org/10.1007/978-3-031-70245-7_16

(e.g., adaptivity of a service or agent or a subset of components) or global perspective (e.g., overall time for adaptation, decentralization degree) [14].

The contribution offered in this paper goes in the direction of gaining further insights on the quality of the adaptation from a local perspective, in particular on the effect of runtime architectural changes, such as the addition of new components, or the ability to remove components that have been shown less attractive than thought at design time. To this purpose, a new adaptivity metric is proposed, based on a runtime statistical analysis of any quality metric (e.g., performance, optimization) defined on a subset of individual components, which exploits the Bell inequality [3,5] to measure how much the individual components actually adapt (to variations of the environment). It measures variations in joint distributions of the selected quality metric related to individual components when new compositions are adopted at runtime. The idea is imported and adapted from [1,4], where concepts originated in Quantum Mechanics are applied to (and in some sense explained through) macroscopic objects. In this respect, the proposed contribution is not a new quality metric (e.g., time needed to change something, as in Table 13.1 [14]) since it combines already defined local quality metrics to evaluate components' adaptivity. Rather, it is a way to translate "adaptivity" in probability/statistics terms regardless of the underling utility metrics semantics, being a purely syntactical procedure.

From a practical viewpoint, this adaptivity metric allows to assess the ability of each individual component, involved in more than one composition, to behave in accordance with which other components are active, i.e., its adaptivity to changes in the configuration as encountered during the system lifetime. It can be exploited as a runtime support to take decision on new system reconfigurations. In addition, the quantities computed as intermediary steps in the adaptivity metric evaluation process can serve as generalized correlation indices among components, thus offering further valuable information about how they adapt. Compute and reason about statistical assertions on self-adaptive systems at runtime [15] or at debug time [6] can be challenging. Testing quality or performance is notoriously hard because of the high degree of uncertainty and variability inherent in an adaptive software application [12]. Likely, the overhead of computing the proposed metric in addition to the already defined quality metrics is expected to be minimal, and there exists a vast literature on how to interpret the metric under different conditions [7]. In our technique, the statistical approach used is simple and efficient, and does not require significant reworking/adjustments at varying the configuration of the system under analysis.

The paper structure is as follows. Background on Bell inequality is presented in Sect. 2. Context and introduced notation are the subject of Sect. 3. The definition of the new adaptivity metric and its application to a case study are in Sect. 4 and Sect. 5, respectively. Conclusions are outlined in Sect. 6.

2 Bell Inequality

Originally conceived within Quantum Mechanics, Bell inequality [3] and its refinements (such as the CHSH inequality [5] adopted in this paper) have been applied in many other contexts. Examples are the macroscopic spin quantum-machine, the vessels of water model, the rubber band model, and the Bertlmann's socks [1]. In all these examples the involved components change their behavior according to which other components are concurrently active, and Bell inequality violation highlights the changes. Thus, it is rather natural to import within the self-adaptive systems context ideas and tools developed around the Bell inequality.

In a nutshell, the Bell-CHSH inequality [5] is given by $|\text{CHSH}| \leq 2$ with:

$$\text{CHSH} = \mathbb{E}[QT|\mathfrak{Z}_2] + \mathbb{E}[RS|\mathfrak{Z}_3] + \mathbb{E}[RT|\mathfrak{Z}_4] - \mathbb{E}[QS|\mathfrak{Z}_1] = \sum_{q,r,s,t} p_2(q,r,s,t)qt$$

$$+ \sum_{q,r,s,t} p_3(q,r,s,t)rs + \sum_{q,r,s,t} p_4(q,r,s,t)rt - \sum_{q,r,s,t} p_1(q,r,s,t)qs, \tag{1}$$

where, $p_j(q,r,s,t) = \mathbb{P}(Q = q, R = r, S = s, T = t|\mathfrak{Z}_j)$ is the conditional joint pmf (probability mass function) of the binary random variables Q, R, S and T (that can take values -1 and $+1$) given[1] the event $\mathfrak{Z}_j$, $\mathbb{P}(\cdot)$ is a probability measure and $\mathbb{E}[\cdot]$ denotes the expected value of a random variable. It is easy to show that, when Q,R,S and T are independent on the event $\mathfrak{Z}_j$, i.e., if

$$p(q,r,s,t) = p_1(q,r,s,t) = \ldots = p_4(q,r,s,t), \tag{2}$$

where $p(q,r,s,t)$ is the unconditional joint pmf, then the Bell-CHSH inequality is satisfied [13]. In fact, from Eq. 2 it is possible to replace $p_j(q,r,s,t)$ with $p(q,r,s,t)$ in Eq. 1, and then factorize it, obtaining

$$|\text{CHSH}| = \left| \sum_{q,r,s,t} p(q,r,s,t)(qt + rs + rt - qs) \right| \leq \sum_{q,r,s,t} p(q,r,s,t)2 = 2. \tag{3}$$

Hence, when the Bell-CHSH inequality is violated, i.e., $|\text{CHSH}| > 2$, at least one of the $p_j(q,r,s,t)$ in Eq. 2 is different from the others[2].

3 Context and Notation

The considered architecture-based self-adaptive system changes its structure and behavior at runtime to continue meeting its goals [8,9]. Although inspired to that for the Emergent Web Server in [8], its logical architecture is general.

The managed system is logically composed of a set of n components $c_1, \ldots, c_n$ (such as incoming request handler, stream processors, cache components, hash tables, compression algorithms, sorting algorithms, cache replacement algorithms, or transfer protocol-serving functions) that can be combined together in different ways and even added and removed on the fly to cope with changes in the environment (e.g., the incoming workload pattern).

[1] The events $\mathfrak{Z}_j$ represent choices that can induce different correlation (joint probability distribution) between the variables.

[2] The opposite is not always true, i.e., when the Bell-CHSH inequality is satisfied then the conditional joint distributions $p_j(q,r,s,t)$ can be different.

Each component c_i implements a list of functions. Many different components are able to implement the same functions, providing a set of component variants (such as different sorting or cache replacement algorithms). These variants are then used as the basis for obtaining m alternative architectural configurations (from now on called *compositions* [8]) A_j of the self-adaptive system [8]. A composition A_j defines the set of the selected components and the interactions between them (i.e., how they are connected) to support the functions of the system. Let $E_1, \ldots, E_m$ be different environmental patterns, corresponding to different changes in the environment in which the system operates (e.g., different incoming load levels and load types). Each composition A_j realizes the system adaptation to a different environmental pattern E_j and provides a different system-level utility or reward when subjected to different environmental patterns. We assume that the system always moves to a new configuration when a new environmental pattern occurs. This ensures that the proposed adaptivity metric measures only the adaptation of the system to environmental conditions and not the effect of the system's failure to adapt.

As a running example, at the level of the system as a whole, let W and $\bar{w}$ be the random variable representing the response time of the system to a random input and the maximum acceptable value of W (adaptation goal), respectively. Any response time over $\bar{w}$ is not considered acceptable and needs to be fixed, by triggering a different architectural configuration. Similarly when W falls significantly below the threshold value $\bar{w}$ then it may be necessary to revert to a previous configuration, for example, to reduce costs. In general, W defines a system-level quality metric (as for example, in a web server, the system average response time or a combination of the latency, revenue and cost in a single value, or, in a cleaning robot system, the amount of surface area cleaned for cleaning session) and is associated with the requirements of the application, so it is not restricted to a specific quality metric, as long as it supports adaptation goal.

In the running example, at the level of individual components, let Y_i and $\bar{y}_i$ be the random variable representing the response time of c_i and threshold value for Y_i, respectively. Note that, while $\bar{w}$ is the maximum acceptable value for W, $\bar{y}_i$ is only a threshold value used to compare the distribution of the response time for alternative component versions defined in different compositions. In fact, for different component versions we use the same threshold. In general, Y_i defines a quality metric (the same for different c_i) representing quality properties meaningful for individual components (e.g., performance, optimization). Thus, just as W also Y_i is not restricted to specific metrics, although they can be different from those used for W, depending on the application[3].

Formally, if c_h and c_k are variants of the same set of functions then we define (i.e., we configure the system so that) $\bar{y}_h = \bar{y}_k$. This ensures[4] that $\mathbb{P}(Y_h \leq \bar{y}_h) \neq$

[3] For instance, in a cleaning robot system, the metric that measures the amount of surface area cleaned for cleaning session is meaningless for individual components.

[4] By allowing $\bar{y}_h \neq \bar{y}_k$, it is always possible to find values for them for which $\mathbb{P}(Y_h \leq \bar{y}_h) = \mathbb{P}(Y_k \leq \bar{y}_k)$, making it impossible to use distributions to discriminate between different variant selections, and thus different system configurations.

$\mathbb{P}(Y_k \le \bar{y}_k)$, being c_h and c_k two different variants of the same function aiming to provide different utility when subjected to different environmental patterns.

The difference between two compositions A_s and A_t is described by the series of individual component hot-swaps performed to reach the new composition A_t from A_s, where a component hot-swap corresponds to use a different component version to implement a function, or add or remove a component version. These hot-swaps represent the ability of the system to adapt, when the environment moves from E_s to E_t. The considerations above suggest that it is possible to derive information on system adaptation to different environmental patterns by observing the differences between the distributions of the events $(Y_{j_1} \le \bar{y}_{j_1}, \ldots, Y_{j_{|A_j|}} \le \bar{y}_{j_{|A_j|}})$ for different A_j, where $|A_j|$ is the number of components $c_{j_1}, \ldots, c_{j_{|A_j|}}$ actually used in A_j. For the sake of simplicity, the utility (or the state) of each component c_i is described by the binary random variable $X_i \in \{+1, -1\}$, where $+1$ and -1 represent the failure (if $Y_i > \bar{y}_i$) or the success (if $Y_i \le \bar{y}_i$) of the component c_i, respectively, in providing its service. In general, much more complex relation among Y_i can be exploited to convey information into X_i. Using the notation adopted in Sect. 2, for a given A_j, let $p_j(x_1, \ldots, x_n)$ be the joint pmf of $X_1, \ldots, X_n$ conditioned on A_j and

$$p_{j,i}(x_i) = \mathbb{P}(X_i = x_i | A_j) = \sum_{x_1,\ldots,x_{i-1},x_{i+1},\ldots,x_n} p_j(x_1, \ldots, x_i, \ldots, x_n) \quad (4)$$

be the pmf of X_i conditioned on A_j. Note that $p_{h,i}(x_i)$ and $p_{k,i}(x_i)$ for the same variable X_i in different configurations may assume different values. We also assume that the configuration A_j adopted in the environment E_j does not worsen the utility of the system with respect to the previous environment E_h. So, for example, we expect that if in E_j the incoming workload increases with respect to E_h, then also $p_{j,i}(-1)$ increases for each c_i involved in the new configuration. This ensures that the metric being proposed measures only the desirable adaptation of the system to environmental conditions.

4 Contribution: A New Adaptivity Metric

In this section we propose a new adaptivity metric which exploits the formulas adopted in the Bell-CHSH inequality [5] to measure how much the system actually adapts to variations of the environment. For a given A_j, a simple summary statistic measuring the relationship between the utility of each component in A_j is given by the generalized correlation index between the random variables $X_{j_1}, \ldots, X_{j_{|A_j|}}$, defined as follows:

$$\mathbb{E}_{j_1,\ldots,j_{|A_j|}} = \mathbb{E}\left[\prod_h X_{j_h} \middle| A_j\right] = \sum_{x_1,\ldots,x_n} p_j(x_1, \ldots, x_n) \prod_h x_{j_h}. \quad (5)$$

The proposed adaptivity metric is obtained through comparing the outcomes of a statistic S_1 defined on the available indicators (quality metrics applied to a subset of individual components) against a given threshold. To ease the reading, consider $n = 4$ components, and the compositions $A_1 = \{1,3\}$, $A_2 = \{1,4\}$, $A_3 = \{2,3\}$ and $A_4 = \{2,4\}$. The statistic S_1 is derived directly from Eq. 1 by replacing Q, R, S and T with X_1, X_2, X_3 and X_4, respectively, $\mathfrak{Z}_j$ with A_j, and adopting the same notation of Eq. 5, as follows:

$$S_1 = \left|\text{CHSH}\right| = \left|\mathbb{E}_{1,4} + \mathbb{E}_{2,3} + \mathbb{E}_{2,4} - \mathbb{E}_{1,3}\right|. \tag{6}$$

Note that $0 \leq S_1 \leq 4$ and each random variable X_i involved in Eq. 6 is shared by two different indexes $\mathbb{E}_{i,h}$ and $\mathbb{E}_{i,k}$ or $\mathbb{E}_{h,i}$ and $\mathbb{E}_{k,i}$. As shown in Sect. 2, if $S_1 > 2$, i.e., Bell-CHSH inequality is violated, then there are at least two different A_h and A_k for which $p_h(\cdot)$ and $p_k(\cdot)$ are different, and so it can be shown also that the distributions $p_{h,i}(\cdot)$ and $p_{k,i}(\cdot)$ of a same variable X_i are different. These differences describe how much the system actually adapts to the environment, and can be captured by the following adaptivity metric $\mathcal{M}$:

$$\mathcal{M} = \max\left\{0, \frac{S_1 - 2}{2}\right\}, \text{ with } 0 \leq \mathcal{M} \leq 1. \tag{7}$$

So $\mathcal{M}$ measures how much a distribution $p_h(\cdot)$ is changed with respect to the $p_k(\cdot)$ of a different composition. We expect that the greater $\mathcal{M}$ is, the larger these differences are.

The main advantage of this metric is its simplicity of implementation. Evaluating Eq. 6 in practice is easy and inexpensive, since adapting the computations detailed in [2] or those of [7] only requires to log the values of $Y_1, \ldots, Y_4$ and perform simple arithmetic operations. Moreover, different variants of $\mathcal{M}$ based on different sets of components (or different quality metrics for Y_i), can contribute to identify Bell-CHSH inequality violations also with respect to specific components, by intersecting the results of these variants of $\mathcal{M}$. Thus, $\mathcal{M}$ can be used at runtime to support the choice of a new composition based, for example, on the ranking obtained by the score of all components (e.g., different versions) involved in Bell-CHSH inequality violations.

5 Example of Application of the New Metric

Let's consider a simplified system based on 4 components (e.g., c_1 = HTTPHandlerCMP, c_2 = HTTPHandlerCHCMP, c_3 = GZip and c_4 = Zlib of the EWS architecture described in [8]) and the configurations $A_1, \ldots, A_4$ (where, for simplicity, only the 4 components used in $\mathcal{M}$ are listed) introduced in Sect. 4.

In the absence of experimental data on X_i, we develop a simple analysis, based on the symbolic quantities[5] $p_{j,i}$ representing the values of the distributions $p_j(\cdot)$, as reported in Table 1 for $p_{1,i}$, aiming to show how, for a specific setting, violating the Bell-CHSH inequality leads to having $p_{1,X_1}(\cdot) \neq p_{2,X_1}(\cdot)$

[5] Note that $p_{j,i}$ is a value that the distribution $p_j(\cdot)$ can take, and $p_{j,i}(\cdot)$ is the distribution of X_i conditioned on the configuration A_j.

Table 1. Values $p_{1,i}$ of the joint distribution $p_1(\cdot)$ of $X_1, \ldots, X_4$ corresponding to A_1

$p_1(x_1, x_2, x_3, x_4)$	x_1	x_2	x_3	x_4	$x_1 x_3$ in A_1
$p_{1,1}$	1		1		1
$p_{1,2}$	−1		1		−1
$p_{1,3}$	1		−1		−1
$p_{1,4}$	−1		−1		1

and $p_{3,X_2}(\cdot) \neq p_{4,X_2}(\cdot)$. Violation of Bell-CHSH inequality is obtained assuming that

$$p_{1,2} = p_{1,3} = p_{2,1} = p_{2,4} = p_{3,1} = p_{3,4} = p_{4,1} = p_{4,4} = \frac{3+e}{8} \text{ with } e > 0, \quad (8)$$

where the expression $\frac{3+e}{8}$ is chosen so that S_1 and $\mathcal{M}$ are derived as follows:

$$S_1 = 2\left|p_{1,2} + p_{1,3} + p_{2,1} + p_{2,4} + p_{3,1} + p_{3,4} + p_{4,1} + p_{4,4} - 2\right| = 2\left|(1+e)\right| > 2,$$
$$\mathcal{M} = e > 0. \quad (9)$$

With this setting, if we assume that $p_{1,X_1}(1) = p_{2,X_1}(1)$ and $p_{1,X_1}(-1) = p_{2,X_1}(-1)$, then from Eq. 4 we obtain that $p_{1,1}+p_{1,3} = p_{2,1}+p_{2,3}$ and $p_{1,2}+p_{1,4} = p_{2,2}+p_{2,4}$, respectively. From this, it is easy to show that we obtain the absurdity that $2e = 0$ with $e > 0$. So when the Bell-CHSH inequality is violated, the probabilities $p_{1,X_1}(1)$ or $p_{1,X_1}(-1)$ must depend on the composition. Here, Eq. 9 means that the system presents a nontrivial adaptivity, and $\mathcal{M}$ increases at increasing the gap between $p_{1,X_1}(\cdot)$ and $p_{2,X_1}(\cdot)$, and the one between $p_{3,X_2}(\cdot)$ and $p_{4,X_2}(\cdot)$. Going deeper, we can identify those components that adapted best by exploiting the generalized correlation indexes: $\mathbb{E}_{1,3} = -0.5 \cdot (1+e)$ and $\mathbb{E}_{1,4} = 0.5 \cdot (1+e)$, meaning that the system switches from a composition where there is negative correlation between X_1 and X_3 (so, if Y_1 increases it is more likely that Y_3 decreases, and vice versa) to a composition where the correlation is positive (so, it is likely that Y_1 and Y_4 move in the same direction). For example, if c_1 and c_3 share a blocking resource, then the faster c_1 is, the slower c_3 is, and vice versa, whereas c_4 does not exploit the same resource. Instead, $\mathbb{E}_{2,3}$ and $\mathbb{E}_{2,4}$ have the same sign, but can have different magnitudes.

6 Conclusion and Future Work

This short paper has introduced a new metric of adaptivity for self-adaptive systems, through which effectiveness of configuration changes in response to environmental changes can be assessed at level of individual components involved in the reconfiguration. The idea behind the metric and its formalization have been presented. A simple case study has been exercised to demonstrate how it can be used in practice. At this preliminary stage, the proposed metric appears to be very interesting, both for its ability to assess the adaptability of components in different architectural configurations, and for the effort needed for its computation. Of course, more investigations are needed to confirm these considerations; directions for advancements include: i) to assess the metric in more realistic scenarios, such as the web system EWS in [8]; ii) to conduct comparison with other metrics tailored to adaptivity proposed in the literature, to understand reciprocal benefits and limitations; iii) to further empower the metric through combining it with performance and cost aspects.

References

1. Aerts, D., Sassoli de Bianchi, M.: When Bertlmann wears no socks. Common causes induced by measurements as an explanation for quantum correlations (2019)
2. Aspect, A.: Bell's theorem: The naive view of an experimentalist. arXiv (2004)
3. Bell, J.S.: On the Einstein Podolsky Rosen paradox. Physics **1**, 195–200 (1964)
4. Sassoli de Bianchi, M.: Using simple elastic bands to explain quantum mechanics: a conceptual review of two of Aerts' machine-models. Open Phys. **11**(2), 147–161 (2013)
5. Clauser, J.F., Horne, M.A., Shimony, A., Holt, R.A.: Proposed experiment to test local hidden-variable theories. Phys. Rev. Lett. **23**, 880–884 (1969)
6. Dinh, M.N., et al.: Debugging scientific applications with statistical assertions. Procedia Comput. Sci. **9**, 1940–1949 (2012)
7. Elkouss, D., Wehner, S.: (Nearly) optimal P values for all bell inequalities. Npj Quantum Inf. **2**(1), 1–8 (2016)
8. Filho, R., Alberts, E., Gerostathopoulos, I., Porter, B., Costa, F.M.: Emergent web server: An exemplar to explore online learning in compositional self-adaptive systems. In: International Symposium on Software Engineering for Adaptive and Self-Managing Systems, pp. 36–42 (2022)
9. Gerostathopoulos, I., Vogel, T., Weyns, D., Lago, P.A.: How do we evaluate self-adaptive software systems?: a ten-year perspective of SEAMS. In: International Symposium on Software Engineering for Adaptive and Self-Managing Systems, pp. 59–70 (2021)
10. Kraaijveld, K., Raibulet, C.: ASMS: a metrics suite to measure adaptive strategies of self-adaptive systems. In: 18th International Conference on Evaluation of Novel Approaches to Software Engineering, pp. 238–249 (2023)
11. Malik, S., Naqvi, M., Moonen, L.: CHESS: a framework for evaluation of self-adaptive systems based on chaos engineering. In: IEEE/ACM 18th Symposium on Software Engineering for Adaptive and Self-Managing Systems, pp. 195–201 (2023)
12. Mandrioli, C., Maggio, M.: Testing self-adaptive software with probabilistic guarantees on performance metrics: extended and comparative results. IEEE Trans. Software Eng. **48**(9), 3554–3572 (2022)
13. Nielsen, M.A., Chuang, I.L.: Quantum Computation and Quantum Information: 10th, Anniversary Edn Cambridge University Press, Cambridge (2010)
14. Raibulet, C., Arcelli Fontana, F., Capilla, R., Carrillo, C.: Chapter 13 - An overview on quality evaluation of self-adaptive systems. In: Mistrik, I., Ali, N., Kazman, R., Grundy, J., Schmerl, B. (eds.) Managing Trade-Offs in Adaptable Software Architectures, pp. 325–352 (2017)
15. Santambrogio, M.D., Todman, T., Stilkerich, S., Luk, W.: Using statistical assertions to guide self-adaptive systems. Int. J. Reconfigurable Comput. (2014)

Advancing Requirements Engineering

Classification of Crowd-Based Software Requirements via Unsupervised Learning

Naimish Sharma and Arpit Sharma(✉)

Indian Institute of Science Education and Research, Bhopal, India
naimish.s2017@gmail.com, arpit@iiserb.ac.in

Abstract. Crowd-based requirements engineering (CrowdRE) involves large scale user participation in RE related tasks. In order to extract meaningful insights, supervised machine learning techniques (SML) have been used in the literature for the classification of crowd-based software requirements. These techniques involve training ML models which requires a lot of time, computational resources and high quality labeled data which is extremely rare to obtain in the context of CrowdRE. We focus on the problem of classifying crowd-based software requirements using unsupervised ML techniques. Our approach involves generating sentence embeddings, evaluating them using information retrieval (IR) measures and applying clustering algorithms on the best performing sentence embeddings. In the last step, we apply topic modeling using BERTopic followed by the manual labeling of clusters. We also provide the option of automated labeling of these clusters using the idea of semantic similarity. We have applied our approach to a large-sized dataset with around 3000 crowd-generated requirements for smart home applications. We have experimented with both binary and multi-class classification problems, e.g., tertiary, quaternary and quinary classification. Our experimental results demonstrate that this approach can be very useful for the classification of crowd-based software requirements in the absence of labeled data. Additionally, our approach can also be used to analyse and identify labeling related issues in the dataset which may be useful for improving the quality of existing ground truth data.

Keywords: Classification · Clustering · Natural Language · Requirements · Word Embedding · CrowdRE · Topic Modeling · BERT

1 Introduction

Software requirements are the specifications of what a software system should do, how it should behave, and what constraints it should satisfy [31]. Requirements engineering (RE) is a critical process which involves identifying, analyzing, documenting and managing the software requirements [20,31]. CrowdRE offers a unique approach for collecting and analyzing requirements relevant information from large and heterogeneous user groups or the so called *crowd* [2,16]. CrowdRE gives the project teams access to a wide diversity of actual users and

A. Bertolino et al. (Eds.): QUATIC 2024, CCIS 2178, pp. 237–252, 2024.
https://doi.org/10.1007/978-3-031-70245-7_17

ensures that requirements represent their actual needs accurately. In addition to improving the overall quality of requirements, it may potentially help in increasing the commercial viability of software requirements elicitation and extraction coverage [8]. CrowdRE involves producing huge volumes of raw, and unorganized natural language (NL) data [30]. This raw and unorganized textual data holds little value until it's analyzed and converted into meaningful insights. Manual extraction of meaningful insights from large amounts of raw NL data is not only expensive but also very time consuming. Additionally, manual extraction is also prone to errors due to the subjective interpretation and human bias associated with the process.

Supervised machine learning (SML) techniques have been successfully applied in the past to extract useful insights from the textual requirements [37]. For instance, they have been deployed to classify requirements into functional vs non-functional [9,19,21], requirements vs non-requirements [1], different sectors [7], errors vs features [22], potential verification methods [35], and fake vs non-fake app reviews [23]. A major limitation of SML-based classification techniques is that it requires a large amount of high quality labeled data which is extremely difficult to obtain in the context of CrowdRE [10,30]. Additionally, training ML models requires a lot of time and computational resources. Finally, SML techniques also suffer from the problem of over-fitting, interpretability, and cannot provide unknown information/trends from the training data.

In this paper, we focus on the problem of classification of crowd-based requirements using unsupervised machine learning techniques. More specifically, the problem in hand is to classify crowd-based software requirements into n classes in the absence of any kind of labeled training data. The only information available is the names of these n classes. We categorize requirements into different sectors using sentence embeddings, clustering and topic modeling techniques. Here, a sector refers to a specialized service or knowledge or technology domain in which the software organizations or their constituent sub-units operate [7]. Sentence embeddings are used to map textual requirements and their semantic information to vectors of real numbers. Clustering is an unsupervised form of ML which focuses on forming groups of homogeneous data points from a heterogeneous dataset. In other words, it aims to group unsorted information according to patterns, similarities or differences without any prior training on data. Topic modeling focuses on the problem of creating topics in an unsupervised manner.

Our approach involves data gathering followed by data pre-processing and generation of sentence embeddings. Next, we perform a detailed evaluation of these sentence embedding techniques using information retrieval (IR) measures, e.g., Mean Reciprocal Rank (MRR), and Mean Normalized Discounted Cumulative Gain (MeanNDCG). This evaluation would allow us to focus on a subset of sentence embedding techniques which are most appropriate for grouping the crowd-based software requirements. Next, we apply two different clustering algorithms, i.e., K-means and Hierarchical Agglomerate Clustering (HAC) to these sentence embeddings, and identify topics for each cluster using BERTopic based topic modeling. Finally, based on the results of the topic modeling, clusters can be manually assigned to different sectors or automated labeling can be performed using the idea of semantic similarity. We have validated our approach on a large-sized CrowdRE dataset which has around 3000 crowd-generated software requirements for smart home application domain. We have performed both binary and multi-class classification, e.g., tertiary, quaternary, and quinary classification. The results of our experiments show that our approach can be particularly useful in those classification scenarios where labeled software requirements are not available, and therefore training a ML model is not an option. Moreover, our approach is able to identify labeling related issues in the CrowdRE dataset, and therefore can also be used for the analysis of the ground truth data.

2 Related Work

Word embedding models have been used in the past for detecting cross-domain ambiguities [13–15, 24] and intra-domain ambiguities [28, 29] present in the software requirements. Additionally, word embedding models have also been used for the automatic identification and extraction of glossary terms from user stories [25, 27], automatic clustering of glossary terms [6], and finding semantic relations between requirements [4]. In [34], authors have proposed an approach based on sentence-BERT for automatic discovery of topics composed of semantically similar user comments. This approach has been evaluated using a large Twitter dataset from the telecommunication domain. The idea of using IR measures for evaluating text embeddings of user comments was recently proposed in [11]. Here, a framework for comparing 4 different types of text embeddings using 7 datasets has been proposed, which enables one to select the most relevant embedding techniques for analysing user feedback. A topic modeling framework which can be used to identify topics within a large set of crowd-generated user stories has been proposed in [18]. In this paper, authors have used three approaches for identifying topics in user stories, namely, Latent Dirichlet Allocation (LDA), Word2vec and Word2vec combined with Word Mover's Distance (WMD). This approach has also been validated on the CrowdRE dataset for smart home applications.

More recently, the potential of large-language models (LLMs) for RE has been explored in [5], where authors have conducted a SWOT analysis for applying LLMs in key RE stages. Authors have also conducted a preliminary evaluation to check the feasibility of using LLMs for requirements elicitation. Similarly, in [33], authors have proposed an evaluation framework for researchers to evaluate different prompt patterns when using LLMs for two RE related tasks, namely, binary classification (functional vs non-functional) and requirements traceability. In [32], authors proposed an approach for the automated classification of deontic modalities from the software contracts using domain adaptation and text generation based techniques. Finally, in [3], authors demonstrate the potential of zero-shot learning (ZSL) for requirements classification. More specifically, authors have performed a series of experiments to classify requirements into functional vs non-functional, security vs non-security requirements, and identification of non-functional classes.

Unlike [11,18,34], which either focus only on evaluating text embeddings or identifying topics in user comments and user stories, our current work proposes an end-to-end framework for the classification of user stories by combining different types of unsupervised learning techniques, e.g., sentence embeddings, clustering, topic modeling and automatic labeling of clusters. Our framework can be used for both binary and multi-class classification problems when the labeled dataset is not available for training the ML model. As in the case of [3], our work also focuses on the long-standing problem of data shortage in RE but is based on an approach which involves clustering, and topic modeling for classifying requirements.

3 Methodology

This section presents the approach used for classifying crowd-based requirements using unsupervised ML techniques.

Data Gathering. This step involves merging the feature and the benefit attributes of the CrowdRE dataset by inserting a comma (,) in between and a full stop (.) at end of benefit attribute. This results in a single textual requirement corresponding to each user story in the CrowdRE[1] dataset.

Data Preprocessing. This step focuses on the transformation of raw NL text into an understandable format. These transformations have been implemented using the NL Toolkit (NLTK) package in the Spyder IDE. Strings such as "[1]", digits, extra white spaces and alphanumeric characters have been removed using regular expressions. Each requirement in the corpus is broken into tokens of words (word tokenization). Note that tokenization preserves the syntactic structure of the sentences. Next, all the tokens are converted into lowercase, stopwords are removed and tokens are lemmatized (to remove inflected forms) using WordNetLemmatizer.

Sentence Embeddings. In word frequency based and transformer based models, textual requirements can directly be converted into numerical vectors. Whereas in word embeddings based models such as Word2vec, FastText and Glove instead of a single numerical vector for a requirement, vector of each word of a requirement is obtained. To obtain the sentence embeddings from these word vectors, the following two approaches were used: *(1) Average of word vectors of a sentence (2) Term Frequency - Inverse Document Frequency (TF-IDF) weighted average of word vectors of the sentence.* Sentence embeddings created by averaging the word vectors are denoted as follows: Word2vec(Self Trained), Word2vec(Pre Trained), FastText(Self Trained), FastText(Pre Trained), Glove(Self Trained), and Glove(Pre Trained). In a similar vein, sentence embeddings based on TF-IDF weighted average of word vectors are denoted as follows: TF-IDF Word2vec(Self Trained), TF-IDF Word2vec(Pre

[1] https://crowdre.github.io/murukannaiah-smarthome-requirements-dataset/.

Trained), TF-IDF FastText(Self Trained), TF-IDF FastText(Pre Trained), TF-IDF Glove(Self Trained), and TF-IDF Glove(Pre Trained). Here, *Self Trained* refers to models trained on the CrowdRE dataset, while *Pre Trained* refers to the publicly available pre-trained variants of these models.

Selection of Sentence Embeddings. There are many different techniques in the NLP literature to generate embeddings i.e., we have considered 19 sentence embedding models in this paper. Therefore, it is important to select a subset of these techniques for generating embeddings which are more relevant for our domain. The challenge of identifying embeddings relevant to our dataset is treated as an IR task [11]. Here, each requirement is treated as a query while every other requirement is regarded as a possible document with whom the query needs to be matched. A "document" (requirement) is considered to be a match if it shares the label with the query requirement, where the labels refer to the application domain of the requirement. Note that the process of selecting sentence embeddings needs to carried out only once for an application domain and can be done by using the requirements documents/user stories of some previous software projects. In case if this is not possible, one can manually label a small fraction of the requirements and evaluate the embedding models on this set. We have used the original labeling information of CrowdRE data-set for evaluating the performance of these sentence embeddings.

Mean Reciprocal Rank (MRR). The Mean Reciprocal Rank (MRR) is determined by ranking all the requirements relative to the query requirement, i.e., f_i. All the requirements except f_i are assigned ranks from 1 to $N-1$ where N is the total number of requirements in the dataset. Ranks are based on the cosine distance of their embeddings to f_i where the closest (or most similar) requirement is assigned the highest rank. Next, the rank of the first requirement in the rankings that shares the same class label (e.g., "health", "energy") with f_i is determined. This rank is referred to as $FirstRank_i$, and subsequently its reciprocal is calculated. This process is repeated for every requirement and the mean of these values is the MRR score (as shown in Eq. 1). The maximum value of this score is 1, indicating a perfect ranking.

$$MRR = \frac{1}{N}\sum_{i=1}^{N}\frac{1}{FirstRank_i} \tag{1}$$

Normalized Discounted Cumulative Gain (NDCG). The NDCG method involves ranking all the requirements based on the embedding distance relative to f_i. Initially, the discounted cumulative gain (DCG) is calculated for f_i by the sum of gains for each ranked requirement within the ranking. The gain for a requirement at rank j in relation to f_i is calculated using rel_j, which is 1 if this requirement shares label with f_i, and 0 otherwise. Next, DCG is calculated as shown in Eq. 2. The ranking effectively scores similar requirements with a high ranking and dissimilar requirements with a 0 ranking. The ideal DCG (IDCG) (Eq. 3) is calculated by determining the DCG if the requirement was ranked perfectly (i.e.

all requirements that share labels with f_i are ranked higher than those that do not). The NDCG is the ratio of the DCG to IDCG, which gives a normalized measure with a maximum value of 1, representing perfect ranking. NDCG is calculated for all the requirements and the mean of these values is taken as shown in Eq. 4.

$$DCG_i = \sum_{j=1}^{p_i} \frac{2^{rel_j} - 1}{log_2(j+1)} \tag{2}$$

$$IDCG_i = \sum_{k=1}^{p_i^{ideal}} \frac{2^{rel_k} - 1}{log_2(k+1)} \tag{3}$$

$$MeanNDCG = \frac{1}{N} \sum_{i=1}^{N} \frac{DCG_i}{IDCG_i} \tag{4}$$

Clustering. The output of the previous step enables us to select the top 3 sentence embedding models which can be used for clustering the crowd-based software requirements. Recall that each requirement has been converted into a numerical vector and these vectors would be given as an input for the clustering algorithm. As mentioned earlier, we focus on using K-means and HAC clustering for grouping these requirements into different clusters. Since our goal is to eventually classify each requirement to a sector in an unsupervised fashion, the value of the number of clusters in both K-means and HAC clustering is selected based on the type of the classification problem, e.g., binary, tertiary etc. Default values of all the other hyperparameters have been used for K-means and HAC clustering algorithms.

Topic Modeling. After obtaining the clusters via K-means and HAC clustering algorithms, we need to identify the sector for every cluster. Manual inspection of requirements present in every cluster and accordingly assigning a label to the cluster is a very time consuming and error-prone task. Therefore, we deploy topic modeling techniques to uncover hidden thematic structures within a collection of requirements. Topic modeling enables us to extract a summary of each cluster which can then be used to label the clusters manually. Since we are trying to solve the classification problem, we already know the names of all the sectors, and therefore it is easy to assign a label to every cluster from the list of sectors based on the results of topic modelling.

We have used the BERTopic [17] model in our experiments to extract a summary of each cluster. BERTopic is a topic modeling technique based on embeddings from the BERT pre-trained models. While using the BERTopic[2] model, we have assumed that each cluster is made up of a single topic as we have used the hard clustering algorithms to cluster the requirements. For tokenizing topics, we have used CountVectorizer with stopwords as English, and for topic representation, we have used ClassTfidfTransformer as the hyperparameters in BERTopic.

[2] https://maartengr.github.io/BERTopic/index.html.

Manual and Automated Labeling. There are two approaches i.e., manual labeling and automatic labeling for assigning labels to the clusters obtained after applying K-means and HAC clustering algorithms on numerical vectors of requirements.

In the process of *manual labeling*, clusters are assigned labels based on the top 10 words extracted from each cluster via topic modeling. More specifically, a label is assigned to a cluster if its top 10 words indicate that it belongs to that particular application domain/sector. The labels have been assigned by the first author, and have been independently reviewed by the second author to check the correctness. The final decision regarding the label of every cluster was determined through consensus after detailed discussions among the authors.

In the process of *automatic labeling*, semantic similarity among the vectors has been used to assign labels to clusters. Initially, a Word2vec model is trained on the unlabeled CrowdRE dataset. Following this, for each sector, a sector-level vector is obtained by taking the mean of vectors of all the requirements belonging to that particular sector in the CrowdRE corpus. Note that sector/domain-specific vectors can be created by mining Wikipedia pages, e.g., see [24–26] and the tool WikiDoMiner [12]. For this preliminary investigation, we have used the original labeling information of the CrowdRE dataset. Next, for the clusters obtained via K-means and HAC, cluster-level vectors are obtained by taking the mean of the vectors of every requirement present in a cluster. To assign a label to a cluster, for each cluster-level vector, semantic similarity is used to find the most semantically similar vector from the set of sector specific vectors.

4 Experimental Results

This section presents the results of our experiments performed for classifying crowd-based requirements using unsupervised machine learning techniques. The experiments can be reproduced using the scripts available on the GitHub repository[3]. Due to space limitations, an online appendix has also been provided on this repository which contains supplementary material and detailed information to support the claims/findings of this paper.

Selection of Sentence Embeddings. The MRR and the NDCG scores of different embedding strategies used to convert textual requirements into numerical vectors can be found in appendix on the GitHub repository. Overall, S-RoBERTa gives the best performance followed by SBERT, and self-trained Word2vec model. In general, it has been observed that transformer based models perform better than the word embedding and word frequency based models in the task of creating high quality sentence embeddings for crowd-based requirements. However, there are two exceptions, firstly, it is surprising to see that self trained Word2vec model which generates context independent embeddings outperforms

[3] https://github.com/naimish3199/Classification-of-Crowd-Based-Software-Requirements-via-Unsupervised-Learning.

Table 1. K-means clustering with different embeddings (Manual Labeling).

	Embedding	SRoBERTa			SBERT			Word2vec (Self Trained)		
		Precision	Recall	F1-score	Precision	Recall	F1-score	Precision	Recall	F1-score
Binary Clustering	Energy, Entertainment	**0.883**	**0.889**	**0.885**	**0.891**	**0.883**	**0.886**	**0.905**	**0.901**	**0.903**
	Energy, Safety	0.873	0.885	0.872	0.867	0.878	0.868	0.876	0.885	0.879
	Entertainment, Safety	0.798	0.829	0.796	0.825	0.854	0.831	0.868	0.879	0.873
	Health, Entertainment	0.821	0.814	0.816	0.826	0.822	0.824	0.811	0.807	0.808
	Health, Safety	0.816	0.829	0.810	0.793	0.804	0.785	0.824	0.836	0.826
	Health, Energy	0.790	0.788	0.786	0.753	0.753	0.753	0.801	0.801	0.801
	Energy, Other	0.791	0.806	0.777	0.761	0.777	0.756	0.797	0.815	0.789
	Entertainment, Other	0.781	0.776	0.765	0.794	0.778	0.761	0.788	0.773	0.757
	Safety, Other	0.708	0.746	0.700	0.672	0.703	0.665	0.673	0.702	0.638
	Health, Other	0.566	0.554	0.493	0.495	0.495	0.495	0.529	0.530	0.528
Tertiary Clustering	Energy, Entertainment, Safety	0.774	0.780	0.760	0.785	0.789	0.779	0.818	0.825	0.819
	Health, Entertainment, Safety	0.743	0.745	0.738	0.715	0.725	0.714	0.742	0.751	0.742
	Health,Energy, Entertainment	0.746	0.733	0.737	0.729	0.720	0.724	0.753	0.739	0.743
	Health,Energy, Safety	0.732	0.730	0.726	0.708	0.708	0.705	0.741	0.743	0.739
	Energy,Entertainment, Other	0.729	0.719	0.711	0.688	0.689	0.684	0.748	0.728	0.721
	Energy,Safety, Other	0.702	0.698	0.686	0.641	0.644	0.642	0.703	0.702	0.682
	Entertainment,Safety, Other	0.697	0.696	0.679	0.657	0.668	0.650	0.659	0.664	0.640
	Health,Safety, Other	0.567	0.536	0.521	0.536	0.519	0.522	0.506	0.442	0.430
	Health,Energy, Other	0.522	0.511	0.515	0.496	0.511	0.493	0.533	0.524	0.527
	Health,Entertainment, Other	0.525	0.529	0.505	0.520	0.530	0.506	0.518	0.501	0.502
Quaternary Clustering	Health, Energy, Entertainment, Safety	0.704	0.696	0.695	0.678	0.675	0.673	0.713	0.708	0.707
	Energy, Entertainment, Safety, Other	0.677	0.663	0.659	0.612	0.617	0.613	0.664	0.658	0.650
	Health, Energy, Safety, Other	0.545	0.536	0.539	0.534	0.528	0.528	0.542	0.503	0.504
	Health, Entertainment, Safety, Other	0.513	0.522	0.515	0.533	0.530	0.522	0.541	0.547	0.542
	Health, Energy, Entertainment, Other	0.525	0.529	0.514	0.481	0.504	0.487	0.551	0.533	0.533
Quinary Clustering	Health, Energy, Entertainment, Safety, Other	0.554	0.549	0.546	0.532	0.531	0.526	0.562	0.549	0.553

USE and LaBSE models both of which are transformer-based models and generate embeddings that are context aware. Similarly, pre-trained Word2vec models also outperforms LaBSE model. Additionally, in case of Word2vec, sentence embeddings obtained by averaging the vectors of words of a sentence are better in quality as compared to the TF-IDF weighted average of vectors of a sentence. It is interesting to observe that simple word frequency based models, e.g., TF-IDF (1,2-gram) and Bag of Words (1,2-gram) have higher MRR and NDCG scores, i.e., perform better as compared to the neural word embedding models like Glove(Self trained), TF-IDF Glove(Self trained), FastText(Self Trained), TF-IDF FastText(Self Trained), and Doc2vec. Finally, self trained Glove models appear to be the worst performers in this comparison. As mentioned earlier, we only use the top three sentence embedding models for the task of clustering crowd-based requirements. More specifically, our top three models are S-RoBERTa, SBERT, and self-trained Word2vec.

Clustering. As mentioned earlier, K-means and HAC clustering algorithms have been applied on the best performing sentence embeddings obtained in the previous step. First, we discuss the set of experiments which involve using K-means and HAC for clustering, and assigning labels to these clusters manually based on the output of the BERTopic model. Next, the results for the second set of experiments which involve using K-means and HAC for clustering followed by the automatic assignment of labels to these clusters using sector-specific vectors, and the idea of semantic similarity have been discussed.

Table 2. HAC clustering with different embeddings (Manual Labeling).

	Embedding	SRoBERTa			SBERT			Word2vec (Self Trained)		
		Precision	Recall	F1-score	Precision	Recall	F1-score	Precision	Recall	F1-score
Binary Clustering	Energy, Entertainment	0.836	0.843	0.837	**0.858**	**0.854**	**0.856**	**0.866**	**0.872**	**0.868**
	Energy, Safety	**0.844**	**0.850**	**0.846**	0.825	0.826	0.802	0.847	0.847	0.847
	Entertainment, Safety	0.842	0.729	0.749	0.856	0.831	0.842	0.727	0.742	0.688
	Health, Entertainment	0.836	0.748	0.749	0.736	0.736	0.727	0.765	0.768	0.764
	Health, Energy	0.775	0.755	0.747	0.791	0.768	0.760	0.717	0.713	0.712
	Energy, Other	0.771	0.778	0.739	0.759	0.772	0.744	0.745	0.760	0.743
	Entertainment, Other	0.722	0.723	0.722	0.771	0.746	0.724	0.773	0.722	0.688
	Health, Safety	0.750	0.721	0.670	0.729	0.738	0.721	0.761	0.739	0.693
	Safety, Other	0.662	0.692	0.641	0.652	0.660	0.655	0.655	0.682	0.651
	Health, Other	0.541	0.523	0.418	0.510	0.509	0.483	0.514	0.514	0.506
Tertiary Clustering	Energy, Entertainment, Safety	0.735	0.745	0.738	0.763	0.736	0.729	0.706	0.713	0.691
	Health, Energy, Entertainment	0.741	0.683	0.691	0.736	0.666	0.675	0.701	0.695	0.692
	Health, Energy, Safety	0.690	0.682	0.678	0.681	0.681	0.681	0.696	0.675	0.680
	Energy, Safety, Other	0.647	0.638	0.637	0.619	0.616	0.616	0.665	0.650	0.646
	Energy, Entertainment, Other	0.615	0.614	0.608	0.583	0.578	0.560	0.667	0.654	0.646
	Health, Entertainment, Safety	0.724	0.628	0.621	0.619	0.624	0.591	0.728	0.607	0.605
	Entertainment, Safety, Other	0.676	0.614	0.616	0.641	0.636	0.628	0.680	0.577	0.568
	Health, Energy, Other	0.522	0.504	0.507	0.530	0.517	0.493	0.542	0.483	0.484
	Health, Entertainment, Other	0.446	0.460	0.419	0.540	0.485	0.498	0.556	0.560	0.547
	Health, Safety, Other	0.502	0.437	0.414	0.469	0.445	0.437	0.527	0.461	0.444
Quaternary Clustering	Health, Energy, Entertainment, Safety	0.659	0.595	0.611	0.589	0.594	0.585	0.676	0.622	0.631
	Energy, Entertainment, Safety, Other	0.623	0.565	0.571	0.622	0.559	0.567	0.654	0.597	0.604
	Health, Entertainment, Safety, Other	0.570	0.476	0.487	0.542	0.460	0.463	0.483	0.495	0.487
	Health, Energy, Safety, Other	0.517	0.456	0.454	0.480	0.479	0.460	0.538	0.485	0.473
	Health, Energy, Entertainment, Other	0.501	0.489	0.471	0.517	0.504	0.486	0.475	0.484	0.462
Quinary Clustering	Health, Energy, Entertainment, Safety, Other	0.525	0.486	0.489	0.505	0.494	0.498	0.600	0.600	0.600

We have conducted experiments involving both binary and multi-class classification, e.g., tertiary, quaternary, and quinary clustering approaches. In case of binary clustering, we have considered all possible combinations of two sectors from the list of sectors. Likewise, in the case of tertiary, quaternary, and quinary clustering, we have considered all possible combinations of three, four, and five sectors, respectively. This not only enables us to do a detailed analysis of our results but also helps us in identifying labeling related issues in the CrowdRE dataset.

Manual Labeling. The results of this set of experiments for the K-means clustering have been shown in Table 1. In case of binary classification problem, K-means returns the best precision (.905), recall (.901), and F1-score (.903) with the self trained Word2vec model when the two classes are: Energy and Entertainment. Moreover, the other two embedding models also return their best scores for the same instance of the binary classification problem, i.e., Energy and Entertainment. This indicates that these two sectors can be easily distinguished from each other and probably have very few overlapping words and semantically similar requirements. Note that the precision, recall, and F1-score drop significantly in the last row of the binary clustering, i.e., Health vs Other. In fact, the F1-score for SRoBERTa and SBERT for this case is even less than .5. This indicates that there may be a great overlap in terms of the words used in the requirements of these two sectors. Additionally, it also means that there may be several requirements present in the Health sector which are semantically more closer to the Other sector, and vice versa.

A similar trend can be observed for the tertiary classification problem where self trained Word2vec model returns the best precision, recall and F1-score. As expected, Energy and Entertainment are also part of the set for which the highest performance measures have been obtained. Again, the performance drops sharply when the set of sectors includes Health and Other, e.g., see the last three rows of the tertiary clustering. In all these cases, F1 score is either less than .5 or close to it. This issue can also be observed for the quaternary classification problem where the performance drops significantly when both the Health and Other sectors are included in the set. For example, see the F1 score of the last three rows of the quaternary clustering. Again, in majority of the cases, the best F1-scores are obtained using the self trained Word2vec model. Finally, even in the case of quinary classification problem, the self trained Word2vec model continues to provide the best performance.

A similar trend can be observed for the results obtained by applying HAC clustering (see Table 2). For example, the performance of binary clustering drops significantly when the sectors are Health and Other. Similarly, in case of tertiary classification, worst performance is obtained for those cases where Health and Other sectors are included in the set. Note that in case of quaternary classification, self trained Word2vec with K-means significantly outperforms self-trained Word2vec model with HAC clustering for all the five instances. In contrast, for the quinary classification problem, HAC clustering combined with self trained Word2vec model returns the best performance among all the quinary clustering techniques used in Table 1 and Table 2.

Put in a nutshell, the highest F1-scores obtained for the binary, tertiary, quaternary, and quinary classification problems are .903, .819, .707 and .600, respectively. First three of these scores are obtained by K-means with self trained Word2vec model, and the last one is obtained by HAC clustering with self trained Word2vec model. This clearly indicates that self trained Word2vec embeddings provide the best choice for sentence to vector conversion, and K-means algorithm turns out to be the most effective clustering approach. In our opinion, these scores are not bad given the fact that we are using an unsupervised learning approach for these classification problems. Additionally, these results also indicate that there may be labeling related issues present in the CrowdRE dataset, i.e., Health and Other sectors may have several overlapping words and semantically similar requirements.

Automated Labeling. Due to space limitations, we only present the results where K-means and HAC clustering algorithms have been combined with the self trained Word2vec embeddings. For K-means, the results have been shown in Table 3. On comparing the results of manual and automatic labeling for the K-means clustering, i.e., Table 1 and Table 3, we can observe that for some cases, e.g., [Energy, Entertainment], [Health, Safety], and [Health, Energy, Entertainment, Safety], F1-scores for both the manual labeling and the automated labeling are very similar. In contrast, for cases like [Health, Entertainment, Safety, Other], and [Health, Energy, Entertainment, Other], F1-scores obtained using manual labeling are better as compared to the automatic labeling of clusters. Interestingly, there are also cases, e.g., [Health, Entertainment, Other] where automatic labeling appears to be performing much better than manual labeling.

Table 3. K-means clustering with self trained Word2vec (Automatic Labeling).

	Embedding	Word2vec(Self Trained)		
		Precision	Recall	F1-score
Binary Clustering	Energy, Entertainment	0.904	0.899	0.901
Binary Clustering	Health, Safety	0.825	0.838	0.827
Binary Clustering	Health, Other	0.522	0.523	0.521
Tertiary Clustering	Energy, Entertainment, Safety	0.812	0.822	0.815
Tertiary Clustering	Energy, Safety, Other	0.707	0.706	0.687
Tertiary Clustering	Health, Entertainment, Other	0.563	0.556	0.558
Quaternary Clustering	Health, Energy, Entertainment, Safety	0.710	0.708	0.706
Quaternary Clustering	Health, Entertainment, Safety, Other	0.474	0.558	0.504
Quaternary Clustering	Health, Energy, Entertainment, Other	0.490	0.549	0.504
Quinary Clustering	Health, Energy, Entertainment, Safety, Other	0.514	0.551	0.517

Table 4. HAC clustering with self trained Word2vec (Automatic Labeling).

	Embedding	Word2vec (Self Trained)		
		Precision	Recall	F1-score
Binary Clustering	Energy, Entertainment	0.832	0.838	0.833
Binary Clustering	Health, Safety	0.736	0.742	0.718
Binary Clustering	Health, Other	0.542	0.542	0.542
Tertiary Clustering	Energy, Entertainment, Safety	0.816	0.723	0.744
Tertiary Clustering	Energy, Safety, Other	0.630	0.626	0.613
Tertiary Clustering	Health, Entertainment, Other	0.408	0.520	0.450
Quaternary Clustering	Health, Energy, Entertainment, Safety	0.661	0.596	0.602
Quaternary Clustering	Health, Entertainment, Safety, Other	0.582	0.479	0.485
Quaternary Clustering	Health, Energy, Entertainment, Other	0.432	0.524	0.471
Quinary Clustering	Health, Energy, Entertainment, Safety, Other	0.558	0.466	0.471

On comparing the results of manual and automatic labeling for the HAC clustering, i.e., Table 2 and Table 4, we can observe that for some cases, e.g., [Health, Other], and [Energy, Entertainment, Safety] results of automated labeling are far better than manual labeling of clusters. On the other hand, for cases like [Energy, Entertainment], [Energy, Safety, Other], and [Health, Entertainment, Other], the results of manual labeling are better (or far better) than the automated labeling of clusters.

By analysing the results of both manual and automatic labeling of clusters, we can see that although automated labeling is supposed to be faster than manual labeling, especially when the number of clusters is huge, it does not always provide the best results. Similarly, for manual labeling, results are not always better than automated labeling, and therefore a semi-automatic approach where some labeling related tasks can be completely automated and others can be completed in a semi-automatic fashion (BERTopic + Manual labeling) seems to be more reasonable.

Analysis of Issues in the Dataset. From the results of our experiments shown in Table 1 and Table 2, one can observe that across all combinations of clustering i.e., binary, tertiary and quaternary clustering whenever [Health, Other] sectors appear together in the set, there is a significant drop in the performance/F1-score of our approach. This trend indicates that it may be possible that requirements of these two sectors have several common words. Additionally, it may also be possible that some of the requirements of the Health sector are semantically very similar to the requirements of Other sector, and vice versa. In order to further investigate this issue, we have computed the percentage of words from the Health sector that are also present in the Other sector, and vice versa. After basic pre-processing and stop word removal, the total number of unique words in the Health category is 1621, and the total number of unique words in the Other category is 1238. Total number of unique words that are common to both the sectors is 678. This essentially means that 54.77% of the words from the Other sector are also present in the Health sector. Similarly, 41.82% of the words from the Health sector are also present in the Other sector. As expected, more than half of the vocabulary of the Other sector is also part of the vocabulary of the Health sector. This overlap is quite high because the Other sector is supposed to contain all those requirements which do not fit well in any other sectors/application domains including the Health sector. This is also true in the other direction where more than 40% of the vocabulary of the Health sector is also present in the vocabulary of the Other sector.

On manually examining these two clusters, we have identified several requirements in the Other sector which seem to be labeled incorrectly and could have been part of the Health sector, and vice versa. For example, consider the following requirement: *my smart home to record my weight, body fat, and my daily calorie intake, I can keep an accurate record.* In our opinion, this requirement should be labeled as part of the Health sector. Consider another requirement from the Other sector: *my toilets and sinks to clean themselves on a schedule, I will not have to clean them as often.* This is a hygiene related requirement and therefore could be labeled as part of the Health sector. Similarly, there are requirements in the Health sector which seem to be labeled incorrectly. For instance, consider the following requirement: *App that lets me know when I need to purchase more of something, I never run out of things.* This requirement does not seem to be concerned with the Health category and therefore should have been part of the Other sector.

In order to verify our hypothesis regarding the labeling related issues in the CrowdRE, we have merged the requirements of the Other sector with the requirements of the Health sector and performed the quaternary clustering based classification of CrowdRE requirements which now has the following sectors:

Table 5. Results obtained after merging Health sector and Other sector (Manual Labeling).

Clustering	Embedding	SRoBERTa			SBERT			Word2vec (Self Trained)		
		Precision	Recall	F1-score	Precision	Recall	F1-score	Precision	Recall	F1-score
K-means	Health, Energy, Entertainment, Safety	0.670	0.684	0.675	0.633	0.648	0.637	0.679	0.694	0.684
HAC	Health, Energy, Entertainment, Safety	0.627	0.593	0.602	0.621	0.641	0.622	0.666	0.636	0.646

Health, Energy, Entertainment, and Safety. The results of K-means and HAC clustering with manual labeling have been shown in Table 5. By comparing the results of quinary clustering with K-means given in Table 1, and K-means based quaternary clustering in Table 5, one can easily verify that the F1-score for all the three embedding models has improved significantly. For example, K-means combined with the self trained Word2vec model returns an F1-score of .553 for the quinary clustering, whereas F1-score after merging the Other sector with the Health sector is .684. Similarly, for K-means with SRoBERTa returns an F1-score of .546 which after merging the two sectors becomes .675. This trend can also be observed for the HAC clustering (see Table 2 and Table 5), where F1-score after merging the sectors has improved significantly for all the embedding models. Note that although merging all the requirements of the Other sector with the Health sector helps in improving the F1-score of our approach, it may not be the case that all the requirements of the Other sector need to be merged with the Health sector. In other words, it is possible that only a subset of the requirements from the Other sector needs to be merged with the Health sector and the remaining requirements can be divided into new sectors which are currently not present in the CrowdRE dataset. Resolving these kinds of issues is outside the scope of this paper as we only focus on detecting labeling related issues in the CrowdRE dataset, and not on identifying new sectors for the smart home applications.

5 Threats to Validity

This section discusses threats to the validity of our experimental results [36]. As we have used an unsupervised ML framework, standard performance metrics like recall, precision, and F1-score cannot be directly used to measure the performance of our approach. We need to first identify the class of each cluster by manually or automatically labeling it, and then use these clusters to compute standard performance measures. This is an indirect measure of performance and the outcome may depend on the method used for labeling the clusters. A major threat to internal validity is the researcher bias, which may be present due to the manual labeling of the clusters. In order to mitigate this threat, labels assigned by the first author by applying topic modeling have been independently checked by the second author, and the decision regarding the label of every cluster has been determined via consensus after conducting detailed discussions among the authors. Another threat to internal validity arises from the fact that the manual labeling of the clusters has not been performed by the domain experts. This threat could not be entirely mitigated. Finally, in the case of automated labeling of clusters, we have used the CrowdRE dataset for generating the domain-specific corpus for each sector but this may not be a good representation of the domain/sector knowledge. In order to completely mitigate this threat, tools like WikiDoMiner [12] need to be used for generating the domain-specific corpus. Since the results of this paper are based on a single case study, we cannot be sure if these results are repeatable on other projects or application domains.

6 Conclusions and Future Work

This paper proposed an approach for the classification of crowd-based requirements using unsupervised ML techniques. Our approach involved generation of sentence embeddings and evaluating them using IR measures. Next, the best performing embedding models have been used for clustering requirements via K-means and HAC clustering algorithms. In the last step, we use the results of topic modeling for the manual labeling of requirements clusters. Additionally, we have also provided the option of automatic labeling of these clusters using the notion of semantic similarity. The efficacy of our approach has been validated on a large-sized CrowdRE dataset, and labeling related issues have also been analyzed in detail. Unlike the Zero-Shot Learning (ZSL) approaches based on Large language models (LLMs), our approach is not prone to hallucinations, and would not require significant computational resources and storage capacity. Our future efforts would focus on improving the F1 score of our approach by investigating new clustering, sentence embedding, and topic modeling techniques. Additionally, we plan to develop a user friendly prototypical tool based on our approach and validate its efficacy by applying it to CrowdRE datasets from different domains.

References

1. Abualhaija, S., Arora, C., Sabetzadeh, M., Briand, L.C., Vaz, E.: A machine learning-based approach for demarcating requirements in textual specifications. In: RE, pp. 51–62. IEEE (2019)
2. Adepetu, A., Ahmed, K.A., Abd, Y.A., Zaabi, A.A., Svetinovic, D.: Crowdrequire: a requirements engineering crowdsourcing platform. In: Wisdom of the Crowd, Papers from the 2012 AAAI Spring Symposium, Palo Alto, California, USA, March 26-28, 2012. AAAI Technical report, vol. SS-12-06. AAAI (2012)
3. Alhoshan, W., Ferrari, A., Zhao, L.: Zero-shot learning for requirements classification: an exploratory study. Inf. Softw. Technol. **159**, 107202 (2023)
4. Alhoshan, W., Zhao, L., Batista-Navarro, R.: Using semantic frames to identify related textual requirements: an initial validation. In: Proceedings of the 12th ACM/IEEE International Symposium on Empirical Software Engineering and Measurement. ESEM 2018, Association for Computing Machinery (2018). 10.1145/3239235.3267441
5. Arora, C., Grundy, J., Abdelrazek, M.: Advancing requirements engineering through generative AI: assessing the role of llms. CoRR **abs/2310.13976** (2023)

6. Bhatia, K., Mishra, S., Sharma, A.: Clustering glossary terms extracted from large-sized software requirements using fasttext. In: ISEC 2020: 13th Innovations in Software Engineering Conference, Jabalpur, India, February 27-29, 2020, pp. 5:1–5:11. ACM (2020)
7. Bhatia, K., Sharma, A.: Sector classification for crowd-based software requirements. In: SAC, pp. 1312–1320. ACM (2021)
8. Breaux, T.D., Schaub, F.: Scaling requirements extraction to the crowd: experiments with privacy policies. In: IEEE 22nd International Requirements Engineering Conference, RE 2014, Karlskrona, Sweden, August 25–29, 2014, pp. 163–172. IEEE Computer Society (2014)
9. Dalpiaz, F., Dell'Anna, D., Aydemir, F.B., Çevikol, S.: Requirements classification with interpretable machine learning and dependency parsing. In: RE, pp. 142–152. IEEE (2019)
10. Dalpiaz, F., Ferrari, A., Franch, X., Palomares, C.: Natural language processing for requirements engineering: the best is yet to come. IEEE Softw. **35**(5), 115–119 (2018)
11. Devine, P., Koh, Y.S., Blincoe, K.: Evaluating unsupervised text embeddings on software user feedback. In: 29th IEEE International Requirements Engineering Conference Workshops, RE 2021 Workshops, Notre Dame, IN, USA, September 20-24, 2021, pp. 87–95. IEEE (2021)
12. Ezzini, S., Abualhaija, S., Sabetzadeh, M.: Wikidominer: wikipedia domain-specific miner. In: Proceedings of the 30th ACM Joint European Software Engineering Conference and Symposium on the Foundations of Software Engineering, ESEC/FSE 2022, Singapore, Singapore, November 14-18, 2022, pp. 1706–1710. ACM (2022)
13. Ferrari, A., Donati, B., Gnesi, S.: Detecting domain-specific ambiguities: an NLP approach based on Wikipedia crawling and word embeddings. In: IEEE 25th International Requirements Engineering Conference Workshops, RE 2017 Workshops, Lisbon, Portugal, September 4-8, 2017, pp. 393–399. IEEE Computer Society (2017)
14. Ferrari, A., Esuli, A.: An NLP approach for cross-domain ambiguity detection in requirements engineering. Autom. Softw. Eng. **26**(3), 559–598 (2019)
15. Ferrari, A., Esuli, A., Gnesi, S.: Identification of cross-domain ambiguity with language models. In: 5th International Workshop on Artificial Intelligence for Requirements Engineering, AIRE@RE 2018, Banff, AB, Canada, August 21, 2018, pp. 31–38. IEEE (2018)
16. Groen, E.C., et al.: The crowd in requirements engineering: the landscape and challenges. IEEE Softw. **34**(2), 44–52 (2017)
17. Grootendorst, M.: Bertopic: neural topic modeling with a class-based TF-IDF procedure. arXiv preprint arXiv:2203.05794 (2022)
18. Gülle, K.J., Ford, N., Ebel, P., Brokhausen, F., Vogelsang, A.: Topic modeling on user stories using word mover's distance. In: 7th IEEE International Workshop on Artificial Intelligence for Requirements Engineering, AIRE@RE 2020, Zurich, Switzerland, September 1, 2020, pp. 52–60. IEEE (2020)
19. Hey, T., Keim, J., Koziolek, A., Tichy, W.F.: Norbert: transfer learning for requirements classification. In: 28th IEEE International Requirements Engineering Conference, RE 2020, Zurich, Switzerland, August 31 - September 4, 2020, pp. 169–179. IEEE (2020)
20. Hull, M.E.C., Jackson, K., Dick, J.: Requirements Engineering, 2nd edn. Springer, Cham (2005)

21. Kurtanovic, Z., Maalej, W.: Automatically classifying functional and non-functional requirements using supervised machine learning. In: RE, pp. 490–495. IEEE Computer Society (2017)
22. Maalej, W., Kurtanovic, Z., Nabil, H., Stanik, C.: On the automatic classification of app reviews. Requir. Eng. **21**(3), 311–331 (2016)
23. Martens, D., Maalej, W.: Towards understanding and detecting fake reviews in app stores. Empir. Softw. Eng. **24**(6), 3316–3355 (2019)
24. Mishra, S., Sharma, A.: On the use of word embeddings for identifying domain specific ambiguities in requirements. In: 27th IEEE International Requirements Engineering Conference Workshops, RE 2019 Workshops, Jeju Island, Korea (South), September 23-27, 2019, pp. 234–240. IEEE (2019)
25. Mishra, S., Sharma, A.: Automatic word embeddings-based glossary term extraction from large-sized software requirements. In: Madhavji, N., Pasquale, L., Ferrari, A., Gnesi, S. (eds.) REFSQ 2020. LNCS, vol. 12045, pp. 203–218. Springer, Cham (2020). https://doi.org/10.1007/978-3-030-44429-7_15
26. Mishra, S., Sharma, A.: Crawling wikipedia pages to train word embeddings model for software engineering domain. In: ISEC 2021: 14th Innovations in Software Engineering Conference, Bhubaneswar, Odisha, India, February 25-27, 2021, pp. 18:1–18:5. ACM (2021)
27. Mishra, S., Sharma, A.: A generalized semantic filter for glossary term extraction from large-sized software requirements. In: ISEC 2021: 14th Innovations in Software Engineering Conference, Bhubaneswar, Odisha, India, February 25-27, 2021, pp. 4:1–4:9. ACM (2021)
28. Moharil, A., Sharma, A.: Identification of intra-domain ambiguity using transformer-based machine learning. In: 2022 IEEE/ACM 1st International Workshop on Natural Language-Based Software Engineering (NLBSE 2022), Co-located with ICSE 2022, Pittsburgh, PA, USA, May 8, 2022, pp. 51–58. ACM/IEEE (2022)
29. Moharil, A., Sharma, A.: TABASCO: a transformer based contextualization toolkit. Sci. Comput. Program. **230**, 102994 (2023)
30. Murukannaiah, P.K., Ajmeri, N., Singh, M.P.: Toward automating crowd RE. In: RE, pp. 512–515. IEEE Computer Society (2017)
31. Pohl, K.: Requirements Engineering - Fundamentals, Principles, and Techniques, 1st edn. Springer, Cham (2010)
32. Rejithkumar, G., Anish, P.R., Ghaisas, S.: Automated identification of deontic modalities in software engineering contracts: A domain adaptation-based generative approach. In: 31st IEEE International Requirements Engineering Conference, RE 2023 - Workshops, Hannover, Germany, September 4-5, 2023, pp. 72–75. IEEE (2023)
33. Ronanki, K., Daniel, B.C., Horkoff, J., Berger, C.: Requirements engineering using generative AI: prompts and prompting patterns. CoRR **abs/2311.03832** (2023)
34. Stanik, C., Pietz, T., Maalej, W.: Unsupervised topic discovery in user comments. In: 29th IEEE International Requirements Engineering Conference, RE 2021, Notre Dame, IN, USA, September 20-24, 2021, pp. 150–161. IEEE (2021)
35. Winkler, J.P., Grönberg, J., Vogelsang, A.: Predicting how to test requirements: an automated approach. In: RE, pp. 120–130. IEEE (2019)
36. Wohlin, C., Runeson, P., Hst, M., Ohlsson, M.C., Regnell, B., Wessln, A.: Experimentation in Software Engineering. Springer, Heidelberg (2012)
37. Zhao, L., et al.: Natural language processing for requirements engineering: a systematic mapping study. ACM Comput. Surv. **54**(3), 55:1–55:41 (2022)

Supporting Q&A Processes in Requirements Elicitation: Bad Smell Detection and Version Control

Yui Imahori[1], Junzo Kato[2], Shinpei Hayashi[3], Atsushi Ohnishi[4], and Motoshi Saeki[1](✉)

[1] Nanzan University, Nagoya, Japan
yui.imahori@apps.nise.org, saeki@nanzan-u.ac.jp
[2] Tokyo, Japan
[3] Tokyo Institute of Technology, Meguro, Japan
hayashi@c.titech.ac.jp
[4] Ritsumeikan University, Kyoto, Japan
ohnishi@is.ritsumei.ac.jp

Abstract. In the process of developing requirements specifications, a requirements analyst conducts question-and-answer (Q&A) sessions iteratively to incrementally make more complete initial requirements preobtained from stakeholders. However, iterated Q&A sessions often have some problems leading to a final requirements specification of lower quality. This paper presents the usage of a graph database system to identify *bad smells* in Q&A processes, which are symptoms leading to a lower quality product, and to control the versions of a list of requirements through the activities. In this system, the records of the Q&A activities and the requirements lists are structured and stored in a graph database Neo4j. Cypher, a database manipulation language, was used to show that we could retrieve *bad smells* in the Q&A process and visualize any version of the requirements list evolving through the processes.

Keywords: Requirements Elicitation · Q&A Process · Bad Smell · Version Control · Graph Database · Object Oriented Modeling

1 Introduction

Requirements elicitation, which is the first activity in a development process, has significant effects on the quality of the developed software, and at the worst cases where its requirements specification of lower quality has been obtained, the developers might re-do the development activities. Usually, a requirements analyst gets an initial list of requirements from stakeholders at first, and then conducts question-and-answer (Q&A) sessions iteratively to incrementally make the initial list more complete. The Q&A sessions are significant to get a resulting requirements specification of higher quality. However, iterated Q&A sessions often contain some problems, e.g., vagueness of the timing when an analyst and

J. Kato—Independent Consultant

A. Bertolino et al. (Eds.): QUATIC 2024, CCIS 2178, pp. 253–268, 2024.
https://doi.org/10.1007/978-3-031-70245-7_18

stakeholders could bring their discussions to a close, no sufficient consensus of discussion conclusions between them, inconsistencies in the resulting requirements list, etc. As a result, the specification, the final product of a requirements elicitation step, may contain the inconsistent requirements and/or unwanted ones, and mandatory requirements may be missing in the specification.

One of the ways to avoid this situation is 1) to keep the records of the activities of the Q&A sessions together with the track of evolving the requirements and 2) to identify the occurrences of so-called *bad smells*, a symptom possible to lead to these problems, by retrieving the stored records. To achieve the above two goals, in this paper we clarify bad smells included in Q&A activities[1], and we realize a database system storing Q&A activities tightly connecting to developed requirements list. We also design database queries to detect the occurrences of *bad smells*. We use a graph database system, Neo4j [10] to store Q&A activities and elicited requirements together. Cypher (a data manipulation language of Neo4j like SQL) is used to represent database queries not only to detect *bad smells* of the Q&A activities but also to control the versions of produced requirements lists, e.g., extract a certain version of the requirements list, differences between its two versions, etc. Our contribution is to 1) define *bad smells* for Q&A activities, 2) model Q&A activities to detect the occurrences of the defined *bad smells* and to realize the model by a graph database system Neo4j, and 3) demonstrate useful database queries for detecting the defined *bad smells*.

The rest of the paper is organized as follows. We first clarify our concrete problems to be addressed and then we refine the problems to *bad smells* and to a rough sketch of queries to detect them. Section 3 presents our data model for the graph database system so that we can realize our queries mentioned in the previous section. In Sect. 4, we pick up a couple of our designed queries and demonstrate their execution results. Our demonstration shows that our queries can work well for detecting bad smells and for controlling versions of requirements lists. Section 5 is for discussions on our contributions. Related work and concluding remarks are mentioned in Sects. 6 and 7, respectively.

2 Our Approach

2.1 Problems in Q&A Activities to be Addressed

Q&A sessions for requirements elicitation may include the following characteristics that provide lower efficiency of development processes and lower quality of developed products.

1. None of an analyst and stakeholders can grasp the whole picture of the process. As a result, sometimes the analyst and stakeholders cannot decide where the end of the activities is.
2. There can be missing implementation of requirements. If the conclusions and consensus on Q&A sessions were neither maintained nor connected to resulting requirements, missing requirement items would occur.

[1] Q&A activities in a session are a sequence of someone's utterances and responses from the others.

3. There can be insufficient communication between an analyst and stakeholders. If this situation happens, opinions of a certain stakeholder may not be reflected in the final version of a requirements list.
4. An analyst and stakeholders cannot come to a consensus, to the end, or their consensus building can take longer time.
5. Multiple discussions on a requirement content on the different agenda topics allow the analyst to list up duplicated requirements that may be inconsistent to each other, and as a result the requirements list can include inconsistency.

2.2 Supporting Q&A Activities Using a Graph Database

To detect the occurrences of the problems mentioned in Sect. 2.1, we record Q&A activities, versions of a requirements list and their relationships in a database system, and by using database queries we automate the detection of their occurrences. An initial requirements list, which has been firstly provided by stakeholders, is stored to the database. An analyst or the stakeholders pick up one of the list items as a topic, and start a Q&A session. For example, the analyst may suggest the details of the picked-up topic and/or propose a new requirement related to the topic. The stakeholders may respond to the analyst's suggestion or proposal. The response allows the analyst to update the requirements list and to produce its newer version. The differences between the older list and the newer one should be identified in the database, i.e., our system should have the function of version control. These Q&A activities are structured and stored in the database, connecting to their related requirements items. During Q&A sessions, the analyst and the stakeholders can access to the database and can retrieve the symptoms of the problems (to be discussed in Sect. 2.3) by using queries represented with a database manipulation language. We use a graph database system Neo4j and its manipulation language Cypher to represent queries. The reasons why we use a graph database system are mainly from implementation view. Firstly, we can update the records of Q&A activities dynamically and flexibly, and secondly we can visualize the results of manipulating data so that the analyst and the stakeholders can understand the results easily at a glance. They are not always an expert of Neo4j or Cypher, so the understandability and the easiness of making queries are very important. We have developed pre-defined templates of queries to retrieve the problems in Q&A activities for each type of their symptoms.

2.3 Bad Smells—Symptoms of the Problems

Next, we should clarify the techniques to detect *bad smells*, a symptom which may cause the problems mentioned in Sect. 2.1, from the recorded Q&A activities are necessary. By using GQM (Goal-Question-Metric) technique [4], where we set "detecting the problems mentioned in Sect. 2.1" as Goals, *bad smells* of the Q&A activities as Questions (Are there bad smells?), and database queries to retrieve the occurrences of *bad smells* as the implementation of calculating Metrics. In our approach, Q&A activities and produced requirements are stored in a database

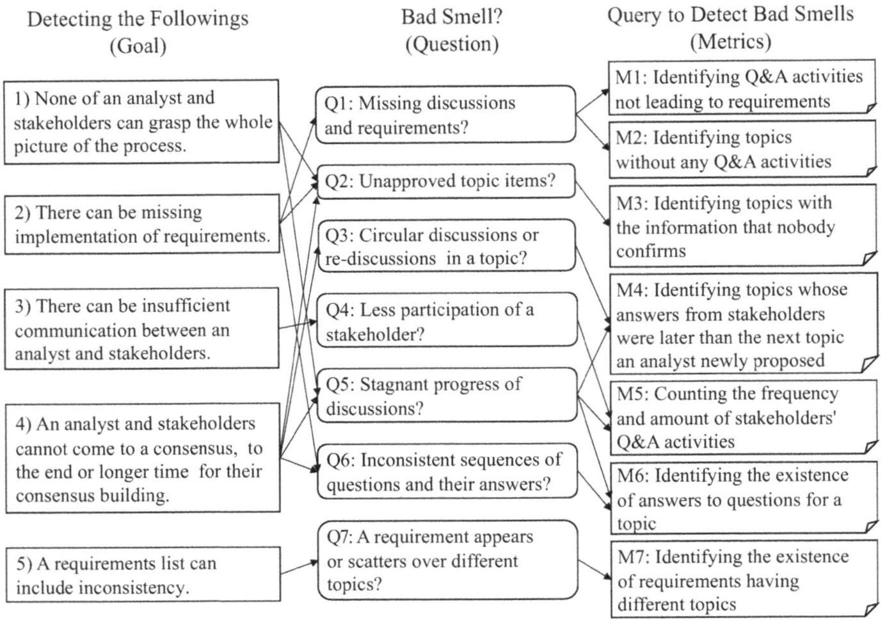

Fig. 1. GQM approach.

system, and therefore the metrics to answer these questions can be defined and calculated with queries on the database system.

Figure 1 illustrates the application of GQM technique. In the example of this figure, one of our goals is to check if Q&A activities do not contain the problem "There can be missing implementation of requirements". To achieve it, we set the three questions "(Are there) Missing discussions and requirements?", "(Are there) Unapproved topic items?" and "(Are there) Inconsistent sequences of questions and their answers?". Consider the case of unapproved topic items as an example. Since an unapproved topic item cannot be usually included in a final requirements list, it will not be implemented in a final product. If the requirement on the unapproved topic item is mandatory to stakeholders, the resulting specification may lose a significant requirement. To find unapproved topic items in our database, we can attach to a discussed and then approved topic a link denoting "confirmed". Our query searches for the occurrences of the link "confirmed" for each discussed topic in the database.

Inconsistent sequences of questions and their answers may be the problem "There can be missing implementation of requirements" as follows. Consider the situation where none of the stakeholders answered to a question from the analyst or the situation where they did not answer to it until the analyst moved to the other new topics. In this situation, the analyst could not find the occurrences of logically consistent sequences of questions and their answers, and as a result, she or he would lose sight of the requirements to be implemented.

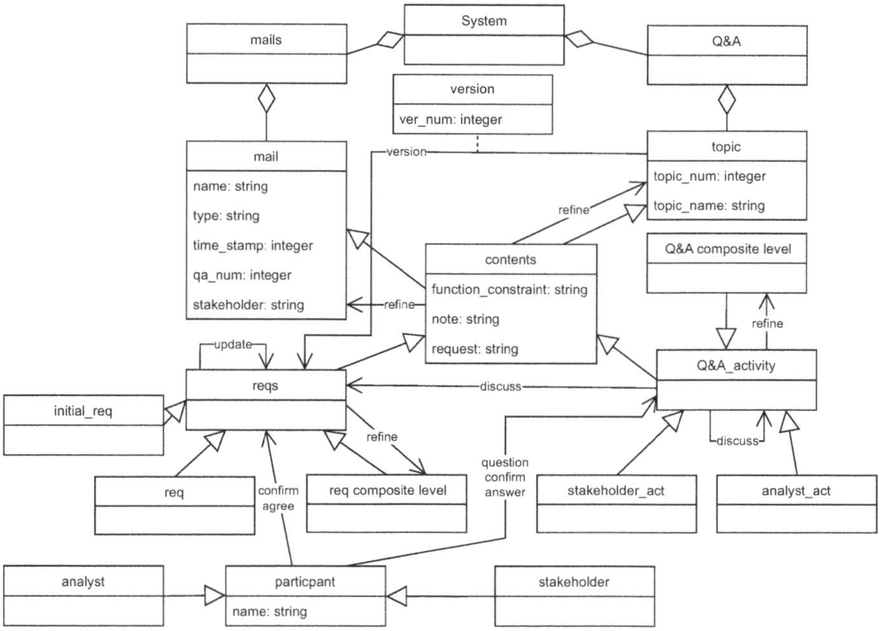

Fig. 2. Object-oriented model of Q&A processes for a graph database model.

2.4 Q&A Activities for Development a Library System

In this subsection, we mention briefly an example to explain our technique in successive sections. This example is a Q&A process to develop a library system, where a practitioner as a requirements analyst conducted it with a library user and a librarian as stakeholders. They communicated with each other by E-mail and through these Q&A activities the analyst gradually made complete a given initial list of requirements of a library system [15]. In this example, we had 43 mails, 7 initial requirements, and 40 requirements that were newly derived from the Q&A sessions.

3 Modeling Q&A Processes

3.1 Object-Oriented Model for Q&A Processes

To realize the queries mentioned in Sect. 2.3, we design an object-oriented model of Q&A processes for a graph database, and uses it as a kind of a schema of graph database systems, as shown in Fig. 2. One of the reasons why we used an object-oriented technique is that we can easily implement a graph database system from the resulting object-oriented model. It is simple how to transform the object model like Fig. 4 to the data of Neo4j. Basically, since classes, associations (including aggregations), and attributes directly corresponds to nodes, edges, and properties of property graph models of Neo4j, the concrete data follows the form of the object model.

The model in the figure is rather an extendable framework by adding subclasses according to Q&A processes. For example, if a Q&A process has more refined types of stakeholders such as users and system administrators etc., we can add them as subclasses of "stakeholder" class. In the case of our library example, we have added "librarian" class and "(library) user" class.

We use "generalization" relationships (super-subclass relationships) to inherit attributes and associations to subclasses. For example, the class "mail" has an attribute "time_stamp", and its subclasses "contents" and "Q&A_activity" can also have it. Since "contents" is a subclass of "topic", the instances of "contents" can have the values of the attributes "topic_name" etc. "Contents" has the attributes "function_constraint", "request", and "notes", which is neither of them. The attribute "function_constraint" specifies whether the content is on a function or a constraint, and "request" can be for a product or for a Q&A session. This kind of usage of generalization is useful to reduce the types of nodes and edges of Neo4j, and as a result we can design simpler queries for retrieving bad smells.

In the model, we use *composite pattern* of Gang-Of-Four to represent a hierarchical nested structure. For example, the classes "reqs", denoting a requirement, and "req composite level" (a set of requirements) for representing the nested requirements, are a component and a composite respectively in a composite pattern. Note that we use the association labelled "refine" instead of aggregation relationship on applying a composite pattern, to differentiate the association "refine" from aggregation used in the non-nested structure. On Neo4j queries, we identify easily that the edges labelled with "refine" can lead to a nested structure. Aggregation can be considered essentially as a kind of association.

The contents of a "Q&A_activity" can also have a nested structure, and we also use a composite pattern for this part. There are some classes having both a generalization and an association such as "refine", except the usage of composite pattern. For example, there are a generalization and a "refine" association between "mail" and "contents". The "refine" association is intuitively considered as an aggregation and is used for pulling from a node of type "mail" its "contents" in retrieving bad smells in Neo4j. Similarly, the classes "topic" and "contents" have a generalization and a "refine" association. The body of a mail, contents, a Q&A activity or requirement is stored in the attribute "name" declared in "mail" class. "Topic" is a kind of a header to identify easily contents and also relates to contents with "refine" association.

A requirement "req" could have its version information itself as an attribute value, but rather we use a link between "reqs" and "topic" having a link attribute "ver_num" to make it easier to retrieve specific versions with links as edges in Neo4j. The class "reqs" has the subclass of initial requirements list "initial_req", which is an input of the Q&A process. The link "update" between "reqs" represents the evolution of requirements through Q&A processes, and we can reason the rationales of the evolution by tracing the link "discuss" from "Q&A_activity".

```
The mail sent from the analyst at 2020/5/6 15:40, whose qa_num is 4.
...
2. Question on Registration of materials to and removal from the library
Does it mean
we register lendable materials to the library system, and
we remove lendable materials from the library system?
...
```

Fig. 3. Example of a part of a mail.

An analyst or a stakeholder (a participant) performs an activity of "question", "answer", or "confirm" to a content of Q&A activity. It is specified with the type of associations "question", "answer" or "confirm" between the participant and her performed Q&A activity, as shown in Fig. 2.

The "discuss" association between "Q&A_activity" shows the relationship from a Q&A activity not only to a requirement but also to another Q&A activity. Suppose that a stakeholder asked a question to an analyst, but after that, the analyst asked another question to this stakeholder's question because the analyst could not understand well the stakeholder's question. The "discuss" association is useful to hold the relationship between these two Q&A activities.

Figures 3 and 4 show an example of a part of a mail for the development of a library system and its object model as the instance of Fig. 2. This mail was sent by the analyst at 15:40 on May 26th in 2020 and had the question-answer number (qa_num) of 4. The time stamp stands for the date when the mail was sent, and we had a 12 digits number "202005261540" as its time stamp. The mail consisted of several contents, and this example shown in the figure is its second part. The topic of the example has a content whose name (topic_name) is "Registration of materials to and removal from the library", whose topic number (topic_num) is 2 as shown in the heading part of the content. The part also tells us that the content is a "question" and refers not to a constraint but to a function of the Library System. Thus, we put the attribute values "question" and "function" as "type" and "function_constraint", respectively. Since this example is a question from the analyst, it is also an instance of "analyst_act" class whose super class is "Q&A_activity".

When the topic refers to a specific version of requirements lists, the reference is specified with a link from the topic[2] to the corresponding requirement. This example refers to the element of the initial requirements list "Registration of books to and removal from the library". The analyst tried to extend the interpretation of word "books" to "lendable materials" in this question. We used as a version number the number derived from the date when the mail was sent, and attached the number 20200526 as its version number in the link to the requirement.

We manually extracted data from 43 E-mails and structured them following this model with ten hours or less. As will be discussed in Sect. 7, some automated techniques are necessary.

[2] In this example, a link from the Q&A_activity whose class is a subclass of "topic".

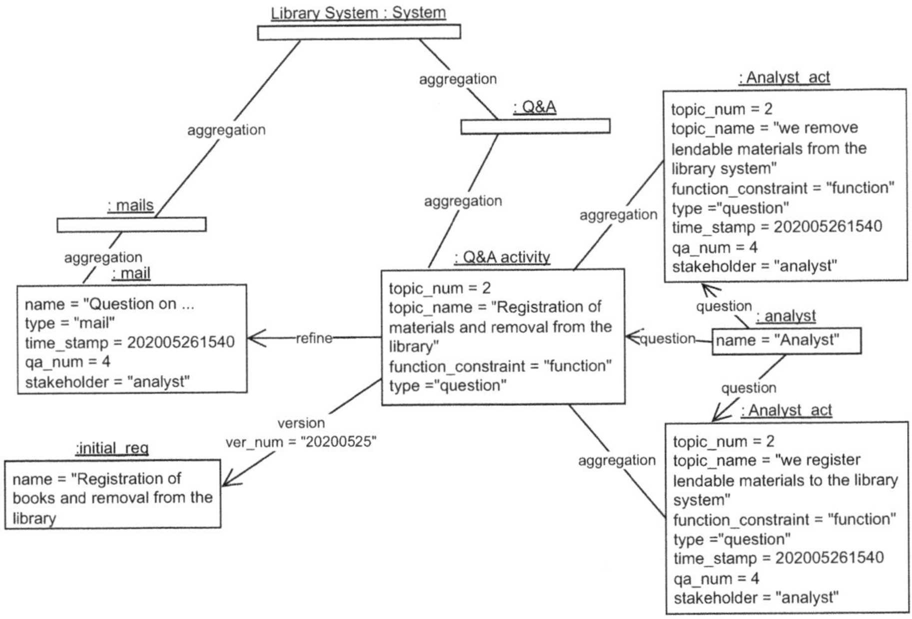

Fig. 4. Object model of the example of Fig. 3.

3.2 Neo4j and Cypher

Figure 5 shows an example of concrete data stored in the graph database Neo4j. It is simple how to transform the object model like Fig. 4 to the data of Neo4j. Basically, since classes, associations including aggregations and attributes directly corresponds to nodes, edges, and properties of property graph models of Neo4j, the concrete data follows the form of the object model. Note that the browser of Neo4j colors nodes and edges to distinguish the types of the nodes and the edges. Instead, for accessibility, we added stereo types denoting the type names in the figures in this paper as needed.

The data manipulation language of Neo4j is Cypher, which is based on SQL. We use `CREATE` statements to create nodes and `MATCH` ones to retrieve subgraphs satisfying a certain condition.

Query 1. Data retrieval.

```
MATCH (n1:stakeholder)-[:confirm]->
    (n2:analyst_act{name:"we register lendable materials"})
    RETURN n1, n2;
```

The above example of a `MATCH` statement outputs the nodes having specific values as their properties and connecting an edge labelled `confirm`. We show a part of templates of Cypher queries to detect bad smells in the next sections.

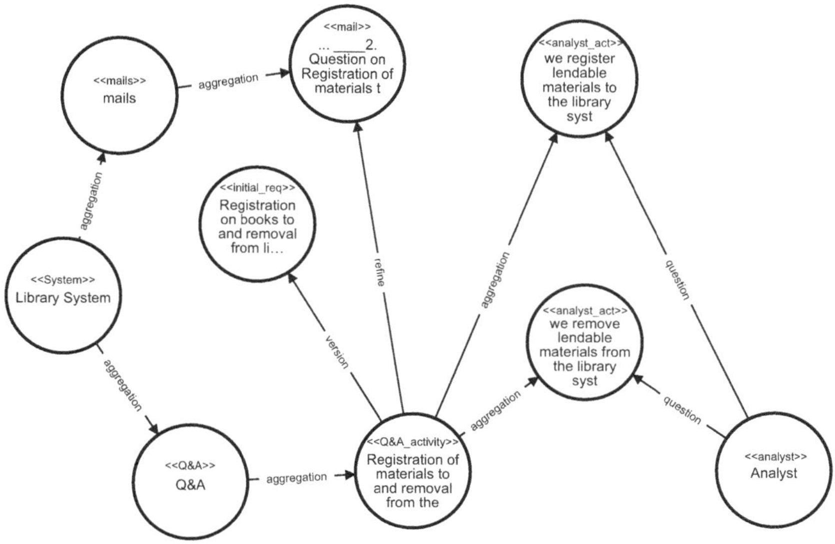

Fig. 5. Graph model of the example of Fig. 3.

4 Detecting Bad Smells and Controlling Versions Using Cypher Queries

4.1 Detecting Missing Discussions and Requirements (Q1 in Fig. 1)

To detect Q1: missing discussions and requirements, we identify 1) the topics that their participants have not discussed (corresponding to M2 in Fig. 1) and 2) the requirement items that had been discussed but are not put in the requirements list (M1 in Fig. 1). As shown in Fig. 1, we have two types of queries and one of them is shown as follows.

Query 2. Identifying Q&A activities not leading to requirements (M1 in Fig. 1).

```
MATCH (n:analyst_act)-[:discuss]->(m)
    WHERE NOT (m:req)
    RETURN n;
```

This query template is used for M1: identifying Q&A activities not leading to requirements. Usually, an analyst starts discussions, maybe utters a question including a proposal, and after some Q&A activities, a requirement related to them is put in the list. However, if the requirement was not put in the list, it could result in a missing one. By using Query 2, we retrieve the nodes of `analyst_act` (analyst's activity) having no edges outgoing to `req` labelled with `discuss`. We can use `stakeholder_act` instead of `analyst_act` as the type of graph node `n`. Figure 6 shows the result of executing Query 2. In the figure, we can see 14 Q&A activities that have not been led to any requirement yet. For example, the graph node "Publisher" (analyst's proposal that "Publisher"

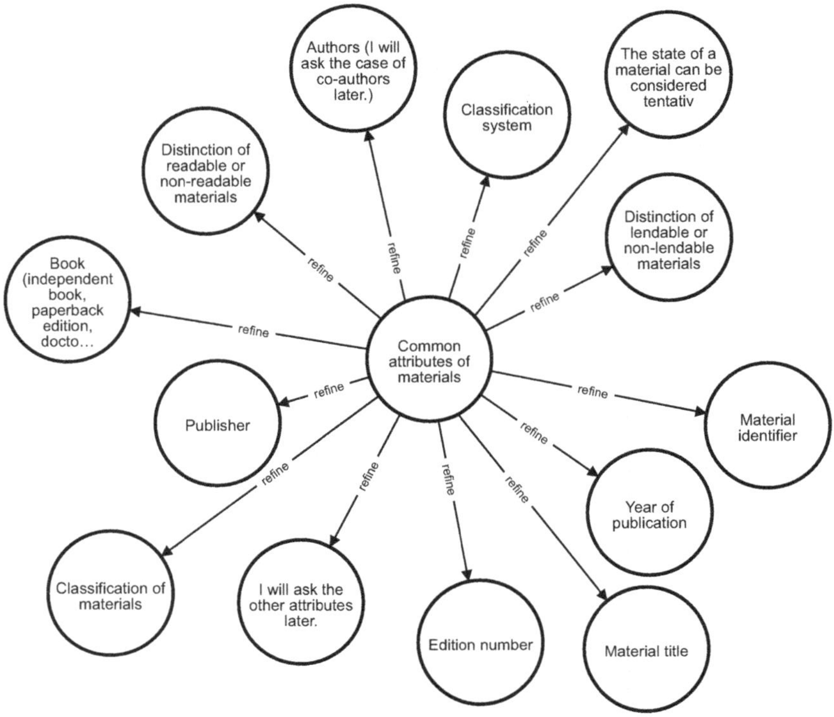

Fig. 6. Result of identifying Q&A activities not leading to requirements.

information should be included in material's attribute data) is proposed to be discussed, but it does not appear as a requirement yet.

4.2 Unapproved Topic Items (Q2 in Fig. 1)

To detect the bad smell "Q2: Unapproved topic items?", we retrieve the graph nodes of requirements (`req`) that have no edges of "confirm" from any stakeholder. Thus, we have the following query template:

Query 3. Identify topics with the information that nobody confirms (M3 in Fig. 1).

```
MATCH (g:analyst_act{type:"confirm"})-[:discuss]->(f:req)
        <-[:discuss]-(h:stakeholder_act)
    WHERE NOT (h)-[:confirm]->(f)
    RETURN g, h, f;
```

The matching pattern in a `MATCH` phrase of Query 3 is to search for the Q&A activity where an analyst asks stakeholders for the confirmation of a requirement and the stakeholders discuss it. The `WHERE` clause specifies the stakeholders have not confirmed it yet. That is to say, the requirement is put in the requirement list without any confirmation from the stakeholders. If you specify a certain stakeholder, e.g., librarian, you can add the condition `h.name="Librarian"` in the `WHERE` clause.

4.3 Circular Discussions or Re-discussions in a Topic (Q3 in Fig. 1)

To detect the occurrences of Q3: circular discussions or re-discussions in a topic, we focus on time sequences of Q&A activities. Our database system holds the information of a time stamp when a Q&A activity was uttered and of temporal ordering on pairs of questions and their answers. As for the latter information, the property "qa_num" (question & answer number) of the model shown in Fig. 2 represents the order of Q&A activities for a topic.

Consider the following scenario. *An analyst asked stakeholders "common attributes of materials" on the topic "Registration of materials to and removal from the library" and its activity was numbered with 7 as "qa_num" property. If the stakeholders answered it immediately, their answer was numbered with the same number. However, actually they did not do anything on the analyst's question and they kept silence. Therefore, the analyst was forced to conduct the other different Q&A activities. Since the analyst conducted the different activities, the "qa_num" was advancing. When the stakeholders finally answered, its "qa_num" was 25. From the view of time sequence, a question and its answer were not successive but the other Q&As was disrupted between them. That is to say, we identify topics or Q&A activities whose answers from stakeholders were later than the next topic an analyst newly proposed. The analyst considered that the discussion on "qa_num" 7 was finished, but the late answer with "qa_num" 25 could cause other discussions on the same topic.* Thus, late answers like this scenario may cause to circular or re-work discussions.

We have a query template to identify them by using "qa_num" as follows.

Query 4. Identifying topics whose answers from stakeholders were later than the next topic an analyst newly proposed (M4 in Fig. 1).

```
MATCH (n)-[:discuss]->(m{type:"answer"})
    WHERE (n.qa_num + DELTA < m.qa_num)
    RETURN (n)-[:discuss]->(m);
```

The parameter `DELTA` stands for the scope where we retrieve late answers. We can specify the types of graph nodes `n` and `m` as `analyst_act` and `stakeholder_act` and vice versa. Figure 7 shows the result with `DELTA` = 3, `analyst_act` as `n` and `stakeholder_act` as `m`[3]. It demonstrated the above scenario where the analyst asked "Common attributes of materials" (Are there any other common attributes of materials?) and where the late answer from the stakeholder "User" contained the proposals of new attributes such as ISBN and Purchase date. The analyst should start re-discussions on "Common attributes of materials" even if she or he considered that its discussions was finished.

4.4 Version Control

The functions of version control are not directly related to detecting bad smells of Q&A activities, but they are necessary to monitor the progress of the

[3] When we click a node on a Neo4j browser, we can see the content of its property values. To make this figure more visible, we paste the property values of the node "Is the following information unnecessary as ...".

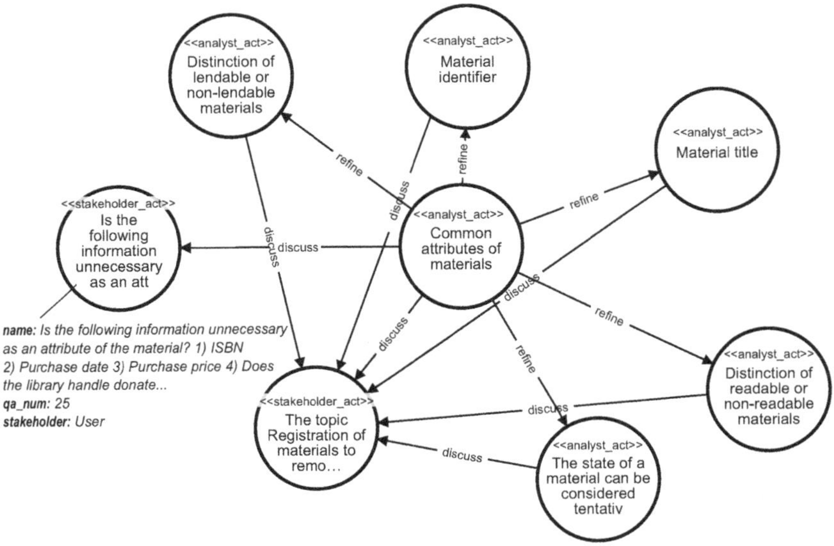

Fig. 7. Circular discussions or re-discussions.

requirements elicitation process. In addition, since the analyst can access to the evolution of the requirements list and can check the rationales why some requirements in the list had been changed and evolved by accessing the linked Q&A activities, it could be useful to avoid circular Q&A activities on the evolved requirements and to capture milestones throughout a Q&A process. In this paper, we list up two types of queries; one is to check-out a certain version of requirements shown in Query 5, and the other is to extract the differences (diffs or delta) between two versions shown in Query 6. The latter is useful to capture the evolution of requirements and its rationales.

Query 5. Check-out.

```
MATCH (n)-[:version{ver_num:XXX}]->(m:req)
    RETURN n, m;
```

Query 5 is used to extract requirements of version number "`XXX`". The node `m` is the extracted requirement, and we can see the content of the requirement by clicking the node on the Neo4j browser.

Query 6. Difference extraction.

```
MATCH (k)-[:version{ver_num:YYY}]->(l:req)
    WHERE NOT (k)-[:version{ver_num:XXX}]->(l)
    RETURN k, l;
```

By using Query 6, we retrieve the requirements which the version "`XXX`" has not but "`YYY`" does, i.e., $Req(\texttt{YYY}) \setminus Req(\texttt{XXX})$ where $Req(\texttt{NNN}) = \{r \mid r$ is a requirement of version number "`NNN`"$\}$. Figure 8 shows the result of the differences between the versions 20200608 and 20220626. In the left side of the figure,

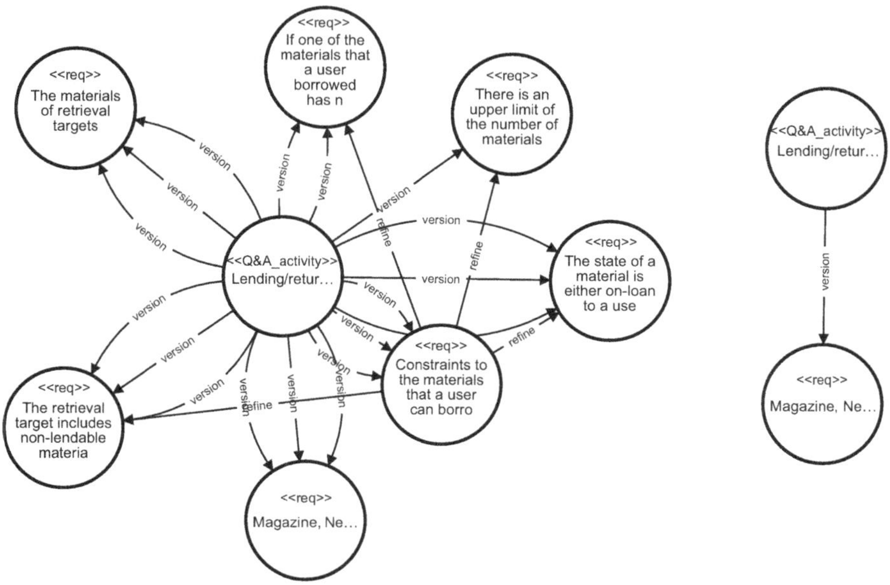

(a) Newly added requirements. (b) Deleted requirement.

Fig. 8. Differences between the versions 20200608 and 20200626.

the nodes of `req` denote the requirements that had been newly added to the newer version 20200626, i.e., the requirements that had not been in the older version 20200608. It resulted from setting 20200628 and 20200608 to `YYY` and `XXX` in Query 6, respectively. On the other hand, Fig. 8(b) shows the requirement that had been deleted in the version 20200626, but that was in the version 20200608. We can retrieve the deleted requirements in the newer version by setting the older one to `YYY` and the newer to `XXX` in Query 6. Note that the `req` node "Magazine, Ne ..." seems to be the same in Figs. 8(a) and 8(b), but their contents were different. Both of the nodes presented the scope of lendable materials and in the newer version, and it was updated and clarified. In Fig. 8, three occurrences of `version` edge between `Q&A activity` and `req` can be found. The Neo4j browser outputs all of the edges between retrieved nodes. One of the three is the version 20200626, and the other two show that the requirements remained in the latter two versions.

5 Discussion

For our Neo4j database system of Library system example, we have designed and executed the queries listed up in Fig. 1. By analyzing the retrieval results, all of the queries except three could identify precisely the subgraphs that we want, which could be used for finding bad smells. These three cases are 1) M1: identifying discussions not leading to requirements, 2) M4: identifying topics whose answers from stakeholders were later than the next topic an analyst newly proposed, and 3) M7: identifying the existence of requirements having different topics. With them we have retrieved unnecessary subgraphs in addition to the subgraphs that we wanted. That is to say, these queries output *false positives.* The reasons why these queries output the unnecessary graphs can be listed up as follows.

- To match the analyst's specific Q&A activities, we might sometimes use weak conditions. In the example of Query 4, we used 3 as the threshold `DELTA`. However, our query found out the answer delayed later than 3 but before the next topic started, and indicated an occurrence of *circular or re-work discussions* bad smell. More sophisticated decision, e.g., comparing topics, may be necessary.
- We used as requirements the sentences appearing in the property "name" values in mails. Although our requirements analyst was a veteran, he sometimes used different words even to express the same meaning or concepts. As a result, we could miss some of the mails including the same topic. This is not a problem on our queries, but on how to construct a Neo4j database.

Neo4j is not the only one system to implement our goal, and other techniques such as simply Excel plus its lining mechanism can realize it. However, comprehensive user interface and the query language Cypher to define bad smells flexibly allowed us to take Neo4j. In Neo4j, we can grasp easily the information connected to each other from bird's eye view, and especially we can capture progress of Q&A sessions. In contrast, for the hierarchical structures of requirement sentences and Q&A activities, in our graph database we should trace nodes and edges to recognize their hierarchical structures. So, it is not so easy to grasp these hierarchical structures at a glance and it is a demerit of using a graph database.

6 Related Work

We can find several studies to support interviews and meetings among analysts and stakeholders. Until the end of 1990s, the application of Searle's speech act theory has often been studied to navigate speakers in Q&A sessions [7,11]. Inquiry Cycle Model [11] is to capture discussions between analysts and stakeholders with Q&A cycles which are patterned with a set of speech acts such as Question, Answer, and Reason. They are navigated following the patterned cycle and their speech acts in the cycle trigger to update a requirements specification. The idea of specific speech acts connecting to evolution of a requirements specification is similar to our model of Neo4j. However, including Inquiry Cycle Model, this category of studies had the idea where analysts and stakeholders are forced into predefined patterns of discussions to avoid *bad smells.* On the other hand, our approach does not force their activities, and instead detect *bad smells* to improve their activities. Since requirements elicitation is one of the most creative tasks of human, over enforcement to its Q&A activities may lead to a specification of lower quality. Rather, we can use the results of this category as complementary ones. In addition, the studies of this category did not mention explicitly the idea nor the definition of *bad smells*, which this paper did. Similarly, interview patterns of expert analysts [2,8,9] can be useful to enhance our approach, especially creating a graph database system. In addition, there are studies of analyzing interviews between analysts and stakeholders to detect ambiguity during the interviews [14]. These results can be applied to design more sophisticated queries to detect bad smells on ambiguity basis. As for combining Q&A activities with artifacts, we used links between Q&A activities and their resulting requirements.

There are several studies on bad smells in requirements engineering [6,12], but many of them are for products, i.e., elicited requirements themselves. This study focuses not on products but on processes to elicit requirements. Ambriola and Gervasi [1] discussed process metrics of requirements analysis using stability of requirements and the efforts of reworks on a part of documents. These metrics are useful to explore new types of metrics to detect bad smells.

7 Conclusion and Future Work

This paper presented an integrated technique of detecting bad smells in Q&A activities between a requirements analyst and stakeholders during requirements elicitation and of controlling the versions of elicited requirements on a graph database Neo4j. The analyst and the stakeholders can access to it using queries in order to detect *bad smells*, symptoms to cause Q&A processes and requirements specifications of low quality, during Q&A sessions. We picked up E-mail bases Q&A activities to develop a library system and constructed a Neo4j database. We designed and executed Cypher queries to detect bad smells and to extract diffs of versions. This is just a proof-of-concept of our technique. The future research agendas, which were obtained from our case study, can be listed up as follows.

- **Tailoring a bad smell catalog:** The bad smells in Fig. 1 resulted from a case study of an expert's E-mail interview, so we can add more new bad smells. To discover them, the analytic results in [3] are very useful.
- **Structuring Q&A activity records for a graph database system:** In this study, we extracted data from a large volume of E-mails and stored them in the database system, with much more human efforts. The technique to summarize interviews like [13] can be applied to reduce human efforts. If we take E-mail based Q&A sessions, we will apply generative AI techniques to automatically classify the texts of E-mails and extract information necessary to generate a graph database system. The annotation tool such as AnnoteREI [5] can support structuring Q&A activities following our model of Fig. 2.

Acknowledgement. This work was partly supported by JSPS Grants-in-Aid for Scientific Research No. JP21K11823 and Nanzan University Pache Research Subsidy I–A–2 for the 2024 academic year.

References

1. Ambriola, V., Gervasi, V.: Process metrics for requirements analysis. In: Conradi, R. (ed.) EWSPT 2000. LNCS, vol. 1780, pp. 90–95. Springer, Heidelberg (2000). https://doi.org/10.1007/bfb0095017
2. Scheinholtz, L.A., Wilmont, I.: Interview patterns for requirements elicitation. In: Berry, D., Franch, X. (eds.) REFSQ 2011. LNCS, vol. 6606, pp. 72–77. Springer, Heidelberg (2011). https://doi.org/10.1007/978-3-642-19858-8_9
3. Bano, M., Zowghi, D., Ferrari, A., Spoletini, P., Donati, B.: Learning from mistakes: an empirical study of elicitation interviews performed by novices. In: Proceedings 26th IEEE International Requirements Engineering Conference, pp. 182–193 (2018)
4. Basili, V.: Software Modeling and Measurement: The Goal/Question/Metric Paradigm. Technical report UMIACS-TR-92-96, University of Maryland (1992)
5. Debnath, S., Subramanian, S.: AnnoteREI! a tool for transcribing and annotating requirements elicitation interviews. In: Proceedings 30th IEEE International Requirements Engineering Conference, pp. 255–256 (2022)
6. Femmer, H., Fernández, D.M., Jürgens, E., Klose, M., Zimmer, I., Zimmer, J.: Rapid requirements checks with requirements smells: Two case studies. In: Proceedings of 1st International Workshop on Rapid Continuous Software Engineering, pp. 10–19 (2014)
7. Kato, J., et al.: A model for navigating interview processes in requirements elicitation. In: Proceedings 8th Asia-Pacific Software Engineering Conference, pp. 141–148 (2001)
8. Malviya, S., Vierhauser, M., Cleland-Huang, J., Ghaisas, S.: What questions do requirements engineers ask? In: Proceedings 25th IEEE International Requirements Engineering Conference, pp. 100–109 (2017)
9. Mohedas, I., Daly, S., Loweth, R., Huynh, L., Cravens, G., Sienko, K.: The use of recommended interviewing practices by novice engineering designers to elicit information during requirements development. Des. Sci. **8**, e16 (2022)
10. Neo4j. https://neo4j.com/
11. Potts, C., Takahashi, K., Anton, A.: Inquiry-based requirements analysis. IEEE Softw. **11**(2), 21–32 (1994)
12. Seki, Y., Hayashi, S., Saeki, M.: Detecting bad smells in use case descriptions. In: Proceedings 27th IEEE International Requirements Engineering Conference, pp. 98–108 (2019)
13. Spijkman, T., de Bondt, X., Dalpiaz, F., Brinkkemper, S.: Summarization of elicitation conversations to locate requirements-relevant information. In: Proceedings 29th International Working Conference on Requirements Engineering: Foundation for Software Quality, pp. 122–139 (2023)
14. Spoletini, P., Ferrari, A., Bano, M., Zowghi, D., Gnesi, S.: Interview review: an empirical study on detecting ambiguities in requirements elicitation interviews. In: Proceedings 24th International Working Conference on Requirements Engineering: Foundation for Software Quality, pp. 101–118 (2018)
15. Wing, J.M.: A study of 12 specifications of the library problem. IEEE Softw. **5**(4), 66–76 (1988)

Goal Model Extraction from User Stories Using Large Language Models

Vaishali Siddeshwar(✉), Sanaa Alwidian, and Masoud Makrehchi

Department of Electrical, Computer and Software Engineering,
University of Ontario Institute of Technology, Oshawa, Canada
{vaishali.siddeshwar,sanaa.alwidian,masoud.makrehchi}@ontariotechu.ca

Abstract. In agile software development, goal modeling is vital for understanding the relationships among user stories, commonly used to capture stakeholders' needs. Manual construction of goal models faces challenges, such as transforming lower-level user stories into higher-level models and capturing implicit goals. This paper presents early research proposing a technique using Large Language Models (LLMs), like GPT-4, to automatically generate goal models from user stories. The approach employs Iterative Prompt Engineering to guide the LLM in extracting intentional elements and generating XML representations using the Goal-oriented Requirements Language (GRL), visualized with the jUCMNav tool. Our primitive qualitative evaluation indicates that GPT-4 can produce GRL models that are acceptable and understandable. Despite the generic nature of LLM-generated models, there is a potential for their use in requirements modeling, particularly in exposing soft goals not immediately apparent to stakeholders new to the domain.

Keywords: Goal-oriented Requirement Language (GRL) · Goal Modeling · User story · Requirements engineering · Large Language Models (LLMs) · GPT-4

1 Introduction

User stories, widely used in agile software development, are concise artifacts capturing stakeholders' intentions, roles, and rationale [10]. User stories are structured in the following format: As a ⟨WHO⟩, I would like to ⟨WHAT⟩, so that ⟨WHY⟩. This format outlines WHO wants WHAT from the system and WHY. Their widespread adoption is due to their simplicity where they are expressed with simple natural language [10].

Goal modeling languages, like Goal-oriented Requirements Language (GRL) [1] can be utilized to express the rationale behind user stories by capturing stakeholder intentions, including actors, goals, softgoals, and tasks. GRL, a part of User Requirements Notation (URN) standard, allows clear articulation of stakeholders' intentions. While both user stories and goal models are valuable in requirements engineering, transforming user stories into goal models is crucial in

A. Bertolino et al. (Eds.): QUATIC 2024, CCIS 2178, pp. 269–276, 2024.
https://doi.org/10.1007/978-3-031-70245-7_19

agile development. Manually extracting goals from user stories and building goal models is a tedious and challenging task for requirements engineers, due to: (1) *"Granularity mismatch"*: user stories are written with a low level of granularity, focusing on specific functionalities or features. Goal models, on the other hand, may require a higher level of abstraction and may need to capture broader objectives. Bridging this is challenging. (2) Converting user stories into explicit, well-formulated goals needs Requirements engineers to fully understand the implicit meaning of the natural language of the user story to extract the implicit goals and articulate them in a way that aligns with goal modeling principles. (3) Lack of explicit capture of dependencies between goals or intentional elements in user stories can hinder the creation of a complete and accurate goal model.

Current approaches on goal model extraction, such as US2Star [12] and ArTu [7], use manual rules and NLP techniques but lack full contextual understanding of user stories. They often struggle to establish the relationship between different story components, which is crucial for uncovering hidden goals and tasks. Moreover, hand-crafted rules may miss subtle nuances in natural language, resulting in incomplete or inaccurate extractions. Another study [6] attempted automatic creation of GRL goal models but relied on a single prompt, leading to less comprehensive models.

Our research aims to leverage the capabilities of LLMs, which are pre-trained on vast amounts of text data, to enhance the extraction and generation of goal models from user stories. LLMs have demonstrated state-of-the-art performance in various tasks, including text summarization and key phrase extraction [11], making them proficient in understanding the context of stakeholders' requirements, crucial for identifying low-level requirements. To address the previously mentioned challenges, we introduce a method to employ GPT-4, a common LLM, for automatically generating GRL goal models. Our approach utilizes iterative prompt engineering to guide GPT-4 in extracting intentional elements and generating XML representations of goal models, which can be visualized using jUCMNav tool [3], an Eclipse plug-in for visualizing and generating goal models. The replication package, including prompts and source code, is available (See footnote 1).

2 Motivating Example

To motivate our work, we use an example of user stories for designing a traffic simulator. They are adopted from [14] and illustrated in Fig. 1.a . We assigned them to three graduate students with experience in goal modeling, and instructed them to construct a comprehensive and explicit goal model. Figure 1.b displays the result of the traffic simulator design exercise. It contains three distinct goal models produced by the modelers for the same user stories. As can be noted from the figure, the user stories were interpreted by modelers at different levels of granularity, which resulted in inconsistent models. The models exhibit varying levels of granularity and interpretation, leading to inconsistencies. Additionally, certain implicit goals (depicted as softgoals) and dependencies or interactions between different goals(e.g., contribution links) are absent in some of the generated models (e.g., the model in the middle).

Our goal is to explore how LLMs can address the granularity mismatch issue and uncover implicit components often overlooked in manual goal modeling. We aim to assess GPT-4's advanced natural language understanding capabilities in interpreting and extracting implicit goals from user stories. Additionally, we seek to evaluate its ability to suggest appropriate levels of abstraction for refining goal granularity in the model and identifying dependencies and interactions between various goals or features mentioned in user stories.

As a Traffic Engineer, I want to simulate traffic flow, so that I can deliver the most efficient road traffic engineering and design. As a Traffic Engineer, I want to see clear visualizations, so that I can quickly aid development. As a Traffic Engineer, I want to use density maps, so that I can highlight congestion. As a Traffic Engineer, I want to view animations, so that I can demonstrate traffic flow and bottlenecks.

(a) User stories of Traffic Simulator

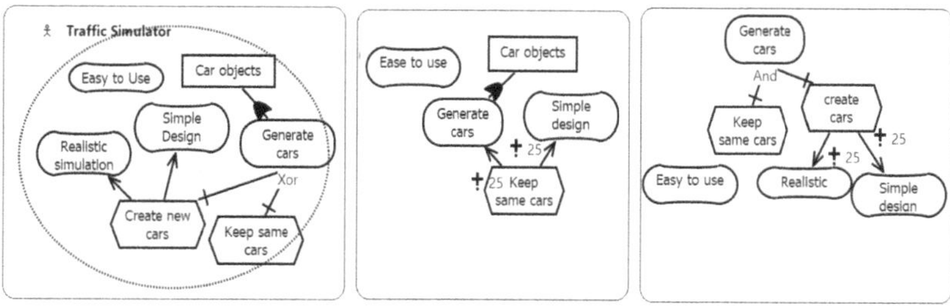

(b) Manually generated GRL models

Fig. 1. User stories of the Traffic Simulator (a), and three manually generated GRL models (b)

3 Proposed Approach

The aim of this study is to address the following research questions (RQs):

RQ1). Is the GPT-4 capable of generating a GRL goal model from a given user story?

RQ2). What is the syntactic and semantic differences between the GRL models generated by GPT-4 and those developed by a requirements engineer?
Towards this end, an overview of our proposed approach with two phases: GRL model generation, and GRL model visualization, is illustrated in Fig. 2.

3.1 GRL Model Generation Phase

This phase generates a GRL Model. In LLMs like GPT, a *prompt* is a textual directive that guides the LLM to generate the desired output. Our technique introduces a novel approach to generate goal models from LLMs, unlike typical single-prompt method. It employs a seven-step iterative prompting strategy combined with few-shot learning. Inspired by chain-of-thought prompting, this technique breaks down complex problems into manageable steps, enhancing the LLM's ability to tackle a complex task effectively [13]. The approach mirrors human problem-solving strategies and surpasses conventional prompting methods [13]. We argue that constructing GRL models mirrors reasoning problems [9], involving a series of steps: extracting actors, identifying goals and resources, pinpointing tasks, and establishing various relationships like means-end, contribution, decomposition, and dependency links. This iterative prompting comprises two main stages: the *Start Prompt* stage comprising of one prompt and the *Iteration Prompt* stage with seven prompts, as depicted in Fig. 2. The exact prompts used in the approach along with the source code is available online[1]. Both steps are explained below:

Start Prompt. This step involves a text prompt that consists of three components: The first segment is a fixed message called *contextual background*, which provides the LLM with the context of the task. This includes a comprehensive description of GRL goal model's components, explaining intentional elements and their relationships. Moreover, we explicitly define the LLM's role as a requirements engineer, who can align with stakeholders' objectives. The second segment contains *user stories* for which a GRL model extraction is required. The final segment defines the *characteristics of the output.* jUCMNav tool uses an XML output template to store and visualize goal models. To produce jUCMNav-compatible outputs, we include three instances of outputs generated by jUCMNav as few-shot examples to allow the LLM replicate the output format.

Iteration Prompt. This phase focuses on refining the goal model created earlier using 'ChainOfThought' [13] technique. The LLM follows a sequence of seven textual prompts, re-evaluating its response after each one to develop a more comprehensive goal model. During each iteration, a list of chat history, referred as *Context*, is updated with previous prompts and their responses. This evolving chat history is also passed to the LLM when generating subsequent responses. Here is the outline of the seven prompts: the first three provide brief instructions to analyse its previous response and to identify hidden actors, goals, and tasks, respectively. The following four prompts encourage the LLM to add additional means-end, decomposition, contribution, and dependency links. The seven-step process of multi-step prompting, as illustrated in Fig. 2, guides the LLM through each stage of goal model creation.

3.2 GRL Model Visualization

The response generated in the previous phase is validated for malformations by the validator module. If errors are detected, the process restarts. If no errors are found, the XML is ready for manual import and visualization in the jUCMNav tool.

[1] https://zenodo.org/records/11562002.

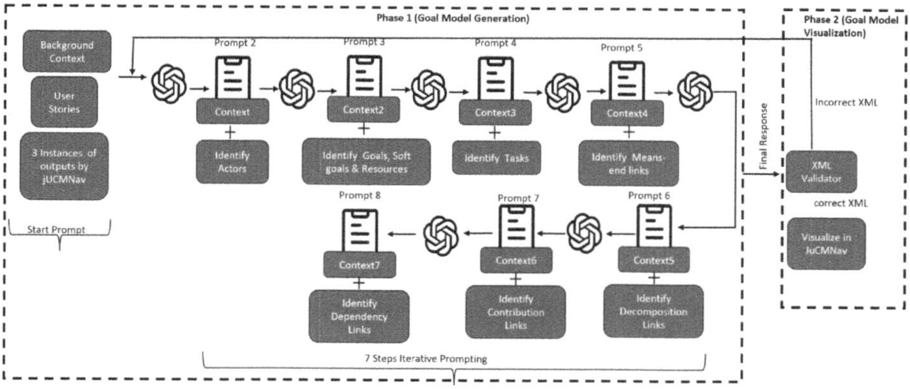

Fig. 2. An overview of the proposed approach

4 Evaluation and Preliminary Results

To evaluate, ten GRL models were randomly selected from the literature, where these models are well-validated. The data adopted from the literature included GRL models and snippets of requirements in natural language which the authors transformed them into the format of user stories. The user stories, their sources, and their goal models are available (See footnote 1). This aids a swift evaluation of the methodology without involving human experts. Two assessments were carried out in order to address the second research question. The first assessment examines the syntactic distinctions between the ground-truth GRL models and the generated outputs, whereas, the second evaluates the semantic similarities between the models.

To assess the syntactic similarities (RQ2), a coverage score is calculated. We define the coverage score as a percentage of intentional elements (i.e. actors, softgoals, goals, tasks, resources, contributions, and dependencies) in the ground-truth model that are included in the response provided by the LLM. Each response model generated by LLM is evaluated manually and a coverage score is calculated. To perform a semantics analysis of the generated models (RQ2), the models were compared manually with the ground-truth models by the authors and assigned a quality score. The intention of this second assessment is to ascertain whether the generated models are coherent and effectively convey the information contained in the user stories. To assess this, each response generated by LLM will be manually evaluated based on three categories: fully correct (=1), partially correct (=0.5, i.e., a model is acceptable, but a few minor faults are found), and incorrect.

Figure 3 depicts a GRL model generated by LLM for the TrafficSimulator example mentioned in Sect. 2. The LLM-generated model surpasses manually created models because it identifies a hidden goal and a softgoal ('Manage Cars' and 'Dependability'), and adds a task ('Run simulation') that contributes to the goal of managing car instances.

The preliminary results of our approach on ten randomly selected GRL models from literature is summarized in Table 1. It displays the average coverage score, indicating the percentage of intentional elements covered by the LLM-generated responses. The complexity column estimates the level of expertise required to develop the model. A GRL model is labeled 'Difficult' if the user stories exceeds four sentences and intentional elements are not discernible. The columns for actors, softgoals, goals, tasks, decompositions, and contributions show the number of intentional elements in the existing GRL models, while the last column, Coverage, indicates the covered elements in the outputs.

The results show that LLMs generated reasonable goal models for all user stories, but with notable variation. While all responses accurately covered actors, goals, and tasks, coverage of soft goals was inconsistent, and few models included resources. Notably, shorter user stories were better synthesized by GPT-4, especially those with clear goals and contributions but lacking soft goals. However, GPT-4 struggled with longer stories, particularly in incorporating soft goals and contributions effectively. Despite lacking quantitative evidence, we observe that the goal models generated were more readable than those in existing literature, attributed to LLMs' advanced natural language understanding capabilities in interpreting and extracting implicit goals and requirements from user stories.

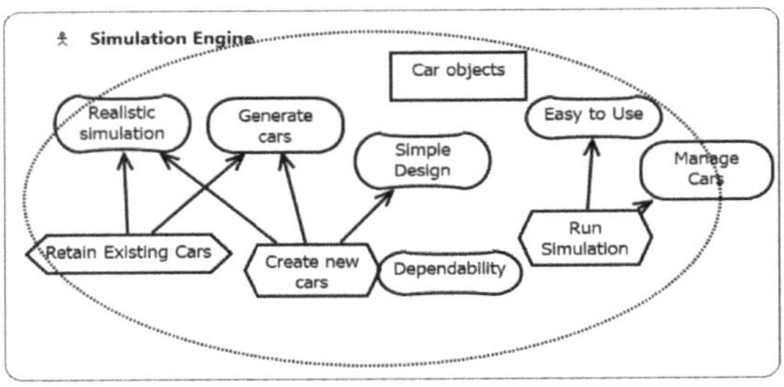

Fig. 3. GRL model generated by GPT-4 API

Table 1. Evaluation of syntactic similarities of the LLM-generated GRL models

Story	Ground Truth							Coverage	Quality
	Complexity	Actors	Soft-goals	Goals	Tasks	Decom-position	Contributions		
1 [14]	Easy	1	0	4	0	0	3	100%	1
2 [7]	Easy	1	0	3	0	0	2	100%	1
3 [4]	Easy	1	0	4	0	0	3	62%	0.5
4 [4]	Easy	1	0	3	1	0	2	71%	0.5
5 [4]	Easy	1	0	1	6	6	0	78%	1
6 [2]	Easy	1	5	1	0	2	4	84%	1
7 [5]	Difficult	1	4	3	5	5	6	50%	0.5
8 [8]	Difficult	1	7	1	2	0	14	72%	0.5
9 [8]	Difficult	1	5	1	2	0	11	30%	0.5
10 [8]	Difficult	1	4	1	2	0	11	73%	0.5

5 Related Work

Various approaches have been proposed to convert user stories into goal models. Mesquita et al. [12] developed the US2StarTool to automatically generate iStar models from user stories. They focus on extracting user story components using hand-crafted rules based on linguistic structures. Other studies use natural language processing (NLP) techniques and heuristics to build goal models by identifying relationships in the stories. In contrast, our approach leverages Large Language Models (LLMs) for a deeper understanding of language, allowing for the capture of implicit relationships within user stories without relying on linguistic rules. Chen et al. [6] also explore automatic creation of GRL goal models using LLMs, but our approach involves an iterative prompting strategy to refine responses and generate more comprehensive models.

6 Research Agenda

So far, we have assessed our approach with a small set of GRL models from existing literature. Although we lack quantitative evidence, our observations indicate that LLM-generated goal models are more comprehensible than manually created ones. The next evaluation phase will compare the semantics of LLM-generated models for user stories sourced from the industry. The focus will be on how well the LLM captures implicit goals and tasks from user stories. We also aim to determine if LLM-generated goal models are more comprehensive than those produced by NLP-based techniques. The final evaluation will involve goal modeling experts who will construct goal models from a series of user stories. They will provide feedback on the output generated by our approach and enhance the generated goal models to fine-tune the LLM. In addition, we recognize that our current evaluation of the syntactical and semantical aspects of the models is simplistic and that we need to establish a gold standard for comparison.

7 Threats to Validity

The presence of two biases in the conducted experiments are acknowledged. First bias is related to manual evaluation of the generated models that arose due to subjectivity and variations in the interpretation of LLM outputs. The second bias is associated with the user stories that were selected. These stories were created by the research team and may not accurately reflect real-world user stories.

8 Conclusion

In this exploratory paper, we investigated the potential of using LLMs to automatically generate GRL models from user stories. We used prompt engineering with output templates to guide LLMs to generate an XML representation of the GRL model that can be visualized using jUCMNav-plugin. Our studies find that employing LLMs for GRL modeling task is a promising approach. This approach not only address the abstraction gap between user stories and goal models but also encourages stakeholders to avail the assistance of LLMs to uncover softgoals and tasks that are not readily visible. Although, LLM-generated goal models are more comprehensive than the manually generated models, they need thorough evaluation by field experts.

References

1. Amyot, D.: Amyot, D.: Introduction to the user requirements notation: learning by example. Comput. Netw. **42**, 285–301 (2003). https://doi.org/10.1016/S1389-1286(03)00244-5
2. Amyot, D.: Introduction to the user requirements notation: learning by example. Comput. Netw. **42**(3), 285–301 (2003). https://doi.org/10.1016/s1389-1286(03)00244-5
3. Amyot, D., Mussbacher, G., Ghanavati, S., Kealey, J.: Grl modeling and analysis with jUCMNav. (2011)
4. Baslyman, M., Almoaber, B., Amyot, D., Bouattane, E.M.: Activity-based process integration in healthcare with the user requirements notation, pp. 151–169 (2017). https://doi.org/10.1007/978-3-319-59041-7_9
5. v. Bochmann, G.: Goal modeling and GRL (2009). Accessed 06 Dec 2023
6. Chen, B., et al.: On the use of GPT-4 for creating goal models: an exploratory study. In: 2023 IEEE 31st International Requirements Engineering Conference Workshops (REW), pp. 262–271 (2023). https://doi.org/10.1109/REW57809.2023.00052
7. Gunes, T., Aydemir, F.B.: Automated goal model extraction from user stories using NLP (2020). https://doi.org/10.1109/re48521.2020.00052
8. Horkoff, J., Yu, E.: Interactive goal model analysis for early requirements engineering. Requirements Eng. **21**(1), 29–61 (2016). https://doi.org/10.1007/s00766-014-0209-8
9. Krishna, S., Agarwal, C., Lakkaraju, H.: Understanding the effects of iterative prompting on truthfulness (2024)
10. Lucassen, G., Robeer, M., Dalpiaz, F., van der Werf, J.M.E.M., Brinkkemper, S.: Extracting conceptual models from user stories with visual narrator. Requirements Eng. **22**(3), 339–358 (2017). https://doi.org/10.1007/s00766-017-0270-1
11. Mars, M.: From word embeddings to pre-trained language models: a state-of-the-art walkthrough. Appl. Sci. **12**(17) (2022). https://doi.org/10.3390/app12178805
12. Mesquita, R., Jaqueira, A., Lucena, M., Filho, C.S., Alencar, F.M.R.: Us2startool: generating i* models from user stories. In: International i* Workshop (2015). https://api.semanticscholar.org/CorpusID:690350
13. Wei, J., et al.: Chain of thought prompting elicits reasoning in large language models. CoRR (2022), arXiv:abs/2201.11903
14. van Zee, M., Bex, F., Ghanavati, S.: Rationalgrl: a framework for argumentation and goal modeling. Argument Comput. **12**, 191–245 (2021). https://doi.org/10.3233/AAC-200527

Quality in Organisations and Practice

Digitalization Impact Evaluation Model: A Case Study

Juhani Heikka[1,2](✉), Sanna Heikkinen[2], Marika Iivari[1], and Timo Koivumäki[1]

[1] Martti Ahtisaari Institute, Oulu Business School, University of Oulu, Oulu, Finland
{juhani.heikka,marika.iivari,timo.koivumaki}@oulu.fi
[2] Istekki Oy, Kuopio, Finland
sanna.heikkinen@istekki.fi

Abstract. Investments in the digital transformation are significant in all sectors of society. However, evaluating the impacts of the digital transformation still needs to be completed due to the lack of comprehensive approaches and empirical evidence. The need for digital transformation impact evaluation models is evident in public and private organizations. Investments are expected to yield a positive impact, and high-quality information is needed for efficient decision-making. This study presents a model for evaluating the effect of digital transformation based on a design science research approach. The model is then explored in a real-world setting through a participatory case study in a large ICT-service provider organization operating in the healthcare sector. The research data is analyzed using a socio-technical framework. The findings offer valuable insights into three perspectives of the model: 1) essential properties and phases, 2) benefits and value for the case organization and its customers, and 3) future development needs. This study also recognizes topics for future research.

Keywords: digital transformation · impact · evaluation · model · value · strategy · decision-making · service management · design science · case study

1 Introduction

Modern societies rely on the wide use of information and communication technologies (ICT). Organizations are adopting new technologies and innovations to improve productivity, develop and automate business processes, and provide modern digital services. Investments in boosting the digital transformation have been remarkable. For instance, the European Union [15] launched The Digital Europe Programme, which provides strategic funding (7.5 billion Euros) to support the digital transformation in the key areas. New technologies and innovations are often expected to have strong economic potential [24]. The underlying assumption of the digital transformation is that technology will positively impact performance, expenses, efficiency, customer satisfaction, well-being, or other desired outcome [46]. However, history indicates that such promises on impact may or may not materialize. Potential benefits may also be accompanied by unintended and negative short-term or long-term impacts [41]. Impact evaluation is complex because the digital transformation can have both direct and indirect effects [10].

A. Bertolino et al. (Eds.): QUATIC 2024, CCIS 2178, pp. 279–294, 2024.
https://doi.org/10.1007/978-3-031-70245-7_20

Prior studies argue that research illustrating or assessing the impact of digital transformation is scant, and multidisciplinary research is needed [8, 12, 16, 24, 36, 43, 48]. It has even been argued that current studies have focused on measuring easily measurable things, and more rigor in the theoretical foundation and empirical evidence on actual value is needed [10, 48]. For instance, widely used cost/benefit analyses need more support in quantifying intangible benefits [11, 46]. Also, extant research has placed limited emphasis on understanding evaluation processes [10, 16]. To fully grasp the impact of technology, the use of qualitative and quantitative approaches is necessary [10, 29, 30]. In addition to exploring new theoretical avenues, methodological contributions are called for.

Technological changes [12] and the digital transformation are wide, systemic phenomena, implying continuous and constant change affecting the whole organization and its way of operating [9, 17, 22, 48]. The problem area is "wicked," where complexity theory and complex adaptive systems could provide a valuable lens for sensemaking [2, 45]. However, there is also a clear need to develop new approaches and multidimensional digitalization impact evaluation models that help us make sense of the complexity and direct us toward potential solutions. Digital transformation is more than a technological shift; it requires aligning strategy, leadership, culture [8, 17, 22], standardization, new knowledge, and partnerships [9]. Digital transformation also enables the emergence of new business models and logic to capture value, which has led to exponential growth of data that can be utilized in effective and data-driven decision-making [14]. Especially understanding how technologies create and capture value through digitalization-enabled change has been called for [18, 43]. The dynamic nature of digital transformation has also been highlighted in strategic management, where the significant influence of incorporating technology into organizations' processes has been discussed [8]. However, more research on the relationship between digital transformation and strategic management is needed [22, 40].

This paper aims to contribute to resolving the complexities of digital transformation by increasing understanding of how value can be created by using impact evaluation models in different stages of companies' digitalization activities. To meet this aim, our specific research question asks *how the use of a digitalization impact evaluation model can create value for companies.*

The rest of the paper is organized as follows: Sect. 2 overviews related work. Section 3 presents the chosen research methodology. Section 4 describes the contents of the constructed digitalization impact evaluation model and illustrates its implementation in an empirical case. In Sect. 5, we present the findings of our research. Section 6 includes a discussion of our study with reflections and our conclusions.

2 Related Work

2.1 Digital Transformation and Impact Evaluation

Positive impacts of digital transformation do not simply happen [3]. To drive positive impacts, a well-defined, up-to-date strategy is needed [22, 40]. To realize the positive impact systematic planning, managing, measuring, and reviewing are necessary [22,

40]. The dynamic nature of the digital transformation has changed strategic management practices by highlighting the significant influence of incorporating technology into organizations' processes [8]. Still, research into the relationship between the digital transformation and strategic management is needed [22, 40].

Prior research introduces various frameworks [10, 14, 16, 18, 29–31, 38] and factors [43] or barriers [9, 42] that aim to describe the impacts and explain a successful digital transformation. Digital transformation is a complex phenomenon, and evaluating its impact is difficult [10, 11, 18]. Impacts are often linked to performance (i.e., cost reductions, increased volumes, new information, increased effectiveness in service production, staff reduction, etc.), which is evidence that digital intervention positively impacted organizations of improved productivity [11]. Eggers and Park [12] define a positive impact through the successful commercialization of new technologies and that this requires necessary knowledge about the new technology and the means to commercialize it. Digital technologies, for example, in healthcare organizations, significantly impacts organizational performance due to increasing accessibility to services, speed of decision-making, transparency, and trust [46]. The focus should be on the impacts, not the technology itself [3, 10].

Prior studies highlight that research illustrating or evaluating the impact of the digital transformation is scant, and multidisciplinary research is needed [8, 12, 16, 24, 36, 48]. Research on the digital transformation's impact is fragmented and lacks systematic empirical evidence [10, 48]. Many approaches have limitations focusing on measuring what is easily measurable while lacking a rigorous theoretical foundation and empirical evidence on the value [10, 48]. The digital transformation and the impact of technologies need to be evaluated not only for their feasibility and acceptance but also for their impact [29, 38]. To understand the impacts, qualitative and quantitative approaches are necessary [10, 30]. Ashurst [8] found that few benefit-oriented practices were adopted because IT professionals focused primarily on technical aspects.

It is crucial to evaluate digitalization-enabled change to understand how technologies create and capture value [18, 43]. Service value chain responds to demand and facilitates value realization by creating and managing products and services [4]. Multidimensional and interactive value chains can be seen as ecosystems or networks [49]. An IT service value network is a multi-staged construct of networked but autonomous service suppliers whose delivery relies on digital systems that generate tangible and intangible value for a consumer through complex exchanges between network participants [21]. IT service providers are increasingly concerned with their ability to co-create digital services with customers in service ecosystems [25].

IT service providers must consider the customer environment when improving and developing digital services. For example, in healthcare, WHO states that quality health services should be effective, safe, people-centered, timely, equitable, integrated, and efficient [50]. From the impact evaluation perspective, IT service providers should consider these quality-of-care perspectives in designing and evaluating IT systems or IT services in the healthcare domain. In Finland, the law on the organization of social and health care states that the well-being counties should monitor impact elements such as the availability, quality, effectiveness, and equality of the social and health care it organizes. These defined elements may be included in the digitization projects of social and healthcare services [31]. In measuring the value and impact of digital services, IT systems or services, the IT service provider may use the Input, Output, Outcome, Impact (IOOI) logic chain [1]. To conclude, there is a need to build and develop new theoretically grounded approaches that provide an overall model for evaluating digitalization impacts in chosen contexts.

2.2 Information Technology and Service Management (ITSM)

Service science is an interdisciplinary approach that includes theories from service, management, engineering, and design (SSMED) [44]. In SSMED, services are used to create knowledge and theories about services, while services management is related to improving service value, and engineering is associated with the practical problems of producing benefits through creating knowledge [35].

ITSM frameworks [5, 26–28, 32, 37] are de facto standards and widely used in the IT industry. ITSM includes capabilities, technological tools, skills, and working practices that IT organizations utilize to assure quality, effectiveness, and efficiency in their services [42]. ITSM frameworks provide a basis for process and service development and support organizations in optimizing their use of resources (personnel, technology, budget). Effective resource management results in cost savings, enhanced staff allocation, and optimal utilization of technology assets, thereby fostering a more economical IT operation.

High-class and impactful ITSM practices are crucial for creating value for the customer in the form of customer-oriented IT services. Typically, ITSM frameworks list a set of requirements for evaluation. For example:

- ISO 9001 [26]. *The organization shall continually improve the suitability, adequacy and effectiveness of the quality management system* (Clause 10.3 Continual improvement).
- ISO/IEC 20000-1 [28]. *The organization shall continually improve the suitability, adequacy and effectiveness of the SMS and the services* (Clause 10.2 Continual improvement).
- ISO/IEC 13485 [27]. *The organization must identify and verify all connections that are functional and to maintain the quality management system's continued suitability, appropriateness and effectiveness as well as medical safety and performance, a functional quality policy, quality is important, follow-up after delivery for audit results, data analysis, corrective and preventive measures and management reviews* (Clause 8.5 Improvement)
- ITIL [5, 32] assists organizations in optimizing their IT resources, encompassing personnel, technology, and budget.
- The Management of Value [37] framework includes a collection of principles, processes, and techniques that will help organization to optimize the benefits of their portfolios, programs, and projects.

ITSM requirements help organizations recognize essential aspects that need to be considered. However, the frameworks rarely provide concrete and practical tools to support, such as evaluation activities. Frameworks typically include an improvement cycle, which is a repetitive activity that works to improve efficiency and effectiveness over time. For example, in the ITIL framework [32], this cycle is a seven-step improvement process, where the implementation of improvements is based on 1) the information collected by the improvement goals and development strategy, 2) the analysis and reporting of the information, and 3) the improvements implemented through the utilization of the information. To help IT service providers to demonstrate their service's impact on customers, new properties or steps could be introduced into the seven-step improvement process (e.g., evaluate the impacts) [20].

ITSM has become the prevalent management approach to providing IT services worldwide. Researchers and practitioners, however, still lack an understanding of which mechanisms and strategic contexts an ITSM capability contributes most to information systems effectiveness [49].

3 Research Methodology

3.1 Design Science and Participatory Case Study

Design approaches such as design theory and design science [23] have been successfully applied in ICT method development [19]. This study was conducted by utilizing a design science research methodology (DSRM) process model [39]. The process includes six steps (Fig. 1) that guide the development and evaluation of an artifact. A participatory case study [51] in a real-life empirical environment was conducted to evaluate the artifact. The case study approach is suitable for investigating qualitative research questions [13] and is therefore utilized.

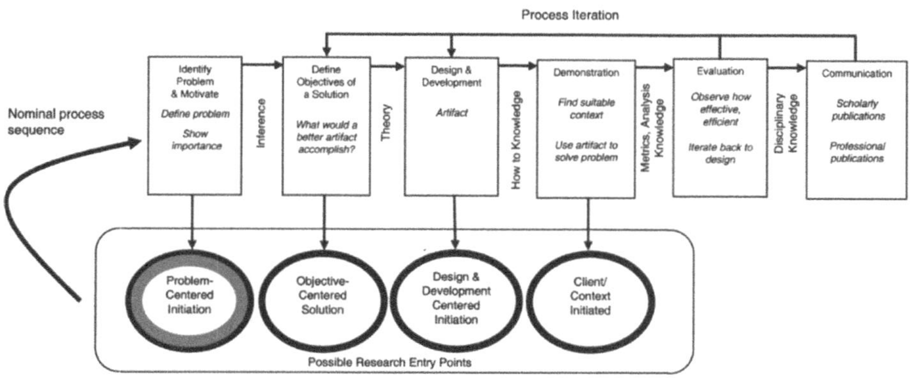

Fig. 1. Design science research methodology [39] utilized in the study.

3.2 Case Organization: A Large ICT Service Provider

The case organization operates in the public sector, providing ICT services in the social and healthcare domains. The company's turnover is about 300 million euros and employs 1,300 ICT specialists. The standards [26–28] used by the company do not provide clear guidance or a model of how the impacts of digitalization should be evaluated. The company has strategic goals that indicate a strong business need to improve evaluation capabilities. 1) the company's ICT services should create measurable value for customers by enhancing the use of public resources, 2) the company aims to develops a method for digitalization impact evaluation, and 3) investment decisions will be made based on the impact evaluation.

3.3 Data Collection Methods

The study utilized multiple sources of evidence throughout the DSRM phases (Table 1). The initial situation was clarified by reviewing the documentation and information in various information systems. Participant observation was used to gain an in-depth understanding of the problem field and the use of the artifact in the case organization. Observation findings were documented as field notes.

The main research instruments were questionnaires and semi-structured interviews. The evaluation data was collected via an evaluation questionnaire and semi-structured interviews. The questionnaire was divided under six themes of the FEDS framework [47]: expected utility, evidence that theory leads to valuable artifact, artifact makes an improvement to state of the art, utility (functionality, consistency, accuracy, performance), side effects (undesirable results), and why artifact works or not. One respondent piloted the questionnaire before launching, and two questions were modified after receiving feedback. To enrich the data, researchers chose four directors working closely on digital transformation into semi-structured interviews. To avoid respondent bias in the interviews, indirect open-ended questions were used. The interviews were implemented utilizing Microsoft Teams meetings, and the discussions were transcribed. The transcripts are in Finnish. Direct quotes have been translated into English. The average duration of the interviews varied between 30–50 min. The observations began to saturate at this point, and the researchers concluded that new interviews were no longer needed.

Table 1. Data collection methods (classification according to Yin [51]).

Research phase	Source
Participant observation (design & development, evaluation)	Field notes from a workshop in April 2023 (9 participants), digitalization impact evaluations (6 cases)
Documents (design & development, demonstration, evaluation)	Case organization ISO 9001 and ISO/IEC 20000-1 standardization documentation, meeting memos, digitalization impact evaluations (pre-evaluation tool)
Physical artefacts (design & development, demonstration)	Quality and service process management and mapping System, the case organization's Intranet

(*continued*)

Table 1. (*continued*)

Research phase	Source
Interviews (I), discussions (identify problem, design & development, demonstration, evaluation)	Discussions with key actors of the company, workshop memos and materials, semi-structured interviews with the Innovation and Development Board (4 interviews: I1–I4)
Questionnaire (Q) (evaluation)	Evaluation questionnaire concerning the artifact (Fig. 2) (11 open and 3 multiple choice questions, 9 answers: Q1–Q9)

3.4 Data Analysis

This study focuses on qualitative data. Multiple data sources were utilized to enable data source triangulation and verification of findings (Table 1). The data analysis was conducted using an inductive strategy and within-case analysis technique suitable to study results from a single case organization [13]. Researchers interacted with data during the research process by reading the data repeatedly to recognize themes. Researchers used a four-step data analysis process: describing, interpreting, drawing conclusions, and determining significance. The descriptive phase included familiarization and reviewing of the data. The data from the questionnaire (Q1–Q9) and interviews (I1–I4) were coded into themes in an Excel table. The empirical data was then tabularized through socio-technical system (STS) components [6, 7, 33] (people, structure, process, technology). The common understanding and consistency were ensured with active dialog between researchers. The findings and emerging themes were categorized under STS components [6], which enabled answering the research question and drawing conclusions. One of the case organization's key informants reviewed the case study report to validate the findings and conclusions.

4 Implementation of DIEM in the Case Organization

Implementing the research in the case organization follows the Problem-Centered Approach of the Design Science Research Methodology Process Model [28]. At the beginning of the study, the problem was identified (the lack of systematic practices for digitalization impact evaluation). The company was **motivated** to solve the problem: the evaluation capability had become one of its main strategic objectives, requested by the owners and customers. In addition, there was public pressure from the ministry responsible for funding. The development of digitalization evaluation capability was defined as one of the company's strategic goals in December 2022.

The **objective** was to develop a model that fulfills the needs for digitalization impact evaluation. First, the model should guide evaluating digitalization initiatives' impact in various settings. Second, the model should be integrated into the organizations' quality and service management processes. Third, the model should support impact evaluation from various perspectives and not focus only on the return on investment or cost efficiency. Fourth, the model should be informal and easy to use, and it should help the company implement its strategy.

Designing and developing a solution to answer the company's strategic needs, the process started with a literature review in February 2023. The digitalization impact evaluation model (DIEM) was introduced to provide needed guidance. The model (Fig. 2) consists of three main phases (A: Pre-Evaluation, B: Leading of Impact Factors, C: Post-Impact Evaluation). To enable comprehensive impact evaluation, researchers introduced four dimensions for impact evaluation (timely, efficiency, safety, and cost-effectiveness) based on the WHO's quality viewpoints. Four evaluation levels were included to observe all relevant stakeholders: 1) clients/patients, 2) professionals, 3) the organization, and 4) society. DIEM provides support for the identification of pertinent impact indicators and data sources that are used data sources that are used throughout the process. In phase A, understanding customers and ICT service goals is recognized to clarify the intended impact. In phase B, the indicators serve as input for the management of measures. In addition, the required abilities and resources (e.g., personnel, knowledge, skills, technologies) for implementation and change are allocated. In phase C, indicators and data validate the impacts (outcome). In this phase, an understanding is developed of how the activity affected and whether the goals were achieved from the perspective of the stakeholders. The phase concretizes the results quantitatively and qualitatively.

The model was enhanced in a workshop in April. The workshop included specialists representing innovation and development, enterprise architecture, service design, quality and process development, and program and change management. An International Consulting Firm facilitated the workshop. During the spring of 2023, the DIEM was integrated by the researchers and the company's specialists into the company's quality and service management processes. This was done in a series of meetings facilitated by the company's quality and development manager. Integration included defining roles, responsibilities, documents, and decision-making in all process phases.

In the **demonstration** phase, the DIEM was introduced to the case organization in June 2023. The model's pre-evaluation became a prerequisite for digitalization initiatives. After the introduction, the company's ITSM processes were audited against ISO standards [26–28] by external auditors in September 2023. The auditors implemented several group interviews to collect data. The auditors were interested in the roles, responsibilities, processes, procedures, instructions, measurements, services, productization, and examples. One external auditor stated: *"Impact evaluation is a central prerequisite for prioritization ability."* The auditing results were reported in a meeting with the auditors, the company's executive committee, unit leaders, and process owners in September 2023. The external audit was successful, and the company was certified.

Evaluation of the DIEM was conducted in April 2024 by utilizing semi-structured interviews and questionnaires. The focus group for evaluation was the company's Innovation and Development Board (IDB), consisting of 18 members (eight directors and ten managers/specialists). The IDB is responsible for the company's development portfolio management and investment decisions. By the time of the evaluation, the DIEM was used for seven months. A link to the questionnaire was sent to all members of the IDB at the beginning of April, resulting in 9 answers (50%). To enrich the data, researchers

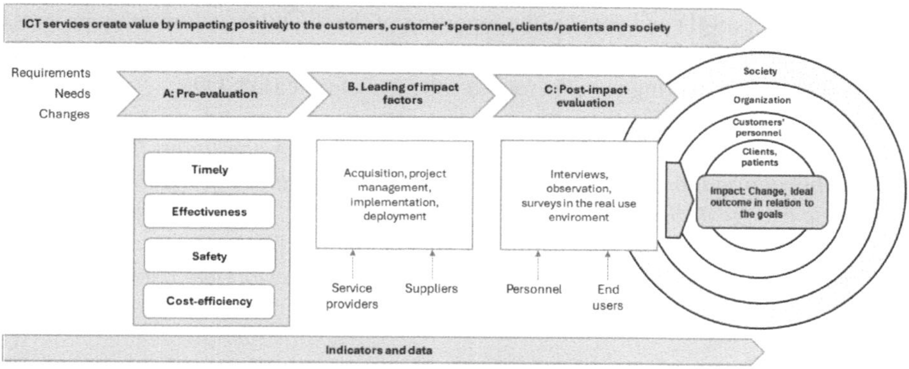

Fig. 2. Digitalization Impact Evaluation Model (DIEM).

chose four director members of IDB working closely with digital transformation into semi-structured interviews.

5 Findings

The study provided a rich set of data that was analyzed using the four perspectives of the socio-technical framework [6]. The data sources have been indicated using abbreviations: '**I**' for **interview** and '**Q**' for **questionnaire**.

People: The model facilitate the evaluation of impact goals from a broader perspective (Q2, Q7, Q8, I3), clarifies goals and responsibility (Q7), supports the strategic guidelines of the case organization (Q4, Q7). In addition, the phases of the model enable measurement and progress monitoring several times during the development and maintenance of the invested solution (Q7, Q8). The respondents highlighted the need for a broader and more diverse reflection on how the impact is seen in practice, as well as a calculation of the benefit or trends of the digitalization initiative and the payback time (Q1, Q2, Q3, I1, I4).

- *Attention in cases is focused on impacts and their aspects, such as efficiency, safety, timeliness, and cost-effectiveness. It helps to prioritize what to do* (Q2).
- *[The model] raises awareness, improves decision-making, promotes responsible business, improves stakeholder relations… [it] helps make more informed, justified, and effective decisions to achieve goals and sustainable success* (Q7).
- *We better remember to evaluate impacts from several angles and times over time* (Q8).
- *Cost-effectiveness and investment payback time are important* (Q3).

An added value of the model is the promotion of a holistic thinking culture (Q4, Q5, I1), which promotes the customer's trust and deepens the partnership (I3). Considering impacts helps to meet customer expectations and increases the value of services for customers (I2). The model guides the consideration of the scalability of services for several customers (Q1) and enables the reporting of the digital transformation progress (I1) while enabling fact-based, high-quality and efficient decision-making that promotes success (Q6, Q7). Ensuring benefits requires the use of time (Q5, Q9).

- *[We get] a comprehensive understanding of the company's operations transparently, available information and trend monitoring with accumulated information to support possible change decisions* (I1).
- *[The model] helps us to create customer understanding* (I2).
- *We get closer to fact-based decision-making, away from emotional decision-making* (Q6).

Process: The model was seen to be useful because there is a need for fact-based post-evaluation (Q1, I2, I3) and realization of qualitative and financial benefits (Q1, Q2, Q6). The analysis revealed essential elements of the pre-evaluation phase: a description of the challenge/need that the investment would solve (Q1, Q6), an assessment of the sales potential (Q1), an understanding of the customer benefit and its alignment with their development goals (Q1), a description of the goals and hypothetical issues that have changed after development (Q1, Q6, I1), metrics (Q1, Q6, Q8, Q9), description of positive and negative effects (Q1, Q9), risks (Q9), the effects of information security and protection on planned operations (Q7), as well as customer and employee satisfaction (Q8, I4).

- *We need to use this effectiveness framework so that we can state that our services are effective for our customers* (I1).
- *I think the post-evaluation perspective was particularly gratifying* (I2).
- *[The model] brings systematicity and uniform assessment throughout the stages... Understand the customer benefit, assess the sales potential, determine whether it aligns with the customers' development goals, and determine opportunities/threats in scalability* (Q1).

The model clarifies the goals and helps allocate resources (Q7, Q9, I4) by introducing systematics and harmonizing the evaluation through the stages (Q1, I3, Q4, Q8). The model helps to focus attention on important aspects such as cost-effectiveness (Q2, Q3, Q8, I4) and national requirements (Q4), which allows for prioritization and the selection of development initiatives (Q2, Q5, I3, Q4). The model produces information and success metrics to support decision-making (Q3, Q4, Q5), in addition to which inspection points and criteria are needed to support decision-making (I3). The process increases awareness, promotes business, and improves stakeholder relations (Q7).

- *Resources can be allocated better* (Q9).
- *[The model] produces a uniform operating model as an added value, through which it is easy to assess how meaningful work is done and whether the action brings about the desired benefit or change... The impact of the activity becomes more visible, making reasoned decisions easier... It certainly helps in many ways in selecting development proposals. One criterion can be the impact of the proposal at the national level or how much the customer will benefit from the proposal* (Q4).

Structure: The case organization can utilize the model from various perspectives: the ability to demonstrate the effectiveness of the case organization's operations, the opportunity to prove that the produced services are effective, and the evaluation of effectiveness as a service. The B phase enables the case organization to offer more versatile impact evaluation services for the customers (Q3). The post-evaluation phase is a new practice that enables the case organization to track and measure the impacts and payback realization in the long-term (I3). From the acquisition point of view, evaluating the impacts would enable the selection of the most impactful solution, which is the participation of suppliers (I2).

- *[The model] produces additional information to support decision-making and measurement possibilities of how we have succeeded* (Q3).
- *We may have products in the service portfolio that are not scientifically effective, and then we have spearhead products that would have such an effectiveness label* (I2).
- *An impact assessment could be included in procurements. We can offer such a framework* (I3).

The model supports strategic alignment by helping the company to outline goals and results (Q4, Q7). One control and decision forum for development ensures positive impacts (I1). The use of the model should be expanded (Q6, I3), the evaluation could be offered as a service to customers, and it could be applied when questioning current operating models (I3). The model produces a competitive advantage - other actors concentrate on evaluating the effectiveness of treatment or treatment chains (I3). The model supports the customers' governance and management processes. To support governance, the impact of a service or product could be shown with the label *"Impact is scientifically proven"* attached to the services (I2).

- *[The model] helps to evaluate and monitor the effects of operations in different areas, clarify goals and strategies, measure and monitor progress, better allocation of resources, and improve accountability* (Q7).
- *Chains of impact come to the fore, which gives an idea of what the company is aiming for and what impacts are achieved* (Q4).
- *The impact of digital services is such that there are no other operators in the field, but they are more concerned about the effectiveness of the treatment or the treatment path* (I3).

Technology: Utilization of technology would increase systematism in the pre-evaluation phase, where every digitalization initiative could be evaluated through a formal/quantitative evaluation process (Q5). The ability to evaluate the impacts of digital services is a competitive advantage (I3).

- *This could be somewhat protectable [IPR]… a competitive advantage in research on this topic and these methods. At least you wouldn't hand it over to outsiders, but you would get the benefit yourself* (I3).

6 Discussion and Conclusions

This study aimed to understand the complexities of digital transformation by developing and empirically exploring an impact evaluation model (DIEM) that was evaluated at different stages of a case company's digitalization activities. We specifically explored how the use of such a model can create value for companies. To ensure a systematic approach, we carefully followed the guidelines by Hevner [23]. 1) This design science study produces a viable artifact in DIEM. 2) The problem relevance was demonstrated via literature analysis, as well as the business needs of the Company and its strategy. 3) The efficacy was demonstrated via a rigorous case study. 4) The study provides a clear research and practical contribution. 5) The study relies on the use of rigorous research methods that are suitable for recognized research problems. 6) The design was conducted as a search process that produced a satisfactory result and set of future improvement initiatives. 7) The research is reported and communicated as a scientific article.

Theoretical Implications. The study increases understanding and provides deep insight into the impact evaluation of digital transformation and organizations' service management. This study directly answers the prior research call for new digitalization impact evaluation approaches that are empirically evaluated [10, 16, 18, 29]. Commonly utilized ITSM standards [5, 26–28, 32] do not provide a systematic model for impact evaluations. This study represents an evidence-based approach to digitalization-related improvement impact evaluation. ISO/IEC 20000-1 [28] defines requirements for continual improvement (e.g., improvements are measured, and improvements are reported). In this study, the DIEM creates a structure to carry out impact evaluations per the ISO/IEC 20000-1 standard requirements. Additionally, DIEM complements the ITIL-based seven-step improvement process [32] by proposing a new Step 8: "Evaluate the impact of the implemented improvement," as Heikkinen [20] proposed. DIEM also supports holistic thinking to overcome the problem of too technical focus among IT specialists in impact evaluation [3, 12, 48]. To theorize even more deeply, modern social science approaches such as complexity theory [2] and the concept of complex adaptive systems [45] might be fruitful. The use of DIEM could be beneficial in the healthcare context to support societies in overcoming current problems such as aging, growing need for services, labor shortages, and organizational performance. However, a clear vision, strategy [8, 18, 22, 40], and evaluation [29, 30, 36, 38, 41, 46] are inevitable to have a significant and notable impact. Hence, our research also contributes to academic research on strategic management [8, 17, 22, 40].

Practical Implications. The main practical contribution of the work includes the DIEM, which was created by utilizing a design science research approach. The developed model was validated empirically through a participatory case study. DIEM answers the strategic need to collect data to increase the current and future IT services improvement and impact of digital services more widely. The DIEM created significant value for the company. The DIEM was integrated into the company's ITSM processes, forming a comprehensive solution that is a crucial success factor [46]. The model is used in the company's strategy implementation and decision-making related to investment decisions and process and service development. The data gathered via DIEM provided notable value for all relevant stakeholders (i.e., Directors, ICT specialists, Innovation & Management Board). The model enables the visualization of the impacts that enhance internal and external communication between stakeholders. The model improves the company's competitive advantage by providing valuable information about customer needs, digitalization activities, benefit potential, and their impact on customers. The DIEM systematizes processes and supports aligning the company's strategy and investments in digital transformation. This study provided data that DIEM provided helpful means to evaluate the impact and improve decision-making. In addition, DIEM focuses on what is important and valuable for the company. While no approach can ever be perfect, given the complexity of digital transformation [18], the DIEM provides a valuable means to evaluate digitalization initiatives and their impacts on companies in practice, thus illustrating an answer to our research question.

Limitations and Future Research Directions. The study utilized design science, case study methods, and versatile qualitative data collection methods that enabled data source triangulation. Still, the study does not come without limitations. In the participatory case study and qualitative research, generalization is challenging because the situation in a unique organizational setting can never be repeated. Internal validation of the research is strengthened with the selected research methodology and the accurate description of the stages of the research: participatory research approaches aim to describe and understand a research phenomenon in question rather than to predict or control it [34]. When the primary goal of qualitative research is to interpret and document the research phenomenon from an individual's viewpoint, a single case study was deemed suitable. As we collected data in the form of an internal questionnaire and four expert interviews with the key personnel responsible for digitalization initiatives within the case company, the validity of the collected data is deemed suitable to answer the research question.

Method triangulation and quantitative approaches would provide an even more robust chain of evidence with mixed-method approaches that could be expanded and tested to provide generalizability of the developed DIEM. The findings and, thus, analysis is based on one organization operating in a specific public healthcare sector. More research and empirical results from various contexts are needed to improve the external validity of findings and generalizability. These limitations naturally feed into many interesting future research avenues. We especially call for future research to focus on designing practices and measurements in each phase of the DIEM or how the developed model could be applied to various digital solutions and industry contexts. Especially linking DIEM with business analytics (BA), artificial intelligence (AI), and machine learning (ML) presents a lucrative research topic, as both theoretical and empirical studies on the application of AI are called for.

This study suggests the necessity of using a digitalization impact evaluation model that can foster holistic thinking within companies by offering systematic guidance for strategy implementation (including alignment, governance, prioritization, and decision-making) and evaluation of digitalization impact (facilitated by fact-based, continuous data flow). This model can enhance stakeholder collaboration and foster a deeper understanding of customers' needs. These can thus lead to enabling the organization to gain a competitive advantage. The benefits of such a model include holistic thinking, improved customer trust, scalable services, high-quality decision-making, clarity of the goals and strategic alignment, scientific proofs, improved resource allocation, and prioritization ability. The value covers the increased value of services to the customers, meeting accurate customers' needs, impact reporting capabilities, development of new services, including impact evaluation itself, and other competitive advantages.

References

1. Aistrich, M.: Is it worth trying to measure impact? (2014). https://www.sitra.fi/en/articles/it-worth-trying-measure-impact/. Accessed 10 Apr 2024
2. Amagoh, F.: Perspectives on organizational change: systems and complexity theories. Innov. J. Public Sect. Innov. J. **13**(3), 1–14 (2008)
3. Ashurst, C., Doherty, N., Peppard, J.: Improving the impact of IT development projects: the benefits realization capability model. Eur. J. Inf. Syst. **17**(4), 352–370 (2008)
4. Axelos: ITIL Foundation, ITIL 4 edition. The Stationery Office (2020)
5. Axelos: ITIL Practitioner Guidance. The Stationery Office, GBR (2016)
6. Baxter, G., Sommerville, I.: Socio-technical systems: from design methods to system engineering. Interact. Comput. **23**(1), 4–17 (2011)
7. Blumberg, M., Cater-Steel, A., Rajaeian, M., Soar, J.: Effective organisational change to achieve successful ITIL implementation: lessons learned from a multiple case study of large Australian firms. J. Enterp. Inf. Manag. **32**(3), 496–516 (2019)
8. Bozintan, A.G., Crisan, E.L., Pinco, O.: The impact of digital transformation on strategic management. Ann. Univ. Oradea **32**(1), 647 (2023)
9. Cichosz, M., Wallenburg, C.W., Knemeyer, M.A.: Digital transformation at logistics service providers: barriers, success factors and leading practices. Int. J. Logist. Manag. **31**(2), 209–238 (2020)
10. Cresswell, K., Anderson, S., Montgomery, C., Weir, C.J., Atter, M., Williams, R.: Evaluation of digitalisation in healthcare and the quantification of the "unmeasurable." J. General Intern. Med. **38**(16), 3610–3615 (2023)
11. DeLone, W.H., McLean, E.R.: Information systems success: the quest for the dependent variable. Inf. Syst. Res. **3**(1), 60–95 (1992)
12. Eggers, J.P., Park, K.F.: Incumbent adaptation to technological change: the past, present, and future of research on heterogeneous incumbent response. Acad. Manag. Ann. **12**(1), 357–389 (2018)
13. Eisenhardt, K.: Building theories from case study research. Acad. Manag. Rev. **14**(4), 532–550 (1989)
14. Elragal, A., Elgendy, N.: A data-driven decision-making readiness assessment model: the case of a Swedish food manufacturer. Decis. Anal. J. **10**, 100405 (2024)
15. European Union: The Digital Europe Programme (2020). https://digital-strategy.ec.europa.eu/en/activities/digital-programme. Assessed 24 Apr 2024
16. Gastaldi, L., Corso, M.: Smart healthcare digitalization: using ICT to effectively balance exploration and exploitation within hospitals. Int. J. Eng. Bus. Manag. **4**, 9 (2012)
17. Gong, C., Ribiere, V.: Developing a unified definition of digital transformation. Technovation **102**, 102217 (2021)
18. Gurbaxani, V., Dunkle, D.: Gearing up for successful digital transformation. MIS Q. Exec. **18**(3), 209–220 (2019)
19. Heikka, J., Baskerville, R., Siponen, M.: A design theory for secure information systems design methods. J. Assoc. Inf. Syst. **7**(11), 31 (2006)

20. Heikkinen, S., Jäntti, M., Tukiainen, M.: Continual service improvement: a systematic literature review. In: Fernandes, J.M., Travassos, G.H., Lenarduzzi, V., Li, X. (eds.) QUATIC 2023. CCIS, vol. 1871, pp. 30–44. Springer, Cham (2023). https://doi.org/10.1007/978-3-031-43703-8_3
21. Heininger, R., Prifti, L., Böhm, M., Krcmar, H.: Towards a model of heterogeneity in IT service value networks: results from a literature review. In: BLED 2016 Proceedings, vol. 37 (2016)
22. Hess, T., Christian, M., Benlian, A., Wiesböck, F.: Options for formulating a digital transformation strategy. MIS Q. Exec. **15**(2), 123–139 (2016)
23. Hevner, A.R., March, S.T., Park, J., Ram, S.: Design science in information systems research. MIS Q. **28**(1), 75–105 (2004)
24. Holand, A., Svadberg, S., Breunig, C.J.: Beyond the hype: a bibliometric analysis deconstructing research on digitalization. Technol. Innov. Manag. Rev. **9**(10), October 2019
25. Iden, J., Eikebrokk, T.R., Marrone, M.: Process reference frameworks as institutional arrangements for digital service innovation. Int. J. Inf. Manag. **54**(99), 1021501–1021514 (2020)
26. ISO 9001: Quality Management Systems, Requirements. European Committee for Standardization, Switzerland (2015)
27. ISO 13485: Medical devices quality management systems requirements for regulatory purposes. International Organization for Standardization (2016)
28. ISO/IEC 20000-1: Information technology. Service management. Part 1: Service management system requirements. International Organization for Standardization (2018)
29. Khosravi, P., Ghapanchi, A.H.: Investigating the effectiveness of technologies applied to assist seniors: a systematic literature review. Int. J. Med. Inf. **85**(1), 17–26 (2016)
30. Koebe, P., Bohnet-Joschko, S.: The impact of digital transformation on inpatient care: mixed methods study. JMIR Public Health Surveill. **9**(1), e40622 (2023)
31. Koivisto, J.: Esiselvitys sosiaali-ja terveydenhuollon kansallisten digitalisaatio-ohjelmien arviointikehikon kehittämiseksi. Finnish Institute for Health and Welfare (2021). https://www.julkari.fi/handle/10024/143248. Accessed 11 Apr 2024
32. Lloyd, V., Wheeldon, D., Lacy, S., Hanna, A.: ITIL Continual Service Improvement. The Stationery Office, London (2011)
33. Luukkonen, I., Toivanen, M., Mursu, A., Saranto, K., Korpela, M.: Researching an activity-driven approach to information systems development. In: Cruz-Cunha, M., Miranda, I., Gonçalves, P. (eds.) Handbook of Research on ICTs and Management Systems for Improving Efficiency in Healthcare and Social Care, pp. 431–450 (2013)
34. Macdonald, C.: Understanding participatory action research: a qualitative research methodology option. Can. J. Action Res. **13**(2), 34–50 (2012)
35. Maglio, P.P., Srinivasan, S., Kreulen, J.T., Spohrer, J.: Service systems, service scientists, SSME, and innovation. Commun. ACM **49**(7), 81–85 (2006)
36. Norine, W.M., Rumsfeld, J.S.: Leading the digital transformation of healthcare. J. Am. Coll. Cardiol. **70**(21), 2719–2722 (2017)
37. Office of Government Commerce (OGC): Management of Value. The Stationery Office (2010)
38. Pedrosa, G.V., et al.: A systematic review of indicators for evaluating the effectiveness of digital public services. Information **11**(10), 472 (2020)
39. Peffers, K., Tuunanen, T., Rothenberger, M., Chatterjee, S.: A design science research methodology for information systems research. J. Manag. Inf. Syst. **24**(3), 45–77 (2007)
40. Rego, B., Shital, J., Ferreira, J.J., Carayannis, E.: Digital transformation and strategic management: a systematic review of the literature. J. Knowl. Econ. **13**, 1–28 (2021)
41. Ricciardi, W., Barros, P., Bourek, A., Brouwer, W., Kelsey, T., Lehtonen, L.: How to govern the digital transformation of health services. Eur. J. Pub. Health **29**(3), 7–12 (2019)

42. Shang, S.S.C., Lin, S.F.: Barriers to implementing ITIL - a multi-case study on the service-based industry. Contemp. Manag. Res. **6**(1), 53–72 (2010)
43. Soltanzadeh, J., Sahebjamnia, N., Khosroshahi, E.M., Bouguerra, A.: Commercializing Covid-19 diagnostic technologies: a review of challenges, success factors, and insights from the profiting from innovation framework. Technovation 102903 (2023)
44. Spohrer, J., Kwan, S.: Service science, management, engineering, and design (SSMED): an emerging discipline - outline and references. Int. J. Inf. Syst. Serv. Sect. **1**(3), 1–31 (2009)
45. Turner, J.R., Baker, M.R.: Complexity theory: an overview with potential applications for the social sciences. Systems **7**(1), 4 (2019)
46. Vărzaru, A.A.: An empirical framework for assessing the balanced scorecard impact on sustainable development in healthcare performance measurement. Int. J. Environ. Res. Public Health **19**(22), 15515 (2022)
47. Venable, J., Pries-Heje, J., Baskerville, R.: FEDS: a framework for evaluation in design science research. Eur. J. Inf. Syst. **25**, 77–89 (2016)
48. Verhoef, P.C., et al.: Digital transformation: a multidisciplinary reflection and research agenda. J. Bus. Res. **122**, 889–901 (2021)
49. Winkler, T.J., Wulf, J.: Effectiveness of IT service management capability: value co-creation and value facilitation mechanisms. J. Manag. Inf. Syst. **36**(2), 639–675 (2019)
50. World Health Organization (WHO): Quality of care (2024). https://www.who.int/health-topics/quality-of-care. Accessed 11 Apr 2024
51. Yin, R.K.: Case Study Research: Design and Methods. SAGE Publications Ltd., Los Angeles (2014)

Improving the Quality of Self-service in an IT Service Provider Organization: A Case Study

Marko Jäntti[1(✉)] and Henri Lindström[2]

[1] School of Computing, University of Eastern Finland,
P.O. Box 1627, 70211 Kuopio, Finland
marko.jantti@uef.fi

[2] Clorient Oy, PL 10, 70101 Kuopio, Finland
henri.lindstrom@clorient.com

Abstract. Customer self-service (CSS) has become a crucial part of IT service provider organizations' business operations. Customer self-service is a type of customer service enabling customers and service users to receive service-related information and submit service requests and incidents 24/7 through a self-service portal as well as perform some routine tasks including reseting passwords or installing low risk configuration items (CI) to their workstations. There are clear business benefits for using self-service portals and self-service enabled processes. They improve customer experience by eliminating the need to communicate with service desk workers and provide a round-the-clock digital channel. From a service provider's perspective, self-service channels increase productivity by ensuring that relevant information is collected from users in structured format. The main contribution of this paper is to show how to organize deployment of self-service portal as a digitalisation initiative. The research problem of this study is: How quality aspects should be taken into account by an IT service provider organization while designing and deploying self-service portals to customers? A case study method with one case organization, a large Finnish IT service provider company, was used to answer the research problem.

Keywords: ICT quality · self-service · IT service management · self-service portal

1 Introduction

During the COVID-19 pandemic, demand for digital customer service, customer self-service and self-service portals exploded. Customer self-service can be defined as a customer service type that enables customers and service users

Supported by Productivity and Digital Services for Business Needs (TUPLA) project S21138 (ESF, South Savo ELY).

A. Bertolino et al. (Eds.): QUATIC 2024, CCIS 2178, pp. 295–310, 2024.
https://doi.org/10.1007/978-3-031-70245-7_21

perform activities without calling service desk, help desk or customer service agents. Different types of self-service technologies (SST), ATMs, online banking platforms, self-service coffee kiosks, self-service flight boarding machines and self-service portals are used daily by millions of users.

In this paper, we focus on customer self-service used in IT service provision. This is typically based on a service catalogue that is visible to customers and can assist in selling and delivering IT services. The service catalogue includes information about service delivery and deliverables, service pricing, contact persons as well as how to order and request those services [23]. The service catalogue acts as a backbone of the self-service portal. The world-wide adoption of cloud service platforms has also boosted self-service revolution. Instead of purchasing and installing infrastructure components to their own facilities, organizations can utilize cloud service portals aka self-service portals to deploy, run and manage infrastructure as a service on-demand. Cloud computing is an excellent example how modern digital technology combined with a self-service delivery model can radically transform customer experience, business processes and business models [9].

Beatson, Lee and Coote [3] state that we need to understand the impact of self-service technology facilities on consumers' assessments of their interactions with the service organisation. They continue emphasizing that while self-service technologies may offer customers several benefits, people will not automatically accept and use them. There might be negative outcomes related to self-service model for both service consumers and providers. Examples of negative outcomes include stealing from supermarkets by using self-service kiosks [19].

The technological solution may decrease or increase the quality of customer service. As an example, poorly implemented customer service chatbots may decrease customer satisfaction remarkably. However, there are a lot of several positive outcomes related to self service, for example, increased efficiency in service encounters, such as in library environments [15], increased accuracy of submitted incident and service request records and 24/7 availability of service channels. In order to succeed, SSTs must be both useful and easy to use [6].

Much has been written on IT service desk improvement and service processes, such as service request management [20], success factors of service process improvement [8] and specific tools assisting customer self-service, including customer support knowledge bases [7,29] and ICT knowledge bases [14] where customers can browse known errors and their solutions, workarounds, release notes and bug fixes. Through a self-service portal, users may also receive service-related information, receive self-help material, such as training videos [22] and submit service requests and incidents 24/7 as well as perform some routine tasks including reseting passwords or installing low risk configuration items (CI) to their workstations.

A study of Wiggins [28] showed that the IT service desk of University of Colorado reduced the number of service requests to the service desk by 63% during the first semester by implementing a self-service portal with a password reset feature. Furthermore, Scherer, Wunderlich and Wagenheim [27] report that customers need multiple service channels instead of one channel. They conclude that absence of multiple service channels might end the service relationship between the service provider and customer. Thus, service providers should definitely pay attention to establishment of service channels in order to stay competitive in their business.

The purpose of the self-service is to engage and activate the customer as part of service delivery and reduce the employee's role in service delivery. Therefore, a customer and a service provider participate together in the creation of value [12]. Kokkinou [17] report that designing and deploying self-service technologies may turn out to be costly and time-consuming. The service provider should therefore understand customer requirements and how to inspire customers and users to use self-service technologies.

Additionally, a study of Considine and Cormigan [5] revealed several concerns in the user adoption of SST technologies, such as their features are not personalized for users' specific requirements and technology is not user centric enough. Employees might also fear that SST makes low skilled workers jobless [25]. Service providers should pay attention on the design and layouts of SST portals as well as customization. While customers and users value the convenience and easy access of self-service technologies, they forget all of these benefits when a self-service channel fails [4].

For this reason, the stakeholders' requirements and the concept of quality they have attached to the self-service portal are important issues to study in more detail. Surprisingly few of the existing SST-related studies have dealt with quality aspects. Othman, Hamzah and Hassan [26] discuss quality aspects of self-service technologies in the context of ATMs by stating that reliability, convenience, and functionality (three of five quality factors) significantly positively affected customer satisfaction. Hossein, Zhou and Rahman [11] compare four SST-based bank channels (mobile, telephone, ATM, online) and customer satisfaction related to those channels. Their study found that mobile banking provides more enjoyment service than other SSTs. Lin and Hsieh [18] have identified seven primary dimensions in the quality of SST: SST functionality, enjoyment, security, assurance, design, convenience, and customization.

In this paper, we see customer self-service technologies as integral part of digital service management and in order to discuss it thoroughly, we need use a cross-disciplined research approach integrating concepts and approaches from several service-related research areas, such as services computing [31], service science [21], service operation management [24] and service process improvement. Typically, a service catalogue is implemented as a database or structured document with information about all live services, including those available for deployment [24].

This catalogue is transformed into the self-service model by establishing a service channel that enables customers and users contacting customer support independent of time and place. The service channel may be implemented with a simple web form, a traditional help desk system, a modern service desk system, an instant messaging channel, a chatbot without intelligence or as an AI-powered smart bot. Some of the existing studies predict that AI-driven customer service is going to critically impact customer experience [16].

The main contribution of this study is to make quality aspects of self-service technologies visible by

- discussing design actitivities related to the introduction of the IT service provider's self-service portal and
- showing how IT service provider organization and its customer organizations are using the self-service portal.

The results of this article are aimed at IT customer support process managers, customer service managers, directors governing the customer support especially in IT service organizations and other roles that may be involved in designing and implementing self-service support channels. Our results may help persons in above mentioned roles to identify functionality needed in self-service portals as well as steps required to introduce a self-service portal successfully to users and customers.

The remainder of the paper is organized as follows. Section 2 describes the research methodology of the study. Section 3 presents the case study results. Section 4 provides an analysis, and conclusions are given in Sect. 5.

2 Research Methods

This study aimed at answering the following research problem: How quality aspects should be taken into account by an IT service provider organization while designing and deploying self-service portals to customers? In this study, we utilized a case study research to answer the research problem with a single case organization, a publicly-owned large Finnish IT service provider company. The research problem was divided into following two research questions:

- How design and introduction of the self-service portal to customers and users is performed by the IT service provider?
- How IT customers and users use and see the self-service portal?

There was a clear rationale for selecting these research questions. The first research question was selected to reveal valuable background activities of self-service portal implementations. Typically, companies are not sharing a lot of information on self-service portal design work if the status is work-in-progress but tend to wait until everything is polished and ready for live operation. Choosing the second research question was quite obvious because making decisions on functions of the self-service portal is a key issue in establishing self-service support portals. However, most self-service studies tend to focus solely on service provider's perspective and ignore customers' and users' viewpoints.

In our study, we focused on exploring a digital transformation initiative conducted in collaboration between case Alfa and the university research teams. The researchers had an easy access to the case organization because it was one of the European Social Fund project partners. Most of the case organization's contact persons were already familiar to the research team which resulted in a smooth start for the project. Case study research can be defined as "an empirical inquiry that investigates a contemporary phenomenon within its real-life context" [30]. The case study research method was a natural choice for the study because it allowed us to investigate the self-service concept (phenomenon) thoroughly within IT service provision (real-life context). The context of the study is described in Fig. 1.

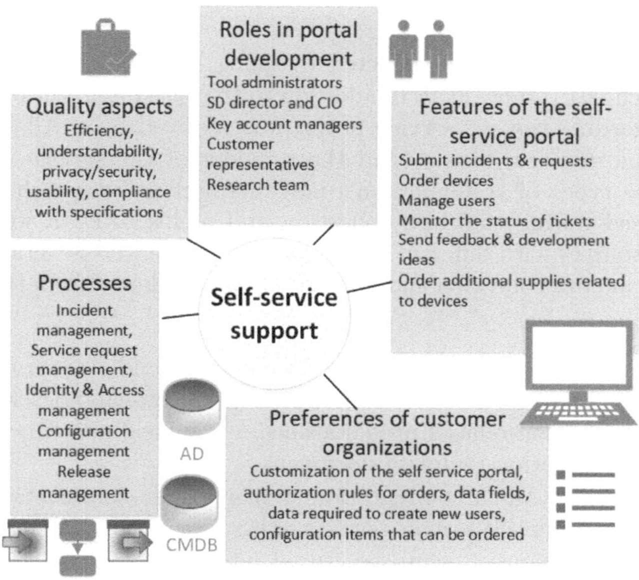

Fig. 1. The context of the case study.

2.1 Case Organization

Our case organization Alfa is a publicly-owned limited company that provides health care information system services, digital operating environments as well as information, communication and medical technology services. Alfa has over 1300 employees and provides information, communication and medical technology services to its customers in Finland. Alfa's user management services cover service desk, user support, user management, on-site support and terminal device services for all customers and customers' end users. The unit is also responsible for solutions on identity management (IDM), single sign-on (SSO) and service management (ITSM).

Main customers of Alfa include 15 wellbeing services counties and 19 cities/municipalities or joint municipalities. The operation system of Alfa is based on ISO/IEC 20000-1 service management system and ISO 9001 quality management system and ISO 13485 quality management system for medical devices. Alfa's service management focuses on a core IT service management system that enables customer self service. During the research period, Alfa had two service management systems. The new service management system with effective identify and access management features and the old service management system that was still used by some service areas.

2.2 Data Collection Methods

Data for this case study was collected by using multiple sources of evidence between March 2019–June 2019. In addition to the case organization Alfa, valuable data regarding the self-service portal was received from Alfa's customers (Beta, Gamma, Omega, Sigma) and the provider of the service management system. Three types of triangulation (data, method and researcher triangulation) were used during the data collection and analysis. Data were collected from several sources with different techniques and there were several researchers participating in data collection and analysis of data gathered from the case organization.

- Documentation: A service description document for end user services, an infoletter of security services, a self-service portal brochure and description of the service, organization-related presentations, a graphical guidelines document, the service description template document
- Archival records: Alfa's configuration item register, comments from Alfa's customer regarding self-service portal testing
- Interviews/discussions: 8 semi-structured interviews with Alfa's customers: Beta, Gamma and Sigma, interviews with Alfa's key account manager representing Omega
- Participative observation: Participative observation in self-service portal work meetings and workshops with the case organization between February-June 2019 (persons from Alfa included two ITSM tool administrators and two managers, persons from the university included three researchers),
- Physical artifacts: Self-service portal
- Direct observation: Alfa's presentation how their self-service portal can be used

2.3 Data Analysis Methods

Data analysis of this study was performed by a within case analysis technique. According to Eisenhardt [10], the key idea of the within case analysis technique is to become intimately familiar with each case as a stand-alone entity and allow the unique patterns of each case to emerge. Pattern matching [30] was used to support data analysis. In pattern matching, empirical patterns are compared to predicted patterns. In our study, we used data from only one case organization and we did not create quality aspect categories in the very beginning to avoid limiting our perspectives. Analysis of research questions 1 and 2 was carried out first and after that we continued to analyze quality aspects.

In order to identify quality aspects that would be relevant for our study, several quality frameworks were studied, including IT Infrastructure Library (ITIL) version 3 [24], ITIL version 4 [2], the international standard on Systems and software engineering—Systems and software Quality Requirements and Evaluation (SQuaRE) [13], and Software and Systems Engineering Vocabulary (SEVOCAB) [1].

3 Results

Next, the results of the case study are presented according to selected research questions. For each research question, a case study narrative is provided to highlight the improvement actions that were taken during the digital transformation initiative related to the deployment of the self-service portal. Additionally, these narratives reveal what types of findings were collected from Alfa's customers or persons belonging to Alfa and providing valuable information to the research team, including two authors of this paper.

3.1 How Design and Introduction of the Self-service Portal to Customers and Users is Performed by the IT Service Provider?

The goal setting meeting for the case study was organized with the case organization on February 25th, 2019. The case organization's representative presented the current state of the self-service support, related challenges and required actions. In the current situation, it was possible for customers to make orders and requests using the electronic service channel, telephone or email. This slowed down the processing of orders and requests, and reduced transparency for the customer and from the user's point of view. The goal of the service provider was to reduce the size of the email channel use by replacing it with a self-service portal. This aimed at reducing a number of contacts to the service point.

In March 2019, we had two work meetings (March 12, March 19) with the case organization to gather information on rationale of the self-service portal project and discuss the current state of self-service technologies in Alfa. The following information was captured in those meetings:

- "Users of our current service channel should be brought into new service management system. Every customer should have their own order templates". (Work meeting, March 12)
- "Every customer has its own way to authorize requests, in the new self-service portal it is possible to define whether it is the supervisor of the employee or somebody else". (Work meeting, March 12)
- "Each customer organization has its own instance of the self-service portal. It can be branded in terms of colors, logo etc." (Work meeting, March 12)

- "For some products to be ordered, there are specific persons that can authorize the order, such as a Chief Information Officer". (Work meeting, March 19)
- "Regarding some customers, order authorization is based on Active Directory (AD). Information on the supervisory person is available in the AD. If the user information is up-to-date in the AD, the self-service system shows only the supervisory person while a person submits a service request, for example, an order for a mobile device."(Work meeting, March 19)
- "Other order is an order that is outside the scope of the service catalogue. For these orders, a rationale for usage is required". (Work meeting, March 19)
- "Some of our customers have two-level authorization for orders". (Work meeting March 19)
- "Login to the portal can be done by using a person's work station account or a locally managed account" (Work meeting March 19)

When discussion on the implementation of the self-service portal started, a representative of Alfa suggested that "the self-service portal should be developed based on the customer's functional needs" and "user-oriented manner avoiding generic presentations on the portal". Thus, in collaboration between the service provider and Alfa, it was decided to conduct interviews with selected persons related to the self-service portal.

The third work meeting with the case organization was held in April, 2019 (April 1). This meeting resulted in valuable information how the research team should introduce the self-service portal to Alfa's customers and which organizations would be considered as pilot customers as well revealed the status of the introduction of the new service management tool in Alfa. Additionally, we interviewed other persons (key account manager) that we considered valuable data sources for pinpointing the trigger for improvement and need for better quality self-service portal:

- "Our current service channel for Beta is outdated and very limited, tickets are not real-time" (Interview with a key account manager of Alfa, March 25)
- "The self-service portal of the new ITSM tool is not used by our customers although they use the self service channel of our existing tool". (Work meeting with Alfa, April 1)
- "Your task is to interview our customers to find out which items they would like to order from the self-service portal and whether there are customer-specific requirements". (Work meeting with Alfa, April 1)
- "There are customer-specific prices for items that can be ordered from the self-service portal". (Work meeting with Alfa, April 1)

The new portal would serve as a one-stop shop for service requests, such as orders, information requests and queries. making it easier for the user to form a clearer overall picture of where the products and services offered by the Service Provider are located. However, this did not mean that the existing service channels should be abandoned completely, but users would be directed to use the modern self-service portal instead of other service channels, such as email. After the second meeting, we had to take a quick look at the existing service channel of Alfa (in this paper, we use abbreviation ESC to refer that channel). ESC was considered difficult to customize for Alfa's customers' needs.

The second work meeting led the research team to explore what are the different types of configuration items customers and users can order from the portal. The list of Configuration Items (document) revealed that there are two charging options for services: contract-based charging and separate charging. According to discussion with the case organization's representatives, also project-based charging was applied sometimes. They commented that there can many pricing options for same configuration items because prices vary between customer contracts. We observed that a wide range of pricing options causes difficulties in charging customers correctly for services and results in reclamations from customer organizations.

According to the service description document, the services of the new self-service portal were: 1) Incident notification submission service, 2) General case submission service, 3) Sending feedback and development ideas service, 4) User ID subscription service, 5) Equipment and product ordering service (workstations, phones, screens, printers, accessories and peripherals), 5) E-mail subscription service and 6) Email calendar subscription service.

Regarding the introduction of the self-service portal to customers, Alfa's staff advised the research team to pay attention to the following facts and limitations while discussing with selected pilot customers: First, record labels of the can be updated to be customer-specific. Second, incident and service requests are presented in their own areas in the portal (these cannot be displayed in the same main view). Third, all portal users must have their own credentials instead of general credentials. Third, the customer can influence the required fields, for example, which datafields are used in mobile phone orders. Fourth, orders for standard software can be done through the portal. Fifth, the new system does not constitute an invoice breakdown. Finally, resetting user passwords has to still go through the service desk of Alfa.

3.2 How IT Customers and Users Use and See the Self-service Portal?

The representatives of Alfa commented that introduction of the new version of the self-service portal provides customers and users of Alfa with enhanced capabilities to receive information on their services and manage and submit orders. The new self-service portal enables users and customers to order services locally from their own workstations and end-users might not even notice that they are ordering services from Alfa due to the customizable outlook of the portal. The portal can also be used as a one-stop shop for frequently asked questions.

The research team started to interview Alfa's customers in March - April 2019 to explore how they are using the self-service portal. The following findings are based on the interview sessions with Alfa's customers: Beta, Gamma, Omega and

Sigma as well as some key account managers working for Alfa but representing above mentioned customer organizations:

- "While ordering user priviledges, the system could use a calendar function to select a date and the current date should be set as a default date". (Interview with Beta, March 27)
- "Regarding laptops, along the laptop, a SIM card shall be delivered to a user. This SIM card can be activated by Beta's Information System department when needed. Thus, data field 'Data plan for a laptop' should be removed". (Interview with Beta, March 27)
- "All laptops that our user order should have a privacy filter, either external or electronic". (Interview with Beta, March 27)
- "While ordering activation for a user account, could this form be auto-filled?" (Interview with Beta, March 27)
- "We hope that we could order user rights to other systems from the portal, not only to AD". (Interview with Beta, March 27)
- "Is it possible to set a different person to the authorization role during a vacation?" (Interview with Beta, March 27)
- "All requests causing costs for our organization should be processed by the admistrative director. " (Interview with Gamma, April 15)
- "Monitoring live status of tickets is an important and long-awaited feature". (Interview with Gamma, April 15)
- "As additional devices, wireless mouses, privacy shields and web cameras can be ordered in our organization". (Interview with Gamma, April 15)
- "While creating a user account, could it be possible to include a cost center, applications, directories and email groups?" (Interview with Gamma, April 15)
- "We shall deliver data on employees and their supervisors to Alfa as Excel/CSV to establish the portal and configure authorization rules". (Interview with Omega, April 25)
- "We shall discuss with the account managers and the service manager whether our workstations and phone models match Alfa's standard models and prices". (Interview with Omega, April 25)
- "Could you check whether Jabra conference speakerphone has been added to 'Additional items' that can be ordered?" (Interview with Omega, April 25)
- "I hate ordering several mobile phones (10 pieces) if I have to enter the order for each phone separately". (Interview with Sigma, June 3)
- "Bundling would be appreciated. Everything could be done with the same order: workstation, monitor, additional equipment and software. Possibility to choose a different mouse, bag, dock and keyboard". (Interview with Sigma, June 4)

The self-service portal was one of the three service channels of Alfa. Other identified service channels included telephone and email. The service channels are open on weekdays from 7 am to 4 pm. As a rule, the self-service portal is open around the clock (24/7) for customers and users. The service channels were provided in two languages: Finnish and English. The research team also organized meeting with the provider of the self-service portal (see Fig. 2). The representative of the tool provider commented that basically all the data records and fields in the portal and ITSM tool are customizable.

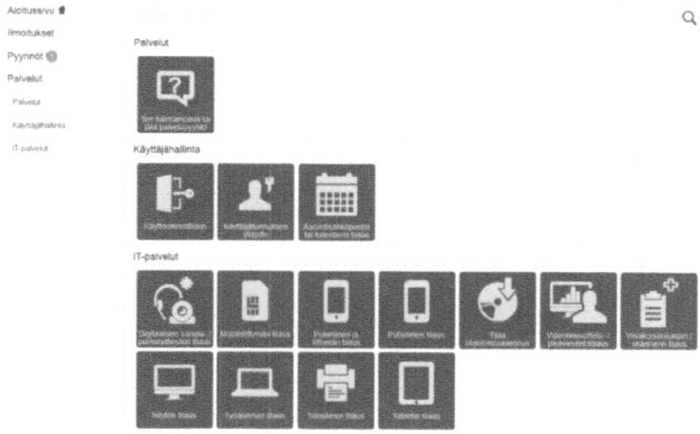

Fig. 2. A self-service portal.

Service providers can provide workarounds and permanent solutions on the portal and their customers and users may browse them and potentially solve problems without contacting the service desk team of Alfa. This, in turn, reduces the number of calls to the service point and makes information gathering more effective. Additionally, Alfa can open various views of the portal which increases the visibility of the service provider's activities. These include, for example, keeping track of user's own orders and service requests. The tool provider emphasized that they are continuously adding new features to the tool based on customer's wishes.

4 Analysis of Findings

The data analysis for the case study results was performed by using a pattern matching technique. The results of the case study are presented in this section according to quality aspects of a self-service portal. In Table 1, analysis of case study results is presented. The source of evidence has been marked by the following abbreviations: IN = Interviews, DI = Discussions, DO = Documentation, PO = Partic. observation, DOB = Direct observation, PA = Physical artefacts.

Regarding the first research question, we analyzed how the self-service portal was designed and introduced. We interpreted that both customers and Alfa's staff were waiting for the change and transition from an old service channel to the modern self-service portal and we did not observe signs of change resistance among those persons that were interviewed during the study. The old service channel was considered as outdated and not providing any possibilities for customizing order forms neither providing opportunities for real time status tracking of service requests and incidents.

Table 1. Design, introduction and usage of the self-service portal by customers and users (RQ1, RQ2, summary on quality aspects).

Finding	Category
Design of the self-service portal (RQ1)	
Our service channel is outdated & very limited	Limited set of features (IN, PO)
Tickets are not real-time	Real time status tracking (IN)
Customer should have their own order templates	Tailoring, order (PO, PA)
There are specific persons that authorize orders	Authorization (PO, IN)
Customers have their own branded portals.	Tailoring (PO)
The self-service portal is first launched to pilot customers	Pilot customers (PO)
Usage of the self-service portal (RQ2)	
Customer-specific prices for items	Pricing (DO, PO, IN)
Order authorization is based on AD	Order, authorization (PO)
Order user rights to other systems	Order, user rights (IN)
Authorization role during a vacation	Authorization (IN)
Cost center, apps, folders & email groups of a user	User data (IN)
For 'Other order' type, a user should put 'Reason'	Order (PO)
Wireless mouses, privacy shields&web cameras	Addit. devices (IN)
All laptops we order should have a privacy filter	Addit. devices (IN)
We deliver authoriz. data to Alfa as Excel/CSV	Authorization (IN)
Do our workst. & phones match Alfa's models & prices	Pricing (IN)
Is Jabra speaker in 'Additional items'?	Addit. devices (IN)
Quality aspects of SST (Research problem)	
Smooth phone orders	Efficiency IN, DI
Automatic filling of fields	Efficiency IN
Tracking requests under processing	Efficiency DI
Create reports on all orders	Efficiency DI, IN
Separate forms for mass orders	Usability IN
We would like to see automated form filling	Usability IN
Links to CMDB and invoices from the portal	Usability IN
Evaluation of incident impact is difficult	Understandability IN
Technical jargon ("corrupted")	Understandability PO, IN
New services cause confusion	Understandability IN, PO
Self-service portal should be GDPR audited	Security&privacy IN
Limited use of social sec number	Security&privacy IN
Orders by using other person's names prohib.	Security&privacy IN
Accurate device data helps user to find right tools	Availability IN
Service channel that is open 24/7	Availability DO, IN, DI, PO

The scope and depth of the portal introduction came as a surprise for the research team. We expected that there is a single self-service portal that all customer organizations would use. Instead of that, every customer of Alfa was provided its own tailored self-service portal instance with various forms of authorization mechanisms and varying set of configuration items that could be ordered from the portal. The selection of pilot customers was done by Alfa's representatives and one of the pilot customers was removed from the list because of complexity of the organization and its services. The research team received a thorough briefing on the self-service portal from the Alfa's staff before interviews.

Concerning the second research question on how IT customers and users see and use the self-service portal, our study revealed that during the SST improvement project, customers and users were more concerned on service request management (orders for mobile devices, orders for user rights, creating new users, configuring authorization rules) than incident management. Identity and Access Management played also larger role than we expected. For some of the customer organizations, introduction of the self-service portal triggered the need to check the status of Active Directory whether data on employees and their supervisors was up-to-date. Some customers had a very simple model with two dedicated persons being responsible for authorizing orders while others showed evidence on multi-level authorization or AD-based authorization. Furthermore, we observed that Alfa's self-service portal should provide users with better means for installing new software or request licences, offer customers with ability to view their own configuration items and browse invoices from the portal through the direct link. Finally, findings from data related to RQ1 and RQ2 were linked into five quality aspect categories: efficiency, usability, understandability, security and privacy, and availability. For one of our initial categories, compliance with specifications, we did not found supporting evidence.

Our interviews resulted in valuable information what IT customers and users want to order from the self-service portal and what types of variations they have in ordering. Especially, in ordering laptops and data plans as SIM cards, a lot of variation was observed. We explored first main level configuration items (mobile phones, workstations, user rights) but also identified a set of additional configuration items (category Additional devices) that customers need in their daily operations including wireless mouses, privacy shields, web cameras and conference speakers.

Although the results of the study revealed many functionality issues related to self-service portals by observation, interviews and documentation of functional needs, we could also capture valuable findings on non-functional requirements and quality aspects concerning the self-service support. The combination of ITIL, SQUARE and SEVOCAB provided good starting point for identifying quality criteria but even with these three frameworks we identified overlapping quality aspects, such as understandability, usability and adequacy of information. Thus, we decided to simplify categorization and captured efficiency from SEVOCAB, understandability and usability from SQUARE and availability, security and privacy from ITIL.

5 Conclusions

This study aimed at answering the research problem: How quality aspects should be taken into account by an IT service provider organization while designing and deploying self-service portals to customers? The main contribution of this paper was to 1) discuss design actitivities related to the introduction of the IT service provider's self-service portal and 2) study how IT service provider organization and its customer organizations are using the self-service portal.

There were two research questions in the study. Regarding the first research question 'How design and introduction of the self-service portal to customers and users is performed by the IT service provider?', we found that main triggers for improving self-service techniques in case Alfa were customer feedback on existing service channels and launch of new IT service management system that included a modern self-service portal. Alfa aimed at designing and introducing their customers with a tailored self-service portal with customized authorization rules for service requests and varying set of configuration items that could be ordered from the portal. The introduction of the portal was performed as a staged approach by using pilot customers.

Concerning the second research question 'How IT service provider organization and its customer organizations are using the self-service portal?', we observed that customers and users paid significantly more attention to service request management than incident management during the introduction of self-service portal. The second important observation was that Identity and Access Management plays an important role in self-service portal projects because order authorization rules are often based on the data stored in Active Directory. In addition to standard configuration items, such as laptops, phones, applications, IT customers need additional devices including SIM cards, wireless mouses, privacy shields, web cameras and conference speakers. These cannot be ignored while designing online service catalogues. As an answer to our research problem, while designing and deploying self-service portals to customers, IT service provider should pay attention at least to the following quality aspects: efficiency, usability, understandability, security and privacy and availability.

The following limitations can be identified related to this study: The first limitation is related to applicability and generalization of our findings on self-service portals results to other service provider organizations nationally or internationally. The case study research method does not allow us to generalize our findings to other organizations because each IT service provider organization is a unique instance with its own processes, technologies, operational system, people and rules. However, we can still use our results to extend the theory of self-service technologies and processes around the self-service customer support.

The second limitation is related to data collection. More end-user representatives could have been interviewed to gather more detailed information on challenges in the existing self-service portal and aspirations for desired state of the self-service support approach of Alfa. The third limitation is related to duration of the case study. The digital transformation initiative under the umbrella of a university-coordinated development project provided us an opportunity of collaboration with case organization. Each digital transformation initiative is relatively short resulting in limited possibilities to interact with the case organization and its customers. However, clear goal setting, familiar contact persons and strong commitment of Alfa's staff with the project helped us to start productive collaboration work and interviews with Beta, Gamma, Omega and Sigma rapidly. Further research could be related to, for example, studying how Artificial Intelligence (AI) impacts customer self-service technologies.

References

1. 24765:2017(E), I: ISO/IEC/IEEE International Standard - Systems and software engineering–Vocabulary. ISO/IEC JTC1/SC7 (2017)
2. Axelos: ITIL 4 Managing Professional: Create, Deliver and Support. Stationary Office Books, UK (2020)
3. Beatson, A., Lee, N., Coote, L.: Self-service technology and the service encounter. Serv. Ind. J. **27**(1), 75–89 (2007)
4. Bitner, M., Ostrom, A., Meuter, M.: Implementing successful self-service technologies. Acad. Manag. Perspect. **16** (2002)
5. Considine, E., Cormican, K.: The rise of the prosumer: an analysis of self-service technology adoption in a corporate context. Int. J. Inf. Syst. Project Manag. **5**, 25–39 (2017)
6. Curran, J., Meuter, M.: Self-service technology adoption: comparing three technologies. J. Serv. Mark. **19**, 103–113 (2005)
7. Davis, K.: Charting a knowledge base solution: empowering student-employees and delivering expert answers. In: SIGUCCS02: Proceedings of the 30th Annual ACM SIGUCCS Conference on User Services, pp. 236–239. ACM Press, New York (2002)
8. Diirr, T., Santos, G.: Improvement of it service processes: a study of critical success factors. J. Softw. Eng. Res. Dev. **2**, 4 (2014)
9. Doukidis, G., Spinellis, D., Ebert, C.: Digital transformation - a primer for practitioners. IEEE Softw. **37**(5), 13–21 (2020)
10. Eisenhardt, K.: Building theories from case study research. Acad. Manag. Rev. **14**, 532–550 (1989)
11. Hossein, M.S., Zhou, X., Rahman, M.F.: Customer satisfaction under heterogeneous services of different self-service technologies. Manag. Mark. Challenges Knowl. Soc. **14**, 90–107 (2019)
12. Hsieh, A.T., Yen, C.H., Chin, K.C.: Participative customers as partial employees and service provider workload. Int. J. Serv. Ind. Manag. **15**, 187–199 (2004)
13. ISO/IEC 25010: Systems and software engineering - Systems and software Quality Requirements and Evaluation (SQuaRE) - System and software quality models. ISO/IEC JTC1/SC7 Secretariat (2011)
14. Jackson, A., Lyon, G., Eaton, J.: Documentation meets a knowledge base: blurring the distinction between writing and consulting (a case study). In: SIGDOC 1998: Proceedings of the 16th Annual International Conference on Computer Documentation, pp. 5–13. ACM Press, New York (1998)
15. Jit, A., Kamhangwong, D., Wicha, S., Yamsa-Ard, S.: Determinants of customer satisfaction with self-service technology (SST): a case study of Mae Fah Luang University's library. In: 2023 International Conference On Cyber Management And Engineering (CyMaEn), pp. 128–131 (2023)

16. Khan, S., Iqbal, M.: AI-powered customer service: does it optimize customer experience? In: 2020 8th International Conference on Reliability, Infocom Technologies and Optimization (Trends and Future Directions) (ICRITO), pp. 590–594 (2020)
17. Kokkinou, A.: Why wait? Impact of waiting lines on self-service technology use. Int. J. Contemp. Hospitality Manag. **27** (2015)
18. Lin, C., Hsieh, P.L.: Assessing the self-service technology encounters: development and validation of SSTQUAL scale. J. Retail. **87**, 194–206 (2011)
19. Linardi, M., Duarte, P., Susana, S.S., Novais, B.: Understanding the implementation of retail self-service check-out technologies using necessary condition analysis. Int. J. Retail Distrib. Manag. **50**, 140–163 (2022)
20. Ludwig, H., et al.: Catalog-based service request management. IBM Syst. J. **46**(3), 1–18 (2007)
21. Maglio, P., Spohrer, J.: Fundamentals of service science. J. Acad. Mark. Sci. **36**, 18–20 (2007)
22. Meuter, M., Ostrom, A., Roundtree, R., Bitner, M.J.: Self-service technologies: understanding customer satisfaction with technology-based service encounters. J. Mark. **64**(3), 50–64 (2000)
23. Office of Government Commerce(b): ITIL Service Design. The Stationary Office, UK (2007)
24. Office of Government Commerce(d): ITIL Service Operation. The Stationary Office, UK (2007)
25. Otekhile, C.A., Milan, Z.: Self service technologies: a cause of unemployment. Int. J. Entrepreneurial Knowl. **4** (2016)
26. Othman, A.K., Hamzah, M.I., Abu Hassan, L.F.: Modeling the contingent role of technological optimism on customer satisfaction with self-service technologies: a case of cash-recycling ATMs. J. Enterp. Inf. Manag. **33**(3), 559–578 (2020)
27. Scherer, A., Wuenderlich, N.V., Von Wangenheim, F.: The value of self-service: long-term effects of technology-based self-service usage on customer retention. MIS Q. Manag. Inf. Syst. **39**(1), 177–200 (2015)
28. Wiggins, C.: Self-service portal solves the forgotten password dilemma. In: Proceedings of the 40th Annual ACM SIGUCCS Conference on User Services, SIGUCCS 2012, pp. 127–130. Association for Computing Machinery, New York (2012)
29. Wood, S., Howlett, R.J.: A web-based customer support knowledge base system. In: Lovrek, I., Howlett, R.J., Jain, L.C. (eds.) KES 2008. LNCS (LNAI), vol. 5177, pp. 349–361. Springer, Heidelberg (2008). https://doi.org/10.1007/978-3-540-85563-7_47
30. Yin, R.: Case Study Research: Design and Methods, 4th edn. Sage Publishing, Beverly Hills (2009)
31. Zhang, L.J., Zhang, J., Cai, H.: Services Computing. Tsinghua University Press, Beijing and Springer-Verlag GmbH Berlin Heidelberg (2007)

Understanding How Power Distance Affects Agile Organizations

Claudio Saraiva Mattos[1], Eliezer Dutra[2], Edna Dias Canedo[3], and Gleison Santos[1](✉)

[1] Universidade Federal do Estado do Rio de Janeiro, UNIRIO, Rio de Janeiro, Brazil
claudio.mattos@edu.unirio.br, gleison.santos@uniriotec.br
[2] Centro Federal de Educação Tecnológica Celso Suckow da Fonseca, CEFET/RJ, Rio de Janeiro, Brazil
eliezer.goncalves@cefet-rj.br
[3] Universidade de Brasília (UnB), Brasília, Brazil
ednacanedo@unb.br

Abstract. Agile methods offer flexibility, collaboration, and responsiveness to rapid changes, making them a popular choice for organizations seeking to adapt to the dynamic business landscape. However, the successful adoption of agile alternatives does not occur uniformly across all cultural and organizational contexts. In an organizational culture with high power distance, there is a clear hierarchy, and team members are less likely to question authority and expose problems, which can affect the adoption of relevant agile principles and practices, thereby potentially compromising the software quality. It is not always trivial to identify the latent behaviors associated with high power distance. Thus, managers may overlook the existence of high power distance and its effects, jeopardizing agile transformation initiatives. We conducted a systematic literature review to characterize power distance in agile organizations. Based on 15 studies, we identified 15 manifestations, 31 effects and 36 possible actions to minimize power distance. Most signs of power distance are associated with human factors such as Decision-Making, Empowerment, Autonomy, and Trust. Managers can use the identified manifestations and effects to diagnose the occurrence of high power distance. Likewise, they can use the identified treatments to define appropriate and contextualized treatment strategies in agile transformation initiatives.

Keywords: Power Distance · National Culture · Agile Methods · Agile Transformation · Agile · Hofstede · Systematic Literature Review

1 Introduction

In recent years, agile methods have been increasingly used as an option to traditional software development methods [7,12,26,29,31] with the aim of facing the continuous changes that characterize the Information Technology (IT) industry. Agility offers flexibility, collaboration, and responsiveness to rapid changes,

A. Bertolino et al. (Eds.): QUATIC 2024, CCIS 2178, pp. 311–327, 2024.
https://doi.org/10.1007/978-3-031-70245-7_22

making it a popular choice for organizations seeking to adapt to the dynamic business landscape [8]. Agile transformations are associated with the transition or migration from the traditional software development process to the agile one and affect all organizations' areas [6]. However, the successful adoption of agile methods does not occur uniformly in all cultural and organizational contexts [4].

Different human factors impact the adoption of agile methods [9]. Among them, "Cultural Aspects" stand out, which generate influence both in agile teams and in organizations. Organizational culture is "the collective programming of the mind that distinguishes the members of one organization from another" [17]. This definition highlights the importance of organizational culture as a set of values, beliefs, and behaviors shared by the members of an organization. On the other hand, national culture is defined as "the collective programming of the mind acquired when growing up in a given country" [17], exerting influence on organizational culture. In many countries, national culture often influences organizational culture, such as in the perception people have about decision-making power and hierarchical consent. Power Distance, defined as "the degree of acceptance of a society in relation to inequality of power among people," is one of the essential elements in Hofstede's Theory of National Cultural Dimensions [16]. In an organizational culture with high power distance, there is a clear hierarchy, and team members are less likely to question authority and expose problems. This aspect can be problematic for the adoption of agile methods, which emphasize collaboration and shared responsibility [4,32,34]. In contrast, in an organizational culture with low power distance, there is a more collaborative approach and team members are encouraged to question authority and make decisions together [4,32,34].

According to SWEBOK [19], software quality can refer to the desirable characteristics of software products, the extent to which a particular software product possesses those characteristics, and the processes, tools, and techniques used to achieve them. It is also noteworthy that the quality of the process influences the quality of the developed software [10,30]. In this paper, we address software quality from the perspective of the process used to create it.

In agile environments, the quality of the process – and therefore the quality of the developed software – is often influenced by the team's ability to collaborate effectively, adapt to changes, and continuously learn. If an organization has a high power distance, this can lead to restricted communication, reduced collaboration, and resistance to change, which in turn can negatively affect the software quality. Alsanoosy et al. [2] investigated how cultural aspects of power distance affect Requirements Engineering (RE) activities. They have conducted 32 interviews with software development and requirements engineering practitioners from two distinct cultures: Saudi Arabia and Australia. Their findings indicate that power distance significantly affects RE collaboration among software stakeholders, particularly during the requirements elicitation and validation phases. This influence can compromise software quality, given that RE activities are crucial for ensuring the quality of the developed product. To mitigate the negative impact of power distance on RE activities, the authors suggested conducting more workshops involving stakeholders and end-users. Additionally, they recommended holding one-on-one discussions with managers to emphasize the organizational benefits of achieving software quality.

According to Šmite et al. [34], effective high power distance mitigation strategies – such as cultural training, adaptive leadership and open communication – can improve the effectiveness of agile transformation in organizations with high power distance. However, it is not always trivial to identify latent behaviors associated with high power distance. Thus, project managers may neglect the existence of high power distance and its effects, putting organizational agile transformation initiatives at risk.

Hofstede [16] measured power distance through an opinion survey undertaken with IBM employees in different countries, in which respondents answered questions related to their perception of the level of equality or inequality in the distribution of power in their organizations. Applying the same questionnaire to an organization (regardless of whether it is agile or not) may not bring adequate results. A possible alternative is the identification of manifestations or symptoms, the presence of high or low power distance during iterations among members or teams of an organization. Based on these manifestations, treatments can be defined to minimize their effects.

A recent tertiary study [9] investigated human factors and their influence on software engineering development teams and agile software development teams. Although they identified studies associated with the human factor "Cultural Aspect," none dealt with aspects associated with national culture or power distance.

We conducted a systematic literature review to characterize power distance in agile organizations. Based on 15 studies, we identified 15 manifestations and 31 effects of high power distance, in addition to 36 possible actions to minimize its impact. Most manifestations of power distance are associated with human factors, such as Decision-Making, Empowerment, Autonomy, and Trust. Examples of effects are an undervalued feedback culture, a lack of agile leadership with leaders being more authoritarian and centralized, a risk-averse culture in which mistakes are punished, and innovation is discouraged. Among the treatment actions identified are creating an environment of psychological safety and trust, paying special attention to socialization and cultural training when integrating new team members, prioritizing the strengthening of autonomous teams, and changing the organizational structure and culture. Project managers can use the identified manifestations and effects to diagnose the occurrence of high power distance in agile transformation initiatives. They can also use some of the treatments we have identified to define appropriate and contextualized treatment strategies.

Besides this introduction, this paper is structured as follows: Sect. 2 presents the research method, Sect. 3 reports the study's results, Sect. 4 presents the discussion and, finally, Sect. 5 offers our final considerations.

2 Research Method

To support the planning and execution of the study, we followed the guidelines proposed in [21,28]. The study *aims* to characterize power distance in agile organizations. Three *research questions* (RQ) were defined:

RQ1: How does power distance manifest in agile organizations?
RQ2: What are the effects of power distance in agile organizations?
RQ3: What strategies and treatments can minimize the effects of power distance in agile organizations?

The *search string* was defined according to two of the five aspects of the PICOC strategy [28]. Our *Population* of interest is agile organizations. *Intervention* references the specific aspect of the investigation, that is, power distance. As our study does not aim to make a *Comparison* of different organizational approaches or capture their *Outcomes*, these fields were not used.

During the initial formulation of the search string, specific criteria were integrated, and tests were conducted on multiple bases to evaluate the accuracy and calibration of the search string. Furthermore, it was ensured that control papers [4,34] were recovered. It was observed, after the initial analysis, that the exclusive use of the term "Power Distance" did not lead to comprehensive results. This result motivated the inclusion of additional terms identified during the informal literature review as relevant synonyms: "cultural barrier" and "national culture." Tests were also carried out with the terms "software development," "lean," and "Software engineering," but only the term "agile" brought satisfactory results for the research. Thus, the final version of the search string is: *("cultural barrier" OR "power distance" OR "national culture") AND (agile).*

To maximize the number of included studies, we searched eight digital databases and supplemented the results with backward and forward snowballing [40]. The digital databases consulted were Scopus, IEEE Xplore, El Compendex, ISI Web Of Science, ACM, SpringerLink, Science Direct, and Wiley. Different databases require different search strategies, as outlined in [25]. For instance, for SpringerLink and Wiley, we considered only Computer Science studies.

We defined the following selection criteria to exclude (EC) and include (IC) relevant studies: IC1 – Studies related to power distance in agile organizations; EC1 – Duplicate study; EC2 – Study not written in English; EC3 – Study not peer-reviewed; EC4 – Study not accessible in full text; EC5 – Study is a short article; and EC6 – Study that does not answer any research question.

Data extraction consisted of categorizing: (i) study data, such as title, author(s), year, publication vehicle, type of publication, search database, country of affiliation of the author(s), conference or journal, citation, country of execution of the study; (ii) answers to research questions, that is, manifestations, effects, strategies and treatments of power distance; and (iii) supporting data for a better understanding of the results, such as the relationship among manifestations and the studies, and additional comments of the researchers. The Parsifal tool was used to catalog each document extracted from the databases.

3 Results

We searched the databases in October 2023 and performed snowballing in February 2024. Figure 1 represents the study search and selection process. Four hundred-ninety studies were identified in the searched databases, of which 39 were duplicates. The first and second authors applied the first selection filter (reading the title, abstract and keywords) to the remaining 451 studies. In total, 424 studies were excluded by the other exclusion criteria, resulting in 27 studies selected for the second filter.

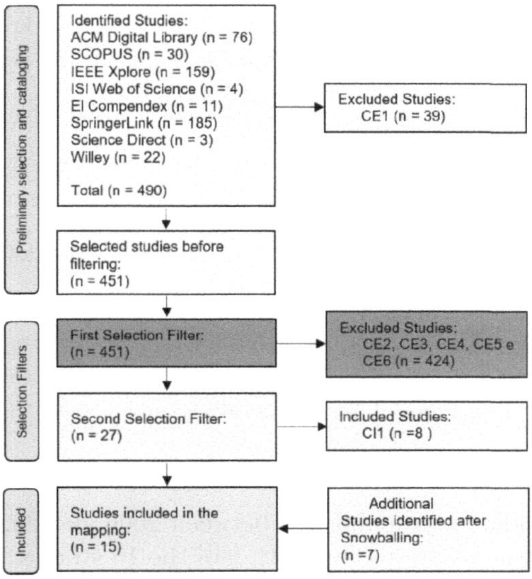

Fig. 1. Search and selection process for studies based on the PRISMA approach [27]

The first author read the 27 studies in full and applied the second filter. One study [33] was excluded due to the availability of an extended version [34]. In the end, 8 studies were selected. Backward snowballing was then applied. Twenty-seven studies were identified, 25 of which were new. Of these, only four were selected by applying the first and second filters. During forward snowballing, 327 studies were identified, of which 323 were new. The application of the first filter resulted in the exclusion of 318 studies. Of the remaining studies, only three were accepted in the second filter. After the second round of snowballing was performed, no additional studies were identified.

In total, 15 studies were selected. The first author extracted information from both. All steps of the study were reviewed and audited by the second and the fourth authors. The final selected studies are presented in Table 1. The extracted results are available in [25].

Table 1. Final List of Selected Studies

ID	Study	Year	Portrayed Countries	Authors Countries
S01	[34]	2021	Sweden and India	Sweden and Norway
S02	[24]	2022	South Africa	South Africa
S03	[4]	2017	Belgium, Malaysia, and Singapore	Belgium
S04	[13]	2022	Türkiye	Türkiye and the United Kingdom
S05	[22]	2023	Germany	Germany
S06	[35]	2019	Germany	Germany
S07	[36]	2009	New Zealand	New Zealand
S08	[14]	2023	India	France and India
S09	[18]	2006	India, Malaysia, New Zealand, Ireland, Poland, and China	Sweden and Ireland
S10	[15]	2011	New Zealand and India	New Zealand
S11	[20]	2010	The United States, India, China, Canada, Sweden, Finland, Bangladesh, The United Kingdom, The Netherlands, Russia, Hong Kong and Poland	Sweden
S12	[39]	2023	Germany, Italy, Azerbaijan, India, Pakistan, and Türkiye	Germany
S13	[5]	2021	England and India	The Netherlands
S14	[3]	2022	Arabia	The United Kingdom and Arabia
S15	[37]	2008	India, Romania and The United Kingdom	The United Kingdom

The selected studies were published between 2006 and 2023. It is important to note that most studies are recent, with 9 of the 15 studies being published in the last five years. Four studies (S08, S09, S13, S14) were published in journals and the others in conferences. As Hofstede et al. [17] indicated, power distance is associated with national culture. Therefore, the countries portrayed in the studies can help to understand part of the described phenomena.

3.1 Power Distance Manifestation (RQ1)

We identified 15 power distance manifestations, answering the first research question, as seen in Table 2. We identified seven manifestations associated with human factors [9], six with elements of organizational culture, and two with the execution and improvement of processes by teams.

Our responses to this research question are derived from our interpretation of the study's text. For example, in S04, the authors highlight the tendency of Turkish culture to favor hierarchical structures and resist changes, which can impact decision-making and the implementation of agile practices. A participant of the study mentioned that managers did not accept questions regarding authority, did not allow teams to self-manage, and requested specific details about the work, such as story points or task completion deadlines. Based on the authors' report,

Table 2. Power Distance Manifestations Identified

ID	Power Distance Manifestations
M01	* *Decision-Making* – Decision-making, when there is a high power distance, limits the ability of agile teams to make decisions independently, as the final decision is made by leaders and managers [S02, S04, S06, S12, S13]
M02	* *Autonomy* – The autonomy of agile teams is reduced in environments with a bureaucratic organizational structure, limiting the ability to make independent and agile decisions [S06, S12, 13]
M03	* *Collaboration* – Collaboration is impaired in contexts with high power distance, especially when there is no psychologically safe environment, in which there may be a reluctance to openly share failures [S04, S05, S06, S07, S12, S13]
M04	+ *Centralized Hierarchical Structure* – Centralized hierarchical structures, characterized by a high power distance, tend to make team members feel less inclined to raise problems, question perceived directives from superiors, and participate in constructive discussions. [S01, S02, S03, S04, S05, S06, S07, S08, S10, S11, S12, S13, S14, S15]
M05	# *Software Process Execution* – In cultures characterized by high power distance, agile teams have less control over the sprint scope and face frequent interruptions imposed by management or leadership. [S02]
M06	* *Empowerment* – Controlling leadership style inhibits the team's initiative and creativity, reflecting a lack of empowerment. [S03, S04, S13]
M07	+ *Lack of Transparency* – The lack of transparency, exemplified by the reluctance to express "no" and the tendency to filter only positive information, is one of the effects of high power distance. This aspect can result in difficulties in assertive communication and honesty when dealing with deadlines and commitments [S03, S04, S09, S11, S15]
M08	+ *Management Behavior* – In cultures characterized by high power distance, management behavior can be described by a more directive and centralizing approach, where managers exercise tighter control over team activities [S03, S04, S07, S08]
M09	+ *Resistance to Sharing Knowledge* – Power distance affects the ability and willingness to share knowledge openly [S04]
M10	* *Feedback* – Feedback is often inhibited in centralized hierarchical structures, in which freedom of expression is limited [S04, S10, S11, S12, S13]. M11
M11	+ *Lack of Access to Stakeholders* – Lack of access to superiors and indirect communication can hinder teams' ability to collaborate openly and flexibly [S01, S03, S04, S05]
M12	* *Trust* – Lack of trust can lead to hesitation in disclosing problems, the continual need to get approval for tasks, and the acceptance of impossible tasks out of respect for superiors [S01, S03, S04, S05, S06, S07, S09, S10, S11, S13, S14, S15]
M13	# *Process Improvement* – In cultures characterized by a high power distance, agile teams face challenges in committing to process improvement due to the lack of time to think about better solutions since improvement initiatives usually originate at the superior levels of the organizational hierarchy [S03]
M14	* *Communication* – Members of agile teams must know how to communicate problems and not just listen, as these professionals may hesitate to express criticism or difficulties, especially when it comes to hierarchical superiors [S01, S02, S03, S04, S05, S06, S07, S09, S10, S11, S13, S14, S15]
M15	+ *Leadership Style* – Leadership behaviors that discourage team members from being open to raising problems and proposing alternatives to superiors' directions can be an obstacle to the successful implementation of agile methods [S01, S04, S05, S06, S07, S08, S11, S12, S13]

Human factors (*), Organizational culture elements (+), Process-related elements (#)

S04 was associated with the M01 – Decision-Making, M04 – Centralized Hierarchical Structure, M06 – Empowerment, M08 – Management Behavior, M09 – Resistance to Sharing Knowledge, M10 – Feedback, M14 – Communication, and M15 – Style of Leadership manifestations.

It is noteworthy that the manifestations coexist and interact with each other. For example, effective decision-making often requires collaboration among team members, while transparency in communication is essential for building trust and fostering a collaborative culture.

3.2 Power Distance Effects (RQ2)

We identified 31 effects of power distance in agile organizations, answering the second research question. Effects are associated with 15 different categories. Ten categories represent human factors [9] (as can be seen in Table 3): Cultural Aspect (E21), Autonomy (E05, E06), Collaboration (E07, E08, E09), Communication (E10), Empowerment (E11), Feedback (E12), Innovation (E13, E14), Fear (E01, E02, E03, E04), Respect (E15), and Decision-Making (E16, E17, E18, E19, E20).

Another five categories represent elements of organizational culture (as can be seen in Table 4): Management Problems (E22, E23, E24, E25, E26), Resistance (E27, E28), Authority (E29), Constraints (E30), and Turnover (E31).

Several effects resulting from power distance in agile organizations were identified and highlighted in the studies. For example, the E01 (*Silence and reluctance to discuss failures*), mentioned in [S01], is evidenced when team members express hesitation in discussing problems openly, as mentioned in the excerpts "*Reluctance to discuss failure*" and "*It depends on who is in the meeting, sometimes we keep silent. It depends on who is asking, and who is running the meeting.*"

Equivalently, effect E07 (*Team members spend time and energy protecting themselves and inspecting each other instead of collaborating*) is derived from the following excerpt about the importance of trust within the team, "*Without sufficient trust, team members will spend time and energy protecting, checking, and inspecting one another, as opposed to collaborating to provide value-added ideas.*" Note that, in some cases, the same effect was mentioned in more than one study.

We must also recognize that the effects cannot be solely attributed to power distance, as other factors or combinations of factors may also contribute. For instance, psychological safety [1,11] might influence the effects associated with Fear (i.e., E01, E02, E03, and E04). Team psychological safety is a shared belief among team members that it is acceptable to take risks in expressing ideas and concerns, asking questions, and admitting mistakes, all without fear of negative consequences [11].

Table 3. Power Distance Effects Associated with Human Factors

ID	Power Distance Effects
	:: Fear
E01	Silence and reluctance to discuss failures [S01, S03, S12, S15]
E02	Hesitation to immediately clarify doubts about tasks motivated by fear of seeming incompetent or inferior in the organizational hierarchy [S01]
E03	A work environment based on employee motivation through fear [S01, S10]
E04	Deadlines not met due to reluctance to warn about unfeasible deadlines [S01, S09, S13]
	:: Autonomy
E05	Team members do not share the authority to make decisions [S01]
E06	Less participation and autonomy of team members in decisions related to deadlines and quality [S02, S06]
	:: Collaboration
E07	Team members spend time and energy protecting themselves and inspecting each other instead of collaborating [S01]
E08	Little flexibility and collaboration between different hierarchical levels [S05]
E09	Authoritarian management inhibits the open spreading of information and knowledge among team members [S11]
	:: Communication
E10	Communication is indirect, as it avoids open conflicts and direct feedback [S04]
	:: Empowerment
E11	Inhibition of team empowerment [S03, S04]
	:: Feedback
E12	Feedback culture is undervalued [S05]
	:: Innovation
E13	Lack of innovation due to hierarchy [S03, S06]
E14	A culture of risk aversion, where mistakes are punished and innovation is discouraged [S05]
	:: Respect
E15	Lack of respectful treatment among organization members [S05]
	:: Decision-Making
E16	Decisions concentrated on team leaders or management [S02]
E17	Decisions during sprint planning are often made by empowered individuals, with less team input and consensus [S02]
E18	Lack of agile leadership, in which leaders can be more authoritarian and centralized [S05]
E19	Decisions made exclusively by top-level management [S05]
E20	The ability for the team to respond quickly to changes and make autonomous decisions [S07]
	:: Cultural Aspect
E21	Culture of valuing titles and positions [S04]

Table 4. Power Distance Effects Associated with Organizational Culture Elements

ID	Power Distance Effects
	:: Management Problems
E22	Greater formalization of agile methods in organizations with high power distance characteristics [S01, S05]
E23	Agile practices can be adapted to maintain some level of hierarchical control [S01]
E24	Teams have less control over the scope and face more interruptions, being frequently interrupted by operational managers [S02]
E25	Negative customer interference [S03, S04, S14]
E16	Impact on team speed [S03, S06]
	:: Resistance
E27	Resistance from top-level managers [S04, S14]
E28	Resistance from employees who feel uncomfortable with uncertainty or the loss of more traditional control structures [S05]
	:: Authority
E29	Superiors maintain a position of authority and the flow of information is selective [S04]
	:: Constraints
E30	Constraints in business choices and priorities [S03]
	:: Turnover
E31	The centralized hierarchical structure can increase the agile teams turnover [S01]

3.3 Strategies and Treatments for the Power Distance Effects (RQ3)

In response to the third research question, we identified 36 strategies and treatments that can minimize the power distance effects in agile organizations. Table 5 presents treatments associated with human factors [9]: Autonomy (T11, T13), Collaboration (T12, T15), Communication (T17), Trust (T08), Cultural Aspects (T07, T10, T18, T21), Feedback (T03, T04, T09), Innovation (T14), Relatedness (T16, T19, T20), Responsibility (T02), and Psychological Safety (T01, T05, T06, T22). Table 6 presents the factors associated with organizational culture elements: Training (T35), Hierarchical Structure (T24, T27, T36), Knowledge Management (T29, T30, T31, T33), and Management Improvements (T23, T25, T26, T28, T32, T34).

Most strategies and treatments of the power distance effects were extracted from the selected studies verbatim. However, some methods and treatments mentioned were ignored when their understanding was not self-contained, as in the case of the recommendation *"schedule more frequent check-ins or updates"* mentioned in [S01]. Although it was featured in the list of recommendations for team leaders and managers struggling to drive an agile transformation and overcome the same cultural barriers, there was not enough context to associate it with a strategy for minimizing the power distance effects.

Table 5. Strategies and Treatments Associated with Human Factors Elements.

ID	Strategies and Treatments
T01	Creating an environment of psychological safety and trust [S01]
T02	Setting an example by taking responsibility for failures safely, showing how teams can learn from mistakes, and rewarding people for making mistakes if/when they lead to valuable lessons [S01]
T03	Searching for individual conversations [S01]
T04	Encouraging offshore members to be more direct [S01]
T05	Encouraging suggestions for better ways of working [S01]
T06	Do not criticize ideas; praise people for their valuable contributions [S01]
T07	Paying special attention to socialization and cultural training when integrating new team members [S01]
T08	Creating a fun environment to build trust [S03]
T09	Explaining openly the details of the transformation process, become clearer, have effective change management, top-level management participation, training, coaching, consultancy, more appropriate office projects, and be strong and determined [S04]
T10	Adopting a gradual approach rather than trying to resolve all cultural challenges at once [S05]
T11	Prioritizing the strengthening of autonomous teams and changes in organizational structure and culture [S06]
T12	Creating protected and isolated environments allows teams, management and surrounding structures to experiment, learn and embrace new forms of collaboration [S06]
T13	Expanding successful autonomous team initiatives to a broader organizational level, integrating individual learnings and activities for less prepared structures [S06]
T14	Promoting an organizational culture that values innovation and experimentation, encouraging employees to explore new technologies and work practices [S08]
T15	Implementing open workspaces to promote interaction and collaboration by removing physical barriers between team members and leaders [S11]
T16	Encouraging the use of first names to promote a more informal culture and facilitate communication without hierarchical barriers [S11]
T17	Encouraging team members to learn each other's body language to understand implicit issues when direct solutions are not found [S11]
T18	Emphasizing specific cultural characteristics that support important aspects such as open communication or feedback [S12]
T19	Promoting personal meetings outside of work [S12]
T20	Involving training and development for managers to understand and respect cultural differences [S13]
T21	Developing culturally aware approaches to support teams in agile adoption [S14]
T22	Fragmenting the work into smaller parts and allowing the daily communication of the team with experienced specialists, as a way to address the team's reluctance to engage in constructive disagreements [S15]

3.4 Limitations and Threats to Validity

This study sought to preserve quality, rigor, and criticality throughout all its stages. However, like any study, it can present threats to the validity of its results. Next, the most important threats are discussed following the classification presented in [28].

Descriptive validity focuses on the precision and impartiality of the observations made. A rigorous protocol was defined and followed to detail the approach, identify data sources, extract information, and present results accurately to address this issue. The search string was tested and revised before searching the digital databases, and control articles were defined to avoid losing important information and ensure a greater scope of results.

Finally, *interpretative validity* concerns the coherent and reasonable interpretation of the results. The data were analyzed by researcher R1 and reviewed by more experienced researchers to deal with possible researcher bias, especially in stages that may be subjective and depend on the reviewer's interpretation. Also, we classified our findings according to the human factors identified in [9]. Other authors might present a different list of human factors.

A possible limitation concerns the variety of examples of manifestations, effects, or treatments due to the low number of selected studies, which may restrict the *results' generalization*. As a treatment, searches were conducted in eight digital libraries, and the results were subsequently complemented through snowballing. Also, we limited our research to academic studies within the agile field. We did not include gray literature or studies discussing power distance manifestations in non-agile contexts, which may have restricted our findings. Furthermore, our research exclusively focused on power distance, omitting consideration of other national culture dimensions [16].

4 Discussion

Thanks to Hofstede's research [16], it has been possible to understand how people in different cultures perceive and respond to authority since the early 1980s. However, the specific perception of power distance in agile environments is a relatively new area of research and practice. It is noteworthy that there is a growing interest from the academic community, as 9 of the 15 studies identified were published less than five years ago, 6 of which were published in the last two years.

Another evident aspect is that the manifestations and effects are latent but sometimes are not explicitly associated with the power distance dimension. This aspect may occur due to a lack of knowledge about the power distance dimension, as defined by Hofstede [17]. For instance, in study S11 [20], the authors mention that "communication between the onshore and offshore teams was not always honest and direct," as the offshore team was only filtering positive information for the onshore team. However, no relationship was established with high power distance. Furthermore, it is notable that the countries of onshore participants are associated with low power distance, while the countries of offshore participants are associated with high power distance.

In multicultural teams, such as agile teams, where some members originate from high power distance backgrounds, these individuals may feel uncomfortable raising questions during refinement meetings to clarify misunderstandings. This discomfort can result in team members not having a unified understanding of

Table 6. Strategies and Treatments for the Power Distance Effects Associated with the Elements of Organizational Culture.

ID	Strategies and Treatments
T23	Letting external leaders focus on mentoring and removing impediments [S01]
T24	Establishing a second level of communication for teams that are reluctant to expose problems such as unfeasible deadlines or technical difficulties in which the manager maintains personal contact with everyone in the structure, allowing everyone to feel important in the organization despite perceived inequalities [S03]
T25	Promoting understanding of the importance of agile transition and acceptance of its benefits with the help of management support and collaboration [S04]
T26	Using models such as the Cynefin Framework or the Deming Circle, adapted to the specific needs of the organization, to provide direction and structure during the process of cultural change [S05]
T27	Involving all organizational levels to optimize both the structure and culture of the company [S05]
T28	Using researchers to facilitate agile transformation and cultural change initiatives in organizations [S05]
T29	Promoting a learning organization that encourages employees to continually share knowledge openly and learn from each other, regardless of their position or functional structure [S06]
T30	Implementing tools and communities that enable transparency and facilitate knowledge sharing among team members [S06]
T31	Encouraging active participation in communities of practice and open space meetings by providing adequate work time for these activities [S06]
T32	Adopting a Scrum approach that allows easy access to different skills and abilities when the team does not have all the necessary skills [S06]
T33	Promoting an open and accessible organization, facilitating access to diverse skills and abilities as needed to achieve sprint goals [S06]
T34	Allowing the offshore team to participate in negotiation meetings with the client to promote understanding of the process and improve negotiation skills [S11]
T35	Increasing awareness and agility knowledge among stakeholders by supporting training and learning events [S14]
T36	Proposing a decentralized hierarchical structure [S14]

the project, which decreases productivity and extends project lead times. This misalignment can compromise the quality of the software being developed [23].

In total, it was possible to identify 15 manifestations that demonstrate the influence of power distance in agile environments. It is noted that most of these manifestations (8) are associated with human factors. The most cited in studies (12 times) is Trust (M12). In the absence of trust, team members tend to hesitate in revealing problems [S01, S03, S04, S06, S13]. Trust is a key element in psychological safety, which is essential for the successful implementation of agile methods [38]. In an environment with high psychological safety, team members feel safe to share ideas, admit mistakes, and ask for help, which is the key to effective collaboration and collective decision-making [38].

One cannot also neglect the importance of elements of organizational culture in the dynamics of power distance. The most cited manifestation among all (14 studies) is the Hierarchical Structure (M04). Countries with a high power distance are associated with a social and organizational structure in which authority is valued, and there is a clear division between those who hold power and those at lower levels in the hierarchy [16]. Power is centralized, even if it does not seem like it, and managers expect obedience from their subordinates. Employees expect to receive clear instructions about their roles and responsibilities [16]. Additionally, as studies [S01, S03, S04, S06, S13] show, in environments where the hierarchy is centralized, team members may be less likely to raise problems, question superiors' guidance, and participate in constructive conversations.

It is important to highlight that these manifestations do not exist in isolation but interact with each other, as evidenced by the manifestations of Trust (M12) and Hierarchical Structure (M04). The lack of trust can be directly influenced by the rigidity of the hierarchical structure in agile organizations [S01].

5 Final Considerations

Power distance refers to the power distribution in an organization and how it affects relationships between team members [17]. The manifestation of power distance can negatively influence agile behaviors such as empowerment, transparency, trust, and communication [4,32,34]. By analyzing and synthesizing the results of multiple studies through a systematic literature review, this research offers insight into the power distance manifestations and effects in agile organizations, as well as identifying strategies and treatments to mitigate these effects. We identified 15 manifestations, 31 effects, and 36 possible treatments for high power distance. Most of the findings refer to human factors such as Decision-Making, Empowerment, Collaboration, Trust, Communication and Relatedness. Other relevant categories of findings refer to elements of organizational culture, such as Hierarchical Structure, Management Behavior, Knowledge Management, and Resistance.

This study brings practical and theoretical contributions to make it possible to understand how power distance influences team dynamics and decision-making in agile organizations. The summarized findings can provide a basis for future research to explore these aspects further, including evaluating the effectiveness of the identified actions and their applicability in different organizational contexts, such as agile organizations or those undergoing an agile transformation journey. Furthermore, by understanding the influence of power distance in organizations that adopt agile methods, practitioners will be able to adopt more effective approaches to implementing agile methods in diverse cultural environments. Besides, the identified strategies and treatments offer practical recommendations to mitigate the negative effects of power distance. These findings provide resources for leaders and managers to improve the dynamics of their agile teams and promote a work environment that is more compliant with agile principles and practices.

In future work, we intend to evaluate the relationships between the manifestations and the indication of specific treatments for their different effects. Finally, we intend to define an instrument supported by a psychometric scale to measure power distance in agile organizations.

Acknowledgement. The authors are grateful for the financial support of FAPERJ (210.231/2021, 211.437/2021).

References

1. Alami, A., Zahedi, M., Krancher, O.: Antecedents of psychological safety in agile software development teams. Inf. Softw. Technol. **162**, 107267 (2023)
2. Alsanoosy, T., Spichkova, M., Harland, J.: The influence of power distance on requirements engineering activities. In: Rudas, I.J., Csirik, J., Toro, C., Botzheim, J., Howlett, R.J., Jain, L.C. (eds.) Knowledge-Based and Intelligent Information & Engineering Systems: Proceedings of the 23rd International Conference KES-2019, Budapest, Hungary, 4–6 September 2019. Procedia Computer Science, vol. 159, pp. 2394–2403. Elsevier (2019). https://doi.org/10.1016/J.PROCS.2019.09.414
3. Altuwaijri, F.S., Ferrario, M.A.: Factors affecting agile adoption: an industry research study of the mobile app sector in Saudi Arabia. J. Syst. Softw. **190**, 111347 (2022)
4. Ayed, H., Vanderose, B., Habra, N.: Agile cultural challenges in Europe and Asia: insights from practitioners. In: 2017 IEEE/ACM 39th International Conference on Software Engineering: Software Engineering in Practice Track (ICSE-SEIP), pp. 153–162. IEEE (2017)
5. Bastiaansen, C.A., Wilderom, C.P.: Agile and generic work values of British vs Indian it workers: a culture-clash case. J. Strateg. Manag. **15**(3), 353–376 (2021)
6. Campanelli, A.S., Bassi, D., Parreiras, F.S.: Agile transformation success factors: a practitioner's survey. In: Dubois, E., Pohl, K. (eds.) CAiSE 2017. LNCS, vol. 10253, pp. 364–379. Springer, Cham (2017). https://doi.org/10.1007/978-3-319-59536-8_23
7. Campanelli, A.S., Parreiras, F.S.: Agile methods tailoring–a systematic literature review. J. Syst. Softw. **110**, 85–100 (2015)
8. Digital.ai: 16th annual state of agile report (2022). https://digital.ai/resource-center/analyst-reports/state-of-agile-report/. Accessed 07 Oct 2023
9. Dutra, E., Diirr, B., Santos, G.: Human factors and their influence on software development teams-a tertiary study. In: Proceedings of the XXXV Brazilian Symposium on Software Engineering, pp. 442–451 (2021)
10. Fuggetta, A.: Software process: a roadmap. In: Proceedings of the Conference on the Future of Software Engineering, ICSE 2000, pp. 25–34. ACM, New York (2000). https://doi.org/10.1145/336512.336521
11. Gallo, A.: What is psychological safety? (2023). https://hbr.org/2023/02/what-is-psychological-safety. Harvard Business Review. Accessed 24 July 2023
12. Geffers, K., Bretschneider, U., Eilers, K., Oeste-Reiß, S.: Leading teams in today's dynamic organizations: the core characteristics of agile leadership. In: Bui, T.X. (ed.) 57th Hawaii International Conference on System Sciences, HICSS 2024, Hilton Hawaiian Village Waikiki Beach Resort, Hawaii, USA, 3–6 January 2024, pp. 4868–4877. ScholarSpace (2024). https://hdl.handle.net/10125/106967
13. Gelmis, A., Ozkan, N., Ahmad, A.J., Guler, M.G.: Impact of Turkish national culture on agile software development in Turkey. In: Przybyłek, A., Jarzębowicz, A., Luković, I., Ng, Y.Y. (eds.) LASD 2022. LNBIP, vol. 438, pp. 78–95. Springer, Cham (2022). https://doi.org/10.1007/978-3-030-94238-0_5
14. Gupta, S., Modgil, S., Bhushan, B., Kamble, S., Mishra, J.: Digital innovation and transformation capabilities in a large company. Expert Syst. e13452 (2023)

15. Hoda, R., Noble, J., Marshall, S.: Supporting self-organizing agile teams. In: Sillitti, A., Hazzan, O., Bache, E., Albaladejo, X. (eds.) XP 2011. LNBIP, vol. 77, pp. 73–87. Springer, Heidelberg (2011). https://doi.org/10.1007/978-3-642-20677-1_6
16. Hofstede, G.: Culture's Consequences: Comparing Values, Behaviors, Institutions and Organizations Across Nations. Sage (1980)
17. Hofstede, G., Hofstede, G.J., Minkov, M.: Cultures and Organizations: Software of the Mind, vol. 3. Mcgraw-Hill, New York (2010)
18. Holmström, H., Fitzgerald, B., Ågerfalk, P.J., Conchúir, E.Ó., et al.: Agile practices reduce distance in global software development. Inf. Syst. Manag. **23**(3), 7–18 (2006)
19. IEEE Computer Society: Guide to the Software Engineering Body of Knowledge (SWEBOK). IEEE Computer Society Press (2014)
20. Kajko-Mattsson, M., Azizyan, G., Magarian, M.K.: Classes of distributed agile development problems. In: 2010 Agile Conference, pp. 51–58. IEEE (2010)
21. Kitchenham, B.A., Budgen, D., Brereton, P.: Evidence-Based Software Engineering and Systematic Reviews, vol. 4. CRC Press (2015)
22. Kuchel, T., Neumann, M., Diebold, P., Schön, E.M.: Which challenges do exist with agile culture in practice? In: Proceedings of the 38th ACM/SIGAPP Symposium on Applied Computing, pp. 1018–1025 (2023)
23. Likhi, T.: Effects of the power distance index on multicultural software engineering teams. Leiden Univ. **1**, 1–40 (2022). https://theses.liacs.nl/pdf/2021-2022-LikhiT.pdf
24. Matthews, K.B., Tanner, M.C.: The influence of national culture dimensions on agile practices: the case of South African software development teams. IADIS Int. J. Comput. Sci. Inf. Syst. **17**(2) (2022)
25. Mattos, C.S., Dutra, E., Santos, G.: Dataset SLR on power distance in agile organizations (2024). https://doi.org/10.17605/OSF.IO/2E6M5, database on OSF
26. Mishra, A., Abdalhamid, S., Mishra, D., Ostrovska, S.: Organizational issues in embracing agile methods: an empirical assessment. Int. J. Syst. Assur. Eng. Manag. **12**(6), 1420–1433 (2021)
27. Page, M.J., et al.: The PRISMA 2020 statement: an updated guideline for reporting systematic reviews. Syst. Rev. **10**(1), 1–11 (2021)
28. Petersen, K., Vakkalanka, S., Kuzniarz, L.: Guidelines for conducting systematic mapping studies in software engineering: an update. Inf. Softw. Technol. **64**, 1–18 (2015)
29. Reginaldo, F., Santos, G.: Challenges in agile transformation journey: a qualitative study. In: Proceedings of the 34th Brazilian Symposium on Software Engineering, pp. 11–20 (2020)
30. Santos, G., et al.: Towards successful software process improvement initiatives: experiences from the battlefield. In: 21st Americas Conference on Information Systems, AMCIS 2015, Puerto Rico, 13–15 August 2015. Association for Information Systems (2015). http://aisel.aisnet.org/amcis2015/GlobDev/GeneralPresentations/13
31. Schüll, M., Hofmann, P., Philipp, P., Urbach, N.: Reporting in large-scale agile organizations: insights and recommendations from a case study in software development. Inf. Syst. E Bus. Manag. **21**(3), 571–601 (2023). https://doi.org/10.1007/S10257-023-00643-1
32. Siakas, K.V., Siakas, E.: The agile professional culture: a source of agile quality. Softw. Process: Improv. Pract. **12**(6), 597–610 (2007)

33. Šmite, D., Gonzalez-Huerta, J., Moe, N.B.: "When in Rome, Do as the Romans Do": cultural barriers to being agile in distributed teams. In: Stray, V., Hoda, R., Paasivaara, M., Kruchten, P. (eds.) XP 2020. LNBIP, vol. 383, pp. 145–161. Springer, Cham (2020). https://doi.org/10.1007/978-3-030-49392-9_10
34. Šmite, D., Moe, N.B., Gonzalez-Huerta, J.: Overcoming cultural barriers to being agile in distributed teams. Inf. Softw. Technol. **138**, 106612 (2021)
35. Spiegler, S.V., Heinecke, C., Wagner, S.: The influence of culture and structure on autonomous teams in established companies. In: Hoda, R. (ed.) XP 2019. LNBIP, vol. 364, pp. 46–54. Springer, Cham (2019). https://doi.org/10.1007/978-3-030-30126-2_6
36. Strode, D.E., Huff, S.L., Tretiakov, A.: The impact of organizational culture on agile method use. In: 2009 42nd Hawaii International Conference on System Sciences, pp. 1–9. IEEE (2009)
37. Summers, M.: Insights into an agile adventure with offshore partners. In: Agile 2008 Conference, pp. 333–338. IEEE (2008)
38. Thorgren, S., Caiman, E.: The role of psychological safety in implementing agile methods across cultures. Res. Technol. Manag. **62**(2), 31–39 (2019)
39. Welsch, D., Burk, L., Mötefindt, D., Neumann, M.: Navigating cultural diversity: barriers and potentials in multicultural agile software development teams. arXiv preprint arXiv:2311.12061 (2023)
40. Wohlin, C.: Guidelines for snowballing in systematic literature studies and a replication in software engineering. In: Proceedings of the 18th International Conference on Evaluation and Assessment in Software Engineering, pp. 1–10 (2014)

AI in GUI-Based Software Testing: Insights from a Survey with Industrial Practitioners

Domenico Amalfitano[1], Riccardo Coppola[2](✉), Damiano Distante[3], and Filippo Ricca[4]

[1] University of Naples Federico II, Naples, Italy
domenico.amalfitano@unina.it
[2] Politecnico di Torino, Turin, Italy
riccardo.coppola@polito.it
[3] UnitelmaSapienza University of Rome, Rome, Italy
damiano.distante@unitelmasapienza.it
[4] Università di Genova, Genova, Italy
filippo.ricca@unige.it

Abstract. In today's technology-driven world, there is a growing interest in leveraging Artificial Intelligence (AI) to streamline software testing processes. Our research delves into GUI-based testing, a prominent technique for verifying software functionality. Preliminary findings from our industrial survey of 45 respondents provide insights into the use of AI in GUI-based software testing. The survey aims to understand how AI supports GUI-based testing, the AI techniques and tools used, and the perceived advantages and limitations.

The collected results suggest a diffuse yet superficial utilization of AI-based mechanisms among GUI-based testers. Practitioners often employ AI techniques in a technology-agnostic way, treating commercial tools as black boxes. These findings underscore the need for additional research aimed at gaining a deeper understanding of the AI techniques and tools employed in industry and their intended purposes.

Keywords: GUI-based testing · Artificial Intelligence · Industrial survey

1 Introduction

As society increasingly depends on technology, the demand for efficient and reliable software development grows. An integral part of this development process is software testing, which ensures the proper functioning of applications and systems. However, conventional testing approaches typically require substantial time commitments, involve tedious tasks, and are prone to human errors [3,4].

In light of the growing complexity of software applications and the desire for quicker development cycles, IT organizations are exploring the potential advantages of integrating Artificial Intelligence (AI) into their testing processes. It's

A. Bertolino et al. (Eds.): QUATIC 2024, CCIS 2178, pp. 328–343, 2024.
https://doi.org/10.1007/978-3-031-70245-7_23

worth noting that leveraging AI might offer the possibility of automating certain testing procedures, which could potentially result in significant time and cost savings, while also potentially enhancing overall productivity.

One of the most commonly utilized techniques in the industry is GUI-based testing [4], which prioritizes verifying the functional conformance of the System Under Test (SUT) through its Graphical User Interface (GUI) [5].

While the gray literature, including blogs and web articles, may suggest the apparent utilization of AI in GUI-based testing [15,16], numerous facets necessitate deeper exploration to comprehend the true potential of AI in revolutionizing software testing. In particular, there exists uncertainty from a researcher's perspective regarding the precise AI techniques, algorithms, and approaches utilized to enhance GUI-based testing.

Over the past few years, we have been researching GUI-based testing, and we are currently seeking to interview industry professionals to better understand the AI phenomenon in this area.

Our team has administered a survey featuring a questionnaire for professionals on the use of AI in GUI-based testing of industrial software. The overarching objective is to gain insights into the extent of AI usage in GUI-based testing activities, identify the prevalent AI techniques and tools utilized, and explore the associated advantages and limitations.

The paper is organized as follows. Section 2 provides a basic background, allowing readers unfamiliar with GUI-based testing and AI to grasp the paper's content. Section 3 presents the relevant aspects of the conducted survey such as the questionnaire design, sample identification, and survey preparation/execution. Section 4 presents the findings and discusses the obtained results. Section 5 briefly sketches related works. Finally, Sect. 6 concludes the paper and presents some future research directions.

2 Background

2.1 GUI-Based Testing

GUI-based testing refers to an end-to-end functional testing technique applied to a specific SUT, where the system's GUI is interacted with. End-to-end testing is a software testing approach that aims to verify the functionality and performance of an entire software application, spanning from initiation to completion. It accomplishes this by simulating real-world user scenarios and replicating live data inputs. The primary goal of end-to-end testing is to detect any bugs or issues that may arise when all components of the application are integrated, ensuring that the application behaves as expected as a unified entity [5]. It can involve the manual execution of the SUT's GUI or the use of automated tools. In the current landscape, automated testing has become predominant thanks to its ability to reduce time and effort required, compared to manual testing.

GUI-based testing has become indispensable in modern software development due to the escalating complexity resulting from numerous interconnected systems. As a result, it is widely utilized in the industry to ensure the quality and reliability of software applications [14]. While individual components may perform flawlessly in isolation, integration issues can arise due to miscommunication between them. GUI-based testing plays a crucial role in verifying the flow of information throughout the SUT, encompassing all possible paths and dependencies to ensure seamless functionality of the integrated system.

Several techniques have been explored by the Software Engineering literature to conduct GUI-based testing. Classifications of GUI-based testing activities have been made according to the way test cases are created, e.g. randomly, by defining test scripts manually, by record and replay or by leveraging models of the GUI of the application [13]. Also, GUI-based testing can be characterized according to the type of locators or oracles used to generate test cases and perform verifications on the application, either using coordinate-based, text-based or visual clues [2].

2.2 Artificial Intelligence in Software Testing

AI encompasses the concept of computers emulating human intelligence, programmed to replicate human-like thinking and actions. This term extends to machines exhibiting traits akin to human cognition, including learning and problem-solving abilities. The core aims of AI include learning, reasoning, and perception [17]. AI has demonstrated its utility across various application domains, with recent advancements extending its capabilities into the realm of software engineering. More recently, AI has also been leveraged in software testing [1,12,20], offering innovative solutions and approaches to enhance testing processes and outcomes.

AI-based testing is emerging as a novel and innovative type of software testing that harnesses artificial intelligence to optimize and streamline the testing processes. Unlike conventional testing automation, AI-based testing automation employs AI models and AI techniques to generate test cases and test input, to adapt seamlessly to changes within the SUT, to identify potential defects in the SUT, to generate test oracles, and, in general, to automate complex tasks in software testing such as self-healing test automation [1,15,16]. Recent secondary studies have shown how AI-based testing has the potential to enhance efficiency and improve test adequacy, representing a notable advancement in the field of software testing [1].

AI has been applied to enhance various software testing activities, including test results evaluation, spanning from unit testing to system testing. It's been integrated into various testing techniques like random, model-based, and mutation testing, covering objectives such as functional, non-functional, regression, and GUI testing [1]. In this study, our objective is to explore the application of AI in supporting GUI-based testing within industrial environments.

3 The Survey

We conducted an industrial survey to assess the extent to which AI techniques and tools are used in GUI-based testing activities in the practice. In particular, the goal of the survey was to understand how, in industrial settings, AI is applied to support GUI-based testing, what are the AI techniques and tools employed, and what are their advantages and limitations. Specifically, we focused on three main testing activities: test case definition, test oracle design, and test case optimization.

To conduct the survey, we followed the guidelines proposed by Kitchenham *et al.* [8], discussing the main activities that need to be considered when undertaking a survey. In the next subsections, we describe the various steps we executed in accordance with these guidelines.

3.1 Questionnaire Design and Implementation

To collect answers from interviewees we designed a questionnaire by adopting the Goal-Question Metric approach [18] to align questions and metrics with our research goals.

The questionnaire was thoughtfully designed to directly address our research goals and optimized for completion within 10–15 min. It comprises six sections for a total of 23 questions. Section 1 focuses on gathering demographic information. It includes questions on the size of the participants' organizations, their experience with AI in GUI-based testing, the used programming languages, application domains, types of software systems tested, and testing tools utilized. Sections 2 through 4 follow a similar structure but explore three distinct aspects of GUI-based software testing: section 2 delves into test case definition, section 3 focuses on test oracles design, and section 4 addresses test case optimization. The questionnaire asks participants to select techniques utilized for each of these testing aspects and indicate the AI techniques (e.g., genetic algorithms, NLP, clustering) they employ. Section 5 identifies the AI tools and platforms utilized for GUI-based testing, while section 6 aims to gather insights into the advantages and limitations of using AI for GUI-based testing.

3.2 Population and Identification of the Sample

The initial step in conducting a survey is to define a target population. For our study, the target population comprises software testers possessing expertise in GUI-based software testing. To sample the population, we employed both probabilistic (random sampling) and non-probabilistic (convenience sampling) methods [8]. More in detail, the sampling was performed in four ways: (i) as a convenience sampling relying on the network contacts of the four research units involved (Turin, Genoa, Naples, and Rome); (ii) using the Scopus search engine to select authors, having industrial affiliations, who coauthored papers on the topic of GUI-based testing; (iii) by sending invitation messages on LinkedIn mailing lists concerning software engineering and software testing; (iv) by selecting participants (e.g., organization and program committee members, keynote speakers) of conferences in software testing having an industrial affiliation.

The questionnaire was introduced to contacts with a concise explanation outlining the goals and motivations of the study. The questionnaire was accompanied by a cover letter providing a brief overview of our research project and emphasizing the importance of getting answers from each participant. We made a deliberate choice to refrain from offering any material incentives for participation. However, to motivate professionals, we assured all participants that they would have received a report containing the analyses and the obtained results.

In the end, our questionnaire received 45 responses, 33 of which (73.3%) were from respondents that declared to apply AI in GUI-based testing. Regrettably, we could not determine the exact number of individuals reached by our invitation messages and advertisements, thus preventing us from calculating the response rate. This issue is common for online questionnaires (see for example, [11,19]).

Many contacts informed us that they did not participate in the survey as they have no experience in using AI in GUI-based testing. This prevents us from being able to estimate the percentage of testing professionals who use AI in GUI-based testing.

3.3 Data Collection and Analysis

Data collection was facilitated through an online questionnaire[1] created using Google Forms. The questionnaire was made available from September 1, 2023 until January 31, 2024, spanning a period of 5 months. During the data collection phase, we monitored the progress of questionnaire submissions. This enabled us to send targeted reminders to individuals who had not responded or completed the questionnaire. Upon collecting the questionnaires, we conducted analyses primarily focused on descriptive statistics, given the survey's descriptive and exploratory nature. Our main findings are presented in the following Sect. 4.

4 Findings

In this section, we present the main findings of our survey. First, we provide an overview of the respondents' background, focusing on the analysis of the responses to questions from the first section of our questionnaire. Subsequently, we delve into responses gathered from questions included in the remaining sections. Finally, we discuss the obtained results and outline the potential threats to the validity of our study.

4.1 Respondents' Background

The geographical distribution of the 45 respondents lacks uniformity, with the majority of them being Italian (75.5%). However, we also received responses from professionals residing in various other parts of the world. In Fig. 1, nations represented in our sample are highlighted in dark blue, indicating those with at least one respondent.

Out of the 45 respondents, 33 (73.3%) indicated experience with AI in GUI-based testing. The remaining 12 respondents (26.7%), although not formally

[1] www.doi.org/10.6084/m9.figshare.26048332.

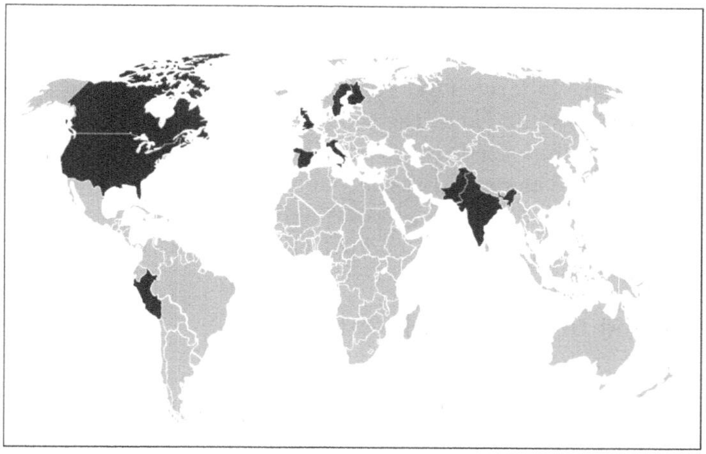

Fig. 1. Nationalities of the Respondents (dark blue means that in our sample we have at least one respondent for that Nation) (Color figure online)

declaring experience in utilizing AI, are professional software testers proficient in traditional GUI-based testing platforms and tools. They possess an awareness of AI within the software testing domain.

Figure 2(a) summarizes the respondents' years of experience focusing on the specific context of the GUI-based testing. We can observe that more than one-quarter of the participants have a long experience in the field, exceeding nine years. The majority (about 53%) of the participants are junior software testers with less than 3 years of experience. Finally, 13% of the respondents have between 3 and 6 years of experience, and 7% have between 6 and 9 years of experience. Overall, we can observe that many respondents are experienced professionals.

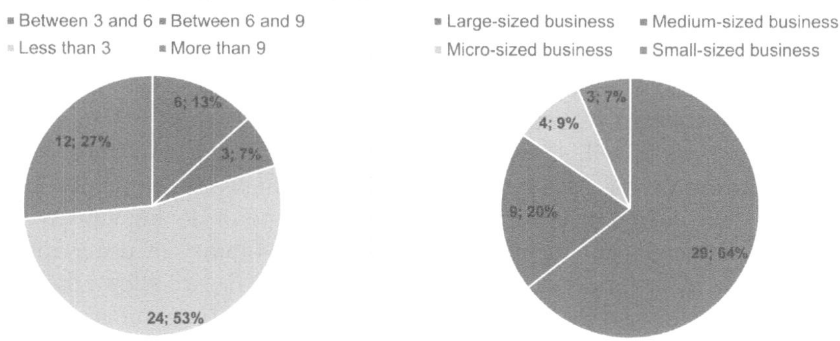

(a) Years of experience of the respondents (b) Company size of the respondents

Fig. 2. Characterization of the respondents

The pie chart reported in Fig. 2(b) provides an overview of the size of the companies where the participants work. Most of the responses were obtained by practitioners working in large-sized companies (i.e., 250+ employees), totaling about 64% of the answers. Then, the second larger group is the one of respondents working in medium-sized companies (i.e., 50–249 employees), corresponding to about 20% of the answers. Finally, only a small fraction of the respondents work in small-sized (i.e., 10–49 employees) and micro-sized companies (i.e., 1–9 employees), respectively, about 7% and 9% of all the participants.

4.2 AI Applied to GUI-Based Testing

In this section, we discuss the primary findings on the use of AI in GUI-based testing, derived from the analysis of the responses provided to questions in sections 2 to 6 of our questionnaire by the subset of participants (33 out of 45) who indicated their use of AI in this context.

AI Techniques to Define Test Cases. In Table 1, the first column lists the AI techniques that respondents of our survey indicated to use for test case definition in GUI-based testing, along with corresponding counts. Natural Language Understanding (NLU) emerges as the most used AI technique, with 42.4% of respondents (14 out of 33), followed by Ontology, Natural Language Generation (NLG), and Text Mining, each mentioned by 36.4% of respondents (12 out of 33). Statistical approaches like Probabilistic Models and Regression were also frequently cited by 33.3% of respondents (11 out of 33). While Genetic Algorithms and Semantic Web technologies show a strong presence with 30% of respondents (10 out of 33) indicating usage for each, Machine Learning (ML) techniques, such as Decision Trees (9 out 33), Artificial Neural Networks (8 out of 33), and Supervised Learning (8 out 33) are less common but still significant, reflecting wide support of ML to test case definition in GUI-based testing. Seven respondents provided insights about how they make use of AI techniques to define test cases for GUI-based testing answering the open question *"Could you please briefly describe how you use AI techniques to define Test Cases in GUI-based testing?"* A respondent emphasized the use of many AI techniques in GUI-based testing, including Natural Language Processing (NLP) for GUI-based test case design and implementation. It noted that while these techniques enhance efficiency, human expertise is still crucial for effective test design. Another respondent mentioned considering AI for generating surrounding test documentation, albeit with a certain degree of uncertainty about the type of documents AI could be useful for. Several respondents highlighted the possibility of using specific AI-based tooling in the phase of test case definition: TestRigor[2] allows the definition of test scripts through the use of natural language; the QLearning deep learning algorithm is used as the basis for test generation for web applications, prioritizing the actions leading to significant GUI changes for high test effectiveness; NLG and NLU tools can be used for generating conversational scenarios; Neural

[2] https://testrigor.com/.

Networks are used to reduce the scope of GUI testing while maximizing coverage; finally, one respondent highlighted the use of NLP techniques to create user stories, which are then translated using manual scripting into test cases.

AI Techniques to Define Test Oracles. The second column of Table 1 lists the AI techniques used by respondents for test oracle definition, along with their counts. Knowledge Representation and Reasoning and Regression are at the forefront, each utilized by 27.3% (9 out of 33) of respondents. Text Mining follows closely with 24.2% (8 out of 33) mentions, reflecting its importance in extracting pertinent information from textual data, such as requirements and specification models. Techniques like Ontology and Image Processing are also commonly employed, with 21.2% (7 out of 33) of developers indicating their use, underscoring their relevance in structuring knowledge and analyzing visual elements respectively. Machine learning techniques, such as Decision Trees, Reinforcement Learning, and Supervised Learning, as well as deep learning techniques, such as Convolutional Neural Networks, are less common, with an average of 15% of respondents indicating the use of each of them, in average. Knowledge Representation and Reasoning techniques can be used to construct a knowledge base describing the composition of GUIs through their constituent widgets, essential for designing and implementing GUI-based oracles. Moreover, Regression techniques are essential for predictive analytics, indicating their dual role in defining test oracles and enabling predictive analysis during testing processes.

Table 1. Number of professionals indicating use of specific AI techniques in GUI-based testing for test case definition, test oracle definition, and test case optimization.

Defining Test Cases		Defining Test Oracles		Optimizing Test Cases	
AI technique	Count	AI technique	Count	AI technique	Count
Natural Lang. Understanding	14	Knowledge Repr. and Reasoning	9	Regression	8
Ontology	12	Regression	9	Semantic Web	7
Natural Lang. Generation	12	Text Mining	8	Clustering	7
Text Mining	12	Ontology	7	Ontology	6
Probabilistic Models	11	Image Processing	7	Text Mining	6
Regression	11	Decision Trees	6	Metaheuristic Optimisation	6
Semantic Web	10	Semantic Web	5	Word Embedding	6
Constraint Satisfaction	10	Ensemble Method	5	Classification	6
Genetic Algorithms	10	Reinforcement Learning	5	Decision Trees	6
Information Extraction	10	Supervised Learning	5	Support Vector Machine	6
Evolutionary Algorithm	9	Genetic Algorithm	4	Evolutionary Algorithm	5
Clustering	9	Graph Plan Algorithm	4	Genetic Algorithm	5
Decision Trees	9	Artificial Neural Network	4	Boosting	5
Intelligent Agent	9	Boosting	4	Artificial Neural Network	5
Q-learning	9	Classification	4	Probabilistic Models	5
Metaheuristic Optimizations	8	Convolutional Neural Network	4	Recurrent Neural Network	5
Artificial Neural Network	8	Support Vector Machine	4	Reinforcement Learning	5
Supervised Learning	8			Supervised Learning	5
Convolutional Neural Network	7			Unsupervised Learning	5
Recurrent Neural Network	7				
Reinforcement Learning	7				
Support Vector Machine	6				

Responses provided by the surveyed developers and testers to the open question *"Could you please briefly describe how you use AI techniques to define Test Oracles in GUI-based testing?"* underlined the successful use of AI techniques to define test oracles for GUI-based testing. The AI-supported activities involve the support for defining expected behaviors and outcomes of the GUI, for example by training AI models, through logs or execution traces, to recognize at runtime the expected GUI responses or to compare the GUI behaviors against learned patterns. AI plays a key role in identifying GUI deviations from expected behavior and flagging potential defects or anomalies. However, human domain knowledge is essential for training AI, establishing initial parameters, and accurately interpreting results. Respondents also emphasized the potential of employing large language models, like OpenAI's ChatGPT, to analyze program documentation and specifications for generating appropriate oracles.

AI Techniques to Optimize Test Cases. In Table 1, the third column presents the AI techniques reported by developers in our survey for optimizing test cases in GUI-based testing, alongside the corresponding counts. Regression techniques stand out as the most utilized, with 24.2% (8 out of 33) of respondents endorsing them, underscoring the use of predictive analytics for test case selection and prioritization to reduce the costs and the resources of the testing processes. Semantic Web and Clustering are also highly esteemed, each mentioned by 22.1% (7 out of 33) of respondents, signifying their importance in deriving meaning from web content and grouping similar test scenarios, respectively. Ontology, Text Mining, Metaheuristic Optimization, Word Embedding, Classification, and Decision Trees, each mentioned by 18.2% (6 out of 33) of respondents, highlight a multifaceted approach to improve the cost-effectiveness of test suites. Support Vector Machine follows suit, demonstrating the value of this method to reduce the testing process costs in high-dimensional spaces. Finally, Evolutionary Algorithm, Genetic Algorithm, Boosting, Artificial Neural Networks, Probabilistic Models, Recurrent Neural Network, Reinforcement Learning, Supervised, and Unsupervised Learning, each mentioned by 15.1% (5 out of 33) of respondents, underscore a broad engagement with machine learning techniques to advance test case optimization.

In answering the open question *"Could you please briefly describe how you use AI techniques for Test Case Optimization in GUI-based testing?"*, respondents highlighted the use of AI techniques to optimize GUI-based test cases by automating selection and generation. This involves using algorithms to prioritize test cases based on historical data, code changes, and critical areas. In particular, a respondent emphasized the use of machine learning for test case prioritization. AI helps in reducing redundancy, increasing coverage, and detecting relevant combinations of user interactions. However, human input is essential to fine-tune AI recommendations, ensuring thorough testing and effective bug detection.

Most Used Combinations of AI and Software Testing (ST) Techniques in GUI-Based Testing. Table 2 shows the AI techniques most commonly used in conjunction with various GUI-based testing techniques, as it results from our survey. We limit our analysis to couples of ST and AI techniques that were indicated by at least 4 participants out of 33.

In Test Case definition, AI is primarily used in combination with Exploratory Testing, Model Based, and Scenario Based techniques. In Exploratory Testing, AI techniques such as Knowledge Representation and Reasoning, Q-learning, and Clustering are utilized to develop intelligent agents capable of autonomously exploring and testing the GUI of the SUT. In Model Based testing, the use of Regression shows the need to define GUI-based test cases starting from predictive models. Finally, employing AI techniques capable of Knowledge Representation, Text Mining, and Natural Language Understanding is very common among practitioners for deriving testing scenarios from software requirements and specifications. As for the Test Oracle definition, since test oracles are often derived from the program documentation, this justifies the use of AI techniques like Knowledge Representation and Reasoning and Natural Language Understanding and Generation for supporting these ST techniques. Ontology is the most used AI technique for Test Case Optimization. It is used in conjunction with ST techniques aimed at reducing the costs of the testing processes, or optimizing the test suites by analyzing the requirements or the risks. Moreover, Regression AI techniques are exploited to apply predictive models on historical testing data to improve the cost-effectiveness of preexisting test suites.

Table 2. Most used combinations of ST and AI techniques in GUI-based testing

Testing Technique	AI technique	Count
Most used combinations of ST and AI techniques for Test Case Definition		
Exploratory Testing	Knowledge representation and reasoning	7
	Natural language understanding	6
	Q-learning	6
	Text mining	6
	Clustering	5
Model Based	Regression	8
	Ontology	6
	Clustering	5
	Knowledge representation	5
	Supervised learning	5
Scenario Based	Knowledge representation and reasoning	5
	Natural language understanding	5
	Probabilistic models	5
	Intelligent agent	4
	Natural language generation	4
Most used combinations of ST and AI techniques for Test Oracle Definition		
Derived from program documentation	Text mining	5
	Ontology	4
	Text mining	4
Most used combinations of ST and AI techniques for Test Case Optimization		
Cost-Effective-based	Ontology	4
History-based	Regression	4
Requirement-based	Ontology	4
Risk-based	Ontology	4
Search-Based	Semantic Web	4

AI Tools and Platforms Used in GUI-Based Testing. In Table 3, we summarize the tools mentioned by the respondents of our survey. We report for each tool a brief description of the tool, if the tool is open-source, if it is test-specific and, if so, if it is specific for GUI-based testing. This distinction is necessary since many respondents mentioned general-purpose AI agents (e.g., large language models like ChatGPT) that are used to support GUI-based testing activities, albeit not specifically developed for that purpose. In the last column of the table, we briefly sketch the main use of the tool. In addition to the tools reported in the table, a respondent to the survey mentioned the use of proprietary deep-learning and search-based tools without providing additional details; other respondents mentioned different versions of OpenAI tools (e.g., AutoGPT).

Perceived Advantages of the Use of AI in GUI-Based Testing. According to our respondents, AI is seen as a valuable help in automated testing as it increases testing accuracy and precision and uncovers blind spots in GUI-based testing. This augmentation enhances the work performed by test automation. One of the examples mentioned by the respondents for the generation of diverse sets of test cases, and thereby an increase of the provided coverage, is the use of large language models (LLM) to ensure multilingual test cases, or the enhancement of existing test cases to provide better conformance towards black-box testing standards. The most important advantage, which is compatible with the principally perceived advantages of the use of AI in Software Engineering tasks in general, is the significant reduction of human effort required, and the capability of easing the work for inexperienced testers. A respondent mentioned the possibility of providing more easily maintained test suites when the AI generators are fed with the modifications applied to the SUT. Another respondent pointed out that in some cases AI tools allow for a quick generation of effective and not easily observable scenarios with respect to other testing techniques, and to extract knowledge from past executions and test experience to reuse it effectively.

Perceived Drawbacks of the Use of AI in GUI-Based Testing. A shared consensus between respondents was the need for training AI engines in a proper way to perform accurate tests. This particularly applies to GUI-based testing, since the training data can be limited or related to some particular SUTs and not generalizable to any available GUI. Another mentioned problem area is the possible lack of domain knowledge, which may render the AI test case generators applicable only to certain categories of software. The respondents also expressed some criticism towards the nature of AI platforms, which are typically offered as PaaS instruments and provide unclear capabilities if limited fees are paid. This can prove an important limit, especially if the benefits of using AI instruments are unclear in the first place, thereby limiting the penetration of these tools in testing teams. The difficulty in evaluating the AI models without subscribing to them can lead testers to give up completely the selection of a tool with such characteristics and instead rely on traditional tools, e.g. scripted, model-based, or automated input generation tools. The respondents also highlighted that sometimes it is difficult to instrument the AI tools to ignore weak test paths or to learn new/more effective paths based on criteria that have been observed

Table 3. Tools mentioned by the respondents to the survey

Tool name	Description	Open source	Test-specific	GUI-specific	Main use
Applitools	An AI-powered testing platform that allows the definition of test cases in natural language, which can then be enriched by scripting capabilities and the use of computer vision to analyze visual oracles and locators in the GUI of the SUT	No	Yes	Yes	Optimization of GUI-based test cases by automating selection and generation, leveraging historical data
AutoBlackTest	A software tool designed to automatically produce test cases for interactive applications. It engages with the application through its graphical user interface (GUI) and utilizes reinforcement learning methods to grasp the nuances of user interaction. By doing so, AutoBlackTest generates testing scenarios that are relevant and reflective of real-world usage patterns	Yes	Yes	Yes	The tool associates high test effectiveness (rewards) to the actions that provide significant GUI changes, thus driving the test generator to exercise the software under test around these paths
Bing Chat	An AI-powered chatbot created by Microsoft, aimed at delivering natural and conversational replies to user inquiries. It utilizes OpenAI's ChatGPT version 4 Large Language Model	No	No	No	Creation of user stories for testing
ChatGPT	Developed by OpenAI is a chatbot built upon a large language model. It allows users to shape conversations according to desired parameters such as length, format, style, detail level, and language. Prompt engineering, involving successive prompts and replies, is employed at each stage of the conversation to maintain context	No	No	No	Create test scenarios from an automator's perspective to find blind spots in automated testing
Claude	An AI ChatBot using Claude 3, the latest large language model developed by Anthropic. It can interpret user input and produce human-like responses. In addition to engaging in conversations, Claude can process uploaded images and documents, provide summaries, or answer questions on particular topics.	No	Yes	Yes	Create test scenarios from an automator's perspective to find blind spots in automated testing
Gemini	Gemini, previously identified as Bard, represents a generative artificial intelligence chatbot crafted by Google. Built upon the expansive language model (LLM) bearing the same moniker, Gemini emerges as a direct counterpoint to the rapid ascent of OpenAI's ChatGPT	Yes	No	No	Description of test scenarios against the GUI by using natural language
Scipy	Library of advanced mathematical algorithms for Python	Yes	No	No	Define methods to obtain more cost-effective coverage
TestRigor	A GUI-testing tool that leverages natural language processing in order to translate natural language instructions to sequences of operations against the GUI of the SUT	No	Yes	No	Run test scripts written in (constrained) natural language
Tosca	Tool for codeless, AI-fueled End-to-End testing for mobile and web applications	No	Yes	No	Efficiently select locators
UserZoom	A testing tool to evaluate the usability of the GUI of applications in several domains. Artificial Intelligence features are used to generate user scenarios throughout the GUI	No	Yes	Yes	Identify critical areas of the GUI for UX-focused testing

by a human tester. Finally, as it is observed in many fields where AI is applied when language models are involved, input queries (a.k.a. prompts) generation is considered a significant effort and a trial-and-error activity, which requires a fine-tuning of the prompts used and implies the possibility of wrong results of the testing activities. In safety-critical scenarios, this uncertainty of the results may be considered unacceptable.

4.3 Needs and Opportunities for Future Research

Based on the findings discussed on the previous sections, we can identify a set of fundamental takes for researchers and practitioners in the field of GUI-based testing wanting to incorporate AI-based methods in their activities:

- Most of the issues mentioned by the interviewed developers are related to the nature of the available tools, which most of the times are completely closed-source or black-box, of which little is know of the way they work and aid in test case generation and execution. Researchers might aid the community by open-sourcing and documenting tools to aid practitioners in understanding their inner working.
- Respondents pointed out that while there are numerous general-purpose tools available in the domain of Large Language Models (LLM), their potential for GUI-based testing tasks remains unproven. Researchers could concentrate on conducting comparative assessments and developing guidelines for efficient creation of prompts in GUI-based testing facilitated by LLMs.
- There is a need for defining workflows that incorporate supervised AI usage, as AI techniques are often considered unreliable, and user control is frequently impossible. Therefore, it is appropriate to discuss techniques that involve both human and AI-based users working together, able to control and fine-tune each other.
- There is a need for defining architectures that involve multiple AI-based agents controlling each other and allowing for iterative fine-tuning. These architectures for software testing have already been theorized and applied and are based on cognitive models [6].
- For tool developers, the creation of training datasets and clear indication of how the tools are "trained" are necessary steps to build trust among testers.

4.4 Threats to Validity

In our assessment, we have identified several factors that could impact the validity of this study. Firstly, there's a concern regarding our sampling techniques. Since we made the survey available online, there's a risk of receiving responses from individuals who may not be adequately qualified in GUI testing and AI to participate and thus obtain results that are not completely reliable. To limit this, we took proactive measures by distributing the survey to specific groups known to have a professional interest in software testing.

Another potential issue is the selection of ST techniques and AI methods we made to prepare the questionnaire. It's possible that we may have overlooked important techniques from both domains in our research. To mitigate this risk, we referred to the AI and the ST taxonomies presented in [1]. Moreover, participants could use the open-ended questions in our survey to specify any techniques they use that were not included in the list of options provided for closed-ended questions.

Additionally, there is the consideration of terminology. Some terms utilized in the questionnaire might be subject to varying interpretations among practitioners. In an effort to enhance clarity, we conducted a thorough evaluation of each term, drawing from the feedback obtained during our pilot study. Regarding our sample size and geographic distribution, while our sample size aligns with previous software testing surveys [10,19], achieving a larger sample size would be beneficial. However, this proves challenging given the specific focus of our survey and the desired level of expertise among participants. Additionally, while we did cover multiple countries in our study, broader geographic distribution would enhance the generalizability of our findings.

Lastly, there's the concern of self-exclusion among participants. It's possible that some individuals chose not to participate in the survey, deeming it irrelevant. This is a known issue in internet surveys [8], especially those promoted online, as was the case with ours.

5 Related Work

Surveys on software testing are common in literature, covering various aspects (see for example [7,9]). However, surveys specifically focusing on AI in software testing are rare, mainly found in web articles and blogs. This scarcity is due to the novelty of AI's application in this field, making it less explored in survey research. Furthermore, there are currently no industry investigations comprehensively understanding AI utilization in GUI-based software testing.

The aim of the Systematic Literature Review (SLR) paper written by Trodova et al. [20] is similar to our but the empirical instrument chosen is different (SLR instead of survey). Their goal is to highlight AI's role in software test automation by categorizing AI techniques and associating them with relevant testing tasks. Analyzing 34 primary studies on AI implementation in software testing, they identified nine testing activities (e.g., test case generation, test repair) improved by AI techniques, primarily from machine learning and computer vision fields. These enhancements include increased test case reusability, reduced manual effort, expanded coverage, and improved fault detection. The review also identified publicly available AI-enhanced testing tools (e.g., Testilizer, Sikuli), summarizing their features succinctly.

The paper by Lima et al. [12] offers a succinct overview of the current landscape of software testing, focusing on the integration of ML and AI algorithms. It assesses the advancements in AI and ML methods for software testing over the past three years, drawing from databases like Scopus Elsevier, Web of Science, and Google Scholar. The algorithms are categorized in white-box, grey-box, and black-box testing, and their application areas are explored. The authors conclude that black-box testing stands out as the predominant method in software testing when AI is involved. Moreover, across black-box testing, all three ML methods-supervised, unsupervised, and reinforcement learning-are frequently employed. Notably, techniques such as clustering, Artificial Neural Networks, and Genetic Algorithms find widespread application in tasks like fuzzing and regression testing.

6 Conclusion and Future Work

This paper reports the results of a survey conducted with practitioners who are experts in GUI-based testing, to collect their opinions and analyze their work practices involving AI-based tools and techniques. The results indicate that GUI-based testers tend to use AI-based mechanisms in a widespread yet superficial manner. Practitioners commonly employ AI techniques in a technology-agnostic way, treating commercial tools as black boxes, thus hindering their ability to comprehend and fine-tune the technical intricacies effectively. To move towards effective and extensive use of AI in GUI-based software testing, respondents indicated that research effort should be mainly devoted to: *i.* open-sourcing and documenting tools to aid practitioners in understanding their inner behavior; *ii.* developing guidelines for the efficient creation of inputs for GUI-based testing using LLMs; *iii.* creating training datasets and defining guidelines to train AI tools for GUI-based testing.

In the future, we plan to conduct an extension of the survey to involve both tool developers and researchers, in addition to GUI-based testing practitioners. Moreover, we also intend to conduct interviews with professional testers to better understand why certain AI techniques are used in conjunction with various GUI-based testing techniques, as not all pairs present in Table 2 are fully clear to us. Finally, we also plan to conduct comparative research on AI technologies applied to different activities of GUI-based software testing.

References

1. Amalfitano, D., Faralli, S., Hauck, J.C.R., Matalonga, S., Distante, D.: Artificial intelligence applied to software testing: a tertiary study. ACM Comput. Surv. **56**(3) (2023). https://doi.org/10.1145/3616372
2. Ardito, L., Coppola, R., Torchiano, M., Alégroth, E.: Towards automated translation between generations of GUI-based tests for mobile devices. In: Companion Proceedings for the ISSTA/ECOOP 2018 Workshops, pp. 46–53 (2018)
3. Bertolino, A.: Software testing research: achievements, challenges, dreams. In: Future of Software Engineering (FOSE 2007), pp. 85–103 (2007). https://doi.org/10.1109/FOSE.2007.25
4. Cerioli, M., Leotta, M., Ricca, F.: What 5 million job advertisements tell us about testing: a preliminary empirical investigation. In: Proceedings of the 35th Annual ACM Symposium on Applied Computing, SAC 2020, pp. 1586–1594 (2020). https://doi.org/10.1145/3341105.3373961

5. Coppola, R., Alégroth, E.: A taxonomy of metrics for GUI-based testing research: a systematic literature review. Inf. Softw. Technol. **152**, 107062 (2022). https://doi.org/10.1016/j.infsof.2022.107062
6. Feldt, R., Kang, S., Yoon, J., Yoo, S.: Towards autonomous testing agents via conversational large language models. In: 2023 38th IEEE/ACM International Conference on Automated Software Engineering (ASE), pp. 1688–1693. IEEE (2023)
7. Garousi, V., Zhi, J.: A survey of software testing practices in Canada. J. Syst. Softw. **86**(5), 1354–1376 (2013)
8. Kitchenham, B.A., Pfleeger, S.L.: Personal opinion surveys. In: Shull, F., Singer, J., Sjøberg, D.I.K. (eds.) Guide to Advanced Empirical Software Engineering, pp. 63–92. Springer, London (2008). https://doi.org/10.1007/978-1-84800-044-5_3
9. Lee, J., Kang, S., Lee, D.: Survey on software testing practices. Softw. IET **6**, 275–282 (2012). https://doi.org/10.1049/iet-sen.2011.0066
10. Leotta, M., García, B., Ricca, F., Whitehead, J.: Challenges of end-to-end testing with selenium webdriver and how to face them: a survey. In: 2023 IEEE Conference on Software Testing, Verification and Validation (ICST), pp. 339–350 (2023). https://doi.org/10.1109/ICST57152.2023.00039
11. Lethbridge, T.C.: A survey of the relevance of computer science and software engineering education. In: Proceedings of the 11th Conference on Software Engineering Education and Training, CSEET 1998, pp. 56–66. IEEE (1998). https://doi.org/10.1109/CSEE.1998.658300
12. Lima, R., da Cruz, A.M.R., Ribeiro, J.: Artificial intelligence applied to software testing: a literature review. In: 2020 15th Iberian Conference on Information Systems and Technologies (CISTI), pp. 1–6 (2020)
13. Linares-Vásquez, M., Moran, K., Poshyvanyk, D.: Continuous, evolutionary and large-scale: a new perspective for automated mobile app testing. In: 2017 IEEE International Conference on Software Maintenance and Evolution (ICSME), pp. 399–410. IEEE (2017)
14. Nass, M., Alégroth, E., Feldt, R.: Why many challenges with GUI test automation (will) remain. Inf. Softw. Technol. **138**, 106625 (2021). https://doi.org/10.1016/j.infsof.2021.106625
15. Ricca, F., Marchetto, A., Stocco, A.: A retrospective analysis of grey literature for AI-supported test automation. In: Fernandes, J.M., Travassos, G.H., Lenarduzzi, V., Li, X. (eds.) QUATIC 2023. CCIS, vol. 1871, pp. 90–105. Springer, Cham (2023). https://doi.org/10.1007/978-3-031-43703-8_7
16. Ricca, F., Marchetto, A., Stocco, A.: AI-based test automation: a grey literature analysis. In: 2021 IEEE International Conference on Software Testing, Verification and Validation Workshops (ICSTW), pp. 263–270 (2021). https://doi.org/10.1109/ICSTW52544.2021.00051
17. Russell, S., Norvig, P.: Artificial Intelligence: A Modern Approach, 3rd edn. Prentice Hall Press (2009)
18. Solingen, R., Basili, V., Caldiera, G., Rombach, D.: Goal Question Metric (GQM) Approach (2002). https://doi.org/10.1002/0471028959.sof142
19. Torchiano, M., Tiso, A., Ricca, F., Reggio, G.: Maturity of software modelling and model driven engineering: a survey in the Italian industry, vol. 2012, pp. 91 –100 (2012). https://doi.org/10.1049/ic.2012.0012
20. Trudova, A., Dolezel, M., Buchalcevova, A.: Artificial intelligence in software test automation: a systematic literature review. In: Proceedings of the 15th International Conference on Evaluation of Novel Approaches to Software Engineering, ENASE, vol. 1, pp. 181–192. INSTICC, SciTePress (2020). https://doi.org/10.5220/0009417801810192

A Preliminary Interview Study on Developers' Perceptions of Code Smell Detection in Industry

Felipe Ribeiro[1(✉)], Eduardo Fernandes[2], and Eduardo Figueiredo[1]

[1] Federal University of Minas Gerais, Belo Horizonte, Brazil
felipelrib@ufmg.br, figueiredo@dcc.ufmg.br
[2] University of Southern Denmark, Odense, Denmark
edmf@mmmi.sdu.dk

Abstract. This paper presents a preliminary interview study aimed to understand i) how practitioners perceive code smells and ii) whether/why developers use code smell detection tools. We carefully designed an structured interview protocol composed of six major questions. We interviewed seven developers, recruited by convenience, who work for major companies worldwide on software maintenance and evolution. We followed strict guidelines for thematic synthesis to analyze the interview texts. The perception of interviewees on code smells is in line with the traditional definition, even when developers lack academic formation. All interviewees were concerned with adding code smells while they produce code, although a half of them feel that their pairs do not share these concerns. Most interviewees use detection tools, but costs with tool setup and company culture may prevent developers from using them.

Keywords: Code smell detection · Software tool · Interview study

1 Introduction

This paper introduces a preliminary interview study on code smell detection in industry. We rely on a six-question interview protocol to ask developers about i) how they perceive code smells, ii) how concerned developers are about adding code smells while they produce source code, and iii) whether/why they use (or do not use) code smell detection tools. We recruited seven developers who work for major companies. We interviewed each developer in isolation, for commodity and to avoid biases, via Telegram Messenger. We performed a qualitative analysis on the interview texts based on thematic synthesis guidelines [1].

Previous work [4,5,7] discusses that developers may be reluctant or too busy to use automated software development tools. This is particularly true in the case of the many tools available [2] that change the internal code structure. For instance, the use of refactoring tools has been neglected by developers [4,7] because developers are afraid that the tools will affect the software functionalities

A. Bertolino et al. (Eds.): QUATIC 2024, CCIS 2178, pp. 344–352, 2024.
https://doi.org/10.1007/978-3-031-70245-7_24

and introduce bugs. In our study, we are specifically interested in understanding why our target developers do not use code smell detection tools.

The research questions are as follows: **RQ1:** *How do developers define code smells?* – Previous work [6,8,9] investigated whether developer's perception on code smells contrasts with the academic wisdom. Unfortunately, the most recent related research study [8] was conducted in 2016, so that the perceptions may not reflect the recent generation of developers. **RQ2:** *Are developers concerned about adding code smells to the source code they produce?* **RQ3:** *Do developers use tools to detect code smells on the source code they produce, consume, or maintain?* We assess the extent to which the recent generation of developers embraces code smell detection tool adoption. Our study artifacts are available online[1].

2 Study Design

The interview questions and follow-up questions are available in our website. We first approached interviewees with the main questions and, depending on their answers, we asked for clarifications or made follow-up questions as needed to deeply explore the subject and proper answer our research questions. For reference, the two first questions aim to collect background information about the interviewees. Likewise, the other four questions, identified as **C1** to **C4**, are related to the goal of our study and its research questions.

We designed core interview questions to address each of the research questions of our study. **C1** (*What do you understand as being a code smell?*) directly asks interviewees about their understanding of code smells, which means that **C1** and its follow-up questions are meant to address RQ1. Both **C2** (*Are you concerned about adding code smells to the source code you produce?*) and **C3** (*Do you believe that your teammates share the same concern?*) ask interviewees about their concerns (or concerns of their teammates) about adding code smells in the source code. Therefore, these interview questions, and their follow-up questions, aim at answering RQ2. Finally, **C4** (*Do you use tools to detect code smells on the code you produce, consume or maintain?*) is about code smell detection tools and, therefore, it is meant to provide answers to RQ3.

All interviewees are from Brazil; most of them work internationally. We selected the interviewees with four to eight years of experience in software development because our goal is to investigate the perception of a new generation of developers since the main related work is about ten years old [6,8,9].

3 Results on Perceptions About Code Smells (RQ1)

Figure 1 depicts our results for the thematic synthesis procedures applied to the tabulated answers on the interviewees understanding of code smells (**C1**). The root node of the tree corresponds to the major theme. All leaves from the trees

[1] https://github.com/felipelrib/preliminary-study-code-smells-in-industry.

corresponds to codes found during the code extraction step, being represented as nodes with a solid border (*concrete codes*), with exception to the root node. Some of the codes were grouped into themes present in the second and third levels, being represented as nodes with dashed borders (*abstract codes*). All leaf nodes have a number annotated to it. The number corresponds to the frequency of the content of the node in the answers, i.e., the amount of times the code was extracted from different answers for the same question.

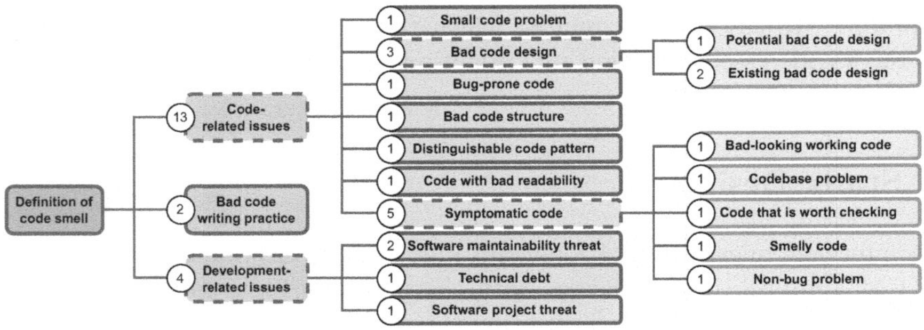

Fig. 1. Perceptions about Code Smells

The first intermediate level includes three elements: *Code-related issues*; *Bad code writing practice*; and the theme *Development-related issues*. The theme *Code-related issues* groups the nodes where the idea is related to the source code of the system. The code *Bad code writing practice* relates code smells to a bad practice from developers, associating the process to the results. The theme *Development-related issues* groups codes where the code smell is seen as an issue to the software development process.

The second intermediate level includes eight codes and two minor themes as follows: *Small code problem*; *Bad code design*; *Bug-prone code*; *Bad code structure*; *Distinguishable code pattern*; *Code with bad readability*; *Symptomatic code*; *Software maintainability threat*; *Technical debt*; and *Software project threat*. The theme *Symptomatic code* is worth noting since it is composed by some vague codes that, when grouped, mean the source code appears to have a problem in the way it was wrote – even if it works as intended. The following quote is an example of answer that specifically relates to this code: "Code smell is [...] not a bug or error – the code works, it is just possibly badly designed" (Interviewee I7). The third level contains the remaining seven codes.

Some of our results stand out as follows. Regarding the code smell definition, we found it curious that developers define code smells in terms of aspects that may not be obvious. For instance, there is this assumption in industry that smelly code can lead to bugs. If confirmed by empirical research, this can support the point of view of Interviewee I6 from which we extracted the code *Bug-prone code*: "Parts of some code [...] that potentially can bring some future bug".

Another code that is worth further discussion is the *Technical debt*, implying a need for refactoring at some point during the life cycle of a software system. It was interesting to get this point of view from at least one of the interviewees because it somehow supports the idea that fixing code smells is relevant to some extent. In the end, we noticed that all answers are in line with the traditional definition of code smells [3], even when some interviewees lacked higher education. This could lead to the perception that the intuition behind code smells might be learned by practice, as developers with some experience can better understand the practical effects of dealing with code smells.

4 Results on Concerns About Adding Code Smells (RQ2)

The interview questions that addresses RQ2 were **C2** and **C3**. For **C2**, all seven interviewees claimed that they are concerned with adding code smells to their source code. On the other hand, **C3** answers were balanced between "Yes," "No," and a half-term "Not all", meaning that some interviewees understand that some of their colleagues share the same concern about code smells as them when coding, but others do not. The table with summarized answers is available in our website. All interviewees answered "Yes" for question **C2**, and there were three "Yes," two "No," and two "Not all" for question **C3**. The answer "Not all" was not literal in the answers from interviewees **I3** and **I6**, but was summarized in this way for a better overview in the table.

Figure 2 is a tree of themes on the reasons the interviewees mentioned not to add a code smell in their source codes. The major theme is represented by the root node, *Reasons not to add code smells*, linked with some ideas extracted in form of codes and themes from the answers of interviewees to the question **C2**.

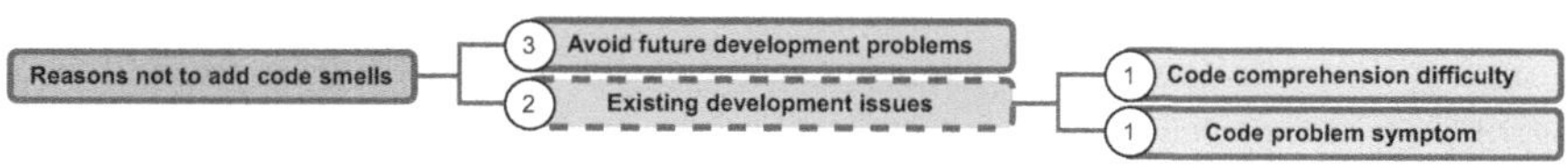

Fig. 2. Reasons Not to Add Code Smells

The first intermediate level corresponds to the code *Avoid future development problems*, illustrated by the quote "Adding [code smells] can potentially make my life harder in the future" (Interviewee I6) and the theme *Existing development issues*. The theme *Existing development issues* groups codes that refer to the issues that are raised during the development when code smells are present.

The second intermediate level has two codes, with emphasis on *Code problem symptom*. As the interviewee explained, the presence of code smells is a symptom of bigger problems in the source code, but leaving the "problems" as something vague. This is illustrated by the following quote: "Code smells exist and are in fact a strong sign of something funky (sic) going on" (Interviewee I7).

Figure 3 is a tree of themes on if the interviewees believe their teammates share the same concerns as them about code smells. The main theme is represented with the root node *Do you believe that your teammates share the same concern? Why?*, being a "yes or no" question. Through this question, interviewees were expected to discuss their points of view on the topic.

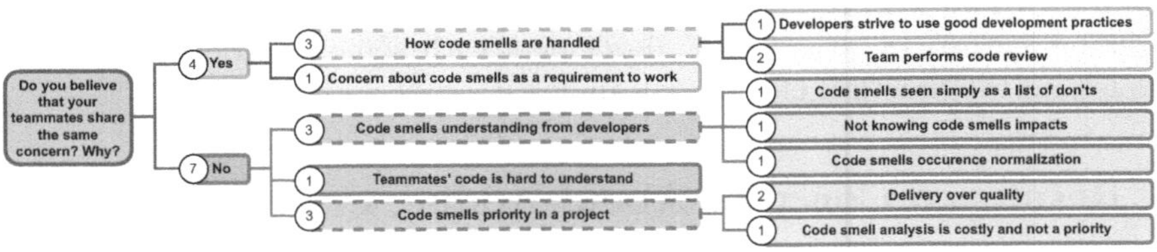

Fig. 3. Why Developers Believe Their Teammates (Do Not) Share Their Concerns

The first intermediate level is composed of the possible answers *Yes* and *No*. Their frequencies follow the previous definition, being the sum of their children frequencies, and does not represent the amount of positive or negative answers. Since these nodes were extracted as part of the answer itself, they are not counted as codes by themselves. Additionally, for both Figs. 3 and 4, the children of the themes from this level is composed only by codes that ratify the theme and where the interviewees gave that initial answer, i.e., if a interviewee answered "No," but provided context that might be encoded into the "Yes" theme, this context was not considered for the taxonomy.

The second intermediate level, for the *Yes* answers, has the theme *How code smells are handled* and the code *Concern about code smells as a requirement to work*. These two elements present reasons why the interviewees believe their teammates are concerned about code smells. Regarding *No*, we have two themes and one code as follows. The theme *Code smells understanding from developers* groups some codes explaining that their teammates might not have enough knowledge about code smells and their impacts, or they simply consider their presence as something normal. The code *Teammates' code is hard to understand* means that the interviewee considers that code with low understandability is a result of a team that does not care about code smells. Finally, the theme *Code smells priority in a project* groups codes reporting that the teammates and the project management are more focused in delivering the functional requirements than in the overall project quality.

The third intermediate level consists of two codes for the *Yes* answers and five codes for the *No* answers. It is worth noting the code *Team performs code review* as a reason why some interviewees believe their teammates are concerned about code smells as they use this process, among other reasons, to analyze the presence of code smells and refactor the code as needed. This is illustrated by the following quote: "We also review each other's code, so 'code smell' normally doesn't make it to the final product" (Interviewee I4). Our perception is that a good quality code review is capable of detecting and resolving code smells.

The interviewees seemed concerned about avoiding inserting code smells in source code, even reassuring some reasons why this addition would be an issue. Some interviewees reported that some of their colleagues appeared to have the same concerns. This claim is sustained by the perception that colleagues would apply good development practices and review code to achieve a better code quality. Others did not seem to share the same concerns, being justified by: i) their apparent lack of understanding of code smells and their impacts; ii) the source code produced by their colleagues being hard to understand; or iii) the lack of prioritization that code smells had in the scope of the project and its tasks.

The code *Delivery over quality*, for instance, refers to the interviewees describing that developers seem to be more focused on the requirements they are asked to implement rather than on the code quality. This may not mean necessarily that the teammates do not have the knowledge on code smells, but they are pressured to put this concern aside to deliver the clients' requirements faster. Meanwhile, the code *Not knowing code smells impacts* presents an idea that the lack of knowledge about code smells from teammates is latent due to this exact behavior, since the delivery is prioritized over this concern, possibly ignoring the future problems that could happen. This is illustrated by the following quote: "Maybe they don't see the direct impact that could cause, and they care more about delivering" (Interviewee I6).

5 Results on the Use of Detection Tools (RQ3)

For question **C4**, two out of the seven interviewees do not use detection tools in their projects, while five of them use. Out of those five, **I7** emphasized that they use tools in their company project, but they do not use any tools in personal projects, giving reasons why not, so we have attributed their answer as "Yes/No". The table with summarized answers is available in our website.

The tools the interviewees said they use in their projects and at which development stages are also available in the website. Interviewee **I7** informed that the tool their team use to detect code smells is developed by their company and only available there, not being publicly available. They also informed that their team uses another public library to detect code smells and detect vulnerabilities while building their projects, but they did not remember the name at the time, thus we attributed their answer as "Unknown". We see that, from all interviewees that said they use detection tools in their projects, all of them use the tools in their produced code, during the development stage.

Figure 4 is a tree of themes on if the interviewees use code smell detection tools and at which development stages, or else why they do not use tools. The main theme is represented with the root node *Do you use tools to detect code smells on the code you produce, consume or maintain? If yes: when? If not: why?*, being a "yes or no" question. Through this question, the interviewees were expected to discuss their points of view on the topic.

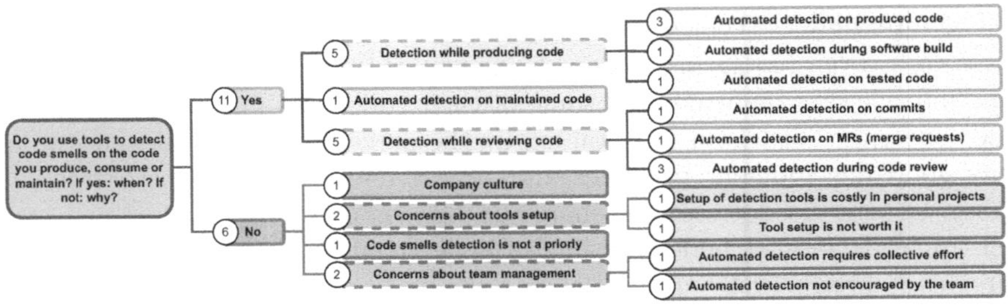

Fig. 4. Use of tools to detect code smells on produced, consumed or maintained code

The first intermediate level has the possible answers *Yes* and *No*. The second intermediate level has the theme *Detection while producing code*; the code *Automated detection on maintained code*; and the theme *Detection while reviewing code*. These three, children of *Yes*, relate the interviewees answers to the stage of the code subject to the tools detection. From the *No* answer, we have the code *Company culture*; the theme *Concerns about tools setup*; the code *Code smells detection is not a priority*; and the theme *Concerns about team management*. These four nodes were extracted from the interviewees' answers to why they do not use code smell detection tools in their projects. The third intermediate level consists of six codes for the *Yes* answers and four codes for the *No* answers.

We observed that the usage of detection tools on produced code can be done in different stages of development while producing the code, as the interviewees reported using tools during the software build or while adding automated tests to the new code. It is very common for the interviewees to use tools for newly produced code that is being reviewed by their peers, be it automatically after pushing code commits or during code reviews on open merge requests (MRs) – also called pull requests (PRs) depending on the GIT tool used. This is illustrated by the following quote: "I do run it again while reviewing code done by teammates to make sure this practice is being followed" (Interviewee I2).

Additionally, from the interviewees that do not use code smell detection tools, we could see scenarios where the usage of tools was not encouraged by the team management due to lack of prioritization in face of other functional and cross-functional requirements. Moreover, specifically for personal projects, some interviewees mentioned the fact that the setup of these tools would be too costly given the size of the projects. Another interviewee mentioned laziness as a factor to prevent them to setup tools in personal projects, justifying that the potential problems would not worth the cost of configuring a tool. This is shown in the following quote: "In personal projects it would be mostly a matter of laziness – there's no easier setup than no setup at all, and it is easy to justify to myself that the potential problems aren't worth the hassle" (Interviewee I7).

None of the interviewees answered that they use detection tools on consumed code, may it be a library or imported code from other projects. **I2** said that they never thought about using tools on this kind of code: "I never thought about doing it in code I consume". **I1** mentioned that they never maintain consumed code, so they would never use tools on it: "I do not run any linting or any testing whatsoever for code I consume (third party, open source projects, etc.) as part of a personal policy of not maintaining code that does not belong to me".

6 Threats to Validity

Construct Validity: To have an interview protocol that is well-structured and sufficient to address our RQs, we decided to define the interview protocol in pairs. One of the authors proposed the first version and we had meetings to iteratively refine the questions and add new questions. We recruited the interviewees based on convenience (industry colleagues) and arbitrarily (as they are experienced, work for different development teams and are trustworthy). We had meetings to set up the way how we approach the developers during the interview conduction.

Internal Validity: We conducted the interviews via Telegram for convenience. This may prevent interviewees from engaging in the interviews, thereby resulting in information loss. In contrast to interviewing people by email, the tool allowed to closely interact with the interviewees and ask questions in a more efficient and reactive way. We tried to keep interviewees engaged with the interview by asking additional/follow-up questions, especially to make sure they understand the questions. The use of email could prevent us from clarifying things to interviewees so they answer questions properly.

Conclusion Validity: Inappropriate extraction and analysis of interview data may lead to information loss and harm the study conclusions. To guide us on performing the textual data analysis, we followed guidelines for thematic synthesis [1]. All procedures were performed in a pair. Three sessions to extract the codes (open coding). Two sessions to sort the codes (axial coding) and build the taxonomies, also based on literature guidelines [1].

Acknowledgements. CAPES, CNPq and FAPEMIG funded this work.

References

1. Cruzes, D., Dyba, T.: Recommended steps for thematic synthesis in software engineering. In: 5th ESEM, pp. 275–284 (2011)
2. Fernandes, E., Oliveira, J., Vale, G., Paiva, T., Figueiredo, E.: A review-based comparative study of bad smell detection tools. In: 20th EASE, pp. 18:1–18:12 (2016)
3. Fowler, M.: Refactoring, 2nd edn. Addison-Wesley Professional (2018)
4. Kim, M., Zimmermann, T., Nagappan, N.: An empirical study of refactoring. IEEE Trans. Softw. Eng. **40**(7), 633–649 (2014)
5. Lethbridge, T., Sim, S., Singer, J.: Studying software engineers. Empir. Softw. Eng. **10**, 311–341 (2005)

6. Palomba, F., Bavota, G., Di Penta, M., Oliveto, R., De Lucia, A.: Do they really smell bad? In: 30th ICSME, pp. 101–110 (2014)
7. Sharma, T., Suryanarayana, G., Samarthyam, G.: Challenges to and solutions for refactoring adoption. IEEE Softw. **32**(6), 44–51 (2015)
8. Taibi, D., Janes, A., Lenarduzzi, V.: How developers perceive smells in source code. Inf. Softw. Technol. **92**, 223–235 (2017)
9. Yamashita, A., Moonen, L.: Do developers care about code smells? In: 20th WCRE, pp. 242–251 (2013)

On Security and Privacy

A Rapid Review on Graph-Based Learning Vulnerability Detection

Rosmaël Zidane Lekeufack Foulefack(✉) and Alessandro Marchetto

University of Trento, Trento, Italy
{rz.lekeufack,alessandro.marchetto}@unitn.it

Abstract. Security testing aims at identifying software vulnerabilities that can be exploited by malicious actors. Software vulnerability detection (SVD), in particular, studies techniques to identify source code weaknesses and bugs that could lead to vulnerabilities. Automated SVD has made significant progress thanks to artificial intelligence tools, including large language models and deep learning. Most of the existing SVD techniques extract a token-based vector representation from the source code under analysis, and then pass it to a learning algorithm inspired by the ones used for natural language processing. The code vulnerability detection is hence considered as a binary classification task: the learned model is used to predict whether new code snippets are vulnerable or not. A recent trend consists in extracting graph-based structures from the source code, and then pass them to a graph-based learning algorithm. The graph-based code representation is expected to be an enabler to search for vulnerabilities by considering syntactic, semantic, and structural information of the source code.

This paper reports on a rapid review conducted to study the literature about code graph-based learning SVD, with the goal of capturing evidence that can be transferred to practitioners. Our analysis reveals that most of the presented graph-based learning SVD techniques: (i) use combinations of graphs extracted from the source code by (almost) employing the same tool; (ii) use frequently Graph Neural Networks (GNN) and Gated Graph Sequence Neural Networks (GGNN); (iii) work at the function level, and only rarely at the statement level. Furthermore, we also noticed that: (iv) only a limited number of tools that support such techniques are available, and (v) several real-world datasets exist and are largely used, however, they are unbalanced, labeled only at the function level, and, in most cases, contain C/C++ source code, thus hampering their adoption with other programming languages.

Keywords: Software vulnerability detection · Deep Learning · Graph-Based model · Source code · Rapid Review

1 Introduction

Software bugs and weaknesses can expose software systems to vulnerabilities that can be potentially exploited by malicious actors with fraudulent intentions.

A. Bertolino et al. (Eds.): QUATIC 2024, CCIS 2178, pp. 355–372, 2024.
https://doi.org/10.1007/978-3-031-70245-7_25

Cyber-attacks towards connected systems are growing and can cause dramatic damage to businesses and persons. Recent statistics[1] show an increased adoption of vulnerability exploitation as an initial access method for attacks that aim at penetrating and compromising a system. Security testing aims at studying methods for identifying software vulnerabilities, thus reducing the possible attack points of software systems. Software vulnerability detection (SVD), in particular, is a critical concern in the security testing field that aims at developing tools for identifying vulnerabilities and code weaknesses, such as the ones described by the MITRE's Common Weakness enumeration system[2].

Traditional static SVD techniques do not require the code execution and: (a) adopt source code parsing and rules to search in source code for patterns that are known to be vulnerable [8]; or (b) apply control and data-flow analysis, e.g., taint analysis [6]. These techniques are effective in detecting vulnerabilities but they produce a large number of false-positive alarms that need to be manually checked by developers. Recently, automated SVD has made significant progresses with the integration of artificial intelligence tools, including Large Language Models (LLMs) and Deep Learning (DL). Several new SVD techniques have been proposed to adopt learning algorithms for vulnerability detection in source code [5]. These techniques apply learning algorithms to a dataset of labeled code snippets to build a model. The model is then used to predict whether new code snippets are vulnerable or not. Most of existing SVD techniques, known as *sequence-based learning techniques*, consider the source code under analysis as text: they extract a token-based representation of the code snippet under analysis (a token can be a code instruction or part of it), and then adopt a learning algorithm inspired to the ones used for natural language processing. These techniques show promising results, in particular when they are applied to identifying vulnerable code snippets (e.g., functions or slices), while they are less precise in the identification of which statements inside the vulnerable snippets are related to the vulnerability. Furthermore, empirical experiences [2,10] showed that the adoption of these SVD techniques in real scenarios is hampered by the spurious information contained in the models learned during the training phase.

A recent trend to overcome such issues consists of representing the source code under analysis through graph structures (e.g., control-flow graphs, data-flow graphs), which are then tokenized and passed to an adequate learning algorithm, in most of cases a graph-based learning algorithm. These techniques are known as *graph-based learning techniques*. The use of such graph structures allows developers to consider semantic, syntactic and structural information of the code when searching for vulnerabilities [13]. Several types of graphs (e.g., Abstract Syntax Tree (AST), Control Flow Graph (CFG)), representations, and learning algorithms (e.g., Graph Neural Networks (GNN), Gated Graph Sequence Neural Networks (GGNN)) have been investigated in the literature.

In this paper, we document a Rapid Review (RR) conducted to study the recent literature on automated graph-based learning SVD by adopting the point

[1] https://www.paloaltonetworks.com/blog/2024/02/unit-42-incident-response-report/.

[2] https://cwe.mitre.org.

of view of developers who have to apply a graph-based SVD technique in a new project. We aim to investigate: (i) the different graph structures used for representing the source code; (ii) the used learning algorithms; (iii) the datasets used to train such learning algorithms; and (iv) the available supporting tools.

Rapid Reviews (RRs) [4] are a recent type of evidence-based review studies for easily and quickly transferring knowledge to practitioners, through evidence. RRs adopt a systematic and rigorous review process, such as the one of the conventional Systematic Literature Reviews (SLRs), but they omit and simplify some steps. The goal of a RR, in fact, consists in identifying early the best evidence from the literature in a specific domain, thus increasing the knowledge that practitioners can use to make decisions in an engineering process. RRs typically take into account practical needs, e.g., the need of delivering evidence quickly and promptly, with low costs, and reporting the evidence in a clear and simple way without formal synthesis. We opted for a RR because it better fits our needs and project schedule with respect to a conventional SLR. In fact, we do not aim at fully capturing and analyzing the state-of-the-art in the specific domain (as done by SLRs), rather we aim at capturing and reporting to developers relevant evidence.

Our analysis reveals that most of the presented graph-based learning SVD techniques: (i) use combinations of graph-based representations extracted from the source code by employing almost the same tool; (ii) use frequently two types of graph-learning architectures: Graph Neural Networks (GNN) and Gated Graph Sequence Neural Networks (GGNN); and (iii) work at the function level, i.e., they can identify vulnerable functions or code snippets but they cannot clearly identify the vulnerable statements that cause the vulnerability. Furthermore, we also found that: (iv) only a limited number of tools supporting the proposed techniques are available; and (v) several real-world datasets exist to train such techniques but they are unbalanced, labeled at the function level only, and, in most cases, based on C/C++ source code, thus hampering their adoption in projects using other programming languages.

2 Related Works

2.1 Background: Sequence and Graph-Based SVD

A cutting-edge technique for deep-learning SVD is based on two main approaches that differ one from another for the source code representation: *sequence-based models* and *graph-based models*. Sequence-based models tackle vulnerability detection by treating source code as sequences of tokens. Leveraging architectures such as Recurrent Neural Networks (RNNs), Long Short-Term Memory (LSTM) networks, and transformers, these models analyze the sequential nature of code, capturing syntax and semantic nuances [13]. Graph-based models for vulnerability detection leverage the power of both graph theory and deep learning techniques to analyse the code structure deeply. They represent source code as graphs by extracting a graph representation such as the Abstract Syntax Tree (AST), the Control Flow Graph (CFG), the Program Dependency Graph

(PDG), or the Code Property Graph (CPG), where nodes represent programming elements such as functions, variables, or statements, and edges represent relationships between them, such as control flow or data dependencies [12]. Generally, graphs are composed of nodes and edges, that can have sets of features and can be directed/ undirected, weighted/ unweighted. DL architectures such as Graph Neural Networks (GNN), Gated Graph Sequence Neural Networks (GGNN), Graph Convolutional Networks (GCN), and Bidirectional Graph Neural Networks (BGNN), are then applied to these graph representations to learn characteristics and patterns and detect vulnerabilities in the code. Several types of architectures exist and they are mainly characterized according to how they propagate and aggregate information in the network, thus capturing both features and topological information. Figure 1 summarizes the generic process of accessing vulnerabilities from source code using a graph-based model. The figure illustrates a comprehensive method for extracting graph structure data, including CFG and PDG, from the source code to train a GNN model. This extraction process begins with parsing the source code using specialized tools like Joern or Java-Parser. Subsequently, vectorization occurs, which entails obtaining the vector representation of the extracted features. This step involves employing embedding techniques such as Word2vec, Doc2vec, and others to transform the extracted data into a vectorized form, while maintaining their relationships to feed the model.

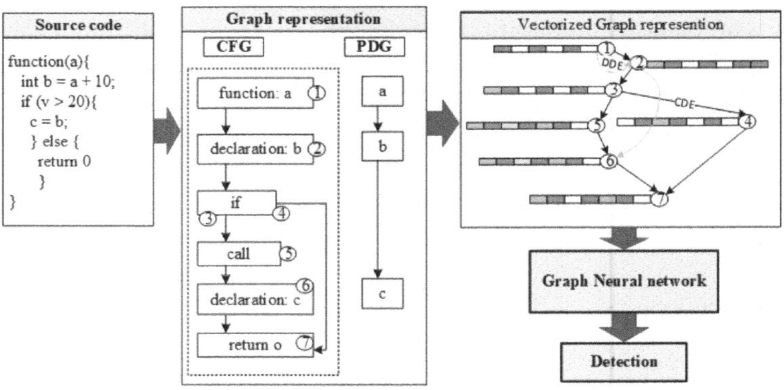

Fig. 1. An illustration of code vulnerability detection using a GNN model. The process involves extracting CFG and PDG from the source code as features. The numbers $1, 2, \ldots, 7$ represent node IDs with the vectors of features extracted from the corresponding codes. CDE (Control Dependency Edge) and DDE (Data Dependency Edge) represent connections between CFG and PDG nodes.

2.2 Secondary Studies

A large effort has been spent by the community in the last years to study and evaluate the adoption of LLMs, DL, and Machine Learning (ML) methods for vulnerability detection in source code. Only to cite a few works, for instance,

VulDeePecker [9] was one of the pioneer works that applies learning algorithms to detect vulnerabilities in code gadgets (i.e., semantically related code statements). Such code gadgets are encoded by using fixed-length vectors of symbols, and a BLSTM neural network is then used to learn a classification model. Devign [17] was one of the first works to represent code snippets with a graph structure (e.g., AST), then passed to a GNN for graph-level classification. LineVul [7] uses a transformers architecture for detecting vulnerable functions and statements within a code snippet.

Several works have surveyed the state-of-the-art in the field. For instance, [1] and [11] provide a comprehensive review of learning-based SVD studies, identify how the proposed techniques leverage the state-of-the-art of neural methods for learning and understanding code structure and semantics, and identify those methods that perform better. [13] investigates and compares how sequence and graph-based DL methods are applied to vulnerability detection in source code. They show that sequence-based methods can also capture quite rich code semantic features, while graph-based methods can represent complex code structural information. Also [14] investigates how existing SVD techniques use neural methods to identify vulnerable code, i.e., how the source code is encoded to be fed into learning algorithms, and both type and configurations of the adopted neural algorithm. [15] empirically compared several code representations and DL-based SVD techniques. Empirical experiences, however, show contrasting results [2,5,10].

These works aim to comprehensively review the literature concerning learning-based SVD, identifying existing trends, and potential open issues that could drive future research directions. Despite these works being related to our RR, they did not address our research goal. Similarly to these works, in fact, we reviewed the state-of-the-art in the field of learning-based SVD techniques, but differently from these works we: (i) focused on graph-based learning techniques; (ii) did not conduct our survey by adopting a research-oriented point of view, as well as done instead by such works; but rather adopting the point of view of practitioners. Existing surveys investigate all types of learning procedures for source code analysis, which leads them to be less precise on graph-based architecture. Additionally, they do not provide related information on the availability of ready-to-use (pre-trained) models and tools, which potentially limits their funding to researchers only, leaving developers looking to apply such detection techniques without clear direction. To the best of our knowledge, this is the first paper that presents a RR on the field of graph-based learning SVD techniques and that reports the result by focusing on the collected evidence.

3 Review Description

According to [4], we designed our RR by defining: (i) the research questions (RQs); (ii) the search strategy; (iii) the set of characterization criteria to analyze the literature; and (iv) the threats to validity for our study.

3.1 Research Questions

The following research questions were developed for our **goal** of *studying and gaining knowledge about graph-based learning techniques proposed to detect vulnerabilities in source code.*

- **RQ1** *What are the graph-based learning architectures employed for SVD?* RQ1 seeks to identify which graph-based learning architectures are employed in SVD, i.e., used to classify the code snippets as vulnerable and non-vulnerable. By understanding the different graph-based architectures utilized, we can gain insights into the methods adopted to learn the model then used to classify new code snippets. To answer this question, we collected information about the used graph-based learning architecture, e.g., Graph Neural Networks (GNN), Gated Graph Sequence Neural Networks (GGNN), Graph Convolutional Networks (GCN), Bidirectional Graph Neural Networks (BGNN), Relational Graph Convolution Networks (R-GCN). We are aware that other architectures (e.g., Transformers and Convolutional Neural Networks) can work with code graph representations. However, in this work, we focus on graph-based learning architectures since they are the natural learning algorithms, and the most diffused ones, to work with graph-based source code representations (e.g., AST, CFG). As future work, we will consider other possible learning algorithms.
- **RQ2** *What are the different source code representations used with the graph-based learning SVD?* RQ2 aims to investigate the different source code representations used within existing graph-based learning algorithms. This research question focuses on the identification of different suitable representations adopted in order to capture semantic and structural information of the source code in the dataset. To answer this question, we investigated the type of information considered (e.g., source code only, commits, external knowledge) and the used graph structures, e.g., Abstract Syntax Tree (AST), Enhanced AST (eAST), Control Flow Graph (CFG), Program Dependency Graph (PDG), and Code Property Graph (CPG).
- **RQ3** *What are the embedding techniques used for code vectorization?* RQ3 objective aims at identifying the different techniques employed in embedding code vectors, then passed as input to the learning algorithms. We intend to gain a comprehensive understanding of the most used techniques employed to convert the source code into vector-based representations, then fed into the learning algorithm. RQ3 aims to offer guidance in knowing and choosing appropriate embedding techniques for the code vectorization task. To answer this question, we collected information about the embedding strategies and techniques used in the literature, e.g., Word2vec (a neural network that produces vector representations of words), transformer-based embeddings, and one-hot encodings.
- **RQ4** *Which datasets are commonly used, and what programming languages do they support?* RQ4 aims to identify commonly used datasets and the programming languages they support. The goal is to gain insights into data sources for related applications.

- **RQ5** *What are the available tools that support graph-based learning SVD techniques in source code?* RQ5 aims at identifying the available tools that support the investigated graph-based learning techniques for detecting vulnerabilities in source code and that can be used by developers to apply such techniques.

These RQs are of interest to both practitioners and researchers. In detail, RQ1 is useful to know which learning graph-based architectures can be used for automated SVD. RQ2 and RQ3 are useful to understand how to analyze and represent the source code, and then analyze it with the learning architectures (captured in RQ1). RQ4 and RQ5 are useful to understand whether the graph-based learning techniques can be applied to new projects or if additional development effort is required. Furthermore, as a side effect of our work, the answers to these RQs can help researchers in identifying open issues in the existing literature that can require further investigation.

3.2 Data Acquisition

To acquire the amount of data required for our comprehensive RR, as suggested by [4], this study leveraged a significant and comprehensive data source, namely Scopus. To establish the search criteria, we extracted and combined relevant terms and phrases from our research questions (RQs), including "Vulnerability", "Detection", "Discovery", "Graph Neural Networks", and "Source Code". An automatic search was conducted using such specified keywords. Initially, a total of 78 relevant papers were gathered from any publication date up until February 2024. Only conference and journal papers written in English were considered, while other sources were excluded. Given our specific focus on vulnerability detection in source code using graph-based DL techniques, we manually filtered the initial list to exclude papers that utilized graph neural networks in other domains, e.g., smart contracts and networks. Furthermore, additional papers that solely proposed datasets for training DL models, as well as inaccessible papers, were removed from the list of considered papers. As a result, a final list of 51 items was obtained, forming the basis for our analysis.

3.3 Analysis Criteria

We followed the literature analysis approach described in [4] for a RR, which involved conducting a thematic analysis [3] on each relevant shortlisted article. This process involved carefully examining the papers to identify and explore specific ideas and concepts based on predetermined criteria established for examining our RQs. We considered the following groups of analysis criteria; their expansion and examples are listed in Table 1:

- **Work and Architecture:** this group considers a short description of what the paper does, the goal of the work (e.g., presenting a new technique, an assessment of existing tools, a survey), the learning architecture investigated, and the used classifier;

- **Feature representation:** this group aims to provide pieces of evidence about how the source code is characterized and represented, as well as the code-feature extractor used in the proposed learning technique, leading the proposed automatic SVD technique to capture relevant information;
- **Feature vectorization:** this group highlights the most commonly used and recent vectorization techniques to transform features into understandable formats by proposed models;
- **Dataset details:** this group includes information related to the datasets, the programming language of the data source snippets inside the dataset, and the detection level (i.e., the level in which the vulnerable code is detected, e.g., code snippets, code gadgets/slices, code functions, and code statements).
- **Tool:** this group of criteria collects information about the supporting tools, if any;
- **Empirical performance:** this group includes information related to results achieved in documented experimentation, if any, and about the effectiveness of the SVD techniques in detecting vulnerable source code. For instance, it details the achieved vulnerability detection Accuracy and F1-score. In the case in which more datasets and setup are applied in the reported experiment, we considered the best performance. Our purpose is not to compare results of different experiments that used different datasets and different setup, but rather we aim at capturing only a first overall feeling with respect to the reported experimentation.

We employed a three-step procedure to establish this set of distinct criteria. Firstly, (i) we created a preliminary set and subsequently (ii) applied this set to a sample of papers, gathering feedback in order to refine the proposed criteria. The final step (iii) encompassed the analysis of all papers and the collection of relevant evidence. These criteria were utilized to explore and extract evidence from the available literature, aligning with our research questions. Specifically, the criteria of **work and architecture** and **empirical performance** were employed for investigating **RQ1**, while **RQ2** focused on **feature representation**. Furthermore, **RQ3** involved **feature vectorization**; **dataset details** served as evidence-based for **RQ4**; and finally **tools** was employed for **RQ5**.

3.4 Limitations of the Study

This study is primarily constrained by the following limitations. Firstly, our reliance on a single data source may have restricted the breadth of available literature analyzed. Additionally, the detailed paper characterization was conducted by only one of the authors, which could potentially introduce bias into the report. We are also aware that different criteria could be utilized to analyze the paper, potentially resulting in divergent outcomes and findings. These factors pose a challenge to the validity of our work but are expected for a RR [4].

Table 1. Evaluation criteria for in-depth analysis.

Work and Architecture
Description: a short description of the paper
Goal: the goal of the work, e.g., presentation of a new technique, an experiment, a survey
Learning architecture: learning algorithms architecture used; e.g., GNN, GCN, GCN, BGNN
Classifier: information on the method used to predict the current status as vulnerable or non-vulnerable, e.g., Multi-layer Perceptron classifier (MLP), Softmax layer, CNN layer
Detection level: the granularity to which the SVD technique is applied, e.g., Code snippets, code functions, code slices or gadgets, code statements, their combinations
Feature representation
Type of information: the type of information used, besides the code, e.g., source code only, code commits, commit logs, expert knowledge
Code representation: how the code is represented, e.g., AST, enhanced-AST (eAST), CFG, data dependency graph (DDG), code property graph (CPG), data flow graph (DFG), natural code sequence (NCS), and attributed control flow graph (ACFG)
Feature extractor: tool or technique used to extract the representation from the source code, e.g., Joern, Joern-Php, Tree-sitter, JavaParser, proprietary code parser
Feature vectorization
Embedding: techniques used to encode the feature representation in a form suitable for the learning algorithm, e.g., Word2vec, Doc2vec, Glove, Node2vec, CodeBERT, structure2vec, UniXcoder
Dataset details
Datasets: the dataset used for learning and testing, e.g., Bigvul, REVEAL, CodeXGLUE, Project KB, proprietary dataset
Type of dataset: if the used dataset contains synthetic, real, or both types of source code
Programming language of the dataset: the code programming language considered by the proposed SVD technique, e.g., Java, C, C++, Php, Python
Availability: the link to the available dataset, if any
Granularity dataset information: the granularity of the information available within the dataset that is used in the proposed SVD technique, e.g., code snippets, code functions, code statements
'**Preparation:** the operations conducted on the data before using it, e.g., resampling, under-sampling to better balance the data, and data augmentation operations
Tool
Name of the tool: the name of the tool, if any
Link of the tool: the link to the tool, if any
Pre-trained: availability of the pre-trained or ready-to-use models, if any
Empirical performance
Effectiveness: the performance in terms of Accuracy and F1-score measured to evaluate the effectiveness of the proposed SVD technique and reported in empirical evaluations

4 Results

As recommended by [4], we report evidence-based concepts and notions that emerged from the study. The full set of collected data is available online[3]

(**RQ1**) Table 2 and Table 3 summarize the collected data about relevant criteria for the group **Work and Architecture** and the criterion **Effectiveness**.

- **Evidence 1.1**. By analyzing the collected descriptions and work goals, we clearly see that all the papers except one (a survey) propose a novel technique for automated SVD in source code based on learning architectures. This seems to indicate that the field is still immature and that open-issues persist.
- **Evidence 1.2** Concerning the used learning architectures, we could observe that the most frequently proposed are based on GNN (27%), followed by the GGNN (20%) and GCN (13%). Even if the large majority of the works (90%) consider only a specific architecture, 5 works (10%) investigated different combinations of two or more architectures, in particular, GNN and GCN are the most frequently combined architectures. Despite their diverse architectures as described in Table 2, we could identify four groups [16]: (i) architectures that predominantly rely on recurrent operations to process information sequences, e.g., GNN, BGNN, and GRNN; (ii) architectures that primarily employ convolutional operations to handle spatial data, e.g., GCN, GTCN, and GIN; (iii) architectures that incorporate additional mechanisms, like gated or attention mechanisms, to control or weight the information flow in the network, e.g., GGNN and GAT; and (iv) other hybrid or advanced architectures that combine elements from multiple groups.
- **Evidence 1.3** Most of the proposed methods use a Multi-layer Perceptron classifier (MLP) as a classifier (32.6%), other use Softmax and CNN layers (6% and 2% of works, respectively). Most of such classifiers are hence based on learning methods, but no details were specified about the used classifier for more than half of the works (53%).
- **Evidence 1.4**. In terms of detection level, we noticed that more than half of the proposed techniques (56%) work at function level, while only few techniques (12%) work at statement-level. This indicates that existing techniques cannot precisely identify the bug statements or the code weakness that causes the vulnerability in a code snippet.
- **Evidence 1.5**. In terms of effectiveness, Table 3 summarizes relevant results about Accuracy and F1-score. The performance observed for the SVD techniques is somewhat variable, contingent upon factors such as the dataset utilized, the embedding method employed, and the granularity level of detection. However, some trends can be identified: (i) the proposed techniques seem to perform better with real-world datasets (higher accuracy and F1-score), but the best F1-score is obtained by considering real-world and synthetic data at the same time; (ii) the proposed techniques exhibit better performance at

[3] Full data about papers and classification is available at: https://tinyurl.com/5n7ffpy6.

Table 2. Work and Architecture

Criterion value	Papers
Learning Architecture	
GNN is the fundamental and general class of neural network that can be applied to graph models (based on simple message/information through nodes). Examples: GCN, Graph Attention Network (GAT), Graph Isomorphism Networks (GIN)	12
GGNN which differs from the GNN in the information flow process by incorporating a gated mechanism to enable more sophisticated reasoning and inference over graph-structured data.	9
GCN is a type of GNN that uses convolutional operations to propagate information between nodes in a graph. Non-linear activation functions are used.	6
GAN is a type of GNN that applies attention mechanisms to weight the contributions of neighboring nodes during message passing.	3
BiGGNN architecture which aims to extend the concept of GNN by enabling bidirectional information propagation in the graph.	2
Combination of architectures such as GNN, GCN, GAT, GGNN, GIN	5
Others architectures: Typed Geometric GNN (TGGNN), Flow-Sensitive-GNN graph tensor convolution neural network (GTCN), Gated Recurrent Unit (GRU), and Graph Representation Learning (GRL), GIN	1 each
Classifier	
MLP	16
Softmax layer	4
CNN and convolutional layer	2
VGG11 (convolutional layer)	1
Extract Slice Code and Extract Slice Subgraph	1
Detection Level	
Function	22
Slice	7
Statement	5
Function, Statement	2
Code snippet	1
Function, File	1
Function, Slice	1

code fragments (functions, slices, and snippets), while there is a decrease of the performance at statement-level (11 and 15 point-percentage for Accuracy and F1-score).

Table 3. Effectiveness

Effectiveness			
	Criteria	Accuracy	F1
Data types	real-world	79.7	70.5
	synthetic	68.8	70.2
	combination	65.9	91.8
Detection Level	Statement	69.7	64.4
	Function	81.4	80.1
	other	73.6	78.7
Embedding	Word2vec	86	81.9
	Doc2vec	58.9	97
	combination	89.2	71.8
Data types & Detection Level	real-world & statement	82.6	49
	real-world & function	76.2	65.7
	real-world & *other*	83.7	83
Data types & Detection Level	synthetic & statement	35	95.1
	synthetic & function	92.2	74.9
	synthetic & *other*	50.7	53.2
Data types & Detection Level	*combination* & statement	–	–
	combination & function	69.4	92.1
	combination & *other*	–	91

Table 4. Feature representation: Code representation

Features	CFG	AST	DFG	PDG	CPG	NCS	ACFG
Papers	31	24	11	9	7	2	2

(**RQ2**) Table 4 and Table 5 report the collected data for criteria of the group **Feature representation**.

- **Evidence 2.1**. Almost all the works (93.3%) use only the code as a source for extracting the information then fed to the learning algorithm. Only a few other works (6.1%) use extra sources such as code commits, the hosting environment, and the binary code.
- **Evidence 2.2** We noticed that to capture syntactic, semantic and structural information from the source code, different types of graphs have been adopted, e.g., AST, CFG, CPG, and PDG. We identified a total of 16 graph types used. However, in most of the works (84%) more than one type of graph is used. Table 4 summarizes the occurrence of the most frequent types of graph used in the investigated combinations. We could observe that the most recurrent representations are: CFG (62%), AST (48%), DFG (22%), and PDG (18%). In detail, (i) CFG represents the flow of control and execution within a pro-

Table 5. Feature representation: Feature extractor

Tool name	Supported Programming language	Papers
Joern/Joern-Php (Code analysis)	Php, C/C++, Python	30
LLVM (Low-Level Virtual Machine)	C/C++	2
PhP-Parser (Language parser)	PhP	1
Java-Parser (Language parser)	Java	1
Tree-sitter (Parser generator)	C/C++	1
ANTLR (Parser generator)	Swift, Php	1
Soot (Binary-code analysis)	Java	1
Eclipse CDT/JDT (Source code development)	C/C++, Java	1

Table 6. Feature vectorization: Embeddings

Techniques	Word2vec	CodeBert	Doc2vec	Glove	Others (e.g., BERT, Structure2vec, Unixcoder, MPNET, Node2vec, FasText)	Others (ad-hoc: LSTM, GNN)
Papers	23	4	3	2	6	6

gram, depicting how the different basic blocks of code are executed. (ii) AST representation captures the syntactic structure of source code, representing the hierarchical relationships between language constructs such as statements and expressions. (iii) DFG depicts the flow of data dependencies between program activities or instructions, demonstrating how data values are generated, consumed, or changed. (iv) PDG captures both data and control dependencies between program elements, focusing on program behaviors. Each type of graph focuses on representing specific code features (control and data flow, dependencies). Hence, the use of different representations allows developers to consider several (code) features of the same type.

- **Evidence 2.3** From the analyzed works, we have identified the techniques used to convert raw source code into a different features representation, then useful for graph construction. Table 5 reports the name of the techniques, the purpose of use, and the list of the supported code languages. The table shows that the technique most widely used (79%) is **Joern**[4], an open-source platform designed for analyzing both source and binary code and generating different types of graphs, e.g., AST, CFG, PDG.

(**RQ3**) Table 6 reports the collected information about the vectorization techniques identified for the criteria in the group **feature representation**.

- **Evidence 3.1** From Table 6, we observe that Word2vec is the most frequently used embedding technique (52%), followed by CodeBERT (9%), Doc2vec (6.8%), and GloVe (4.5%). These techniques differ from one another in terms

[4] https://joern.readthedocs.io.

Table 7. Dataset Details

Dataset										
Name	SARD	public proj.	BigVul	NIST	CodeXGLUE	Github	REVEAL	NVD	D2A	Others (Juliet)
Papers	14	8	6	3	3	3	3	2	2	11
Type of dataset										
Type	real-world		synthetic			real-world, synthetic			Not clear	
Papers	22		9			7			4	
Programming language of the dataset										
Lang.			C/C++	Php	Java	JavaScript	Swift	Python		
Papers			37	4	2	2	1	1		
Lang. combination			C/C++, Java, Swift, Php				C/C++, Java			C, Python
Papers			3							
Availability										
Link		Online					Not online			
Papers		15					10			
Granularity dataset information										
Gran.		Function		NF		Code line		Script files		
Papers		29		15		2		1		
Gran.		Code snippet		Function, file		Function, line				
Papers		1		1		1				
Preparation										
Prep.		unbalanced			resample (balancing)				undersampling	
Papers		19			4				2	
Prep.		combinations (balancing)					unbalanced (statement-level)			
Papers		1					1			

of their structure, the size of the embedding vectors produced, and the type of embedding. For instance, CodeBERT and Doc2vec can produce contextualized embeddings, in contrast to Word2vec and GloVe. Besides the prominent feature encoding method outlined in Table 6, we also highlight several supplementary feature vectorization techniques utilized uniquely within the considered works, e.g., Unixcoder, Node2vec, Structure2vec, MPNET, and FasText. Even though these techniques have been used only once, they also have certain advantages. For example, Node2vec can capture nonlinear neighborhood information, which is not the case for some other techniques as they are based on the linear nature of the text. For most of these techniques, pretrained models exist and can be directly used. However, they were mostly retrained in the analyzed works, by adopting a corpus extracted from specific data source, aiming at acquiring a specific coding context.

- **Evidence 3.2** A significant proportion of the research (38%) employed a combination of the techniques listed in Table 6 with the aim of improving the performance of models based on the embedding techniques utilized. They aim at improving the parameters' selection or contextualizing better the embeddings. Half of these combinations involve CodeBERT, which can produce contextualized embeddings.

(**RQ4**) Table 7 summarizes the data about the used datasets collected for the criteria of the group **Dataset details**.

- **Evidence 4.1** Several datasets exist, we counted 21 datasets used in 43 works. Most of the works (70%) use only one dataset, while others (30%) use more than one datasets. The most used datasets are: SARD (24%) and BigVul (10%). Conversely, a non-trivial number of works (14%) assemble its dataset by collecting ad-hoc data from open-source projects. Overall, more than half of datasets used (60%) are available online.
- **Evidence 4.2** Most of the used datasets (52%) are composed of real-world code and vulnerabilities (e.g., Reveal, Big-Vul, and CodeXGlue), even if a non-trivial percentage of datasets (21%) are based only on synthetic data. Some works (16%) use both types of data (see *Evidence 4.4*).
- **Evidence 4.3** Almost all datasets contain source code related to C/C++ programming languages (78%), a low percentage relate to Php (8%), while other languages less present in the datasets are: Java, Swift, JavaScript, Python (on average, 3% each one). We can observe that several existing programming languages still lack available datasets.
- **Evidence 4.4** Existing datasets are mostly labeled at function level (58%), while only few datasets (6%) declare to be labeled at statement-level. However, an open issue that impacted on the proposed SVD techniques is that such datasets suffer of (strong) class imbalance (74% of the works declared to use unbalanced datasets), i.e., they contain a different number of vulnerable and non-vulnerable code snippets. As balanced datasets are crucial for learning models to avoid generalization issues such as underfitting and overfitting, few works (16% of the 43 works declaring the use of a dataset) investigated the use of additional synthetic data or adopted resampling methods to address this challenge.

(**RQ5**) We collected data about the tools' availability. In fact, a key aspect to let developers adopt existing techniques for SVD is the availability of ready-to-use tools. Unfortunately, we can observe that only 14 tools (29%) are available (via Github). In terms of pre-trained models and pre-trained embedding models the availability further decreases: only 1 and 4 models are available (via Zenodo or Google Drive shared folders). These very low numbers hamper the adoption of the presented SVD techniques not only for developers and in real projects, but also limit the capability of the scientific community to replicate experiments and conduct empirical assessments. In fact, none of the considered papers present an empirical assessment of existing techniques and tools.

5 Discussion and Conclusion

This paper reports a RR conducted to get evidence on existing graph-based learning SVD techniques. According to our analysis, we could answer our RQs as follows.

- **RQ1**. GGNN and GCN with MLP as classifiers are the most used learning architectures to detect vulnerabilities at function-level; GGNN and GNN are widely used with code slices/gadgets; and GNN are mostly used also at statement-level. However, existing works mainly focus on function-level and only rarely at statement-level.

- **RQ2**. The analyzed source code is represented by using several graphs, starting from CFG and AST, for capturing syntactic, semantic, and structural information of the code then fed into learning algorithms. However, almost all works use the same tool to extract such graphs from the code.
- **RQ3**. Word2vec is largely the most frequently used embedding technique, others techniques widely used are CodeBERT and Doc2vec. Some works require the use of different techniques at the same time, mainly to optimize the parameters' selection (all techniques are, in fact, based on learning algorithms) or to better contextualize the embeddings.
- **RQ4**. Several datasets are available and most of them resort to real-world code and vulnerabilities collected in C/C++ projects. Such datasets are mostly unbalanced, hence, some works use both real-world and synthetic data, aiming at working with more balanced datasets (data augmentation). Furthermore, almost all datasets are labeled at the function level, thus hampering their adoption at statement-level techniques.
- **RQ5**. Only a limited number of tools are available and almost all use C/C++ datasets. Among them only one (VulChecker) is ready to use.

With the aim of further analyzing the collected data, we built several Sankey diagrams by putting together the information related to (different sub-groups of) the criteria considered in our analysis. A Sankey diagram shows the flow (link) connecting different types of nodes (entities) organized in layers. The link between entities is represented with an arc having width proportional to the relevance of the flow. Figure 2 shows an example of a diagram representing the flow among: learning architectures, embeddings, detection levels, graph-based code representations, and effectiveness. In order to make the diagram readable, we did not include unspecified elements, ("Other" category), and we consider only F1-score for the effectiveness. Furthermore, we identified three classes for the F1-score: high (F1-score > 80%), medium (F1-score > 40% and <80%), and low (F1-score < 40%). Table 8 reports the graph-based learning techniques that most frequently reach high F1-score. We can observe that to achieve a high F1-score: (i) AST is the key graph-based code representation for all detection levels, even if PDT is also relevant at function-level, and other graphs such as PDG, NCCS, and DFG, are also important for the slice detection level; (ii) Word2vec is the key technique for embeddings, especially for statement-level, while for other levels other techniques can play a relevant roles; and (iii) GCN is the key learning architecture for function and statement level, while GGNN for the slice detection level. Summing up, it seems that the fundamental aspects we observed concern: the adoption of AST graphs to hierarchically represent the syntactic structure of code and the relationships among language structures (statements, expressions); the use of Word2vect as learning technique to produce vectorized representations of the code; and the adoption of graph neural networks architectures that employ convolutional operations for analyzing fine-grain code input (statement detection

Table 8. Frequent configurations with high F1

Detection Level	Code Representation	Embedding	Architecture
Function	AST, PDT	Word2vec, Glove, FastTex	GGNN, GCN, GIN
Slice	AST, PDG, NCCS, DFG	Word2vec, CodeBert, GNN, Doc2vect, GGNN	GGNN, GNN, GAN
Statement	AST	Word2vec	GCN, R-GCN

level), or architectures that rely on recurrent operations for analyzing coarse-grain code input characterized by semantic relations (code slice detection level).

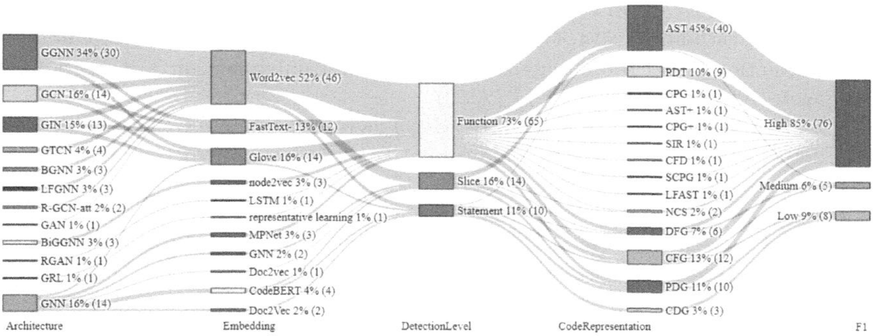

Fig. 2. A SankeyDiagram

This paper shows that graph-based learning SVD techniques are promising, but some more effort and experimentation are still required in order to make datasets, models, and tools available and useful for different programming languages. In our future work, we plan to conduct experiments with different configurations to adopt graph-based learning SVD in our project.

Acknowledgments. The work was supported by the European Union Horizon Europe Research and Innovation Programme under Grant 101120393 (Sec4Ai4Sec).

Disclosure of Interests. The authors have no competing interests to declare.

References

1. Ahmed, S., Taha, D.: Machine learning for software vulnerability detection: a survey. In: Proceedings of the of International Conference on Contemporary Information Technology and Mathematics. IEEE (2022)
2. Arp, D., et al.: Dos and don'ts of machine learning in computer security. In: Proceedings of USENIX Security Symposium, pp. 3971–3988 (2022)
3. Braun, V., Clarke, V.: Using thematic analysis in psychology. Qual. Res. Psychol. **3**(2), 77–101 (2006)
4. Cartaxo, B., Pinto, G., Soares, S.: Rapid reviews in software engineering. In: Felderer, M., Travassos, G. (eds.) Contemporary Empirical Methods in Software Engineering, pp. 357–384. Springer, Cham (2020). https://doi.org/10.1007/978-3-030-32489-6_13
5. Chakraborty, S., Krishna, R., Ding, Y., Ray, B.: Deep learning based vulnerability detection: are we there yet? IEEE Trans. Softw. Eng. **48**(09), 3280–3296 (2022)
6. Chen, X., et al.: Vulchecker: achieving more effective taint analysis by identifying sanitizers automatically. In: Proceedings of International Conference on Trust, Security and Privacy in Computing and Communications, pp. 774–782 (2021)
7. Fu, M., Tantithamthavorn, C.: LineVul: a transformer-based line-level vulnerability prediction. In: Proceedings of International Conference on Mining Software Repositories, pp. 608–620. ACM (2022)
8. Li, Z., Zou, D., Xu, S., Jin, H., Qi, H., Hu, J.: VulPecker: an automated vulnerability detection system based on code similarity analysis. In: Proceedings of Annual Conference on Computer Security Applications. ACM (2016)
9. Li, Z., et al.: VulDeePecker: a deep learning-based system for vulnerability detection. In: Proceedings of Network and Distributed System Security Symposium, San Diego, CA. Internet Society (2018)
10. Marchetto, A.: Can explainability and deep-learning be used for localizing vulnerabilities in source code? In: Proceedings of International Conference on Automation of Software Test (2024)
11. Sonnekalb, T., Heinze, T.S., Mäder, P.: Deep security analysis of program code: a systematic literature review. Empir. Softw. Eng. **27**(1), 2 (2022)
12. Vagavolu, D., Swarna, K.C., Chimalakonda, S.: A mocktail of source code representations. In: 2021 36th IEEE/ACM International Conference on Automated Software Engineering (ASE), pp. 1296–1300 (2021)
13. Wu, B., Zou, F.: Code vulnerability detection based on deep sequence and graph models: a survey. Secur. Commun. Netw. **2022** (2022)
14. Zeng, P., Lin, G., Pan, L., Tai, Y., Zhang, J.: Software vulnerability analysis and discovery using deep learning techniques: a survey. IEEE Access **8** (2020)
15. Zhang, Y., Zhu, J., Yang, Y., Wen, M., Jin, H.: Comparing the performance of different code representations for learning-based vulnerability detection. In: Proceedings of Asia-Pacific Symposium on Internetware. ACM (2023)
16. Zhou, J., et al.: Graph neural networks: a review of methods and applications. AI Open **1**, 57–81 (2020)
17. Zhou, Y., Liu, S., Siow, J., Du, X., Liu, Y.: Devign: effective vulnerability identification by learning comprehensive program semantics via graph neural networks. In: Advances in Neural Information Processing Systems, vol. 32 (2019)

Towards the Use of Domain Knowledge to Enhance Transformer-Based Vulnerability Detection

Alessandro Marchetto(✉) and Rosmaël Zidane Lekeufack Foulefack

University of Trento, Trento, Italy
{alessandro.marchetto,rz.lekeufack}@unitn.it

Abstract. In the last years, several software vulnerability detection techniques based on learning methods, such as deep-learning and large language models, have been proposed to detect vulnerabilities in source code. These techniques build code classification models from datasets of code snippets labeled as vulnerable and non-vulnerable, with the purpose of predicting the presence of vulnerabilities in new code snippets. Experiments documented in the literature, however, show that such techniques can achieve promising results only under specific context and conditions.

In this paper, we document a preliminary investigation on the impact of the use of domain-specific knowledge information on vulnerability detection tasks. To this aim, a transformer-based vulnerability detection method has been enhanced with domain-specific knowledge information and an experiment has been performed to understand whether such additional domain knowledge information can increase the detection performance of the learning-based method.

Keywords: Software vulnerability detection · Deep Learning · Domain Knowledge · Source code

1 Introduction

Cyber-attacks against interconnected software systems are nowadays frequently and widely diffused. In the last decade, a strong increase of the number of attacks has been observed. For instance, between 2021 and 2023, data breaches episodes increased by 72%[1]. Malicious attackers exploit software security vulnerabilities, such as the one identified by the Common Vulnerabilities and Exposures identifiers (CVE[2]), for bypassing organizations' security measures. Software vulnerabilities are often caused by the exploitation of software bugs and code weaknesses, such as the ones described in the MITRE system by the Common Weakness Enumeration (CWE[3]). The CWE is a community-developed taxonomy that lists the common software security weaknesses: it is a common language for identifying, mitigating, and preventing the weaknesses that may become exploitable

[1] https://www.forbes.com/advisor/education/it-and-tech/cybersecurity-statistics.
[2] https://cve.mitre.org.
[3] https://cwe.mitre.org.

A. Bertolino et al. (Eds.): QUATIC 2024, CCIS 2178, pp. 373–390, 2024.
https://doi.org/10.1007/978-3-031-70245-7_26

vulnerabilities if not detected and controlled adequately. Software vulnerability detection is the field of Security Testing devoted to study methods, techniques, and tools to early identify, in the software development life cycle, code bugs and weaknesses that could lead to vulnerabilities. Static vulnerability detection methods do not require the system execution but rather use code parsing, pattern matching, data and control-flow analysis to identify such code bugs and weaknesses. For instance, taint analysis [3] applies data-flow analysis to identify vulnerabilities due to missing data sanitization (e.g., SQL Injection). SAST techniques are known to be fast and easy to apply, but they produce a large number of false positive alarms that have to be checked manually by developers. In the last years, several vulnerability detection techniques based on deep-learning and large language models have been presented [24]. These techniques usually require fragments of source code (also known as *code snippets*) labeled as vulnerable or non-vulnerable as dataset of input. For each code snippet, a token-based vectorized representation is then extracted from code and code properties (e.g., control and data dependencies), and fed to a learning algorithm. In the training phase, the algorithm generates a classification model that can be used to classify new code snippets as vulnerable or non-vulnerable.

Despite the proposed techniques show promising results, empirical studies [2,18] discuss controversial results and issues that hamper their adoption in real scenarios. For instance, among the most relevant limitations we could consider: (i) their limited capability of capturing and working with syntax, semantics, and deep-structure characteristics of source code and vulnerabilities; (ii) their strong dependency on the training dataset; and (iii) the limited knowledge about the types of vulnerability and their characteristics that is available to the learning methods. The first limitation is mainly due to the intrinsic capability of the used code representation and learning methods, and it could strongly impact on the difficulty of such methods in accurately locating the root cause of vulnerabilities (e.g., identification of the statements that contain the bug). The other two limitations are mainly due to the existing datasets (e.g., BigVul, ProjectKB, and CVEfixes)[4] and the limited availability of methods that use domain-specific knowledge information on the vulnerability detection task. Often, existing datasets are imbalanced (they contain only few vulnerable code samples), and contain a lot of spurious information, then reflected in the learned models. Moreover, often, datasets are composed only of code snippets and their corresponding labels. Hence, the existing vulnerability detection techniques have only a limited capability of understanding and characterizing what they are looking for. In other terms, they have a quite limited access to domain knowledge information, and they simply look at the code snippets for identifying (explicit or implicit) characteristics and patterns that could be used to identify the presence of vulnerable code.

In this paper, we documented a preliminary investigation in which we applied different approaches to enhance an existing transformer-based vulnerability

[4] {https://github.com/} ZeoVan/MSR_20_Code_vulnerability_CSV_Dataset, SAP/project-kb, secureIT-project/CVEfixes.

detection method named VDet [17], based on JavaBert [21], with domain-specific knowledge information. We opted for VDet since it is a recent method that achieved promising results in previous evaluations as a binary classifier [17,18], and since it can be used as multi-label classifier, thus going beyond the traditional binary classifiers. The goal of this work is understanding whether, by providing additional domain knowledge information, we can improve the detection performance of an existing vulnerability detection technique.

2 Transformer-Based Vulnerability Detection

JavaBert [21] leverages a specific type of neural network based system, named Bidirectional Encoder Representation from the Transformer architecture (BERT), to work with Java code. BERT is a well-known learning algorithm typically applied in natural language processing (NLP) tasks. JavaBert is a BERT version specialized for Java. JavaBert considers the source code (typically, Java functions) as a sequence of text that is splitted in tokens by the tokenizer. The tokens are then encoded by using a vectorized representation of the embeddings (sequences of tokens and their positions). The JavaBert's tokenizer uses three special tokens, $[MASK]$, $[UNK]$, $[PAD]$ to manage respectively: (i) masked tokens used in token-prediction tasks for improving the model prediction performance; (ii) unknown tokens; and (iii) tokens used for short sequences (longer sequences are split into chunks). The vectors are passed to a multi-layer (JavaBert uses 12 layers) structure of transformers that implements the sequence-to-sequence transformation for taking into account contextual information of each considered token thanks to the attention blocks. JavaBert dynamically adapts the token embeddings based on the input sequence, thus capturing the code token dependencies. A loss function is used to compute the distance between the predicted probability distribution and the true binary labels. JavaBert uses BCE with Logits Loss function as loss function: it combines a sigmoid layer and the binary-cross-entropy loss. JavaBert provides a pre-trained model [21]. VDet [17] is a JavaBert-based model fine tuned for detecting vulnerable code, i.e., for classifying code snippets as vulnerable or non-vulnerable. VDet can work as binary or multi-label classification: in the first case, the code is classified as vulnerable or non-vulnerable, in the second one the code is also classified according to the considered CWEs [16].

Explainable AI [1] is used to comprehend the decision function (i.e., the set of key features) used by an AI model. Explainability methods allow indeed to capture relevant features (code tokens) used by an AI model to make decisions (the code classification) [20]. These methods can be: model-agnostic, if they approximate the decision function with a surrogate function, or model-specific, if they leverage the knowledge of the model itself. *SHAP* is a model-agnostic explainability method that computes the SHAP values (ranging from -1 to 1) to estimate how much each feature of an AI model contributes to the model's decisions. The absolute SHAP value indicates the estimated impact of a feature, while the sign of the value indicates whether a feature impacts positively (negatively) on the model's decisions. By prioritizing the features according to their

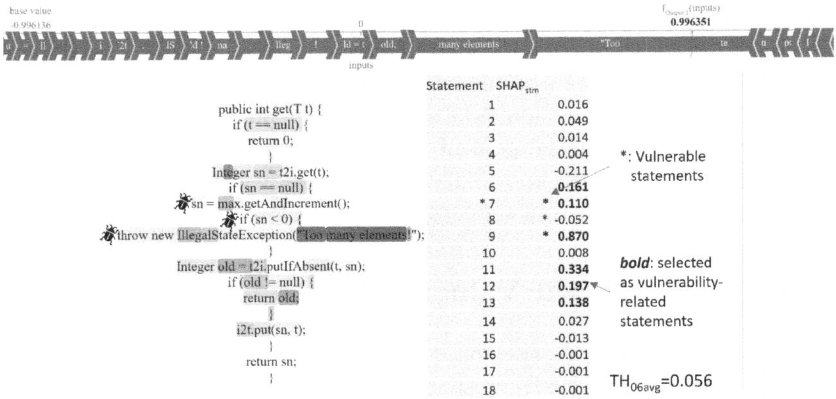

Fig. 1. Example of SHAP applied to a Java function code

SHAP value, we can identify the most relevant features. To compute such SHAP values: first, SHAP computes a base value by masking all (input) tokens with the tag [$MASK$] and obtaining the value without features. Second, SHAP iteratively adds features and computes the SHAP values, thus estimating the contribution of each feature to the observed value changes. Figure 1 shows a simple function with tokens highlighted according to their SHAP value (intense color represents higher SHAP value). For instance, the features "*Too*" and "*many elements*" (positive SHAP values: red) have a positive impact on the decision of classifying the code as vulnerable, while "($sn < 0$)" (negative SHAP value: blue) has a negative impact. In this paper, we adopt SHAP on top of VDet (we call this variant **SVDet**) aiming at localizing the vulnerability-related code statements (in Fig. 1 lines with bugs and '*'). Our approach, coherently with the existing literature [16,18,20], consists in computing the SHAP value for each code statement of the code snippet under test, and select the statements with (positive) SHAP values higher than a **selection threshold** (TH) as the ones related to the vulnerability (i.e., statement causing the vulnerability). To identify **TH**, given a code snippet: (1) for each statement, we compute the statement-level SHAP value (SHAP_{stm}) as the sum of the SHAP values of all tokens of the statement divided by the number of tokens; (2) we compute the average value of the SHAP_{stm} of the code snippet (called $\text{SHAP}_{stm-avg}$); and (3) the statements with the SHAP value higher than or equal to 60% of $\text{SHAP}_{stm-avg}$ (threshold called: $THavg$) are selected as vulnerability-related statements. As example, Fig. 1 shows the calculated SHAP_{stm} and TH_{06avg}, as well as (in bold) the statements classified as vulnerability-related.

3 Domain Knowledge Enhancement of Vulnerability Detection

Domain-specific knowledge refers to the knowledge of a specific discipline or field. People with domain knowledge in a field are considered specialists or experts in

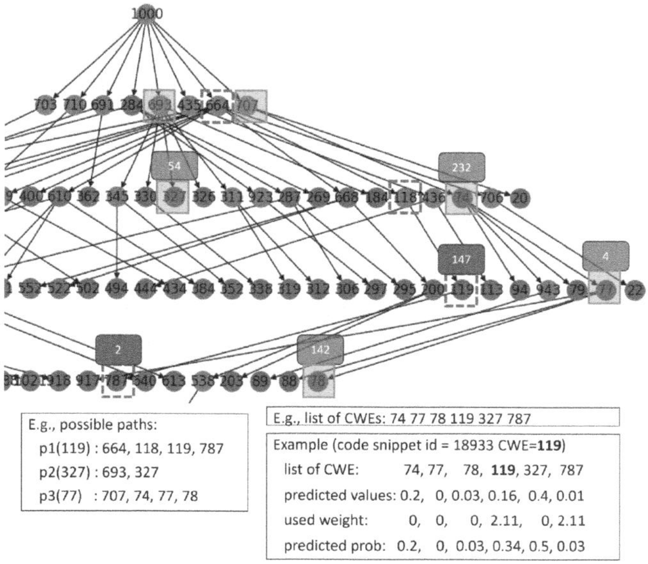

Fig. 2. CWE hierarchy for ProjectKB (green nodes represent CWEs in the dataset): the number inside each node represents the CWE, blue boxes report the number of code snippets in the dataset (Color figure online)

such a field. For instance, a security expert who has knowledge on computer security and vulnerability detection in source code, has expertise and knowledge about the CWE. CWEs are, in fact, weaknesses that are known to lead to security vulnerabilities. In this work, we carry out a preliminary study on four approaches to enhance SVDet with domain-specific knowledge concerning CWEs' information and their occurrence in code snippets.

(1) **Multi-label (Mu).** As baseline for enhancing SVDet with domain knowledge, we consider that SVDet can be used as multi-label classification by labeling each input code snippet, not only with a label that expresses the vulnerability of the snippet (vulnerable or non-vulnerable) but also with the specific implemented CWE, if any. The assumptions are that: (i) the presence of a CWE in a code snippet can lead to a vulnerability, but this is not always guaranteed; (ii) a code snippet can implement more than one CWEs; and (iii) by providing the information about the CWE(s) implemented in a code snippet, we are providing a domain-specific information that enriches the knowledge of the learning method with respect to the code under analysis. The information about the CWE is encoded as a label for the SVDet by means of a one-hot encoding representation in which the length of the vector is given by the number of the CWEs in the used dataset.

(2) **CWE hierarchy (CWEh).** As a further method to add domain knowledge to the multi-label version of SVDet, we considered that the CWEs are hierarchically defined in the MITRE system[5] by means of properties such as:

[5] https://cwe.mitre.org/data/slices/1000.html.

CWE-x is *ParentOf* CWE-y (CWE-x is of the same type of CWE-y, but it is less-specific) and CWE-y is *ChildOf* CWE-x (CWE-y is of the same type and more-specific than CWE-x). For instance, CWE-22 (*Improper Limitation of a Pathname to a Restricted Directory - Path Traversal*) is a code weakness more specific than CWE-706 (*Use of Incorrectly-Resolved Name or Reference*), so CWE-22 is *ChildOf* CWE-706. The CWE hierarchy can be represented with a Directed Acyclic Graph (DAG) having a neutral root node (node 1000 is the root node in the CWEs hierarchy). For instance, Fig. 2 shows a fragment of the hierarchy composed of the CWEs in the ProjectKB dataset [19] (the one used in this work). Overall, the DAG is composed of 5 layers for a total of 85 nodes (CWEs) connected by 84 edges (CWEs' relationships). In the DAG, green nodes represent CWEs in the dataset, while gray nodes represent CWEs that are not in the ProjectKB dataset but that are in relationship, in the CWEs hierarchy, with the CWEs in the dataset. The CWE hierarchy allows us to capture the inter-relationships between CWEs. Moreover, it is worth noticing that each node of the DAG can be enriched with extra-information about the CWE it represents, such as the frequency of the CWE in the dataset (i.e., the number of code snippets in the dataset that contains the CWE), which is depicted as a blue box on top of the green circles in Fig. 2.

Specifically, we used the CWE hierarchy to weigh the output (probabilities) predicted by SVDet for each CWE in each iteration of SVDet and input to the computation of the loss function. We essentially weigh the CWE's predictions according to the position of the predicted CWE with respect to the actual one, in the CWE hierarchy. In detail, *first*, we measured the frequency of each CWE in the dataset, and we add this information to the nodes of the built CWE hierarchy[6]. *Second*, for each CWE c in the dataset, we: (i) identified all nodes (CWEs) in the DAG paths from the root node of the hierarchy to the leaves that pass through such c; (ii) we weighed c with 1 plus the (normalized) sum of the inverse frequency of all nodes/CWEs contained in the identified paths of c. The result is that we characterized each CWE c in the dataset with a (normalized) weight value that estimated the inter-dependence relationships of c with others nodes/CWEs in the hierarchy. *Third*, during the running of the SVDet learning algorithm, we use the computed weights to weigh the CWEs' probability predictions produced from the learning method and used for the computation of the loss function. In particular, we added the weights computed to the predicted probability only if the CWE predicted is contained in at least one path of the CWE hierarchy extracted from the actual CWE label. In this way, we aim at increasing the "relevance" of the CWE's prediction given by the algorithm, depending on the position in the hierarchy and the frequency in the database of the predicted CWEs with respect to the actual ones (ground truth in the dataset).

Figure 2 shows an example for the Java code in Fig. 1. For instance, the code in Fig. 1 is labeled with the CWE-119 (green node in the hierarchy), and

[6] We aim at using the inverse frequency for balancing the different numbers of code snippets per CWE in the dataset.

let's us consider a (small) set of CWEs such as: CWE-74, CWE-77, CWE-78, CWE-119, CWE-327, and CWE-787 (as a set representative, in this example, of the 64 CWEs of the considered dataset). (*First*) The frequency for the CWE-119 is 147, thus the inverse frequency is 0.75 (by considering, e.g., 581 code snippets). (*Second*(i)) One path from root to leaves that pass through the node 119 (dashed nodes in the figure) is: CWE-664, CWE-118, CWE-119, and CWE-787. (*Second*(ii)) The computed weights for the CWEs in the identified path are: 1 for CWE-664 and CWE-118[7], 0.75 for CWE-119, and 0.99 for CWE-787. The obtained sum for the path is: 2.11. (*Third*) By considering for example that the probabilities predicted by the algorithm are: 0.2 for CWE-74, 0 for CWE-77, 0.03 for CWE-78, 0.16 for CWE-119, 0.4 for CWE-327, 0.01 for CWE-787, we can weigh such predicted probabilities by considering the CWE in the identified path with the computed weights, thus increasing the weigh of the CWEs that have a position related to the one of CWE-119 in the CWEs' hierarchy. The new probability in the example are: for CWE-119 is 0.33 and for CWE-787 is 0.02, while the other predicted probabilities remain unchanged since they are not in the path related to CWE-119.

(3) **CWE hierarchy and probability form dataset (CWEhp).** As a method to further add domain knowledge with respect to **CWEh**, we also considered the probability that, in the given dataset, the presence of a CWE in a code snippet makes the snippet vulnerable or non-vulnerable. We computed these two probabilities for each vulnerability in the dataset, and we used them in the learning algorithm to weight the output (probabilities) prediction of SVDet for the vulnerability prediction of each analyzed code snippet. We aim at weighing the prediction produced from SVDet by considering the correlation in the dataset between the presence of the CWE(s) in the code and the code vulnerability.

(4) **Similarity with samples (Sim).** As a further alternative method to add domain knowledge to SVDet, we extracted all Java samples used to characterize each CWE in the MITRE's system. We obtained a set of 74 Java samples that characterize 41 different CWEs, of which 60 samples related to 33 CWEs are in the ProjectKB dataset. We analyzed and tokenized the Java samples, as done by SVDet for the code snippets to analyze, and then computed the cosine similarity between such samples and the code snippets in the dataset. The underlying idea is to weigh the prediction of CWEs obtained from the learning algorithm according to the similarity between code snippets and MITRE's samples, i.e., we use such samples for corroborating the predictions done by SVDet.

4 Evaluation

We aim at conducting a preliminary evaluation of the SVDet enhanced with domain knowledge information for detecting and localizing vulnerability-related code. To this aim, we considered (1) *Bin*, binary classifier, as our baseline corresponding to SVDet without any enhancement, and we considered the following SVDet-enhanced methods (overall named eSVDet variants): (2) *Mu*, multi-label

[7] We consider the fixed value of 1 for each gray node in the DAG hierarchy.

classifier; (3) *CWEh*, multi-label classifier with the CWE hierarchy; (4) *CWEhp*, multi-label classifier with the CWE hierarchy and probability extracted from the dataset; (5) *Sim*, multi-label classifier with similarity of MITRE's samples. The research questions we aim at investigating are the following ones:

RQ1. *What is the impact of the domain knowledge information on the detection of vulnerable code snippets?* RQ1 aims at evaluating the impact of the use of domain knowledge information in the capability of the deep-learning method to detect vulnerable code snippets. In our case, a code snippet is a Java function from the dataset (see below). To answer RQ1, we measured the performance of our baseline and of eSVDet variants in the classification of code snippets as vulnerable or non-vulnerable.

RQ2. *What is the impact of the domain knowledge information on the localization of the source code statements related to vulnerabilities?* RQ2 aims at evaluating the impact of the use of domain knowledge information in the capability of the deep-learning method to localize vulnerability-related code statements inside the vulnerable code snippets. To answer RQ2, we measured the performance of our baseline and of eSVDet variants in the identification of the vulnerability-related code statements, i.e., the capability of classifying the code statements inside each snippet as related or not to a vulnerability.

4.1 Metrics

For RQ1, we compared the classification obtained from the considered methods, with the gold standard (ground truth in the dataset). We then calculated the following metrics.

- Balanced accuracy $bAcc = \frac{(Sensitivity+Specificity)}{2}$ indicates the number of correctly classified code snippets; it is often used with imbalanced datasets (i.e., when one class is more frequent than the other one), and it is computed starting from sensitivity and specificity, where:
- Sensitivity (or Recall) $Sen = \frac{TP}{TP+FN}$ indicates the portion of vulnerable code snippets correctly identified.
- Specificity $Spec = \frac{TN}{TN+FN}$ indicates the portion of non-vulnerable code snippets identified.
- $nMCC = (\frac{TP*TN-FP*FN}{\sqrt{(TP+FP)*(TP+FN)*(TN+FP)*(TN*FN)}} + 1)/2$, the normalized Matthews Correlation Coefficient, is a correlation coefficient that summarizes the trend of the data by considering TP, FP, TN, and FN at the same time; it is often used with imbalanced datasets instead of F1-scores (the harmonic mean of precision and recall) since it is less sensitive to the result of the majority class [4].

For RQ2, we calculated the same set of metrics, but at statement-level. In this case, the used gold standard has been defined by the authors by analyzing the commits of the source code provided in the dataset. In detail, according to [10], we considered all statements that have been removed in vulnerability fixing commits as vulnerability-related statements. Other works suggested also that other potential vulnerability-related statements can be derived by applying control and data -flow analysis to the statements added in the fixing commits. However, to be conservative in our results, we decided to consider only the removed statements as related to the vulnerabilities. All metrics can be applied to both binary and multi-label classification. In particular, in this latter case, we considered the macro-average [9] by averaging the metric scores of individual measure. The macro-average is often used with imbalanced datasets since it is not influenced by the number of items in the dataset classes. The considered vulnerability detection methods aim at achieving high metrics values, i.e., close to 1 for all metrics.

4.2 Object

ProjectKB is the vulnerability dataset used in this experiment. It provides a set of security-relevant commits extracted, and manually curated, from real-world Java software and GitHub commits. The dataset provides several information: the vulnerable code, the vulnerabilities' type (according to the National Vulnerability Database and CVE), and the fixed code. The dataset is composed of: (i) 3770 Java files with more than 1.3M/1.4M lines of code (e.g., statements, comments) respectively before/after the vulnerability fixes. (ii) 20155 Java functions, out of which 2467 are labeled as vulnerable (12.2%), i.e., they contain at least one statement related to one of the 496 CVEs and that refer to 64 different CWEs. The top-4 most frequent CWEs in the dataset are: CWE-20 "Improper Input Validation" (11.9% of the 64 CWEs, of which 18.8% are vulnerable), CWE-22 "Improper Limitation of a Pathname to a Restricted Directory (Path Traversal)" (8.8% of the 64 CWEs, of which 5.1% are vulnerable), CWE-502 "Deserialization of Untrusted Data" (6% of the 64 CWEs, of which 4.8% are vulnerable), Other CWEs achieve a frequency around or lower than 5% each one.

4.3 Process

1. We randomly shuffled and splitted the Java functions of the dataset for training (80%), validation (10%), and test (10%) – each set contains about 12% of the actually vulnerable Java functions.
2. We used the training set to set-up the baseline and the four eSVDet variants (described above).
3. We provided training and validation sets to the five methods for building their AI models. The configuration used is the same for all used methods:

epoch: 4; input vector length: 512; Loss Function: BCE with logits loss; Optimizer: Adamax; Recurrent Activation: sigmoid; Vocabular Size: 30522; Training steps: size(input)*epoch; Hidden layers: 12; and Batch size: 12. We obtained five AI models, one for the baseline and one for each considered eSVDet variant.
4. We provided our test set of 2014 Java functions (code snippets) to the built AI models for classifying them.
5. On the obtained results, we computed the performance metrics (*bAcc* and *nMCC*) for answering RQ1.
6. We then ran SHAP on top of the five AI models to obtain the SHAP values for each code statement in a subset of 300 randomly selected Java functions of the test set.
7. By considering the identified vulnerability-related code statements, we computed the metrics to answer RQ2.

4.4 Threats to Validity

The adoption of only one (imbalanced) dataset clearly limits the generalization of the obtained results. However, the dataset we used is a real-world dataset that lets us apply the methods in real conditions, e.g., it is a common scenario to have large portions of code with only few lines that contain bugs. Another threat concerns the use of only one AI method, which could limit the generalization of the achieved results. We opted for SVDet since it achieves reasonable and representative results according to the existing literature. We are conscious that more datasets and methods could strengthen the results. We hence we plan to extend the experimentation in our future work.

5 Results

RQ1. Figure 3 shows the boxplots and Table 1 (first column) reports the average values of the performance metrics *bAcc* and *nMCC* for the five methods considered. The metrics show that *Mu*, *CWEh*, and *CWEhp* obtain results comparable to the ones of *Bin*. In detail, *Mu* tends to be slightly better than *Bin*, e.g., the average *nMCC* is 0.88 for *Mu* and 0.81 for *Bin*, and *Mu* is more stable than *Bin*. However, *Bin* is slightly better than *CWEhp*, the average values of *bAcc* *nMCC* for *CWEh* are 0.77 and 0.79, respectively. Finally, *Sim* is notably worse than the other approaches, e.g., the average *nMCC* for *Sim* is 0.53. This last result is expected since the used MITRE's Java samples are few and cover only partially the CWEs of the dataset (only 60 samples for 33 CWEs).

Table 1. RQ1 and RQ2: average value of $bAcc$ and $nMCC$

	RQ1		RQ2	
	$bAcc$	$nMCC$	$bAcc$	$nMCC$
Bin	0.82	0.81	0.44	0.46
Mu	0.86	0.88	0.51	0.54
CWEh	0.81	0.83	0.48	0.52
CWEhp	0.77	0.79	0.44	0.45
Sim	0.57	0.53	0.64	0.64

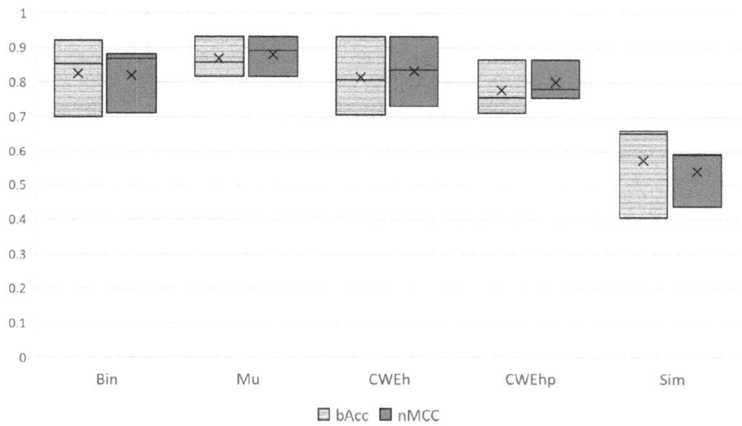

Fig. 3. RQ1: boxplots of $bAcc$, $F1$, and $nMCC$

RQ2. Figure 4 shows the boxplots and Table 1 (second column) reports the average values of $bAcc$ and $nMCC$ for the five methods considered. The metrics show that *Sim* almost outperforms all the other methods, while *Mu* and *CWEh* tend to slightly overcome *Bin* and *CWEhp*, on average. Overall, we can observe that on average the domain-enriched variants of SVDet tend to overcome *Bin*. For all the cases, we can note from the boxplots a quite large variability of the metrics. This is also due to the fact that the used dataset is imbalanced in terms of vulnerable and non-vulnerable Java functions and statements. For instance, more than 10% of the code snippets classified in the test set do not contain vulnerability-related statements. This is expected since in software applications, bugs are due to a limited number of lines of code (statements). We, however, argue that this does not compromise our experiment with the goal of investigating the possible impact of adding domain knowledge information to a transformer-based vulnerability detection method.

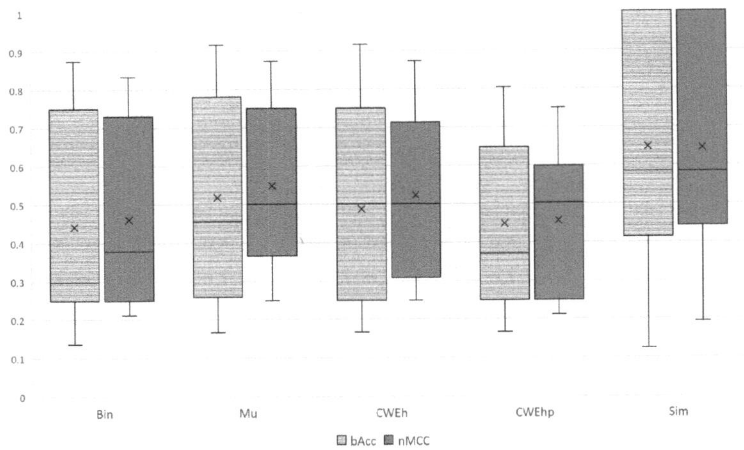

Fig. 4. RQ2: boxplots of *bAcc* and *nMCC*

RQ1 The experiment shows that *Mu*, *CWEh*, and *CWEhp* can achieve classification performance comparable to the binary classifier. In particular, *Mu* shows slightly better results. Low performance can instead occur for *Sim* if a limited set of additional samples is considered (such as in our case).
RQ2 The experiment shows that all domain-enhanced methods can achieve results comparable or slightly better than the ones obtained with the binary classifier. *Sim*, in particular, shows promising results in the detection of vulnerability-related statements.

6 Further Analysis and Discussion

With the aim of better comprehending the observed results, we conducted two further analyses in the collected data.

Capability of the (Domain-Enhanced) Vulnerability Detection Methods to Classify CWEs in Code Snippets. For evaluating the capability of the learning methods to recognize the presence of CWEs in code snippets, we measured the classification performance metrics used for RQ1, but comparing the CWEs predicted for each code snippet by eSVDet with respect to the CWEs in the dataset (ground truth).

Table 2 and Fig. 5 report the (macro) average values for the performance metrics calculated for the CWE predictions. In particular, we considered two cases: (i) *all_ CWEs*: in which we considered all the predictions; and (ii) *top**X**_ CWEs* (where ***X*** is equal to 10, 5, and 3): in which we considered three subsets of predictions for each of these subsets we compared the metrics by taking inot account only ***X*** most frequent (vulnerable) CWEs in the dataset, e.g., *top10_ CWEs* contains the top-10 most frequent and vulnerable CWEs. In the case of *Sim*, we additionally considered as further criterion to have at least two MITRE's

Table 2. CWEs classification: average value of *bAcc* and *nMCC* for *all_CWEs*, *top10_CWEs*, *top5_CWEs* and *top3_CWEs*

	all_CWEs		top10_CWEs		top5_CWEs		top3_CWEs	
	bAcc	*nMCC*	*bAcc*	*nMCC*	*bAcc*	*nMCC*	*bAcc*	*nMCC*
Mu	0.041	0.32	0.12	0.41	0.189	0.67	0.31	0.79
CWEh	0.044	0.34	0.13	0.42	0.187	0.68	0.3	0.81
CWEhp	0.043	0.34	0.12	0.42	0.19	0.676	0.31	0.8
Sim	0.52	0.49	0.58	0.5	0.58	0.49	0.59	0.5

samples per CWE. The table shows that *CWEh* and *CWEhp* achieved comparable or slightly better results than *Mu*. Moreover, *Sim* outperforms the other variants in terms of *bAcc* (always) and *nMCC* in *all_CWEs* and *top10_CWEs*. We can observe that the obtained results are low, if we consider all or a large set of the CWEs of the dataset, while they increase, if we consider only the most vulnerable and frequent CWEs. Hence, the results observed in the experiment are influenced by the used (imbalanced) dataset in which, for instance, 1.4% and 0.86% of Java functions (about 291 and 174 functions) are vulnerable for the presence of the CWE-20 and CWE-863 respectively, while all the others CWEs (e.g., CWE-22) have a number of vulnerable functions lower than 0.65% (e.g., 0.63% for CWE-22 corresponding to 126 functions).

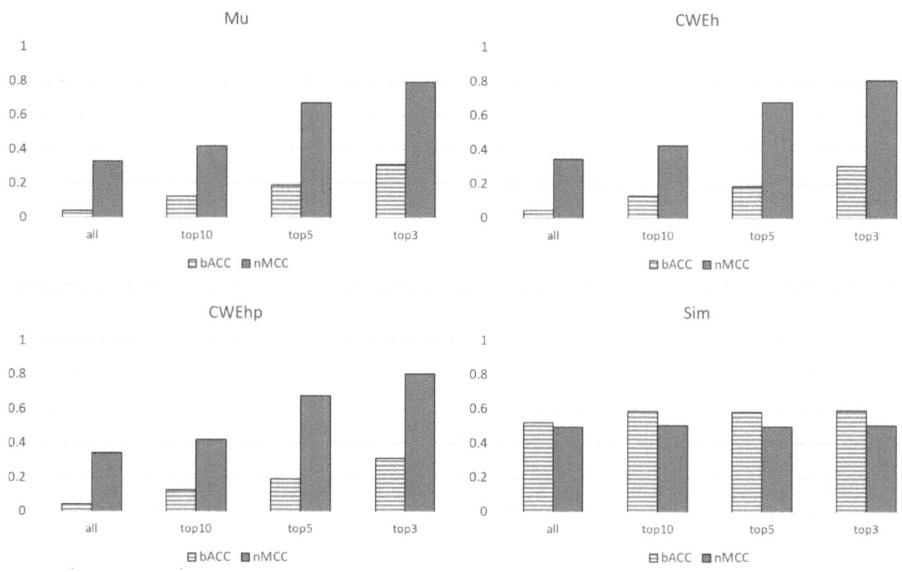

Fig. 5. CWEs classification: plots of average value of *bAcc* and *nMCC* for *all_CWEs*, *top10_CWEs*, *top5_CWEs* and *top3_CWEs*

Table 3. Impact of the CWE's classification: average value of *bAcc* and *nMCC*

	function-level				statement-level			
	top5_ CWEs		*top3_ CWEs*		*top5_ CWEs*		*top3_ CWEs*	
	bAcc	*nMCC*	*bAcc*	*nMCC*	*bAcc*	*nMCC*	*bAcc*	*nMCC*
Mu	0.83	0.88	0.85	0.90	0.55	0.56	0.51	0.25
CWEh	0.8	0.83	0.81	0.84	0.52	0.44	0.48	0.47
CWEhp	0.81	0.85	0.82	0.87	0.42	0.44	0.39	0.43
Sim	0.59	0.54	0.62	0.57	0.79	0.8	0.79	0.8

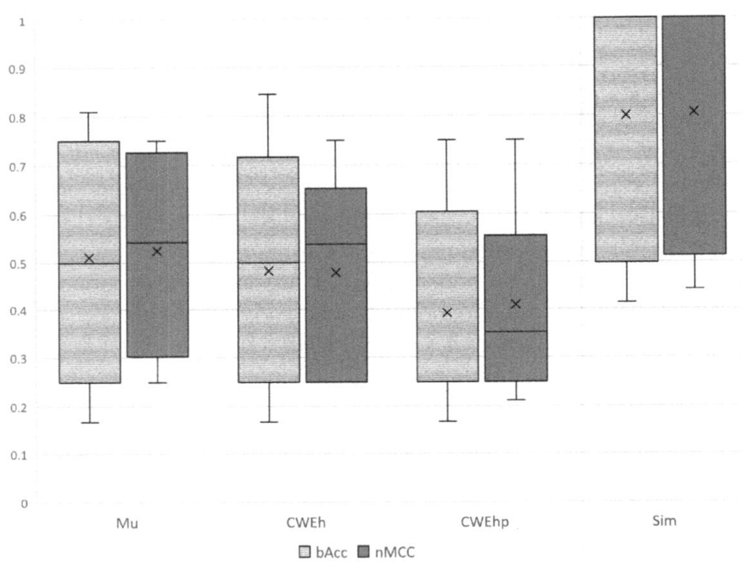

Fig. 6. Impact of the CWE's classification: boxplots of *bAcc* and *nMCC* at statement-level for *top3_ CWE*

Impact of the CWE's Classification Accuracy on the Vulnerability Detection Performance. For evaluating the impact of the accuracy of the CWE's classification on the capability of eSVDet to detect vulnerable code snippets, we computed the performance metrics focusing on the only CWEs that obtained better results in the previous further analysis (in terms of *top5_ CWE* and *top3_ CWE*).

Table 3 reports the average value of the metrics calculated for detecting vulnerable functions (function-level) and code statements (statement-level), by considering only the *top5_ CWEs* and *top3_ CWEs*. The table shows that, almost all *top3_ CWEs* eSVDet variants improves the function-level prediction performance with respect to RQ1, while only *CWEhp* and *Sim* improves for *top5_ CWEs*. Figure 6 details the boxplots obtained for the statement-level prediction (statement-level) for *top3_ CWEs*. From Table 3 and Fig. 6, we can observe that the statement-level predictions are almost inline with the ones achieved for RQ2, although sometimes slightly better (e.g., *Mu* for*top5_ CWEs*), sometimes slightly worst (e.g., *CWEh* for*top5_ CWEs*), except for *Sim* that outperforms the other variants and all results achieved for RQ2. This seems to confirm that the relevance of an adequate classification of the CWEs for all eSVDet variants has an impact on the vulnerability detection. We could also note that this result is related to the performance observed in previous further analysis, thus showing that the domain-enhancement of deep-learning vulnerability detection methods could increase the performance of such methods, but the used dataset (ProjectKB in our study) probably does not allow to achieve relevant results.

– The experiment shows that the domain-enhancement methods achieves low performance in the identification of the CWEs in the code snippets. We argue that this is mainly due to the large number of CWE considered with few vulnerable code snippets in the used (imbalanced) dataset.
– The experiment shows that when CWEs are classified well, the capability of the domain-enhanced methods in detecting vulnerabilities at function level improves (it seems that a correlation exists), while such an improvement is observed only for *Sim* at statement level.

7 Related Work

Existing works, e.g., [24], survey the literature in the field of SAST methods for detecting vulnerabilities in source code.

In the last years, several works explored in particular the usage of deep-learning and large language models for detecting vulnerabilities. For instance, VulDeePecker [12] detects vulnerabilities in code "gadgets", i.e., sets of semantically-related code statements, by encoding them in fixed-length vectors of symbols then fed into a Bidirectional Long Short-Term Memory (BLSTM) neural network. SySeVR [11] extends VulDeePecker by additionally considering semantic relationships among code statement within gadgets and by using Bidirectional Recurrent Neural Networks instead of BLSTM. VDet [17] and LineVul [6] are two transformer-based methods for vulnerability detection tools for Java functions and code statements. IVDetect [10], VulGraB [23], and Funded [22] use graph-based code representations (e.g., program dependency graphs and abstract syntax trees) and learning architectures (e.g., feature-attention graph convolutional networks and gated graph neural networks) to capture code syntax, semantics, and structure while learning the classification model.

Some effort has been spent by the community to adopt domain knowledge in vulnerability detection. For instance, [14] uses learning algorithms with cross-domain adaptation to overcome the cross-domain issues that hamper the vulnerability detection. [5] presents a transformer-based approach that achieves promising performance to map CVE (natural language) descriptions to CWEs.

[15] presents a model that uses two learning algorithms to detect code vulnerabilities by strengthening the combination of local and global information, i.e., information of a specific code snippet and information from all snippets in the dataset. [7] proposes a graph-based extension of a transformer-based learning model to detect vulnerabilities based on source code, data flow analysis, and natural language descriptions of code commits, thus considering both structural and semantics information while searching for vulnerabilities. [13] incorporates external knowledge into a learning algorithm used for predicting code vulnerabilities. The external knowledge used is composed of natural language text that describes the CVEs that label the (training) code in the used dataset. The goal was to predict the vulnerable code based on the combination of source code and descriptions of semantic features. [8] proposes a probabilistic model to integrate the domain knowledge derived from the CWE hierarchy into transformer-based models then used for predicting vulnerabilities.

In this work, we preliminary investigated a set of representative approaches that could be used to enhance SVDet [18] with domain-specific knowledge information. Inspired from the existing literature, we investigated Sim, which uses external knowledge to enhance SVDet, but differently from [13], we use the MITRE's samples as source of such an external knowledge. We also investigated CWEh, which considers the CWE hierarchy to enhance SVDet, but differently than [8], we defined our approach to estimate the inter-dependency among the CWEs in the used dataset of real vulnerabilities. Furthermore, in CWEhp, we additionally considered the probability information related to the frequency between CWE(s) and vulnerabilities in the dataset.

8 Conclusions

We conducted a preliminary investigation in which we considered different possible approaches to enhance a transformer-based vulnerability method with domain-specific information. Our investigation shows that adding some extra information, in addition to the source code, can help the deep-learning methods. However, we also observed that the used datasets can play a fundamental role by amplifying or hampering the results. We showed that more investigation and effort have to be spent both in the dataset preparation and in the way in which the domain-knowledge information is used into deep-learning methods in order to make these approaches usable in real application scenarios.

On the one side, hence, our future work will be devoted to study how to produce a new and better balanced dataset or how to improve existing datasets, e.g., by considering for instance practices of data augmentation. On the other side, we will try to go beyond this preliminary investigation by working on a more structured approach to represent domain-specific knowledge useful for enhancing existing deep-learning methods.

Acknowledgements. The work was supported by the European Union Horizon Europe Research and Innovation Programme under Grant 101120393 (Sec4Ai4Sec).

Disclosure of Interests. The authors have no competing interests to declare.

References

1. Burkart, N., Huber, M.F.: A survey on the explainability of supervised machine learning. J. Artif. Intell. Res. **70**, 245–317 (2021)
2. Chakraborty, S., Krishna, R., Ding, Y., Ray, B.: Deep learning based vulnerability detection: are we there yet? IEEE Trans. Softw. Eng. **48**(09), 3280–3296 (2022)
3. Chen, X., et al.: Vulchecker: achieving more effective taint analysis by identifying sanitizers automatically. In: Proceedings of International Conference on Trust, Security and Privacy in Computing and Communications, pp. 774–782 (2021)
4. Chicco, D.: Ten quick tips for machine learning in computational biology. BioData Min. **10**(35) (2017)
5. Das, S.S., Serra, E., Halappanavar, M., Pothen, A., Al-Shaer, E.: V2W-BERT: a framework for effective hierarchical multiclass classification of software vulnerabilities. In: Proceedings of IEEE International Conference on Data Science and Advanced Analytics (DSAA), pp. 1–12 (2021)
6. Fu, M., Tantithamthavorn, C.: LineVul: a transformer-based line-level vulnerability prediction. In: Proceedings of International Conference on Mining Software Repositories, pp. 608–620. ACM (2022)
7. Guo, D., Ren, S., Lu, S., et al.: GraphCodeBERT: pre-training code representations with data flow. In: Proceedings of International Conference on Learning Representations, ICLR 2021, Virtual Event, Austria, 3–7 May 2021. OpenReview.net (2021)
8. Jeong, S.: Integrating domain knowledge into transformer-based approaches to vulnerability detection. Master's thesis, Ludwig-Maximilians-Universität München, Ge (2023)
9. Kanae, T., Kouji, Y., Aya, K., Tatsuki, K.: Confidence interval for micro-averaged F1 and macro-averaged F1 scores. Appl. Intell. **52**(5), 4961–4972 (2022)
10. Li, Y., Wang, S., Nguyen, T.N.: Vulnerability detection with fine-grained interpretations. In: Proceedings of ACM Joint Meeting on European Software Engineering Conf. and Symposium on the Foundations of Software Engineering, ESEC/FSE 2021, pp. 292–303. Association for Computing Machinery (2021)
11. Li, Z., Zou, D., Xu, S., Jin, H., Zhu, Y., Chen, Z.: SySeVR: a framework for using deep learning to detect software vulnerabilities. IEEE Trans. Dependable Secure Comput. **19**(04), 2244–2258 (2022)
12. Li, Z., et al.: VulDeePecker: a deep learning-based system for vulnerability detection. In: Proceedings of Network and Distributed System Security Symposium, San Diego, CA. Internet Society (2018)
13. Liu, J., Ai, J., Lu, M., Wang, J., Shi, H.: Semantic feature learning for software defect prediction from source code and external knowledge. J. Syst. Softw. **204**(C) (2023)
14. Liu, S., et al.: CD-VuLD: cross-domain vulnerability discovery based on deep domain adaptation. IEEE Trans. Dependable Secure Comput. **19**(1), 438–451 (2022)
15. Lu, Z., Du, P., Nie, J.-Y.: VGCN-BERT: augmenting BERT with graph embedding for text classification. In: Jose, J.M., et al. (eds.) ECIR 2020. LNCS, vol. 12035, pp. 369–382. Springer, Cham (2020). https://doi.org/10.1007/978-3-030-45439-5_25

16. Mamede, C., Pinconschi, E., Abreu, R., Campos, J.: Exploring transformers for multi-label classification of Java vulnerabilities. In: Proceedings of IEEE International Conference on Software Quality, Reliability and Security (QRS), pp. 43–52 (2022)
17. Mamede, C., Pinconschi, E., Abreu, R.: A transformer-based ide plugin for vulnerability detection. In: Proceedings of International Conference on Automated Software Engineering. ASE, ACM (2023)
18. Marchetto, A.: Can explainability and deep-learning be used for localizing vulnerabilities in source code? In: Proceedings of International Conference on Automation of Software Test (2024)
19. Ponta, S.E., Plate, H., Sabetta, A., Bezzi, M., Dangremont, C.: A manually-curated dataset of fixes to vulnerabilities of open-source software, pp. 383–387. MSR, IEEE Press (2019)
20. Sotgiu, A., Pintor, M., Biggio, B.: Explainability-based debugging of machine learning for vulnerability discovery. In: Proceedings of International Conference on Availability, Reliability and Security, USA. ARES, ACM (2022)
21. Sousa, N.D., Hasselbring, W.: JavaBERT: training a transformer-based model for the Java programming language. In: Proceedings of International Conference on Automated Software Engineering Workshops (ASEW), USA, pp. 90–95. IEEE (2021)
22. Wang, H., et al.: Combining graph-based learning with automated data collection for code vulnerability detection. IEEE Trans. Inf. Forensics Secur. **16**, 1943–1958 (2021)
23. Wang, S., Chen, Y., Dongjin, X.: VulGraB: graph-embedding-based code vulnerability detection with bi-directional gated graph neural network. Softw. Practi. Experience **53** (2023)
24. Zeng, P., Lin, G., Pan, L., Tai, Y., Zhang, J.: Software vulnerability analysis and discovery using deep learning techniques: a survey. IEEE Access **8** (2020)

Black-Box Reconstruction Attacks on LLMs: A Preliminary Study in Code Summarization

Marco Russodivito, Angelica Spina, Simone Scalabrino(✉), and Rocco Oliveto

University of Molise, Campobasso, Italy
{marco.russodivito,angelica.spina,simone.scalabrino,
rocco.oliveto}@unimol.it

Abstract. Large Language Models (LLMs) have demonstrated effectiveness in tackling coding tasks, leading to their growing popularity in commercial solutions like GitHub Copilot and ChatGPT. These models, however, may be trained on proprietary code, raising concerns about potential leaks of intellectual property. A recent study indicates that LLMs can memorize parts of the source code, rendering them vulnerable to extraction attacks. However, it used *white-box* attacks which assume that adversaries have partial knowledge of the training set.

This paper presents a pioneering effort to conduct a *black-box* attack (reconstruction attack) on an LLM designed for a specific coding task – code summarization. The results achieved reveal that while the attack is generally unsuccessful (with an average *BLEU score* below 0.1), it succeeds in a few instances, reconstructing versions of the code that closely resemble the original.

Keywords: LLMs for Coding Tasks · Security · Reconstruction Attacks

1 Introduction

Large Language Models (LLMs) are increasingly integral to software engineering research, proving particularly effective in coding tasks such as bug fixing and code summarization [14]. These models operate by inputting a sequence of textual tokens and outputting another sequence, which may include source code or natural language depending on the task. Modern LLMs employed for coding typically leverage the Transformer architecture [21] and undergo a two-stage training process: initial *pre-training* on extensive codebases to learn language patterns semi-supervised, followed by task-specific *fine-tuning* in a supervised manner (*i.e.,* by providing examples of input and output sequences).

The effectiveness of these models has led to their integration into commercial tools like CoPilot[1] and ChatGPT[2], which are becoming indispensable coding

[1] https://www.microsoft.com/en-us/microsoft-copilot (Verified on April 26th, 2024).
[2] https://chat.openai.com.

A. Bertolino et al. (Eds.): QUATIC 2024, CCIS 2178, pp. 391–398, 2024.
https://doi.org/10.1007/978-3-031-70245-7_27

assistants [26]. While research-oriented LLMs are often trained on open-source datasets, commercial variants might use proprietary code that companies wish to keep confidential.

Consider a company that wants to develop a coding assistant from an LLM fine-tuned on its proprietary data from 1,000 software projects and over 5,000 developers, aiming to commercialize this tool without exposing the underlying source code. This introduces potential confidentiality issues if methods exist that can extract specific data instances from the trained model without any other dataset information.

Let us call the (confidential) dataset used for fine-tuning the LLM D_p. If there is a methodology that can extract any instance $p \in D_p$ given only the trained model (as a *black-box*) and no other instance of D_p, we say that the LLM violates confidentiality. Al-Kaswan *et al.* [2] recently proved that LLMs for coding tasks memorize token sequences. Especially, the authors tested whether such LLMs are vulnerable to *white-box* attacks, which assume that the adversary has partial knowledge of the D_p. In most cases, however, adversaries might not have such information. Previous work highlighted that other types of privacy attacks are possible for DNNs [7,18–20,22]. *Reconstruction Attacks* (or *Model Inversion Attack*) are a specific type of such attacks that aim to recreate one or more training samples [18] assuming that the adversary has no information about the training instances. It is still unclear, however, to what extent such attacks are effective on LLMs for coding tasks.

In this paper, we present an empirical study assessing the feasibility of a *black-box* attack (*Reconstruction Attack*) to compromise confidentiality in LLMs used for coding tasks. We specifically analyze the T5 model by Mastropaolo *et al.* [14] trained for the task of code summarization ($T5_{summ}$), where the model generates textual descriptions from code snippets. Our experiment involved constructing an *inverse model* that takes textual descriptions and attempts to output original code snippets. To build an *inverse model* for $T5_{summ}$ ($T5^{-1}_{summ}$), we first collected a set S of ~700k open-source code snippets from state-of-the-art datasets [11–13]. Then, we gave each snippet $s \in S$ to the trained $T5_{summ}$, which generated its textual summary s_c and trained $T5^{-1}_{summ}$ on the pairs $\langle s_c, s\rangle$. Finally, we tried to extract the code snippets in D_p by giving textual summaries s_c to $T5^{-1}_{summ}$.

The obtained results revealed that in almost all the cases it is not possible to extract training instances (*BLEU score* < 0.1). Still, we found some cases in which the *BLEU score* is high and the attack generated closely-resembling versions of the source code in D_p. Our results call for future work aimed at investigating more in depth the possibility of running such attacks on other tasks and propose solutions to mitigate such a problem.

2 Related Work

Reconstruction Attacks have been extensively studied in both *black-box* and *white-box* settings. In the former, the adversary lacks information about the model parameters, architecture, and training data. In the latter, the adversary has complete knowledge of the target model [18]. Such a concept was first introduced by Fredrikson *et al.* [6], who showed that an attacker could predict a patient's genetic markers using only demographic information and model access.

This led to a broader application of model inversion attacks, as demonstrated by Fredrikson *et al.* [5] in subsequent work. In this work, the authors proposed a more generic model inversion attack applicable either in *black-box* or *white-box* settings and against different models (*e.g.*, decision trees and neural networks for face recognition) which exploits confidence values obtained from prediction APIs. Hidano *et al.* [9] introduced a *black-box* technique targeting online prediction systems that adapt over time, demonstrating that these systems could be influenced by poisoning attacks to make them more susceptible to *Reconstruction Attack*. Some attacks can even involve Generative Adversarial Networks (GANs) [10]. Their approach uses real-time learning in collaborative deep learning models to train a GAN to generate private and prototypical examples of the training set. Another example is the attack by Zhang *et al.* [24], which leverages partial public data (*e.g.*, blurred or corrupted images) to learn a distributional prior using GANs and employs it to guide the inversion process.

Recently, many studies have focused on the security of LLMs, to understand the degree of training data storage that these models achieve. This type of attacks is called *Training Data Extraction Attacks*. Like Model Inversion Attacks, Training Data Extraction Attacks aim to reconstruct training samples, but in a *verbatim* way [4,25]. A popular approach [4] consists of two main steps: a generation phase where different potential suffixes are obtained by querying several times the model with a set of prefixes, and an inference step used to infer if each suffix, or just some of them [1], belongs to the target training set. This can be done in different ways: one can perform fuzzy match like 3-gram fuzzy match or using BLEU-4 score, he can apply an exact match, or even a combination of all the techniques [2,4]. The exact match check also includes the case of Type-1 clone detection to identify code memorization presented by Yang *et al.* [22], which tries to reconstruct small snippets belonging to the training set. Another interesting approach involves the use of canaries, *i.e.*, the insertion of N clones of predefined samples into the training set, which researchers then attempt to reconstruct. This reconstruction can be performed either by employing a canary completion task [16] or by exploiting the *exposure* concept illustrated by Carlini *et al.* [3].

Yang *et al.* [23] tested the execution of a *Reconstruction Attack* for Large Language Models. Such an attack (i) is a *black-box* attack that works without special assumptions on adversary knowledge; (ii) can be applied at inference time (*i.e.*, when the target model is already trained); (iii) is effective against complex models, such as CNNs. To the best of our knowledge, our work is the first attempt to use an adaptation of the work by Yang *et al.* [23] to exploit LLMs for coding tasks.

3 Empirical Study Design

Our study aims to determine the feasibility of a *Reconstruction Attack* on LLMs for code summarization tasks. addressing the following Research Question (RQ):

To what extent is a code summarization model vulnerable to a Reconstruction Attack?

3.1 The Reconstruction Attack Method

In the context of our study we exploit the *Reconstruction Attack* methodology proposed by Yang *et al.* [23], originally designed for CNNs, adapting it to LLMs for coding tasks. The core concept involves training an *inverse model* ($M_{inverse}$) that functions oppositely to the target model (M_{target}), enabling the extraction of training instances by querying $M_{inverse}$. We assume that the adversary lacks knowledge of the dataset used to train M_{target} (*i.e.,* the one we want to reconstruct), and she has *black-box* access to M_{target}, allowing her to input data and receive prediction outputs. Additionally, the adversary understands the semantics of the input and has access to the *tokenizer* used by M_{target}, which converts textual data into numerical vectors. We assume that the target model uses a publicly available tokenizer that the adversary can access.

The attack process is structured around the phases of the *Kill Chain.* Initially, in the *Reconnaissance phase*, the adversary analyzes the target model to understand its input and output characteristics. Next, during the *Weaponization phase*, the adversary compiles an auxiliary set (D_{aux}) of semantically compatible samples, in our case, source code snippets. This set is used to probe M_{target}, creating an attack set (D_{atk}) during the *Delivery phase.* This set consists of pairs $\langle M_{target}(a), a\rangle$, which are then used to train the *inverse model* ($M_{inverse}$) in the Exploitation phase. Ultimately, the adversary queries $M_{inverse}$ with the intention of reconstructing original training instances.

3.2 Context of the Study

The context of our study is composed of two types of *objects*: (i) a target model and a dataset that we use as the *auxiliary dataset.*

As for the former, we focus on the T5 model [17] adapted to support coding tasks [14]. The authors introduced specialized models to supports four tasks: *Automatic Bug Fixing*, *Injection of Code Mutants*, *Generation of Assertions*, and *Code Summarization.* We focus on the model that tackles the code-summarization task, $T5_{summ}$. The dataset we want to reconstruct (*i.e.,* the one used to train $T5_{summ}$) is a variation of the dataset provided by Haque *et al.* [8]. Specifically, the instances of their dataset are tuples $\langle s, a_s, c_s, d\rangle$, where s is the source code, a_s is the AST, c_s is the remaining code of the Java class, and d is the textual description of the method. Instead, our set consists of pairs $\langle s, d\rangle$. We focus on code summarization because it is the only task that assumes that the adversary has no information about the source code. Ideally, the adversary only needs a textual description that is close to the one used in the training set to retrieve the protected source code.

We use as the *auxiliary dataset* a combination of three state-of-the-art dataset of code snippets. The first one is CodeSearchNet [13], which contains about 6M functions from open-source code involving six different programming languages. We only focus on Java instances. The second one is TL-CodeSum [12], which has been collected from GitHub mining Java projects with at least 20 stars and create from 2015 to 2016.

Such a dataset is frequently used for code-summarization tasks, but it is different from the dataset used in the target model. The third one is DeepCom [11], which has been built from 9,714 open-source projects from GitHub and is used as a benchmark for comment generation tasks. We merged these datasets, removing duplicate entries and code comments, and leveraged the tokenizer from the target model to adapt all auxiliary set samples to the input format of the target model. After preprocessing, the final auxiliary dataset comprised 722,067 instances.

3.3 Experimental Procedure

To construct the *inverse model* of $T5_{summ}$ ($T5^{-1}_{summ}$), we chose to use the same architecture of the *target model* (*i.e.*, T5). We fine-tuned such a model using the *attack dataset* built using the procedure reported in Sect. 3.1.

In order to address our research question, we optimistically assume that the adversary can access the exact summaries used in the training set. We then run $T5^{-1}_{summ}$ once for each summary and evaluate the similarity between the code generated by $T5^{-1}_{summ}$ and the original code from the training set. It is important to note that this scenario relaxes the conditions described in Sect. 3.1, as it assumes prior knowledge about the training set. Therefore, our findings should be considered an upper bound of potential outcomes, given that such information might not be available to an adversary in practice.

To quantify the reconstruction quality, we utilized the *BLEU score* (Bilingual Evaluation Understudy) [15], which measures the similarity of n-grams between the reconstructed and original sequences on a scale from 0 to 1. A value closer to 1 indicates a higher similarity between the two code snippets.

4 Empirical Study Results

This section provides a discussion on the results achieved and the limitations of our study.

4.1 Analysis of the Results

Figure 1 shows the distribution of the *BLEU score* between the reconstructed code and the actual code in the training set. The average score is lower than 0.1. Nevertheless, there are several outliers with relatively high *BLEU score*, suggesting that our reconstruction attack can sometimes recover significant portions of the original training data.

We conducted a manual analysis of some reconstructions with high *BLEU score* to determine if the reconstruction attack was successful in these instances. Figure 2 presents examples of Java methods that were partially reconstructed.

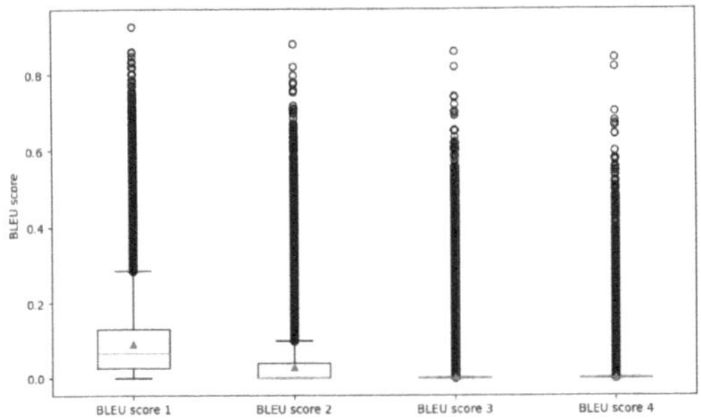

Fig. 1. Box plots for the *BLEU score* among all performed *Reconstruction Attacks*

(a) PROMPT: Adds new attribute

ORIGINAL
```
public void putAttribute(String name, String value){
    attributes.put(name, value);
}
```

RECONSTRUCTED
```
public void addAttribute(String name, String value){
    attributes.put(name, value);
}
```

(b) PROMPT: Log the given message with the tag of info

ORIGINAL
```
public void info(String message) {
    writeInfoToken(message);
}
```

RECONSTRUCTED
```
public static void log(String message) {
    log(message, null);
}
```

(c) PROMPT: Deletes the named file

ORIGINAL
```
public void delete(String filename) {
    new File(filename).delete();
}
```

RECONSTRUCTED
```
public void deleteFile(String filename)
                                throws IOException {
  if (filename == null) {
    throw new IllegalArgumentException("File name cannot be null");
  }
  if (filename.endsWith(File.separator)) {
    filename = filename.substring(0,
                    filename.length() - File.separator.length());
  }
  new File(filename).delete();
}
```

Fig. 2. Examples of partially reconstructed Java methods

Notably, all examples are concise (three lines of code). Even though the reconstructions are not perfect, they always allow to get the core logic of the methods. In detail, Fig. 2-a displays a method with a different (but semantically similar) name.

The reconstructed code in Fig. 2-b is more generic compared to the reference one. The reconstruction in Fig. 2-c exhibits additional logic in method body. These findings indicate that while the reconstruction attack does not always replicate the training data verbatim, in some cases it is able to produce meaningful and logically coherent code snippets.

4.2 Threats to Validity

As for the threats to **construct validity**, we assumed the adversary could access the tokenizer to encode and decode raw input and output data. In practical scenarios, an adversary might might not have such a piece of information. In terms of **internal validity**, merging three datasets to create the auxiliary set (*auxiliary dataset*) might introduce duplicates, as all datasets were sourced from

GitHub. However, we found that the overlap of common samples was under 4%, and these were subsequently removed. Finally, as for the threats to **external validity**, our study focused on a single code summarization model. Testing the attack against other models could enhance the generalizability of our results.

5 Conclusion and Future Work

We present an initial exploration of performing a *Reconstruction Attack* on an LLM designed for a coding task – specifically, code summarization – with the objective of reconstructing the source code used for training. The results indicate that the attack fails on most instances, suggesting that state-of-the-art LLMs for coding tasks largely maintain confidentiality and do not disclose source code. However, there were some instances where the attack successfully reconstructed versions of the source code that closely resembled the original. Future research should focus on developing training methods for LLMs that further reduce the likelihood of successful reconstruction attacks, even in these rare successful instances.

Acknowledgment. This publication is part of the project PNRR-NGEU which has received funding from the MUR - DM 118/2023. This work has been supported by the European Union - NextGenerationEU through the Italian Ministry of University and Research, Projects PRIN 2022 "QualAI: Continuous Quality Improvement of AI-based Systems", grant n. 2022B3BP5S, CUP: H53D23003510006.

References

1. Al-Kaswan, A., Izadi, M., van Deursen, A.: Targeted attack on GPT-neo for the SATML language model data extraction challenge. arXiv:2302.07735 (2023)
2. Al-Kaswan, A., Izadi, M., Van Deursen, A.: Traces of memorisation in large language models for code. In: IEEE/ACM International Conference on Software Engineering, pp. 1–12 (2024)
3. Carlini, N., Liu, C., Erlingsson, Ú., Kos, J., Song, D.: The secret sharer: evaluating and testing unintended memorization in neural networks. In: USENIX Security Symposium, pp. 267–284 (2019)
4. Carlini, N., et al.: Extracting training data from large language models. In: USENIX Security Symposium, pp. 2633–2650 (2021)
5. Fredrikson, M., Jha, S., Ristenpart, T.: Model inversion attacks that exploit confidence information and basic countermeasures. In: ACM SIGSAC Conference on Computer and Communications Security (CCS), pp. 1322–1333 (2015)
6. Fredrikson, M., Lantz, E., Jha, S., Lin, S., Page, D., Ristenpart, T.: Privacy in pharmacogenetics: an {End-to-End} case study of personalized warfarin dosing. In: USENIX Security Symposium, pp. 17–32 (2014)
7. Ganju, K., Wang, Q., Yang, W., Gunter, C.A., Borisov, N.: Property inference attacks on fully connected neural networks using permutation invariant representations. In: Computer and Communications Security Conference, pp. 619–633 (2018)
8. Haque, S., LeClair, A., Wu, L., McMillan, C.: Improved automatic summarization of subroutines via attention to file context. In: International Conference on Mining Software Repositories, pp. 300–310 (2020)

9. Hidano, S., Murakami, T., Katsumata, S., Kiyomoto, S., Hanaoka, G.: Model inversion attacks for prediction systems: without knowledge of non-sensitive attributes. In: IEEE International Conference on Privacy, Security, and Trust, pp. 115–11509 (2017)
10. Hitaj, B., Ateniese, G., Perez-Cruz, F.: Deep models under the GAN: information leakage from collaborative deep learning. In: ACM SIGSAC Conference on Computer and Communications Security, pp. 603–618 (2017)
11. Hu, X., Li, G., Xia, X., Lo, D., Jin, Z.: Deep code comment generation. In: IEEE/ACM International Conference on Program Comprehension, pp. 200–210 (2018)
12. Hu, X., Li, G., Xia, X., Lo, D., Lu, S., Jin, Z.: Summarizing source code with transferred API knowledge. In: International Joint Conference on Artificial Intelligence, pp. 2269–2275 (2018)
13. Husain, H., Wu, H.H., Gazit, T., Allamanis, M., Brockschmidt, M.: Codesearchnet challenge: evaluating the state of semantic code search. arXiv:1909.09436 (2019)
14. Mastropaolo, A., et al.: Studying the usage of text-to-text transfer transformer to support code-related tasks. In: IEEE/ACM International Conference on Software Engineering, pp. 336–347 (2021)
15. Papineni, K., Roukos, S., Ward, T., Zhu, W.J.: BLEU: a method for automatic evaluation of machine translation. In: Annual Meeting of the ACL, pp. 311–318 (2002)
16. Parikh, R., Dupuy, C., Gupta, R.: Canary extraction in natural language understanding models. In: Annual Meeting of the ACL (2022)
17. Raffel, C., et al.: Exploring the limits of transfer learning with a unified text-to-text transformer. J. Mach. Learn. Res. (JMLR) **21**(1), 5485–5551 (2020)
18. Rigaki, M., Garcia, S.: A survey of privacy attacks in machine learning. ACM Comput. Surv. **56**(4), 1–34 (2023)
19. Shokri, R., Stronati, M., Song, C., Shmatikov, V.: Membership inference attacks against machine learning models. In: IEEE Symposium on Security and Privacy (SP), pp. 3–18 (2017)
20. Tramèr, F., Zhang, F., Juels, A., Reiter, M.K., Ristenpart, T.: Stealing machine learning models via prediction APIs. In: USENIX Security Symposium, pp. 601–618 (2016)
21. Vaswani, A., et al.: Attention is all you need. Adv. Neural Inf. Process. Syst. **30** (2017)
22. Yang, Z., et al.: Unveiling memorization in code models. In: IEEE/ACM International Conference on Software Engineering, pp. 856–856 (2024)
23. Yang, Z., Zhang, J., Chang, E.C., Liang, Z.: Neural network inversion in adversarial setting via background knowledge alignment. In: ACM SIGSAC Conference on Computer and Communications Security, pp. 225–240 (2019)
24. Zhang, Y., Jia, R., Pei, H., Wang, W., Li, B., Song, D.: The secret revealer: generative model-inversion attacks against deep neural networks. In: IEEE/CVF Computer Vision and Pattern Recognition Conference, pp. 253–261 (2020)
25. Zhang, Z., Wen, J., Huang, M.: ETHICIST: targeted training data extraction through loss smoothed soft prompting and calibrated confidence estimation. In: Annual Meeting of the ACL (2023)
26. Ziegler, A., et al.: Measuring github copilot's impact on productivity. Commun. ACM **67**(3), 54–63 (2024)

Do Static Analysis Tools Improve Awareness and Attitude Toward Secure Software Development?

Sabato Nocera(✉), Simone Romano, Dario Di Nucci, Rita Francese, Fabio Palomba, and Giuseppe Scanniello

Department of Computer Science, University of Salerno, Fisciano, Italy
{snocera,siromano,ddinucci,francese,fpalomba,gscanniello}@unisa.it

Abstract. We conducted a preliminary qualitative investigation into the Bachelor's students' perception of the usefulness of a Static Analysis Tool (*i.e.,* SonarCloud) in assessing software security. The results revealed that the students considered SonarCloud user-friendly, simple to set up, and easy to learn. Additionally, the students recognized an improvement in their awareness and attitude toward secure software development, as well as with the use of a tool widely adopted in both open-source communities and the software industry. The results suggest that the use of SonarCloud improves students' software security skills, which are demanded by the labor market.

Keywords: Software Security · Software Vulnerability · Secure Software Development · Static Analysis Tool · Focus Group · Empirical Study

1 Introduction

Software security is a non-functional requirement that must be addressed throughout the design, development, and maintenance of software systems [6]. Software security might be threatened by *security concerns* (also known as *security issues*), which are risks whose occurrence would compromise the confidentiality, integrity, or availability of a software system. Among security concerns, *software vulnerabilities* are holes or weaknesses within software systems (*e.g.,* design flaws or implementation bugs) that attackers could exploit to damage stakeholders.

While introducing some security concerns in the source code is unavoidable (*e.g.,* vulnerability still unknown), others can be fixed before the deployment of software systems, or even developers could avoid their introduction. Supporting tools can help developers manage security concerns as many can be easily detected and do not require security experts to be resolved [5]. Among them, *Static Analysis Tools* (*SATs*) can be used to identify security concerns in three scenarios: *(i)* while developers code by highlighting their presence in Integrated Development Environments (IDEs); *(ii)* within Continuous-Integration/Continuous-Delivery (CI/CD) pipelines, which could make a build

A. Bertolino et al. (Eds.): QUATIC 2024, CCIS 2178, pp. 399–407, 2024.
https://doi.org/10.1007/978-3-031-70245-7_28

fail if the code is not compliant with given security criteria; and *(iii)* during code reviews.

In a previous research [9], we conducted a study to comprehend whether Bachelor's CS students in a *Software Technologies for the Web* (STW) course were equipped to manage (*i.e.,* detect and resolve) security concerns in the development of e-commerce web apps. We found that in the academic year (a.y.) 2021–22 students were not equipped to develop secure web apps, although they recognized security as extremely important. Security concerns (also related to severe vulnerabilities like SQL injection) were widespread in the web apps they developed. Then, we devised a security training intervention to fill this gap for the a.y. 2022–23 STW students. It involved lessons on software security and *SonarCloud* as a SAT; in this respect, we chose SonarCloud because it is likely to be used by them in the future (*i.e.,* once they graduate, as the next generation of professional developers) due to its popularity [2,8]. We asked the students (who were different from those enrolled in the a.y. 2021–22) to use SonarCloud to detect security concerns but we did not force them to remove these concerns. One of the most important results shown in [10] was that the number of security concerns in the web apps developed in a.y. 2022–23 was significantly less than those produced in a.y. 2021–22. The presented investigations were quantitative. This is to say that we did not collect their perspective about whether the use of SATs changes CS students' attitudes toward secure software development.

Our work builds on top of these previous findings and advances state-of-the-art by conducting a *preliminary* qualitative study aimed at understanding *(i)* the opinions of CS students on the use of a SAT to manage security concerns and *(ii)* whether its use improved their awareness and attitude toward secure software development.

We used a focus group as a qualitative research method. It involved some of the a.y. 2022–23 students who had used SonarCloud while developing their e-commerce web apps and had passed the STW exam. While the study has a preliminary connotation due to the limited sample of students we could involve, it provides already interesting findings that we argue may be beneficial for the research community. The focus group session took place one semester after the students had passed the STW exam.

2 Related Work

There is a shortage of personnel with expertise in software security [7]. CS students still graduate with little or no secure software development knowledge [1]. To provide adequate security training to the next generation of professional developers, one proposed approach is incorporating software security into university courses not devoted to security [14].

Past studies investigated integrating security practices into web development pipelines. Zhu *et al.* [16] experimented using an *Eclipse* plug-in integrated within an IDE during a web programming course. This tool provides instant security alerts along with descriptions of security concerns. The results involving 20 students revealed that this kind of support could potentially help software security learning in the context of programming assignments. A similar approach was proposed by Tabassum *et al.* [12], who also adopted an Eclipse plug-in to provide instant security alerts while coding in Java. The results suggest the need for incentives to motivate students to adopt secure development techniques.

Taeb and Chi [13] analyzed the gap in software security education and proposed a framework based on three categories of hands-on labs. The proposed framework was then evaluated through a user study using questionnaires involving 39 and seven Bachelor's and master's students, respectively. The results indicated an improvement in students' knowledge of software security.

Yilmaz and Ulusoy [15] studied the security concerns within the source code of two programming tasks over six semesters. The two tasks were performed by students of a course non-devoted to software security (*i.e.*, a *Database Management Systems* course). From a didactic perspective, the results revealed that students did not consider security for time reasons.

3 Study Design

The design of our focus group follows the guidelines by Kontio *et al.* [4].

3.1 Goals

We conceived our focus group to pursue the following goals.

Goal 1. To comprehend the positive and negative points regarding the use of a SAT like SonarCloud when securing web apps. In this respect, we intend to unveil possible side effects and challenges related to the use of SonarCloud, as well as improvements to mitigate the negative points.
Goal 2. To understand the perceived effects of the use of a SAT like SonarCloud toward secure development, including software security awareness and attitude.

3.2 Participants

The focus group participants were five Bachelor's CS students enrolled in the a.y. 2023–24. They had all passed the STW exam during the a.y. 2022–23. To pass the exam, they had to undergo a written test and fulfill a software project consisting of an e-commerce web app. The participants passed the STW exam one semester before the focus group session. The STW course took place in the second semester of the second year of the Bachelor's program in CS, after students had attended courses on procedural (C) and object-oriented programming (Java), databases, computer architecture, and operating systems.

The STW course provides theoretical lessons and practical exercises on web app development. The topics covered by the course are: HTTP/S; HTML and CSS; Java-based server-side technologies (*i.e.*, Servlets, JavaBeans, and JSPs);

Table 1. Focus group script

Questions
1. Why did you use SonarCloud in your projects?
2. Did you experience any difficulty in using SonarCloud in your projects?
3. Do you think it was easy to use SonarCloud?
4. Did you resolve hotspots and vulnerabilities detected by SonarCloud?
5. Did you have any difficulties resolving hotspots and vulnerabilities identified by SonarCloud?
6. Did you think resolving the hotspots and vulnerabilities suggested by SonarCloud was helpful?
7. Did you feel that SonarCloud has improved your awareness and attitude toward software security?

JavaScript and DHTML; XML and JSON to exchange data in asynchronous AJAX requests; Git and GitHub to version software and work collaboratively; and the Model-View-Controller (MVC) as a reference architectural pattern. The reference IDE for the course was Eclipse.

The students enrolled in the STW course for the a.y. 2022–23 received a security training intervention (lasting five hours). It involved basic software security concepts and an overview of the OWASP Top 10 security risks [11]. The STW students enrolled in the a.y. 2022–23 were invited (but not forced) to use SonarCloud when developing the course mandatory project. The focus group participants had all used SonarCloud when developing the STW project.

Before the focus group took place, the participants (two women and three men) filled in a pre-questionnaire regarding their experience as professional and open-source developers. The participants had experience neither as professional nor as open-source developers, except for one who acknowledged having expertise, especially as an open-source developer.

3.3 Execution Plan

The focus group was conducted in a research laboratory at the University of Salerno. It lasted about 40 min and was audio-recorded. At the beginning, the facilitator (first author) explained the purpose and guidelines of the study to the participants. Additionally, the facilitator assured that all information gathered during the session, including the participants' identities and audio recordings, would remain confidential and anonymized. Then, the facilitator guided the discussion according to a predefined script (see Table 1). The discussion followed a semi-structured approach (*i.e.*, deviations from the script were allowed as long as the discussion was consistent with the objectives of the study) as usual in the focus-group research method. We used a *Thematic Analysis Template* (TAT) approach to analyze the transcripts of the audio recording of the focus group. The initial template was created based on our experience and knowledge. We updated the initial template until reaching a consensus on the final one.

4 Results

In the following, we present the results concerning the themes and sub-themes of the final template.

Theme 1) Positive/Negative Points with SonarCloud. This theme includes five sub-themes related to the positive and negative points of using SonarCloud. As far as the positive points are concerned, the participants indicated the usability and usefulness of SonarCloud. They also appreciated that they gained skills and that SonarCloud allows them to prevent mistakes due to distractions. The only negative point is the detection of false-positive security concerns.

a) Usability. The participants found SonarCloud easy to use. For example, one participant asserted that he did not encounter any problems configuring or using it, although he had never used SonarCloud before. Another participant acknowledged having encountered some minor difficulties, which were the same as when approaching a new technology.

b) Usefulness. The participants perceived SonarCloud as helpful in finding security concerns and then useful for securing web apps. The participants also appreciated the tips provided by SonarCloud on how to remove the identified security concerns (*i.e.*, suggestions and practical examples).

c) Gained Skills on SonarCloud. The learning experience allowed the students to acquire skills on SonarCloud that are useful in the labor market. Indeed, two participants stated that the use of SonarCloud during the STW course was a remarkable experience as they were introduced to a SAT that is used extensively.

d) Preventing the Introduction of Security Concerns due to Distractions. The participants highly praised SonarCloud as being able to provide support to prevent the introduction of security concerns into the code of their application due to distraction.

e) False Positives. The participants were not particularly troubled by the false-positive security concerns detected by SonarCloud. The participants found that almost all detected security concerns were harmful. However, we have to mention that SonarCloud can also be used to detect code smells. The participants freely used this feature in their projects and were disappointed to discover a high number of false-positive code smells.

Theme 2) Perceived Effects of Using SonarCloud. This theme includes two sub-themes related to the perceived effects of using SonarCloud. The two sub-themes focus on improving awareness and attitude toward security.

a) Improving Awareness Toward Security. The participants agreed that the use of SonarCloud improved their awareness concerning software security. The participants also mentioned that, after passing the STW exam, their use of SonarCloud was improved, and they started to be even more proactive in resolving security concerns.

g) Improving Attitude Toward Security. The participants affirmed that SonarCloud helped them improve their attitude toward secure software development. Overall, the participants believed that, at least, they would be more careful about the kinds of security concerns that they had previously resolved.

Based on these considerations, the participants agreed that the use of a tool such as SonarCloud could be useful for learning secure software development and, more generally, good development practices. In this respect, novice developers could avoid acquiring and establishing bad habits, while a developer with several years of experience may be less willing to change his/her approach to software development due to established habits.

5 Findings and Implications

In this section, we discuss the findings and implications of our study.

Finding #1: A SAT like SonarCloud is easy to use, configure, and learn, as well as helpful in managing security concerns.

The participants appreciated SonarCloud. They acknowledged its usability and usefulness in detecting and then resolving security concerns, as well as valuable support to improve the security of the software systems they develop. These points are of interest to **educators**. Moreover, since the participants faced, in their projects, mostly dangerous security concerns, this could be relevant for **practitioners**. That is, developers with adequate tool support produce more secure software. However, what we observed is not completely consistent with the results by Johnson *et al.* [3], who reported dissatisfaction with the use of SATs due to their low understandability and lack of issue resolution support. We can postulate that this difference is due to the security training that our participants received and the different issues they focused on (*i.e.*, security concerns). This point could interest **researchers** and be subject to further investigations.

Finding #2: A SAT like SonarCloud allows preventing the introduction of security concerns due to distraction.

Since software development is an error-prone process that involves high human efforts, SATs like SonarCloud are useful because they can warn developers about security concerns introduced due to distractions that would otherwise go unnoticed. As for SonarCloud, these warnings refer to security concerns that have already been in the source code for some time because the analysis is triggered later by a CI/CD event. To notify developers about security concerns introduced while coding (*i.e.*, in real-time), SATs plugged within IDEs should be used. Nevertheless, SonarLint—a free IDE extension that integrates with SonarCloud—has limitations in detecting the same kinds of security concerns as SonarCloud. Therefore, we advise **SAT vendors** to improve their SATs to provide better support to developers, and, in particular, the results seem to suggest SonarSource to improve SonarLint to detect more different kinds of security concerns.

Finding #3: SonarCloud's security concerns are unlikely to be false positives.

It is unlikely that the security concerns returned by SonarCloud are false positives. This finding confirms, from a qualitative perspective, that by Elder *et al.* [2], who compared different security testing strategies and supporting tools, and then concluded that SonarCloud identified a high number of security concerns with the best correctness (*i.e.*, the least number of false positives). Such a low false-positive rate should help **practitioners** to make a more informed decision on the SAT to be integrated into the development pipeline.

Finding #4: A SAT like SonarCloud can support students' learning experience, leading them to improve awareness and attitude toward secure software development.

SonarCloud can be a valuable learning support for students, as it can support them by providing constant feedback on their work. In a previous research [10], we observed that the use of SonarCloud has a significant and large positive effect on the security of web apps. The results of this focus group clarify that the use of SonarCloud also positively affects students' awareness and attitude toward secure software development and, more generally, good development practices. In this respect, the participants also recognized that the labor market demands security skills. Moreover, having previously resolved a certain kind of security concern detected by SonarCloud could lead to avoiding reintroducing it (even without using SonarCloud). Therefore, SonarCloud can help students acquire secure software development skills and habits. After learning about SonarCloud, the participants also changed their attitude toward its use, passing from procrastinating to being more direct and responsive in resolving issues. To a large extent, the focus group fills the gap of our previous investigation from a qualitative perspective [10].

6 Threats to Validity

The threats to validity are presented based on the guidelines by Kontio *et al.* [4].

Researcher Bias. Researcher bias could occur during the planning, execution, or data analysis of empirical studies due to the influence of researchers' expectations. A possible threat could be the selection of the participants.

Group Dynamics. Focus group sessions (as usual) do not have a formal predefined format; thus, group dynamics or communication styles might influence the participants' activity level. To mitigate this threat, we used a semi-structured discussion approach, and the facilitator balanced the discussion and kept less active participants.

Social Acceptability. Social acceptability threatens the themes discussed during the focus group session. Social acceptability weakness was mitigated by laying out appropriate ground rules at the beginning of the focus group session.

Number of Participants. We recognize that the number of participants involved could threaten the validity of the overall investigation. However, our study's connotation is preliminary and provides interesting insights that may be beneficial for the research community. Also, we involved five participants, which is within the typical range (three to 12) according to Kontio *et al.* [4].

Generalization. We recognize that our results may not hold outside the case of Bachelor's CS students taking the STW course (*e.g.,* in the case of students with a different academic background).

7 Conclusion

We conducted a focus group with Bachelor's students in Computer Science to investigate their opinions on using a Static Analysis Tool (*i.e.,* SonarCloud). The participants found SonarCloud easy to use, configure, and learn, as well as helpful in detecting security concerns (which were, based on their experience, mostly true positives). They also found SonarCloud a valuable learning support for improving their awareness and attitude toward secure software development.

References

1. Almansoori, M., Lam, J., Fang, E., Mulligan, K., Soosai Raj, A.G., Chatterjee, R.: How secure are our computer systems courses? In: Proceedings of the Conference on International Computing Education Research, pp. 271–281. ACM (2020)
2. Elder, S., et al.: Do i really need all this work to find vulnerabilities? Empir. Softw. Eng. **27**(6), 154:1–154:78 (2022)
3. Johnson, B., Song, Y., Murphy-Hill, E., Bowdidge, R.: Why don't software developers use static analysis tools to find bugs? In: Proceedings of the International Conference on Software Engineering, pp. 672–681. IEEE (2013)
4. Kontio, J., Lehtola, L., Bragge, J.: Using the focus group method in software engineering: obtaining practitioner and user experiences. In: Proceedings of the International Symposium on Empirical Software Engineering, pp. 271–280. IEEE (2004)
5. Lam, J., Fang, E., Almansoori, M., Chatterjee, R., Soosai Raj, A.G.: Identifying gaps in the secure programming knowledge and skills of students. In: Proceedings of the Technical Symposium on Computer Science Education, pp. 703–709. ACM (2022)
6. McGraw, G.: Software security. IEEE Secur. Priv. **2**(2), 80–83 (2004)
7. Muncaster, P.: Global security skills shortage falls to 2.7 million workers (2021)
8. Nocera, S., Romano, S., Francese, R., Burlon, R., Scanniello, G.: Managing vulnerabilities in software projects: the case of NTT data. In: 2023 49th Euromicro Conference on Software Engineering and Advanced Applications (SEAA), pp. 247–253 (2023). https://doi.org/10.1109/SEAA60479.2023.00046
9. Nocera, S., Romano, S., Francese, R., Scanniello, G.: Training for security: planning the use of a sat in the development pipeline of web apps. In: 2023 IEEE/ACM 45th International Conference on Software Engineering: Software Engineering Education and Training (ICSE-SEET), pp. 40–45 (2023). https://doi.org/10.1109/ICSE-SEET58685.2023.00010

10. Nocera, S., Romano, S., Francese, R., Scanniello, G.: Training for security: results from using a static analysis tool in the development pipeline of web apps. In: Proceedings of the 46th International Conference on Software Engineering: Software Engineering Education and Training, pp. 253–263. ICSE-SEET '24, Association for Computing Machinery, New York, NY, USA (2024). https://doi.org/10.1145/3639474.3640073
11. OWASP: Owasp top ten (2022)
12. Tabassum, M., Watson, S., Chu, B., Lipford, H.R.: Evaluating two methods for integrating secure programming education. In: Proceedings of the Technical Symposium on Computer Science Education, pp. 390–395. ACM (2018)
13. Taeb, M., Chi, H.: A personalized learning framework for software vulnerability detection and education. In: Proceedings of the International Symposium on Computer Science and Intelligent Controls, pp. 119–126. IEEE (2021)
14. White, G., Nordstrom, G.: Security across the curriculum: using computer security to teach computer science principles. In: Proceedings of the National Information Systems Security Conference, pp. 483–488 (1996)
15. Yilmaz, T., Ulusoy, Ö.: Understanding security vulnerabilities in student code: a case study in a non-security course. JJSS **185**, 111150 (2022)
16. Zhu, J., Lipford, H.R., Chu, B.: Interactive support for secure programming education. In: Proceedings of the Technical Symposium on Computer Science Education, pp. 687–692. ACM (2013)

A User-Centric Privacy Control Framework for Decentralized IoT Platforms

Xu Tao[1], Rui Zhao[2], Salim Chehida[3(✉)], Davide Conzon[4], Enrico Ferrera[4], and Saddek Bensalem[3]

[1] University of Kentucky, Lexington, KY, USA
[2] Polytechnic University of Catalonia, Barcelona, Spain
[3] Univ. Grenoble Alpes, Grenoble, France
salim.chehida@univ-grenoble-alpes.fr
[4] LINKS Foundation, Turin, TO, Italy

Abstract. We propose a sticky-policy based distributed privacy control system, namely BRAIN-IoT Privacy Control System, under strict compliance with General Data Protection Regulation (GDPR). It empowers users to set privacy policies and decide how the data should be managed. Furthermore, the proposed architecture aims to offer policy matching services to continuously and automatically enforce privacy protection in fully decentralized Internet of Things (IoT) environments i.e., the BRAIN-IoT platform, which focuses on the interoperability between heterogeneous IoT systems and secure data transmission. We validate the BRAIN-IoT Privacy Control System in real-life large-scale public events. Experiments results show that the system can quickly perform match checking of the privacy policies transmitted with personal data.

Keywords: Privacy Control · Privacy As a Service · IoT · GDPR · Sticky Policy · User Awareness

1 Introduction

Today, IoT has greatly facilitated people's lives in various aspects. Many applications such as smart home, and healthcare are driven by collecting and analyzing a large amount of personal information. Some public authorities launch new legal frameworks considering data privacy and protection to mitigate the threats posed by misusing personal data. For example, The European Union (EU) has established GDPR regulation to protect the privacy of individuals by regulating how their personal data is collected, processed, and stored by organizations. However, these regulations cannot anticipate every possible scenario and address individual privacy needs and concerns. Besides, substantial research aims to only provide management mechanisms for privacy data and policies.

IoT frameworks need new technological infrastructures to provide appropriate privacy control over the flow of information and empower individuals to manage their own privacy in a digital environment. The main challenges for

A. Bertolino et al. (Eds.): QUATIC 2024, CCIS 2178, pp. 408–415, 2024.
https://doi.org/10.1007/978-3-031-70245-7_29

building such infrastructure include: *(C1)* giving data owners the power to control their information; *(C2)* giving data owners the right of rectification; *(C3)* establishing measures to enforce privacy policies when data is going to utilized by heterogeneous IoT service providers and administrations. These issues are even more extractive with decentralized IoT platforms due to cross-platform data exchange and communications.

To accomplish the aforementioned challenges, we propose BRAIN-IoT Privacy Control System as technological means to guarantee privacy compliance with user awareness for decentralized IoT platforms. First, BRAIN-IoT Privacy Control System provides IoT platform users direct fine-grained control of their personal data generated from personal IoT devices through a graphical user interface, e.g., the data owner can register their personal devices into the system and set up the privacy policies of how their data should be stored, processed and managed. On the other hand, the IoT service provider can configure the privacy policies required to provide the demand services. Second, the system employs a "sticky policy" concept [4], in which, authorization policies are attached to the data itself, instead of being managed by the services provider which consumes the data. Third, our system provides a Policy Enforcement Point (PEP) based architecture to enforce the compliance of the accessibility of personal data required by services with the privacy settings of data owners. Finally, the system is able to be flexibly adopted by a wide number of IoT solutions without requiring them to change existing trusted parties or storage providers. The implementation of the system is open-sourced in Eclipse Research GitHub[1].

2 BRAIN-IoT Privacy Control System

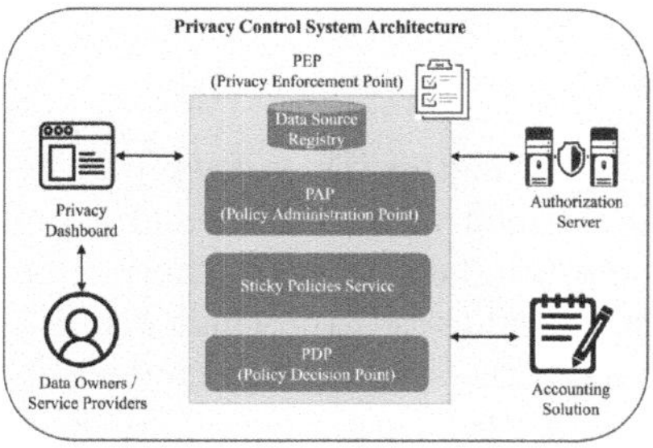

Fig. 1. Privacy Control System Architecture

The proposed Privacy Control System is composed of four main components as shown in Fig. 1: *PEP*, *Authorization Server*, *Privacy Dashboard*, and *Accounting Solution*. **PEP** is the main component used to make enforcement decisions leveraging Distributed Ledger Technologies (DLT), e.g., whether a service is authorized to access the data in transit. It has four sub-components: Data Source Registry, Policy Administration Point (PAP), Sticky Policies Service, and Policy Decision Point (PDP). The data Source Registry stores the map between Data Owner and owned Data resources. PAP is in charge of querying the data owner through Identity (ID) of devices and caches the privacy-related information. Sticky Policies Service manages the privacy policies requests and signs the privacy policies. PDP is responsible for privacy policy compliance verification. **Authorization Server** stores privacy policies configured by both data owners

[1] https://github.com/eclipse-researchlabs/brain-iot-privacy-control-system.

and service providers. PEP queries Authorization Server to obtain the privacy policies associated with the data generated by specific personal devices. **Privacy Dashboard** is a web-based graphical user interface that allows data owners to register and configure policies associated with their personal devices. Service providers can also set data access requirements to provide services. The policies defined by data owners and service providers through the Privacy Dashboard are stored in the Authorization Server. **Accounting Solution** maintains all the policy settings as well as policy enforcement decisions made by the BRAIN-IoT PEP. It is designed to support accounting feature. It is exploited whenever litigation on possible data misusing happens.

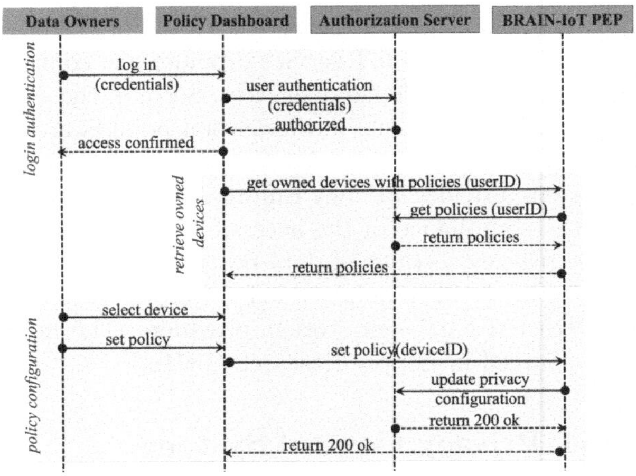

Fig. 2. Privacy Policy Setup

Figure 2 represents the sequence diagram for setting up the privacy policies by a data owner. A similar procedure is also performed when a service provider registers its service within the system, describing the data access authorization it needs for providing the service. This procedure addresses the challenge *C1, C2* introduced in Sect. 1. The data owner first login the system with credentials from the Policy Dashboard, which then requests Authorization Server to check the credentials and grant access to the Privacy Control System. Once the Data Owner is authorized, Policy Dashboard queries PEP to retrieve the information of owned devices, along with their privacy configurations. After receiving the request, PEP forwards the requests to Authorization Server where the privacy settings are stored. Finally, the policies associated with the devices belonging to the data owner are returned and displayed in the Policy Dashboard. The data owner can set up privacy policies for a newly registered device or update existing policies for the devices that are already registered through Policy Dashboard. If the operations are successfully processed, the policy settings will be updated and stored in Authorization Server.

2.1 Sticky Policy Message Generation

We now illustrate the process of sticky policy message generation within an actual IoT platform, i.e., the BRAIN-IoT platform [1,2]. Nonetheless, it can also be easily adapted to any other IoT platforms. We first present the three relevant components in the BRAIN-IoT platform, that interact with the privacy control system. *BRAIN-IoT EventBus* is a distributed publish/subscribe communication channel to transfer data and control messages in the decentralized BRAIN-IoT infrastructure. *Edge Node* [6] is a component providing interoperability for heterogeneous IoT devices/platforms. The southbound of Edge Node interacts with IoT devices/platforms with their desired communication protocol. The northbound of Edge Node injects the data generated by end IoT devices/platforms into BRAIN-IoT EventBus or delivers the messages from the BRRAIN-IoT environment in EventBus to the end IoT devices/platforms. *BRAIN-IoT PEP Adapter* is an interface to integrate the BRAIN-IoT Privacy Control System for the BRAIN-IoT platform, assuring the data flows between these two systems.

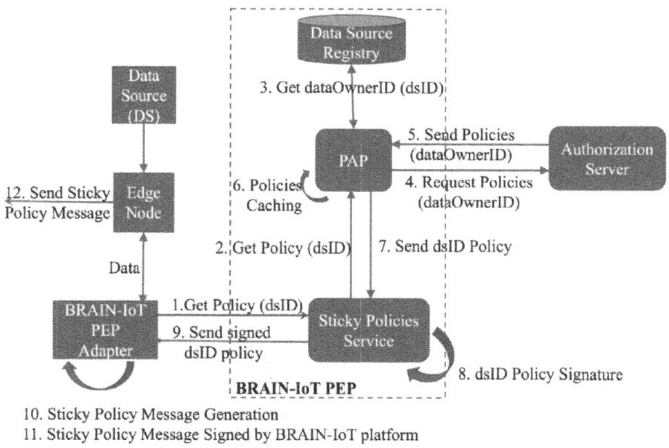

Fig. 3. Sticky Message Generation

During the process of stick policy message generation, PEP is in charge of different functional tasks, which are represented in Fig. 3. Edge Node first calls PEP Adapter before releasing the data to the BRAIN-IoT Communication Infrastructure. The PEP asks for the policy set by the data owner for a given data source represented by its identifier 'dsID'. The Sticky Policy Service of the PEP then forwards the request to a PAP, responsible for managing the policy and other relevant information. The PAP skims through the Data Source Registry, which stores a map between the data owners and the owned data sources. Such information is stored in the registry every time a data owner registers a new device and inserts the policy related to the data sourced by it. The registry returns the identifier of the data owner who owns the specified Data Source. In order to gather the privacy policies, the PAP requests the privacy policies associated with the devices of the given Data Owner to an Authorization Server. The Authorization Server returns the data owner's devices with privacy policies back to the PAP. In order to improve the processing efficiency of future similar requests, the PAP caches this information internally for a certain amount of time or until a new policy is set by the Data Owner. The PAP returns the privacy policies of the corresponding device to the Sticky Policy Service. The Sticky Policy Service signs the policies, which is then returned back to the BRAIN-IoT PEP adapter. BRAIN-IoT PEP Adapter generates the sticky message by attaching the privacy policies to the generated data. The sticky policy message can then be signed by the IoT platform through its own security mechanism. The sticky message is finally published by the Edge Node to the distributed communication infrastructure, i.g., BRAIN-IoT EventBus.

2.2 Privacy Policy Enforcement

Once the sticky message is sent out, the BRAIN-IoT EventBus acts as a broker toward all the available services which subscribe to the type of data in transit on the EventBus. Before delivering the data to the subscribed services, the BRAIN-IoT EventBus performs privacy control leveraging PEP. The detailed procedure is shown in Fig. 4.

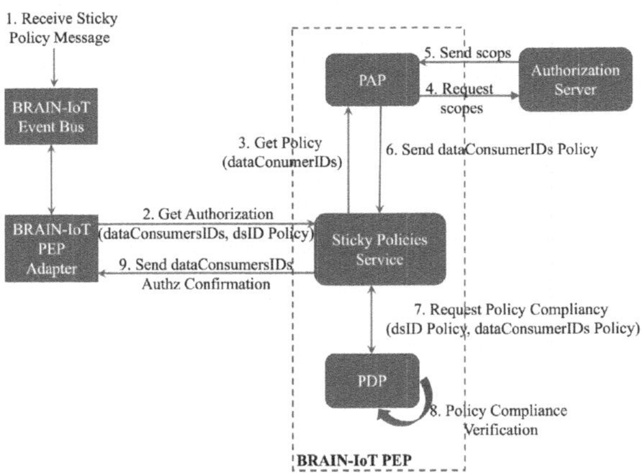

Fig. 4. Privacy Policy Enforcement

After receiving the sticky message, BRAIN-IoT EventBus cooperates with PEP to perform privacy enforcement. The communications are through BRAIN-IoT PEP adapter. The BRAIN-IoT PEP adapter asks for authorization to deliver the data to a list of data consumer services subscribing to the data. Along with the identifiers of the data consumer services, the BRAIN-IoT PEP adapter provides also the policies attached to the data, stripped from the Sticky Policy Message. The Sticky Policy Service receives the request and asks for the privacy policies required by the data consumers to provide the services. The PAP queries the Authorization Server to request the privacy policies associated to the services within the scope of BRAIN-IoT PEP. The service privacy policies are stored when the service provider registers the service to the platform. The Authorization Server returns back the privacy policies of the services registered in the scope of BRAIN-IoT PEP to the PAP. The PAP returns the requested service policies, identified by data consumer ID, back to the Sticky Policies Service. The Sticky Policy Service requests the PDP to validate a possible match between the policies related to the Data Source and the ones related to the Data Consumer. The PDP checks whether the policy specified by the service provider is consistent with the policy configured by the data owner. It then returns the result back to the Sticky Policy Service. Finally, the Sticky Policy Service returns to the BRAIN-IoT PEP adapter a list of conformation or denials for each service that subscribes to utilize the data. Such information is used by BRAIN-IoT EventBus to enforce the decision of whether to deliver the message to the service. If the privacy policies required by the service do not violate the policies set by the data owner, BRAIN-IoT EventBus will deliver the data to the service. Otherwise, it denies sending the data. Together with the sticky policy message generation procedure, privacy policy enforcement addresses the challenge *C3*.

3 Experiment

The performance of our privacy system has been evaluated through an international fair use case provided by the project MONICA [5]. At the international fair, privacy risks are high, so according to GDPR regulations, privacy control strategies must be implemented to protect attendees' personal information while ensuring the operation of public services. This includes monitoring crowds to prevent incidents and allowing exhibitors to use personal data for personalized experiences. Exhibitors sign an agreement with organizers about expected data usage. To comply with GDPR, organizers inform attendees about data collection and allow them to set privacy preferences at ticketing. During the event, everyone will be provided with a wearable device based on Ultra-Wideband (UWB) technology for collecting positioning data. Each device has a BRAIN-IoT Wearable Edge Node deployed on it. Then, the security personnel can monitor the situation at the fair. Moreover, the positioning data will be used by exhibitors to detect which of the stands a participant decides to stop by in order to infer the specific interests.

The architecture of the demonstrator is represented in Fig. 5. The localization data during the visit is continuously sent to the BRAIN-IoT wearable Edge Node using the Message Queuing Telemetry Transport (MQTT) protocol. The Edge Node is dedicated to wrapping and sending the localization data to the Privacy Control System through the distributed BRAIN-IoT EventBus. Then, if the policies set by data owners and data consumers (organizations and exhibitors) are matched, the localization data will be delivered by the system to the consumer services through EventBus again. The policy checking follows the process

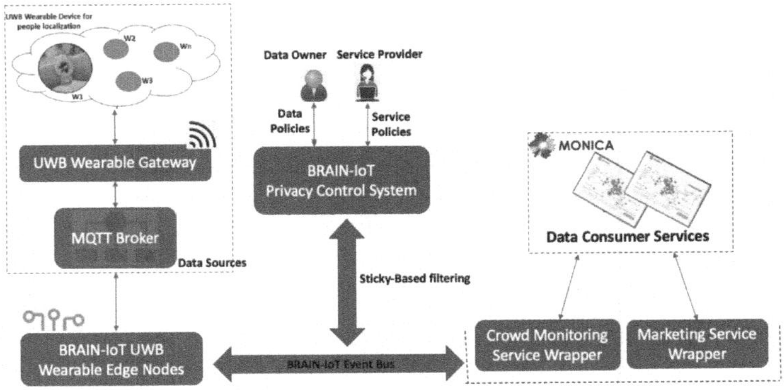

Fig. 5. Architecture of Demonstrator

presented in Sect. 2. Finally, the localization data are required by two types of different services: *(i)* the Crowd Monitoring Services - visualizes a map of the exhibition area with the real-time position of all the attendees. It is used by the safety staff to monitor critical situations. *(ii)* the Marketing Services - visualizes and stores the information about which exhibitor has been visited by the attendees. It is used by exhibitors to profile people and to make commercial offerings tailored to the customers. These services are integrated within the BRAIN-IoT Eco-System through two adapters which represent the counterparts of the so-called Edge Nodes for the external IoT Services/Platforms which would like to exploit IoT Data handled by the BRAIN-IoT Platform. In this demonstration site, the Privacy Control System filters the delivery of personal data to services by checking if data-related policies match service-related policies. Only services with matching policies receive the required data. The system has been validated to operate in a fully distributed environment, offering consistent services and staying updated to meet real-world demands.

To evaluate our system, we have tested the performance with different built-in metrics using the professional load testing tool Grafana k6 [3] in a simulation environment for stressing the system with high volumes of requests. Figure 6 presents the statistics for each tested metric during the validation of the system. In the experiments, a large number of users between 50 to 500 have been simulated to access to the system at the same time, and the overall system performances do not have much differences. As we can see that, for example, when there are 100 users in the fair, a total number of 53847 personal data associated with the privacy policies have been successfully transmitted and checked, and the data with unmatched policies set by audiences and exhibitors will be discarded. Moreover, no threshold is breached causing any risks to the services. The results revealed that the system is reliable and robust enough to handle a significant workload. Furthermore, to do the load testing on the available Representational State Transfer (REST) API, we have also used the main HTTP-specific performance metrics to evaluate an individual HTTP request in various phases in a large scenario. The system API was able to rapidly respond to service requests.

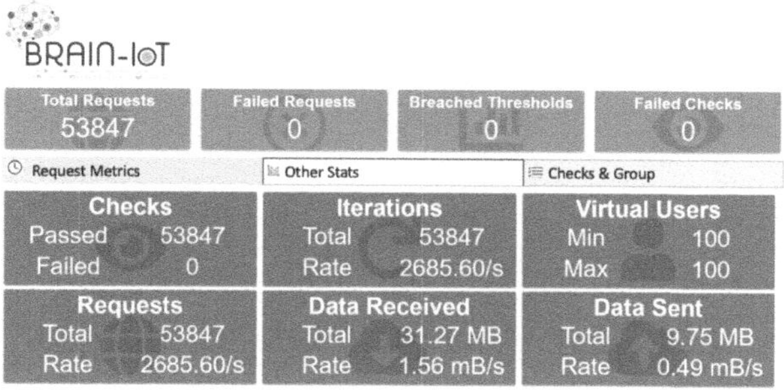

Fig. 6. Performance Statistics for System

4 Conclusion

We presented the BRAIN-IoT Privacy Control System that allows data owners to manage their own data control preferences in real-time and enforces the policies matching among heterogeneous IoT platforms. We release the implementation in the Eclipse Research Github. Experiments show that the system is robust enough in the sense that it's capable of not only enforcing the privacy strategies in compliance with GDPR but also providing enough logging information leveraging on the accounting solution to avoid fraud by evidencing the historical decisions. In the future, we will validate the scalability of the system varying the number of end users and consider more large-scale scenarios.

References

1. Chehida., S., Bensalem., S., Conzon., D., Ferrera., E., Tao., X.: Brain-IoT architecture and platform for building IoT systems. In: Proceedings of the 7th International Conference on Internet of Things, Big Data and Security - IoTBDS, pp. 67–77. INSTICC, SciTePress (2022). https://doi.org/10.5220/0011086000003194
2. Conzon, D., Rashid, M.R.A., Tao, X., Soriano, A., Nicholson, R., Ferrera, E.: BRAIN-IoT: model-based framework for dependable sensing and actuation in intelligent decentralized IoT systems. In: 2019 4th International Conference on Computing, Communications and Security (ICCCS), pp. 1–8 (2019)
3. Labs, G. https://k6.io/docs/
4. Pearson, S., Casassa-Mont, M.: Sticky policies: an approach for managing privacy across multiple parties. Computer **44**(9), 60–68 (2011)
5. Vincent, B., et al.: Monica, a European project focused on the internet of things for the acoustic quality and safety of outdoor large scale events (2018). https://publica.fraunhofer.de/handle/publica/407737
6. Zhao, R., et al.: A cross-platform communication mechanism for ROS-based cyber-physical system. In: Eclipse Research International Conference on Security, Artificial Intelligence and Modeling for the Next Generation Internet of Things (2020)

Doctoral Symposium (SEDES)

Towards Cyber-Physical-Ethical Systems

Yelyzaveta Kurkchi(✉)

Gran Sasso Science Institute, 67100 L'Aquila, Italy
yelyzaveta.kurkchi@gssi.it

Abstract. The increasing complexity of Cyber-Physical Systems poses the challenge of managing dynamic and heterogeneous components, even more so when ethical concerns are explicitly specified and may affect the system's behaviour. This paper aims to address ethical considerations as first-class concerns for the development of Cyber-Physical Systems. To this end, we plan to embed ethical requirements in the formal modelling of Cyber-Physical Systems with the goal of enabling a rigorous and quantitative analysis. Four main activities are foreseen to achieve this goal. First, the specification of a language that captures users' requirements. Second, the development of a modelling formalism that embeds the specification of design elements in Cyber-Physical Systems. Third, a framework that enables the evaluation of these types of systems and produces metrics that quantify their quality. Fourth, a feedback mechanism will be designed to interpret results and provide suggestions to improve the quality of the systems under analysis. This way, we aim to pursue the specification of a new class of systems, namely Cyber-Physical-Ethical systems, where ethics plays a key role in driving the interaction between the cyber and physical components.

Keywords: Cyber-Physical Systems · Ethics · Quantitative Modelling

1 Introduction

Today's life has been significantly transformed in the age of Cyber-Physical Systems (CPS). These systems show the peculiar characteristics of integrating cyber, hence software, components with physical, i.e., hardware, constituent elements. As a consequence, CPS need to manage complex and heterogeneous components while facilitating the digitalisation of intricate business processes. In fact, CPS play a significant role in modern society, whether conducting e-commerce transactions, accessing information, or engaging in social interactions. As these systems become deeply intertwined with our daily existence, their ethical implications become more urgent than ever. The decisions made within CPS can have far-reaching consequences on individuals, entire communities, and societies.

Recently, a series of real-life incidents demonstrate why we must prioritise *ethics* in CPS. For instance, robots were capturing and sharing intimate moments of people, hence exhibiting privacy breaches [4] or cyber assistants like Siri [5] and Alexa [7] made available some private information, hence violating confidentiality

A. Bertolino et al. (Eds.): QUATIC 2024, CCIS 2178, pp. 419–426, 2024.
https://doi.org/10.1007/978-3-031-70245-7_30

in personal data. These incidents raise questions about consent, privacy, and the responsible use of technology in our daily lives. In essence, these scandals demonstrate that the ethical aspects of the CPS are not only theoretical but have a deep influence on individuals and society.

State of the art literature has intensively studied Cyber-Physical Systems [2,8], along with the formal modelling and analysis of these systems [6,11,12,14]. However, to the best of our knowledge, ethics seems to be a concern that has not been extensively considered. This is the reason why we think it is relevant to contribute with a framework that fills the identified gap.

This paper aims to contribute in two directions: (i) embedding ethics in the specification of Cyber-Physical Systems and (ii) evaluating the quality of Cyber-Physical Systems, including ethics in their specification. Aligned with our research goals, we have identified four research questions. Beginning with **RQ1**, we investigate how to effectively gather ethical principles from diverse stakeholders in CPS and formulate precise ethical requirements. Building on this foundation, **RQ2** delves into integrating ethical aspects within CPS modelling, exploring suitable frameworks for representing the intricate interplay between cyber, physical, and ethical components. **RQ3** focuses on the practical aspect of quantifying the quality of these systems, examining methodologies and metrics to evaluate CPS with embedded ethics accurately. Finally, **RQ4** addresses the challenge of improving the quality of CPS with ethic-based concerns by translating quantitative findings into actionable feedback, thus pinpointing shortcomings and offering constructive recommendations. We are aware that these research questions cover a broad range of topics that is too ambitious for a PhD thesis, but we plan to focus on the first two research questions and leave the remaining ones as time permits.

The remainder of the paper is organised as follows. Section 2 defines our research goals and questions, emphasises our significant contributions, and describes the research methodologies. In Sect. 3, we review current literature and practices to provide context for our study and demonstrate gaps that our research addresses. The last Sect. 4 describes our preliminary findings and the estimated timelines for future research, including expected outcomes.

2 Research Plan

The importance of upholding quality while embedding ethics in Cyber-Physical Systems (CPS) is steadily increasing, particularly in the healthcare, transportation, and infrastructure sectors [2]. To make the concept of quality more concrete, in the following, we refer to *trustworthiness* as one example of the quality aspects to be achieved in this context. This choice is motivated by the state of the art literature for CPS since we found many approaches dealing with trustworthiness in such systems [1,9,10,13].

The central goal of this paper is to investigate the incorporation of ethical considerations into Cyber-Physical Systems, resulting in the establishment of Cyber-Physical-Ethical Systems (CPES). We will analyse and define potential trust-related challenges arising from the complex interaction among these systems' cyber, physical, and ethical aspects. Consequently, we aim to develop fundamental conceptual frameworks that can be used as models for assessing the level of trustworthiness inherent in CPES.

Our research encompasses an extensive investigation into establishing a comprehensive design methodology that incorporates various influences affecting the overall trustworthiness of CPES. The aim is to equip stakeholders with in-depth insights, enabling them to gain a nuanced understanding and enhance the inherent trustworthiness attributes of these systems. Additionally, our objectives culminate in evaluating CPS through rigorous methodologies that not only improve existing systems but also drive future developments focused on creating trustworthy infrastructure, all while upholding ethical considerations.

In pursuit of our research goals, we have formulated a set of precise research questions:

Research Question 1 (RQ1 - Requirements): *How can ethical principles be effectively gathered from the diverse stakeholders involved in CPS? Furthermore, what are the essential considerations for formulating and formalising ethical requirements in CPS, and which methodologies best address these considerations?*

To address **RQ1**, a comprehensive approach is needed to collect ethical principles from stakeholders in CPS and translate them into actionable requirements. In this regard, our contribution will be an innovative formalism that is designed to specify ethical requirements within CPS. This formalism will serve as a structured framework that enables collecting and formalising diverse ethical perspectives. It should be user-friendly and accessible to developers, ethicists, policymakers, and end-users. Moreover, the proposed framework aims to facilitate the translation of these principles into tangible ethical requirements. This entails establishing mechanisms for aligning broad ethical principles with specific implementable guidelines that can guide CPS development efforts.

Research Question 2 (RQ2 - Modelling): *How can ethical considerations be successfully incorporated into the modelling of CPS? What models, formalisms, and frameworks are well-suited for representing the intricate interplay between cyber, physical, and ethical components within CPES?*

In response to the challenge posed by **RQ2**, we aim to contribute innovative modelling abstractions specifically tailored to incorporate ethical dimensions in CPS. These specialised modelling abstractions will serve as a bridge, establishing connections between the technical aspects of CPS and the underlying ethical considerations that shape their behaviour. Through creating a structured representation of the intricate interaction between cyber, physical, and ethical components within CPES, these abstractions ensure that ethical principles are not mere additions but integral elements of system modelling. This solution promotes a more comprehensive and transparent approach to modelling CPS, fostering alignment with ethical norms and values while enhancing trust in the ethically sound operation of such systems.

Research Question 3 (RQ3 - Analysis): *How can the trustworthiness of CPES be accurately measured and evaluated? What methodologies and trustworthiness metrics can effectively assess the complex dynamics of CPES, encompassing their ethical dimensions?*

In order to respond to **RQ3** concerning how to measure and evaluate trustworthiness in CPES, our contribution is a comprehensive evaluation framework. This framework will encompass a range of methodologies and metrics for trustworthiness that are specifically designed to effectively capture the complex dynamics of CPES, including their ethical aspects. It will offer a structured method for assessing these systems' ethical behaviour and usability. Additionally, to encourage user participation and accommodate different ethical perspectives, the framework will allow users to define and customise their own trustworthiness metrics.

Research Question 4 (RQ4 - Feedback): *What techniques can be used to enhance the trustworthiness of CPES? How can the results obtained from CPES analysis be converted into actionable feedback that effectively guides improvements in trustworthiness? Specifically, how can this feedback be presented in a manner that not only identifies shortcomings but also provides practical and constructive recommendations for improving trustworthiness in CPES?*

In response to **RQ4**'s challenge of enhancing the trustworthiness of CPES, our expected contribution is the integration of a specialised feedback module into the existing analysis framework. This module is intended to convert CPES analysis insights and outcomes into actionable feedback. It goes beyond simply identifying shortcomings by offering practical and constructive recommendations to improve trustworthiness. This approach not only guarantees that CPES shortcomings are corrected but also offers stakeholders clear guidance on how to improve stakeholders' trust and ethical behaviour of this system. The feedback module plays a critical role in increasing the trustworthiness of CPES, promoting their responsible integration across various domains, and fostering trust among users and stakeholders.

3 State of the Art

This section aims to provide an overview of the state of the art in the field so that readers can understand the landscape of existing works. The first Subsect. 3.1, extensively reviews the existing literature and developments related to Cyber-Physical Systems (CPS) within the ethical context. The following Subsect. 3.2, delves into existing works on trustworthiness within CPS. Our initial literature review focuses on CPS, however, we plan to extend the search to critical or embedded systems, thus learning about approaches in closely related domains.

3.1 CPS with Ethics

Table 1 summarizes the most relevant papers that have been found in the direction of embedding ethical concepts in the specification of Cyber-Physical systems. For each approach, we briefly mention the pros and cons.

Table 1. Summary of Papers on Embedding Ethical Concepts in CPS Specification.

Approach	Pros	Cons
[11], 2015	The framework effectively distinguishes responsibilities between decision-making software and human agents in AI-based CPS	Practical implementation may face challenges in defining responsibility boundaries and may not comprehensively cover all ethical dimensions and complexities in AI-based CPS
[6], 2020	The two-dimensional framework provides a systematic approach to evaluate ethical considerations at different developmental stages	Quantifying and ranking ethical concerns precisely in real-world scenarios may pose challenges, given the complexity of ethical issues and evolving technologies
[12], 2021	The framework, prioritizing fundamental ethical properties and considering the entire lifecycle of industrial CPS, is complemented by the practical tool Dathali16, facilitating the identification and mitigation of ethical risks in this context	The framework primarily focuses on certain ethics aspects and its effectiveness relies on early CPS development stages, potentially limiting its use in established CPS. Furthermore, Dathali16 is in the "proof-of-concept" stage, indicating early development
[8], 2022	The authors provide recommendations for adopting ethical AI applications in Cyber-Physical Production Systems (CPPS)	Suggested frameworks may require regular updates to align with advancements in AI and production technologies
[14], 2023	The data-driven design framework allows for enhanced adaptability, responsiveness to user needs, and optimisation of CPSS, leading to improved practicality and user satisfaction	Data privacy concerns may restrict the collection of extensive data, limiting the framework's applicability in scenarios with stringent data privacy regulations
[3], 2023	The framework allows iterative elicitation of normative requirements with formal automated reasoning support	The tool identifies normative concerns, but it is part of future research to provide concrete resolution mechanisms

Although significant progress has been made in the existing literature on ethics in CPS, significant gaps still need to be discovered. These deficiencies encompass difficulties in practical implementation, insufficient attention to ethical dimensions, and the possibility of becoming outdated in light of technological advancements. As a result, our research can contribute to making ethical concerns a key priority in CPS development by providing all-encompassing and flexible solutions for addressing intricate ethical considerations across various stages of development and application scenarios.

3.2 Trustworthiness for CPS

Table 2 reports the most related papers that have been found in the direction of evaluating the trustworthiness of software systems. We provide a brief summary of the pros and cons of each approach.

Table 2. Summary of Papers on Evaluating Trustworthiness in CPS.

Approach	Pros	Cons
[1], 2017	The paper emphasises the importance of trustworthiness attributes, particularly dependability and cybersecurity, which are critical for ensuring system reliability and resistance to cyber threats	The approach may overlook some ethical considerations of users, potentially impacting the broader ethical dimensions of CPS design and usage
[13], 2018	The approach provides a probabilistic model for assessing trustworthiness in CPS, considering key metrics like ability, benevolence, and integrity, which offer a comprehensive view of trustworthiness factors	The model relies on historical data and prediction probabilities, which can be resource-intensive and may not always reflect real-time conditions, potentially limiting its applicability in dynamic CPS environments
[9], 2022	The approach offers a formal definition of CPS and a structured framework, facilitating precise formalization and problem-solving for various CPS concerns	The framework primarily focuses on technical attributes and may not comprehensively cover ethical considerations, potentially leading to gaps in addressing ethical aspects in CPS
[10], 2023	The approach introduces a comprehensive framework for evaluating trust in CPS, providing a quantitative perspective and considering engineering, CPS, trust, and business aspects	The framework's focus on trustworthiness guarantees may not comprehensively cover ethical considerations and user-centric trust factors, potentially overlooking critical aspects of trust in CPS

Existing approaches to CPS evaluation may not adequately address ethics. They often prioritise technical aspects over broader ethical concerns, potentially overlooking crucial trustworthiness factors in dynamic contexts. In response, our research can enhance the evaluation of CPS' trustworthiness, including ethical dimensions in their specification, for a more holistic approach to development.

4 Time Plan

Figure 1 shows the time plan for this research. It is structured into multiple stages, each focusing on a specific research question mentioned in Sect. 2. Each RQ is allocated a distinct research phase, commencing with an essential literature review to gain profound insights into the existing knowledge on the subject matter. Since the main focus is on the first two research questions, we plan to

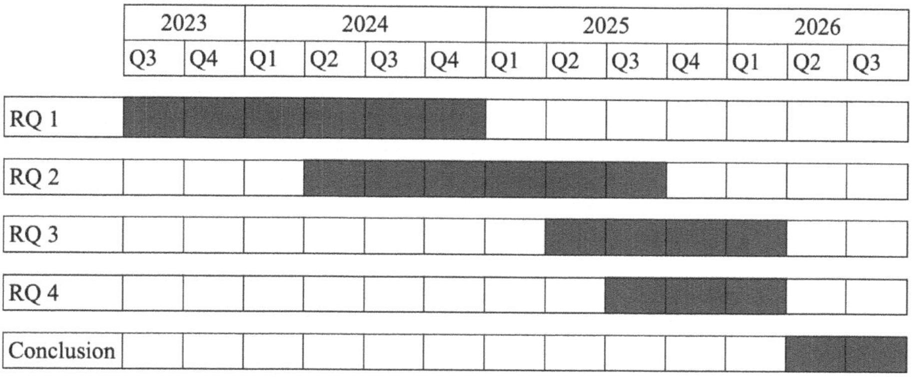

Fig. 1. Research Plan Timetable: Strategic Allocation of Investigative Phases Across Research Questions.

allocate more time, as reflected in the timetable, see Fig. 1. The first step, encompassing an extensive literature review, seeks to comprehensively understand how ethical principles are gathered from diverse CPS stakeholders. Subsequently, the investigation delves into developing methodologies for formulating and formalising these ethical requirements, emphasising novel approaches. Following a similar pattern, the next step begins with an extensive literature review on ethical considerations within CPS modelling. Subsequently, the research explores and extends existing modelling formalisms and frameworks or devises new abstractions that effectively incorporate ethical aspects into CPS modelling. Similarly to the previous steps, the third step begins with an exhaustive literature review to grasp the state of the art trustworthiness measurement and evaluation in CPES. The research then develops trustworthiness metrics and an evaluation framework tailored to CPES, focusing on their ethical dimensions. Finally, after a literature review, we are interested in designing a feedback mechanism capable of translating CPES analysis results into actionable improvements for trustworthiness. This innovative feedback approach considers user perspectives, offering customisation and practical, constructive recommendations for trustworthiness enhancement. These steps culminate in the "Conclusion" phase, synthesising the cumulative knowledge and findings.

Preliminary results. We started to perform a literature search by collecting all the papers, including "ethics", "requirements", and "cyber-physical systems" as keywords. As an outcome of this review process, we are working on producing a catalogue of non-functional requirements that have been considered relevant for CPS. At the current stage, we found that some of the key requirements to be guaranteed are: *Trust*, *Privacy*, *Safety*, *Responsibility*, *Transparency*, and *Justice*. Although such a catalogue cannot be exhaustive by definition since it strongly depends on the selected papers, we think that it may represent an initial attempt to raise attention to some specific non-functional requirements when developing

CPS, thus pushing forward the specification of a new class of systems, namely the Cyber-Physical-Ethical systems.

Acknowledgement. This work has been partially funded by the MUR-PRIN project DREAM (20228FT78M).

References

1. Babiceanu, R.F., Seker, R.: Trustworthiness requirements for manufacturing cyber-physical systems. Procedia Manuf. **11**, 973–981 (2017)
2. EU: Ethical Aspects of Cyber-Physical Systems (2016). https://www.europarl.europa.eu/thinktank/en/document/EPRS_STU(2016)563501
3. Feng, N., et al.: Towards a formal framework for normative requirements elicitation. In: 38th IEEE/ACM International Conference on Automated Software Engineering (ASE), pp. 1776–1780 (2023)
4. Guoarchive, E.: A Roomba recorded a woman on the toilet. How did screenshots end up on Facebook? MIT Technology Review (2022). https://www.technologyreview.com/2022/12/19/1065306/roomba-irobot-robot-vacuums-artificial-intelligence-training-data-privacy/
5. Hern, A.: Apple contractors 'regularly hear confidential details' on Siri recordings. The Guardian (2019). https://www.theguardian.com/technology/2019/jul/26/apple-contractors-regularly-hear-confidential-details-on-siri-recordings
6. Khargonekar, P.P., Sampath, M.: A framework for ethics in cyber-physical-human systems. IFAC-PapersOnLine **53**(2), 17008–17015 (2020)
7. Lynskey, D.: 'Alexa, are you invading my privacy?' The dark side of our voice assistants. The Guardian (2019). https://www.theguardian.com/technology/2019/oct/09/alexa-are-you-invading-my-privacy-the-dark-side-of-our-voice-assistants
8. Mezgár, I., Váncza, J.: From ethics to standards - a path via responsible AI to cyber-physical production systems. Ann. Rev. Control **53**, 391–404 (2022)
9. Nguyen, T.H., Bundas, M., Son, T.C., Balduccini, M., Garwood, K.C., Griffor, E.R.: Specifying and reasoning about CPS through the lens of the NIST CPS framework. In: Theory and Practice of Logic Programming, pp. 1–41 (2022)
10. Oudina, Z., Derdour, M., Boudour, R., Dib, A., Yakoubi, M.A.: Trust cyber physical systems: trust degree framework and evaluation. Int. J. Saf. Secur. Eng. **13**(2), 213–225 (2023)
11. Thekkilakattil, A., Dodig-Crnkovic, G.: Ethics aspects of embedded and cyber-physical systems. In: Annual Computer Software and Applications Conference, vol. 2 (2015)
12. Trentesaux, D., Caillaud, E., Rault, R.: A framework fostering the consideration of ethics during the design of industrial cyber-physical systems. In: Borangiu, T., Trentesaux, D., Leitão, P., Cardin, O., Joblot, L. (eds.) SOHOMA 2021. SCI, vol. 1034, pp. 349–362. Springer, Cham (2021). https://doi.org/10.1007/978-3-030-99108-1_25
13. Wang, Y.: Trustworthiness in designing cyber-physical systems. In: Proceedings of International Symposium on Tools and Methods of Competitive Engineering (TMCE) (2018)
14. Zhang, S., Yang, L.T., Zhang, Y., Zhou, X., Cui, Z.: Data-driven system-level design framework for responsible cyber-physical-social systems. Computer **56**(4), 80–91 (2023)

Designing for Sustainability - The Effect of Software Sustainability on Quality-in-Use

Jennifer Gross(✉)

Department of Information Technology, Uppsala University, Uppsala, Sweden
jennifer.gross@it.uu.se

Abstract. In recent years, the surge in society's use of information and communication technology solutions has increased the importance of software sustainability. Despite increasing attention and publications in this field, challenges persist due to the newness of the domain and the ambiguity surrounding a common definition of sustainability. The complexity of software sustainability extends to its categorization and effects, including first-order impacts from software production and broader consequences on global systems. Sustainability challenges are also noted when users interact with the software, which identifies the gap in user-focused perspectives and models integrating sustainability evaluation. To address this, my thesis aims to achieve four objectives over four years: (1) investigate the incorporation of user perspectives in current software sustainability practices, (2) explore user perceptions regarding software sustainability, (3) co-design a conceptual framework to integrate user perspectives into software sustainability evaluation and (4) empirically validate the framework. The thesis plan involves a mixed-method approach including systematic literature reviews, interviews, questionnaires, empirical evaluations, and participatory design. My preliminary findings reveal research gaps on the user perspective in software sustainability, emphasizing the need for further investigation and the potential impact of this research on software sustainability and user experience. The result of this research has the potential to assist software engineers in considering the user perspective when designing for sustainability in software systems.

Keywords: Software and its Engineering · Human-centered computing · Social and professional topics Sustainability

1 Introduction

In recent years, the significance of software sustainability has surged alongside society's increasing dependence on information and communication technology (ICT) solutions. Though there is increasing importance and publications in software sustainability, there are still challenges within the field due to its newness

A. Bertolino et al. (Eds.): QUATIC 2024, CCIS 2178, pp. 427–434, 2024.
https://doi.org/10.1007/978-3-031-70245-7_31

and the complicated task of a standard definition for sustainability and the ability to identify a single correct answer for how to deal with sustainability [1–5].

Typically, software sustainability has been identified as encompassing several dimensions. Some researchers [6,7] align it with the economic, social, and environmental dimensions outlined in the Brundtland report for sustainable development [8], while others, like the creators of the Karlskrona Manifesto [9], include also individual and technical dimensions. The five sustainability dimensions in the manifesto are the following [9]:

- Social sustainability focuses on preserving societies and communities.
- Economic sustainability works to maintain capital and added value.
- Environmental sustainability aims to protect natural resources.
- Technical sustainability focuses on the ability of the system to endure and evolve with changing needs.
- Individual sustainability focuses on individual humans and their capacity to maintain their livelihood with access to healthcare, knowledge, leadership and access to services.

McGuire et al. proposed to define sustainability into four dimensions, by combining the individual dimension into the social dimension [10]. For this paper and further research, I will align the definition and focus of software sustainability to four dimensions: social, technical, environmental and economic as stated by McGuire et al. [10]. Regarding a specific definition of sustainable software, this thesis considers it as software that seeks to minimize its environmental impact and maximize resource efficiency across all stages of its lifecycle, while also taking into account economic and social considerations [11,12].

The pursuit of sustainability in software systems faces challenges, echoing the long-term focus advocated in the Brundtland Report from the EU and the United Nations' Sustainable Development Goals (SDGs) [13]. The SDGs delineate 17 categories that can be seen in Table 1, each addressing critical global issues. The ISO/IEC 25010:2011 standard [14] offers a framework for defining software quality, including quality-in-use (QiU), which refers to software quality perceived by end-users in a specific context. It considers effectiveness, efficiency, satisfaction, risk, and context coverage. The ISO/IEC 25010:2011 aligns with SDG 9. This thesis aligns with SDG 3, SDG 9, and SDG 11.

Software sustainability is also categorized as sustainability-in (software developed with sustainability as a primary goal) and sustainability-by (software used to achieve environmental sustainability through external actions) [15,16]. In the same way, if the work is only in the environmental dimension of sustainability, it is referred to as green-in and green-by. Software sustainability also encompasses positive and negative effects. These can be identified as first-order effects (the direct impact of the existence of the software), second-order (indirect impacts from using the ICT which can change the impact), and third-order effects (impacts that can be observed from changed behaviors due to the ICT) [17]. For example, secure software can enhance global trade [18]. The focus for this research is on sustainability-in with the plan to include first, second and third-order impacts that can be connected to QiU.

Table 1. Sustainable development goals (SDGs) as defined by the United Nations [13].

Goal ID	Purpose
SDG 1	End all forms of poverty
SDG 2	Achieve food security and sustainable architecture
SDG 3	Ensure healthy lives and well-being for all
SDG 4	Ensure equitable and inclusive education
SDG 5	Achieve gender equality
SDG 6	Ensure sustainable water and its management
SDG 7	Access to affordable, reliable and sustainable energy
SDG 8	Promote sustained economic growth; with decent work for all
SDG 9	Build resilient infrastructures
SDG 10	Reduce inequalities globally and within countries
SDG 11	Make society safe, inclusive and sustainable
SDG 12	Ensure sustainable consumption and production
SDG 13	Take urgent action to combat client change
SDG 14	Conserve and use sustainably water resources
SDG 15	Reverse land degradation and sustainable use land
SDG 16	Provide access to justice for all; have accountable and inclusive institutions
SDG 17	Strengthen methods for global partnership for sustainability

The focus on QiU is important for understanding user needs and preferences to inform sustainable software development. My thesis focuses on three research questions (RQs) to address this gap:

RQ1: Do current software sustainability practices consider the user perspective?
RQ2: What is the user perception of software sustainability?
RQ3: How can the user perspective be integrated into software sustainability practices?

The answers to RQ1 and RQ2 will support the work for RQ3. Since QiU is context-dependent, this thesis will be framed within the connected health (CH) domain. CH term encompasses terms such telecare, telehealth, telemedicine, m-health, digital health, and e-health services [19]. CH represents a conceptual model for health management tailored around patient needs [20]. CH relies on patient-facing devices to proactively support patients [21]. The increasing need for CH is motivated by an aging population and limited healthcare resources, necessitating efficient healthcare delivery through technology. While CH enhances engagement, coordination among stakeholders, and clinical decision-making, it also poses risks such as psychological, physical, and social harm. Therefore, understanding and mitigating these risks are needed in its implementation [22].

Evaluating software sustainability through CH is a way to research two relevant issues; addressing societal health challenges while considering the broader implications of technology use. The main contributions of this research are a conceptual framework and recommendations for the software engineering community which can assist in the development of sustainable CH solutions in particular and software solutions in general.

2 Research Plan

The research plan consists of four different objectives that build on each other.

2.1 Research Objectives

In my thesis, I plan to focus on the attributes that are important for including in software requirements that are relevant towards sustainability and which consider end-users perspectives, hence relevant to QiU.

- **Objective 1:** Investigate the extent to which current software sustainability practices incorporate user perspective. This will be done by identifying research gaps in literature and industry and work done with software sustainability and QiU. This objective is connected to RQ1.
- **Objective 2:** Explore user perceptions including different stakeholders of sustainability in the software systems industry such as requirements engineers, software engineers, designers, end-users, social scientists, economists, and healthcare professionals regarding current software sustainability practices. This objective is connected to RQ2.
- **Objective 3:** Co-design a conceptual framework which aims to integrate the user perspective into software sustainability practices. This objective is connected to RQ3.
- **Objective 4:** Empirically evaluate the proposed framework. This objective is connected to RQ3.

2.2 Research Contributions

My goal is to co-design a conceptual framework that integrates the end user perspective into sustainable software within the CH domain.

2.3 Research Methods

There is a mixed-method approach to the research which unexclusively includes the following:

- **Systematic literature review:** Systematic literature reviews will align with the paper by Kitchenham et al. [23]. A good resource for identifying literature is Scopus [24], a peer-reviewed database of research literature. Prisma [25], will be used to ensure a systematic transparent review is used in the process with a clearly defined methodology. The SMS will be done using Petersen et al. as a resource [26]. This work is done to support Objective 1.

- **Semi-structured interviews** Interviews will give qualitative information that can supplement questionnaires for a mixed method approach [27]. Throughout this thesis, there will be interviews with stakeholders including end-users and different roles in the software industry. This work is done to support Objective 2.
- **Questionnaires** Questionnaires will be used to supplement the interviews and get quantitative data [28]. This work is done to support Objective 2.
- **Empirical evaluations.** This can include energy evaluations and other metrics important towards sustainability to look for relationships with end-users. This work is done to support Objectives 2–4.
- **Prototyping.** The framework will be co-created using participatory design (PD) [29]. A prototype will be developed to assess the simplicity and feasibility of the framework and the recommendations generated from PD. This work is done to support Objective 3.
- **Delphi study.** The Delphi technique is an iterative process to find a group consensus across experts [30]. This will include at least 12 experts working in sustainability and quality from software engineering and human-computer interaction communities. The strength of this method is that the experts have to understand the perceptions of the other experts and perhaps change their minds about how their expertise fits into the end goal. This work is done to support Objective 4.

3 State-of-the-Art

I have completed two literature reviews to better understand previous research and gaps related to my thesis topic. A systematic mapping study (SMS) was completed, now under review, to evaluate what work has been done towards understanding the relationship between QiU and sustainability. There were 27 papers identified that covered the topic when excluding papers focused on green-by. The second review [31], accepted in the 2030 Software Engineering Workshop, is a tertiary study focusing on software sustainability literature reviews that were published in the last five years and indexed in Scopus. This study included 18 papers.

The following gaps and trends were identified from the two studies.

- **Limited Research.** Despite ongoing efforts, research in software sustainability and QiU remains relatively scarce. While there have been 1–4 publications a year since 2012, they are dispersed across various venues, indicating that the field is still emerging and lacks a centralized focus.
- **Ambiguity in Definitions.** A challenge facing researchers is the lack of clear definitions and standardized assessment methods for software sustainability. This can lead to variations in the selection of metrics and evaluation criteria.
- **Ambiguity in Assessment Methods.** Existing evaluation methods for software sustainability are not comprehensive, with no clear consensus on which metrics to include. While some models offer specific metrics, they often fail to address all relevant dimensions or a comprehensive evaluation in a dimension, particularly with including QiU.

- **Incomplete Consideration of Energy Usage.** Evaluations of software sustainability often overlook critical factors such as overall energy usage, including cloud utilization and lifecycle energy consumption. This oversight limits the accuracy of sustainability assessments.
- **Emphasis on Environmental Sustainability.** A notable emphasis exists on environmental sustainability, particularly concerning power usage. This focus follows the growing concerns over increasing emissions and the need for energy-efficient software solutions.
- **Integration of Software Sustainability and Quality.** Researchers increasingly view software sustainability as an integral component of product quality and QiU. This integration shows the connection of software attributes and their impact on overall system performance and user experience.
- **Need for Education and Awareness.** There is a recognized need to educate end-users about software sustainability to help them make informed decisions. This has also been identified as being an issue within the software industry.

4 Time Plan

Each research objective will take approximately one year. Each objective is dependent on the previous milestone's results, so they will be completed in a waterfall fashion. The objectives will result in publications in scientific publications which will be disseminated in international venues.

4.1 Preliminary Results

As of now, I have completed two studies to analyse the current literature about software sustainability, with one mapping study focusing on the relationship of QiU and software sustainability in research as mentioned in Sect. 3. A lack of studies considering the user perspective in software sustainability was identified.

4.2 Future Work and Expected Results

I am currently working on a questionnaire study focused on industry to better understand the current perception and practices in industry toward software sustainability. I have received ethics approval to complete the interviews in industry in the fall which will complete my first year. My second year will focus on analyzing the results from the interviews and conducting studies to understand the end-users' perspectives on software sustainability. The third year will focus on co-creating a framework using a participatory design approach and the understandings that were found from the work done towards Objective 2. The fourth and final year will focus on prototyping and validating the framework identified during objective three using a Delphi study, thus completing the final objective for my thesis.

Acknowledgement. This research is only possible with the support of my supervisor, Sofia Ouhbi. Her consistent feedback, insights and support on this research are invaluable.

Disclosure of Interests. The author has no competing interests to declare that are relevant to the content of this article.

References

1. Verdecchia, R., Lago, P., Ebert, C., de Vries, C.: Green IT and green software. IEEE Softw. **38**(6), 7–15 (2021). https://doi.org/10.1109/MS.2021.3102254
2. Venters, C.C., et al.: Sustainable software engineering: reflections on advances in research and practice. Inf. Softw. Technol. **164**, 107316 (2023)
3. Bremer, C., Knowles, B., Friday, A.: Have we taken on too much?: A critical review of the sustainable HCI landscape. In: Proceedings of the 2022 CHI Conference on Human Factors in Computing Systems, pp. 1–11 (2022)
4. McGuire, S., Schultz, E., Ayoola, B., Ralph, P.: Sustainability is stratified: toward a better theory of sustainable software engineering. In: 2023 IEEE/ACM 45th International Conference on Software Engineering (ICSE), pp. 1996–2008. IEEE (2023)
5. Venters, C.C., et al.: Software sustainability: beyond the tower of babel. In: 2021 IEEE/ACM International Workshop on Body of Knowledge for Software Sustainability (BoKSS), pp. 3–4. IEEE (2021)
6. Taina, J., Mäkinen, S.: Green software quality factors. In: Calero, C., Piattini, M. (eds.) Green in Software Engineering, pp. 129–154. Springer, Cham (2015). https://doi.org/10.1007/978-3-319-08581-4_6
7. Calero, C., Moraga, M.Á., Bertoa, M.F., Duboc, L.: Green software and software quality. In: Calero, C., Piattini, M. (eds.) Green in Software Engineering, pp. 231–260. Springer, Cham (2015). https://doi.org/10.1007/978-3-319-08581-4_10
8. Brundtland, G.H.: Report of the world commission on environment and development: "our common future.", UN (1987)
9. Becker, C., et al.: Sustainability design and software: the karlskrona manifesto. In: 2015 IEEE/ACM 37th IEEE International Conference on Software Engineering, vol. 2, pp. 467–476. IEEE (2015)
10. McGuire, S., Schultz, E., Ayoola, B., Ralph, P.: Sustainability is stratified: toward a better theory of sustainable software engineering. In: 2023 IEEE/ACM 45th International Conference on Software Engineering (ICSE), pp. 1996–2008 (2023). https://doi.org/10.1109/ICSE48619.2023.00169
11. Calero, C., Moraga, M.Á., Piattini, M.: Introduction to software sustainability. In: Calero, C., Moraga, M.Á., Piattini, M. (eds.) Software Sustainability, pp. 1–15. Springer, Cham (2021). https://doi.org/10.1007/978-3-030-69970-3_1
12. Majuntke, V., Obermaier, F.: Towards sustainable software a structured map of techniques and best practices for organizations and development teams to enhance sustainability. In: Lecture Notes in Informatics (LNI). Proceedings Series of the Gesellschaft fur Informatik (GI), vol. P-337, pp. 149–164 (2023)
13. D. o. E. United Nations, S. A. S. Development: Transforming our world: the 2030 agenda for sustainable development (2015). https://sdgs.un.org/2030agenda
14. ISO/IEC 25010, ISO/IEC 25010:2011, systems and software engineering systems and software quality requirements and evaluation (square) system and software quality models (2011)

15. Hilty, L., Lohmann, W., Huang, E.M.: Sustainability and ICT-an overview of the field. Notizie di POLITEIA **27**(104), 13–28 (2011)
16. Penzenstadler, B., Raturi, A., Richardson, D., Calero, C., Femmer, H., Franch, X.: Systematic mapping study on software engineering for sustainability (SE4S), pp. 1–14 (2014)
17. Hilty, L.M., Arnfalk, P., Erdmann, L., Goodman, J., Lehmann, M., Wäger, P.A.: The relevance of information and communication technologies for environmental sustainability-a prospective simulation study. Environ. Model. Softw. **21**(11), 1618–1629 (2006)
18. Oláh, J., Kitukutha, N., Haddad, H., Pakurár, M., Máté, D., Popp, J.: Achieving sustainable e-commerce in environmental, social and economic dimensions by taking possible trade-offs. Sustainability **11**(1), 89 (2018)
19. Taylor, K.: Connected health: how digital technology is transforming health and social care. Deloitte Centre for Health Solutions, London (2015)
20. Caulfield, B.M., Donnelly, S.C.: What is connected health and why will it change your practice? QJM: Int. J. Med. **106**(8), 703–707 (2013)
21. Colorafi, K.: Connected health: a review of the literature. Mhealth **2**, 13 (2016)
22. Fitzgerald, S., et al.: The dark side of connected health technology: how connectivity creates exercise addiction among conscientious users. Adv. Consum. Res. **44**, 731 (2016)
23. Kitchenham, B., Brereton, O.P., Budgen, D., Turner, M., Bailey, J., Linkman, S.: Systematic literature reviews in software engineering-a systematic literature review. Inf. Softw. Technol. **51**(1), 7–15 (2009)
24. Thelwall, M., Sud, P.: Scopus 1900–2020: growth in articles, abstracts, countries, fields, and journals. Quant. Sci. Stud. **3**(1), 37–50 (2022)
25. Page, M.J., et al.: The PRISMA 2020 statement: an updated guideline for reporting systematic reviews. BMJ **372** (2021). arXiv: https://www.bmj.com/content/372/bmj.n71.full.pdf. https://doi.org/10.1136/bmj.n71. https://www.bmj.com/content/372/bmj.n71
26. Petersen, K., Feldt, R., Mujtaba, S., Mattsson, M.: Systematic mapping studies in software engineering. In: 12th International Conference on Evaluation and Assessment in Software Engineering (EASE). BCS Learning & Development (2008)
27. Clarke, V., Braun, V.: Successful qualitative research: a practical guide for beginners (2013)
28. Krosnick, J.A.: Questionnaire design. In: The Palgrave Handbook of Survey Research, pp. 439–455 (2018)
29. Gregory, J.: Scandinavian approaches to participatory design. Int. J. Eng. Educ. **19**(1), 62–74 (2003)
30. McPherson, S., Reese, C., Wendler, M.C.: Methodology update: delphi studies. Nurs. Res. **67**(5), 404–410 (2018)
31. Gross, J., Ouhbi, S.: Clearing the path for software sustainability. arXiv preprint arXiv:2405.15637 (2024)

Facilitating Interoperability in Digital Twin Solutions: A Path Forward

Enxhi Ferko(✉)

Mälardalen University, Västerås, Sweden
enxhi.ferko@mdu.se

Abstract. Digital Twin technology has emerged as a pivotal tool in digital transformation, offering virtual representations of physical components, systems, or processes to enable remote monitoring and control. The functional suitability of digital twin systems relies on accurately capturing, modeling, and exchanging data from their corresponding assets or processes. Consequently, achieving interoperability among various components of digital twins and among different digital twins is crucial. However, this remains an open challenge due to the diversity of data models employed by current digital twin solutions. This thesis proposal addresses this challenge by proposing a model-driven engineering approach, utilizing higher-order transformations alongside the Asset Administration Shell standard as a pivotal model. The approach aims to automate translations to and from the Asset Administration Shell standard, eliminating manual crafting of model transformations.

Keywords: Digital Twin · Architecture · Interoperability · Model-driven engineering

1 Introduction

A Digital Twin (DT) is a virtual representation of a physical component, system, or process (the physical twin) that functions as a digital equivalent for the remote monitoring and controlling of the physical twin [10]. Both academia and industry recognise a variety of benefits from the adoption of DTs, including cost savings, enhanced efficiency, improved safety and reliability, and the fostering of innovation.

The widespread recognition fueled exponential growth in interest in DTs, followed by various practical applications in different domains [7]. Initially, the predominant focus has been on product-specific implementations, often evaluated on prototypes. This approach arises from the maturity level of the DTs, where organizations primarily develop DTs tailored to their specific business goals [9,16]. Consequently, modeling these systems with different in-house technologies, resulting in DTs developed ad-hoc, lacking interoperability mechanisms [22]. However the vision forward is moving from product-specific to larger-scale DTs that cover entire supply chains or even entire cities [8]. This might require a modular structure, where different components of the DT are developed by different teams within a company or across companies, necessitating interoperability

A. Bertolino et al. (Eds.): QUATIC 2024, CCIS 2178, pp. 435–443, 2024.
https://doi.org/10.1007/978-3-031-70245-7_32

within components of the same DT system. On top of that, in today's dynamic business landscape, the demand for interconnected DTs is imperative [16,22]. Organizations operate within complex ecosystems comprising diverse stakeholders and processes. Interconnected DTs would provide a holistic view of entire systems, enabling optimisation of operations on a larger scale. Nonetheless, resolution of the interoperability for DTs is still in its early stages [16] and there is a lack of developed mechanisms to achieve seamless interoperability [21].

Achieving interoperability for DTs is a multifaceted task, considering the landscape of data models and languages existing and still being proposed from different DT platforms (open source or commercial) [10]. Ideally, a universally accepted semantic model could resolve these complexities. Recent initiatives such as the ISO 23247 reference architecture[1] and the Asset Administration Shell (AAS) framework[2] have made significant strides in standardization efforts. However, current DT solutions encompass a diversity of data models. Addressing interoperability challenges might involve direct peer-to-peer translation or through a central pivotal model for DTs [21] like the AAS. While peer-to-peer translation appears straightforward, they introduce scalability challenges due to the increasing complexity of DTs and the wide range of models used in their development and operation. Alternatively, employing a pivotal model could enhance scalability, although it would still require the development and maintenance of numerous translations.

We propose a Model-driven Engineering (MDE) [3] approach that leverages Higher-Order Transformations (HOT) [29] in conjunction with AAS acting as the pivotal model to simplify the interoperability challenges associated with DT systems.

2 Research Plan

In light of the outlined research problem and motivation explained in Sect. 1, in this section, we present the adopted research plan that includes the research goal, challenges, contributions, process, and methods.

2.1 Overall Research Goal and Challenges

Overall research goal: *To provide mechanisms supporting and facilitating the interoperability of digital twin solutions.*

We broke down the above goal into three specific research challenges, each contributing to different and unique aspects of the goal.

Research Challenge 1: *Classify, structure and analyse state-of-the-art architectural solutions for digital twins.* The rapid evolution of DT technology resulted

[1] https://www.iso.org/standard/75066.html.

[2] https://www.plattform-i40.de/IP/Redaktion/EN/Downloads/Publikation/Details_of_the_Asset_Administration_Shell_Part1_V3.html.

in a proliferation of architectural approaches, which complicates systematic categorization due to the diverse methodologies, frameworks, and terminologies utilized in their engineering.

Research Challenge 2: *Analyse data interoperability for digital twin solutions.* DTs operate within complex ecosystems with diverse stakeholders, processes, and data sources, each using different formats, structures, and standards, complicating seamless data exchange and integration. Additionally, DTs interact with various systems, including legacy and proprietary platforms, each with unique interoperability requirements.

Research Challenge 3: *Enable semantic interoperability among digital twin solutions.* This presents a challenge due to the diverse ways in which information is represented and interpreted across different systems and domains. Semantic interoperability involves ensuring that data exchanged between systems can be accurately understood and utilized, regardless of the underlying data structures or formats.

2.2 Research Contributions

Research Contribution 1: *Systematic identification, classification, and analysis of digital twin solutions with ISO 23247 standard as a baseline.* We first provide a detailed snapshot of different architectural solutions aspects of DTs that includes i) publication trends over time, venue and venue type, ii) types of research and validation according to the taxonomies by Wieringa et al. [32] and Shaw [27], iii) relevant quality attributes for DTs, iv) types of architectural solutions according to the characterisation by Bass et al. [1], and v) architectural patterns used for DTs. In addition, we extend ISO/IEC 25010 - System and software quality model with additional quality attributes identified by state-of-the-art DT solutions[3]. Furthermore, we delve deeper into analysing DTs solutions with respect to the reference architecture of the ISO 23247 standard, identifying the functional entities of the standard that are lacking in existing DTs solutions. We conducted surveys and interviews with industry experts to understand the reasons for these discrepancies. Eventually, we pointed out the open challenges for DTs solutions. At the same time this serves as a basis for comprehending the ISO 23247 reference architecture, tracking the progress of standardization efforts, and influencing its potential evolution. This contributions spans in the published journal [9] and the conference paper [11] and address research challenge 1.

Research Contribution 2: *Assessment of digital twins interoperability and trade-off analysis of reaching different interoperability levels referencing LCIM interoperability model.* With this contribution, we provide a thorough examination of the various interfaces, including physical-to-digital, digital-to-digital, and digital-to-physical, existing among the components comprising DT solutions. For each interface, we identified the set of technologies used for data transmission

[3] https://iso25000.com/index.php/en/iso-25000-standards/iso-25010.

and the set of technologies used for data representation and management. Furthermore, we investigated the required interoperability levels for each interface in accordance with the LCIM interoperability model. We used the descriptive view of the LCIM to indicate the interoperability levels that existed for each of the interfaces. Additionally, we used the prescriptive view to discuss the requirements necessary to achieve higher interoperability levels and possible trade-offs. This contribution intends to provide design decision guidelines for DT architects to achieve the desired level of interoperability. With this contribution we tackle research challenge 2 and the results are published in the conference paper [10].

Research Contribution 3: *A model-based approach to facilitate the interoperability of digital twin solutions.* We introduced an approach grounded in model-driven engineering that employs higher-order transformations to alleviate interoperability challenges in digital twin systems. We have showcased the applicability of our approach through an automotive use case described using Systems Modeling Language version 2 (SysML v2). We have proposed mapping rules between SysML v2 concepts and AAS concepts. We are planning the full-scale development of the framework, which involves completing the mapping of SysML v2 and AAS, including behavioral concepts. Additionally, we aim to conduct a thorough validation of our methodology by applying both quantitative and qualitative techniques to evaluate its efficiency, effectiveness, and relevance. For instance, we will utilize official SysML examples and AAS templates as test suites for the mappings. With this contribution we tackle research challenge 3. The conceptual idea behind this contribution has been accepted for publication in a workshop paper [12], which is intended to be expanded into a journal paper featuring including the full-scale implementation and validation.

2.3 Research Process and Methods

Our research process is grounded in constructive research techniques [5,18]. As depicted in Fig. 1, it is an iterative process which comprises five steps.

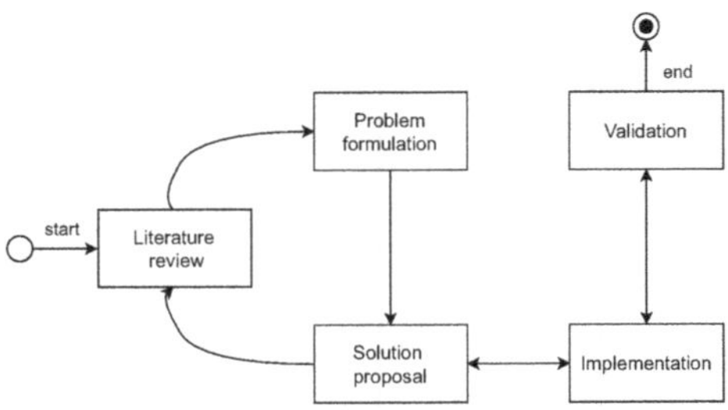

Fig. 1. Research process.

Literature Review: We started by conducting an extensive and critical analysis of state-of-the-art that helped us formulate the research goal and challenges. We followed the guidelines for performing literature reviews from Kitchenham et al. [15] and systematic mapping studies from Petersen et al. [19]. We analysed data using various methods For instance, we used thematic synthesis [6] or grounded theory techniques to identify, analyse, and report patterns within the collected data. In addition, we employed descriptive statistics [33] to understand the prevalence of the presented data and to illustrate the results graphically.

Problem Formulation: We formulated the overarching research goal and identified key research challenges based on the findings of the literature review. Our goal aimed to hold significance both theoretically and practically. Recognizing its critical importance in the literature, we focused on facilitating interoperability within DT solutions. To gain practical insights and validate our problem formulation, we conducted surveys and interviews with field experts and practitioners. We developed the surveys using the guidelines from Kasunic [14], and conducted online interviews following the guidelines from Shull et al. [28].

Solution Proposal: Following problem formulation, our focus shifted towards proposing mechanism to facilitate DTs interoperability. Initially, this involved a thorough analysis of the components of DTs in existing solutions that exchange data, identifying the technologies use to exchange the data and to model and manage the data. This allowed us to have an understanding of the interoperability needs and barriers. We opted for a model-driven approach that employs higher-order transformations to address interoperability challenges. We illustrate our approach through a vehicle use case proposed and documented by SysML v2 specification[4] and available in the SysML v2 repository[5].

Implementation: In the third phase of the research, we plan to implement the solution based on the framework defined previously. We will ulilise or extend existing mapping models to write the conceptual mapping rules among DTs languages, stating by SysML v2 to AAS and exploring other languages proposed by different DTs such as Microsoft Azure Digital Twin Definition Language[6], Eclipse Vortolang[7], and Twinmaker by Amazon Web Service[8]. We plan to use the metamodel provided by Object Management Group for the SysML v2[9] and metamodels provided in the paper from Pfeiffer et al. for the other above mentioned languages [20] to map concepts with AAS. We plan to implement or modify existing HOTs to generate the model transformations to and from AAS.

Validation: After completing the implementation phase, the research process is planned to advance to the validation phase. The primary objective at this stage is to confirm that the implemented solution meets the predefined goals and expectations. A concrete plan for the validation of the approach is using the examples in SysML v2 repository and having translated models in AAS. For the other languages we plan to validate with the use case from Pfeiffer et al. [20].

---

[4] https://www.omg.org/spec/SysML/2.0/Beta1/About-SysML.

[5] https://github.com/Systems-Modeling/SysML-v2-Pilot-Implementation.

[6] https://github.com/Azure/opendigitaltwins-dtdl/blob/master/DTDL/v2/dtdlv2.md.

[7] https://eclipse.dev/vorto/.

[8] https://docs.aws.amazon.com/iot-twinmaker/latest/guide/what-is-twinmaker.html.

[9] https://github.com/Systems-Modeling/SysML-v2-Pilot-Implementation/blob/master/org.omg.sysml/model/SysML.ecore.

3 State-of-the-Art

In this section, we provide an overview of the fundamental concepts underpinning this research and related work.

3.1 Background

Digital Twin and Interoperability. We adopt the definition of DT proposed in the ISO 23247 standard, which describes *"a digital twin in manufacturing as a fit for purpose digital representation of an observable manufacturing element with synchronisation between the element and its digital representation [...]"*[10]. The ISO 23247 standard proposed a reference architecture encapsulating the functionalities of DTs in 23 functional entities. The functional suitability of DTs relies on achieving high levels of interoperability among the diverse comprising entities as well as external systems or other DTs. Interoperability is defined as *"the degree to which two or more systems, products or components can exchange information and use the information that has been exchange"*[11]. We use the Levels of Conceptual Interoperability Model (LCIM) framework by Wang et al. [31], to asses interoperability levels of DTs solutions, due to its successful application in several domains [30]. Interoperability presents a complex challenge due to variations in syntactic and semantic formats across tools, components, and systems. Initial attempts at bridging systems focused on connecting their interfaces directly, but these approaches have proved to be insufficient [3]. With the advent of MDE, interoperability challenges can be addressed at a higher abstraction level.

Model-Driven Engineering and Interoperability. MDE is an approach in software engineering that mitigates platform complexity and efficiently expresses domain concepts, through the systematic use of models, metamodels, and model transformations [25]. Models serve as abstract representations of the software, created in conformance with metamodels [2]. Model transformations are specialized software programs designed to automatically manipulate models [26]. More precisely, a model transformation can automatically manipulate a target model, beginning with a source model, by utilizing the syntactic and semantic information contained in the source and target metamodels. Metamodels provide the necessary framework and guidelines for the transformation process. Model-driven techniques can be used at defining bridges to facilitate interoperability between two or more systems [3]. This can be achieved by first making explicit the metamodels (internal data schema) of each system (or system component). Then, metamodels are aligned by matching related concepts. After that, model-to-model transformations exploit this matching information to export data (i.e., models) created with the first component to data conforming to the second component's metamodel. Finally, HOTs can be used to generate model-to-model transformations. HOTs are a specific type of model transformation,

[10] https://www.iso.org/standard/75066.html.

[11] https://iso25000.com/index.php/en/iso-25000-standards/iso-25010.

characterised by their input and/or output models being model transformations themselves [29].

Asset Administration Shell. AAS is an information model utilised to describe different types of assets in a production environment (See footnote 2). The standard promotes seamless interoperability across organisations for both intelligent and non-intelligent systems and is quickly being adopted in both small and large manufacturing companies [23,24]. Details of the AAS structure are given in (See footnote 2).

3.2 Related Work

Below we discuss several studies that have explored the combination and integration of languages used to model DTs. However, most of them are focused on peer-to-peer integration strategies. To the best of our knowledge, there is no other work addressing DTs interoperability through the use of HOT together with a pivotal model. Lüder et al. recognised AAS as the default standard to represent Industry 4.0 components [17]. They proposed an approach to collect and integrate data from different sources to populate sub models of AAS. In their approach, they used AutomationML to model data from different sources and used these models to specify the sub-models of AAS. Similar to our work, the ultimate goal is to have data represented in the AAS standard. However, unlike our approach, they do not discuss automated translation mechanisms. Several studies investigated the integration of OPC UA with AAS. For instance, Cavalieri et al. described in detail the information model of OPC UA and metamodel of AAS [4]. They reasoned on how to define OPC UA information models exposing the information of the metamodel defined by AAS. In addition, they proposed mappings between the two languages and provided a tool that can be used to map AAS into OPC UA. The main difference with our approach is that we do not reason on how to define information models so they can be easily integrated with AAS. Rather, we propose mechanisms for translating existing information models to AAS by means of MDE. Similarly, Fuchs et al. provided insights on translating descriptions based on the OPC UA information model into AAS [13]. Their contribution primarily revolves around proposing mapping rules between these two languages. Existing DTs platforms, which offer commercial or open-source solutions for DTs, rely on proprietary languages. Pfeiffer et al. conducted a comparative analysis of three modelling languages for DT, i.e., Digital Twin Definition Language (DTDL), Vortolang, and TwinMaker, respectively, from Microsoft Azure, Eclipse, and Amazon Web Service platforms. They extracted conceptual metamodels and compared them with the common object-oriented modelling concepts of UML. In addition, they provided insights about the portability of the models by performing an experiment to transform DTDL to TwinMaker by using UML as a pivot language [20]. Platenius-Mohr et al. proposed a solution to facilitate interoperability based on model transformations and illustrated the application of the solution in an industrial context [21]. Our solution is complementary as we also aim to use model transformations to enable on-demand interoperability. However, our approach goes further by proposing mechanisms to generate model transformations using HOTs.

4 Time Plan

With respect to the research process in Fig. 1, we have concluded the phases of literature review, problem formulation and solution proposal. We aim to finalise the implementation and validation of our approach by the end of 2024, with plans to submit the results for publication in a journal. Following this, we anticipate a period of 6–8 months dedicated to crafting the thesis and preparing for its defense, leading up to the presentation day scheduled for the post-summer of 2025. The preliminary and expected results are elaborated in Sect. 2.1.

References

1. Bass, L., Clements, P., Kazman, R.: Software Architecture in Practice. Addison-Wesley Professional (2003)
2. Bézivin, J.: On the unification power of models. Softw. Syst. Model. **4**, 171–188 (2005)
3. Brambilla, M., Cabot, J., Wimmer, M.: Model-Driven Software Engineering in Practice. Morgan & Claypool Publishers (2017)
4. Cavalieri, S., Salafia, M.G.: Insights into mapping solutions based on OPC UA information model applied to the industry 4.0 asset administration shell. Computers **9**(2), 28 (2020)
5. Crnkovic, G.D.: Constructive research and info-computational knowledge generation. In: Magnani, L., Carnielli, W., Pizzi, C. (eds.) Model-Based Reasoning in Science and Technology. SCI, vol. 314, pp. 359–380. Springer, Heidelberg (2010). https://doi.org/10.1007/978-3-642-15223-8_20
6. Cruzes, D.S., Dyba, T.: Recommended steps for thematic synthesis in software engineering. In: Proceedings of ESEM (2011)
7. Dalibor, M., et al.: A cross-domain systematic mapping study on software engineering for digital twins. J. Syst. Softw. **193**, 111361 (2022)
8. Dembski, F., Wössner, U., Letzgus, M., Ruddat, M., Yamu, C.: Urban digital twins for smart cities and citizens: the case study of Herrenberg, Germany. Sustainability **12**(6), 2307 (2020)
9. Ferko, E., Bucaioni, A., Behnam, M.: Architecting digital twins. IEEE Access **10**, 50335–50350 (2022)
10. Ferko, E., Bucaioni, A., Pelliccione, P., Behnam, M.: Analysing interoperability in digital twin software architectures for manufacturing. In: Tekinerdogan, B., Trubiani, C., Tibermacine, C., Scandurra, P., Cuesta, C.E. (eds.) ECSA 2023. LNCS, vol. 14212, pp. 170–188. Springer, Cham (2023). https://doi.org/10.1007/978-3-031-42592-9_12
11. Ferko, E., Bucaioni, A., Pelliccione, P., Behnam, M.: Standardisation in digital twin architectures in manufacturing. In: 2023 IEEE 20th International Conference on Software Architecture (ICSA), pp. 70–81 (2023)
12. Ferko, E., Berardinelli, L., Bucaioni, A., Behnam, M., Wimmer, M.: Towards interoperable digital twins: Integrating SysML into AAS with higher-order transformations. In: 2024 IEEE 21st International Conference on Software Architecture Companion (ICSA-C), pp. 324–349. IEEE (2024)
13. Fuchs, J., Schmidt, J., Franke, J., Rehman, K., Sauer, M., Karnouskos, S.: I4.0-compliant integration of assets utilizing the Asset Administration Shell. In: 2019 24th IEEE International Conference on Emerging Technologies and Factory Automation (ETFA), Zaragoza, Spain, pp. 1243–1247. IEEE (2019)
14. Kasunic, M.: Designing an effective survey. Technical report (2005)

15. Kitchenham, B., Brereton, P.: A systematic review of systematic review process research in software engineering. Inf. Softw. Technol. **55**(12), 2049–2075 (2013)
16. Klar, R., Arvidsson, N., Angelakis, V.: Digital twins' maturity: the need for interoperability. IEEE Syst. J. **18**(1), 713–724 (2023)
17. Luder, A., Behnert, A.K., Rinker, F., Biffl, S.: Generating industry 4.0 asset administration shells with data from engineering data logistics. In: 2020 25th IEEE International Conference on Emerging Technologies and Factory Automation (ETFA), Vienna, Austria, pp. 867–874. IEEE (2020)
18. Lukka, K.: The constructive research approach. In: Case Study Research in Logistics, pp. 83–101. Publications of the Turku School of Economics and Business Administration, Series B 1:2003 (2003)
19. Pfeiffer, J., Lehner, D., Wortmann, A., Wimmer, M.: Modeling capabilities of digital twin platforms-old wine in new bottles?. J. Object Technol. **21**(3), 3–1 (2022)
20. Pfeiffer, J., Lehner, D., Wortmann, A., Wimmer, M.: Modeling capabilities of digital twin platforms-old wine in new bottles?. J. Object Technol. **21**(3), 3–1 (2022)
21. Platenius-Mohr, M., Malakuti, S., Grüner, S., Schmitt, J., Goldschmidt, T.: File- and API-based interoperability of digital twins by model transformation: an IIoT case study using asset administration shell. Future Gener. Comput. Syst. **113**, 94–105 (2020)
22. Reiche, L.T., Gundlach, C.S., Mewes, G.F., Fay, A.: The digital twin of a system: a structure for networks of digital twins. In: 2021 26th IEEE International Conference on Emerging Technologies and Factory Automation (ETFA), pp. 1–8. IEEE (2021)
23. Rongen, S., Nikolova, N., van der Pas, M.: Modelling with AAS and RDF in industry 4.0. Comput. Ind. **148**, 103910 (2023)
24. Schäfer, S., Schöttke, D., Kämpfe, T., Lachmann, O., Zielstorff, A.: Synchronizing devices using asset administration shells. In: Smirnov, A., Panetto, H., Madani, K. (eds.) IN4PL IN4PL 2020 2021. CCIS, vol. 1855, pp. 70–92. Springer, Cham (2020). https://doi.org/10.1007/978-3-031-37228-5_5
25. Schmidt, D.C.: Guest editor's introduction: model-driven engineering. Computer **39**(02), 25–31 (2006)
26. Sendall, S., Kozaczynski, W.: Model transformation: the heart and soul of model-driven software development. IEEE Softw. **20**(5), 42–45 (2003)
27. Shaw, M.: What makes good research in software engineering? STTT **4**, 1–7 (2002)
28. Shull, F., Singer, J., Sjøberg, D.I.: Guide to Advanced Empirical Software Engineering. Springer, London (2007)
29. Tisi, M., Jouault, F., Fraternali, P., Ceri, S., Bézivin, J.: On the use of higher-order model transformations. In: Paige, R.F., Hartman, A., Rensink, A. (eds.) ECMDA-FA 2009. LNCS, vol. 5562, pp. 18–33. Springer, Heidelberg (2009). https://doi.org/10.1007/978-3-642-02674-4_3
30. Tolk, A.: The elusiveness of simulation interoperability–what is different from other interoperability domains? In: 2018 Winter Simulation Conference (WSC), pp. 679–690. IEEE (2018)
31. Wang, W., Tolk, A., Wang, W.: The levels of conceptual interoperability model: applying systems engineering principles to M&S. arXiv preprint arXiv:0908.0191 (2009)
32. Wieringa, R., Maiden, N., Mead, N., Rolland, C.: Requirements engineering paper classification and evaluation criteria: a proposal and a discussion. Requirements Eng. **11**, 102–107 (2006)
33. Wohlin, C., Höst, M., Henningsson, K.: Empirical research methods in software engineering. In: Conradi, R., Wang, A.I. (eds.) Empirical Methods and Studies in Software Engineering. LNCS, vol. 2765, pp. 7–23. Springer, Heidelberg (2003). https://doi.org/10.1007/978-3-540-45143-3_2

Facilitating β-Factor Estimation for Common Cause Failures of Safety-Related System

Sirisha Bai Govardhan Rao[1,2](✉)

[1] Alstom, Västerås, Sweden
[2] Mälardalen University, Västerås, Sweden
sirisha.bai.govardhan.rao@mdu.se

Abstract. Common Cause Failures (CCF) have the potential to make safety-related systems fail. Hence, the safety-critical industries identify and quantify the probability of CCF using different methodologies. For example, industries like railways rely on a β-factor methodology suggested by the IEC 61508 standard, in which defense measures are established against CCF and β-factor (used in the estimation of the probability of CCF) quantified based on the application of those measures. However, this methodology had two main research problems (RP) they are, RP1: The standard's inception was in 2010, and due to this the measures against the CCF that arose from the emerging new technologies were absent in the standard. Moreover, the methodology has not provided any means to permit new measures. RP2: The methodology is generalized and applicable to all safety-related systems using Electrical/Electronic/Programmable Electronic-based systems across different industries. However, the impact of CCF and the required defense measures against them would be distinct in each industry. Eventually, the negligence of these problems leads to conservative β estimations. Therefore this research aims to provide possible solutions for these two problems. For RP1, by proposing a methodology that enhances the IEC 61508 standard methodology in β-factor estimation and adopts a way that could consider new defense measures in addition to the existing measures. For RP2, we planned to demonstrate an approach to develop an industry-specific β-factor methodology focusing on railways. Later, the methodology is applied to a system i.e., Electro-dynamic braking of railway propulsion systems for β-factor estimation. This research would provide insights to industrial practitioners and researchers to develop industry-specific β-factor methodology to estimate more realistic β, by analyzing appropriate defense measures.

Keywords: IEC 61508 standard · β-factor · System Safety · Common Cause Failure · Redundancy · Railways · Safety-critical industries

A. Bertolino et al. (Eds.): QUATIC 2024, CCIS 2178, pp. 444–451, 2024.
https://doi.org/10.1007/978-3-031-70245-7_33

1 Introduction

Redundancy supports the reliability of safety systems in performing the needed safety functions despite a single failure. Hence, safety-critical industries adopt redundancy in the design of safety systems. However, common-cause failures (CCF) are a major threat to the redundancy of the systems, because CCF is an event leading to the failure of a component due to a cause and that cause has the potential to fail the other redundant components in the system. The failure of those multiple redundant components consecutively leads to system failure [7]. These CCF create a greater impact on the overall probability of system failure. Hence, they are identified and quantified in probabilistic risk assessments of safety systems using the CCF models. There are different varieties of models available for CCF quantification. Among these, the β-factor model [4] is one of the prominent CCF models and has been used by various safety-critical industries. The estimation of the β-factor (i.e., a factor used in the quantification of CCF) could be made following the quantitative or qualitative approaches available in the literature [13].

The IEC 61508 standard [2] suggested a qualitative β-factor estimation methodology for the CCF quantification. The methodology establishes certain defense measures against the CCF to minimize their probability of occurrence. The implementation of each measure leads to the reduction of the β-factor value. The defense measures are provided in the form of 37 checklist questions and each question has an associated value based on engineering judgment to quantify the β-factor value. There are two research problems (RP) with this methodology. The first problem (RP1) is the inability to include new measures to the pre-existed measures in the methodology. Since the methodology is from 2010, there is a need to add new measures against the probability of CCF emerging with the latest technological developments in the industry. In this context, a recent study [12] highlighted and considered the importance of including new measures related to the latest technologies, and developed a CCF score table on the IEC 61508 standard methodology. However, the values assigned to the measures in the proposed table are based on the failure data of the nuclear power plant.

The problem (RP2) is that many safety-critical industries such as railways comply with the IEC 61508 standard as a safety practice. However, the established defense measures in the IEC 61508 standard methodology apply to all industries using Electrical/Electronic/Programmable Electronic (E/E/PE) - based systems and not especially for any application/industry. Hence, there is a need to analyze the industry-specific factors and identify the essential defense measures against the CCF to derive more appropriate application-specific β. In this context, the standard IEC 62061 [3], highlighted that not all measures from the IEC 61508 standard apply to the machinery application. Therefore, a few measures are considered for the β-factor estimation. In the same way, the IEC 61131-6 standard [1] considered some specific defense measures for the programmable controllers. However, there is a lack of studies/standards that focus on the defense measures against the probability of occurrence of CCF in railway applications. Even though certain studies like [5] adopted a distinct method for the CCF analysis of railway applications. However, it is not specifically made for the railway systems. Moreover, it considers the same defense measures from the IEC 61508 standard method. Hence, these two problems (RP1 and RP2) could cause uncertainty in the estimated β, which leads to the adoption of inadequate/inessential safety requirements in the industry. Therefore, this research aims to provide possible solutions for these problems by proposing a methodology that enhances the IEC 61508 standard methodology which could consider additional defense measures and estimate β without the need for historical failure data. Then, we plan to demonstrate an approach to develop an industry-specific methodology focusing on one industry i.e., the railway industry, and perform a railway case study. The solution for RP1 is a demonstration of a generic method that applies to all safety-critical industries which could permit new measures. The solution for RP2 is not only useful for railways but also beneficial for those industries that intend to develop application-specific methodology by following our steps. In this research, we established five goals and adopted five research methodologies to achieve them.

In this paper, Sect. 2 presents our research plan which includes the research goals, research contributions, and the adopted research methods. Section 3 discusses the state-of-art. Section 4 presents our time plan, preliminary results, expected results, and our future work.

2 Research Plan

In this section, we present our research plan including the research goals, research contributions, and research methods. This research aims to provide possible solutions for the two main research problems (see Sect. 1) by making five main research goals (*RG*). The *RG1* is to do an in-depth study of the β-factor methodology and its evolution for a strong background knowledge and academic contribution. The *RG2* is to propose a β-factor methodology built over the IEC 61508 standard methodology, that could adopt additional defense measures and estimate β without the need for historical failure data. For *RG3*, we plan to demonstrate a way to develop industry-specific β-factor methodology focusing on the railway industry, by analyzing the needed defense measures from the insights of railway practitioners. In *RG4*, we planned to do a railway case study by adopting the developed railway-specific β-factor methodology and IEC 61508 standard methodology and compare their β-factor estimations. In *RG5*, we plan to study the Electro-dynamic braking of a railway-propulsion system, the CCF analysis of the system, and how the β-factor estimation is performed by the industry and conduct an experimental study using our developed methodology.

2.1 Research Goals

In this research, we made five main research goals (RG), and we discussed each goal in this section.

- **RG1 - Systematic study of β-factor methodology:** The industries like nuclear and railways adopted the β-factor methodology for CCF analysis. However, there is a lack of studies in the literature focusing entirely on this methodology. Hence, we aim to do an in-depth analysis of the evolution of the β-factor methodology (see Sect. 2.3).
- **RG2 - Proposal of a new generic β-factor methodology:** The IEC 61508 standard suggested a β-factor methodology which estimates β based on the applied CCF defense measures. However, the challenge is that the methodology was from 2010, and the measures concerning newly evolved technologies are not included. Moreover, there is no way to permit them. Hence, to overcome this challenge we proposed a new generic methodology.
- **RG3 - Approach to develop industry-specific β-factor methodology:** We plan to develop a railway-specific β-factor methodology by conducting a survey and getting insights from the railway practitioners about the needed defense measures. Since there are no known existing railway-specific β-factor methodologies, this methodology would support practitioners in estimating appropriate railway-specific β-factor value.
- **RG4 - Evaluation and comparison of two β-factor estimation methods:** We plan to compare the developed railway-specific β-factor estimation method in RG3 with the already existing methodology at the industry[1] by doing a case study of a railway sub-system. The goal is to demonstrate the positives and negatives of using both methodologies.
- **RG5 - Study of Electro-dynamic braking of railway propulsion system:** The electro-dynamic braking of railway propulsion system has the probability of CCF. Hence practitioners performed the CCF analysis and estimated the β-factor using the β-factor methodology from the IEC 61508 standard. However, the methodology has been in use for more than a decade, and practitioners determined to do a re-evaluation of this β estimation. For this purpose, we plan to do an experimental study of this system to estimate the β value using the railway-specific β-factor methodology.

2.2 Research Contributions

In this section, we present our Research contributions (RC) so far in achieving the research goals RG1 and RG2.

- **RC1:** We conducted a systematic literature review (see Sect. 2.3) for RG1 and identified 20 different qualitative and quantitative β-factor estimation methods. Our findings are published in the SEAA[2] conference [13].
- **RC2.** We proposed an enhanced IEC 61508 methodology for β-factor estimation to achieve RG2. We submitted our work for the Euro SPI conference[3] and the paper was accepted for publication in the conference proceedings.

---

[1] https://www.alstom.com/.
[2] https://dsd-seaa2023.com/.
[3] https://conference.eurospi.net/index.php/en/.

- We prepared PhD symposium paper for the Quatic conference[4]. Our research problem comes under the software quality concepts under the *Reliability* topic mentioned in the SWEBOK guide[5] because the research problem is all about a CCF methodology which is used as a part of the reliability assessment of safety systems including hardware and software.

2.3 Research Methods

The research methods (RM) that we planned to adopt to achieve our research goals are discussed in this section.

- **RM1 - Systematic Literature Review:** We conducted the *Systematic Literature Review* proposed by Kitchenham and Charters [9] to achieve RG1. This methodology supports identifying the existing β-factor estimation methods in the literature studies.
- **RM2 - Design Science Methodology:** We proposed a methodology for enhancing the β-factor methodology of the IEC 61508 standard following the guidelines of *Design Science Methodology* [15].
- **RM3 - Survey:** We plan to conduct *Survey Methodology* in the process of achieving RG3, by following the survey guidelines in software engineering [11] to get insights from the railway practitioners regarding the applicable defense measures against the CCF.
- **RM4 - Case Study:** We plan to perform *Case Study Research* to achieve the RG4 by following the guidelines of conducting and reporting case study research in software engineering [14]. This case study planned to analyze the applicability of two different β-factor methodologies.
- **RM5 - Experimental Study:** The research method chosen for achieving the RG5 is the *Experimentation* following the guidelines proposed in [16]. Experimentation is planned for the Electro-dynamic braking of the railway propulsion system to analyze their CCF and β-factor estimation.

3 State-of-the-Art

In the literature, many studies discussed the β-factor estimation using qualitative approaches. These approaches are based on the analysis of the defense measures and the β-factor quantification is made by assigning the values to the defense measures. For example in the [8], the values are assigned to the defense measures based on experiences from the past. In [6], the defense measures are weighted with five different values, and the β-factor is estimated based on the applicability of those measures. In the [2], defense measures are analyzed by establishing 37 checklist questions and assigning values based on the engineering judgment to estimate the β. All these studies evolved between 1987–2010, and the defense measures considered in the studies are assigned with certain pre-defined values

[4] https://2024.quatic.org/phd-symposium-sedes.

[5] https://www.computer.org/education/bodies-of-knowledge/software-engineering.

based on the engineering judgment to use in the quantification of β. For this reason, we are incapable of including/excluding needed defense measures as per the industry-specific requirement. In this context, a recent study [12] evolved based on the IEC 61508 standard which considered the additional defense measures considering the latest technologies. However, the scores assigned for the measures in this methodology are based on past nuclear power plant failure data. In contrast to these studies, in our research, we assigned the values to the defense measures in a simpler way according to their applicability in the system by making a checklist questionnaire, and no historical failure data was used. This would be beneficial in including additional defense measures against the CCF. This is also useful for industries that lack historical failure data and intend to develop domain-specific β-factor methodology.

4 Time Plan

The time plan is made for the entire PhD considering the spring term and autumn terms of each year between 2022 and 2026. We made a brief time plan (see Table 1) with the conducted and planned research activities. The spring term refers to the time between mid-January to the beginning of June and the autumn term refers to the time between the beginning of September to mid-January. The research work has been funded by the Knowledge Foundation[6] within the framework of INDTECH Graduate School.

4.1 Preliminary Results

The preliminary results of our research are identified in RC1 and RC2 (see Sect. 2.2). Our main research revolves around the β-factor methodology identified in the IEC 61508 standard. However, proper background details of the β-factor methodology are absent in the standard and there is also a lack of research studies that explicitly focus on this methodology. Hence, we aim to conduct a systematic literature review of β-factor models and identify 20 types of β-factor models that provide us with a strong background knowledge to achieve the research goals and contribute to RC1. Based on the knowledge gained from RC1 about the historical evolution of the β-factor methodology and the pros & cons of different identified methodologies. We proposed a methodology that enhances the IEC 61508 standard β-factor methodology and serves as a generic method that could adopt new defense measures easily and contribute to RC2. This RC2 provides a solution to our RP1 (see Sect. 1).

4.2 Future Work and Expected Results

Expected Results: The expected results would be our expected contributions RC3, RC4 and RC5.

[6] https://www.kks.se/en/start-en/.

Table 1. Timeline

Timeline		
Year	Research Activities - Spring term (ST) and Autumn term (AT)	Research Contributions and Expected outcomes
2022	ST. Setting the research goals AT. Research Planning and the start of writing the research paper A	Finalized research goals and initiated research paper A to do a systematic literature review of β-factor models
2023	ST. Writing and submitting paper A for the SEAA conference AT. Presented Paper A at the conference and it was published in IEEE Xplore Digital Library	Presented paper A at the SEAA conference in Albania Publication of paper A "A Systematic Review of β-factor Models in the Quantification of Common Cause Failures"
2024	ST. For RG2, worked on paper B and submitted it for the EuroSPI conference and submitted PhD symposium paper for Quatic conference AT. Plan to present paper B and symposium paper at conferences, plan to work on paper C for RG3, and prepare the Licentiate proposal	Submitted paper B "A Proposal for Enhancing IEC 61508 Methodology for the β-Factor Estimation" for Euro SPI conference and got accepted Submitted PhD symposium paper "Facilitating β-factor estimation for Common Cause Failures of safety-related system" to Quatic 2024 conference Submission of paper C "Development of railway-specific β-factor methodology"
2025	ST. Writing Licentiate thesis and preparing paper D for RG4 AT. Writing paper E for RG5 and preparation for the licentiate defense seminar	Submission of paper D - "Evaluation and comparative analysis of two β-factor estimation methodologies - A case study" The public defence of my Licentiate thesis
2026	ST. Writing paper E and submitting it to a conference, preparing PhD proposal AT. Completion of writing PhD thesis, making the future goals, and presentation of PhD defense seminar	Submission of paper E - "β-factor estimation of electro-dynamic braking in railway-propulsion system" Completion of writing the PhD thesis The public defense of Doctoral thesis work

- **RC3** - In this, we would propose a railway-specific β-factor methodology by analyzing the needed defense measures for railway applications from the insights of railway practitioners by conducting a survey.
- **RC4** - In this, we would do a comparison of the developed railway-specific methodology in RG3 with the already existing methodology in the industry through a railway case study and demonstrate the results.
- **RC5** - In this, we would do an experimental study of the Electro-dynamic braking of a railway-propulsion system and its β-factor estimation by adopting our developed railway-specific β-factor methodology.

Future Goals: Two main future goals would add benefit to our research and be beneficial, especially for the railway industry.

- **FG1 - Project on CCF data collection focusing railways:** The collection of CCF data of railway sub-systems and maintaining its database would be beneficial in estimating more accurate β-factor values. Industries like nuclear plants have sources like [10] that provide information on how the

CCF data is gathered and evaluated. The nuclear industry also has support from an ongoing project called the International Common Cause Failure Data Exchange Project, where they are collecting CCF data from different countries and analyzing methods to prevent CCF in nuclear plants. The railway industry lacks this kind of support, hence the initiation of a project for CCF data collection would be the first future goal.

- **FG2 - Development of a tool to facilitate our β- factor methodology:** The methodology we developed in RG2 facilitated by a tool would be an add-on benefit. Hence we plan to develop a tool as our second future goal.

References

1. IEC 61131-6:2012 programmable controllers - part 6: functional safety. https://webstore.iec.ch/publication/4555. Accessed 16 June 2024
2. IEC 61508-6: Functional safety of electrical/electronic/programmable electronic safety-related systems part 6: guidelines on the application of parts 2 and 3. https://webstore.iec.ch/publication/5520. Accessed 31 Mar 2024
3. IEC 62061: Safety of machinery - functional safety of safety-related control systems. https://webstore.iec.ch/publication/59927. Accessed 16 June 2024
4. Fleming, K.N.: Reliability model for common mode failures in redundant safety systems. Technical report, General Atomics, San Diego, CA, United States (1974)
5. Hokstad, P., Håbrekke, S., Lundteigen, M.A., Onshus, T.: Use of the PDS method for railway applications. SINTEF Technol. Soc. **15**, 5–23 (2009)
6. Humphreys, R.: Assigning a numerical value to the beta factor common cause evaluation. In: Reliability 1987 (1987)
7. Jin, H., Lundteigen, M.A., Rausand, M.: Common-cause failures in safety-instrumented systems. In: PSAM, vol. 11, pp. 6121–6131
8. Johnston, B.: A structured procedure for dependent failure analysis (DFA). Reliab. Eng. **19**(2), 125–136 (1987)
9. Kitchenham, B., Charters, S., et al.: Guidelines for performing systematic literature reviews in software engineering (2007)
10. MarshaU, F.U.: Common-cause failure database and analysis system: overview (1998)
11. Molléri, J.S., Petersen, K., Mendes, E.: Survey guidelines in software engineering: an annotated review. In: Proceedings of the 10th ACM/IEEE International Symposium on Empirical Software Engineering and Measurement, pp. 1–6 (2016)
12. Park, J., Park, K., Lee, C.J.: The development of a common cause factor score table on IEC 61508 Part 6 Edition 2.0. J. Loss Prev. Process Ind. **68**, 105270 (2024)
13. Rao, S.B.G., Castellanos-Ardila, J.P., Punnekkat, S.: A systematic review of β-factor models in the quantification of common cause failures. In: 2023 49th Euromicro Conference on Software Engineering and Advanced Applications (SEAA), pp. 262–269. IEEE (2023)
14. Runeson, P., Höst, M.: Guidelines for conducting and reporting case study research in software engineering. Empir. Softw. Eng. **14**, 131–164 (2009)
15. Wieringa, R.J.: Design Science Methodology for Information Systems and Software Engineering. Springer, Heidelberg (2014)
16. Wohlin, C., Runeson, P., Höst, M., Ohlsson, M.C., Regnell, B., Wesslén, A.: Experimentation in Software Engineering. Springer, Heidelberg (2012)

Mobile-Based Crowd Monitoring and Management: Assessment and Improvement

Tomás Mestre Santos(✉)

Instituto Universitário de Lisboa (ISCTE-IUL), Lisbon, Portugal
tmmss1@iscte-iul.pt

Abstract. Crowding is a troublesome phenomenon due to safety concerns, public health risks, social tensions, degraded quality of experience for visitors, infrastructure strain, environmental impact, among other reasons. Overcrowding management requires crowd monitoring, the main topic to be addressed in this PhD research plan. In particular, it focuses on developing a machine-learning crowd-monitoring approach based on the detection of mobile device's trace elements from their wireless technologies, namely Wi-Fi and Bluetooth. The expected major challenges are coping with (i) devices' address randomization to derive unified fingerprints in each observation period, (ii) the combination of counting obtained from diverse wireless technologies, and (iii) the combination of data from multiple sources. It also aims to rely on user contributions, to enhance the quality of detection, by developing a mobile application. The latter will also help with real-time management of overtourism, promoting mitigation actions. The research plan builds upon preliminary results on developing a Smart Tourism Toolkit to monitor crowding levels in real-time in the scope of the European RESETTING project.

Keywords: Crowd monitoring · Smart Tourism · Wireless activity detection · Software architecture quality · Detection quality

1 Introduction

The phenomenon of overcrowding follows the increasing development of the tourism sector. If the pre-pandemic trend continues from 2024, it will reach 3 billion arrivals by 2027, based on the World Bank Development Indicators.

Crowding situations degrade visitors' quality of experience, reducing their feeling of safety, making it difficult to move around, enjoy the attractions, and use basic services, such as transportation and restoration, due to long wait times, while reducing destinations' authenticity on the perspective of tourists [1]. Overtourism also deteriorates the lives of residents, due to an increase in urban noise, less effective urban cleaning, higher prices for basic goods and services (as businesses seek to capitalize on the increased demand), displacement caused by local accommodation, and cultural clashes when visitors fail to respect local customs,

A. Bertolino et al. (Eds.): QUATIC 2024, CCIS 2178, pp. 452–460, 2024.
https://doi.org/10.1007/978-3-031-70245-7_34

traditions, and privacy, sometimes leading to the former expressing negatively against the latter [2]. Last, but not least, the environmental sustainability, structures, and cultural heritage of overcrowded destinations are also jeopardized, leading to a loss of authenticity [3].

Overtourism mitigation actions, such as promoting the visitation to less occupied but equally attractive areas, can be applied in recreational, cultural, or religious spots, both in indoor scenarios like palaces, museums, monasteries, or cathedrals, or in outdoor ones such as public parks, camping parks, concerts, or fireworks. Besides assuring a better visiting experience, those actions are also necessary for security reasons (e.g., to prevent works exhibited in a museum from deteriorating or even vandalized by exceeding room capacity), health reasons (e.g., preventing infection in pandemic scenarios by not exceeding the maximum people density specified by health authorities), or even for resource management (e.g., to reduce the intervention of security and cleaning teams).

This plan builds upon preliminary results of a Smart Tourism Toolkit to monitor crowding levels in real-time in the scope of the European RESETTING project. This toolkit uses overcrowding sensors capable of detecting the number of nearby mobile devices, thus measuring how crowded the surrounding location is. The sensors can detect crowding trends and highly populated events over time, however, crowding estimations can be more accurate. Additionally, the system architecture can also be optimized for an easier and faster installation and operation by users, and also to trigger overcrowding mitigation actions.

As so, the goals of this research plan are: (i) improving crowd monitoring based on the mobile device's wireless activity, namely Wi-Fi and Bluetooth, and (ii) developing a system architecture for overcrowding mitigation actions.

2 Research Plan

2.1 Research Goals and Questions

The main objective of this PhD research plan is to improve crowd monitoring based on the wireless activity of mobile devices, to scaffold overcrowding mitigation actions. To reach that objective we have identified two research goals:

- *RG1: Produce accurate crowd estimations* - precise estimates of the real number of mobile devices are required to effectively assess the crowding phenomena. This comprises (i) deriving and calibrating unique device fingerprints to mitigate address randomization processes, (ii) combining measurements obtained from heterogeneous wireless technologies, and (iii) combining crowd information from multiple sources.
- *RG2: Develop a system architecture for crowd information harvesting and mitigation actions* - we aim at a crowding information system that considers several concerns such as reusability, scalability, adaptability, and security. Aspects to be considered include (i) the use of multiple communication options to mitigate local network limitations, (ii) the use of adaptive mechanisms to facilitate the systems' control and operation, and (iii) data protection

to ensure users' privacy rights. It also comprises (iv) overcrowding mitigation actions, by taking actions after its detection.

Based on the previously identified research goals, this PhD plan aims to answer the following research questions:

- RQ1 - What are the pros and cons of existing crowd-monitoring approaches?
- RQ2 - What is the best approach to uniquely identify mobile devices, by tackling address randomization processes used in communication?
- RQ3 - To what extent can mobile devices' activity monitoring be used effectively for overcrowding mitigation actions?

2.2 Research Contributions

The main expected contributions of this PhD research plan are the following:

1. A systematic literature review on crowd monitoring based on the mobile devices' activity;
2. An innovative approach to monitor crowding in a given location, addressing recent address randomization processes from mobile devices by adopting advanced machine-learning techniques;
3. The provision of labelled datasets of mobile device's messages, allowing other authors with similar approaches to train and test their algorithms;
4. A low-cost, flexible, scalable, adaptive, maintainable, and installable system architecture for monitoring crowding at several locations in real-time, also enabling overcrowding mitigation actions;
5. The application and deployment of our solution in real crowded scenarios, with relevant impact for their mitigation.

2.3 Research Method

After outlining the research goals and questions, we will now detail the adopted research method. Its first and crucial step is to obtain a clear and comprehensive overview of the different approaches that can be used for crowd monitoring based on the activity of mobile devices. To this end, a systematic literature review (SLR) on the topic will be conducted. This SLR will identify, aggregate and summarize the different approaches that will serve as a baseline and will be used to determine the best approach for producing accurate crowd estimates.

Besides the outcomes of the SLR, and since this PhD work plan builds upon preliminary results, a machine-learning crowd-monitoring approach is already envisaged to enhance the quality of detection. In particular, a Semi-Supervised Learning (SSL) approach will be used to determine which message fields should be considered to generate unique device fingerprints. It will use data from public datasets of device messages, and data from our dataset collections performed in controlled environments as input. A clustering algorithm will then combine the fingerprints with other properties of the device's messages to leverage accurate crowd estimations (accomplishes goal RG1.i). This approach will be implemented on both Wi-Fi and Bluetooth detection technologies, and further combined to leverage more accurate crowd estimations by eliminating the trade-offs of each technology (accomplishes goal RG1.ii).

After implementation, it is necessary to prosecute testing and validation to assess the effectiveness and reliability of detecting the crowding phenomena. For this, the accuracy of the detection algorithm will be determined, based on the difference between the number of devices detected from the sensors with the real and ground-truth number of devices in a given period. These validations will be undertaken in two different scenarios, with different scales of dimension: (i) in a controlled and laboratory environment, with a small number of mobile devices during a short period; (ii) in real crowded application scenarios, with a large number of mobile devices during large periods.

If a high accuracy (to be determined) is obtained in both scenarios, then we conclude that the crowding sensors are capable of producing accurate crowd estimations by passively detecting mobile devices. If the contrary, it will be necessary to determine and implement a new approach and execute the same previous steps. Additionally, the research outcomes of the SLR may also refine the initial proposed approach to achieve higher accuracy. Additionally, we also plan to rely on user feedback to enhance the quality of detection through a mobile application. The latter will allow users to gain access to the occupancy of spaces by consenting to being monitored by the application. This active detection of the mobile users, together with the passive detection from the sensors, will leverage a more accurate crowd estimation (accomplishes goal RG1.iii).

Apart from producing accurate crowd estimation, this PhD work plan also envisages the development of a system architecture for crowd monitoring harvesting and mitigation actions. As claimed in [4], distributed, real-time applications require an early definition of the system architecture to fulfil functional and non-functional quality requirements, such as those defined in [5]. To promote software *reusability* and reap its benefits [6], we will use open-source components whenever possible. For the sake of *interoperability* and *reliability*, we aim to test and validate multiple communication protocols for data exchanges from the sensors, either uplink or downlink, such as LoRaWAN, Wi-Fi mesh, and Narrowband Internet of Things, to mitigate the network limitations at the installation of the sensors (accomplishes goal RG2.i). Regarding *adaptability*, we plan to implement an auto-healing mechanism to dynamically change the communication protocol in use in case of failure, ensuring resilience and data continuity (accomplishes goal RG2.ii). As for *security*, we will guarantee data protection by anonymizing collected data from sensors and anonymizing users' identification on the mobile application (accomplishes goal RG2.iii).

Lastly, real-time crowding data provided by sensors deployed in real application scenarios and the mobile application will be used to trigger overcrowding mitigation actions. These actions may be notification alerts to suggest people exit currently overcrowded areas, providing alternative routes to other less-occupied but equally attractive areas, or even triggering actuators, prohibiting people from entering certain areas or rooms (accomplishes RG2.iv sub-goal).

3 State-of-the-Art

Several approaches can be used for crowd detection and crowd monitoring, such as image capturing, sound capturing, mobile operator's data, and wireless spectrum analysis [7]. Some authors have relied on capturing sound from microphones and acoustic sensors to detect crowds [8,9], however, low precision and detection ranges were achieved, as well as sound analysis requires high processing and network bandwidth, and can also raise privacy issues since conversations could be recorded. Alternatively, some authors have used massive volumes of data from mobile operators [10,11]. Nevertheless, these methods focus on retrieving patterns and predictions from past gathered data, making it inconvenient to generate relevant metrics in real time from those massive datasets.

The use of image and video processing has been extensively used to monitor crowds, where cameras provide visual information from a location, and images are processed, usually with the aid of learning techniques [12]. Nevertheless, this approach has significant drawbacks for detecting crowds in real-time: processing images and videos is very computationally demanding and, therefore lacks scalability; implementations and communication costs and bandwidth can be considerable; and also privacy issues arise since images of persons are being captured. Nevertheless, research on crowd detection has evolved from vision-based approaches towards sensor-based systems [13]. Sensing wireless communication traces from mobile devices has gradually been an adopted approach to crowd monitoring, since most persons usually carry a mobile phone, also complying with users' privacy rights by its passive and non-intrusive detection. In particular, research has advanced toward the exploration of specific fields and properties of device messages to tackle Media Access Control (MAC) address randomization processes that led to inaccurate estimations. Several strategies have already been adopted to address this issue, some authors have employed a fingerprinting technique to generate unique identifiers for each device [14,15], while others combined fingerprints with other properties of messages in a clustering algorithm, where each cluster should represent a device [16–18].

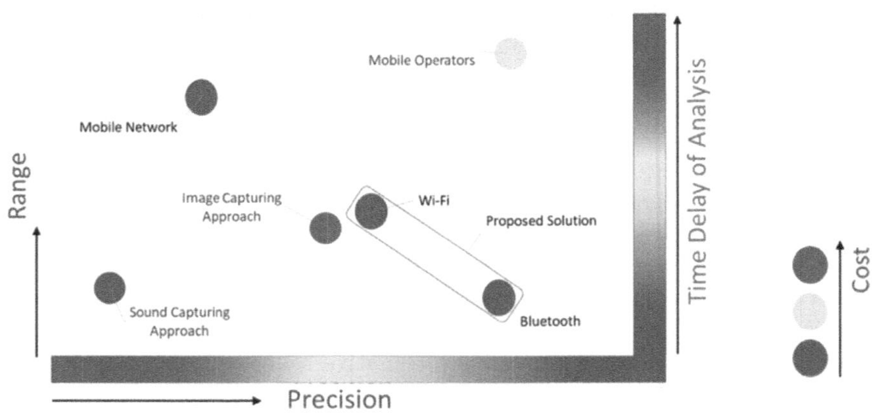

Fig. 1. Crowd monitoring approaches comparison.

Figure 1 summarizes and compares the previous approaches in terms of range, precision, analysis delay, and implementation cost. As can be seen, the best option in terms of the previous criteria, while respecting privacy rights, is the one based on the collection of wireless communication traces.

4 Time Plan

The planned research was split into four work packages, as shown in Table 1.

Table 1. PhD research plan work packages and timeline.

WP	Name	Description	Start date	End date
WP1	Multiple intelligent and adaptive crowd detection	Contribute to achieve RG1.i–ii sub-goals	01/11/2023	31/10/2025
WP2	System architecture for crowd monitoring	Contribute to achieve RG2.i–iii sub-goals	01/11/2023	31/10/2024
WP3	User contribution to crowd monitoring and mitigation	Contribute to achieve RG1.iii and RG2.iv sub-goals	01/11/2025	01/09/2026
WP4	Scientific Articles & Thesis Writing	The outcomes of WP1, WP2, and WP3 will be disseminated through scientific papers that will be converted into PhD thesis chapters	01/11/2023	31/10/2026

4.1 Preliminary Results

Although this PhD program has started recently, some preliminary results have already been obtained. With a total score of 295 out of 300 points, the current Wi-Fi fingerprinting algorithm has won the international CONFRONT challenge, thus dictating a good starting point for reliability and effectiveness on crowd estimations. A new sensor's prototype version was also created, including new hardware components for greater performance and a new custom-made case, and will be used in our future deployments. Efforts have also been made to improve and facilitate the control and operation of the system concerning RG2.i–iii sub-goals. In particular, bidirectional communication (uplink and downlink) was implemented for both Wi-Fi and LoRaWAN protocols, which allows users to remotely and quickly change the system operation from a single point. In addition, an adaptive network auto-healing mechanism was implemented on the crowd sensors, which are now able to quickly and autonomously recover from link failures, ensuring resilience and data continuity.

According to the ISO/IEC 25010 software product quality characteristics [5], adaptability is a sub-characteristic of flexibility and is defined as *"the degree to which a product or system can effectively and efficiently be adapted for or transferred to different hardware, software or other operational or usage environments"*. In our road to providing adaptability features to our system architecture, we are implementing an auto-healing mechanism that detects communication protocol failures and dynamically switches from Wi-Fi to LoRa or vice-versa as required. It can autonomously recover previously lost connections, demonstrating self-configuration and self-organization capabilities. This adaptability ensures communication resilience and data continuity without human intervention or performance degradation. Additionally, over-the-air updates and custom downlink communication enable quick and efficient system reconfiguration.

Last, but not least, it is worth mentioning that this PhD program is also intertwined with other ongoing research threads carried out at the ISTAR Research Unit as described in [19].

4.2 Future Work and Expected Results

Future research will aim to perform the aforementioned SLR on crowd monitoring and management approaches based on mobile device activity. Efforts will also be made to implement the envisioned SSL learning approach for more accurate crowd estimation. To this end, a custom-built Faraday cage is nearing completion. This cage will block electromagnetic radiation from the outside and will be used to generate a large dataset of device messages, which will be used together with other publicly available datasets as input for the SSL algorithm.

In addition, field experiments will be conducted, mostly at popular tourist locations prone to overcrowding situations. These experiments will be crucial to test and validate the latest research advances, either the detection algorithms, the system architecture and new features, the mobile application, as well as the overcrowding mitigation measures, which will also allow tourism managers to make more informed decisions regarding overcrowding.

Expected case studies include the Pena Palace, the Palace of Queluz, the Palace of Monserrate, Quinta da Regaleira, and the Tagus Estuary Bird watching and Conservation Area (EVOA), from partnerships established between our University and the respective entities.

Acknowledgements. This work has been developed in the scope of the RESETTING project, funded by the European COSME Programme (EISMEA), under grant agreement COS-TOURINN 101038190. The cloud-based infrastructure was provided by the INCD, funded by FCT and FEDER under project 01/SAICT/2016 nº022153. The current work has also been supported by FCT under project UIDB/EEA/50008/2020. This work was also funded by GEOTA - Grupo de Estudos de Ordenamento do Território e Ambiente under the partnership and scientific patronage agreement with Iscte - Instituto Universitário de Lisboa (ref. SUSTENTURIS).

References

1. Tokarchuk, O., et al.: How much is too much? Estimating tourism carrying capacity in urban context using sentiment analysis. Tour. Manag. **91**, 104522 (2022). https://doi.org/10.1016/j.tourman.2022.104522
2. Biendicho, M., et al.: Tourists go home! Examining antitourism in Barcelona from an emotions perspective. Tour. Cult. Commun. **22**(3), 275–295 (2022). https://doi.org/10.3727/109830421x16345418234010
3. Seraphin, H., et al.: Over-tourism and the fall of Venice as a destination. J. Destination Mark. Manag. **9**, 374–376 (2018). https://doi.org/10.1016/j.jdmm.2018.01.011
4. Losavio, F., et al.: Quality characteristics for software architecture. J. Object Technol. **2**(2), 133–150 (2003)
5. ISO/IEC. Systems and software engineering – Systems and software Quality Requirements and Evaluation (SQuaRE) – Product quality model. Technical report 25010:2023. International Organization for Standardization, Geneva (2023)
6. Mohagheghi, P., Conradi, R.: Quality, productivity and economic benefits of software reuse: a review of industrial studies. Empirical Softw. Eng. **12**, 471–516 (2007). https://doi.org/10.1007/s10664-007-9040-x
7. da Silva, R.D., et al.: Crowding detection combining trace elements from heterogeneous wireless technologies. In: 22nd International Symposium on Wireless Personal Multimedia Communications (WPMC), pp. 1–6. IEEE (2019). https://doi.org/10.1109/wpmc48795.2019.9096131
8. Agarwal, R., et al.: Algorithms for crowd surveillance using passive acoustic sensors over a multimodal sensor network. IEEE Sens. **15**(3), 1920–1930 (2015). https://doi.org/10.1109/jsen.2014.2369474
9. Kannan, P.G., et al.: Low cost crowd counting using audio tones. In: 10th Conference on Embedded Network Sensor Systems, pp. 155–168. ACM (2012). https://doi.org/10.1145/2426656.2426673
10. De Nadai, M., et al.: The death and life of great Italian cities. In: 25th International Conference on WWWW (2016). https://doi.org/10.1145/2872427.2883084
11. Park, S., et al.: MobInsight: understanding urban mobility with crowd-powered neighborhood characterizations. In: 16th International Conference on Data Mining Workshops (ICDMW) (2016). https://doi.org/10.1109/icdmw.2016.0192
12. López-Cifuentes, A., et al.: Semantic-driven multi-camera pedestrian detection. Knowl. Inf. Syst. **64**(5), 1211–1237 (2022). https://doi.org/10.1007/s10115-022-01673-w
13. Singh, U., et al.: Crowd monitoring: state-of-the-art and future directions. IETE Tech. Rev. **38**(6), 578–594 (2020). https://doi.org/10.1080/02564602.2020.1803152
14. Vega-Barbas, M., et al.: AFOROS: a low-cost Wi-Fi-based monitoring system for estimating occupancy of public spaces. Sensors **21**(11), 3863 (2021). https://doi.org/10.3390/s21113863
15. Bravenec, T., et al.: What your wearable devices revealed about you and possibilities of non-cooperative 802.11 presence detection during your last IPIN visit. In: 12th International Conference on Indoor Positioning and Indoor Navigation (IPIN). IEEE (2022). https://doi.org/10.1109/ipin54987.2022.9918134
16. Cai, Y., et al.: MAC address randomization tolerant crowd monitoring system using Wi-Fi packets. In: Asian Internet Engineering Conference. ACM (2021). https://doi.org/10.1145/3497777.3498547

17. He, T., et al.: Self-supervised association of Wi-Fi probe requests under MAC address randomization. IEEE Trans. Mob. Comput. **22**(12), 7044–7056 (2022). https://doi.org/10.1109/tmc.2022.3205924
18. Uras, M., et al.: MAC address de-randomization for WiFi device counting: Combining temporal-and content-based fingerprints. Comput. Netw. **218**, 109393 (2022). https://doi.org/10.1016/j.comnet.2022.109393
19. Brito e Abreu, F., et al.: A digital transformation approach to scaffold tourism crowding management: pre-factum, on-factum, and post-factum. In: Joint International Conference on ECTI DAMT & NCON, pp. 586–591 (2024). https://doi.org/10.1109/ECTIDAMTNCON60518.2024.10480056

Author Index

A. Bertolino et al. (Eds.): QUATIC 2024, CCIS 2178, pp. 461–462, 2024.
https://doi.org/10.1007/978-3-031-70245-7

SPRINGER NATURE

GPSR Compliance

The European Union's (EU) General Product Safety Regulation (GPSR) is a set of rules that requires consumer products to be safe and our obligations to ensure this.

If you have any concerns about our products, you can contact us on ProductSafety@springernature.com

In case Publisher is established outside the EU, the EU authorized representative is:

Springer Nature Customer Service Center GmbH
Europaplatz 3
69115 Heidelberg, Germany

The manufacturer's authorised representative in the EU is Springer Nature Customer Service Centre GmbH, Europaplatz 3, 69115 Heidelberg, Germany. If you have any concerns regarding our products, please contact ProductSafety@springernature.com

Printed and bound by CPI Group (UK) Ltd, Croydon, CR0 4YY
23/09/2026
02221530-0004